RANDOM Zits®

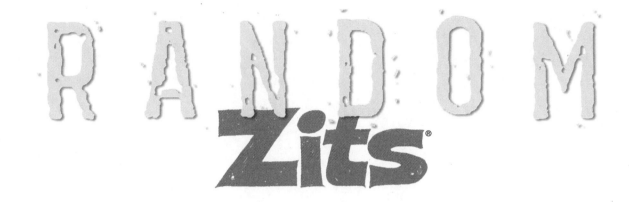

Also by Jerry Scott and Jim Borgman

Zits: Sketchbook 1
Growth Spurt: Zits Sketchbook 2
Don't Roll Your Eyes at Me, Young Man!: Zits Sketchbook 3
Are We an "Us"?: Zits Sketchbook 4
Zits Unzipped: Zits Sketchbook 5
Busted!: Zits Sketchbook 6
Road Trip: Zits Sketchbook 7
Teenage Tales: Zits Sketchbook 8

Treasuries
Humongous Zits
Big Honkin' Zits
Zits: Supersized

RANDOM

Zits®

by JERRY SCOTT and JIMBORGMAN

**Andrews McMeel
Publishing**

Kansas City

Zits® is syndicated internationally by King Features Syndicate, Inc. For information, write King Features Syndicate, Inc., 888 Seventh Avenue, New York, New York 10019.

04 05 06 07 08 BAM 10 9 8 7 6 5 4 3 2 1

ISBN: 0-7407-4669-3

Library of Congress Catalog Card Number: 2004103573

Zits® may be viewed online at
www.kingfeatures.com.

——————————— **ATTENTION: SCHOOLS AND BUSINESSES** ———————————

Andrews McMeel books are available at quantity discounts with bulk purchase for educational, business, or sales promotional use. For information, please write to: Special Sales Department, Andrews McMeel Publishing, 4520 Main Street, Kansas City, Missouri 64111.

To the awesome Barn Girls of Rancho Sea Air, with love and pride.
—J.S.

For Sarah, who made it all happen.
—J.B.

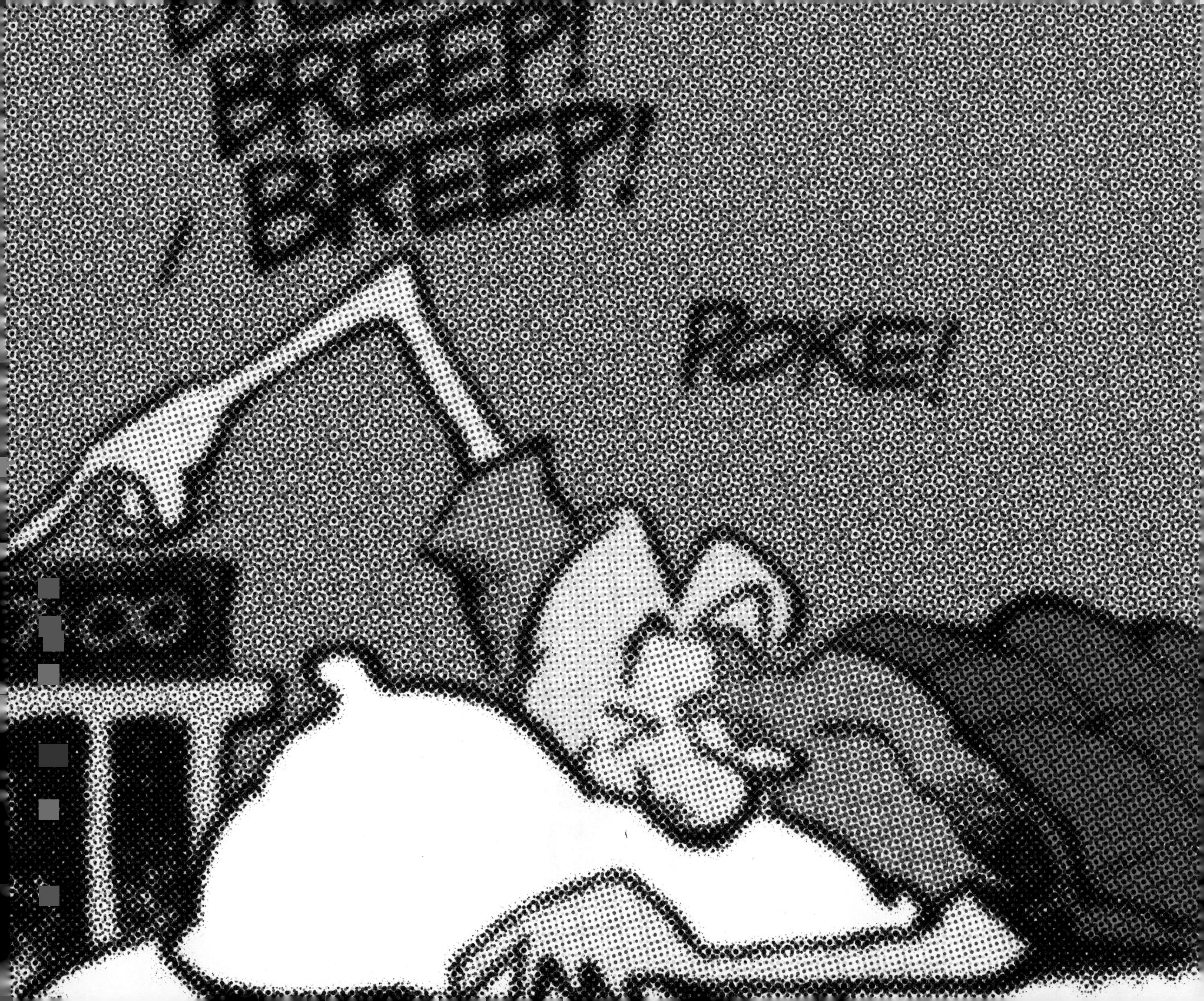
BEEP BEEP!
POKE!

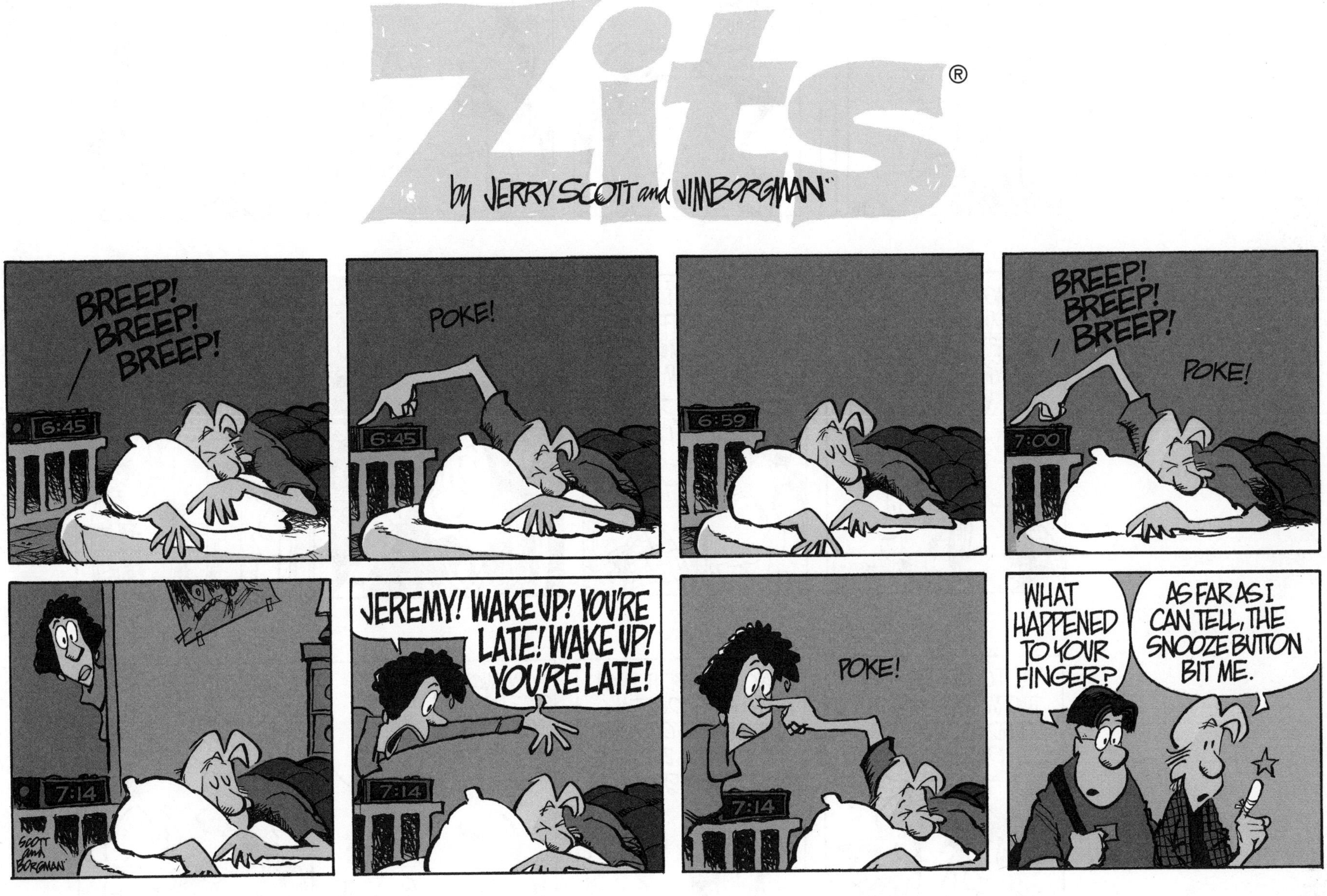
Zits®
by JERRY SCOTT and JIM BORGMAN
BREEP! BREEP! BREEP!
6:45
POKE!
6:45
6:59
BREEP! BREEP! BREEP!
POKE!
7:00
7:14
SCOTT AND BORGMAN
JEREMY! WAKE UP! YOU'RE LATE! WAKE UP! YOU'RE LATE!
7:14
POKE!
7:14
WHAT HAPPENED TO YOUR FINGER?
AS FAR AS I CAN TELL, THE SNOOZE BUTTON BIT ME.

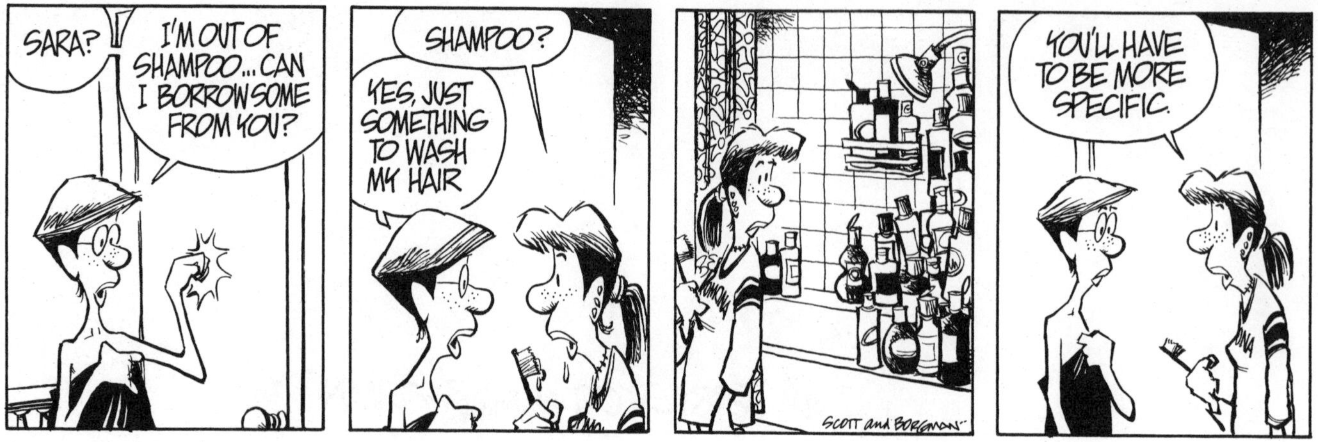
SARA?
I'M OUT OF SHAMPOO... CAN I BORROW SOME FROM YOU?
SHAMPOO?
YES, JUST SOMETHING TO WASH MY HAIR
SCOTT and BORGMAN
YOU'LL HAVE TO BE MORE SPECIFIC.

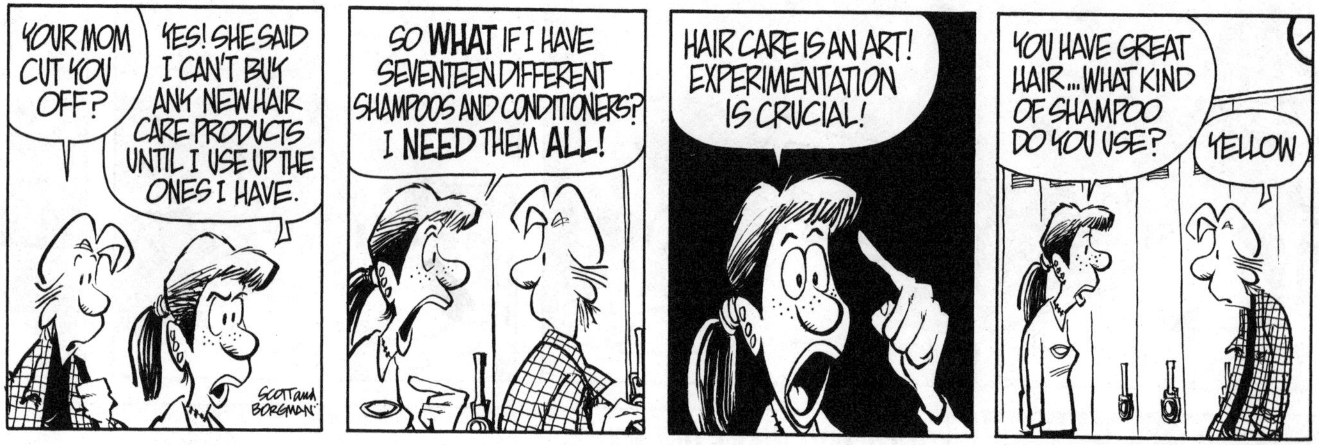
YOUR MOM CUT YOU OFF?
YES! SHE SAID I CAN'T BUY ANY NEW HAIR CARE PRODUCTS UNTIL I USE UP THE ONES I HAVE.
SCOTT and BORGMAN
SO WHAT IF I HAVE SEVENTEEN DIFFERENT SHAMPOOS AND CONDITIONERS? I NEED THEM ALL!
HAIR CARE IS AN ART! EXPERIMENTATION IS CRUCIAL!
YOU HAVE GREAT HAIR... WHAT KIND OF SHAMPOO DO YOU USE?
YELLOW

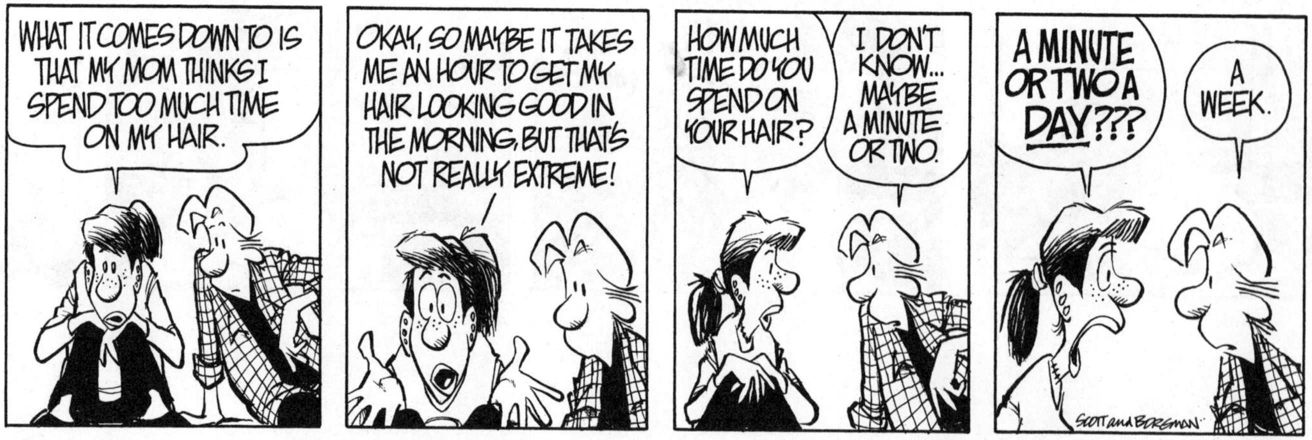
WHAT IT COMES DOWN TO IS THAT MY MOM THINKS I SPEND TOO MUCH TIME ON MY HAIR.
OKAY, SO MAYBE IT TAKES ME AN HOUR TO GET MY HAIR LOOKING GOOD IN THE MORNING, BUT THAT'S NOT REALLY EXTREME!
HOW MUCH TIME DO YOU SPEND ON YOUR HAIR?
I DON'T KNOW... MAYBE A MINUTE OR TWO.
A MINUTE OR TWO A DAY???
A WEEK.
SCOTT and BORGMAN

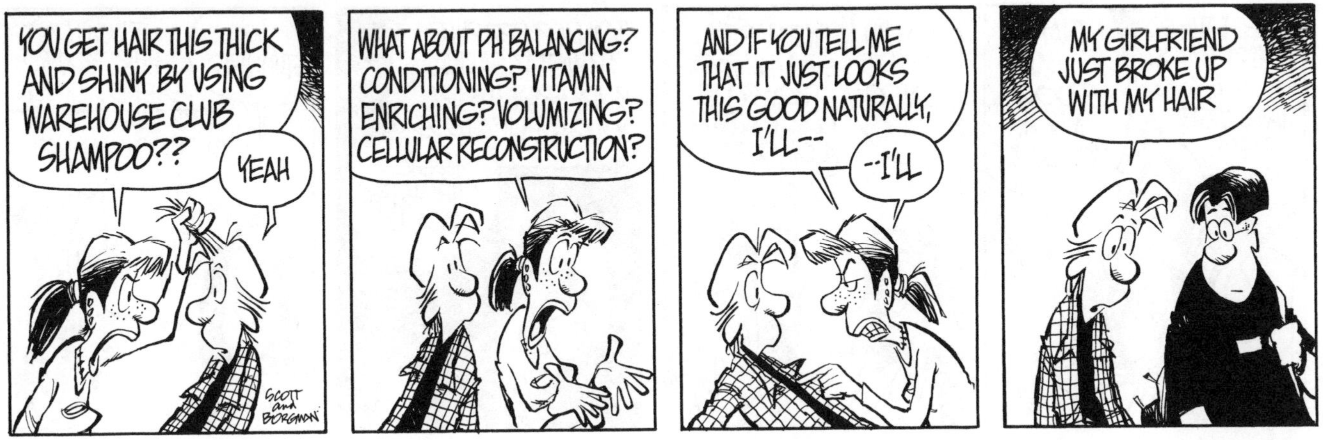
YOU GET HAIR THIS THICK AND SHINY BY USING WAREHOUSE CLUB SHAMPOO??
YEAH
SCOTT and BORGMAN
WHAT ABOUT PH BALANCING? CONDITIONING? VITAMIN ENRICHING? VOLUMIZING? CELLULAR RECONSTRUCTION?
AND IF YOU TELL ME THAT IT JUST LOOKS THIS GOOD NATURALLY, I'LL--
--I'LL
MY GIRLFRIEND JUST BROKE UP WITH MY HAIR

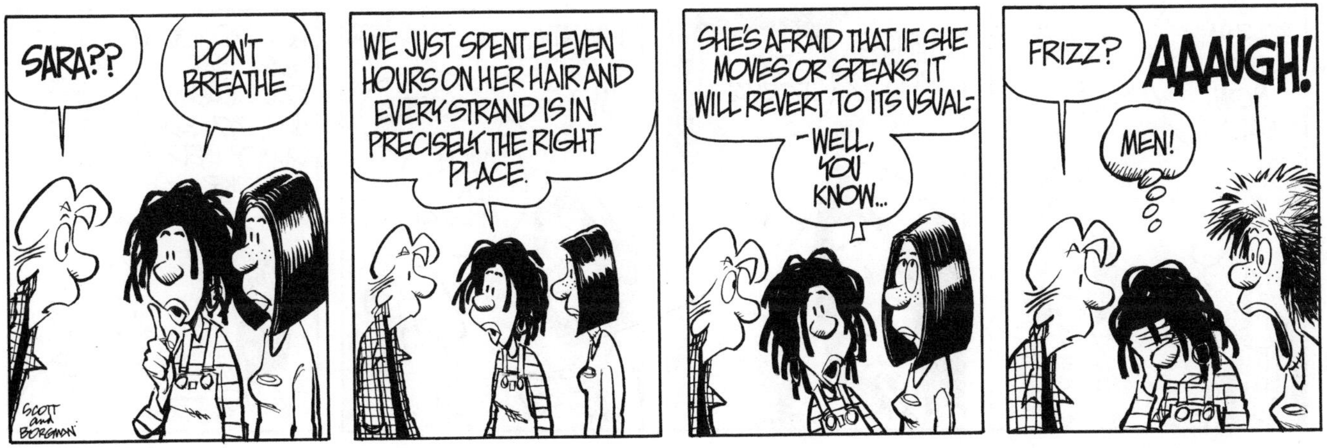
SARA??
DON'T BREATHE
SCOTT and BORGMAN
WE JUST SPENT ELEVEN HOURS ON HER HAIR AND EVERY STRAND IS IN PRECISELY THE RIGHT PLACE.
SHE'S AFRAID THAT IF SHE MOVES OR SPEAKS IT WILL REVERT TO ITS USUAL-
-WELL, YOU KNOW...
FRIZZ?
AAAUGH!
MEN!

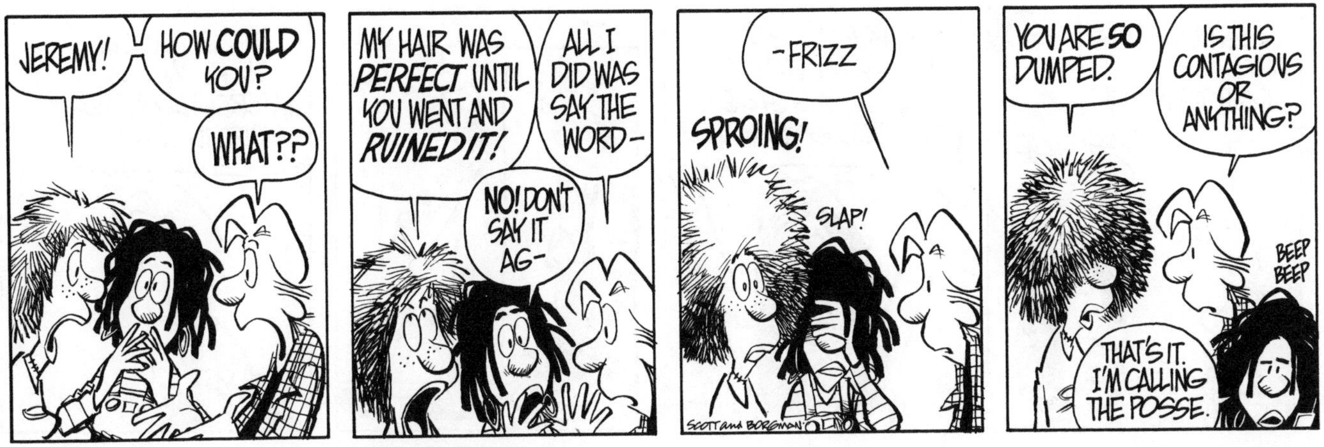
JEREMY!
HOW COULD YOU?
WHAT??
MY HAIR WAS PERFECT UNTIL YOU WENT AND RUINED IT!
ALL I DID WAS SAY THE WORD-
NO! DON'T SAY IT AG-
-FRIZZ
SPROING!
SLAP!
SCOTT and BORGMAN
YOU ARE SO DUMPED.
IS THIS CONTAGIOUS OR ANYTHING?
BEEP BEEP
THAT'S IT. I'M CALLING THE POSSE.

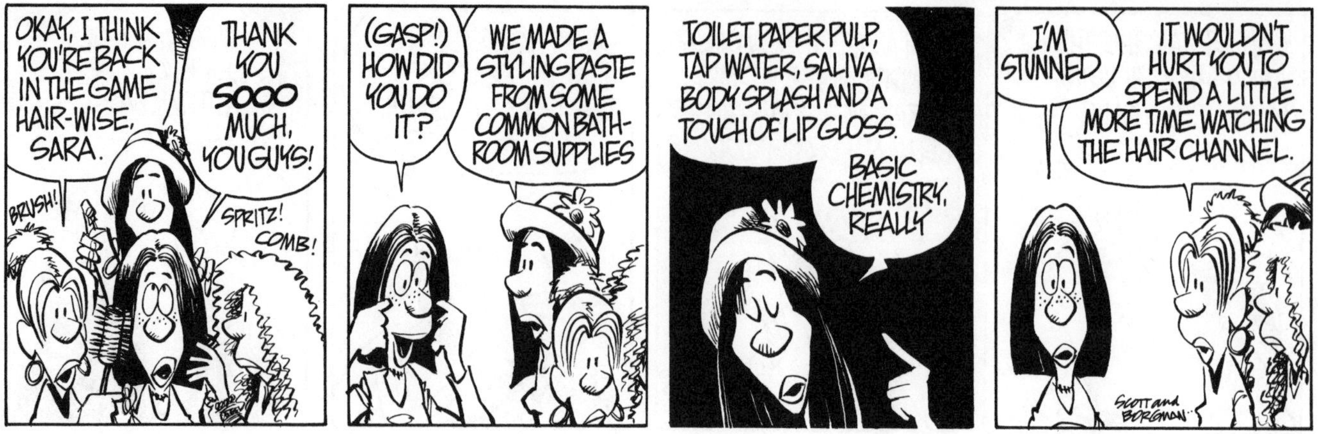
OKAY, I THINK YOU'RE BACK IN THE GAME HAIR-WISE, SARA.
THANK YOU SOOO MUCH, YOU GUYS!
BRUSH!
SPRITZ!
COMB!
(GASP!) HOW DID YOU DO IT?
WE MADE A STYLING PASTE FROM SOME COMMON BATH-ROOM SUPPLIES
TOILET PAPER PULP, TAP WATER, SALIVA, BODY SPLASH AND A TOUCH OF LIP GLOSS.
BASIC CHEMISTRY, REALLY
I'M STUNNED
IT WOULDN'T HURT YOU TO SPEND A LITTLE MORE TIME WATCHING THE HAIR CHANNEL.
SCOTT and BORGMAN

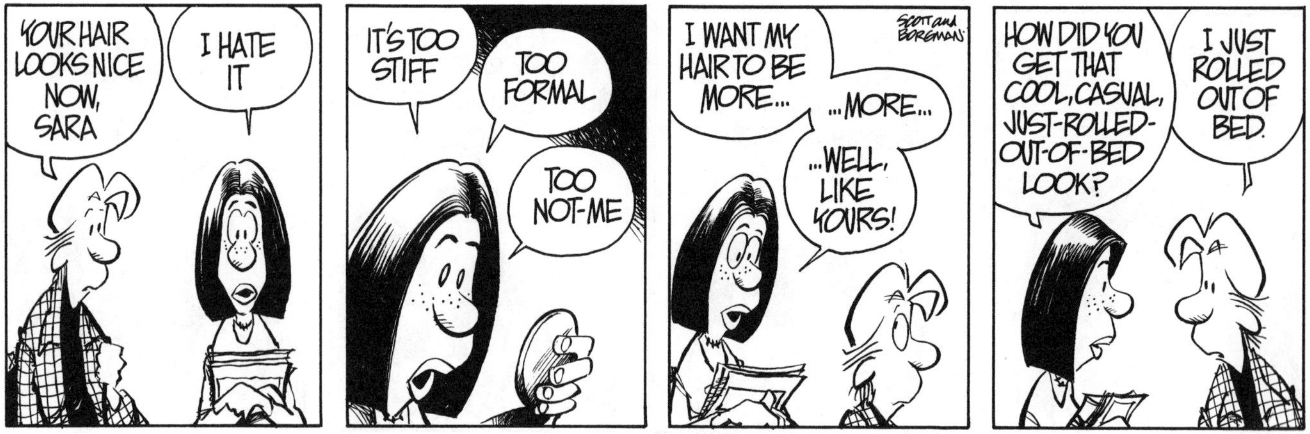
YOUR HAIR LOOKS NICE NOW, SARA
I HATE IT
IT'S TOO STIFF
TOO FORMAL
TOO NOT-ME
I WANT MY HAIR TO BE MORE...
...MORE...
...WELL, LIKE YOURS!
SCOTT and BORGMAN
HOW DID YOU GET THAT COOL, CASUAL, JUST-ROLLED-OUT-OF-BED LOOK?
I JUST ROLLED OUT OF BED.

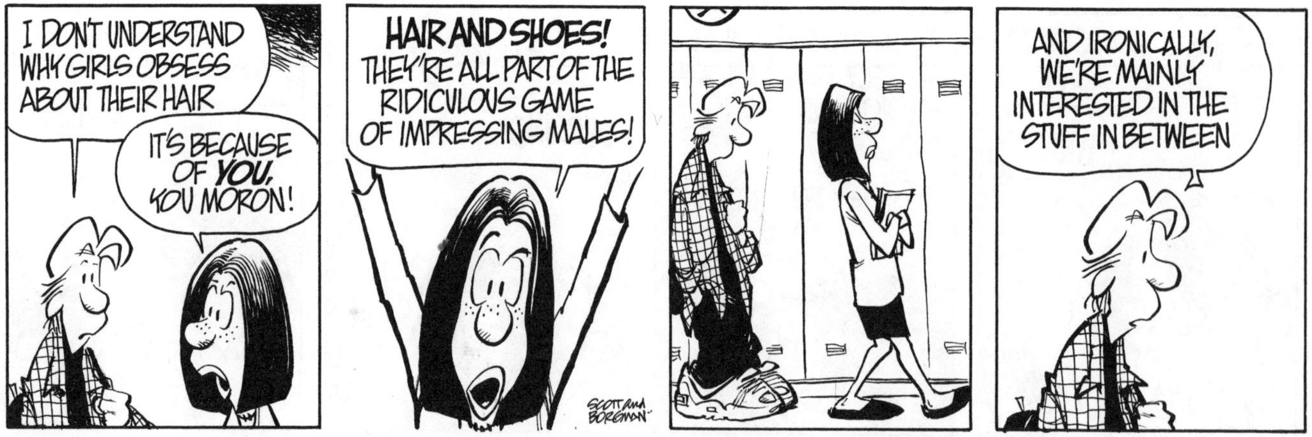
I DON'T UNDERSTAND WHY GIRLS OBSESS ABOUT THEIR HAIR
IT'S BECAUSE OF YOU, YOU MORON!
HAIR AND SHOES! THEY'RE ALL PART OF THE RIDICULOUS GAME OF IMPRESSING MALES!
SCOTT and BORGMAN
AND IRONICALLY, WE'RE MAINLY INTERESTED IN THE STUFF IN BETWEEN

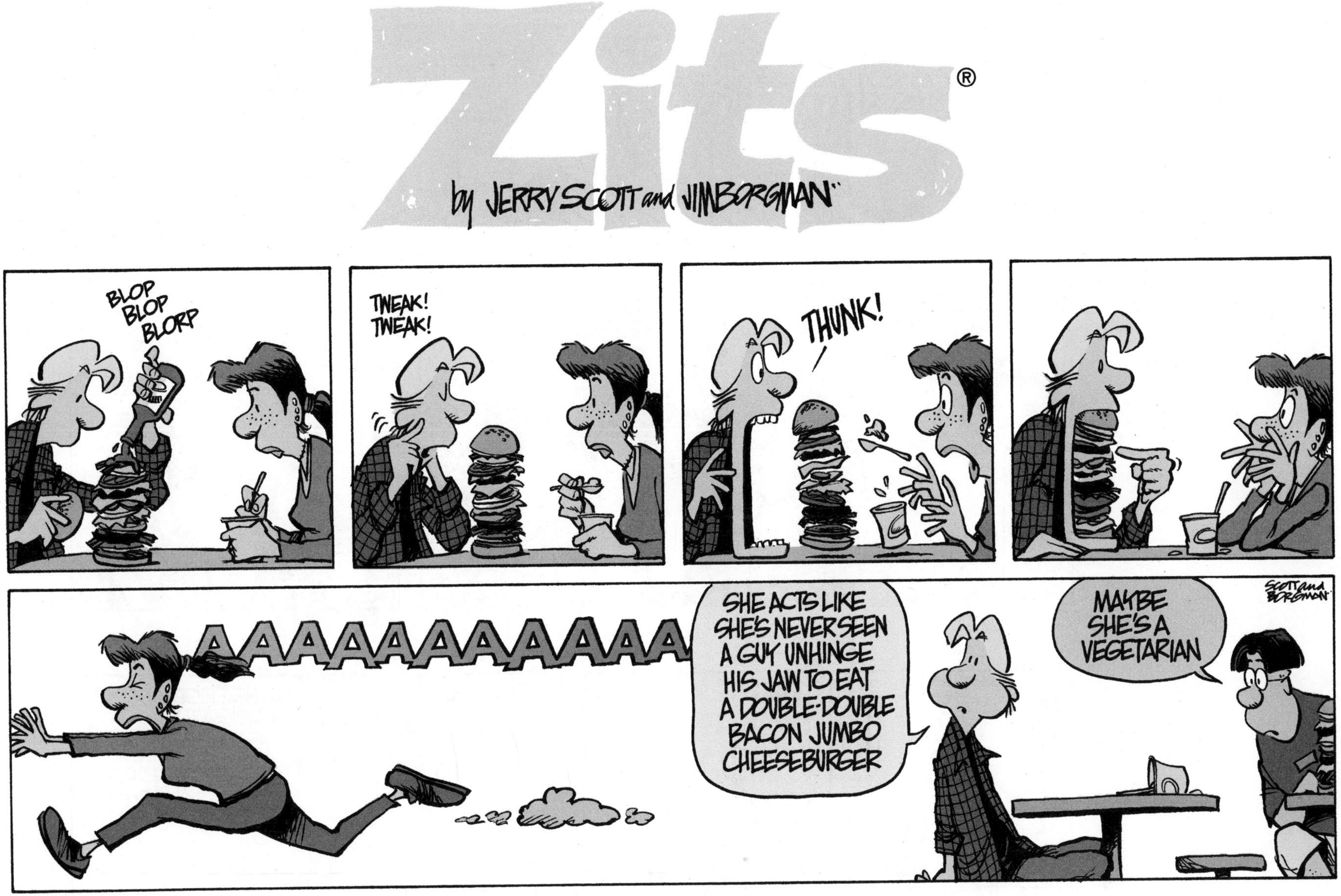
Zits®
by JERRY SCOTT and JIM BORGMAN
BLOP BLOP BLORP
TWEAK! TWEAK!
THUNK!
AAAAAAAAAAA
SHE ACTS LIKE SHE'S NEVER SEEN A GUY UNHINGE HIS JAW TO EAT A DOUBLE-DOUBLE BACON JUMBO CHEESEBURGER
MAYBE SHE'S A VEGETARIAN
SCOTT and BORGMAN

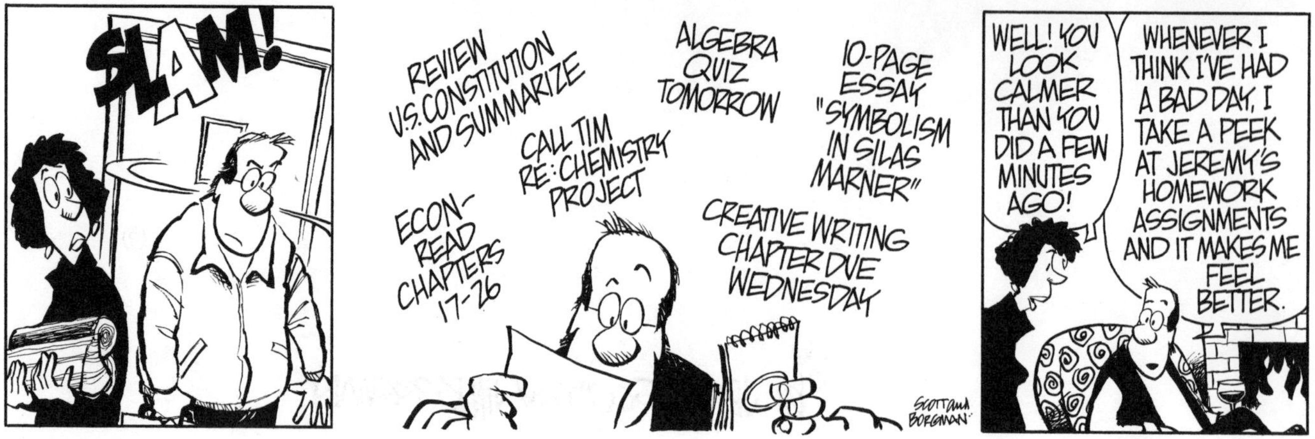
SLAM!
REVIEW U.S. CONSTITUTION AND SUMMARIZE
CALL TIM RE: CHEMISTRY PROJECT
ECON-READ CHAPTERS 17-26
ALGEBRA QUIZ TOMORROW
10-PAGE ESSAY "SYMBOLISM IN SILAS MARNER"
CREATIVE WRITING CHAPTER DUE WEDNESDAY
WELL! YOU LOOK CALMER THAN YOU DID A FEW MINUTES AGO!
WHENEVER I THINK I'VE HAD A BAD DAY, I TAKE A PEEK AT JEREMY'S HOMEWORK ASSIGNMENTS AND IT MAKES ME FEEL BETTER.

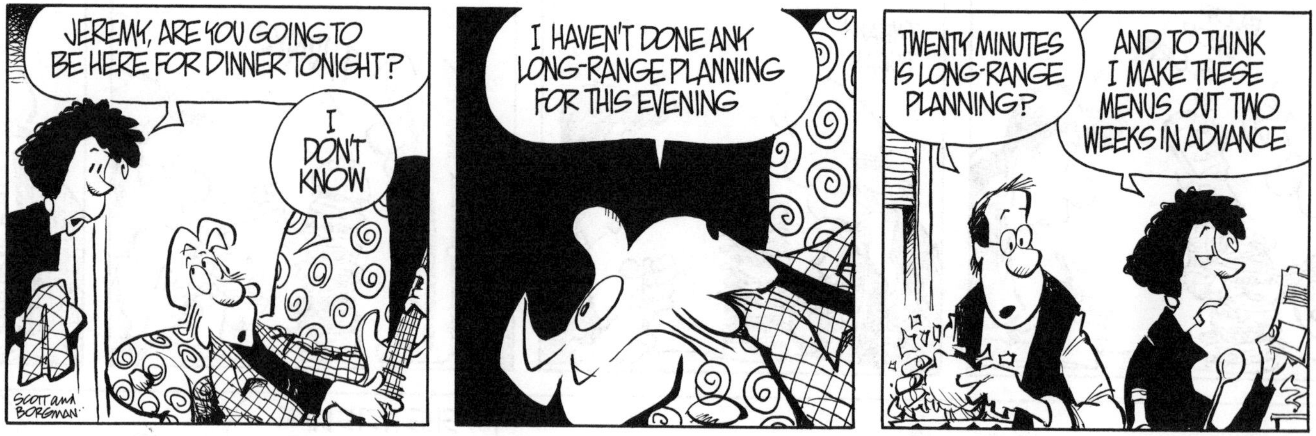
JEREMY, ARE YOU GOING TO BE HERE FOR DINNER TONIGHT?
I DON'T KNOW
I HAVEN'T DONE ANY LONG-RANGE PLANNING FOR THIS EVENING
TWENTY MINUTES IS LONG-RANGE PLANNING?
AND TO THINK I MAKE THESE MENUS OUT TWO WEEKS IN ADVANCE

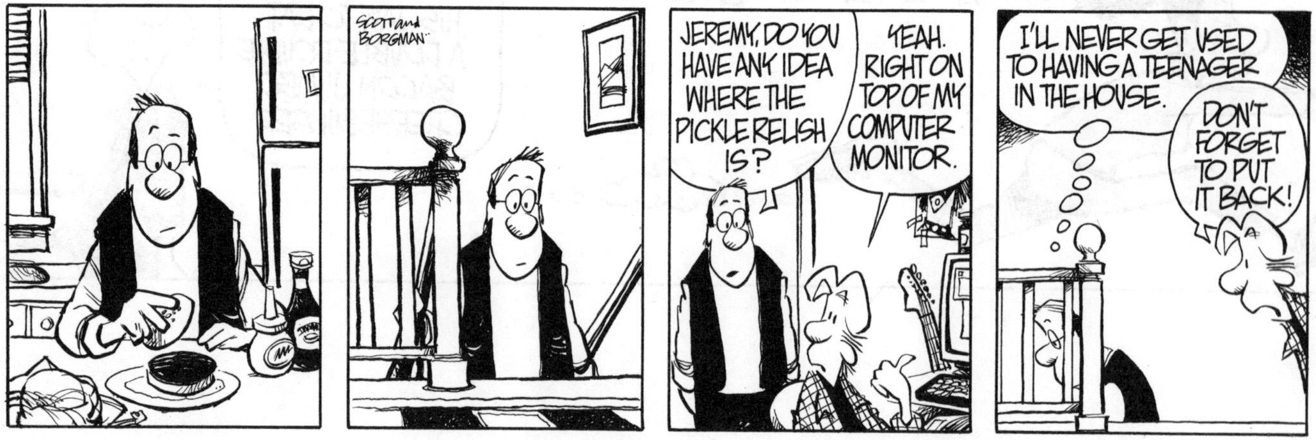
JEREMY, DO YOU HAVE ANY IDEA WHERE THE PICKLE RELISH IS?
YEAH. RIGHT ON TOP OF MY COMPUTER MONITOR.
I'LL NEVER GET USED TO HAVING A TEENAGER IN THE HOUSE.
DON'T FORGET TO PUT IT BACK!

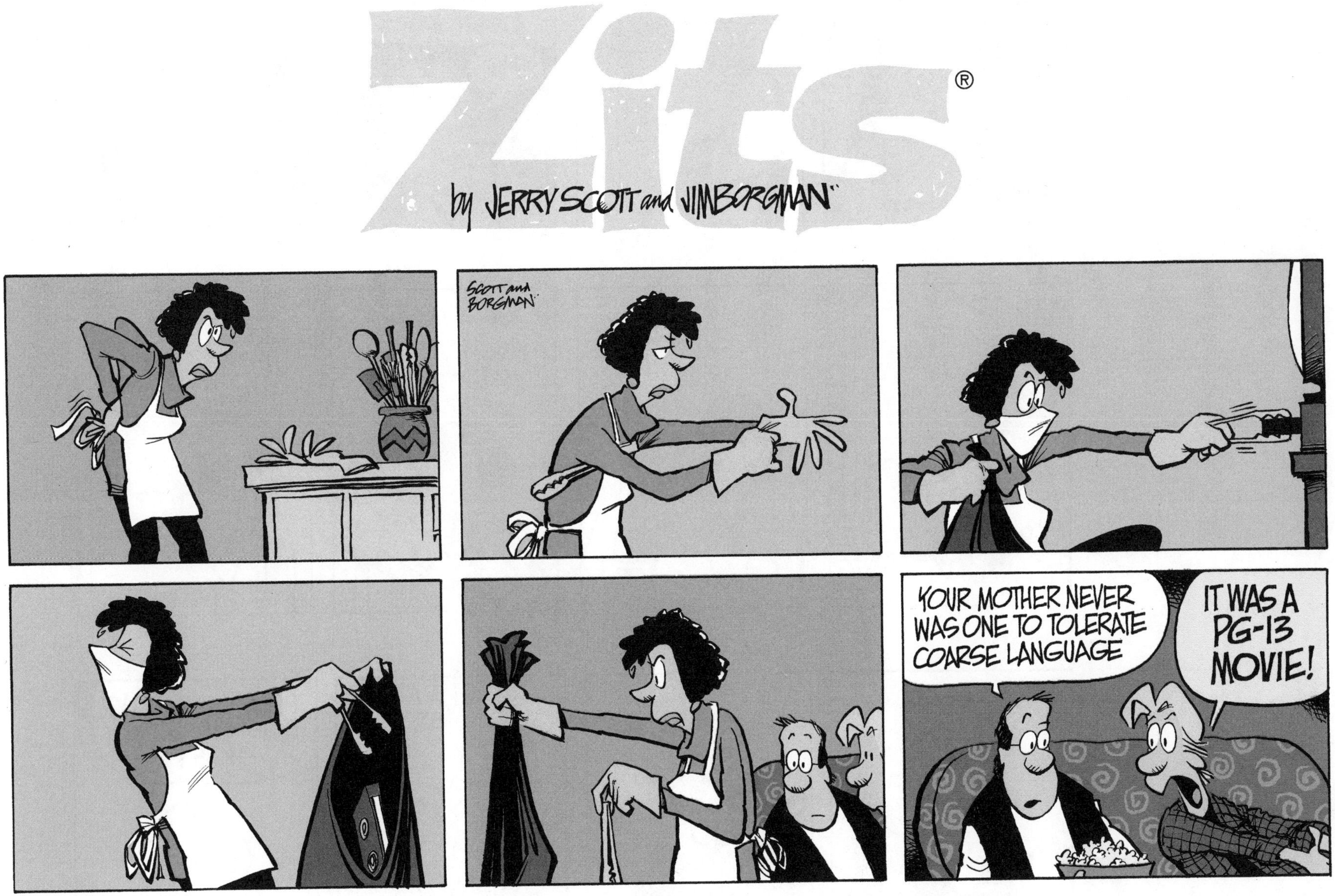
Zits®
by JERRY SCOTT and JIM BORGMAN
SCOTT and BORGMAN
YOUR MOTHER NEVER WAS ONE TO TOLERATE COARSE LANGUAGE
IT WAS A PG-13 MOVIE!

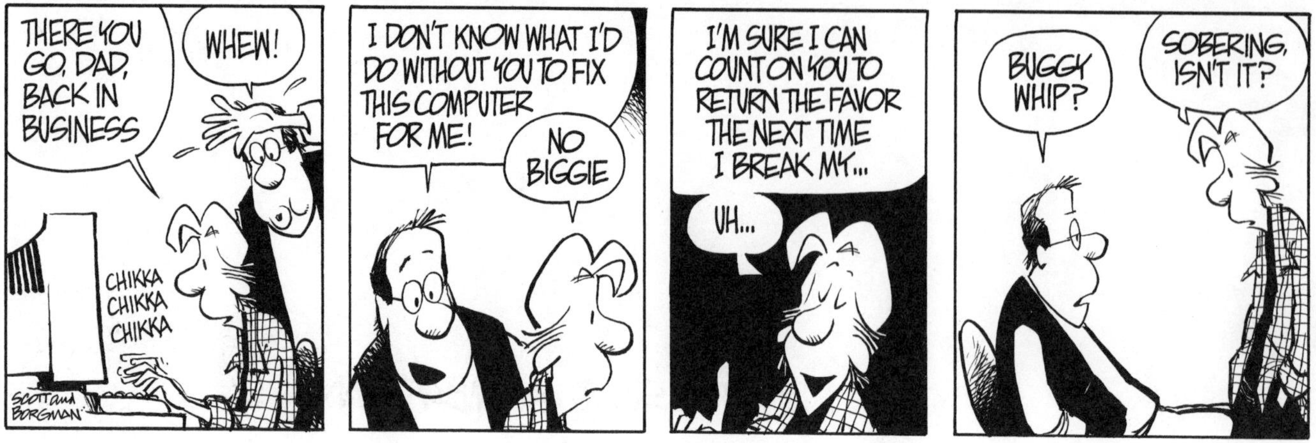
THERE YOU GO, DAD, BACK IN BUSINESS
WHEW!
CHIKKA CHIKKA CHIKKA
SCOTT and BORGMAN
I DON'T KNOW WHAT I'D DO WITHOUT YOU TO FIX THIS COMPUTER FOR ME!
NO BIGGIE
I'M SURE I CAN COUNT ON YOU TO RETURN THE FAVOR THE NEXT TIME I BREAK MY...
UH...
BUGGY WHIP?
SOBERING, ISN'T IT?

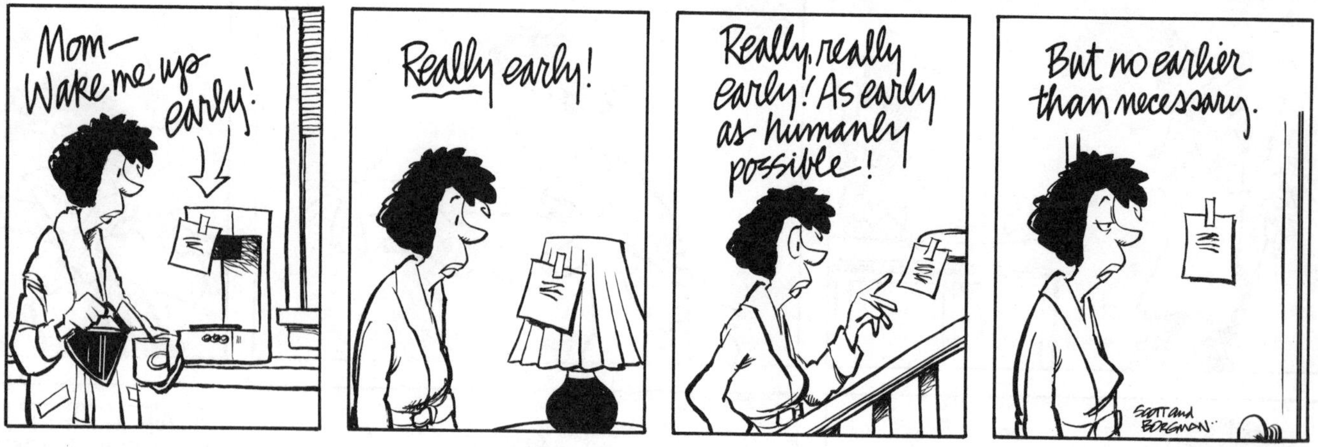
Mom— Wake me up early!
Really early!
Really, really early! As early as humanly possible!
But no earlier than necessary.
SCOTT and BORGMAN

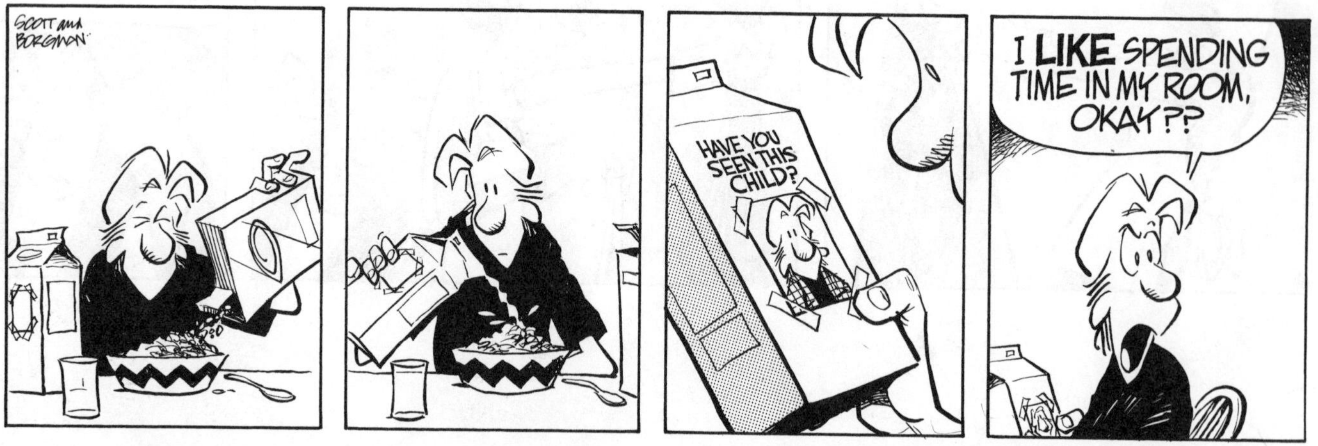
SCOTT and BORGMAN
HAVE YOU SEEN THIS CHILD?
I LIKE SPENDING TIME IN MY ROOM, OKAY??

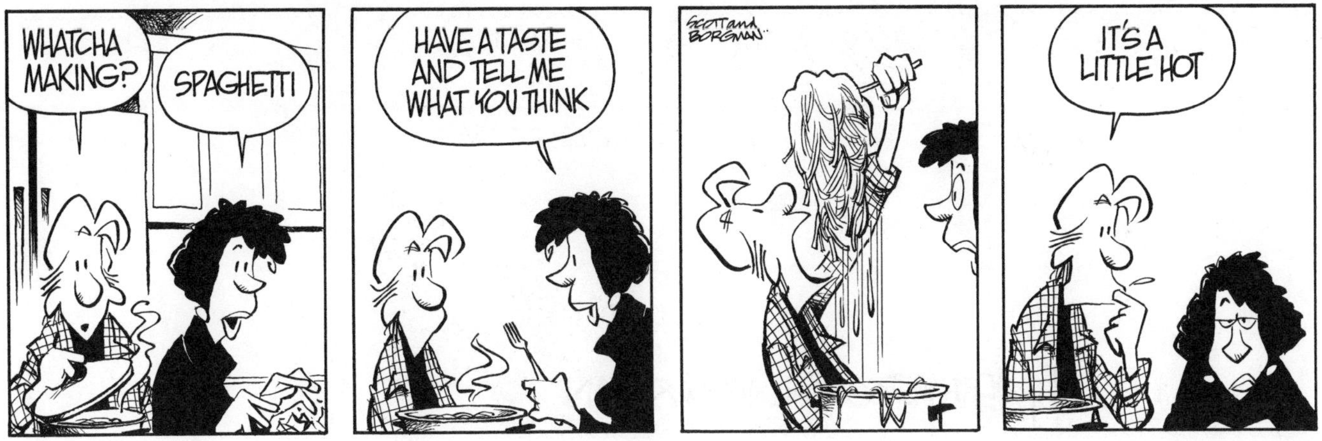
WHATCHA MAKING?
SPAGHETTI
HAVE A TASTE AND TELL ME WHAT YOU THINK
SCOTT and BORGMAN
IT'S A LITTLE HOT

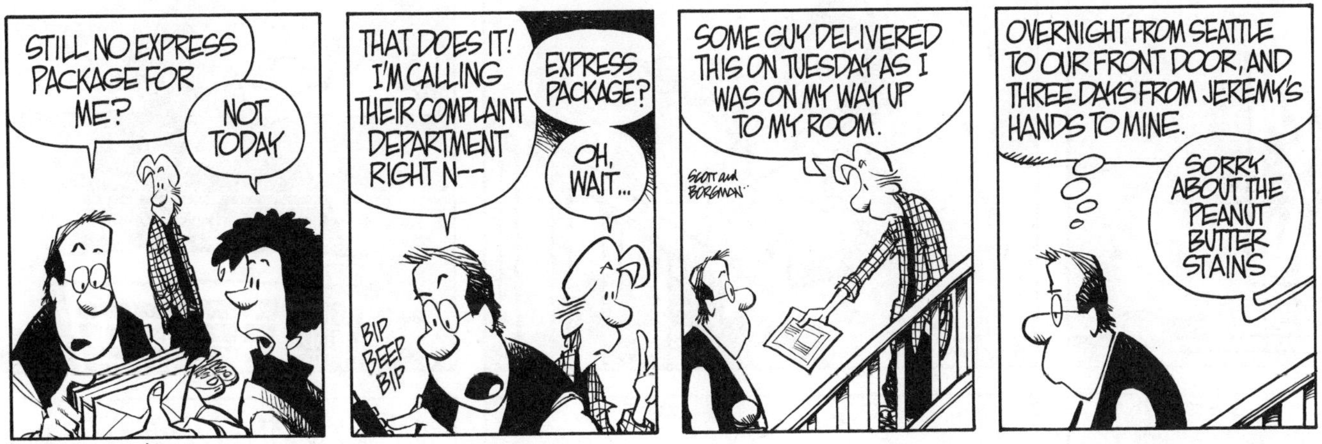
STILL NO EXPRESS PACKAGE FOR ME?
NOT TODAY
THAT DOES IT! I'M CALLING THEIR COMPLAINT DEPARTMENT RIGHT N--
EXPRESS PACKAGE?
OH, WAIT...
BIP BEEP BIP
SOME GUY DELIVERED THIS ON TUESDAY AS I WAS ON MY WAY UP TO MY ROOM.
SCOTT and BORGMAN
OVERNIGHT FROM SEATTLE TO OUR FRONT DOOR, AND THREE DAYS FROM JEREMY'S HANDS TO MINE.
SORRY ABOUT THE PEANUT BUTTER STAINS

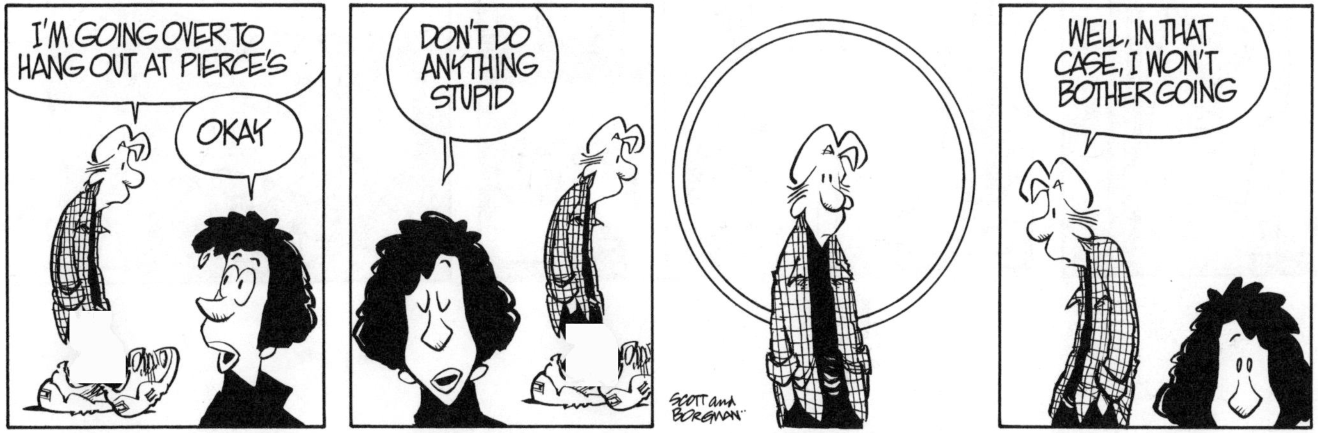
I'M GOING OVER TO HANG OUT AT PIERCE'S
OKAY
DON'T DO ANYTHING STUPID
SCOTT and BORGMAN
WELL, IN THAT CASE, I WON'T BOTHER GOING

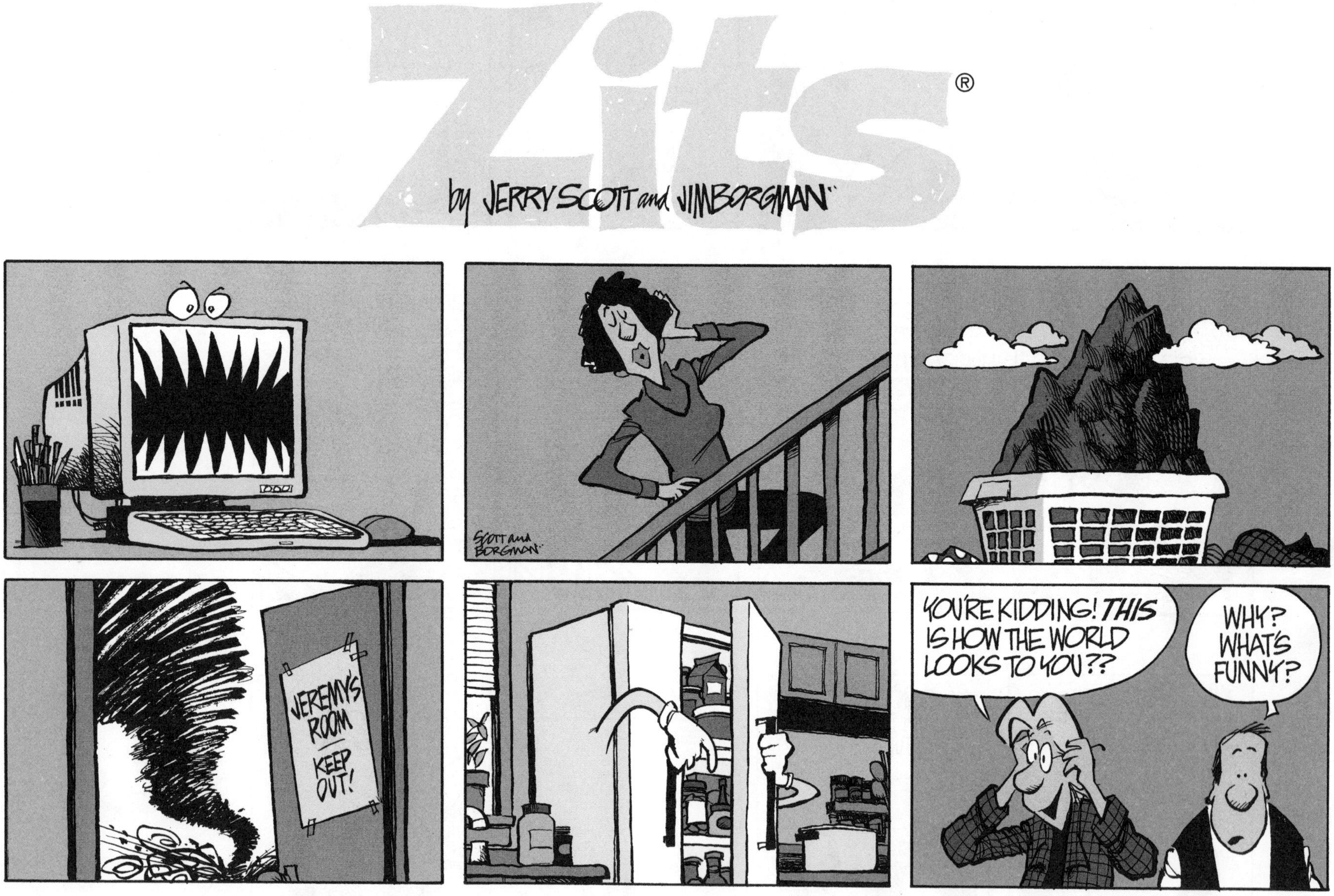
Zits®
by JERRY SCOTT and JIM BORGMAN
SCOTT AND BORGMAN
JEREMY'S ROOM — KEEP OUT!
YOU'RE KIDDING! THIS IS HOW THE WORLD LOOKS TO YOU??
WHY? WHAT'S FUNNY?

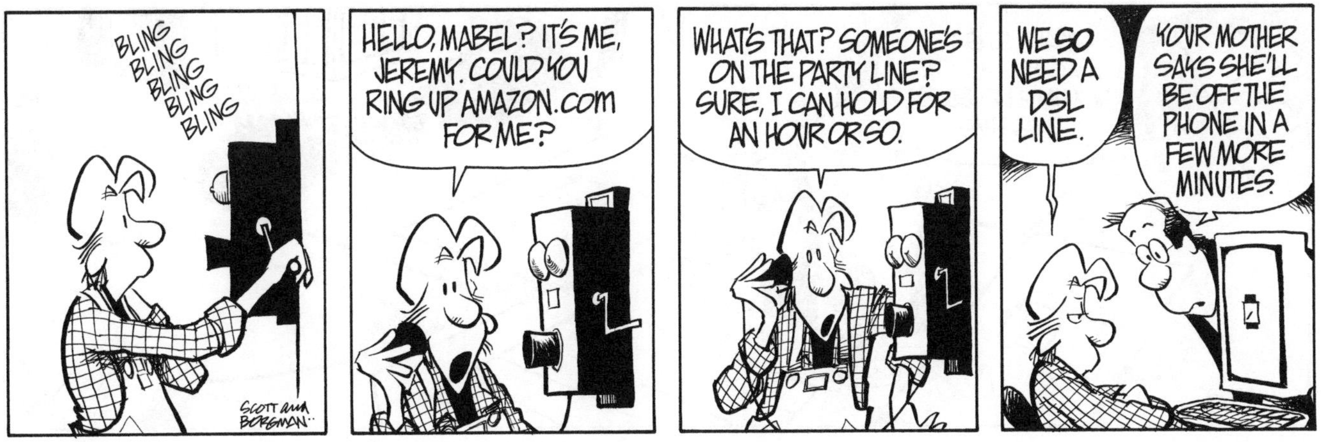
BLING BLING BLING BLING BLING
SCOTT and BORGMAN
HELLO, MABEL? IT'S ME, JEREMY. COULD YOU RING UP AMAZON.com FOR ME?
WHAT'S THAT? SOMEONE'S ON THE PARTY LINE? SURE, I CAN HOLD FOR AN HOUR OR SO.
WE SO NEED A DSL LINE.
YOUR MOTHER SAYS SHE'LL BE OFF THE PHONE IN A FEW MORE MINUTES.

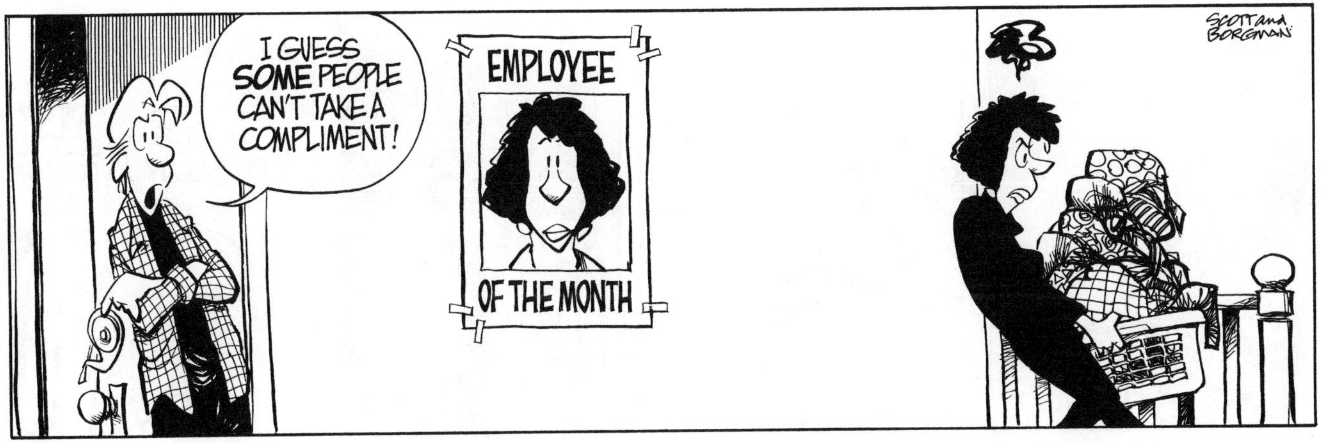
I GUESS SOME PEOPLE CAN'T TAKE A COMPLIMENT!
EMPLOYEE
OF THE MONTH
SCOTT and BORGMAN

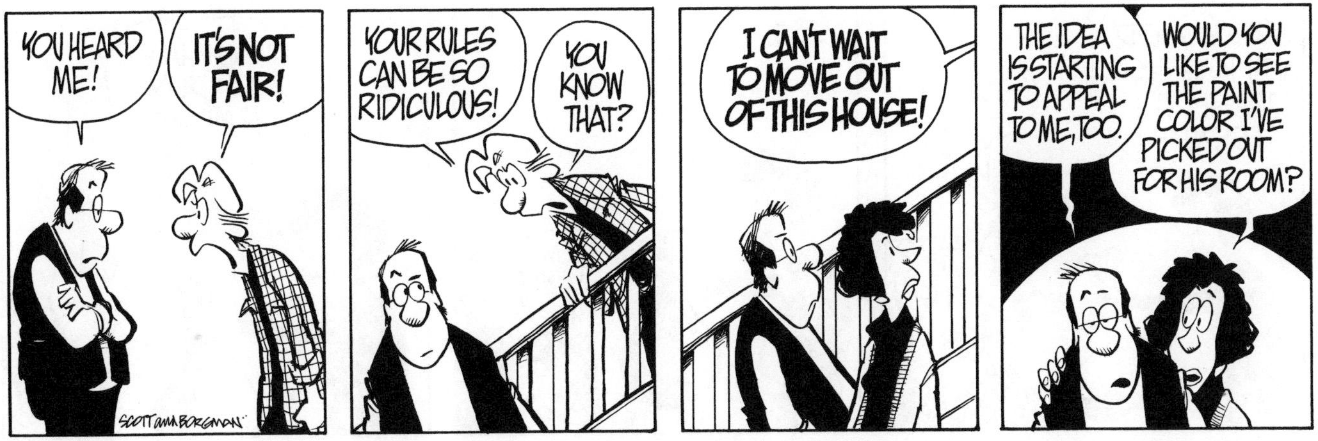
YOU HEARD ME!
IT'S NOT FAIR!
SCOTT and BORGMAN
YOUR RULES CAN BE SO RIDICULOUS!
YOU KNOW THAT?
I CAN'T WAIT TO MOVE OUT OF THIS HOUSE!
THE IDEA IS STARTING TO APPEAL TO ME, TOO.
WOULD YOU LIKE TO SEE THE PAINT COLOR I'VE PICKED OUT FOR HIS ROOM?

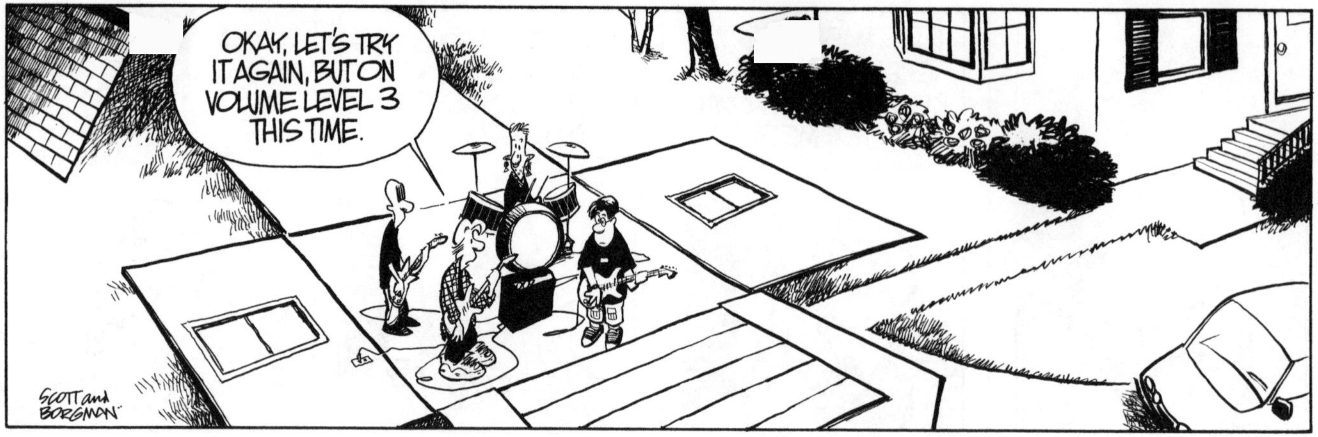
OKAY, LET'S TRY IT AGAIN, BUT ON VOLUME LEVEL 3 THIS TIME.
SCOTT and BORGMAN

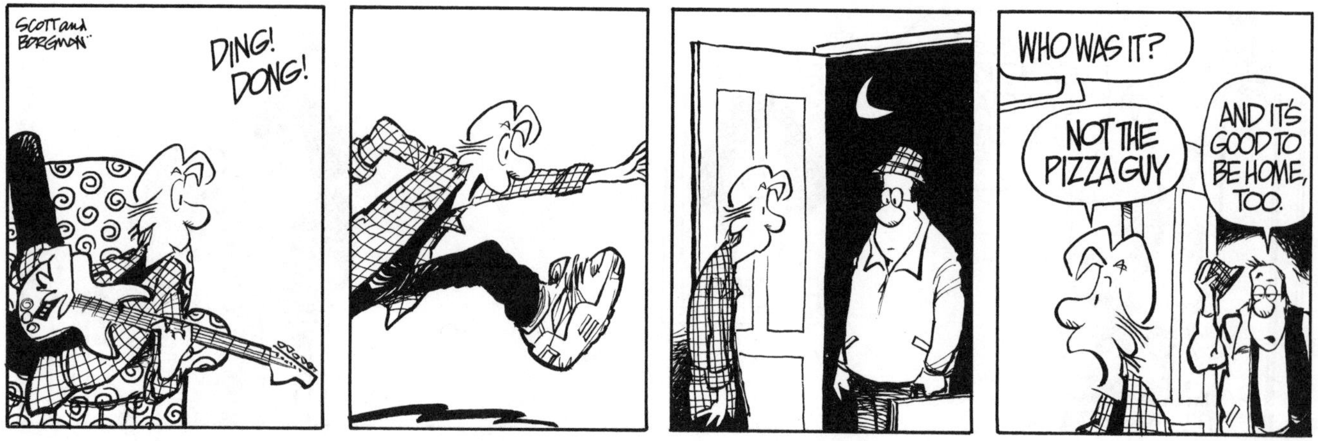
SCOTT and BORGMAN
DING! DONG!
WHO WAS IT?
NOT THE PIZZA GUY
AND IT'S GOOD TO BE HOME, TOO.

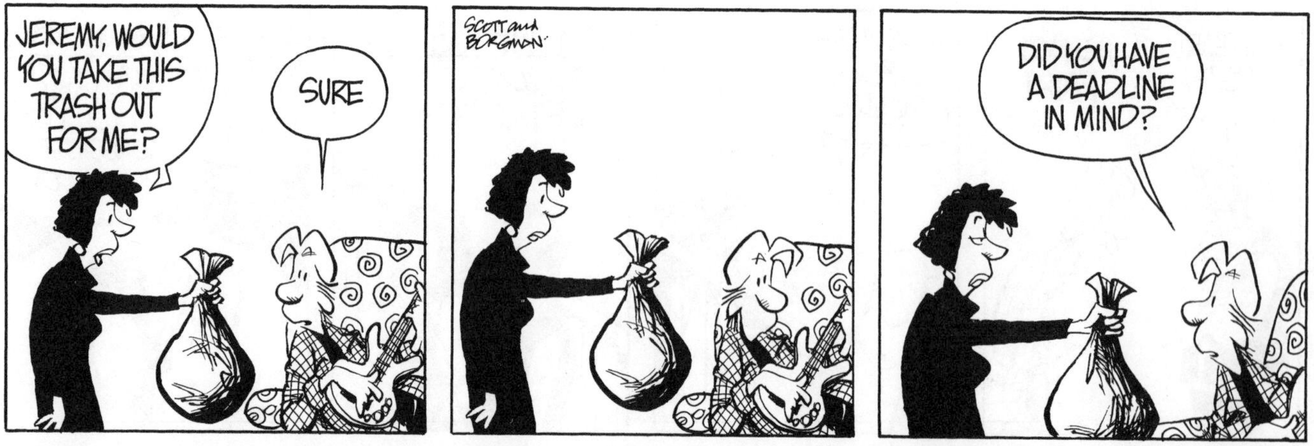
JEREMY, WOULD YOU TAKE THIS TRASH OUT FOR ME?
SURE
SCOTT and BORGMAN
DID YOU HAVE A DEADLINE IN MIND?

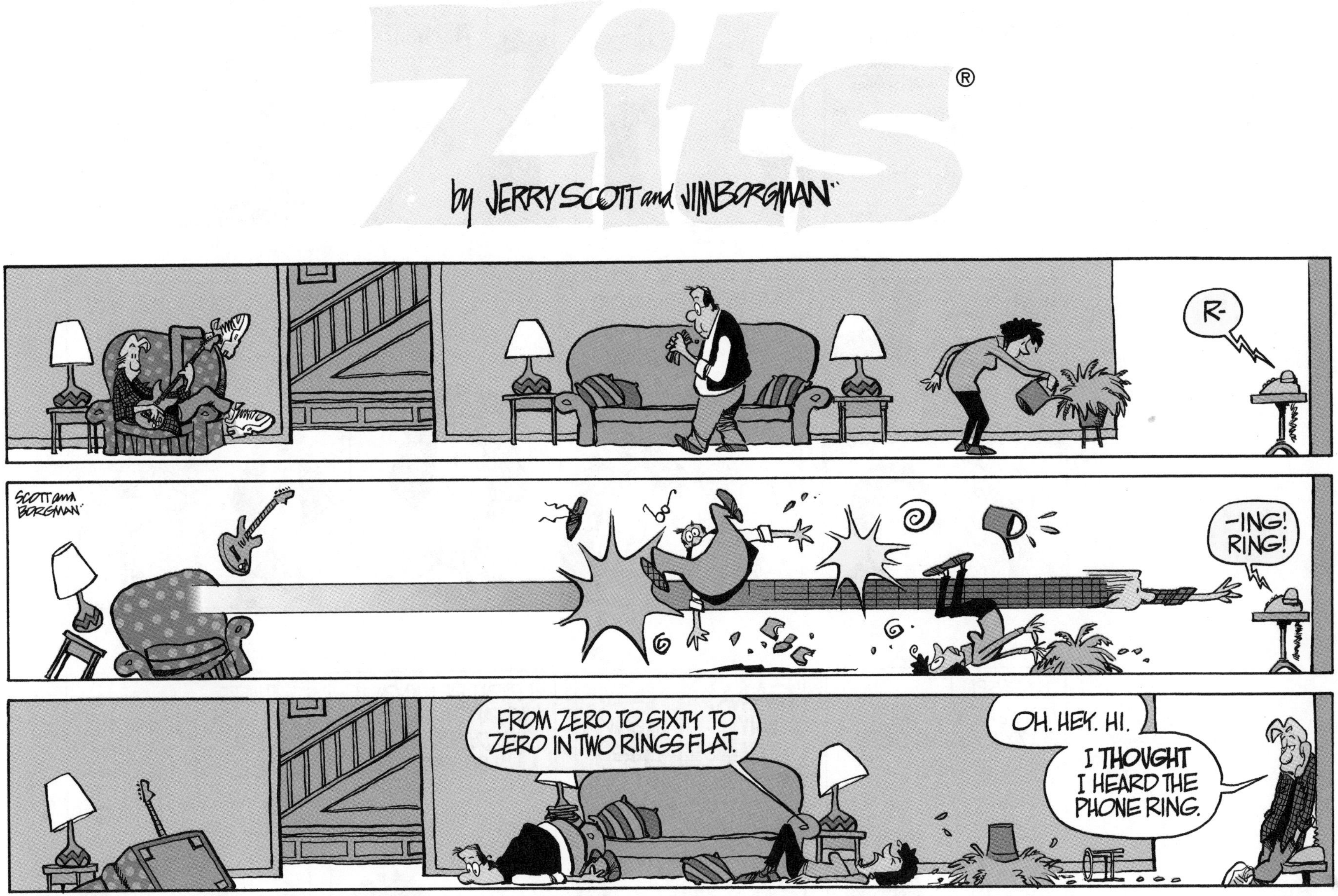
Zits®
by JERRY SCOTT and JIM BORGMAN
R-
SCOTT and BORGMAN
-ING! RING!
FROM ZERO TO SIXTY TO ZERO IN TWO RINGS FLAT.
OH. HEY. HI.
I THOUGHT I HEARD THE PHONE RING.

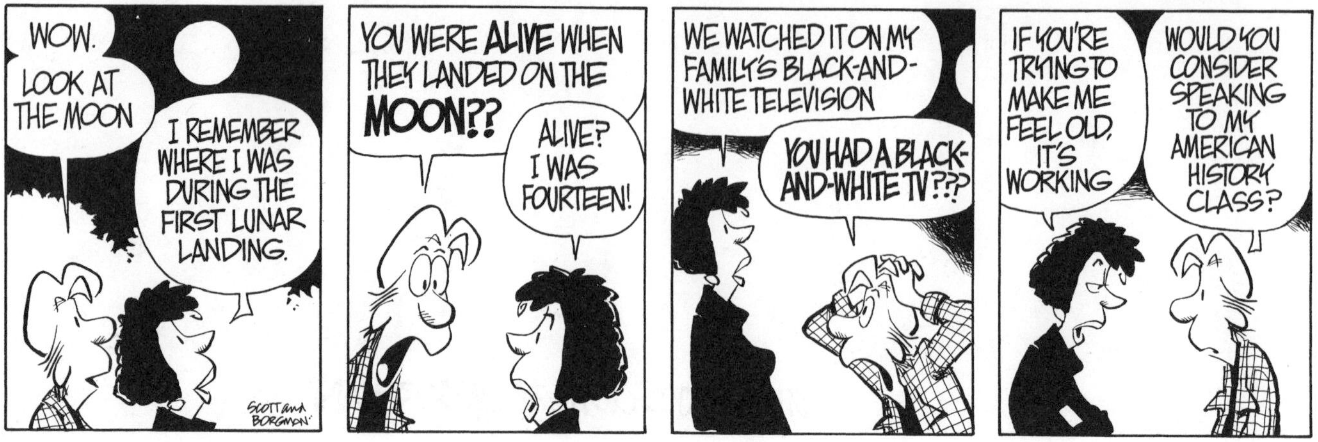
WOW.
LOOK AT THE MOON
I REMEMBER WHERE I WAS DURING THE FIRST LUNAR LANDING.
YOU WERE **ALIVE** WHEN THEY LANDED ON THE **MOON??**
ALIVE? I WAS FOURTEEN!
WE WATCHED IT ON MY FAMILY'S BLACK-AND-WHITE TELEVISION
YOU HAD A BLACK-AND-WHITE TV???
IF YOU'RE TRYING TO MAKE ME FEEL OLD, IT'S WORKING
WOULD YOU CONSIDER SPEAKING TO MY AMERICAN HISTORY CLASS?

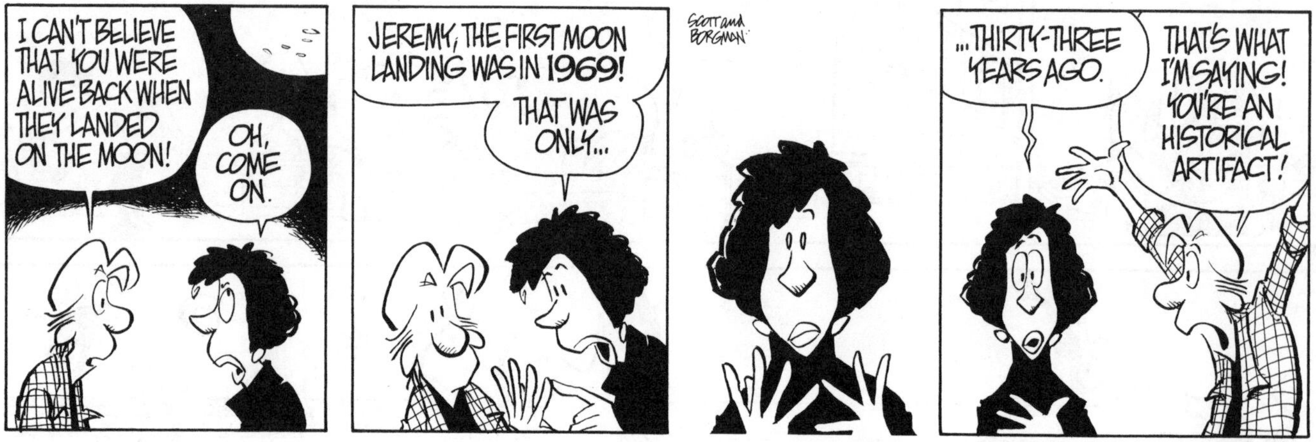
I CAN'T BELIEVE THAT YOU WERE ALIVE BACK WHEN THEY LANDED ON THE MOON!
OH, COME ON.
JEREMY, THE FIRST MOON LANDING WAS IN 1969!
THAT WAS ONLY...
...THIRTY-THREE YEARS AGO.
THAT'S WHAT I'M SAYING! YOU'RE AN HISTORICAL ARTIFACT!

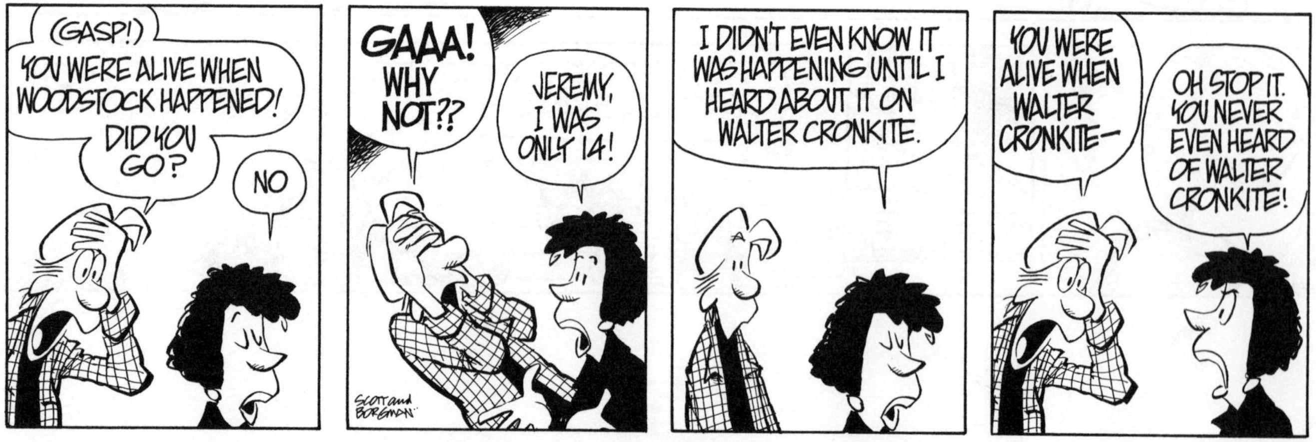
(GASP!)
YOU WERE ALIVE WHEN WOODSTOCK HAPPENED!
DID YOU GO?
NO
GAAA! WHY NOT??
JEREMY, I WAS ONLY 14!
I DIDN'T EVEN KNOW IT WAS HAPPENING UNTIL I HEARD ABOUT IT ON WALTER CRONKITE.
YOU WERE ALIVE WHEN WALTER CRONKITE—
OH STOP IT. YOU NEVER EVEN HEARD OF WALTER CRONKITE!

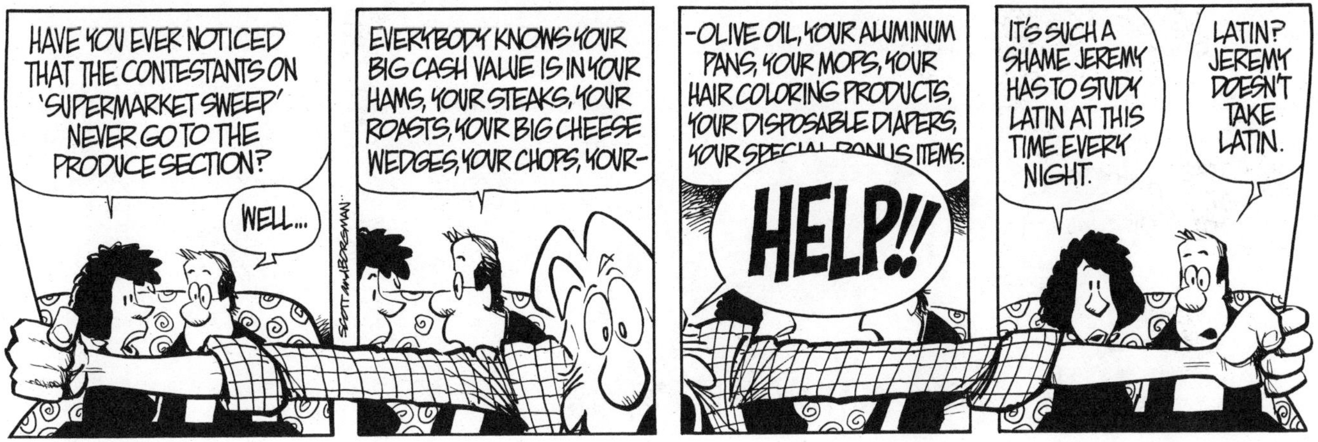
HAVE YOU EVER NOTICED THAT THE CONTESTANTS ON 'SUPERMARKET SWEEP' NEVER GO TO THE PRODUCE SECTION?
WELL...
EVERYBODY KNOWS YOUR BIG CASH VALUE IS IN YOUR HAMS, YOUR STEAKS, YOUR ROASTS, YOUR BIG CHEESE WEDGES, YOUR CHOPS, YOUR-
-OLIVE OIL, YOUR ALUMINUM PANS, YOUR MOPS, YOUR HAIR COLORING PRODUCTS, YOUR DISPOSABLE DIAPERS, YOUR SPECIAL BONUS ITEMS.
HELP!!
IT'S SUCH A SHAME JEREMY HAS TO STUDY LATIN AT THIS TIME EVERY NIGHT.
LATIN? JEREMY DOESN'T TAKE LATIN.

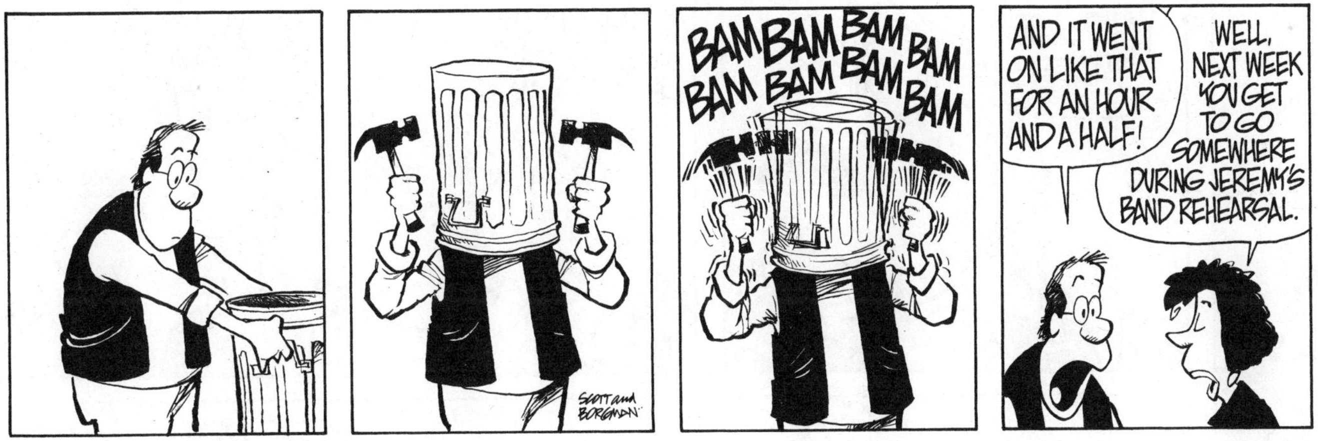
BAM BAM BAM BAM BAM BAM BAM BAM BAM BAM
AND IT WENT ON LIKE THAT FOR AN HOUR AND A HALF!
WELL, NEXT WEEK YOU GET TO GO SOMEWHERE DURING JEREMY'S BAND REHEARSAL.

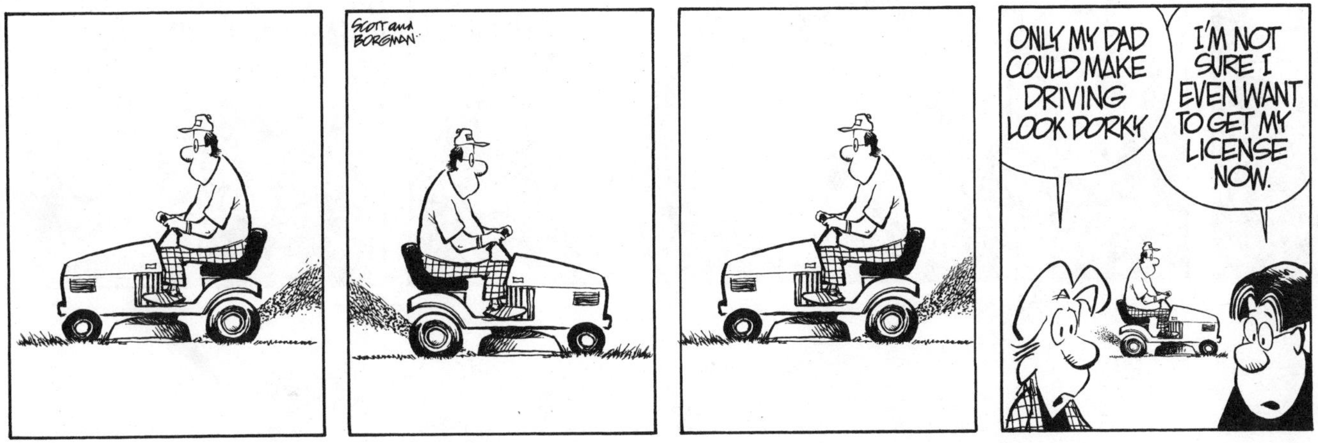
ONLY MY DAD COULD MAKE DRIVING LOOK DORKY.
I'M NOT SURE I EVEN WANT TO GET MY LICENSE NOW.

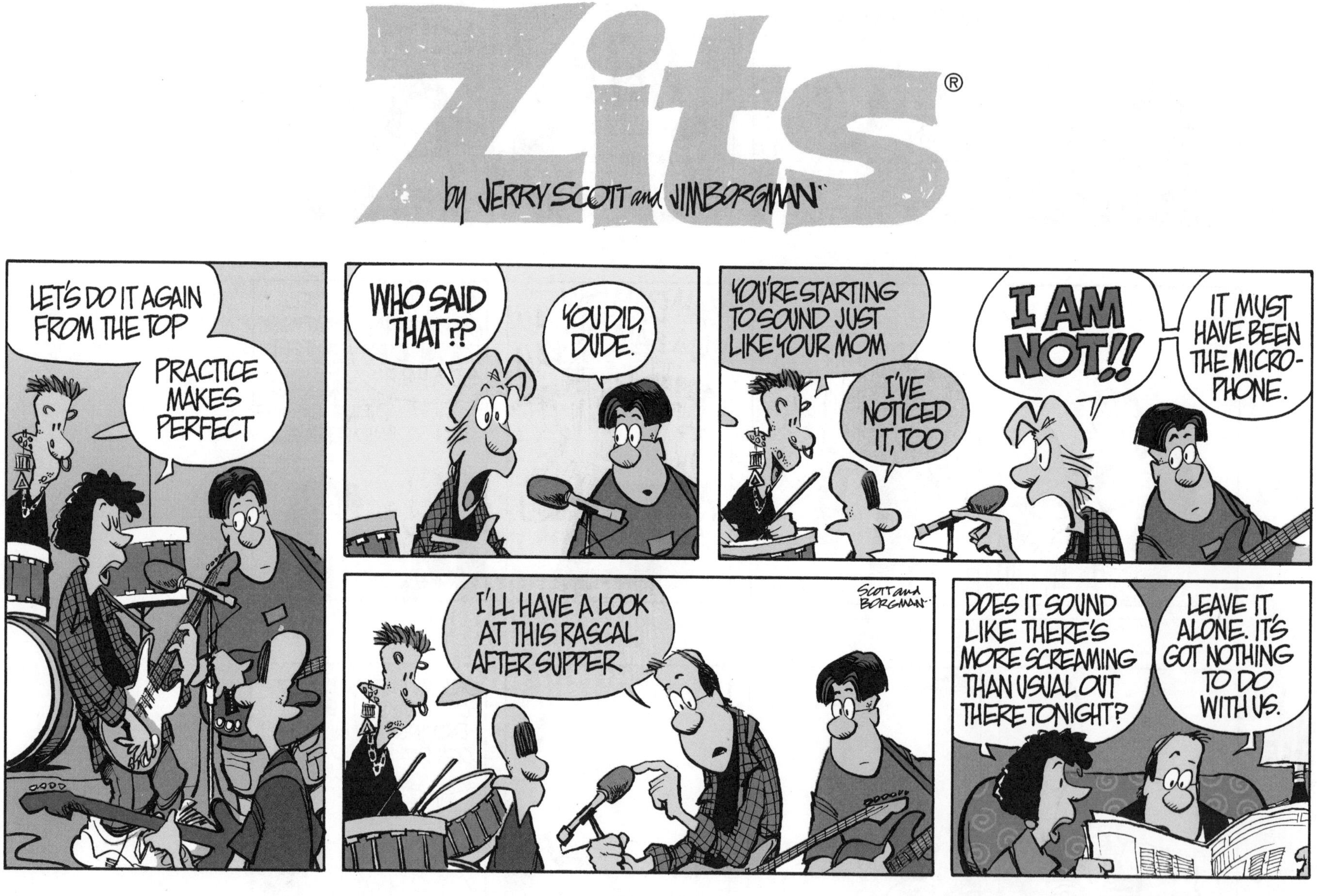

Zits®
by JERRY SCOTT and JIM BORGMAN
LET'S DO IT AGAIN FROM THE TOP
PRACTICE MAKES PERFECT
WHO SAID THAT??
YOU DID, DUDE.
YOU'RE STARTING TO SOUND JUST LIKE YOUR MOM
I'VE NOTICED IT, TOO
I AM NOT!!
IT MUST HAVE BEEN THE MICROPHONE.
SCOTT and BORGMAN
I'LL HAVE A LOOK AT THIS RASCAL AFTER SUPPER
DOES IT SOUND LIKE THERE'S MORE SCREAMING THAN USUAL OUT THERE TONIGHT?
LEAVE IT ALONE. IT'S GOT NOTHING TO DO WITH US.

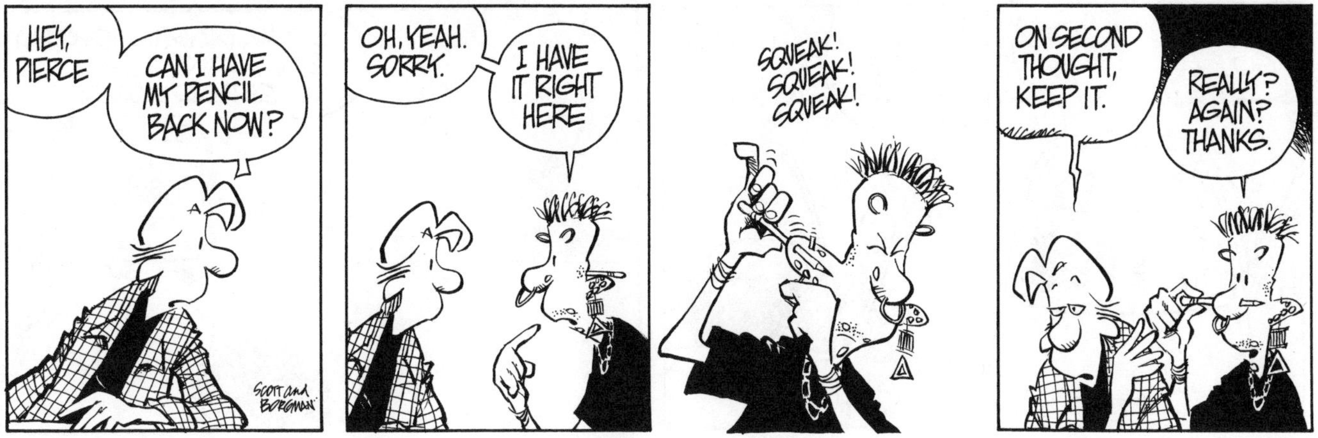
HEY, PIERCE
CAN I HAVE MY PENCIL BACK NOW?
SCOTT and BORGMAN
OH, YEAH. SORRY.
I HAVE IT RIGHT HERE
SQUEAK! SQUEAK! SQUEAK!
ON SECOND THOUGHT, KEEP IT.
REALLY? AGAIN? THANKS.

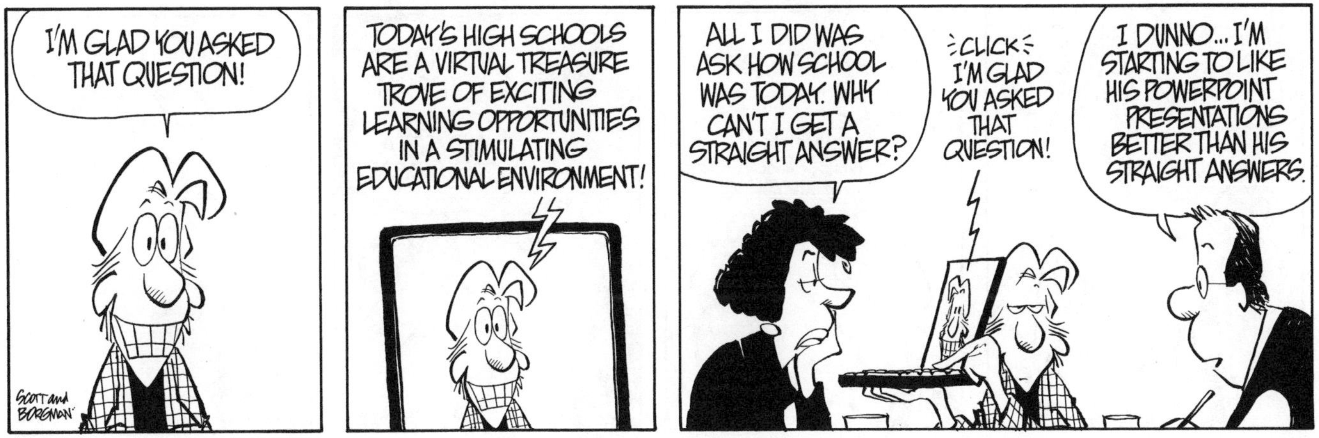
I'M GLAD YOU ASKED THAT QUESTION!
SCOTT and BORGMAN
TODAY'S HIGH SCHOOLS ARE A VIRTUAL TREASURE TROVE OF EXCITING LEARNING OPPORTUNITIES IN A STIMULATING EDUCATIONAL ENVIRONMENT!
ALL I DID WAS ASK HOW SCHOOL WAS TODAY. WHY CAN'T I GET A STRAIGHT ANSWER?
CLICK
I'M GLAD YOU ASKED THAT QUESTION!
I DUNNO... I'M STARTING TO LIKE HIS POWERPOINT PRESENTATIONS BETTER THAN HIS STRAIGHT ANSWERS.

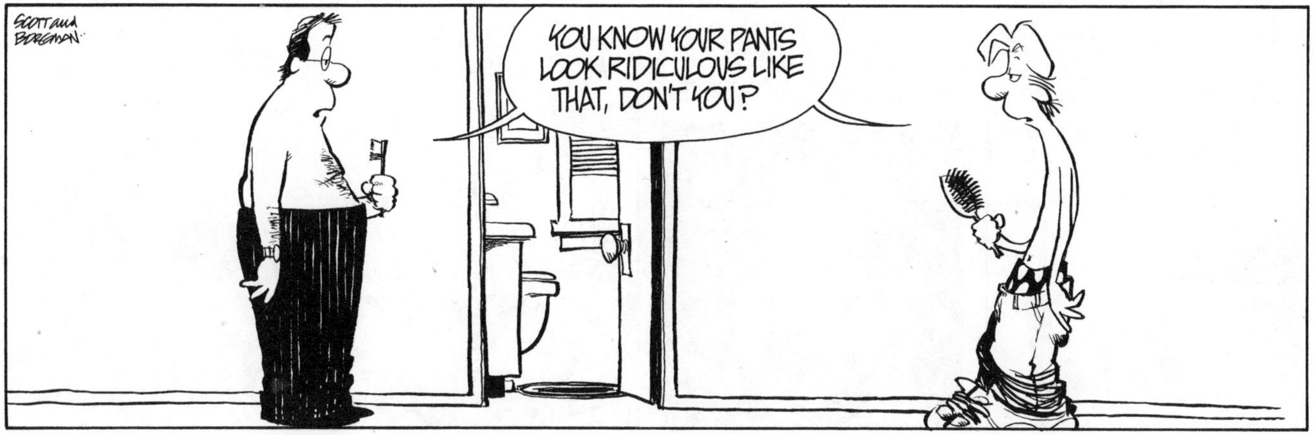
SCOTT and BORGMAN
YOU KNOW YOUR PANTS LOOK RIDICULOUS LIKE THAT, DON'T YOU?

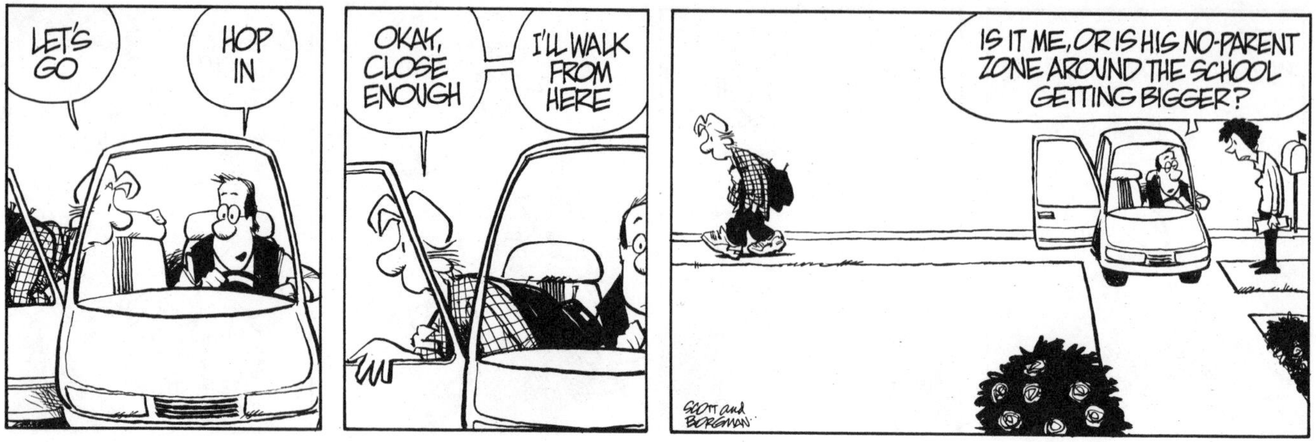
LET'S GO
HOP IN
OKAY, CLOSE ENOUGH
I'LL WALK FROM HERE
IS IT ME, OR IS HIS NO-PARENT ZONE AROUND THE SCHOOL GETTING BIGGER?
SCOTT and BORGMAN

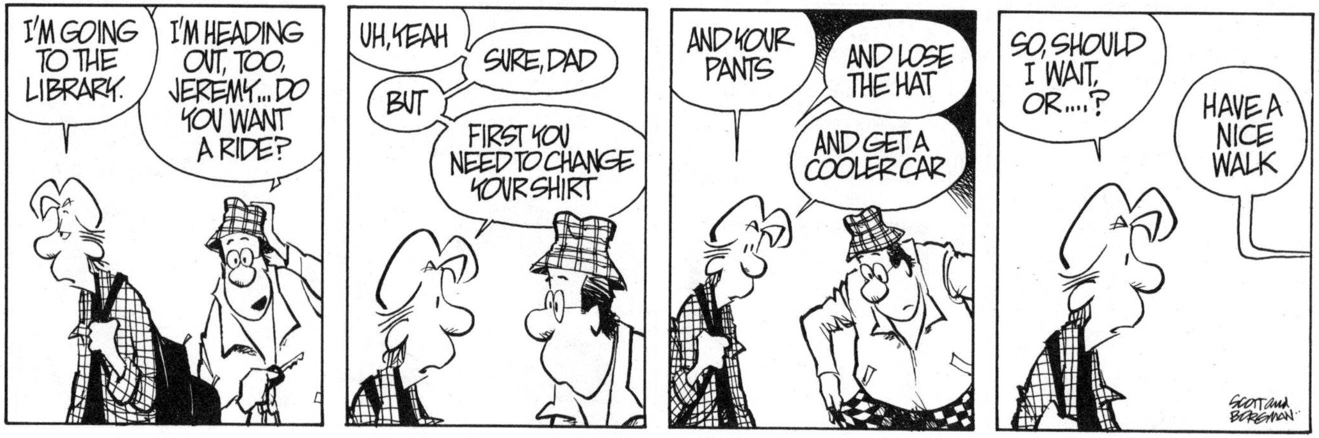
I'M GOING TO THE LIBRARY.
I'M HEADING OUT, TOO, JEREMY... DO YOU WANT A RIDE?
UH, YEAH
SURE, DAD
BUT
FIRST YOU NEED TO CHANGE YOUR SHIRT
AND YOUR PANTS
AND LOSE THE HAT
AND GET A COOLER CAR
SO, SHOULD I WAIT, OR....?
HAVE A NICE WALK
SCOTT and BORGMAN

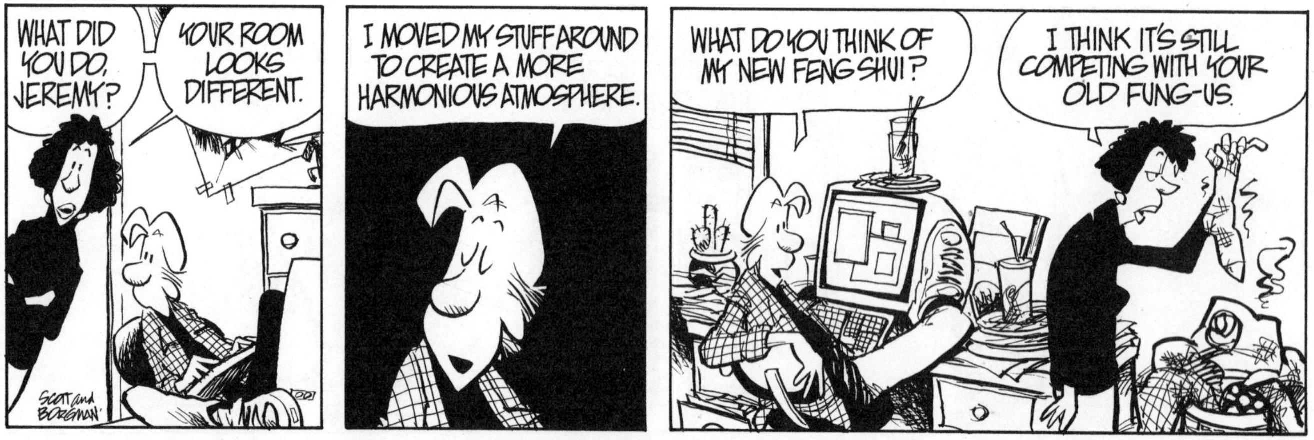
WHAT DID YOU DO, JEREMY?
YOUR ROOM LOOKS DIFFERENT.
I MOVED MY STUFF AROUND TO CREATE A MORE HARMONIOUS ATMOSPHERE.
WHAT DO YOU THINK OF MY NEW FENG SHUI?
I THINK IT'S STILL COMPETING WITH YOUR OLD FUNG-US.
SCOTT and BORGMAN

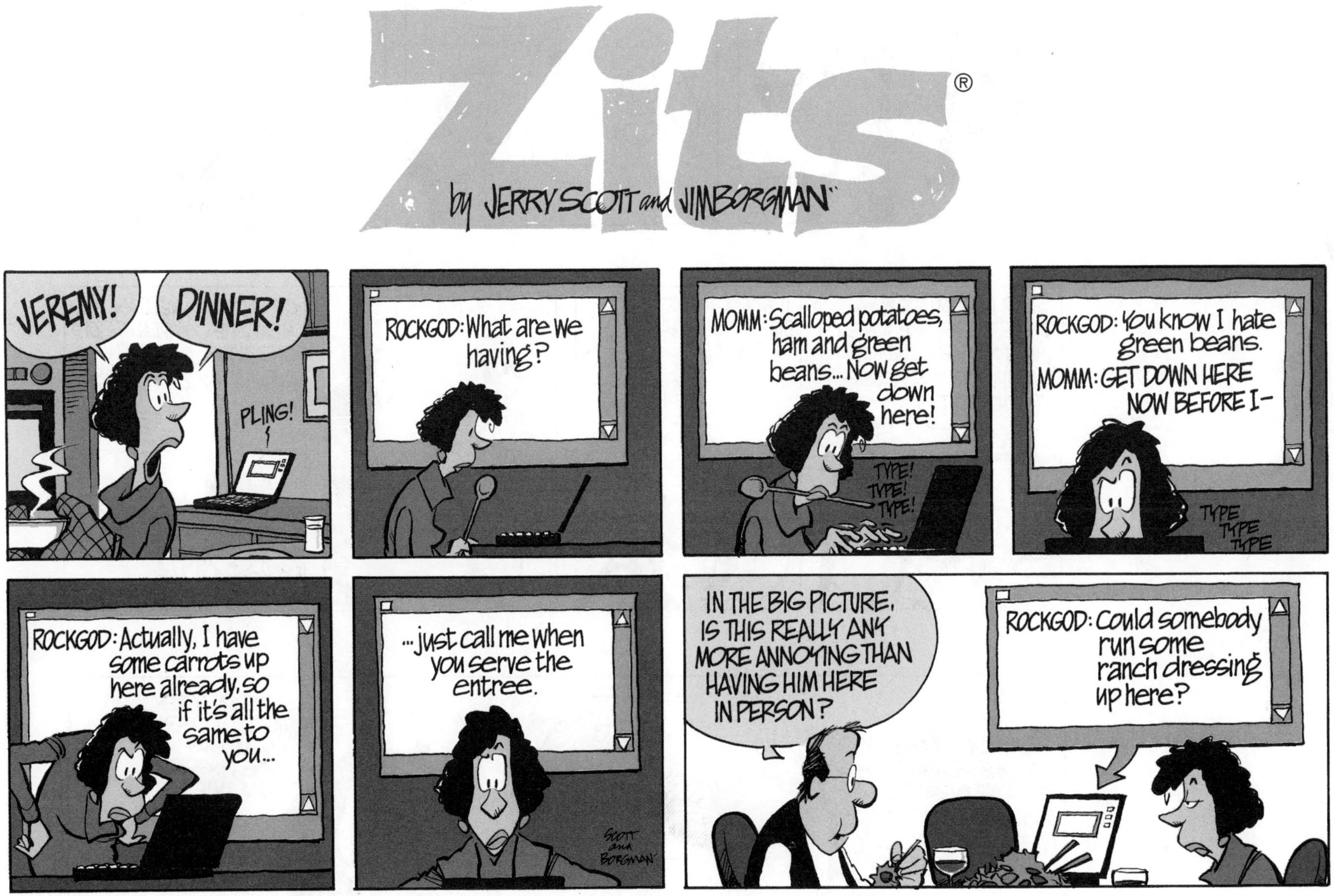
Zits®
by JERRY SCOTT and JIM BORGMAN
JEREMY!
DINNER!
PLING!
ROCKGOD: What are we having?
MOMM: Scalloped potatoes, ham and green beans... Now get down here!
TYPE! TYPE! TYPE!
ROCKGOD: You know I hate green beans.
MOMM: GET DOWN HERE NOW BEFORE I-
TYPE TYPE TYPE
ROCKGOD: Actually, I have some carrots up here already, so if it's all the same to you...
...just call me when you serve the entree.
SCOTT and BORGMAN
IN THE BIG PICTURE, IS THIS REALLY ANY MORE ANNOYING THAN HAVING HIM HERE IN PERSON?
ROCKGOD: Could somebody run some ranch dressing up here?

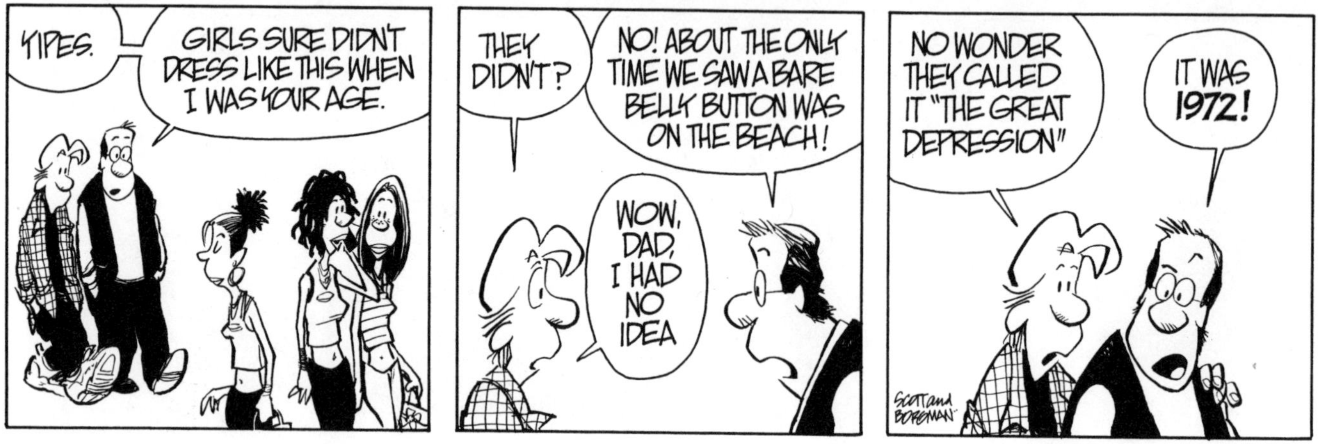
YIPES.
GIRLS SURE DIDN'T DRESS LIKE THIS WHEN I WAS YOUR AGE.
THEY DIDN'T?
NO! ABOUT THE ONLY TIME WE SAW A BARE BELLY BUTTON WAS ON THE BEACH!
WOW, DAD, I HAD NO IDEA
NO WONDER THEY CALLED IT "THE GREAT DEPRESSION"
IT WAS 1972!
SCOTT and BORGMAN

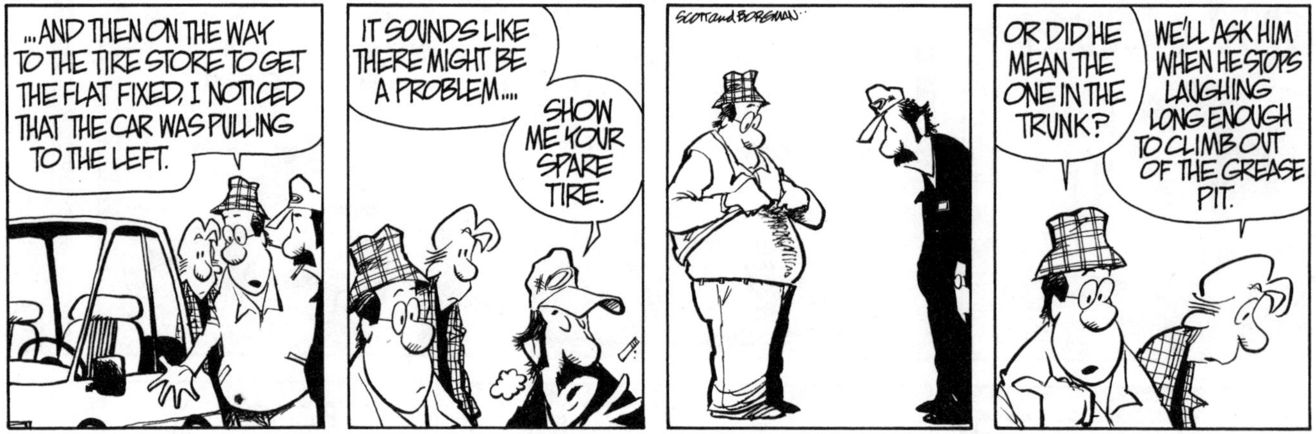
...AND THEN ON THE WAY TO THE TIRE STORE TO GET THE FLAT FIXED, I NOTICED THAT THE CAR WAS PULLING TO THE LEFT.
IT SOUNDS LIKE THERE MIGHT BE A PROBLEM....
SHOW ME YOUR SPARE TIRE.
SCOTT and BORGMAN
OR DID HE MEAN THE ONE IN THE TRUNK?
WE'LL ASK HIM WHEN HE STOPS LAUGHING LONG ENOUGH TO CLIMB OUT OF THE GREASE PIT.

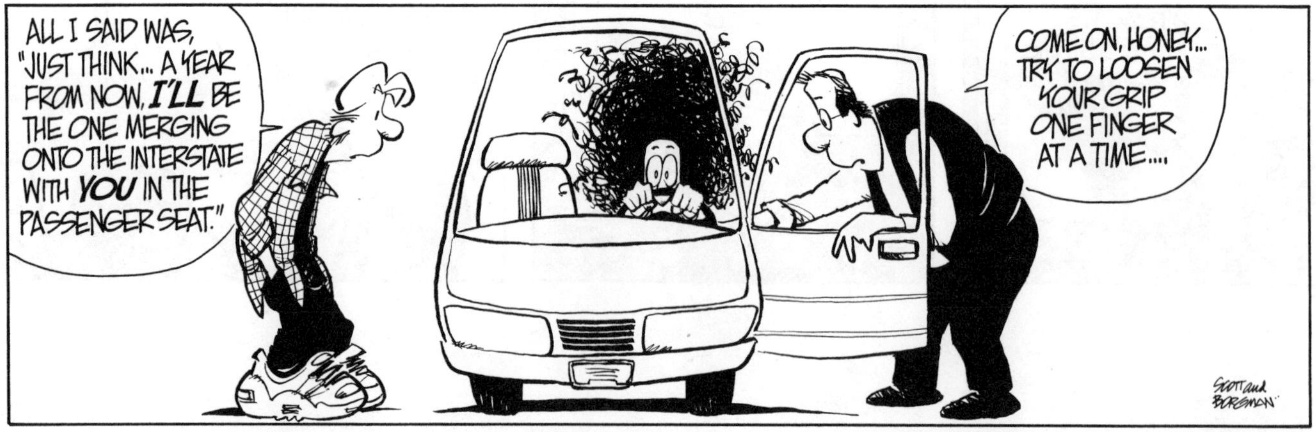
ALL I SAID WAS, "JUST THINK... A YEAR FROM NOW, I'LL BE THE ONE MERGING ONTO THE INTERSTATE WITH YOU IN THE PASSENGER SEAT."
COME ON, HONEY... TRY TO LOOSEN YOUR GRIP ONE FINGER AT A TIME....
SCOTT and BORGMAN

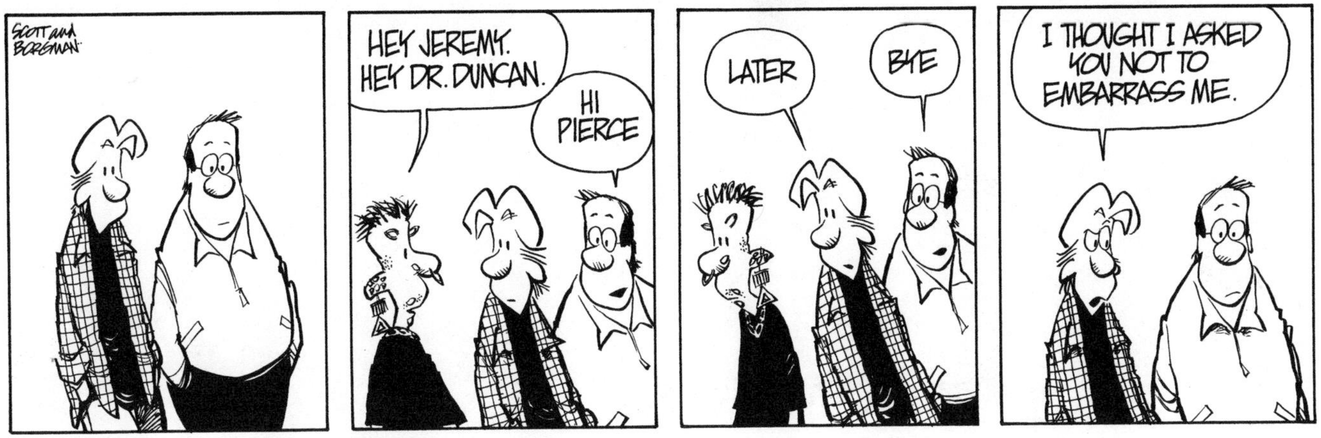
SCOTT AND BORGMAN
HEY JEREMY. HEY DR. DUNCAN.
HI PIERCE
LATER
BYE
I THOUGHT I ASKED YOU NOT TO EMBARRASS ME.

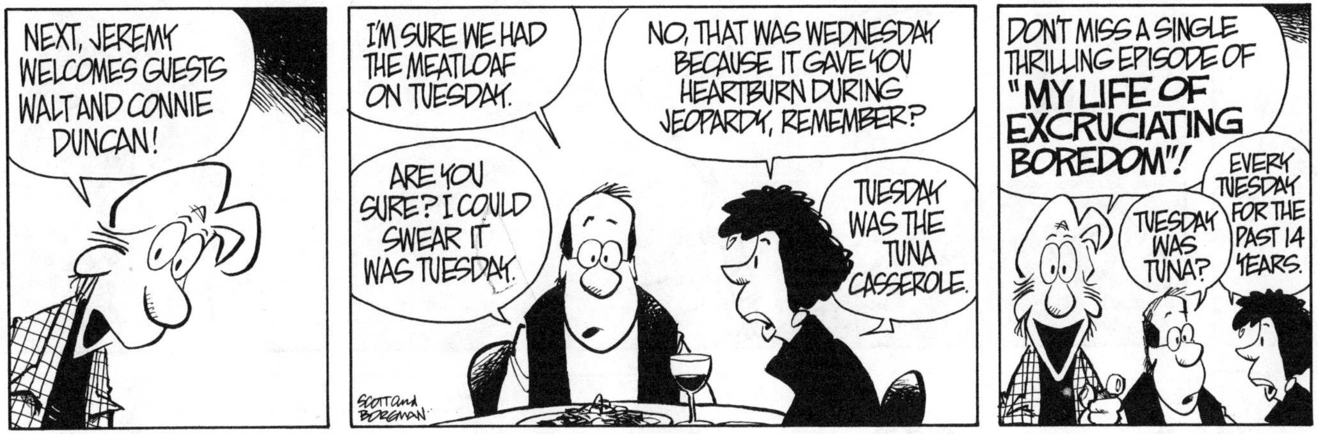
NEXT, JEREMY WELCOMES GUESTS WALT AND CONNIE DUNCAN!
I'M SURE WE HAD THE MEATLOAF ON TUESDAY.
NO, THAT WAS WEDNESDAY BECAUSE IT GAVE YOU HEARTBURN DURING JEOPARDY, REMEMBER?
ARE YOU SURE? I COULD SWEAR IT WAS TUESDAY.
TUESDAY WAS THE TUNA CASSEROLE.
SCOTT AND BORGMAN
DON'T MISS A SINGLE THRILLING EPISODE OF "MY LIFE OF EXCRUCIATING BOREDOM"!
TUESDAY WAS TUNA?
EVERY TUESDAY FOR THE PAST 14 YEARS.

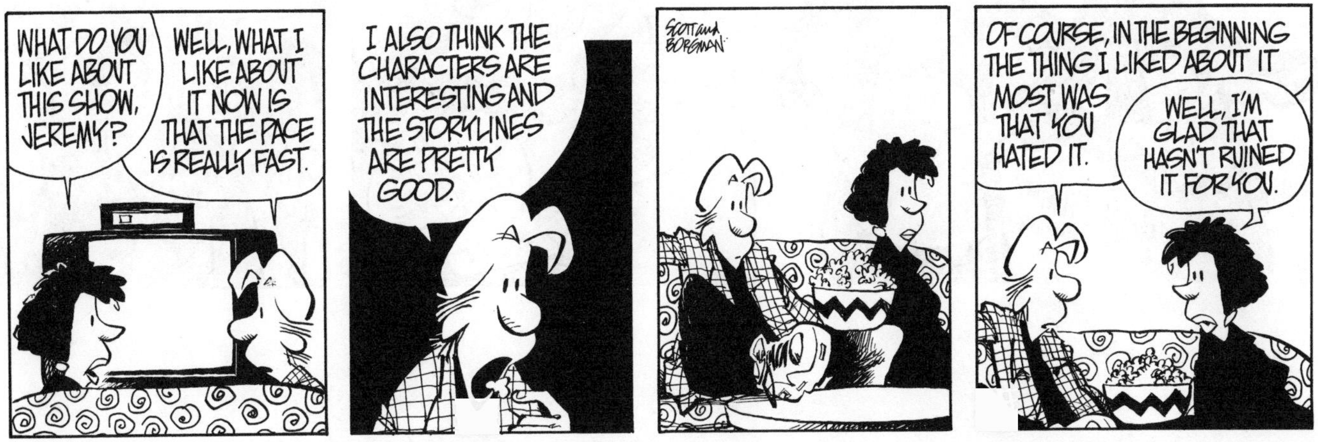
WHAT DO YOU LIKE ABOUT THIS SHOW, JEREMY?
WELL, WHAT I LIKE ABOUT IT NOW IS THAT THE PACE IS REALLY FAST.
I ALSO THINK THE CHARACTERS ARE INTERESTING AND THE STORYLINES ARE PRETTY GOOD.
SCOTT AND BORGMAN
OF COURSE, IN THE BEGINNING THE THING I LIKED ABOUT IT MOST WAS THAT YOU HATED IT.
WELL, I'M GLAD THAT HASN'T RUINED IT FOR YOU.

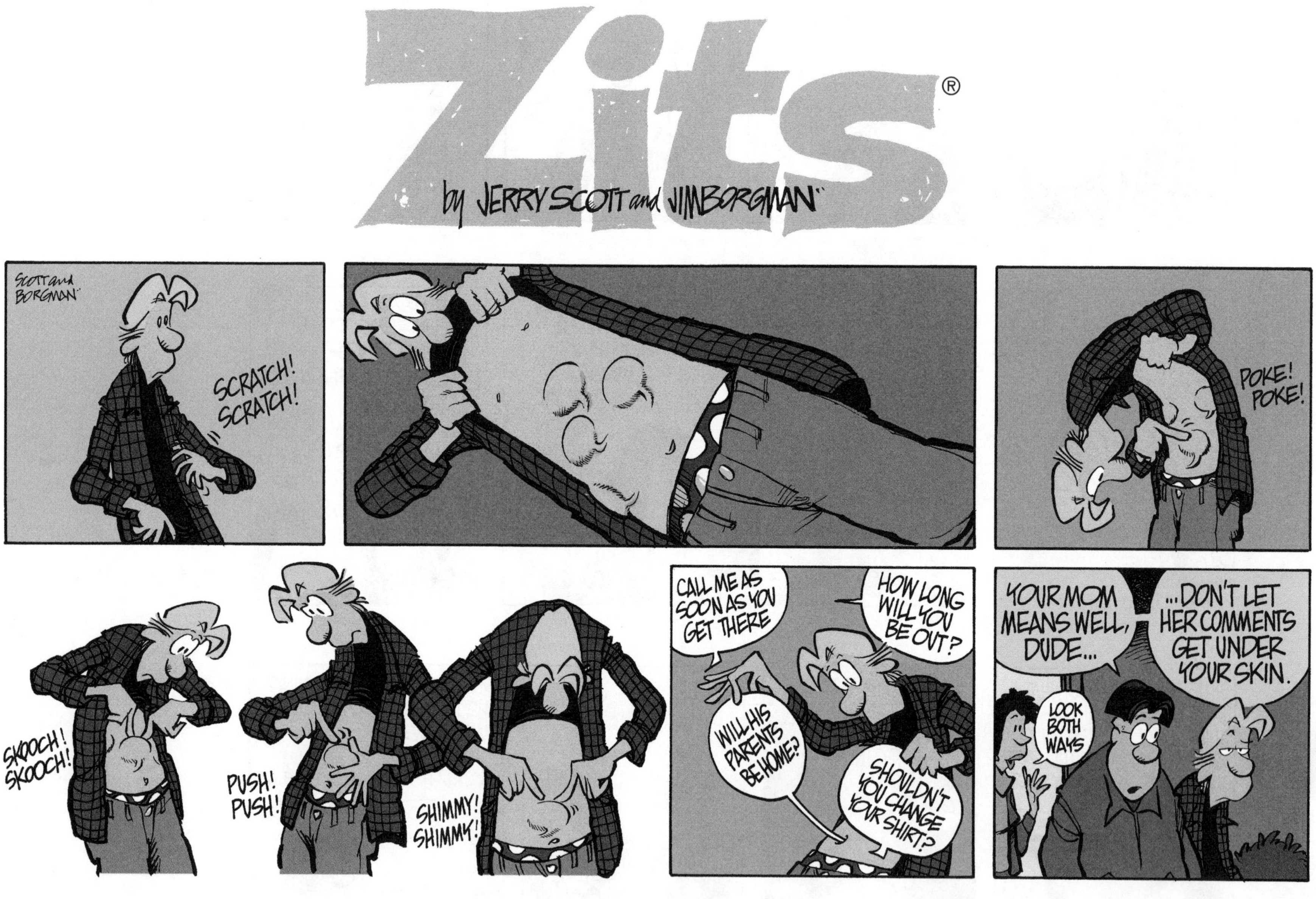
Zits®
by JERRY SCOTT and JIM BORGMAN
SCOTT and BORGMAN
SCRATCH! SCRATCH!
POKE! POKE!
SKOOCH! SKOOCH!
PUSH! PUSH!
SHIMMY! SHIMMY!
CALL ME AS SOON AS YOU GET THERE
HOW LONG WILL YOU BE OUT?
WILL HIS PARENTS BE HOME?
SHOULDN'T YOU CHANGE YOUR SHIRT?
YOUR MOM MEANS WELL, DUDE...
LOOK BOTH WAYS
...DON'T LET HER COMMENTS GET UNDER YOUR SKIN.

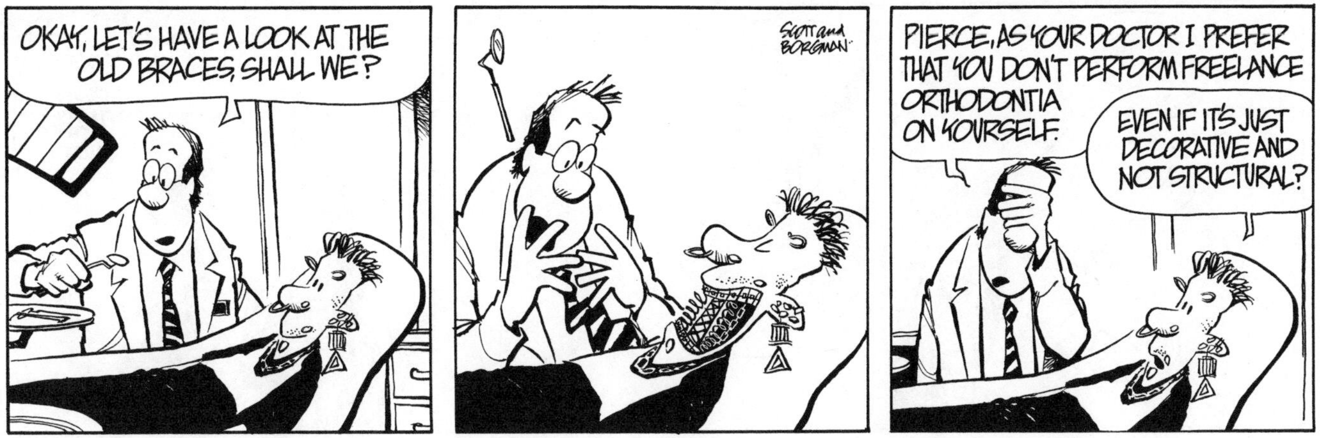
OKAY, LET'S HAVE A LOOK AT THE OLD BRACES, SHALL WE?
SCOTT and BORGMAN
PIERCE, AS YOUR DOCTOR I PREFER THAT YOU DON'T PERFORM FREELANCE ORTHODONTIA ON YOURSELF.
EVEN IF IT'S JUST DECORATIVE AND NOT STRUCTURAL?

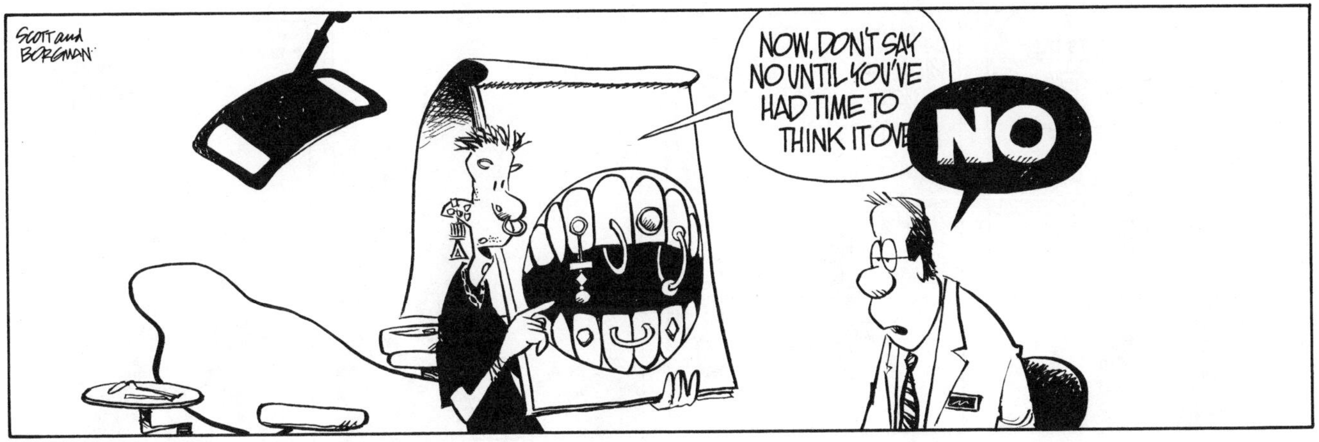
SCOTT and BORGMAN
NOW, DON'T SAY NO UNTIL YOU'VE HAD TIME TO THINK IT OVE
NO

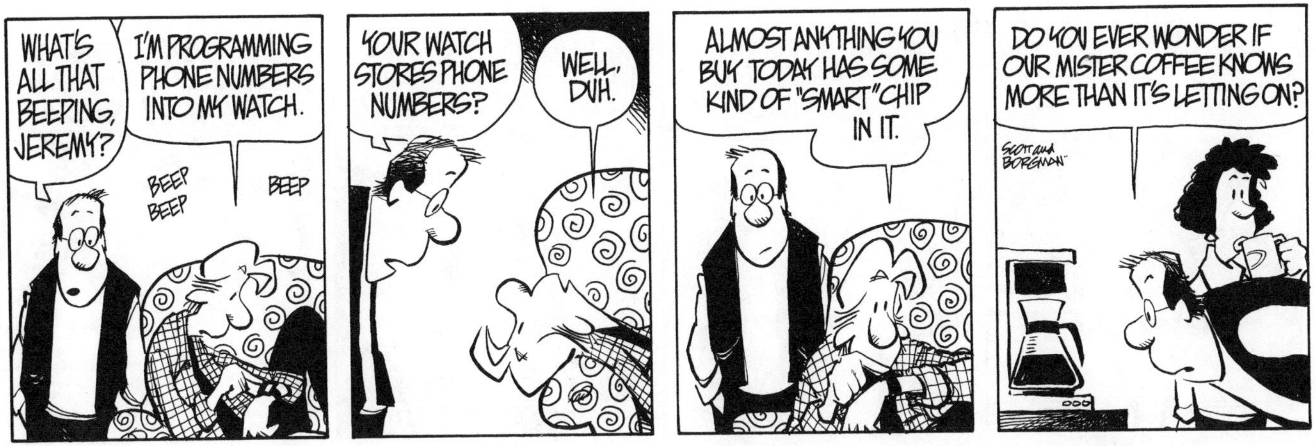
WHAT'S ALL THAT BEEPING, JEREMY?
I'M PROGRAMMING PHONE NUMBERS INTO MY WATCH.
BEEP BEEP
BEEP
YOUR WATCH STORES PHONE NUMBERS?
WELL, DUH.
ALMOST ANYTHING YOU BUY TODAY HAS SOME KIND OF "SMART" CHIP IN IT.
DO YOU EVER WONDER IF OUR MISTER COFFEE KNOWS MORE THAN IT'S LETTING ON?
SCOTT and BORGMAN

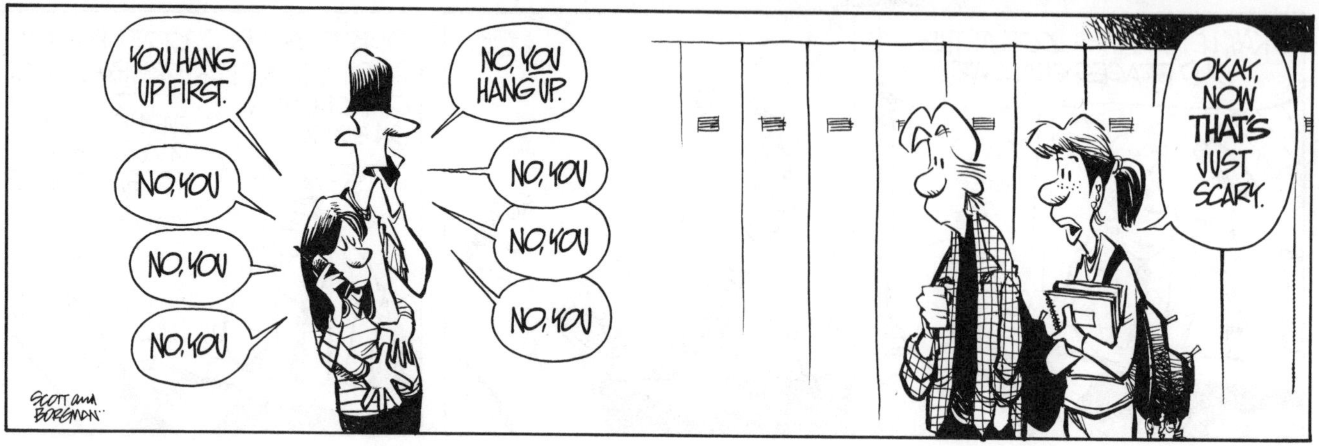
YOU HANG UP FIRST.
NO, YOU HANG UP.
NO, YOU
NO, YOU
NO, YOU
NO, YOU
NO, YOU
NO, YOU
OKAY, NOW THAT'S JUST SCARY.

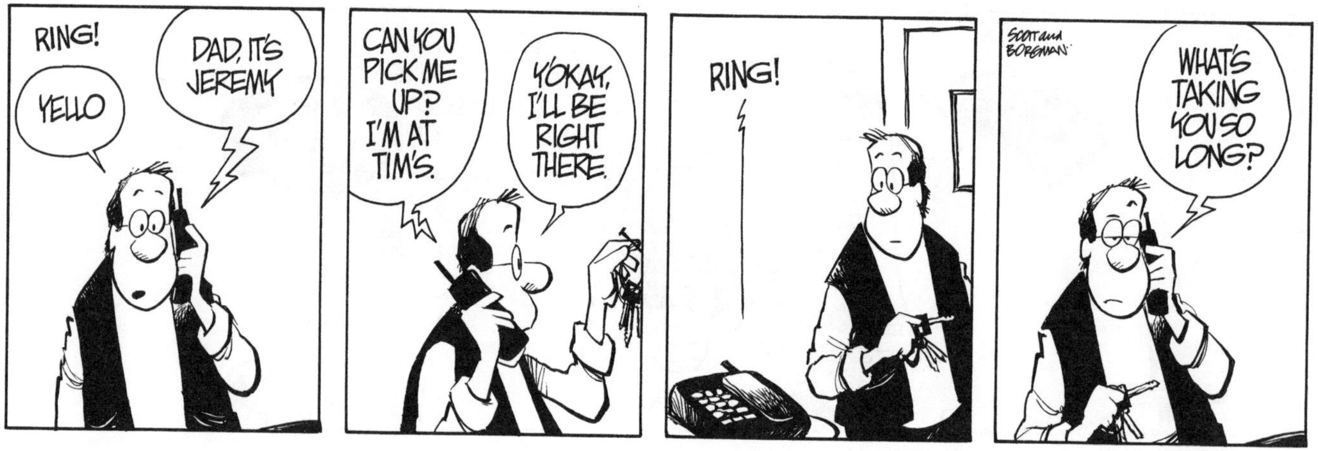
RING!
YELLO
DAD, IT'S JEREMY
CAN YOU PICK ME UP? I'M AT TIM'S.
Y'OKAY, I'LL BE RIGHT THERE.
RING!
WHAT'S TAKING YOU SO LONG?

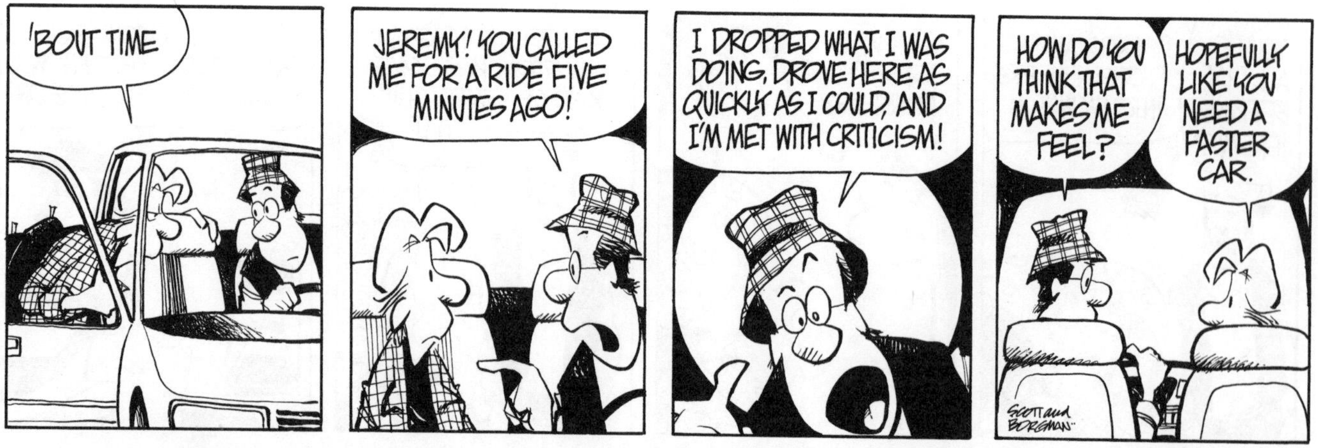
'BOUT TIME
JEREMY! YOU CALLED ME FOR A RIDE FIVE MINUTES AGO!
I DROPPED WHAT I WAS DOING, DROVE HERE AS QUICKLY AS I COULD, AND I'M MET WITH CRITICISM!
HOW DO YOU THINK THAT MAKES ME FEEL?
HOPEFULLY LIKE YOU NEED A FASTER CAR.

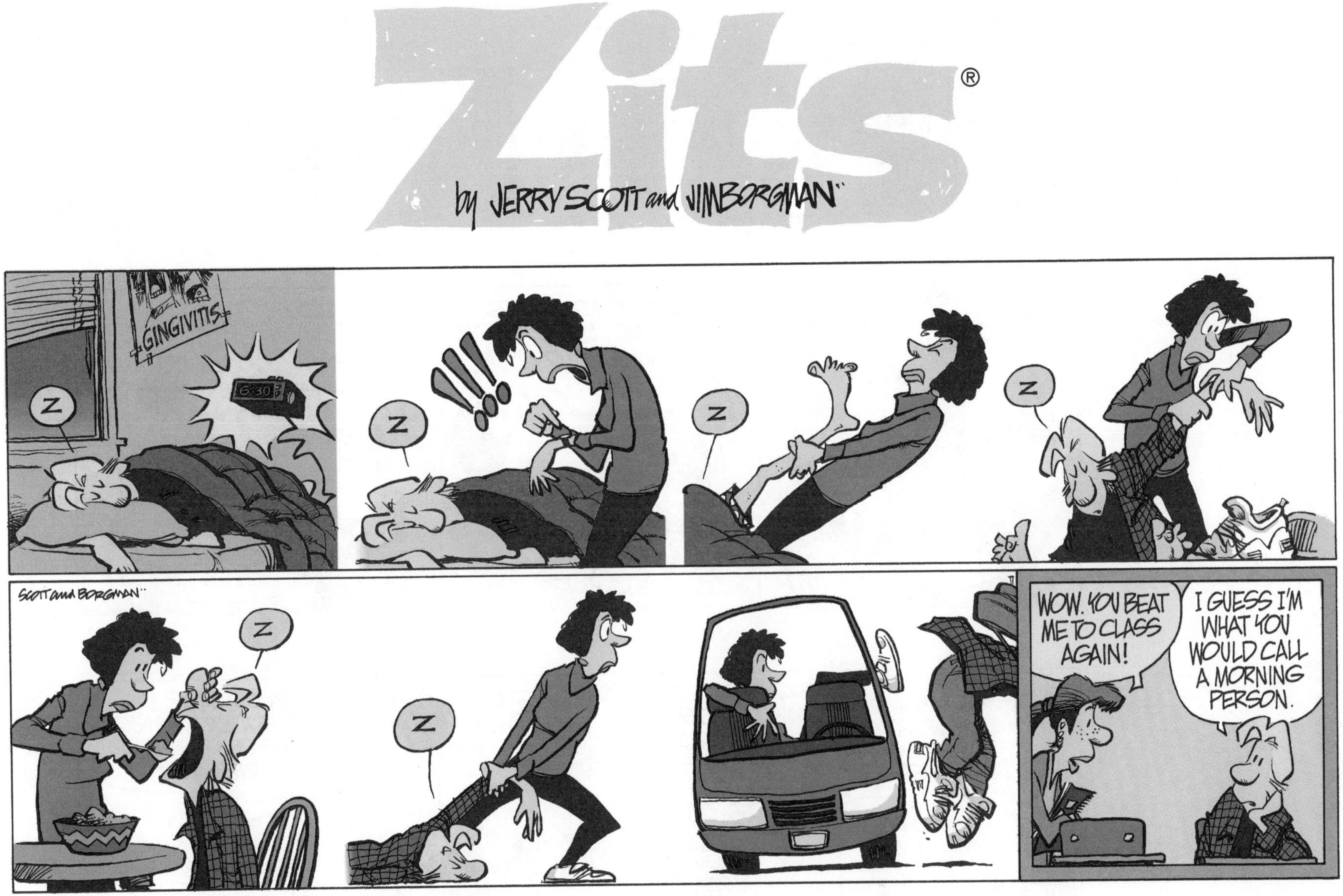
Zits®
by JERRY SCOTT and JIM BORGMAN
GINGIVITIS
6:30
Z
Z
Z
Z
SCOTT and BORGMAN
Z
Z
WOW. YOU BEAT ME TO CLASS AGAIN!
I GUESS I'M WHAT YOU WOULD CALL A MORNING PERSON.

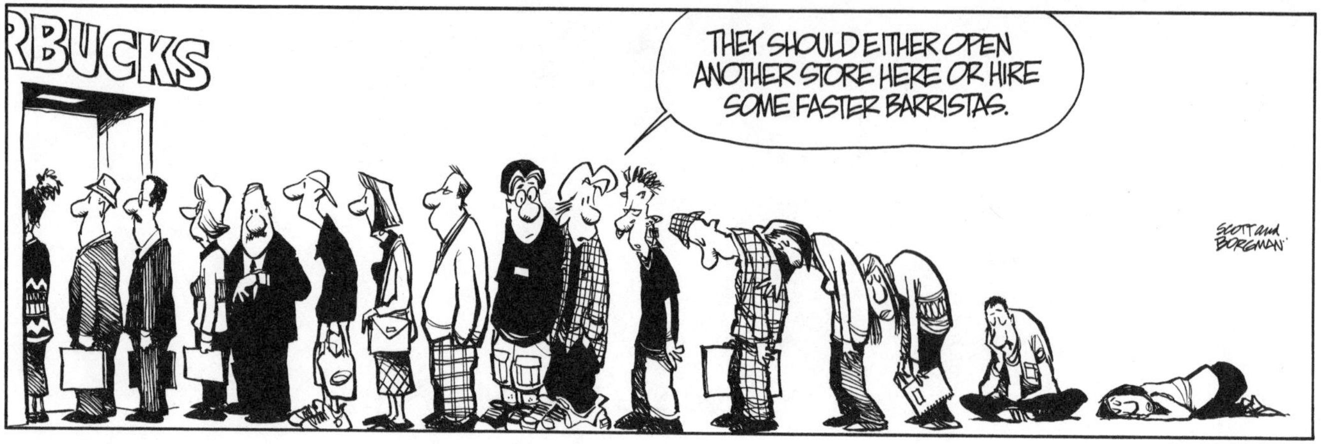
RBUCKS
THEY SHOULD EITHER OPEN ANOTHER STORE HERE OR HIRE SOME FASTER BARRISTAS.
SCOTT and BORGMAN

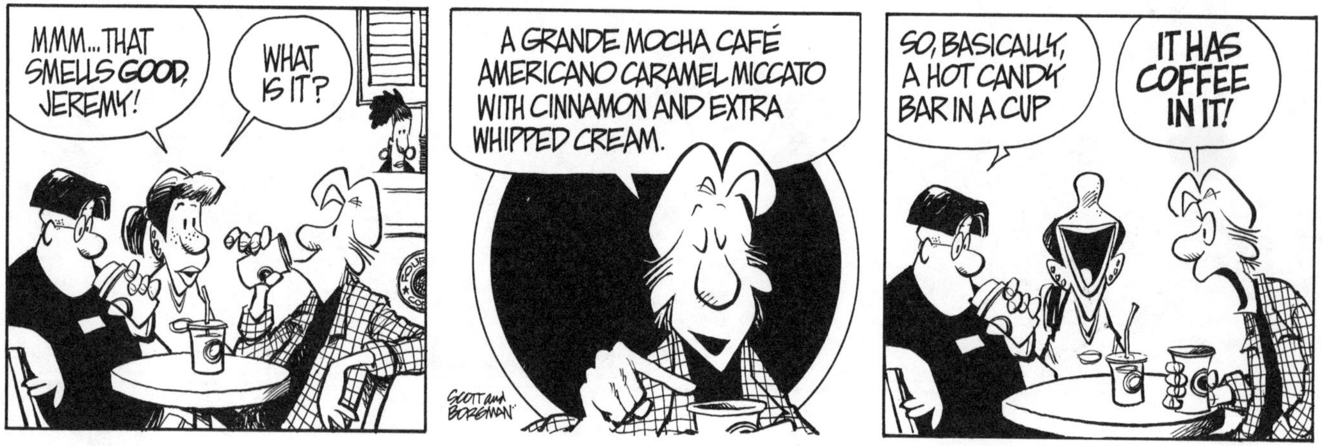
MMM... THAT SMELLS **GOOD**, JEREMY!
WHAT IS IT?
A GRANDE MOCHA CAFÉ AMERICANO CARAMEL MICCATO WITH CINNAMON AND EXTRA WHIPPED CREAM.
SCOTT and BORGMAN
SO, BASICALLY, A HOT CANDY BAR IN A CUP
IT HAS COFFEE IN IT!

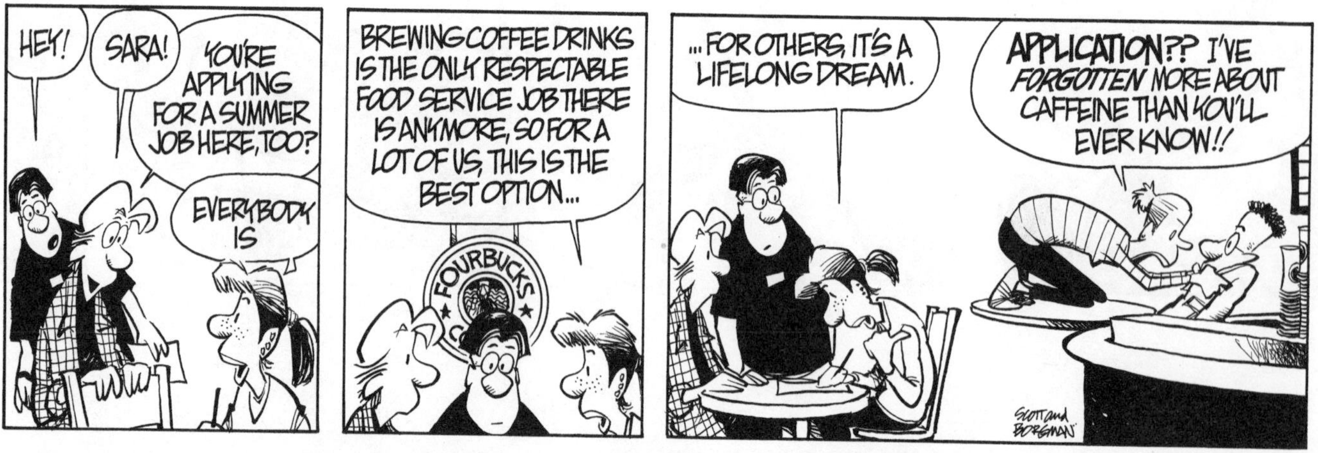
HEY!
SARA!
YOU'RE APPLYING FOR A SUMMER JOB HERE, TOO?
EVERYBODY IS
BREWING COFFEE DRINKS IS THE ONLY RESPECTABLE FOOD SERVICE JOB THERE IS ANYMORE, SO FOR A LOT OF US, THIS IS THE BEST OPTION...
FOURBUCKS
...FOR OTHERS, IT'S A LIFELONG DREAM.
APPLICATION?? I'VE *FORGOTTEN* MORE ABOUT CAFFEINE THAN YOU'LL EVER KNOW!!
SCOTT and BORGMAN

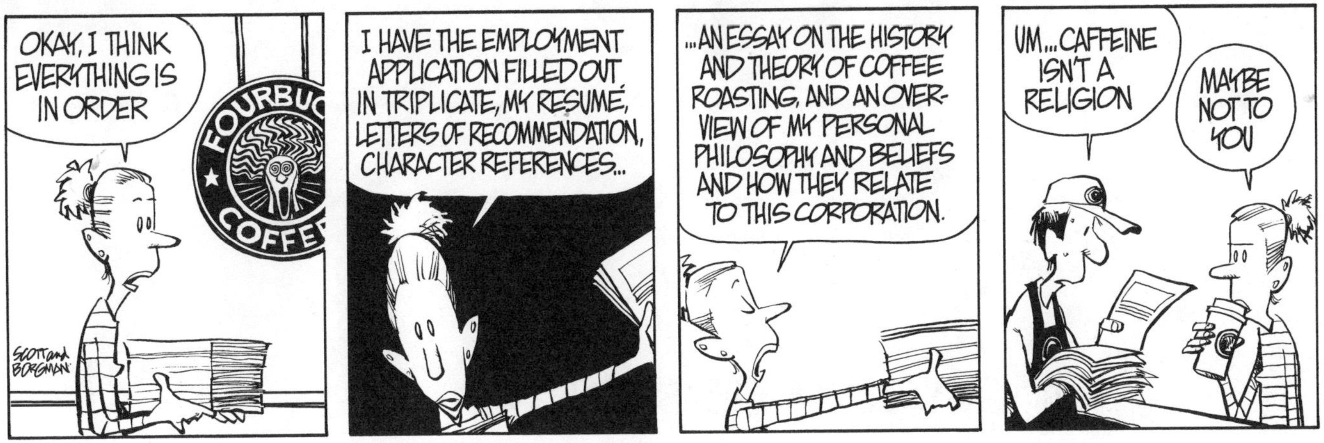
OKAY, I THINK EVERYTHING IS IN ORDER
I HAVE THE EMPLOYMENT APPLICATION FILLED OUT IN TRIPLICATE, MY RESUMÉ, LETTERS OF RECOMMENDATION, CHARACTER REFERENCES...
...AN ESSAY ON THE HISTORY AND THEORY OF COFFEE ROASTING, AND AN OVERVIEW OF MY PERSONAL PHILOSOPHY AND BELIEFS AND HOW THEY RELATE TO THIS CORPORATION.
UM... CAFFEINE ISN'T A RELIGION
MAYBE NOT TO YOU

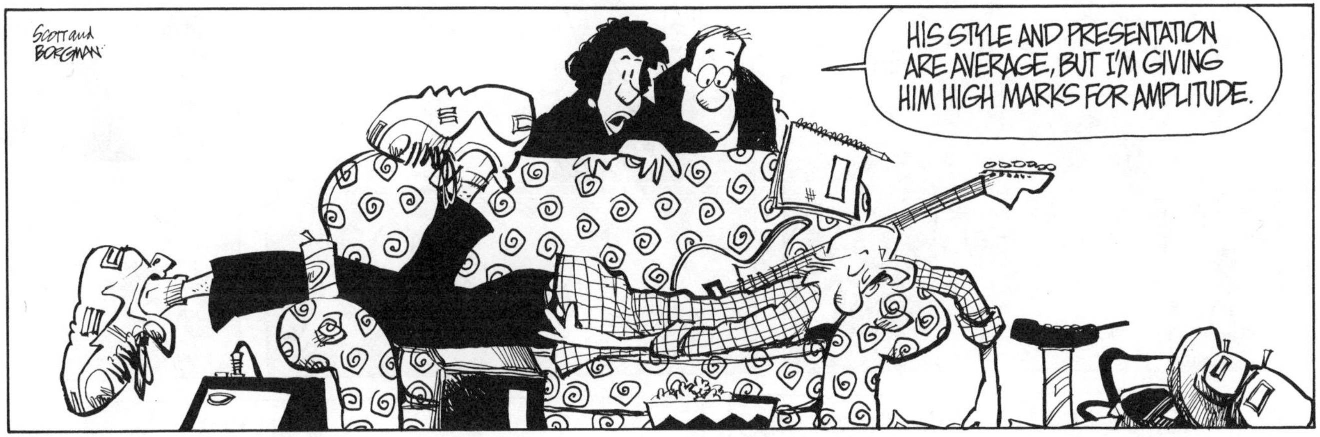
HIS STYLE AND PRESENTATION ARE AVERAGE, BUT I'M GIVING HIM HIGH MARKS FOR AMPLITUDE.

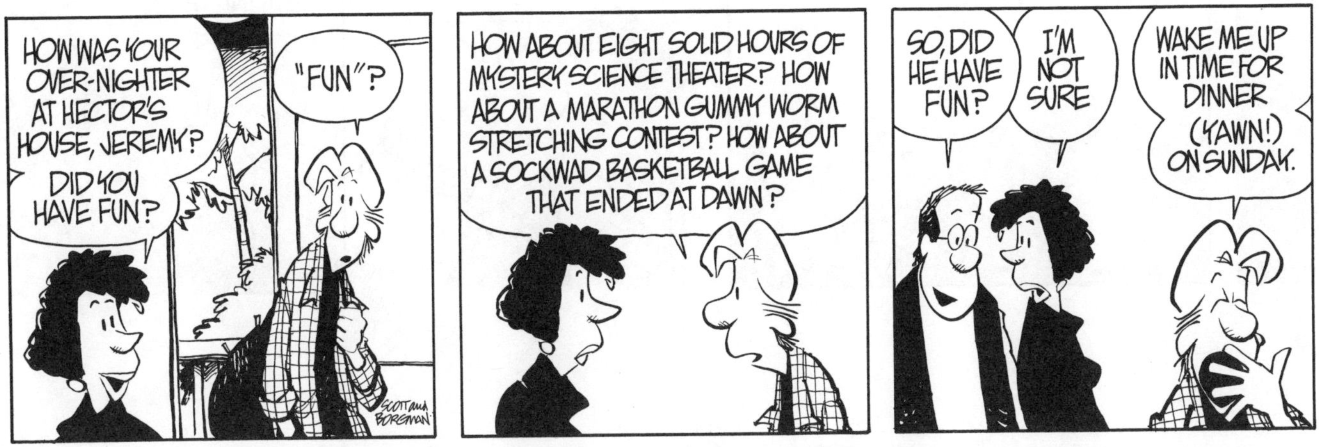
HOW WAS YOUR OVER-NIGHTER AT HECTOR'S HOUSE, JEREMY?
DID YOU HAVE FUN?
"FUN"?
HOW ABOUT EIGHT SOLID HOURS OF MYSTERY SCIENCE THEATER? HOW ABOUT A MARATHON GUMMY WORM STRETCHING CONTEST? HOW ABOUT A SOCKWAD BASKETBALL GAME THAT ENDED AT DAWN?
SO, DID HE HAVE FUN?
I'M NOT SURE
WAKE ME UP IN TIME FOR DINNER (YAWN!) ON SUNDAY.

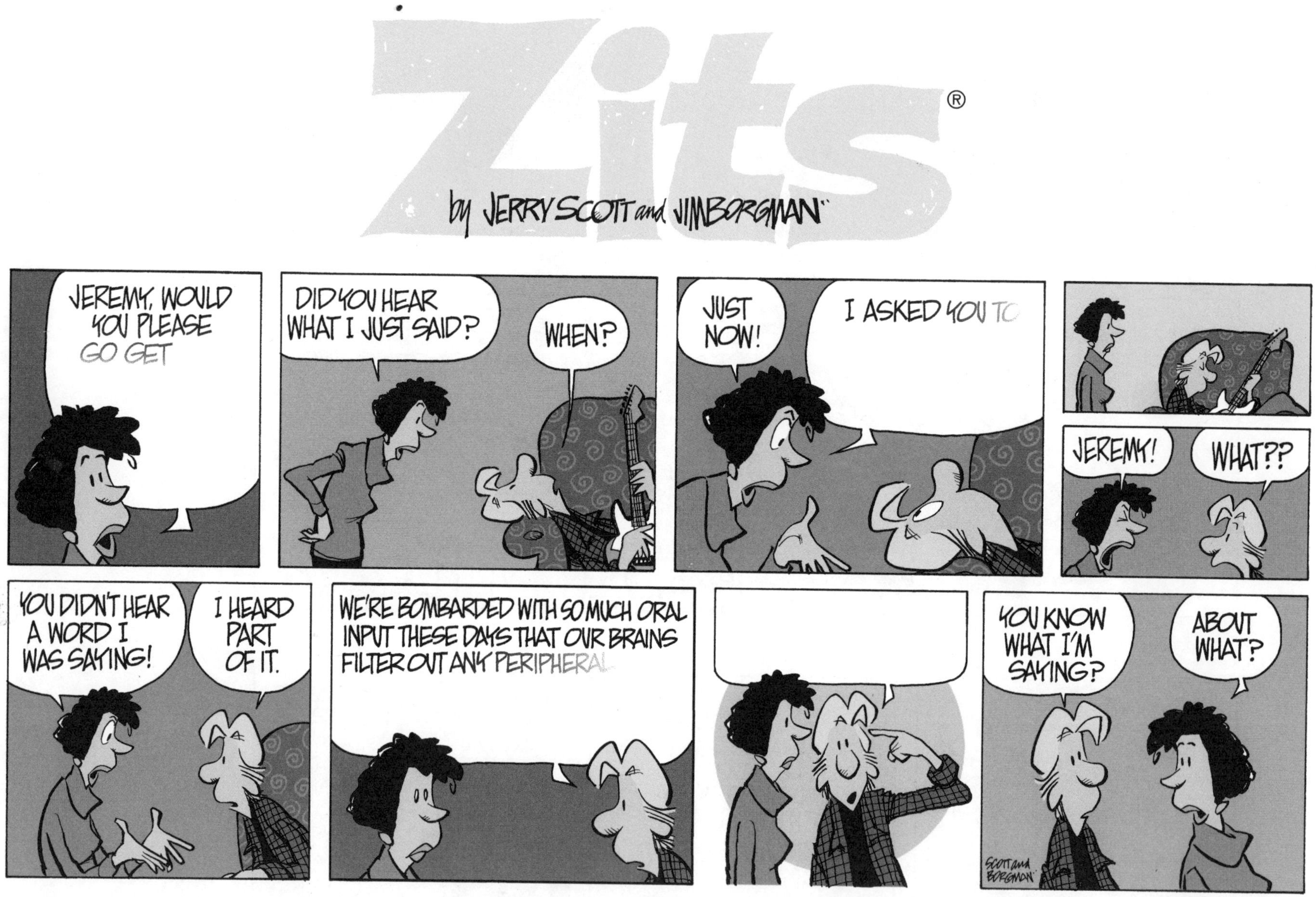
Zits®
by JERRY SCOTT and JIM BORGMAN
JEREMY, WOULD YOU PLEASE GO GET
DID YOU HEAR WHAT I JUST SAID?
WHEN?
JUST NOW!
I ASKED YOU TO
JEREMY!
WHAT??
YOU DIDN'T HEAR A WORD I WAS SAYING!
I HEARD PART OF IT.
WE'RE BOMBARDED WITH SO MUCH ORAL INPUT THESE DAYS THAT OUR BRAINS FILTER OUT ANY PERIPHERAL
YOU KNOW WHAT I'M SAYING?
ABOUT WHAT?
SCOTT and BORGMAN

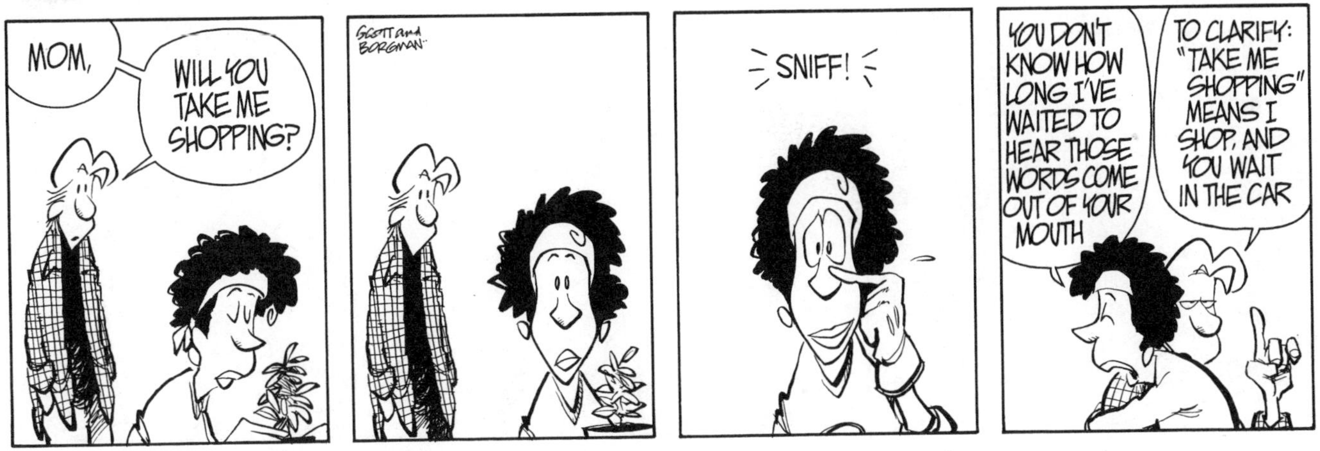
MOM,
WILL YOU TAKE ME SHOPPING?
SNIFF!
YOU DON'T KNOW HOW LONG I'VE WAITED TO HEAR THOSE WORDS COME OUT OF YOUR MOUTH
TO CLARIFY: "TAKE ME SHOPPING" MEANS I SHOP, AND YOU WAIT IN THE CAR

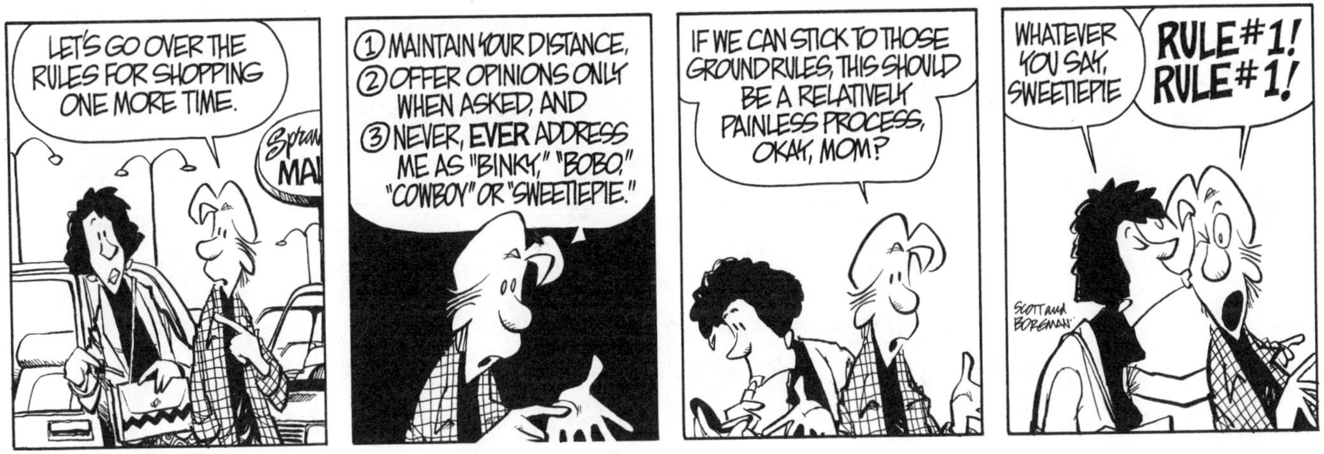
LET'S GO OVER THE RULES FOR SHOPPING ONE MORE TIME.
① MAINTAIN YOUR DISTANCE, ② OFFER OPINIONS ONLY WHEN ASKED, AND ③ NEVER, EVER ADDRESS ME AS "BINKY," "BOBO," "COWBOY" OR "SWEETIEPIE."
IF WE CAN STICK TO THOSE GROUND RULES, THIS SHOULD BE A RELATIVELY PAINLESS PROCESS, OKAY, MOM?
WHATEVER YOU SAY, SWEETIEPIE
RULE #1! RULE #1!

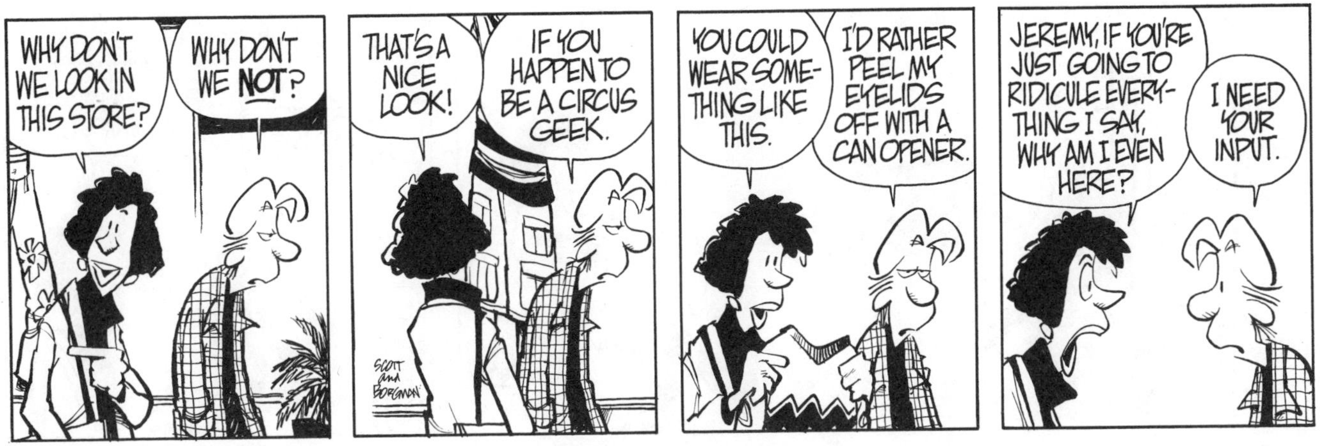
WHY DON'T WE LOOK IN THIS STORE?
WHY DON'T WE NOT?
THAT'S A NICE LOOK!
IF YOU HAPPEN TO BE A CIRCUS GEEK.
YOU COULD WEAR SOMETHING LIKE THIS.
I'D RATHER PEEL MY EYELIDS OFF WITH A CAN OPENER.
JEREMY, IF YOU'RE JUST GOING TO RIDICULE EVERYTHING I SAY, WHY AM I EVEN HERE?
I NEED YOUR INPUT.

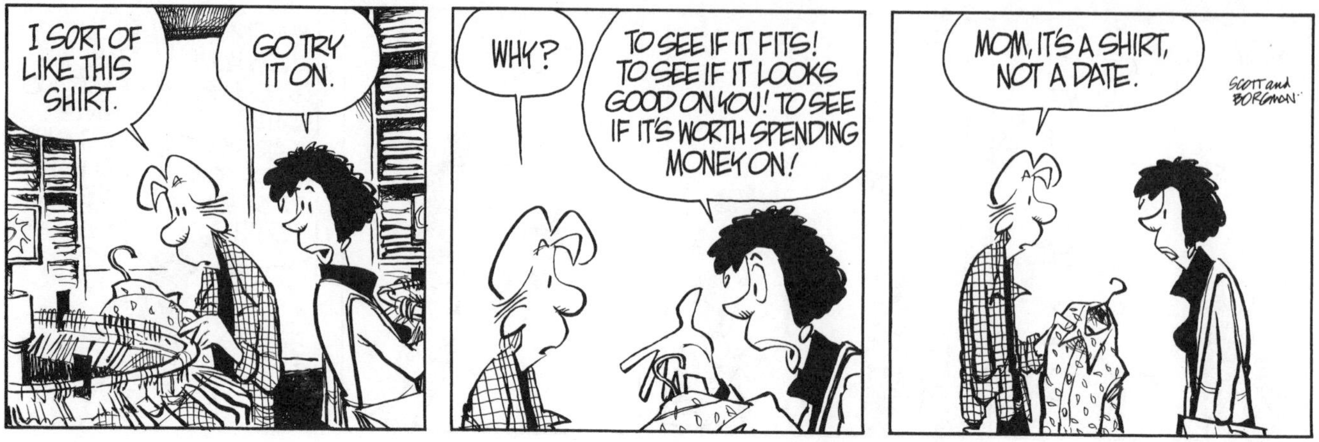
I SORT OF LIKE THIS SHIRT.
GO TRY IT ON.
WHY?
TO SEE IF IT FITS! TO SEE IF IT LOOKS GOOD ON YOU! TO SEE IF IT'S WORTH SPENDING MONEY ON!
MOM, IT'S A SHIRT, NOT A DATE.
SCOTT and BORGMAN

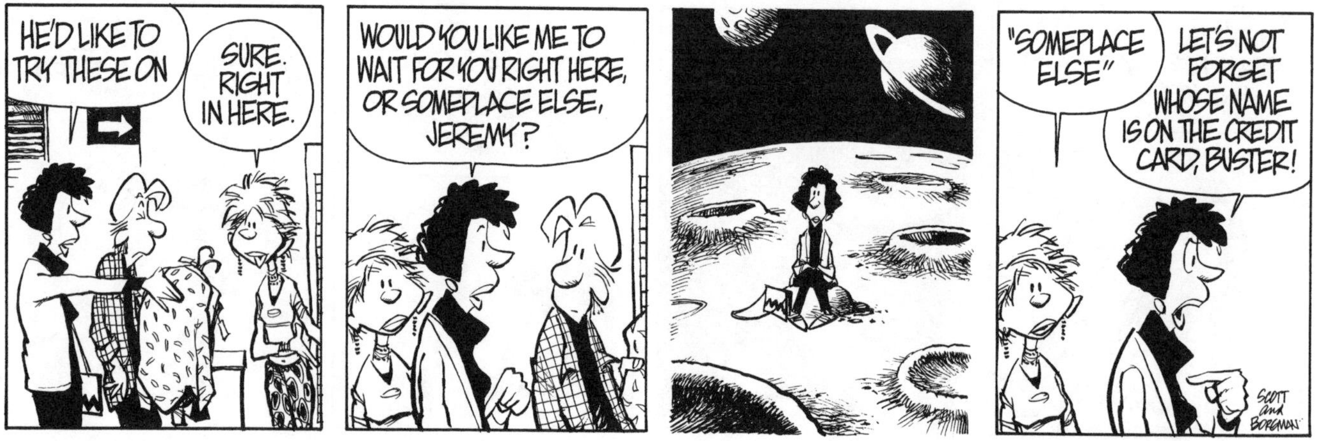
HE'D LIKE TO TRY THESE ON
SURE. RIGHT IN HERE.
WOULD YOU LIKE ME TO WAIT FOR YOU RIGHT HERE, OR SOMEPLACE ELSE, JEREMY?
"SOMEPLACE ELSE"
LET'S NOT FORGET WHOSE NAME IS ON THE CREDIT CARD, BUSTER!
SCOTT and BORGMAN

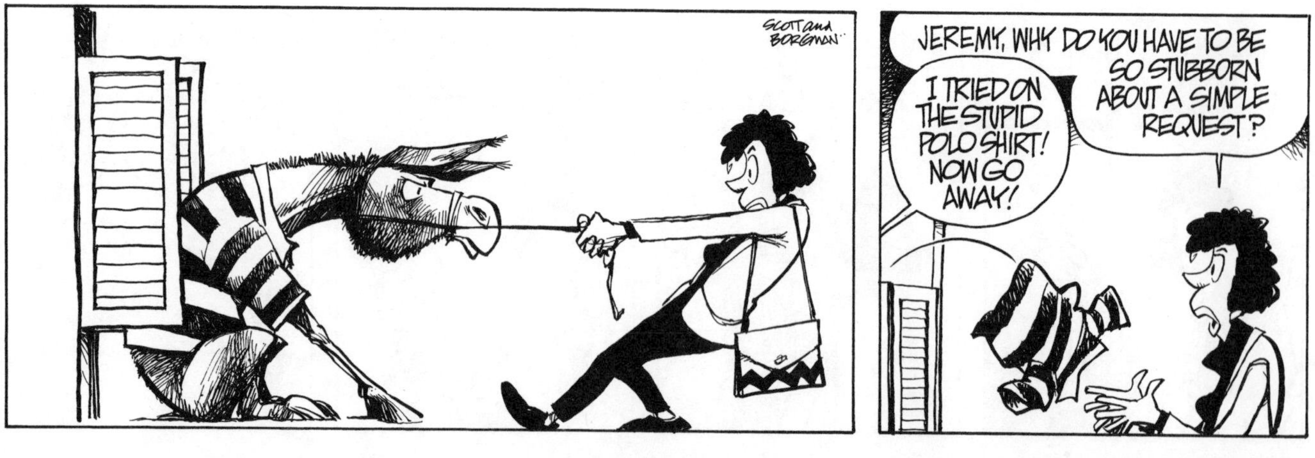
SCOTT and BORGMAN
JEREMY, WHY DO YOU HAVE TO BE SO STUBBORN ABOUT A SIMPLE REQUEST?
I TRIED ON THE STUPID POLO SHIRT! NOW GO AWAY!

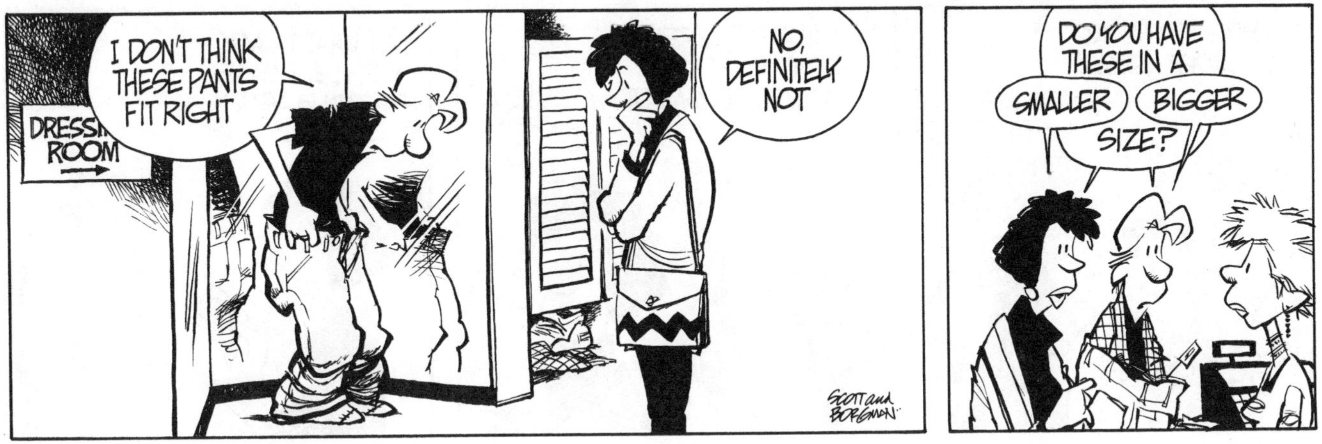
I DON'T THINK THESE PANTS FIT RIGHT
ROOM
NO, DEFINITELY NOT
DO YOU HAVE THESE IN A
SMALLER
BIGGER
SIZE?
SCOTT and BORGMAN

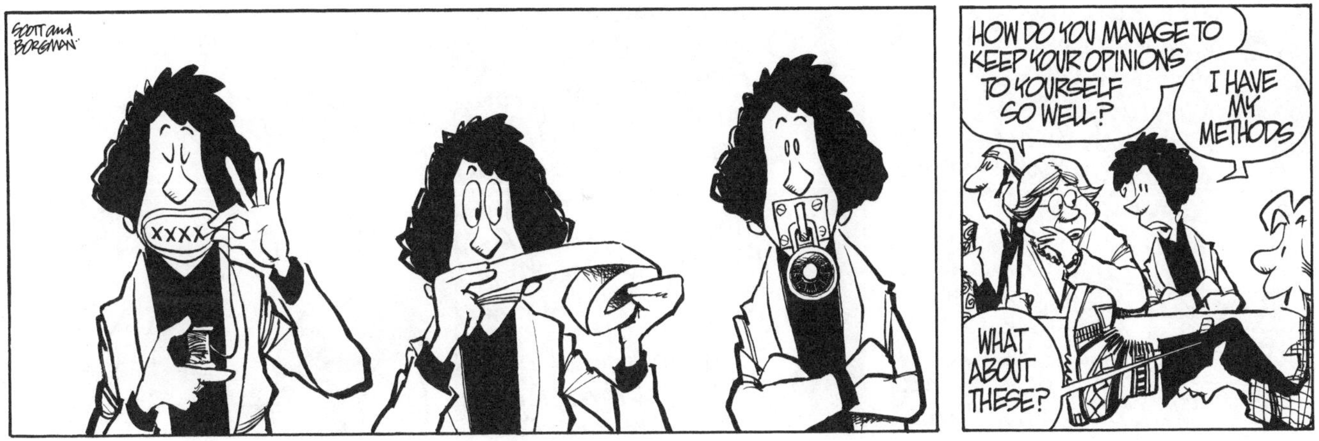
SCOTT and BORGMAN
XXXX
HOW DO YOU MANAGE TO KEEP YOUR OPINIONS TO YOURSELF SO WELL?
I HAVE MY METHODS
WHAT ABOUT THESE?

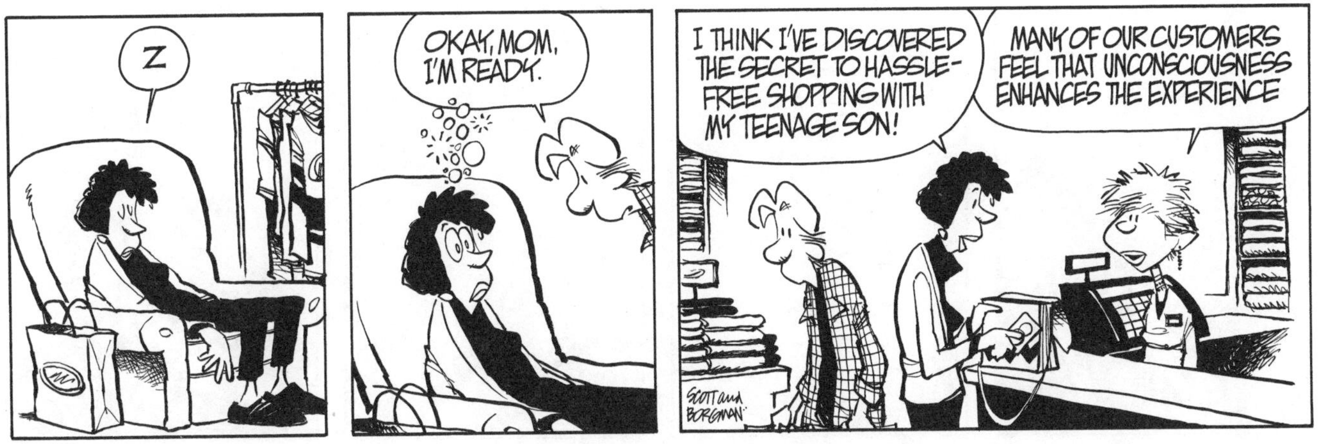
Z
OKAY, MOM, I'M READY.
I THINK I'VE DISCOVERED THE SECRET TO HASSLE-FREE SHOPPING WITH MY TEENAGE SON!
MANY OF OUR CUSTOMERS FEEL THAT UNCONSCIOUSNESS ENHANCES THE EXPERIENCE
SCOTT and BORGMAN

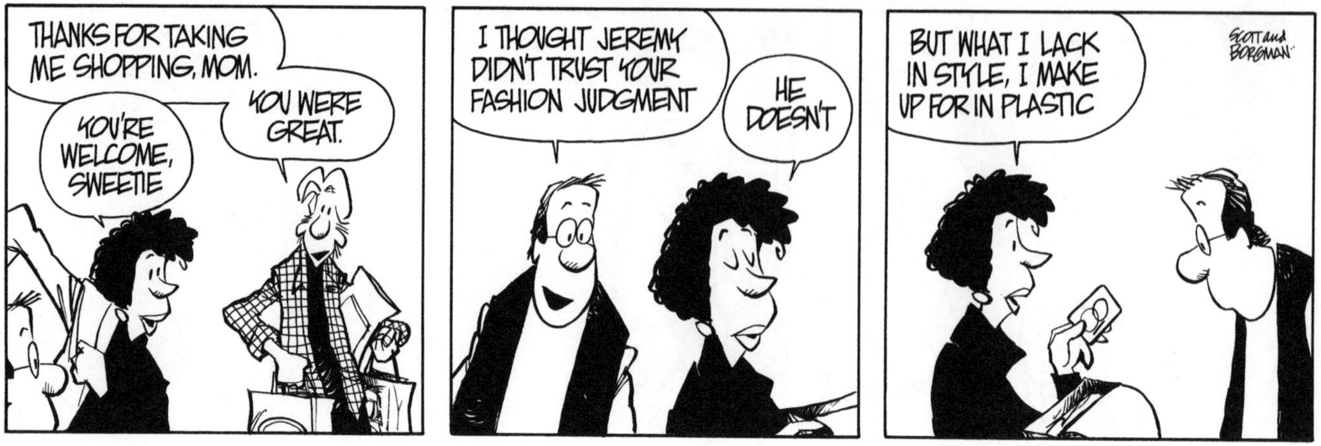
THANKS FOR TAKING ME SHOPPING, MOM.
YOU WERE GREAT.
YOU'RE WELCOME, SWEETIE
I THOUGHT JEREMY DIDN'T TRUST YOUR FASHION JUDGMENT
HE DOESN'T
BUT WHAT I LACK IN STYLE, I MAKE UP FOR IN PLASTIC
SCOTT and BORGMAN

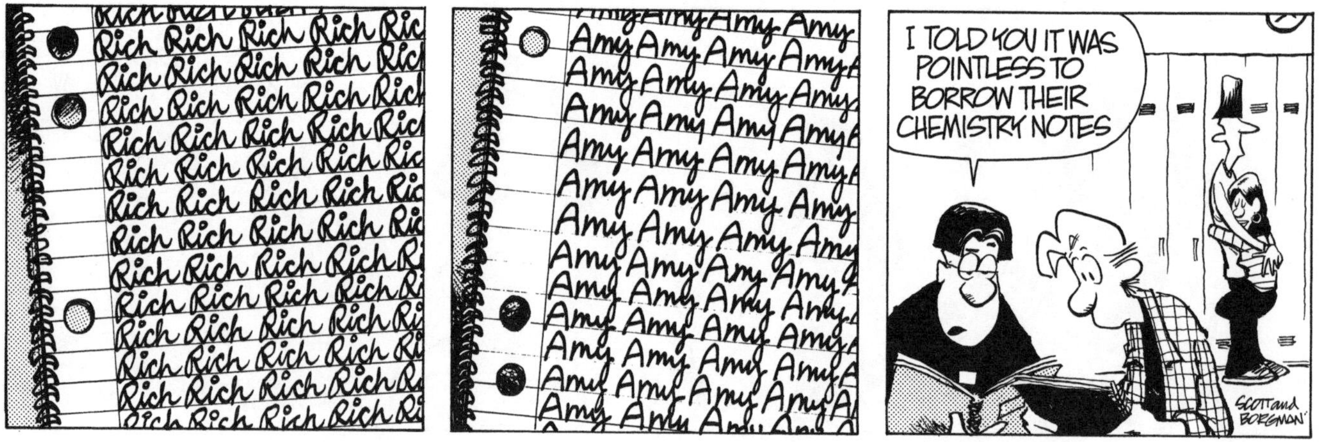
I TOLD YOU IT WAS POINTLESS TO BORROW THEIR CHEMISTRY NOTES
SCOTT and BORGMAN

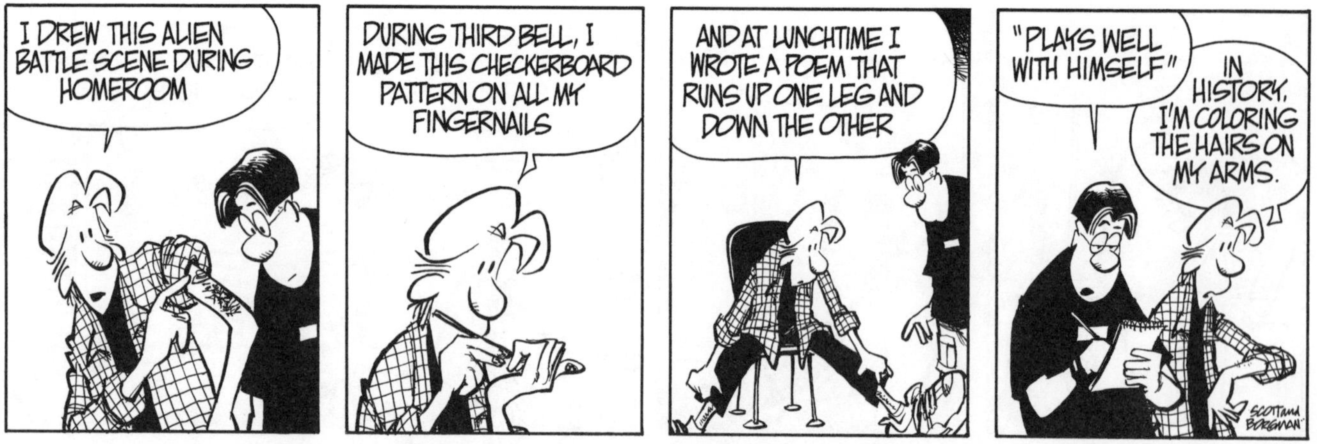
I DREW THIS ALIEN BATTLE SCENE DURING HOMEROOM
DURING THIRD BELL, I MADE THIS CHECKERBOARD PATTERN ON ALL MY FINGERNAILS
AND AT LUNCHTIME I WROTE A POEM THAT RUNS UP ONE LEG AND DOWN THE OTHER
"PLAYS WELL WITH HIMSELF"
IN HISTORY, I'M COLORING THE HAIRS ON MY ARMS.
SCOTT and BORGMAN

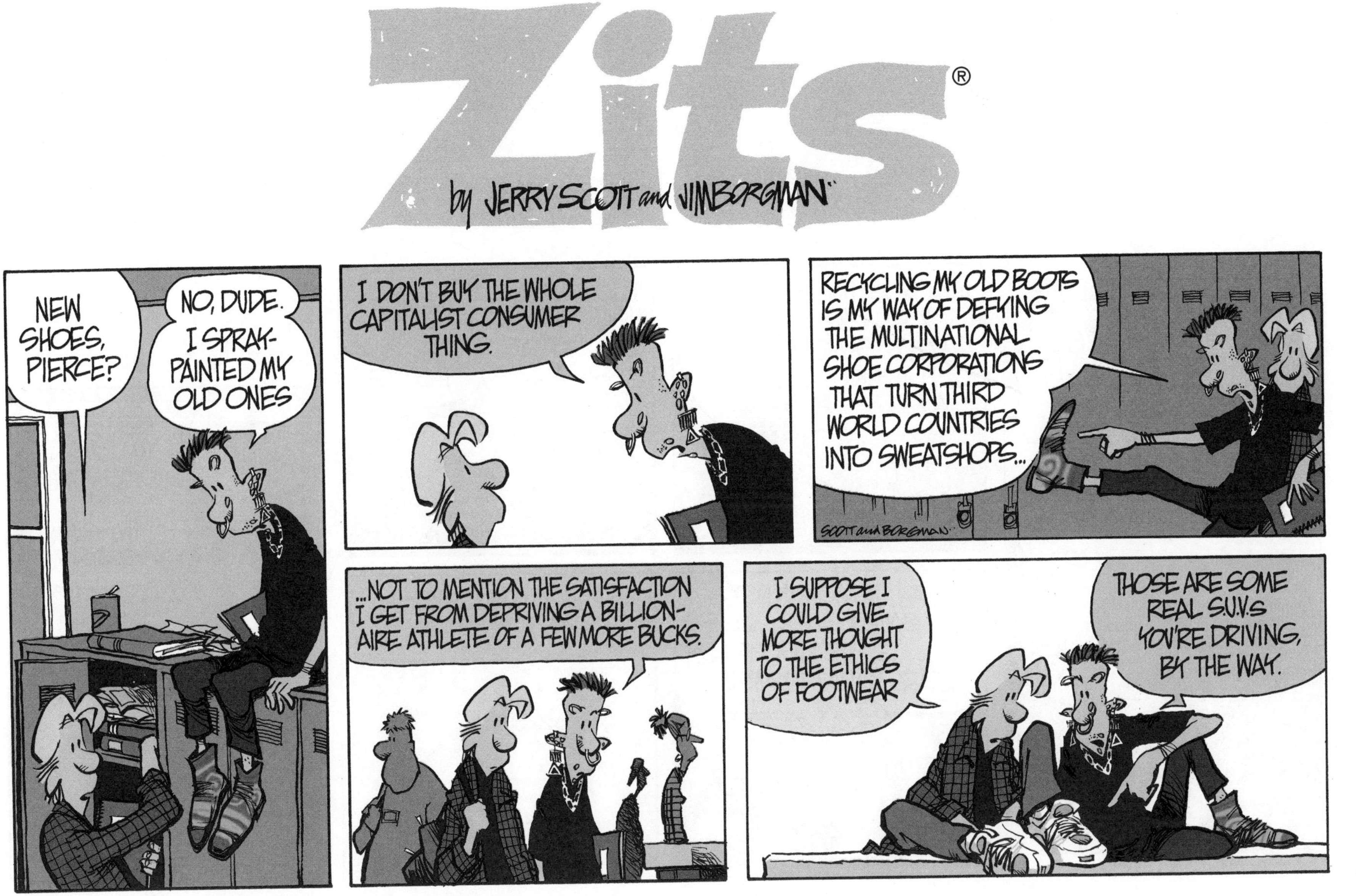
Zits®
by JERRY SCOTT and JIM BORGMAN
NEW SHOES, PIERCE?
NO, DUDE. I SPRAY-PAINTED MY OLD ONES
I DON'T BUY THE WHOLE CAPITALIST CONSUMER THING.
RECYCLING MY OLD BOOTS IS MY WAY OF DEFYING THE MULTINATIONAL SHOE CORPORATIONS THAT TURN THIRD WORLD COUNTRIES INTO SWEATSHOPS...
SCOTT and BORGMAN
...NOT TO MENTION THE SATISFACTION I GET FROM DEPRIVING A BILLIONAIRE ATHLETE OF A FEW MORE BUCKS.
I SUPPOSE I COULD GIVE MORE THOUGHT TO THE ETHICS OF FOOTWEAR
THOSE ARE SOME REAL S.U.V.s YOU'RE DRIVING, BY THE WAY.

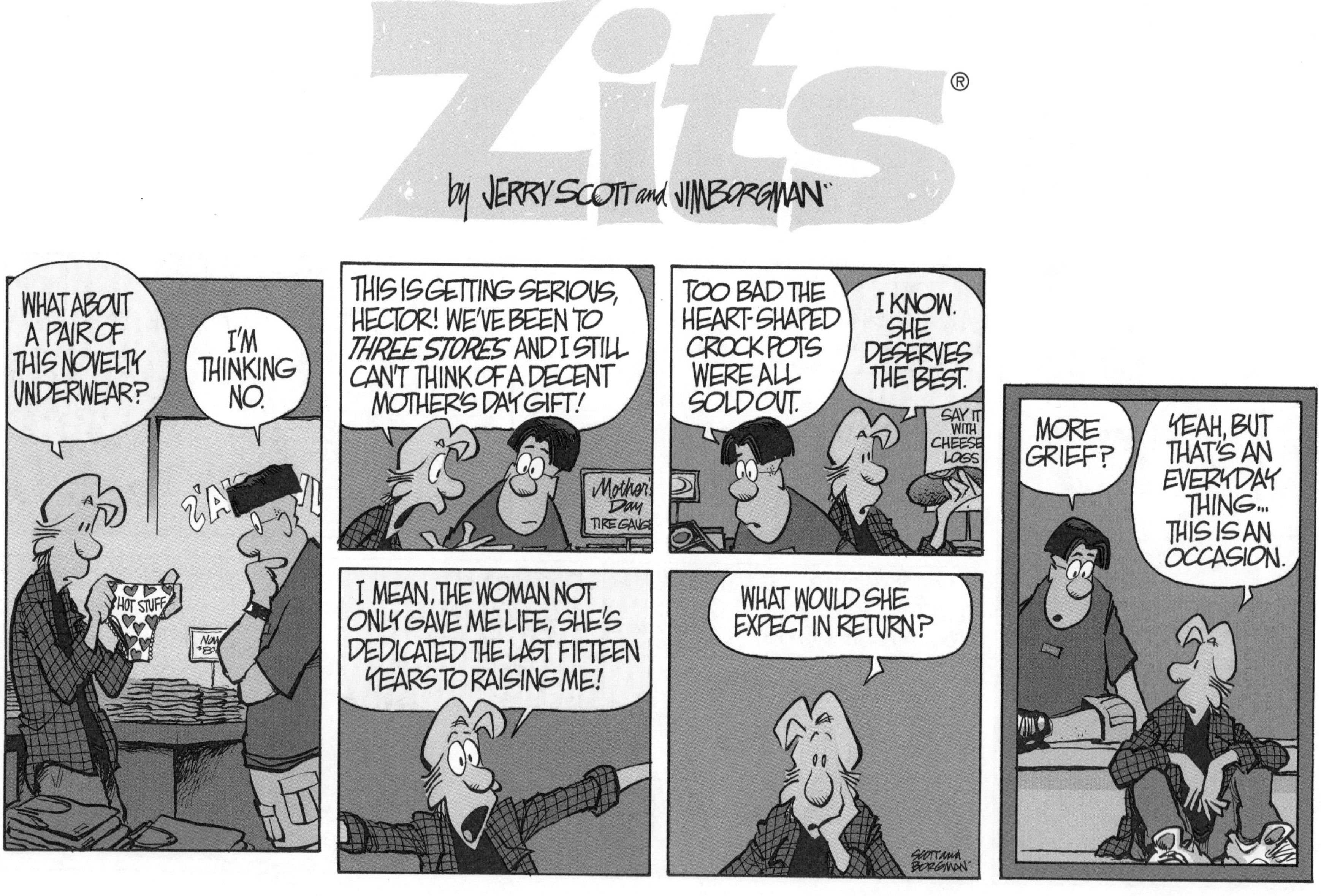
Zits®
by JERRY SCOTT and JIM BORGMAN
WHAT ABOUT A PAIR OF THIS NOVELTY UNDERWEAR?
HOT STUFF
I'M THINKING NO.
THIS IS GETTING SERIOUS, HECTOR! WE'VE BEEN TO *THREE STORES* AND I STILL CAN'T THINK OF A DECENT MOTHER'S DAY GIFT!
TOO BAD THE HEART-SHAPED CROCK POTS WERE ALL SOLD OUT.
I KNOW. SHE DESERVES THE BEST.
SAY IT WITH CHEESE LOGS
I MEAN, THE WOMAN NOT ONLY GAVE ME LIFE, SHE'S DEDICATED THE LAST FIFTEEN YEARS TO RAISING ME!
WHAT WOULD SHE EXPECT IN RETURN?
SCOTT AND BORGMAN
MORE GRIEF?
YEAH, BUT THAT'S AN EVERYDAY THING... THIS IS AN OCCASION.

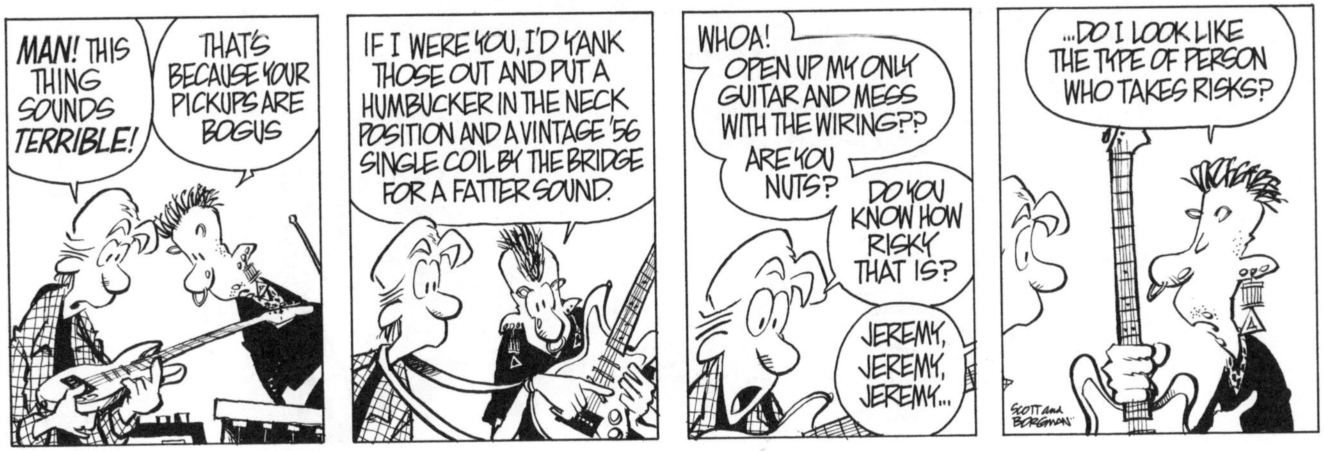
MAN! THIS THING SOUNDS TERRIBLE!
THAT'S BECAUSE YOUR PICKUPS ARE BOGUS
IF I WERE YOU, I'D YANK THOSE OUT AND PUT A HUMBUCKER IN THE NECK POSITION AND A VINTAGE '56 SINGLE COIL BY THE BRIDGE FOR A FATTER SOUND.
WHOA! OPEN UP MY ONLY GUITAR AND MESS WITH THE WIRING??
ARE YOU NUTS?
DO YOU KNOW HOW RISKY THAT IS?
JEREMY, JEREMY, JEREMY...
...DO I LOOK LIKE THE TYPE OF PERSON WHO TAKES RISKS?
SCOTT and BORGMAN

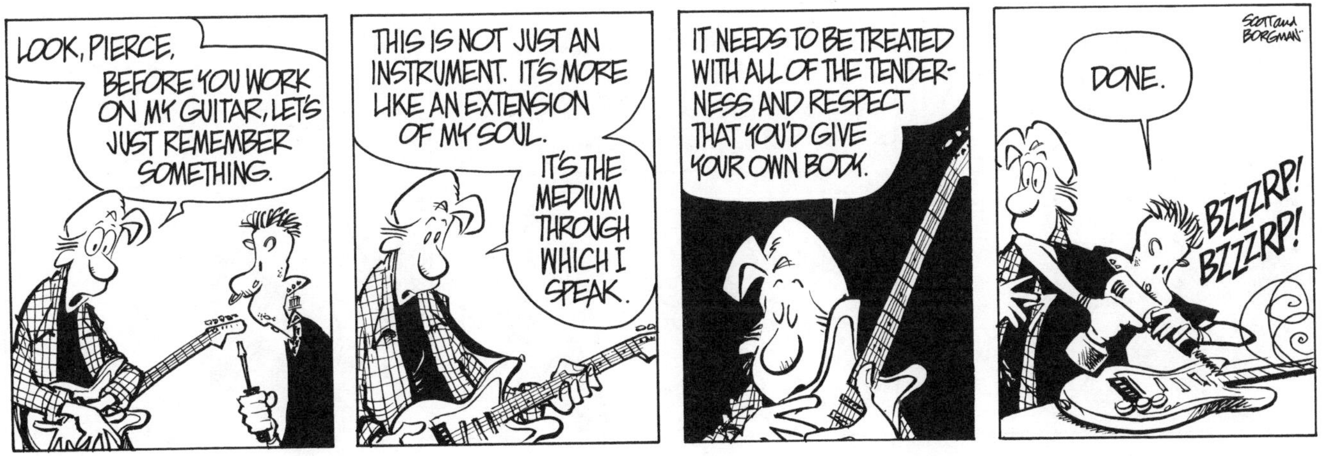
LOOK, PIERCE,
BEFORE YOU WORK ON MY GUITAR, LET'S JUST REMEMBER SOMETHING.
THIS IS NOT JUST AN INSTRUMENT. IT'S MORE LIKE AN EXTENSION OF MY SOUL.
IT'S THE MEDIUM THROUGH WHICH I SPEAK.
IT NEEDS TO BE TREATED WITH ALL OF THE TENDERNESS AND RESPECT THAT YOU'D GIVE YOUR OWN BODY.
SCOTT and BORGMAN
DONE.
BZZZRP! BZZZRP!

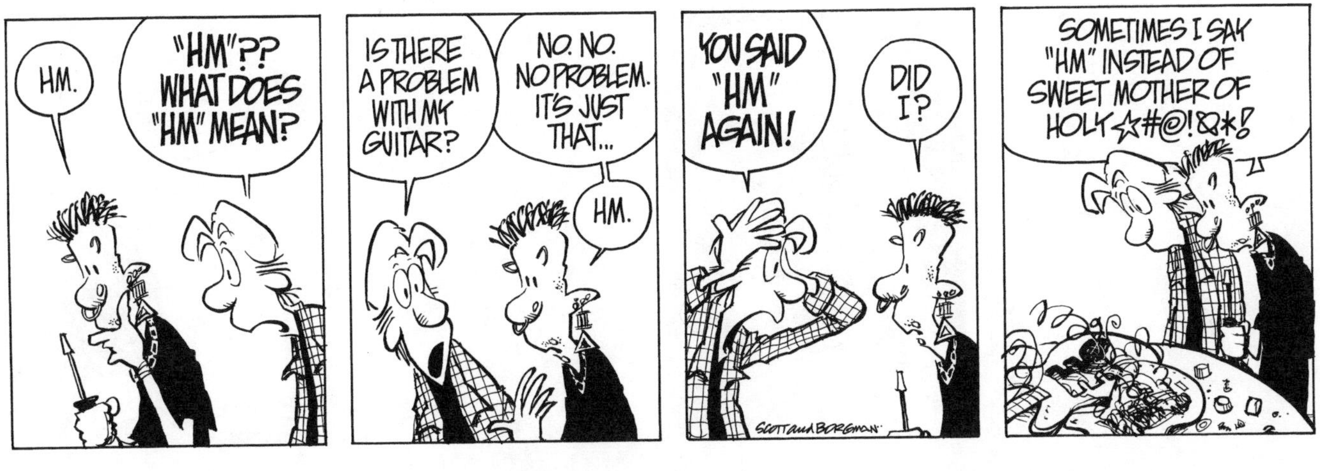
HM.
"HM"?? WHAT DOES "HM" MEAN?
IS THERE A PROBLEM WITH MY GUITAR?
NO. NO. NO PROBLEM. IT'S JUST THAT...
HM.
YOU SAID "HM" AGAIN!
DID I?
SCOTT and BORGMAN
SOMETIMES I SAY "HM" INSTEAD OF SWEET MOTHER OF HOLY☆#@!♀*!

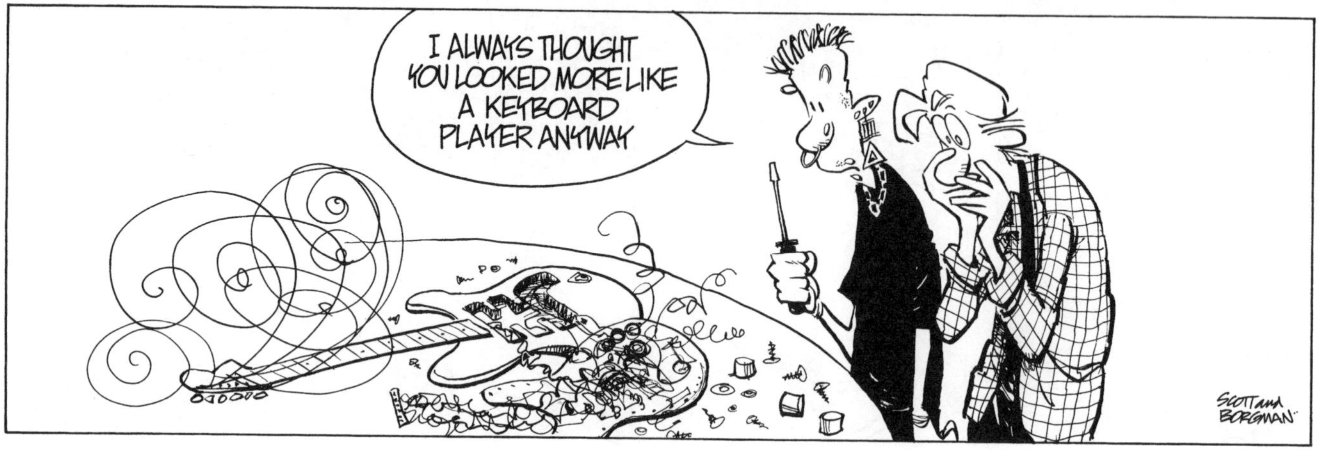
I ALWAYS THOUGHT YOU LOOKED MORE LIKE A KEYBOARD PLAYER ANYWAY

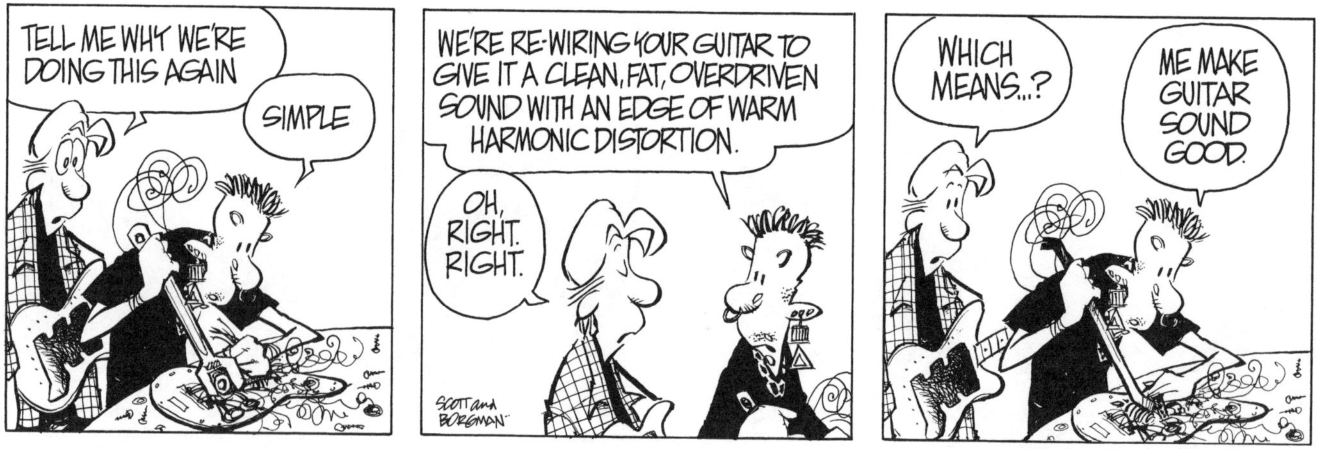
TELL ME WHY WE'RE DOING THIS AGAIN
SIMPLE
WE'RE RE-WIRING YOUR GUITAR TO GIVE IT A CLEAN, FAT, OVERDRIVEN SOUND WITH AN EDGE OF WARM HARMONIC DISTORTION.
OH, RIGHT. RIGHT.
WHICH MEANS...?
ME MAKE GUITAR SOUND GOOD.

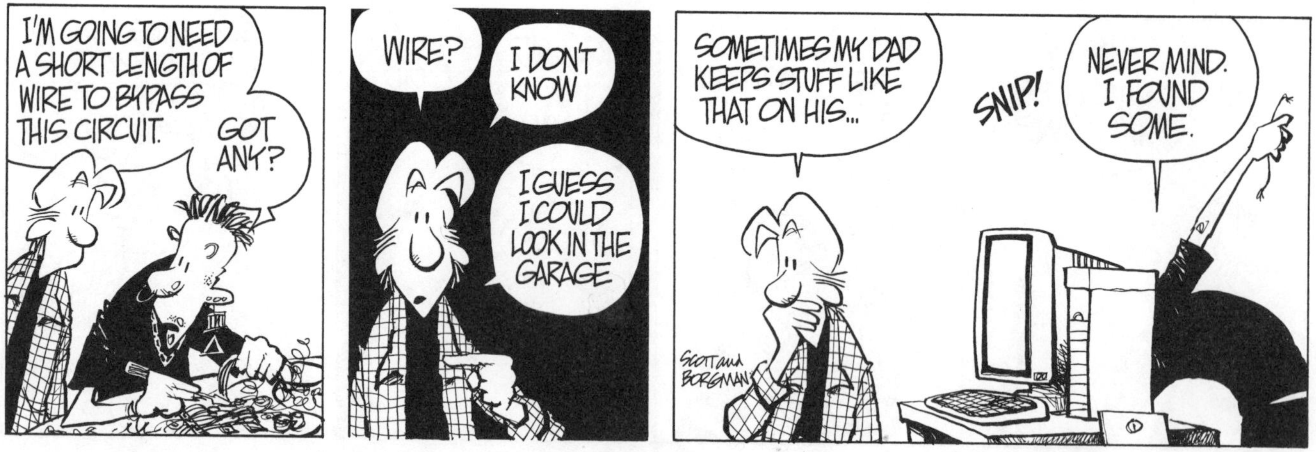
I'M GOING TO NEED A SHORT LENGTH OF WIRE TO BYPASS THIS CIRCUIT.
GOT ANY?
WIRE?
I DON'T KNOW
I GUESS I COULD LOOK IN THE GARAGE
SOMETIMES MY DAD KEEPS STUFF LIKE THAT ON HIS...
SNIP!
NEVER MIND. I FOUND SOME.

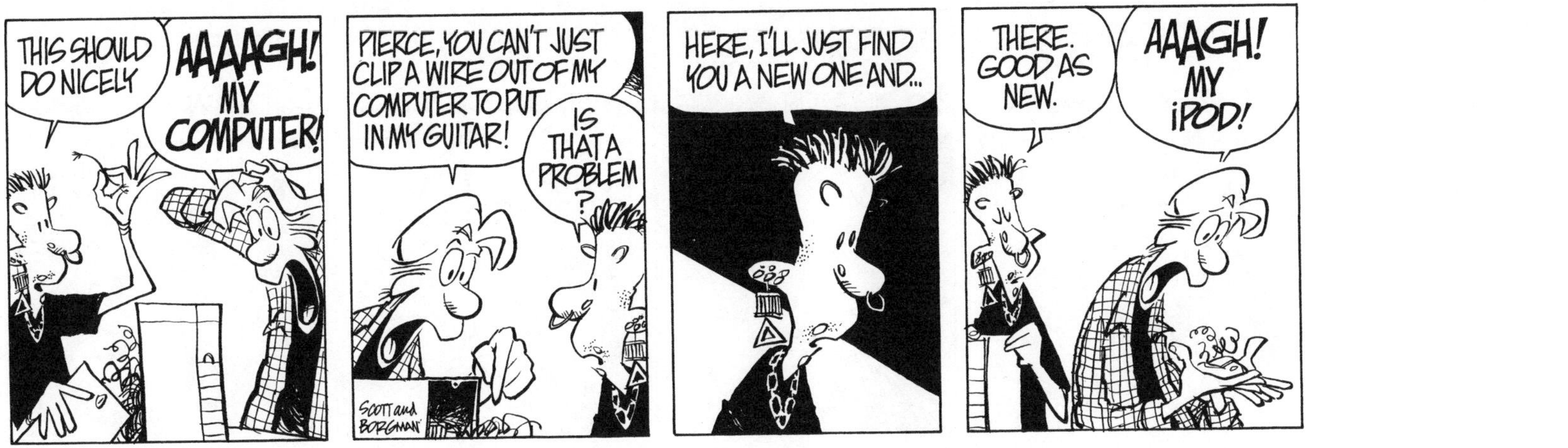
THIS SHOULD DO NICELY
AAAAGH! MY COMPUTER!
PIERCE, YOU CAN'T JUST CLIP A WIRE OUT OF MY COMPUTER TO PUT IN MY GUITAR!
IS THAT A PROBLEM?
SCOTT and BORGMAN
HERE, I'LL JUST FIND YOU A NEW ONE AND...
THERE. GOOD AS NEW.
AAAGH! MY iPOD!

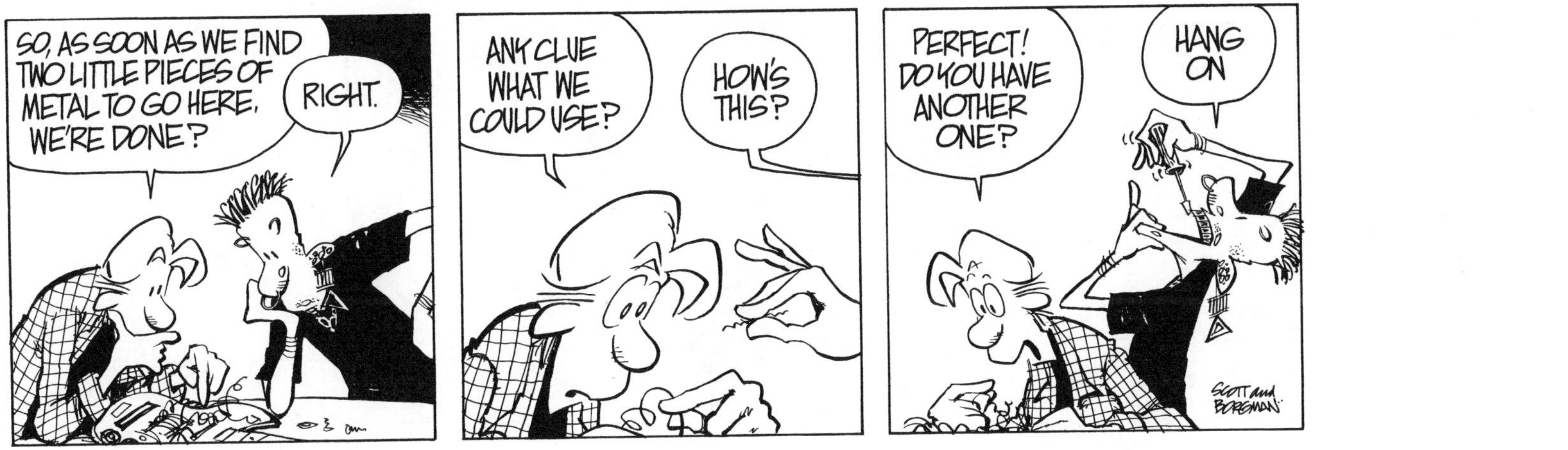
SO, AS SOON AS WE FIND TWO LITTLE PIECES OF METAL TO GO HERE, WE'RE DONE?
RIGHT.
ANY CLUE WHAT WE COULD USE?
HOW'S THIS?
PERFECT! DO YOU HAVE ANOTHER ONE?
HANG ON
SCOTT and BORGMAN

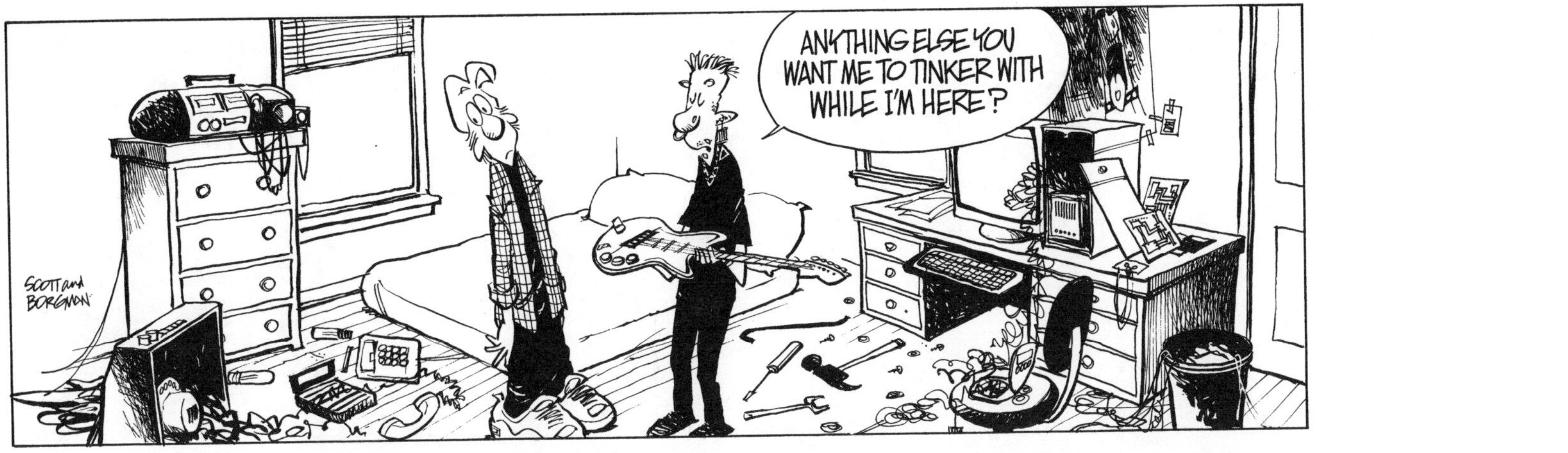
ANYTHING ELSE YOU WANT ME TO TINKER WITH WHILE I'M HERE?
SCOTT and BORGMAN

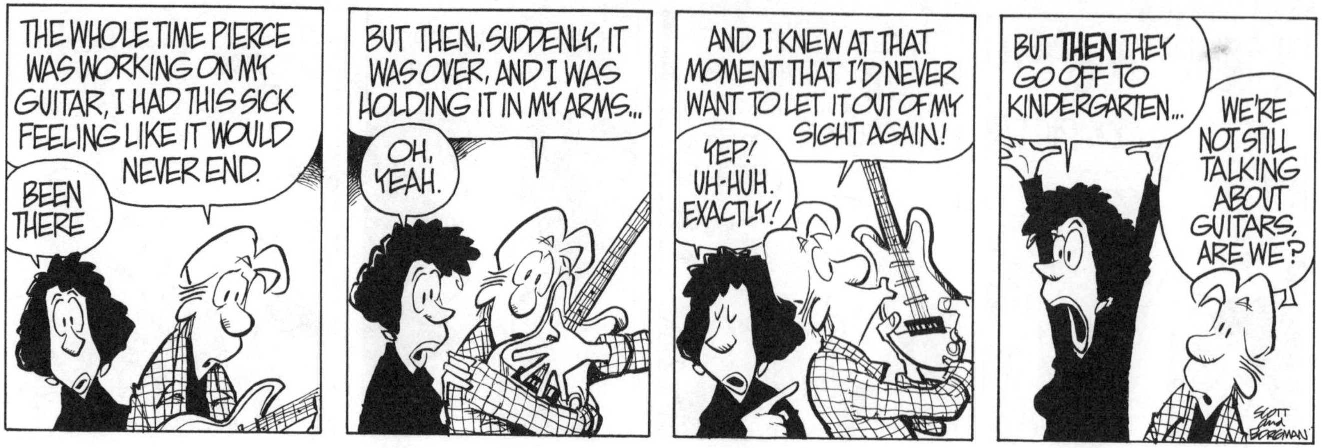
THE WHOLE TIME PIERCE WAS WORKING ON MY GUITAR, I HAD THIS SICK FEELING LIKE IT WOULD NEVER END.
BEEN THERE
BUT THEN, SUDDENLY, IT WAS OVER, AND I WAS HOLDING IT IN MY ARMS...
OH, YEAH.
AND I KNEW AT THAT MOMENT THAT I'D NEVER WANT TO LET IT OUT OF MY SIGHT AGAIN!
YEP! UH-HUH. EXACTLY!
BUT **THEN** THEY GO OFF TO KINDERGARTEN...
WE'RE NOT STILL TALKING ABOUT GUITARS, ARE WE?
SCOTT and BORGMAN

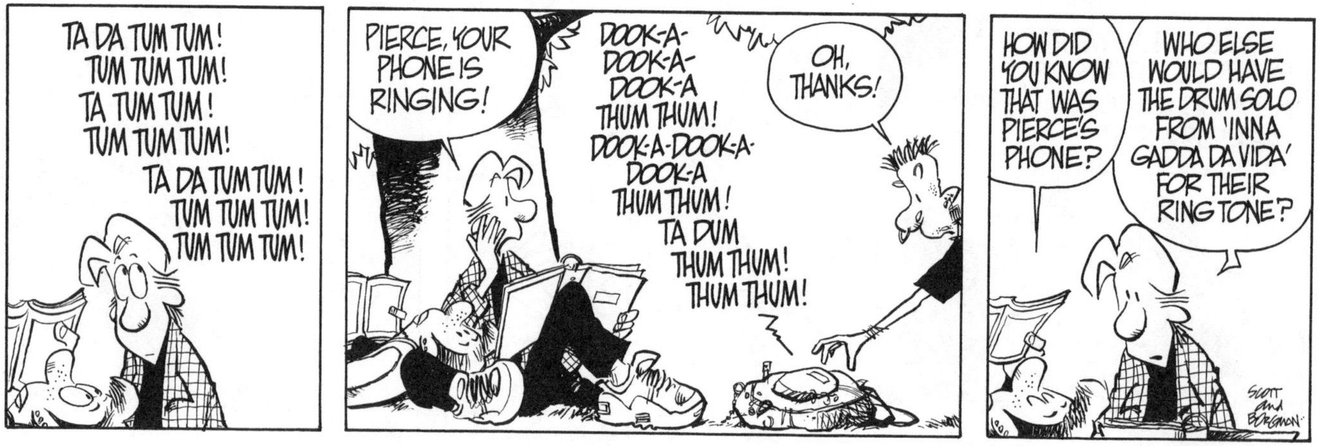
TA DA TUM TUM! TUM TUM TUM! TA TUM TUM! TUM TUM TUM! TA DA TUM TUM! TUM TUM TUM! TUM TUM TUM!
PIERCE, YOUR PHONE IS RINGING!
DOOK-A-DOOK-A-DOOK-A THUM THUM! DOOK-A-DOOK-A-DOOK-A THUM THUM! TA DUM THUM THUM! THUM THUM!
OH, THANKS!
HOW DID YOU KNOW THAT WAS PIERCE'S PHONE?
WHO ELSE WOULD HAVE THE DRUM SOLO FROM 'INNA GADDA DA VIDA' FOR THEIR RING TONE?
SCOTT and BORGMAN

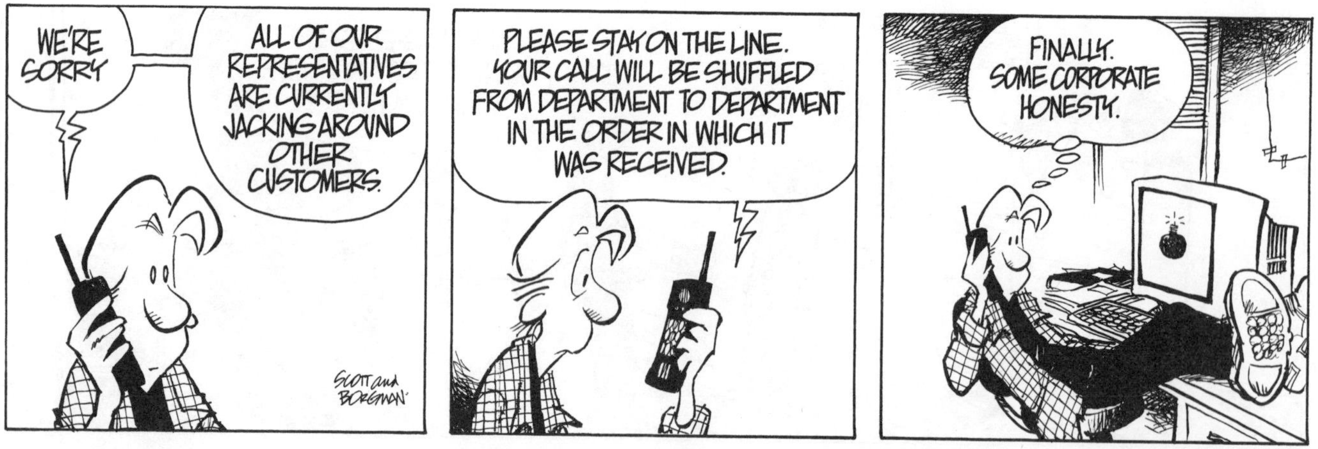
WE'RE SORRY
ALL OF OUR REPRESENTATIVES ARE CURRENTLY JACKING AROUND OTHER CUSTOMERS.
SCOTT and BORGMAN
PLEASE STAY ON THE LINE. YOUR CALL WILL BE SHUFFLED FROM DEPARTMENT TO DEPARTMENT IN THE ORDER IN WHICH IT WAS RECEIVED.
FINALLY. SOME CORPORATE HONESTY.

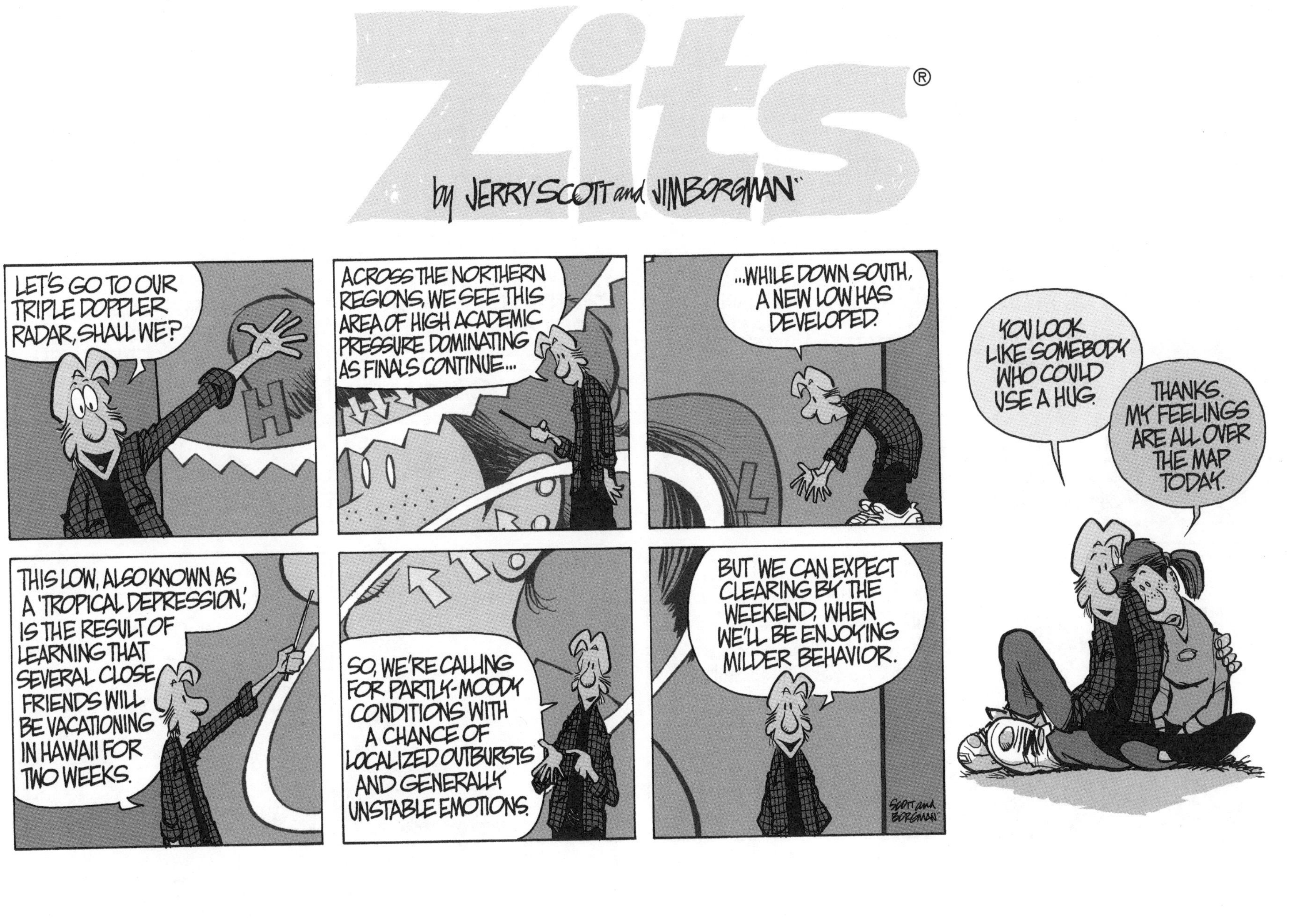
Zits®
by JERRY SCOTT and JIM BORGMAN
LET'S GO TO OUR TRIPLE DOPPLER RADAR, SHALL WE?
ACROSS THE NORTHERN REGIONS, WE SEE THIS AREA OF HIGH ACADEMIC PRESSURE DOMINATING AS FINALS CONTINUE...
...WHILE DOWN SOUTH, A NEW LOW HAS DEVELOPED.
YOU LOOK LIKE SOMEBODY WHO COULD USE A HUG.
THANKS. MY FEELINGS ARE ALL OVER THE MAP TODAY.
THIS LOW, ALSO KNOWN AS A 'TROPICAL DEPRESSION,' IS THE RESULT OF LEARNING THAT SEVERAL CLOSE FRIENDS WILL BE VACATIONING IN HAWAII FOR TWO WEEKS.
SO, WE'RE CALLING FOR PARTLY-MOODY CONDITIONS WITH A CHANCE OF LOCALIZED OUTBURSTS AND GENERALLY UNSTABLE EMOTIONS.
BUT WE CAN EXPECT CLEARING BY THE WEEKEND, WHEN WE'LL BE ENJOYING MILDER BEHAVIOR.
SCOTT and BORGMAN

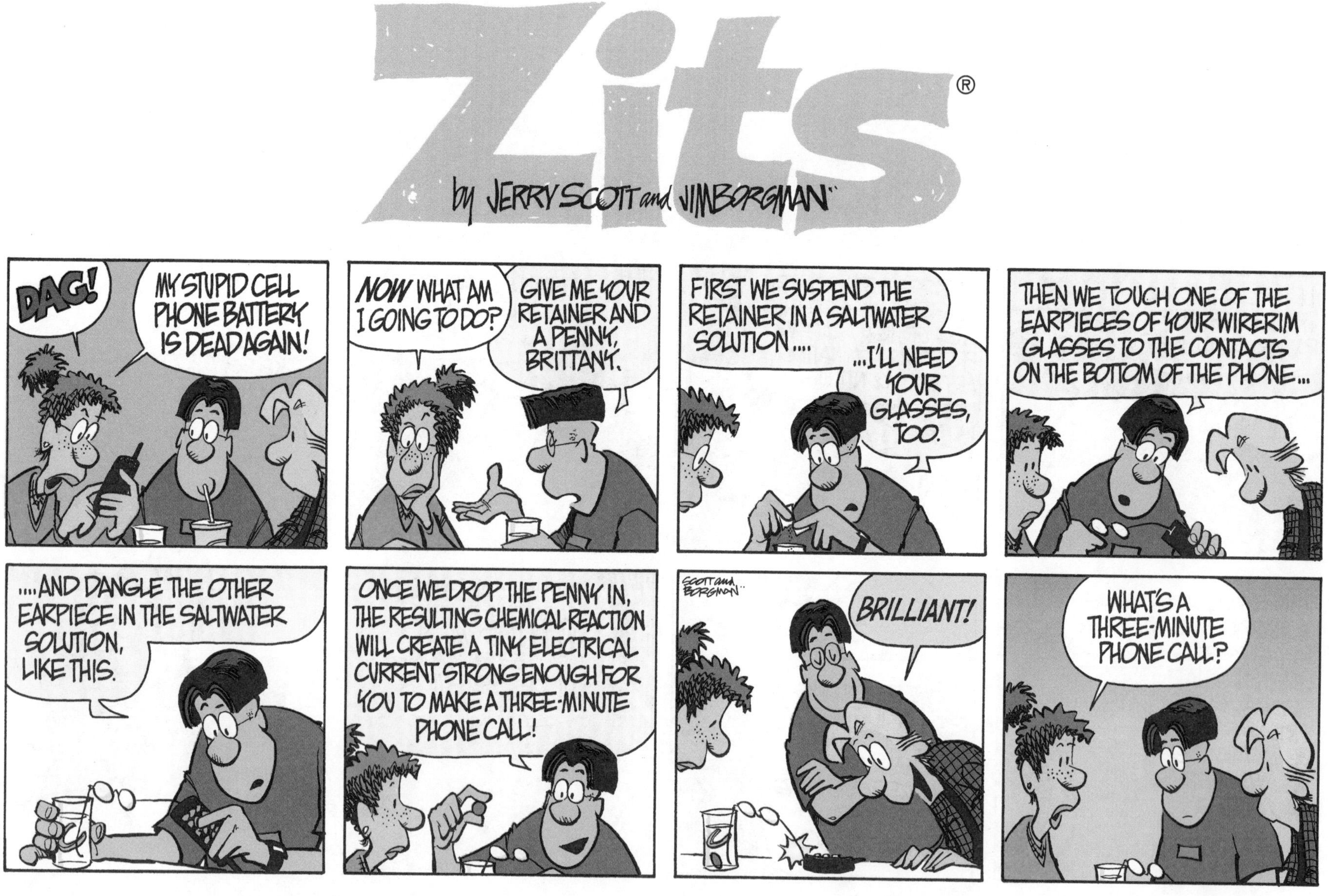
Zits®
by JERRY SCOTT and JIM BORGMAN
DAG!
MY STUPID CELL PHONE BATTERY IS DEAD AGAIN!
NOW WHAT AM I GOING TO DO?
GIVE ME YOUR RETAINER AND A PENNY, BRITTANY.
FIRST WE SUSPEND THE RETAINER IN A SALTWATER SOLUTION....
...I'LL NEED YOUR GLASSES, TOO.
THEN WE TOUCH ONE OF THE EARPIECES OF YOUR WIRERIM GLASSES TO THE CONTACTS ON THE BOTTOM OF THE PHONE...
....AND DANGLE THE OTHER EARPIECE IN THE SALTWATER SOLUTION, LIKE THIS.
ONCE WE DROP THE PENNY IN, THE RESULTING CHEMICAL REACTION WILL CREATE A TINY ELECTRICAL CURRENT STRONG ENOUGH FOR YOU TO MAKE A THREE-MINUTE PHONE CALL!
BRILLIANT!
WHAT'S A THREE-MINUTE PHONE CALL?

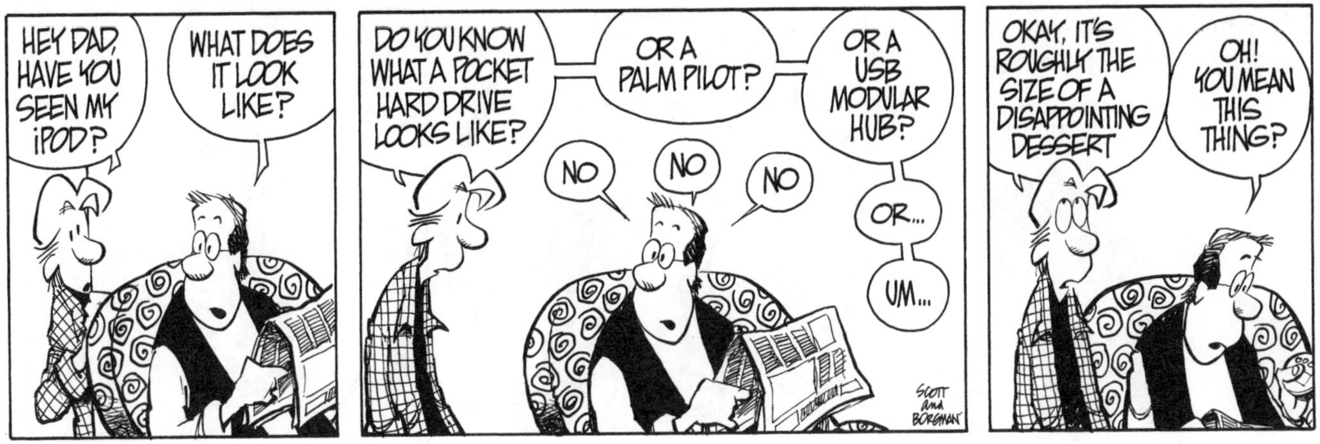
HEY DAD, HAVE YOU SEEN MY iPOD?
WHAT DOES IT LOOK LIKE?
DO YOU KNOW WHAT A POCKET HARD DRIVE LOOKS LIKE?
NO
OR A PALM PILOT?
NO
OR A USB MODULAR HUB?
NO
OR...
UM...
OKAY, IT'S ROUGHLY THE SIZE OF A DISAPPOINTING DESSERT
OH! YOU MEAN THIS THING?

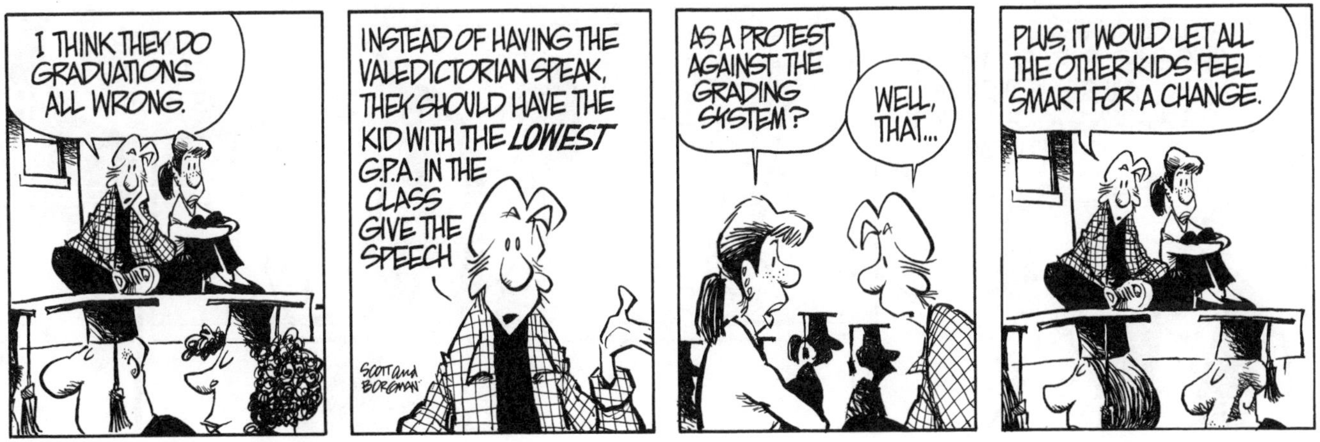
I THINK THEY DO GRADUATIONS ALL WRONG.
INSTEAD OF HAVING THE VALEDICTORIAN SPEAK, THEY SHOULD HAVE THE KID WITH THE ***LOWEST*** G.P.A. IN THE CLASS GIVE THE SPEECH
AS A PROTEST AGAINST THE GRADING SYSTEM?
WELL, THAT...
PLUS, IT WOULD LET ALL THE OTHER KIDS FEEL SMART FOR A CHANGE.

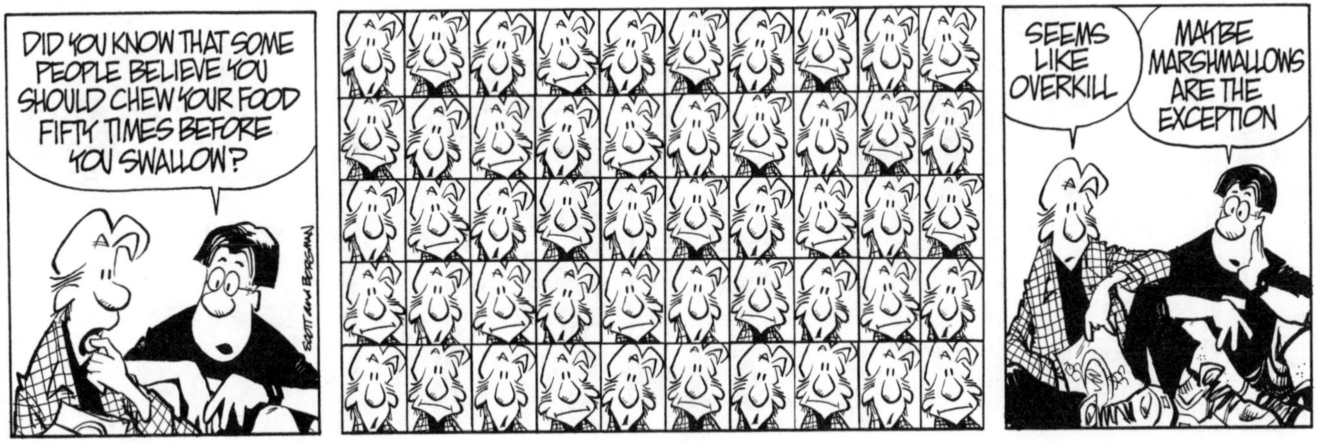
DID YOU KNOW THAT SOME PEOPLE BELIEVE YOU SHOULD CHEW YOUR FOOD FIFTY TIMES BEFORE YOU SWALLOW?
SEEMS LIKE OVERKILL
MAYBE MARSHMALLOWS ARE THE EXCEPTION

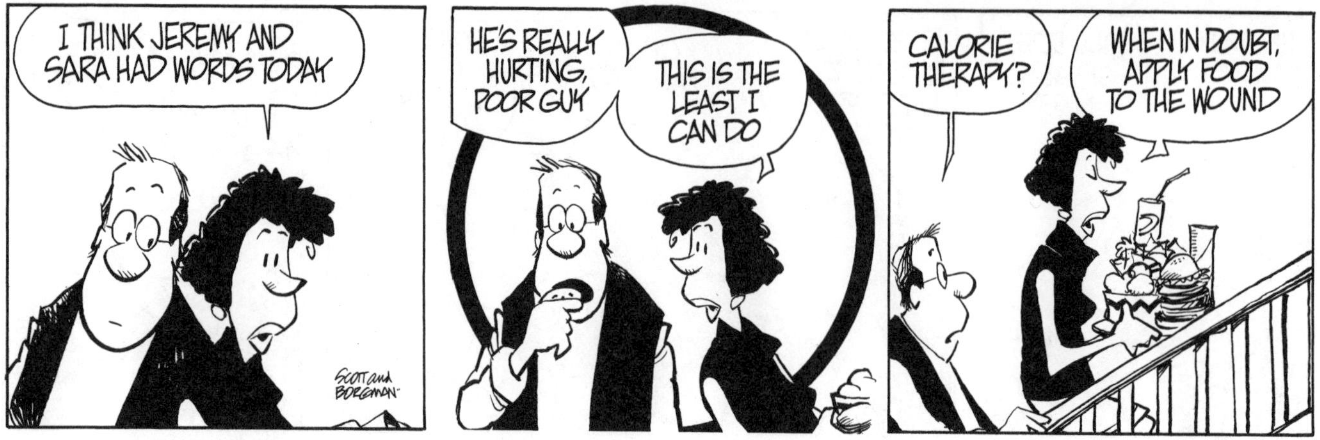
I THINK JEREMY AND SARA HAD WORDS TODAY
HE'S REALLY HURTING, POOR GUY
THIS IS THE LEAST I CAN DO
CALORIE THERAPY?
WHEN IN DOUBT, APPLY FOOD TO THE WOUND

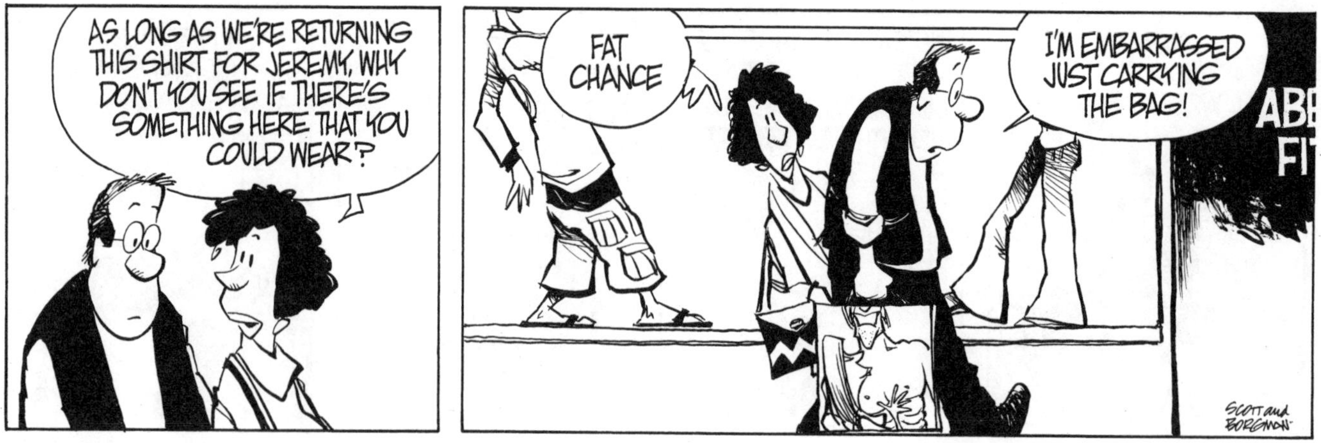
AS LONG AS WE'RE RETURNING THIS SHIRT FOR JEREMY, WHY DON'T YOU SEE IF THERE'S SOMETHING HERE THAT YOU COULD WEAR?
FAT CHANCE
I'M EMBARRASSED JUST CARRYING THE BAG!

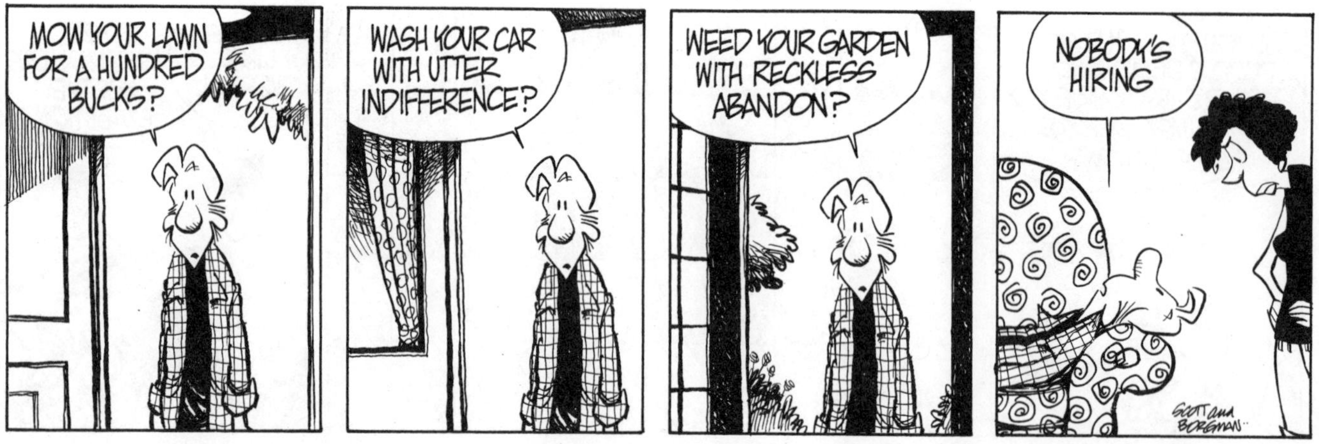
MOW YOUR LAWN FOR A HUNDRED BUCKS?
WASH YOUR CAR WITH UTTER INDIFFERENCE?
WEED YOUR GARDEN WITH RECKLESS ABANDON?
NOBODY'S HIRING

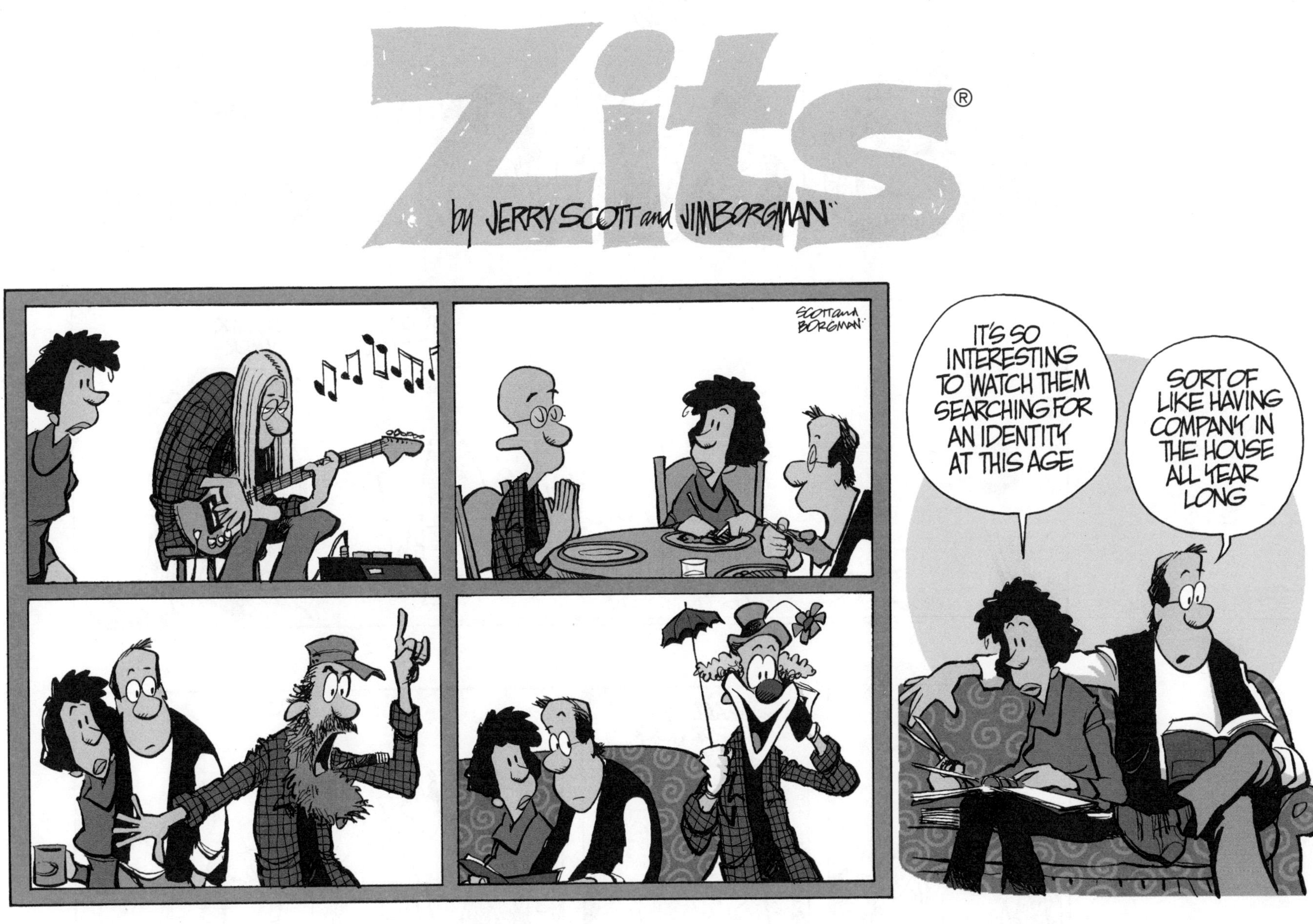
Zits®
by JERRY SCOTT and JIM BORGMAN
SCOTT and BORGMAN
IT'S SO INTERESTING TO WATCH THEM SEARCHING FOR AN IDENTITY AT THIS AGE
SORT OF LIKE HAVING COMPANY IN THE HOUSE ALL YEAR LONG

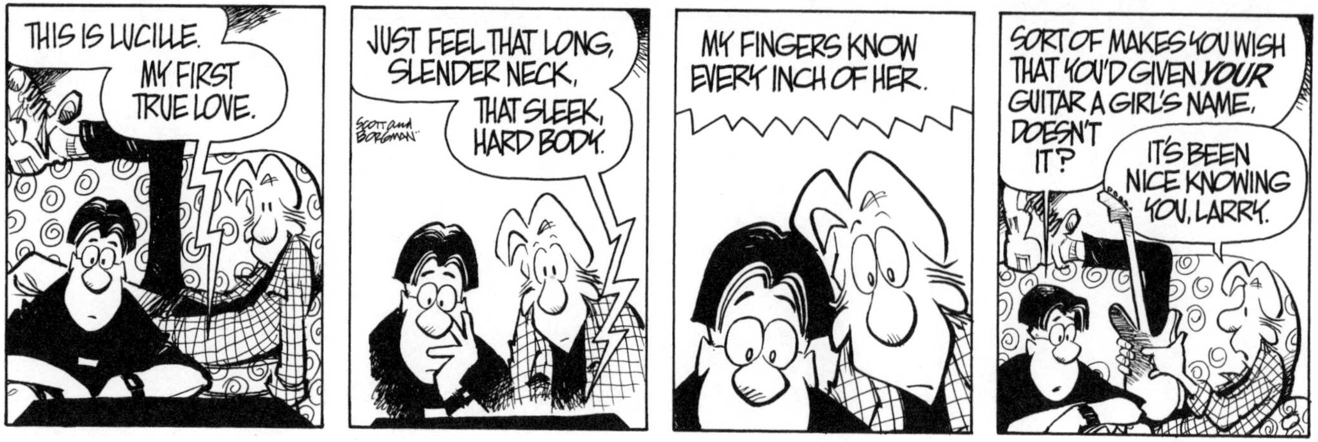
THIS IS LUCILLE.
MY FIRST TRUE LOVE.
SCOTT and BORGMAN
JUST FEEL THAT LONG, SLENDER NECK,
THAT SLEEK, HARD BODY.
MY FINGERS KNOW EVERY INCH OF HER.
SORT OF MAKES YOU WISH THAT YOU'D GIVEN ***YOUR*** GUITAR A GIRL'S NAME, DOESN'T IT?
IT'S BEEN NICE KNOWING YOU, LARRY.

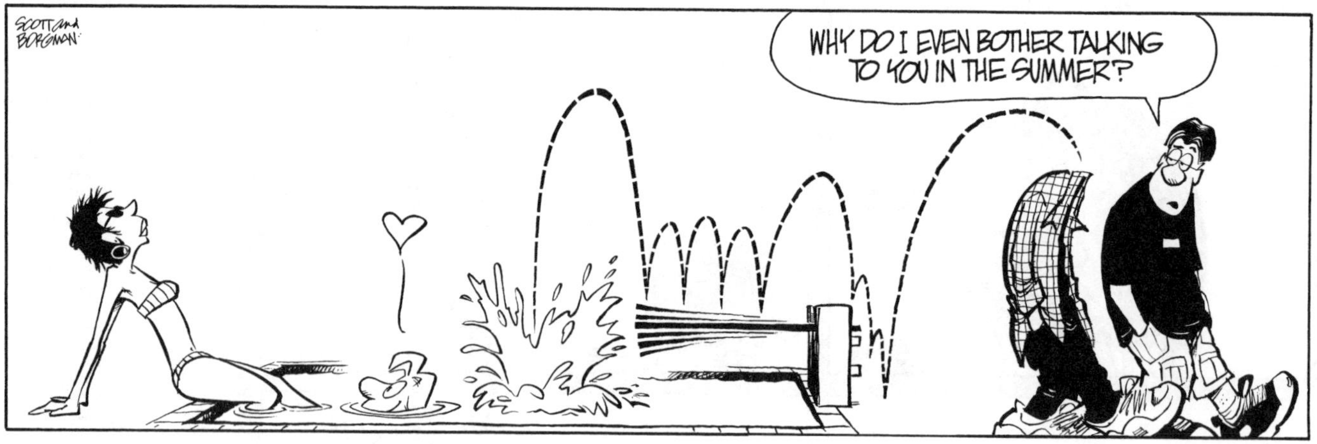
SCOTT and BORGMAN
WHY DO I EVEN BOTHER TALKING TO YOU IN THE SUMMER?

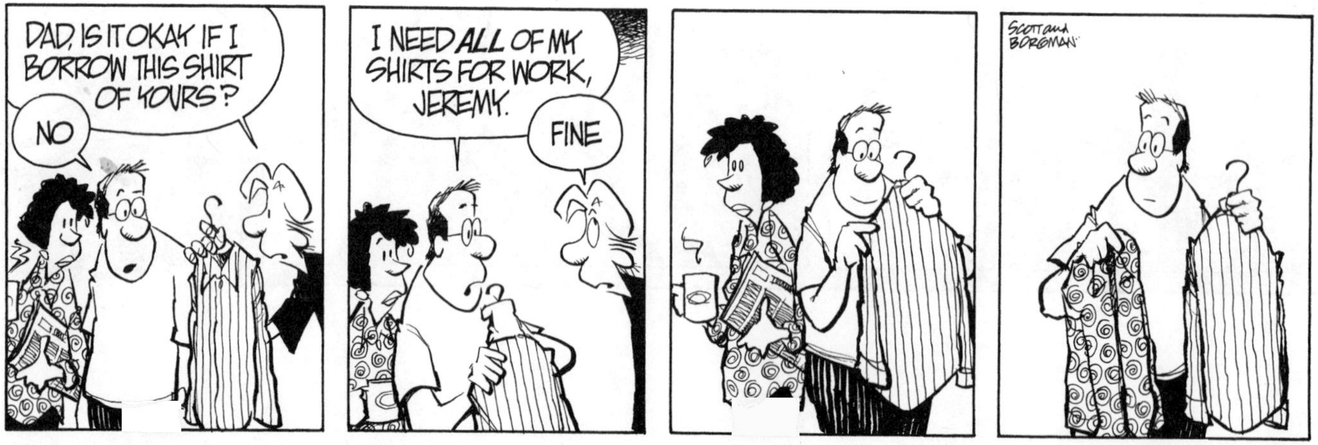
DAD, IS IT OKAY IF I BORROW THIS SHIRT OF YOURS?
NO
I NEED ***ALL*** OF MY SHIRTS FOR WORK, JEREMY.
FINE
SCOTT and BORGMAN

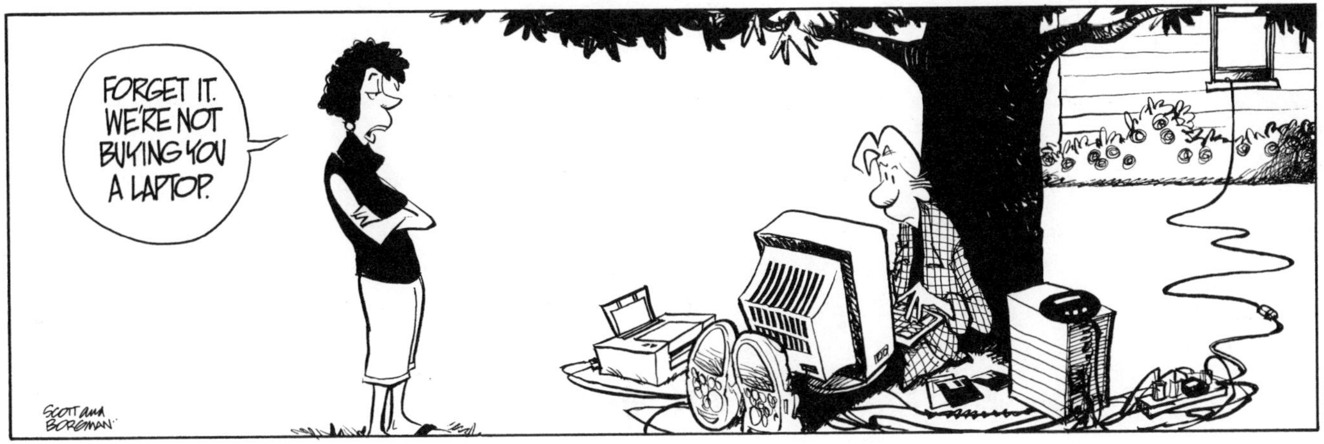
FORGET IT. WE'RE NOT BUYING YOU A LAPTOP.
SCOTT and BORGMAN

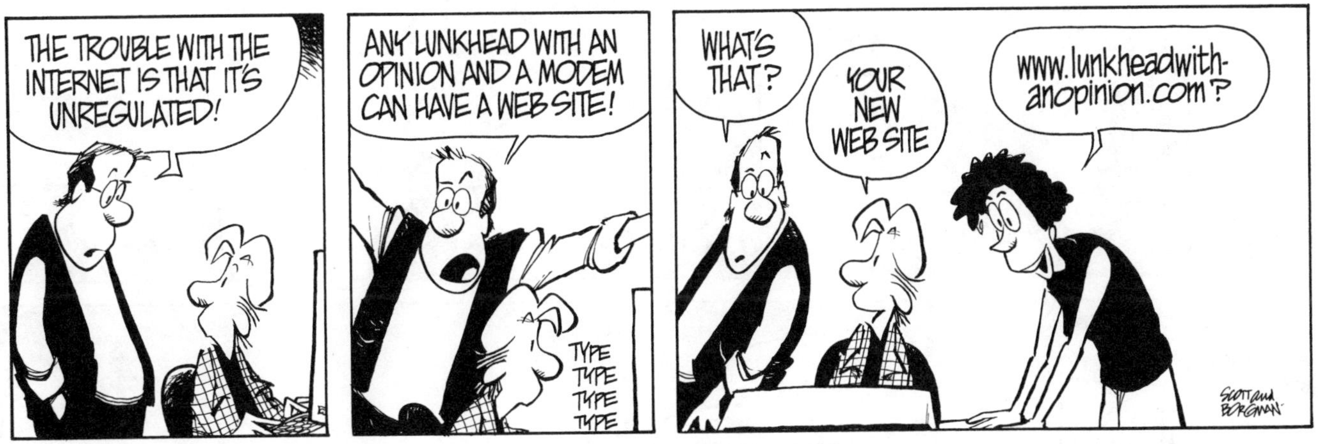
THE TROUBLE WITH THE INTERNET IS THAT IT'S UNREGULATED!
ANY LUNKHEAD WITH AN OPINION AND A MODEM CAN HAVE A WEB SITE!
TYPE TYPE TYPE TYPE
WHAT'S THAT?
YOUR NEW WEB SITE
www.lunkheadwith-anopinion.com?
SCOTT and BORGMAN

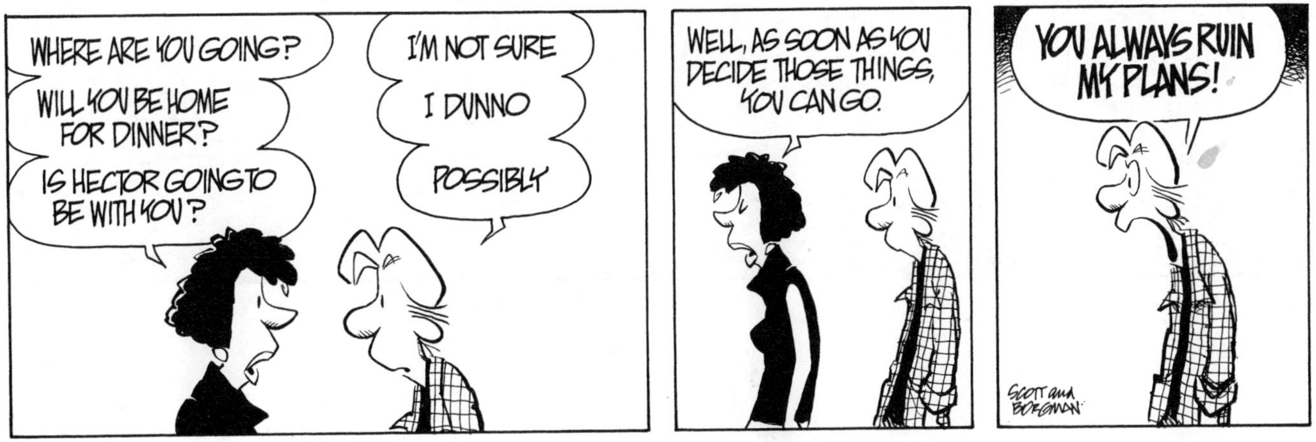
WHERE ARE YOU GOING?
I'M NOT SURE
WILL YOU BE HOME FOR DINNER?
I DUNNO
IS HECTOR GOING TO BE WITH YOU?
POSSIBLY
WELL, AS SOON AS YOU DECIDE THOSE THINGS, YOU CAN GO.
YOU ALWAYS RUIN MY PLANS!
SCOTT and BORGMAN

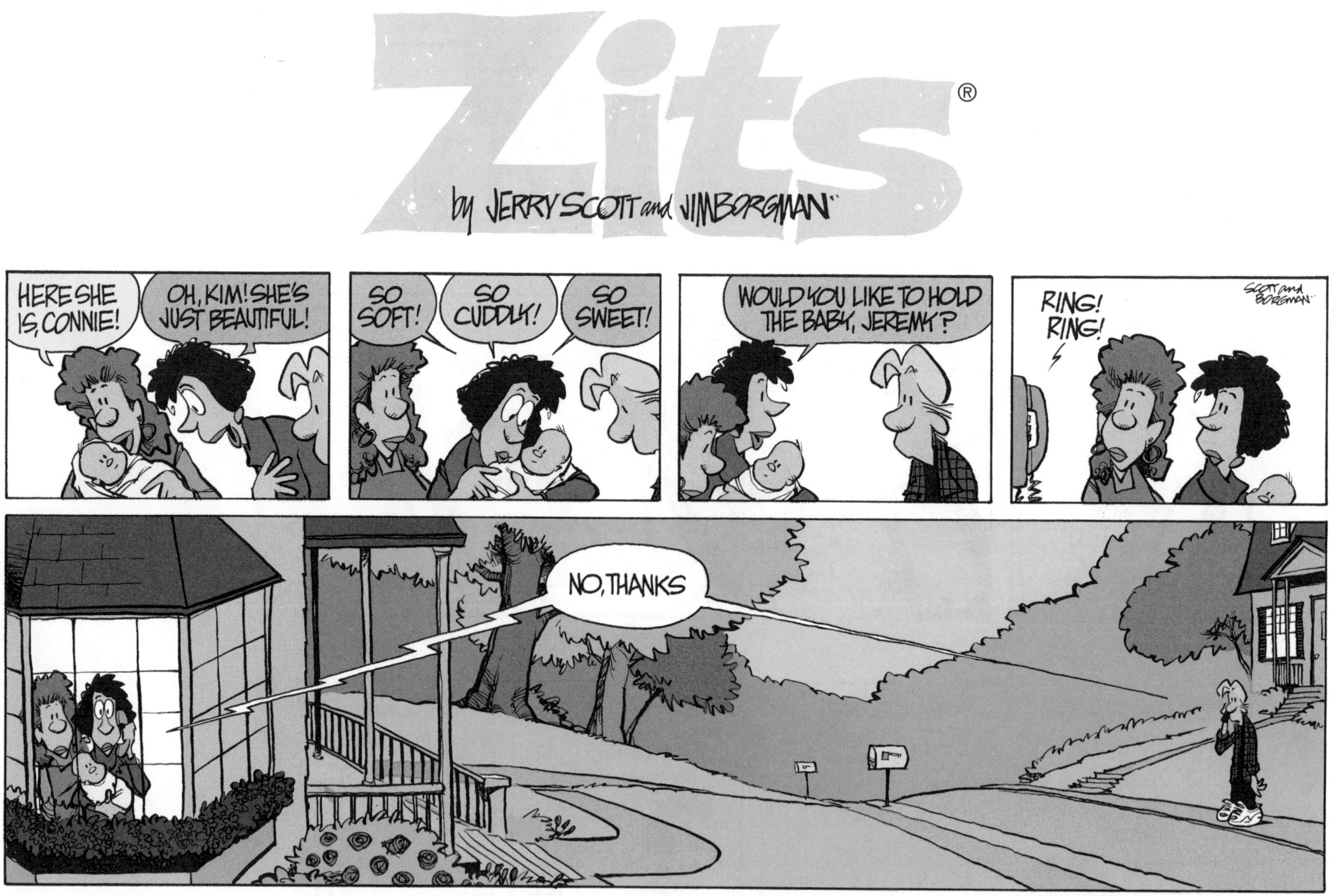
Zits®
by JERRY SCOTT and JIM BORGMAN
HERE SHE IS, CONNIE!
OH, KIM! SHE'S JUST BEAUTIFUL!
SO SOFT!
SO CUDDLY!
SO SWEET!
WOULD YOU LIKE TO HOLD THE BABY, JEREMY?
SCOTT and BORGMAN
RING! RING!
NO, THANKS

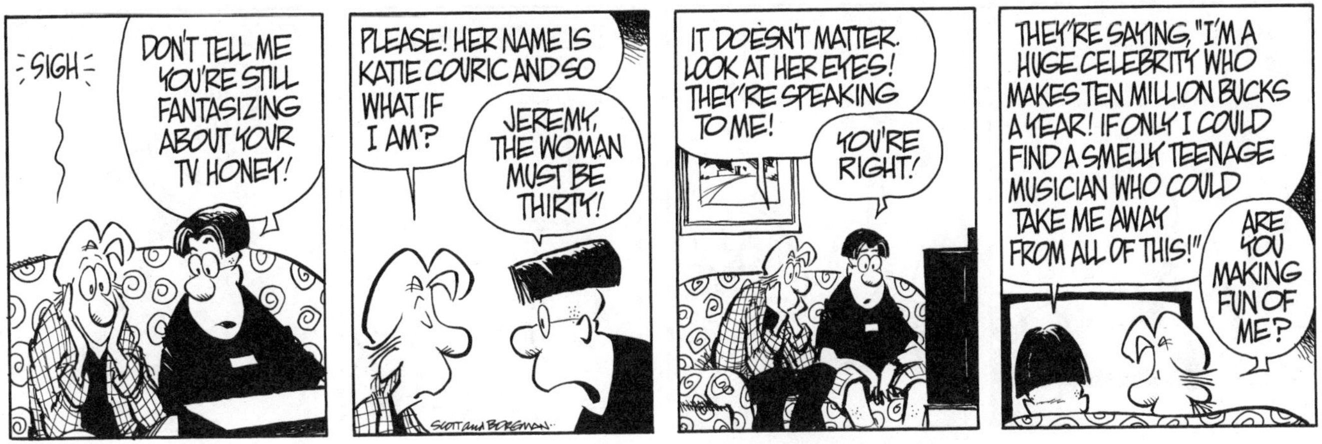
SIGH
DON'T TELL ME YOU'RE STILL FANTASIZING ABOUT YOUR TV HONEY!
PLEASE! HER NAME IS KATIE COURIC AND SO WHAT IF I AM?
JEREMY, THE WOMAN MUST BE THIRTY!
IT DOESN'T MATTER. LOOK AT HER EYES! THEY'RE SPEAKING TO ME!
YOU'RE RIGHT!
THEY'RE SAYING, "I'M A HUGE CELEBRITY WHO MAKES TEN MILLION BUCKS A YEAR! IF ONLY I COULD FIND A SMELLY TEENAGE MUSICIAN WHO COULD TAKE ME AWAY FROM ALL OF THIS!"
ARE YOU MAKING FUN OF ME?

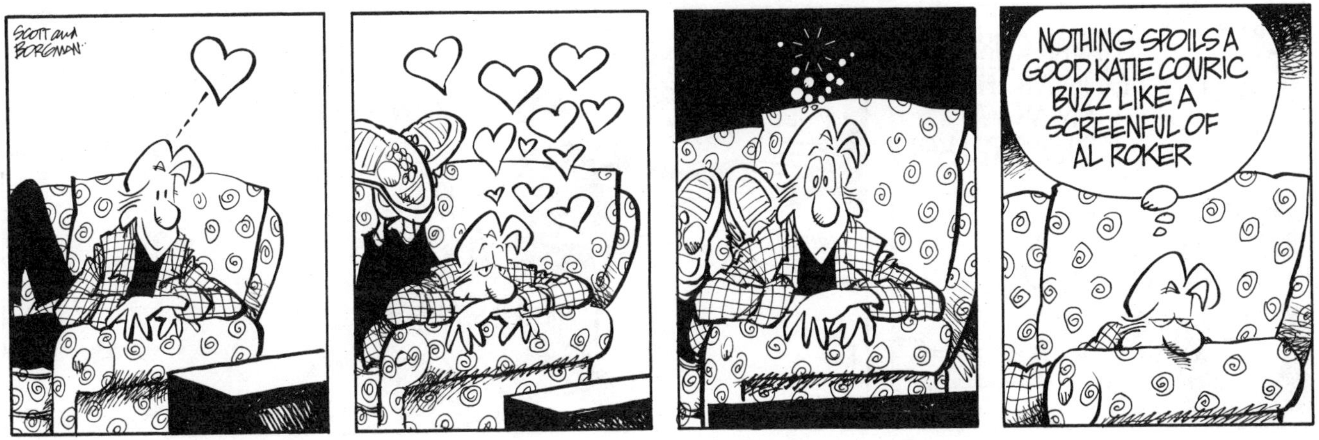
NOTHING SPOILS A GOOD KATIE COURIC BUZZ LIKE A SCREENFUL OF AL ROKER

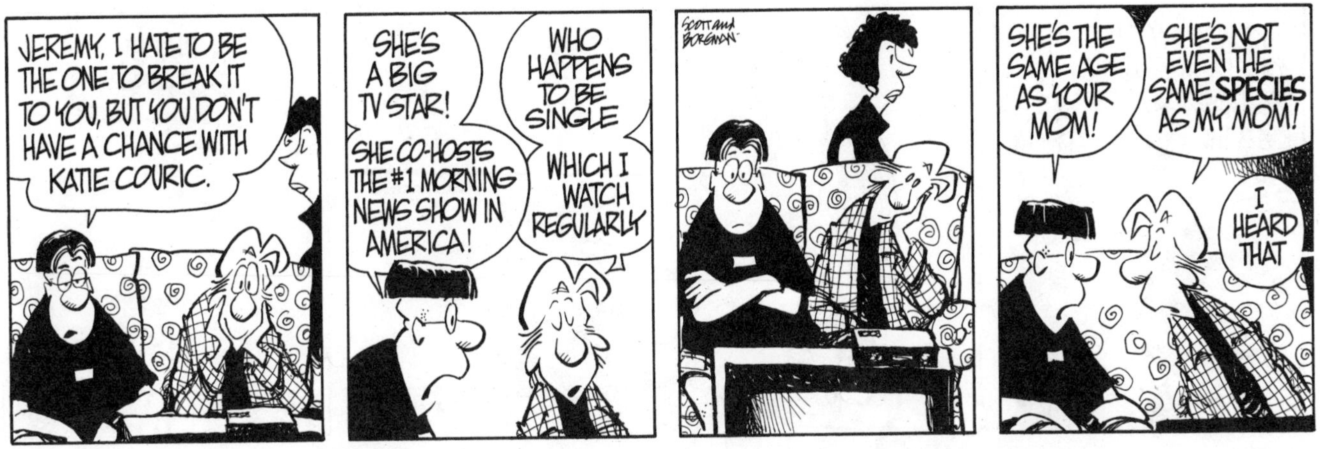
JEREMY, I HATE TO BE THE ONE TO BREAK IT TO YOU, BUT YOU DON'T HAVE A CHANCE WITH KATIE COURIC.
SHE'S A BIG TV STAR!
WHO HAPPENS TO BE SINGLE
SHE CO-HOSTS THE #1 MORNING NEWS SHOW IN AMERICA!
WHICH I WATCH REGULARLY
SHE'S THE SAME AGE AS YOUR MOM!
SHE'S NOT EVEN THE SAME **SPECIES** AS MY MOM!
I HEARD THAT

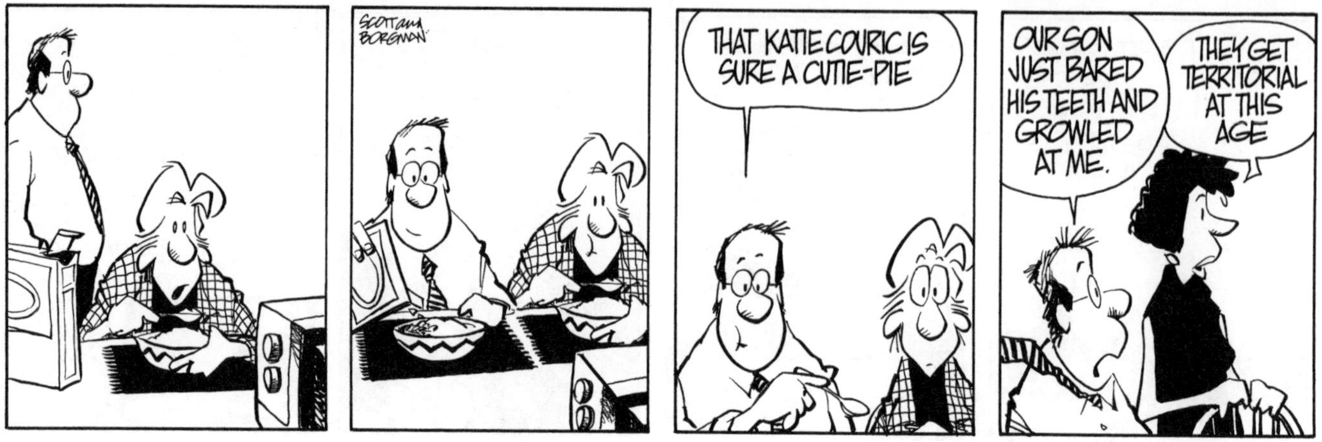
SCOTT and BORGMAN
THAT KATIE COURIC IS SURE A CUTIE-PIE
OUR SON JUST BARED HIS TEETH AND GROWLED AT ME.
THEY GET TERRITORIAL AT THIS AGE

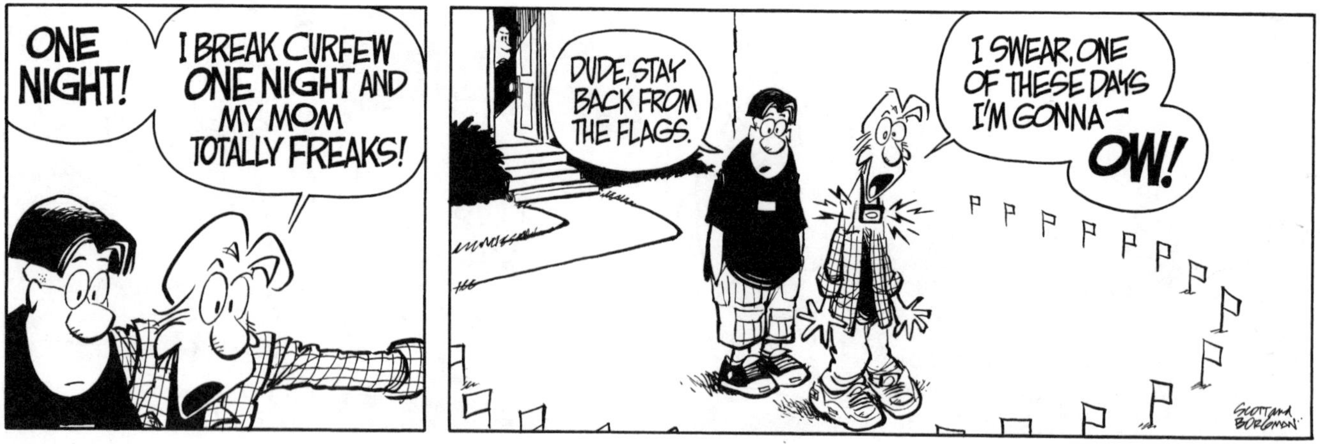
ONE NIGHT!
I BREAK CURFEW ONE NIGHT AND MY MOM TOTALLY FREAKS!
DUDE, STAY BACK FROM THE FLAGS.
I SWEAR, ONE OF THESE DAYS I'M GONNA—
OW!
SCOTT and BORGMAN

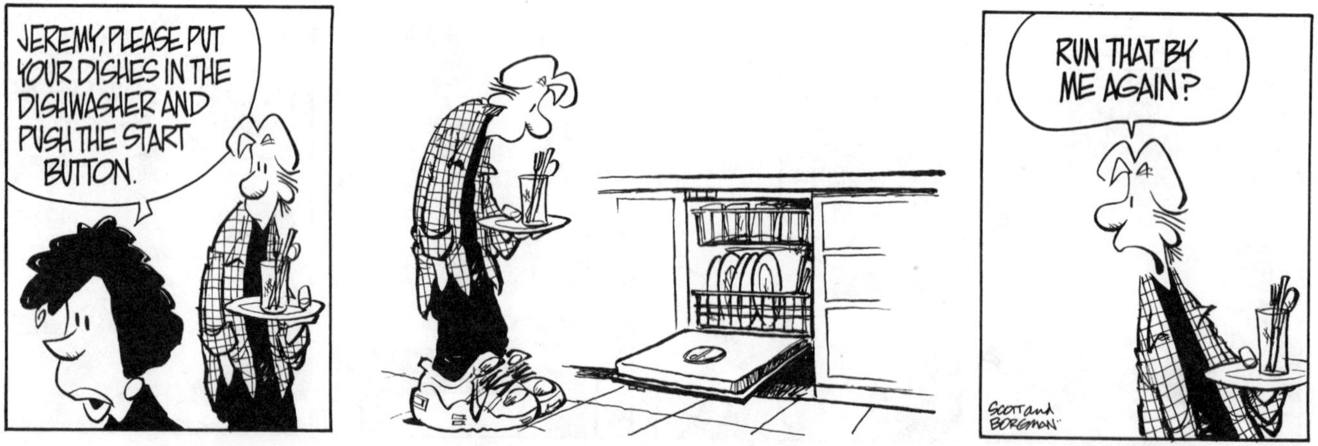
JEREMY, PLEASE PUT YOUR DISHES IN THE DISHWASHER AND PUSH THE START BUTTON.
RUN THAT BY ME AGAIN?
SCOTT and BORGMAN

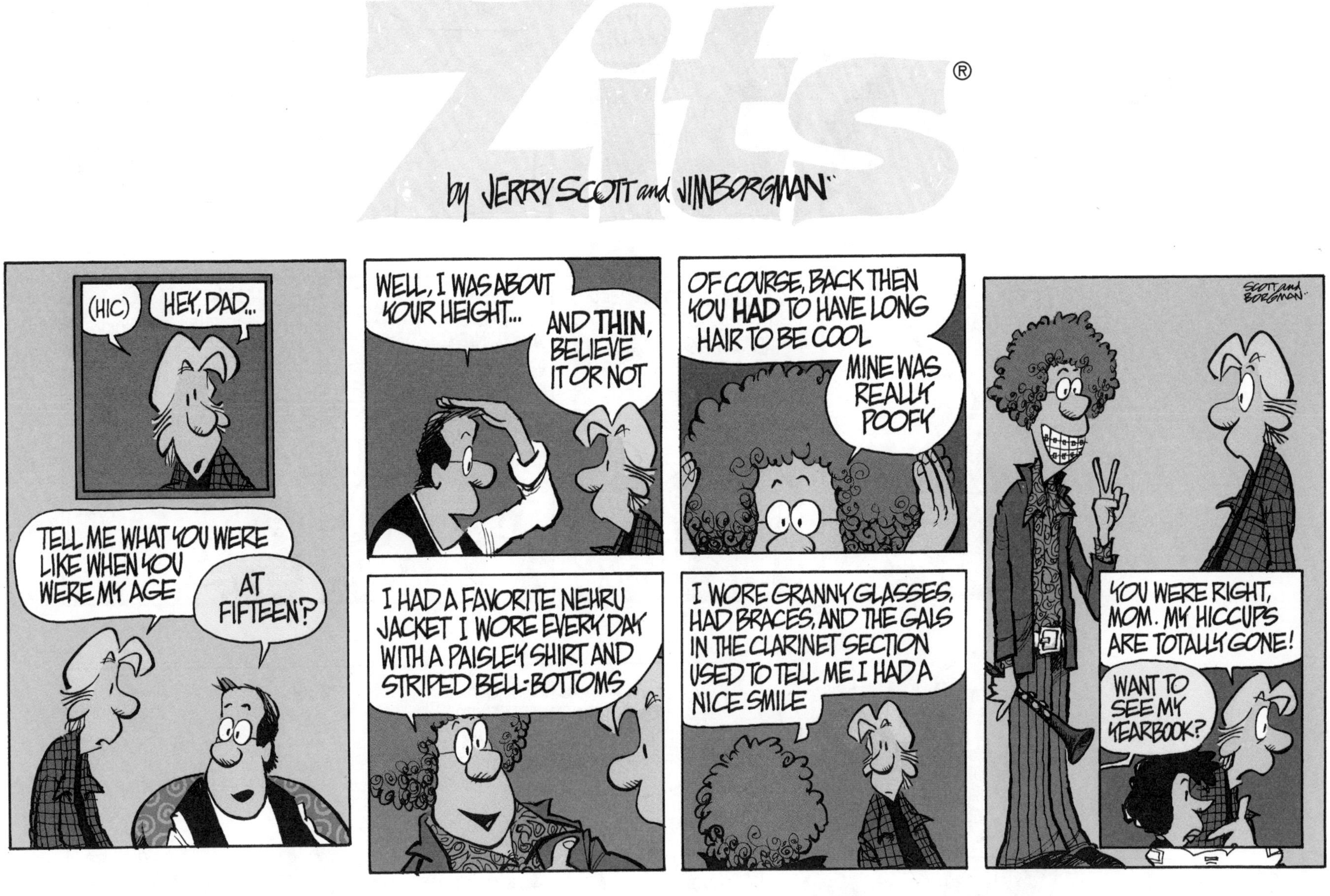

Zits®
by JERRY SCOTT and JIM BORGMAN
(HIC)
HEY, DAD...
TELL ME WHAT YOU WERE LIKE WHEN YOU WERE MY AGE
AT FIFTEEN?
WELL, I WAS ABOUT YOUR HEIGHT...
AND THIN, BELIEVE IT OR NOT
OF COURSE, BACK THEN YOU HAD TO HAVE LONG HAIR TO BE COOL
MINE WAS REALLY POOFY
I HAD A FAVORITE NEHRU JACKET I WORE EVERY DAY WITH A PAISLEY SHIRT AND STRIPED BELL-BOTTOMS
I WORE GRANNY GLASSES, HAD BRACES, AND THE GALS IN THE CLARINET SECTION USED TO TELL ME I HAD A NICE SMILE
SCOTT and BORGMAN
YOU WERE RIGHT, MOM. MY HICCUPS ARE TOTALLY GONE!
WANT TO SEE MY YEARBOOK?

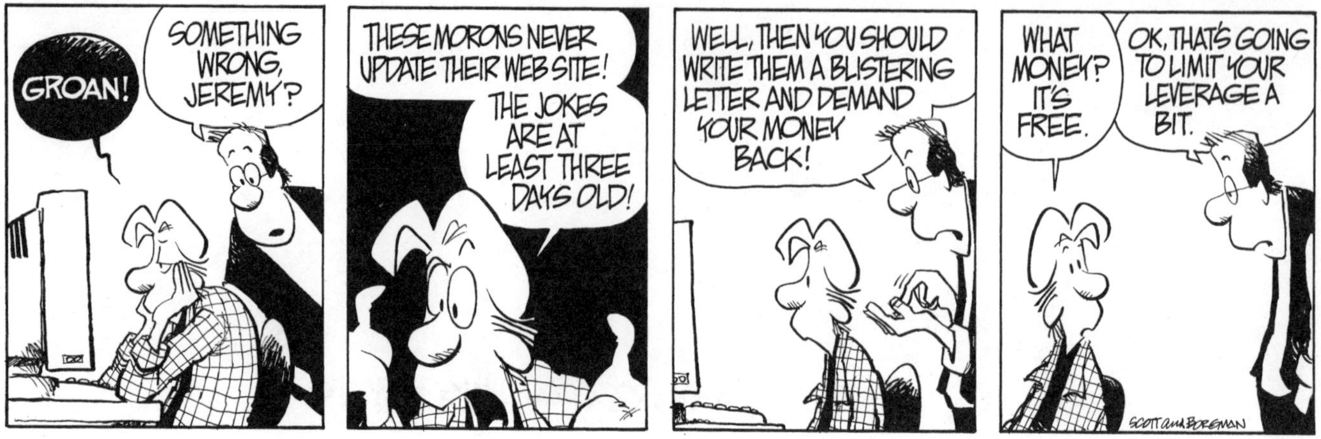
GROAN!
SOMETHING WRONG, JEREMY?
THESE MORONS NEVER UPDATE THEIR WEB SITE!
THE JOKES ARE AT LEAST THREE DAYS OLD!
WELL, THEN YOU SHOULD WRITE THEM A BLISTERING LETTER AND DEMAND YOUR MONEY BACK!
WHAT MONEY? IT'S FREE.
OK, THAT'S GOING TO LIMIT YOUR LEVERAGE A BIT.
SCOTT AND BORGMAN

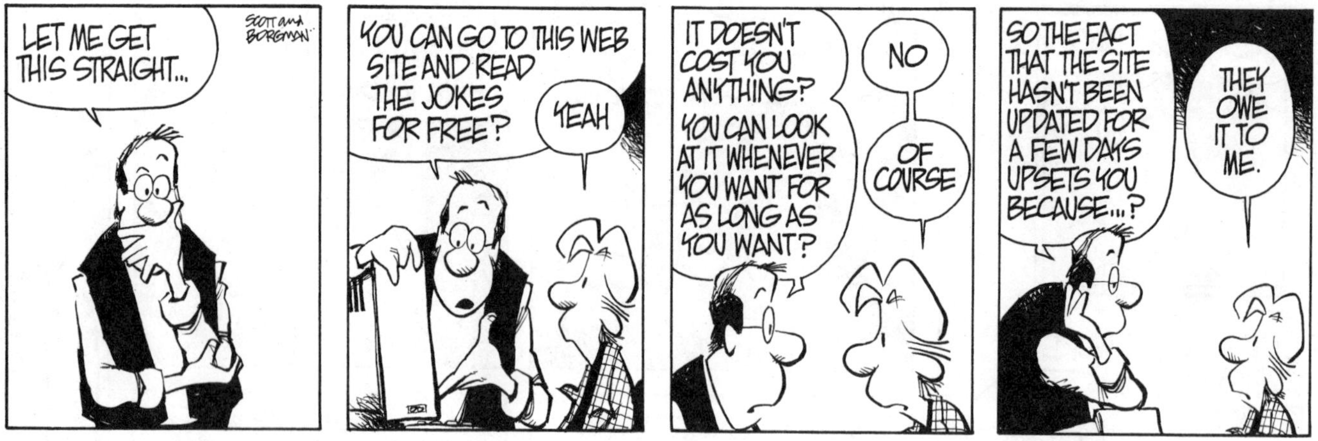
LET ME GET THIS STRAIGHT...
SCOTT AND BORGMAN
YOU CAN GO TO THIS WEB SITE AND READ THE JOKES FOR FREE?
YEAH
IT DOESN'T COST YOU ANYTHING?
YOU CAN LOOK AT IT WHENEVER YOU WANT FOR AS LONG AS YOU WANT?
NO
OF COURSE
SO THE FACT THAT THE SITE HASN'T BEEN UPDATED FOR A FEW DAYS UPSETS YOU BECAUSE...?
THEY OWE IT TO ME.

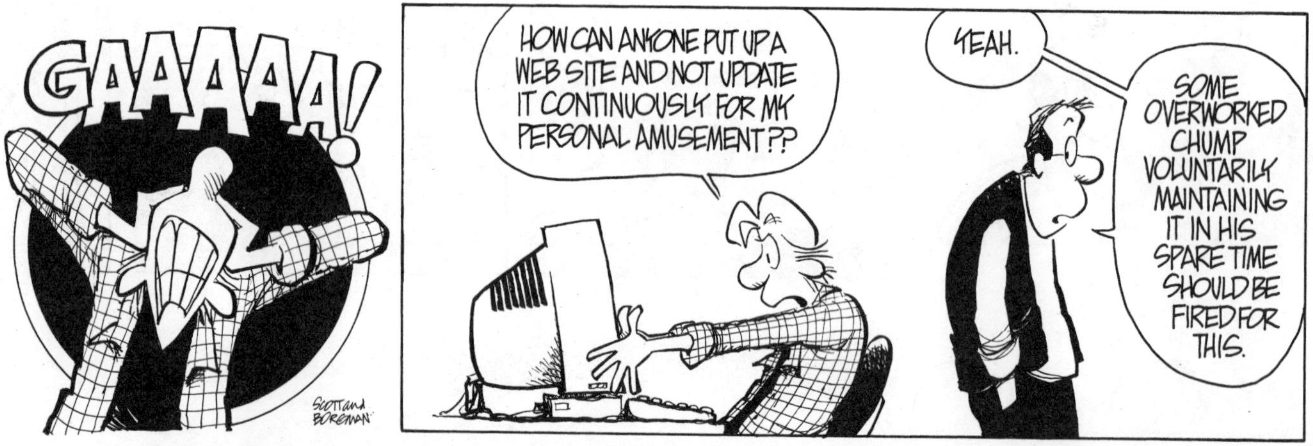
GAAAAA!
SCOTT AND BORGMAN
HOW CAN ANYONE PUT UP A WEB SITE AND NOT UPDATE IT CONTINUOUSLY FOR MY PERSONAL AMUSEMENT??
YEAH.
SOME OVERWORKED CHUMP VOLUNTARILY MAINTAINING IT IN HIS SPARE TIME SHOULD BE FIRED FOR THIS.

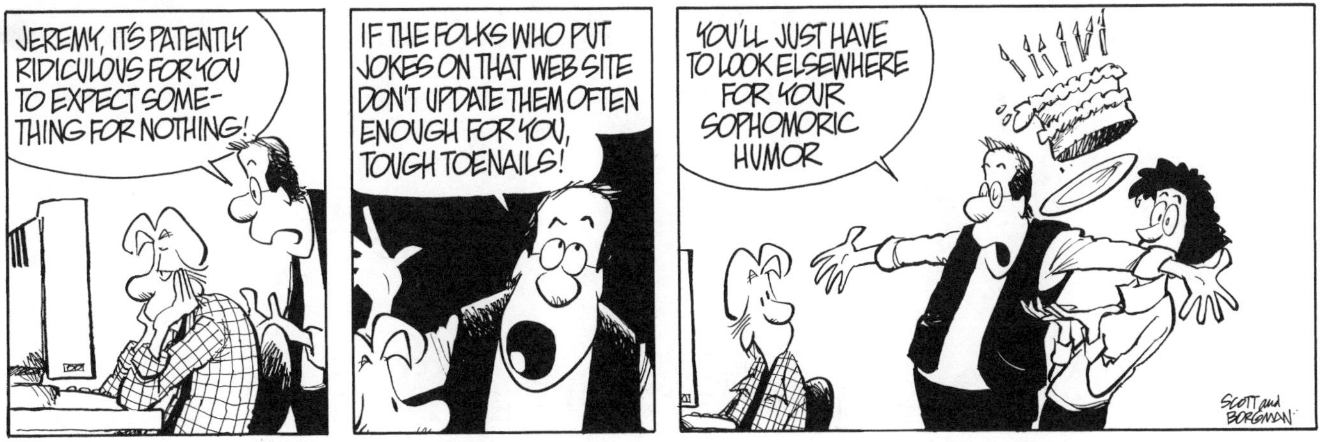
JEREMY, IT'S PATENTLY RIDICULOUS FOR YOU TO EXPECT SOME-THING FOR NOTHING!
IF THE FOLKS WHO PUT JOKES ON THAT WEB SITE DON'T UPDATE THEM OFTEN ENOUGH FOR YOU, TOUGH TOENAILS!
YOU'LL JUST HAVE TO LOOK ELSEWHERE FOR YOUR SOPHOMORIC HUMOR
SCOTT and BORGMAN

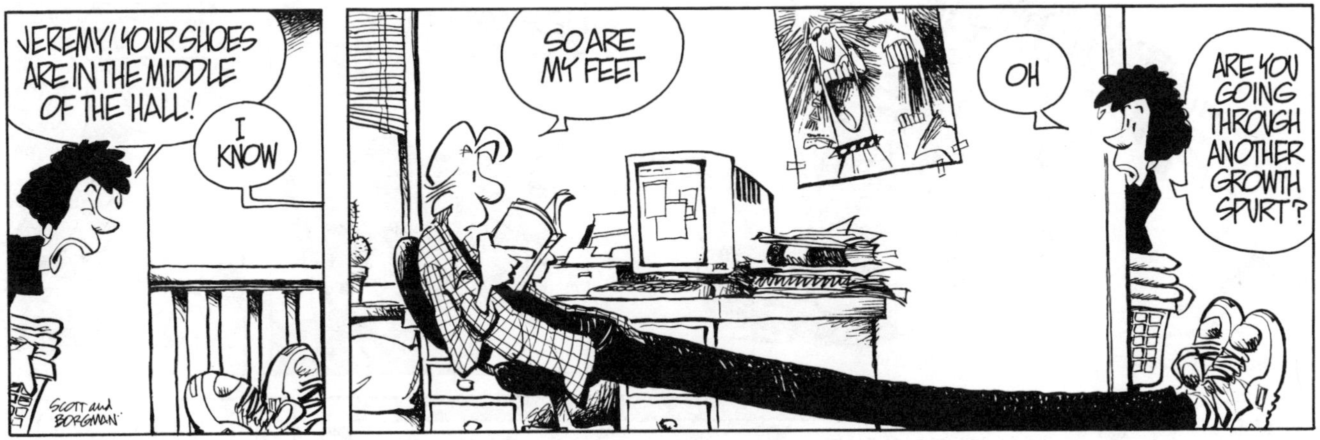
JEREMY! YOUR SHOES ARE IN THE MIDDLE OF THE HALL!
I KNOW
SCOTT and BORGMAN
SO ARE MY FEET
OH
ARE YOU GOING THROUGH ANOTHER GROWTH SPURT?

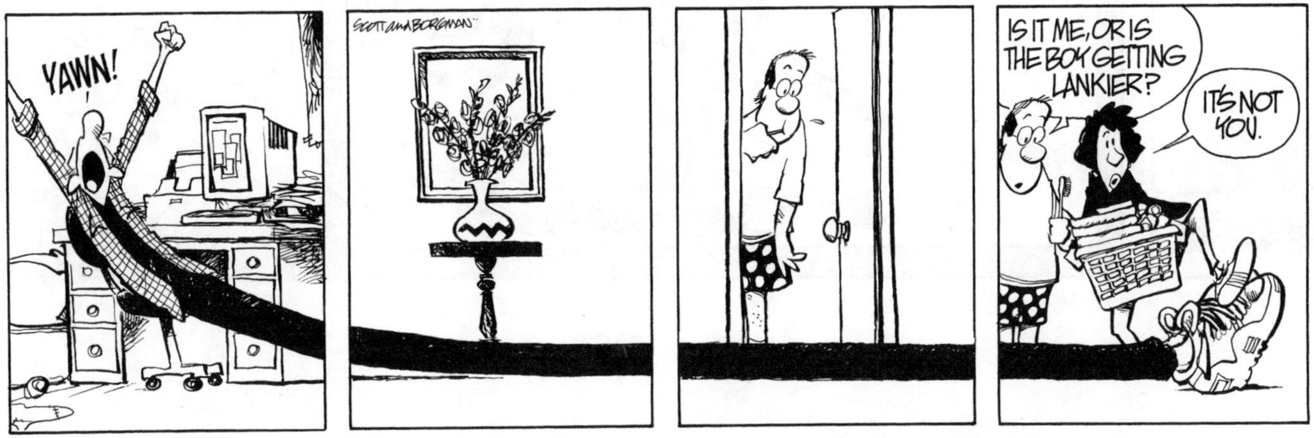
YAWN!
SCOTT and BORGMAN
IS IT ME, OR IS THE BOY GETTING LANKIER?
IT'S NOT YOU.

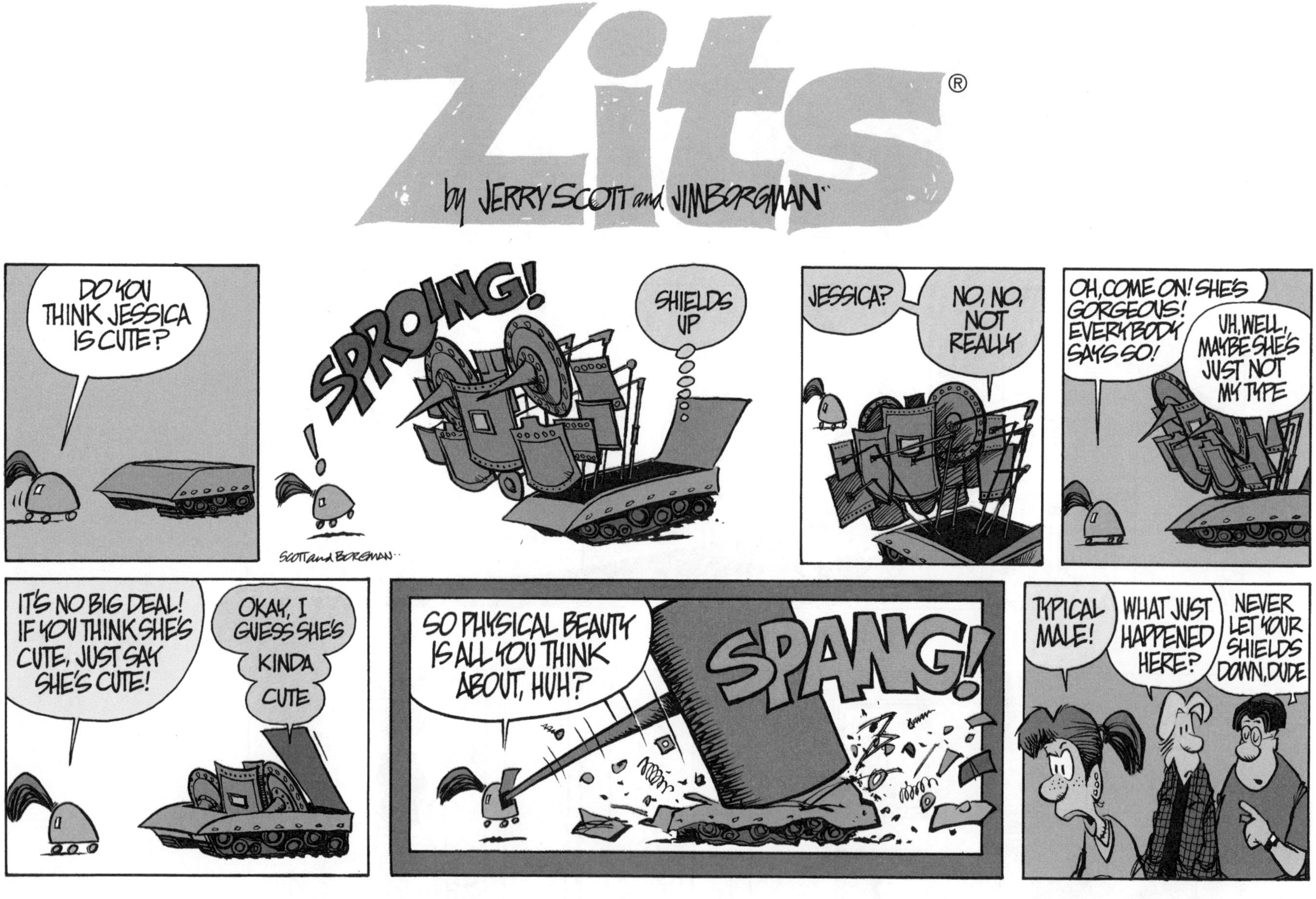
Zits®
by JERRY SCOTT and JIM BORGMAN
DO YOU THINK JESSICA IS CUTE?
SPROING!
!
SHIELDS UP
SCOTT and BORGMAN
JESSICA?
NO, NO, NOT REALLY
OH, COME ON! SHE'S GORGEOUS! EVERYBODY SAYS SO!
UH, WELL, MAYBE SHE'S JUST NOT MY TYPE
IT'S NO BIG DEAL! IF YOU THINK SHE'S CUTE, JUST SAY SHE'S CUTE!
OKAY, I GUESS SHE'S KINDA CUTE
SO PHYSICAL BEAUTY IS ALL YOU THINK ABOUT, HUH?
SPANG!
TYPICAL MALE!
WHAT JUST HAPPENED HERE?
NEVER LET YOUR SHIELDS DOWN, DUDE

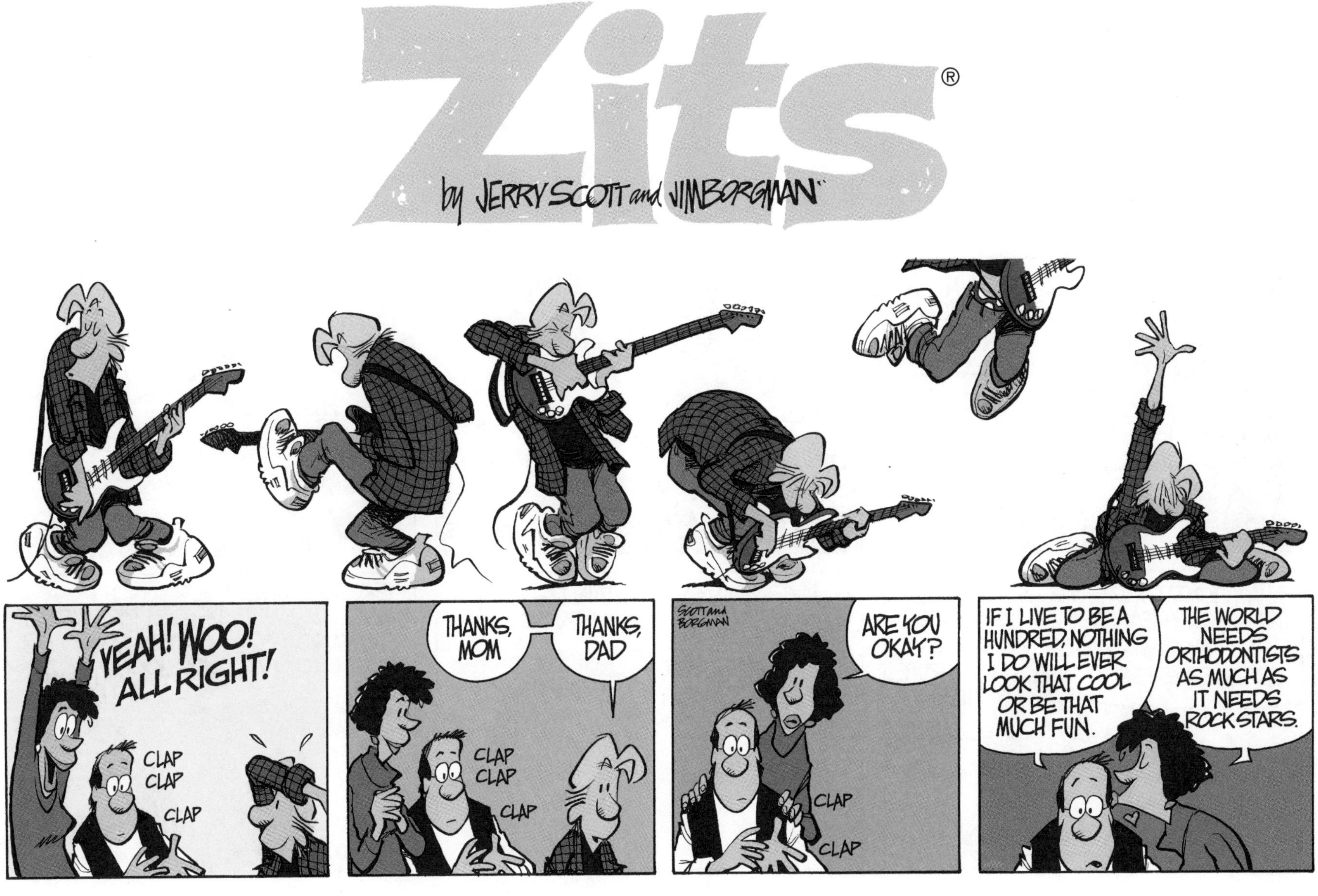
Zits®
by JERRY SCOTT and JIM BORGMAN
YEAH! WOO! ALL RIGHT!
CLAP CLAP
CLAP
THANKS, MOM
THANKS, DAD
CLAP CLAP
CLAP
SCOTT and BORGMAN
ARE YOU OKAY?
CLAP
CLAP
IF I LIVE TO BE A HUNDRED, NOTHING I DO WILL EVER LOOK THAT COOL OR BE THAT MUCH FUN.
THE WORLD NEEDS ORTHODONTISTS AS MUCH AS IT NEEDS ROCK STARS.

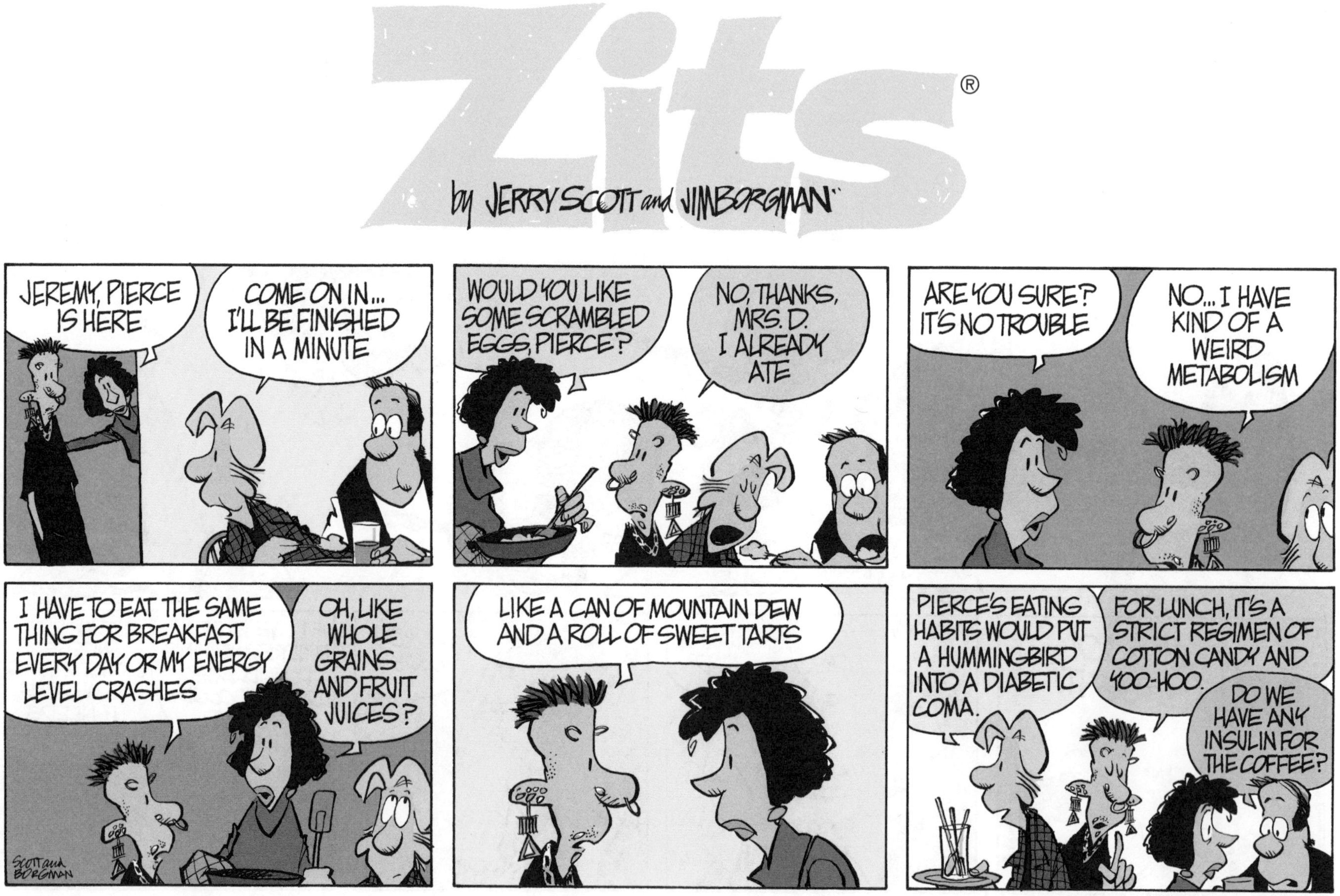

Zits®
by JERRY SCOTT and JIM BORGMAN
JEREMY, PIERCE IS HERE
COME ON IN... I'LL BE FINISHED IN A MINUTE
WOULD YOU LIKE SOME SCRAMBLED EGGS, PIERCE?
NO, THANKS, MRS. D. I ALREADY ATE
ARE YOU SURE? IT'S NO TROUBLE
NO... I HAVE KIND OF A WEIRD METABOLISM
I HAVE TO EAT THE SAME THING FOR BREAKFAST EVERY DAY OR MY ENERGY LEVEL CRASHES
OH, LIKE WHOLE GRAINS AND FRUIT JUICES?
SCOTT and BORGMAN
LIKE A CAN OF MOUNTAIN DEW AND A ROLL OF SWEET TARTS
PIERCE'S EATING HABITS WOULD PUT A HUMMINGBIRD INTO A DIABETIC COMA.
FOR LUNCH, IT'S A STRICT REGIMEN OF COTTON CANDY AND YOO-HOO.
DO WE HAVE ANY INSULIN FOR THE COFFEE?

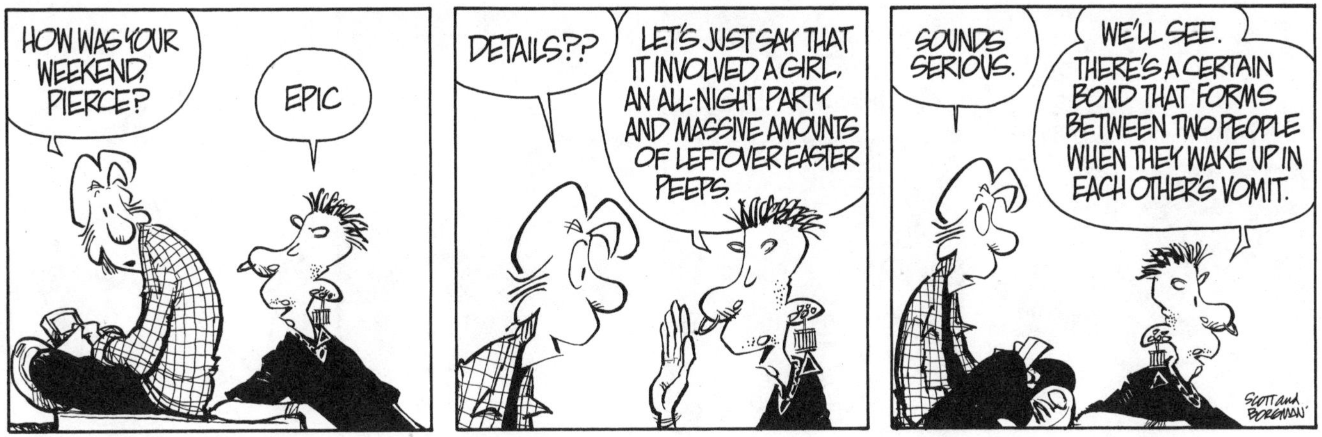
HOW WAS YOUR WEEKEND, PIERCE?
EPIC
DETAILS??
LET'S JUST SAY THAT IT INVOLVED A GIRL, AN ALL-NIGHT PARTY AND MASSIVE AMOUNTS OF LEFTOVER EASTER PEEPS.
SOUNDS SERIOUS.
WE'LL SEE. THERE'S A CERTAIN BOND THAT FORMS BETWEEN TWO PEOPLE WHEN THEY WAKE UP IN EACH OTHER'S VOMIT.
SCOTT and BORGMAN

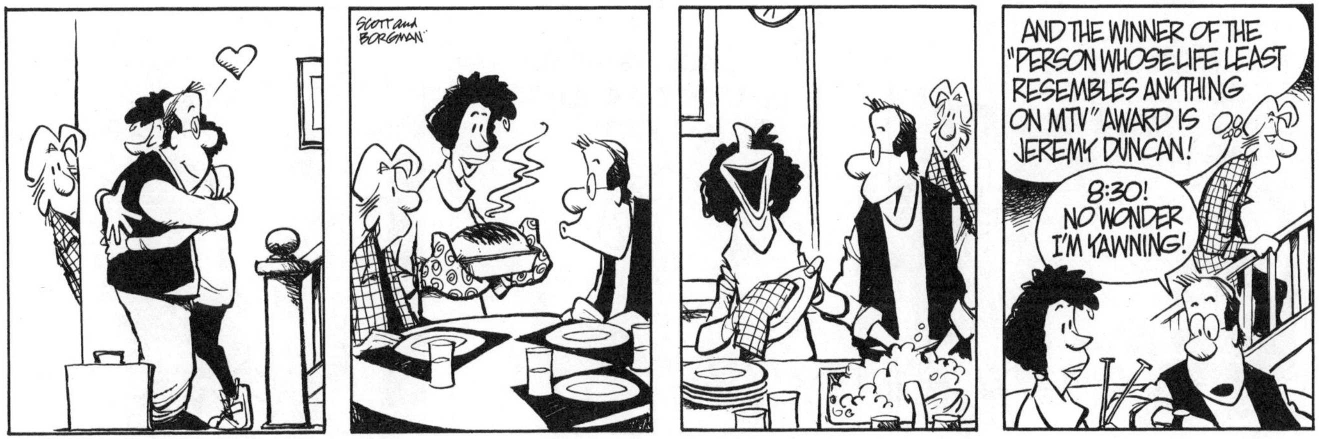
SCOTT and BORGMAN
AND THE WINNER OF THE "PERSON WHOSE LIFE LEAST RESEMBLES ANYTHING ON MTV" AWARD IS JEREMY DUNCAN!
8:30! NO WONDER I'M YAWNING!

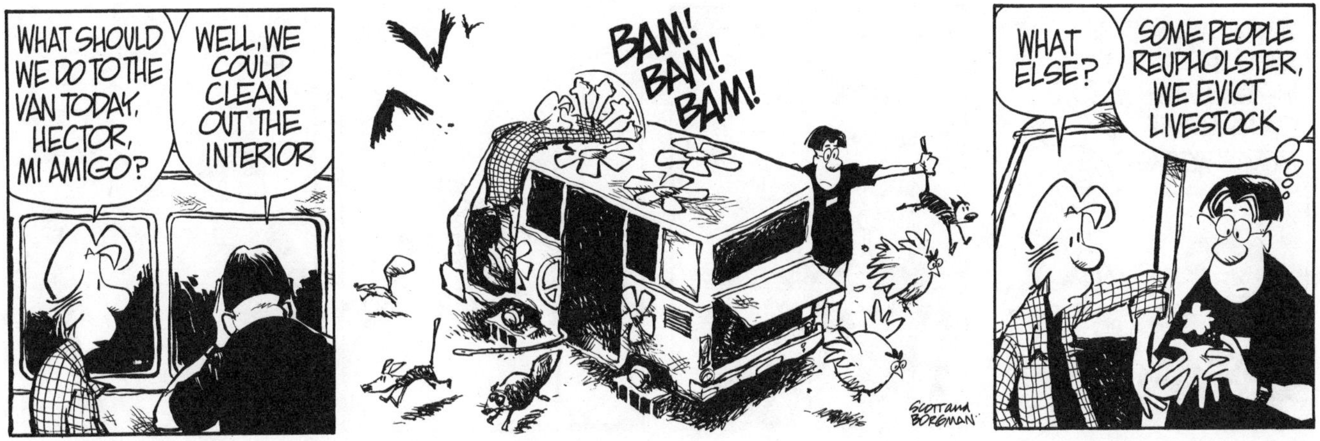
WHAT SHOULD WE DO TO THE VAN TODAY, HECTOR, MI AMIGO?
WELL, WE COULD CLEAN OUT THE INTERIOR
BAM! BAM! BAM!
SCOTT and BORGMAN
WHAT ELSE?
SOME PEOPLE REUPHOLSTER, WE EVICT LIVESTOCK

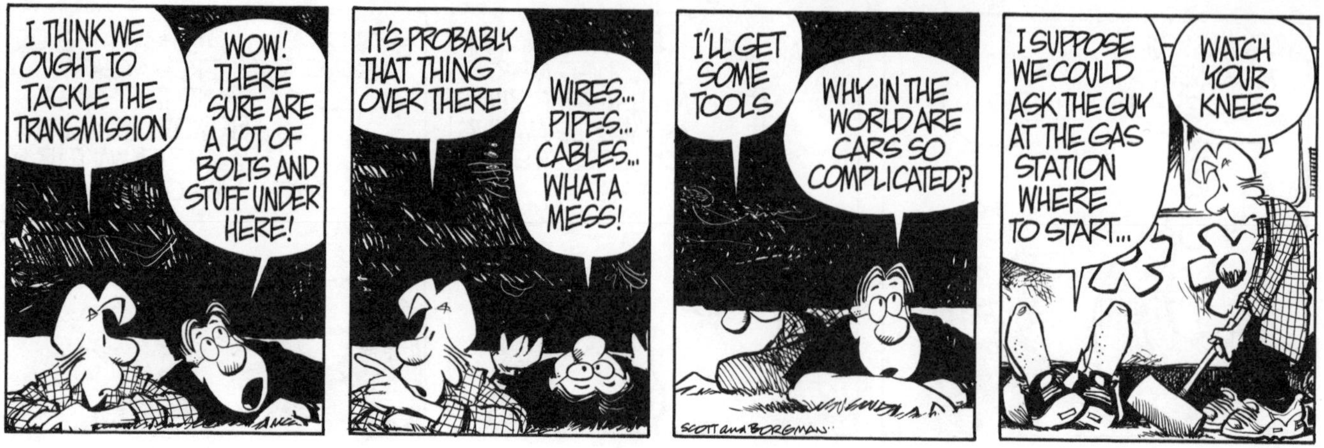
I THINK WE OUGHT TO TACKLE THE TRANSMISSION
WOW! THERE SURE ARE A LOT OF BOLTS AND STUFF UNDER HERE!
IT'S PROBABLY THAT THING OVER THERE
WIRES... PIPES... CABLES... WHAT A MESS!
I'LL GET SOME TOOLS
WHY IN THE WORLD ARE CARS SO COMPLICATED?
SCOTT and BORGMAN
I SUPPOSE WE COULD ASK THE GUY AT THE GAS STATION WHERE TO START...
WATCH YOUR KNEES

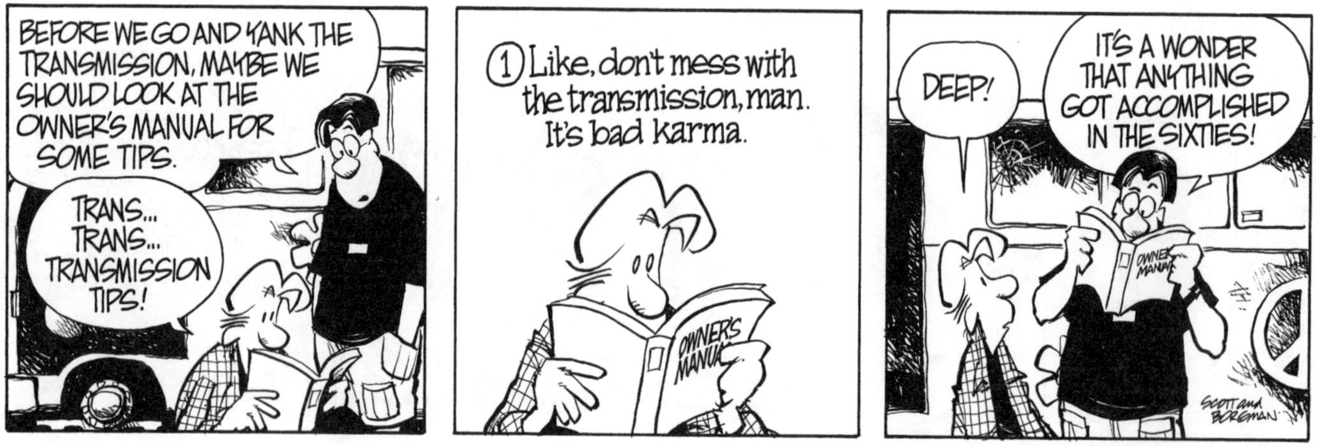
BEFORE WE GO AND YANK THE TRANSMISSION, MAYBE WE SHOULD LOOK AT THE OWNER'S MANUAL FOR SOME TIPS.
TRANS... TRANS... TRANSMISSION TIPS!
(1) Like, don't mess with the transmission, man. It's bad karma.
OWNER'S MANUAL
DEEP!
IT'S A WONDER THAT ANYTHING GOT ACCOMPLISHED IN THE SIXTIES!
SCOTT and BORGMAN

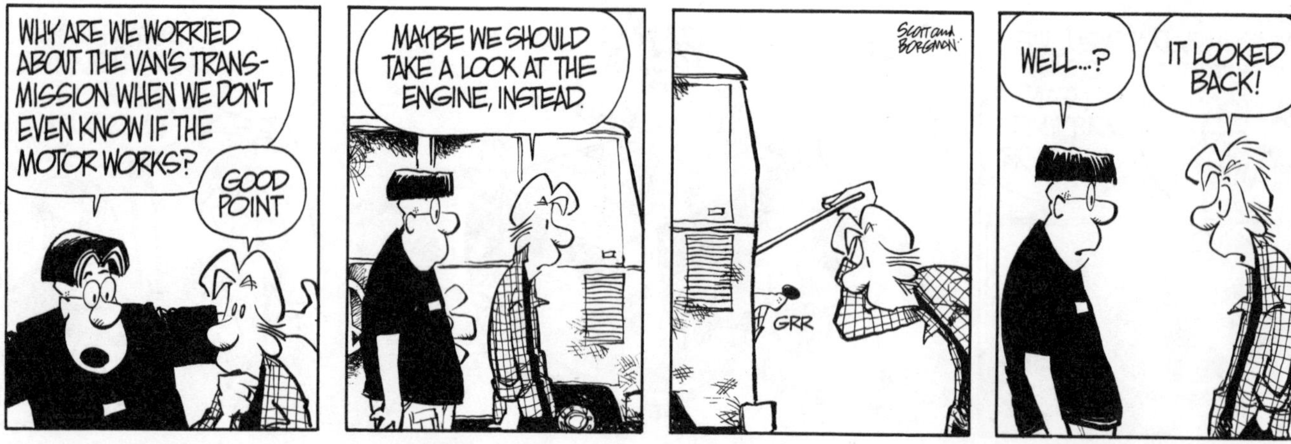
WHY ARE WE WORRIED ABOUT THE VAN'S TRANS-MISSION WHEN WE DON'T EVEN KNOW IF THE MOTOR WORKS?
GOOD POINT
MAYBE WE SHOULD TAKE A LOOK AT THE ENGINE, INSTEAD.
SCOTT and BORGMAN
GRR
WELL...?
IT LOOKED BACK!

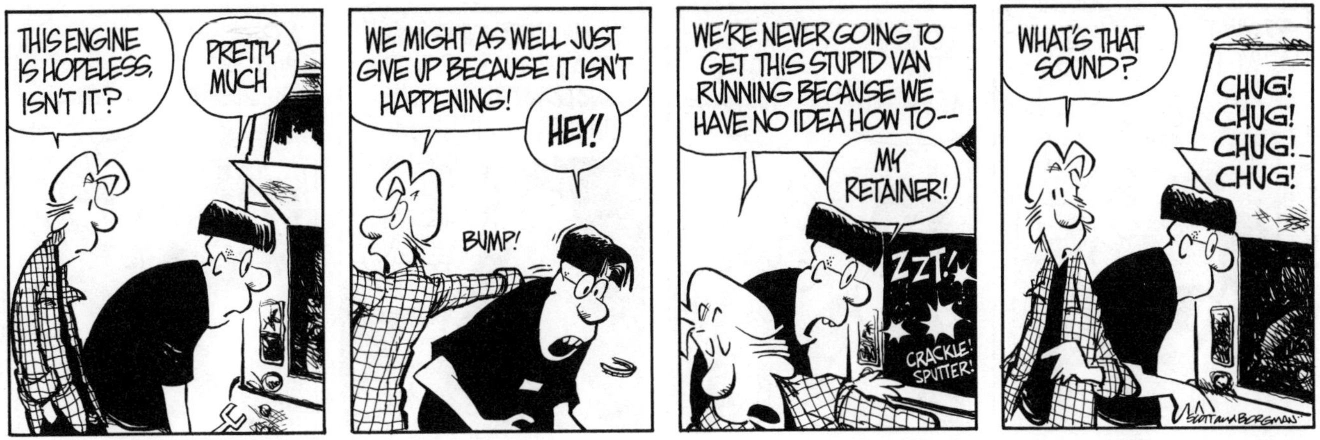
THIS ENGINE IS HOPELESS, ISN'T IT?
PRETTY MUCH
WE MIGHT AS WELL JUST GIVE UP BECAUSE IT ISN'T HAPPENING!
HEY!
BUMP!
WE'RE NEVER GOING TO GET THIS STUPID VAN RUNNING BECAUSE WE HAVE NO IDEA HOW TO--
MY RETAINER!
ZZT!
CRACKLE! SPUTTER!
WHAT'S THAT SOUND?
CHUG! CHUG! CHUG! CHUG!

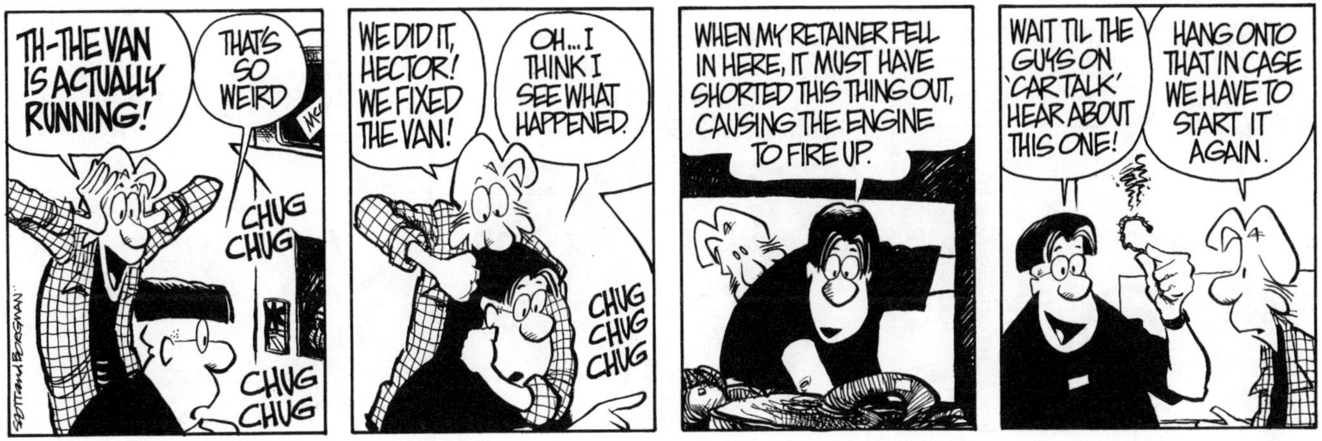
TH-THE VAN IS ACTUALLY RUNNING!
THAT'S SO WEIRD
CHUG CHUG
CHUG CHUG
WE DID IT, HECTOR! WE FIXED THE VAN!
OH... I THINK I SEE WHAT HAPPENED.
CHUG CHUG CHUG
WHEN MY RETAINER FELL IN HERE, IT MUST HAVE SHORTED THIS THING OUT, CAUSING THE ENGINE TO FIRE UP.
WAIT TIL THE GUYS ON 'CAR TALK' HEAR ABOUT THIS ONE!
HANG ONTO THAT IN CASE WE HAVE TO START IT AGAIN.

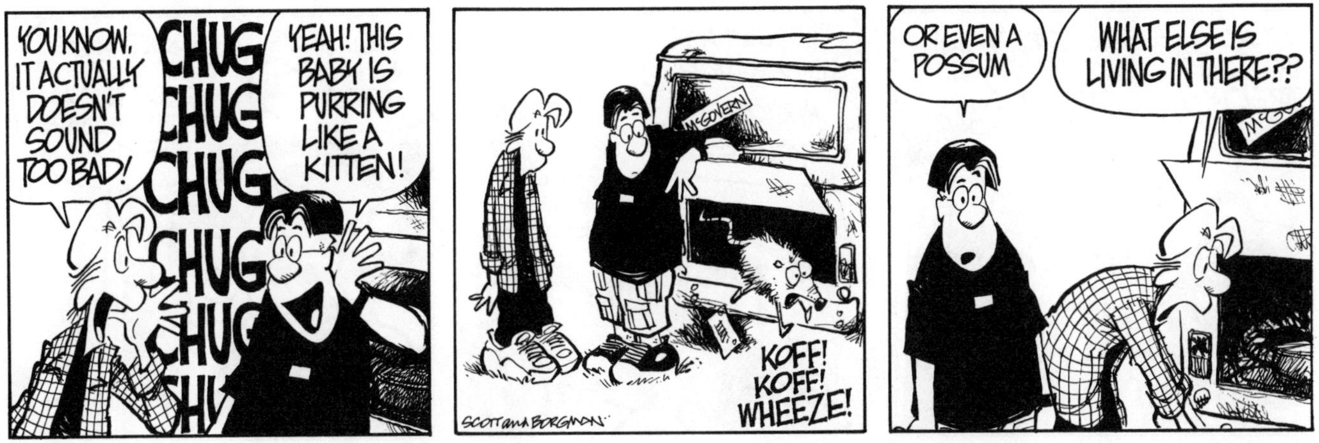
YOU KNOW, IT ACTUALLY DOESN'T SOUND TOO BAD!
CHUG CHUG CHUG CHUG CHUG
YEAH! THIS BABY IS PURRING LIKE A KITTEN!
McGOVERN
KOFF! KOFF! WHEEZE!
OR EVEN A POSSUM
WHAT ELSE IS LIVING IN THERE??

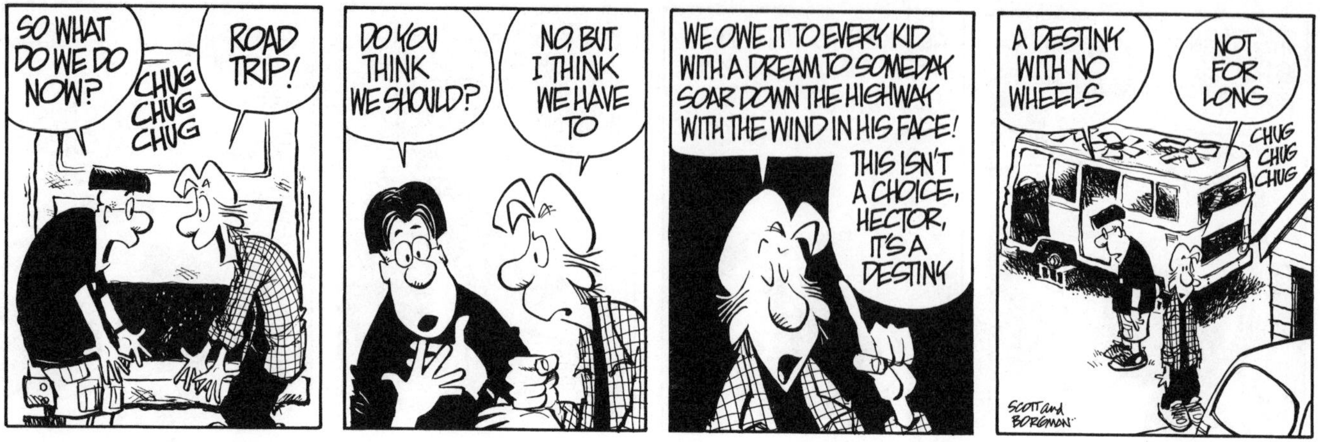
SO WHAT DO WE DO NOW?
CHUG CHUG CHUG
ROAD TRIP!
DO YOU THINK WE SHOULD?
NO, BUT I THINK WE HAVE TO
WE OWE IT TO EVERY KID WITH A DREAM TO SOMEDAY SOAR DOWN THE HIGHWAY WITH THE WIND IN HIS FACE!
THIS ISN'T A CHOICE, HECTOR, IT'S A DESTINY
A DESTINY WITH NO WHEELS
NOT FOR LONG
CHUG CHUG CHUG
SCOTT and BORGMAN

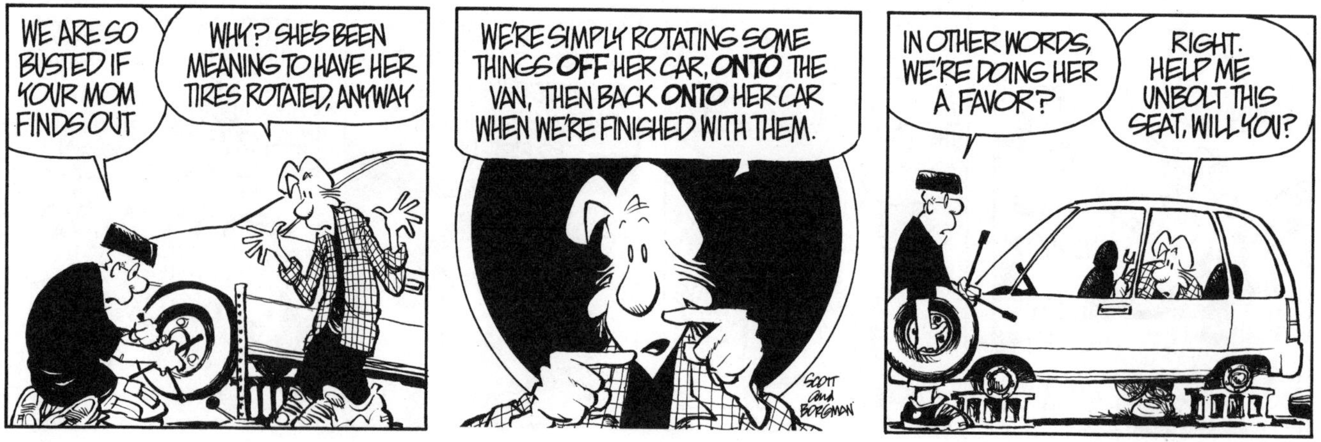
WE ARE SO BUSTED IF YOUR MOM FINDS OUT
WHY? SHE'S BEEN MEANING TO HAVE HER TIRES ROTATED, ANYWAY
WE'RE SIMPLY ROTATING SOME THINGS **OFF** HER CAR, **ONTO** THE VAN, THEN BACK **ONTO** HER CAR WHEN WE'RE FINISHED WITH THEM.
SCOTT and BORGMAN
IN OTHER WORDS, WE'RE DOING HER A FAVOR?
RIGHT. HELP ME UNBOLT THIS SEAT, WILL YOU?

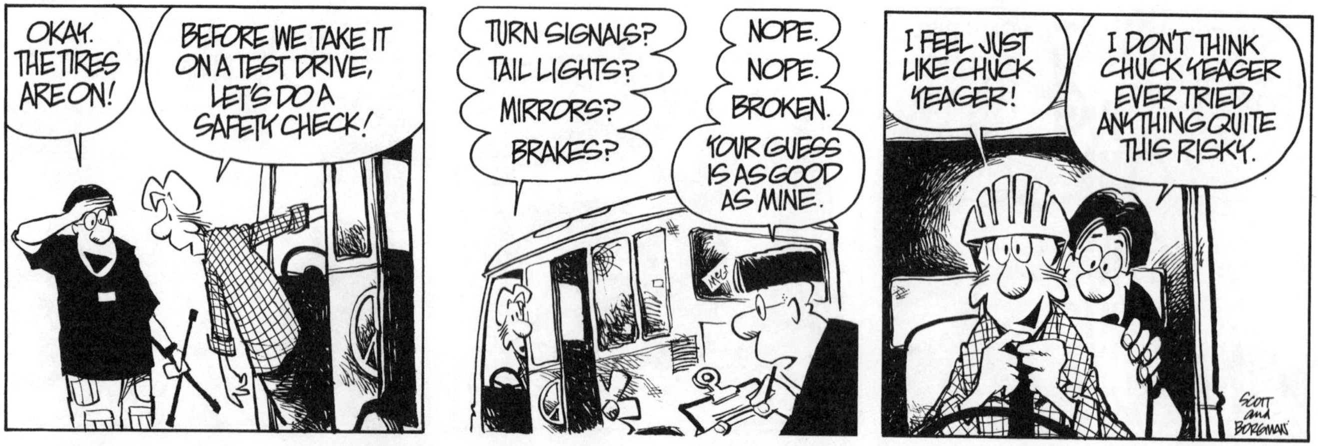
OKAY. THE TIRES ARE ON!
BEFORE WE TAKE IT ON A TEST DRIVE, LET'S DO A SAFETY CHECK!
TURN SIGNALS?
TAIL LIGHTS?
MIRRORS?
BRAKES?
NOPE.
NOPE.
BROKEN.
YOUR GUESS IS AS GOOD AS MINE.
I FEEL JUST LIKE CHUCK YEAGER!
I DON'T THINK CHUCK YEAGER EVER TRIED ANYTHING QUITE THIS RISKY.
SCOTT and BORGMAN

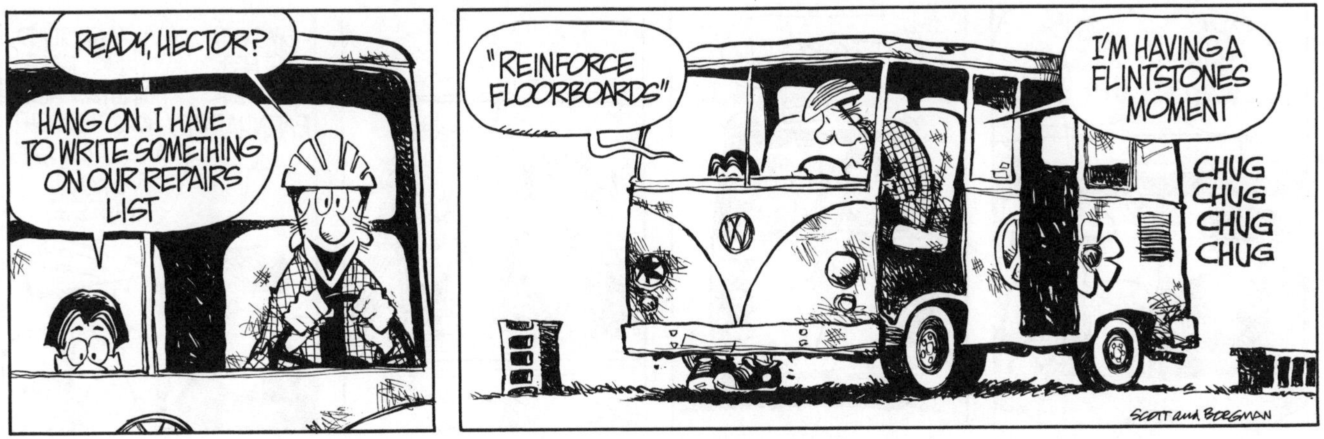
READY, HECTOR?
HANG ON. I HAVE TO WRITE SOMETHING ON OUR REPAIRS LIST
"REINFORCE FLOORBOARDS"
I'M HAVING A FLINTSTONES MOMENT
CHUG CHUG CHUG CHUG
SCOTT and BORGMAN

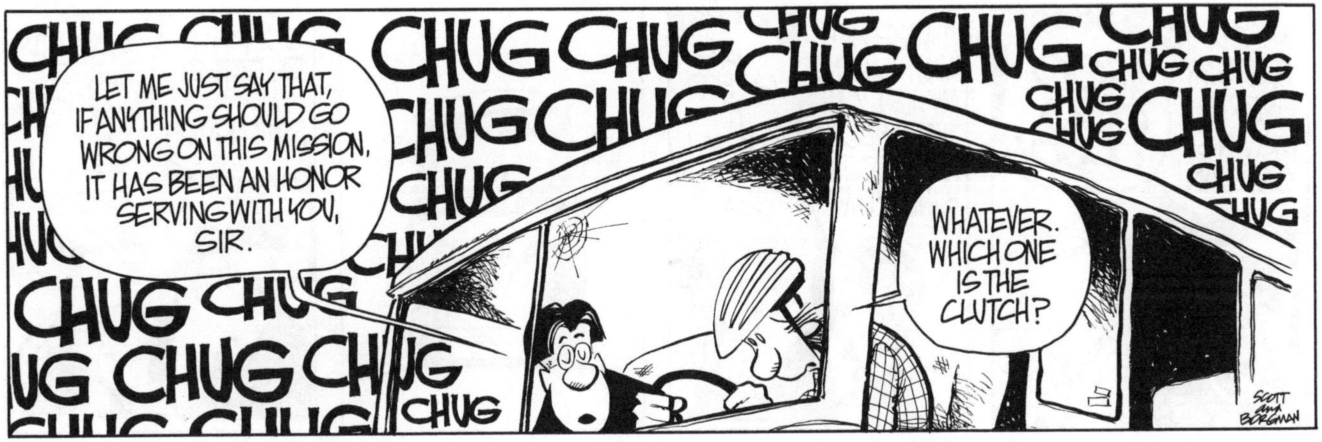
CHUG CHUG CHUG CHUG CHUG
LET ME JUST SAY THAT, IF ANYTHING SHOULD GO WRONG ON THIS MISSION, IT HAS BEEN AN HONOR SERVING WITH YOU, SIR.
WHATEVER. WHICH ONE IS THE CLUTCH?
CHUG
SCOTT and BORGMAN

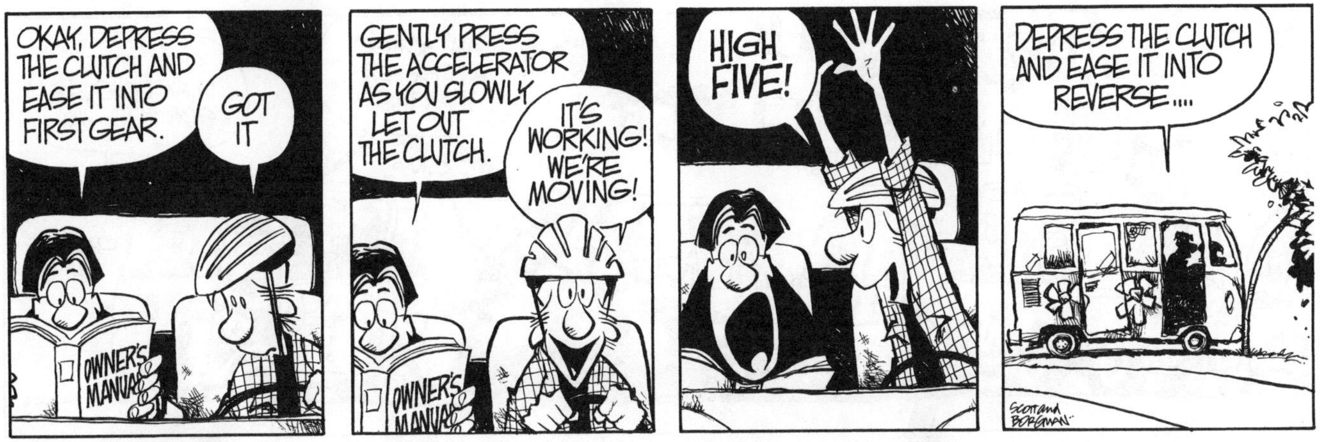
OKAY, DEPRESS THE CLUTCH AND EASE IT INTO FIRST GEAR.
GOT IT
OWNER'S MANUAL
GENTLY PRESS THE ACCELERATOR AS YOU SLOWLY LET OUT THE CLUTCH.
IT'S WORKING! WE'RE MOVING!
OWNER'S MANUAL
HIGH FIVE!
DEPRESS THE CLUTCH AND EASE IT INTO REVERSE.....
SCOTT and BORGMAN

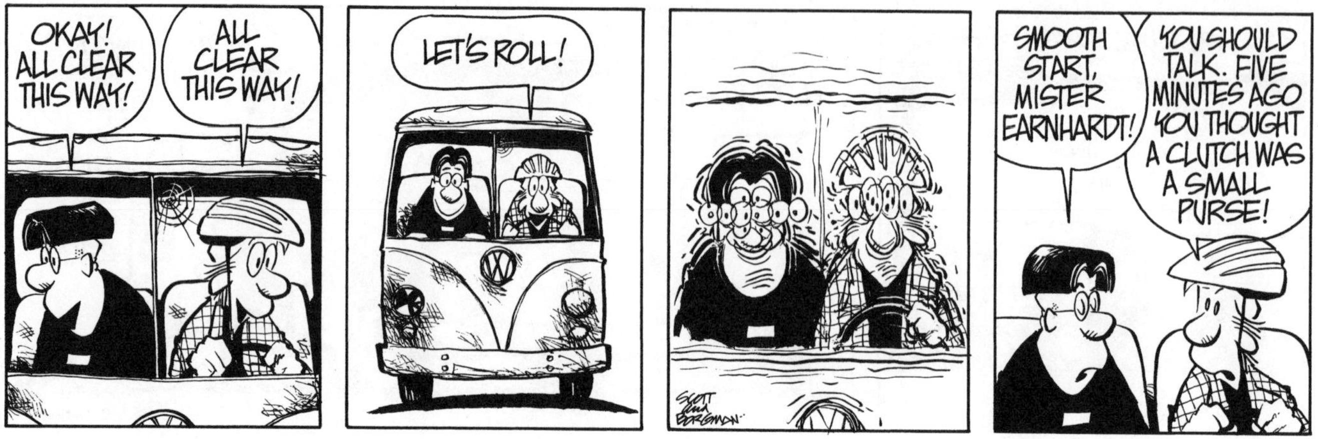
OKAY! ALL CLEAR THIS WAY!
ALL CLEAR THIS WAY!
LET'S ROLL!
SCOTT and BORGMAN
SMOOTH START, MISTER EARNHARDT!
YOU SHOULD TALK. FIVE MINUTES AGO YOU THOUGHT A CLUTCH WAS A SMALL PURSE!

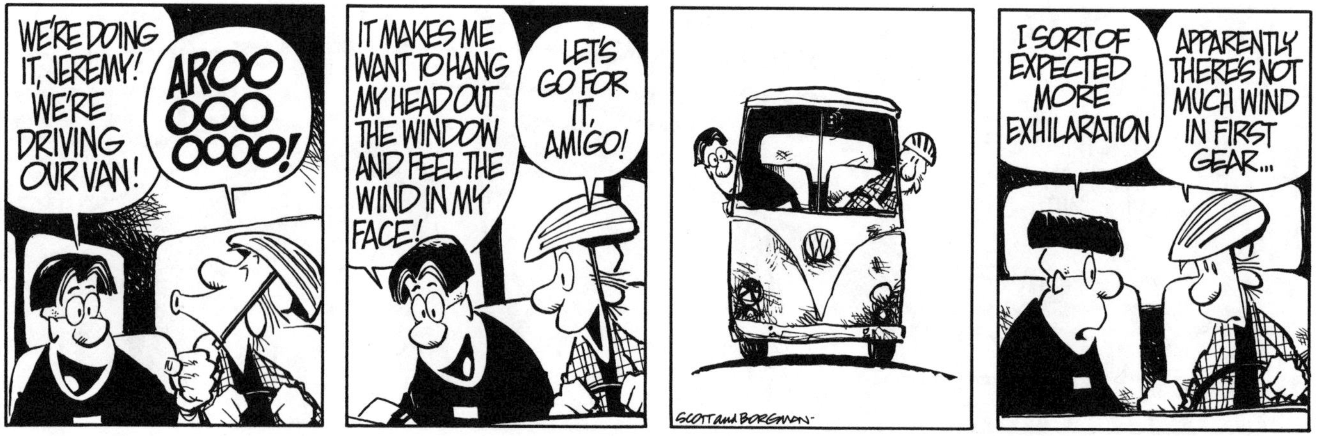
WE'RE DOING IT, JEREMY! WE'RE DRIVING OUR VAN!
AROOOOOOOOOO!
IT MAKES ME WANT TO HANG MY HEAD OUT THE WINDOW AND FEEL THE WIND IN MY FACE!
LET'S GO FOR IT, AMIGO!
SCOTT and BORGMAN
I SORT OF EXPECTED MORE EXHILARATION
APPARENTLY THERE'S NOT MUCH WIND IN FIRST GEAR...

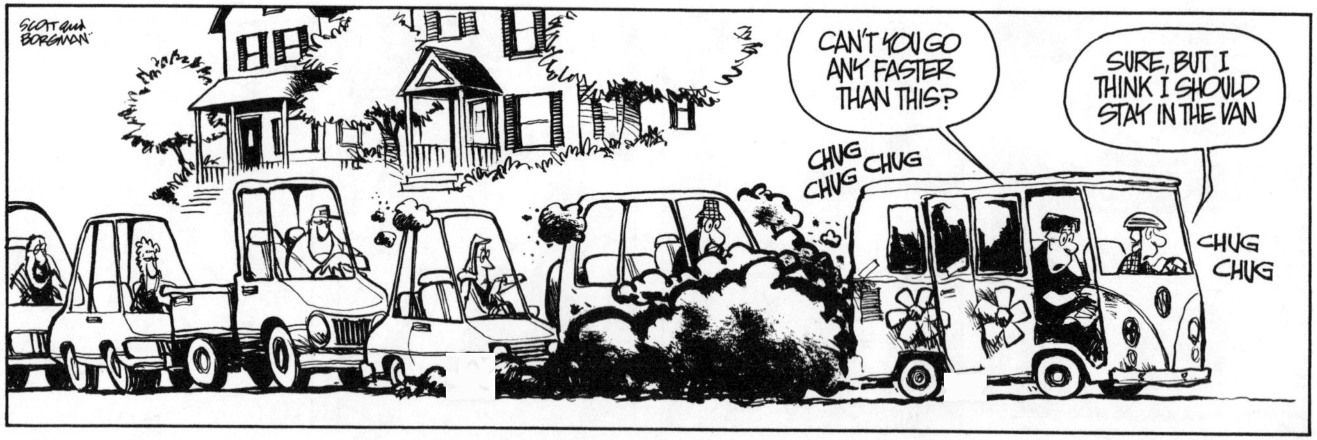
SCOTT and BORGMAN
CAN'T YOU GO ANY FASTER THAN THIS?
SURE, BUT I THINK I SHOULD STAY IN THE VAN
CHUG CHUG CHUG
CHUG CHUG

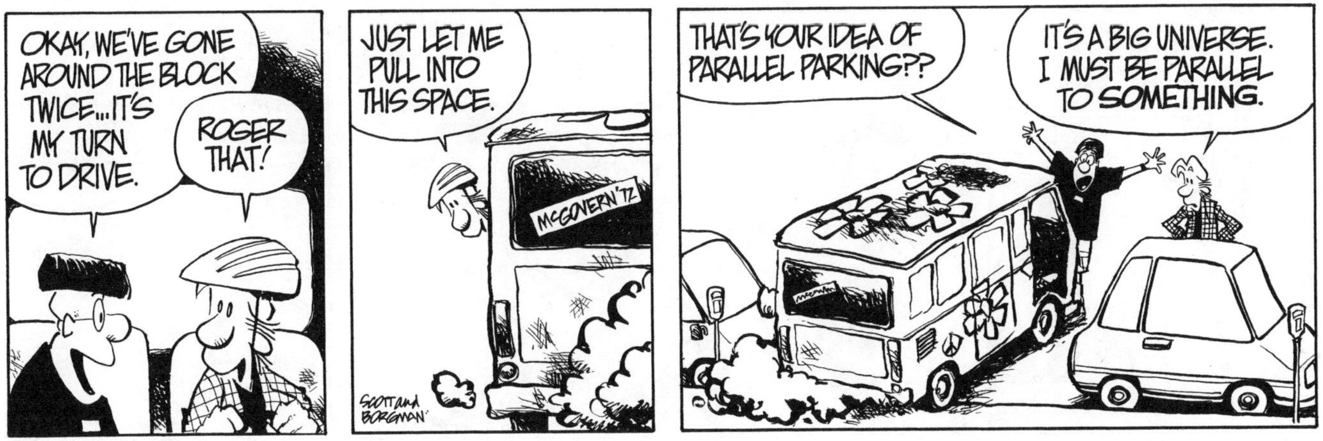
OKAY, WE'VE GONE AROUND THE BLOCK TWICE...IT'S MY TURN TO DRIVE.
ROGER THAT!
JUST LET ME PULL INTO THIS SPACE.
McGOVERN '72
SCOTT and BORGMAN
THAT'S YOUR IDEA OF PARALLEL PARKING??
IT'S A BIG UNIVERSE. I MUST BE PARALLEL TO SOMETHING.

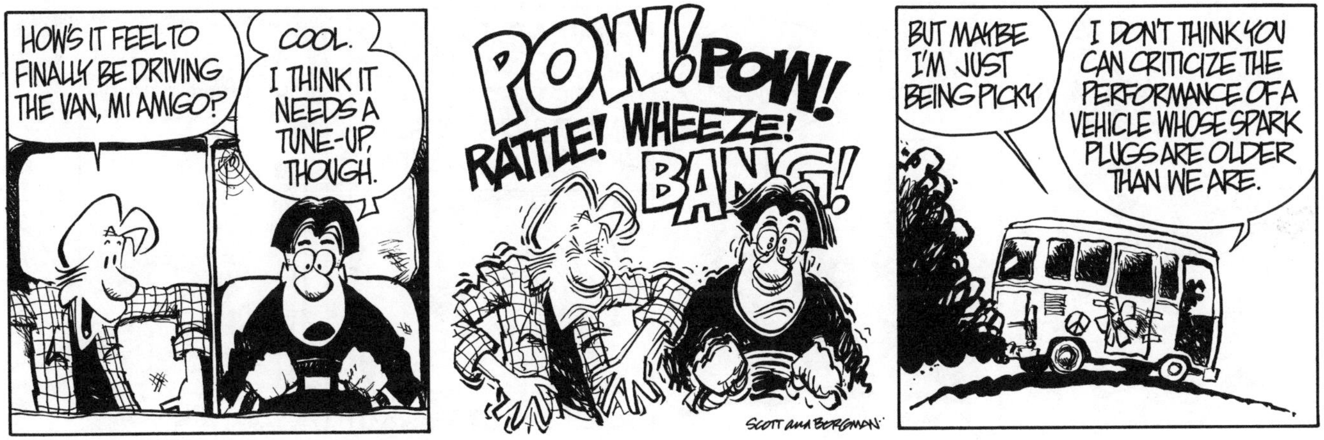
HOW'S IT FEEL TO FINALLY BE DRIVING THE VAN, MI AMIGO?
COOL. I THINK IT NEEDS A TUNE-UP, THOUGH.
POW! POW! RATTLE! WHEEZE! BANG!
SCOTT and BORGMAN
BUT MAYBE I'M JUST BEING PICKY
I DON'T THINK YOU CAN CRITICIZE THE PERFORMANCE OF A VEHICLE WHOSE SPARK PLUGS ARE OLDER THAN WE ARE.

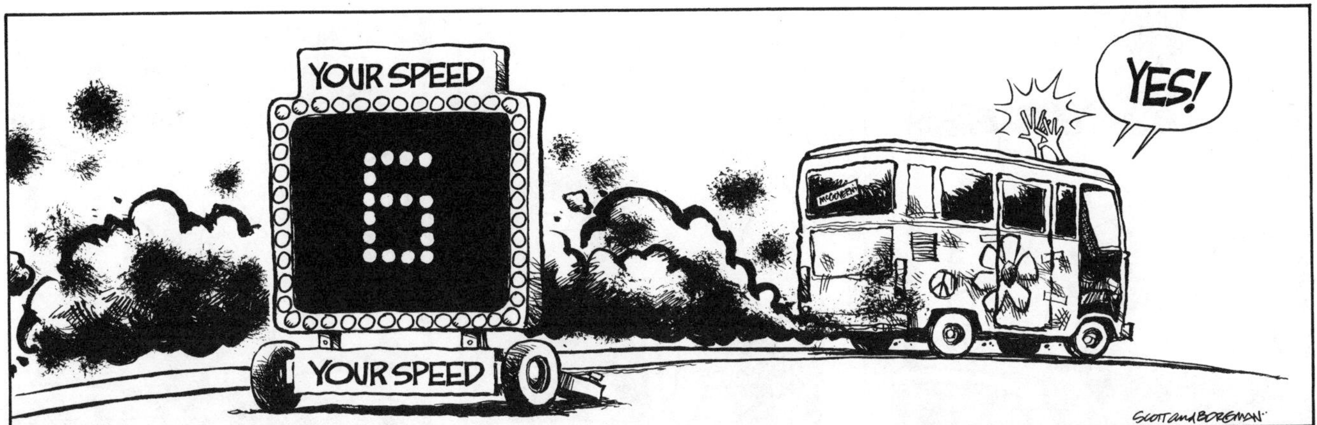
YOUR SPEED
6
YOUR SPEED
YES!
SCOTT and BORGMAN

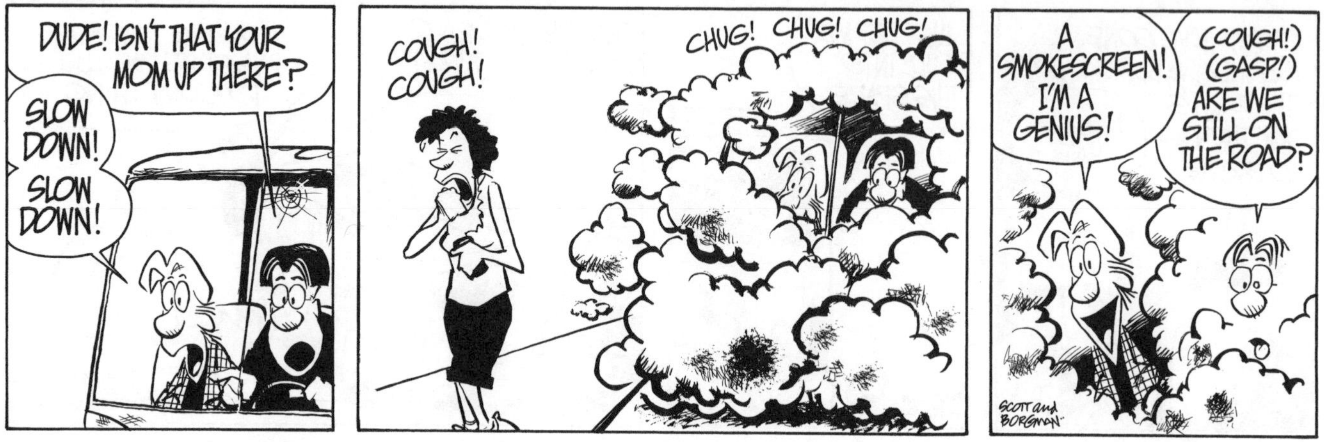
DUDE! ISN'T THAT YOUR MOM UP THERE?
SLOW DOWN!
SLOW DOWN!
COUGH! COUGH!
CHUG! CHUG! CHUG!
A SMOKESCREEN! I'M A GENIUS!
(COUGH!) (GASP!) ARE WE STILL ON THE ROAD?
SCOTT and BORGMAN

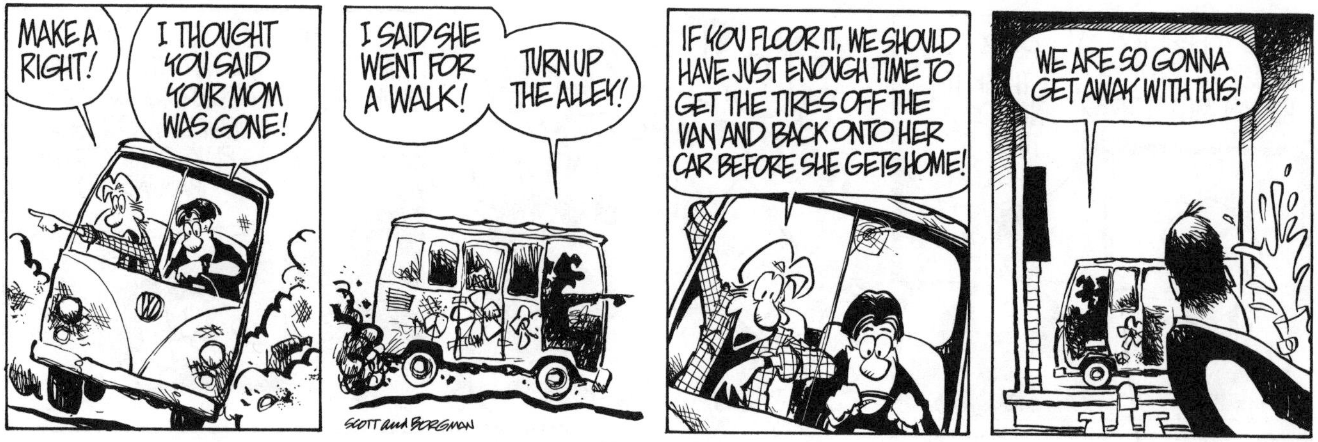
MAKE A RIGHT!
I THOUGHT YOU SAID YOUR MOM WAS GONE!
I SAID SHE WENT FOR A WALK!
TURN UP THE ALLEY!
SCOTT and BORGMAN
IF YOU FLOOR IT, WE SHOULD HAVE JUST ENOUGH TIME TO GET THE TIRES OFF THE VAN AND BACK ONTO HER CAR BEFORE SHE GETS HOME!
WE ARE SO GONNA GET AWAY WITH THIS!

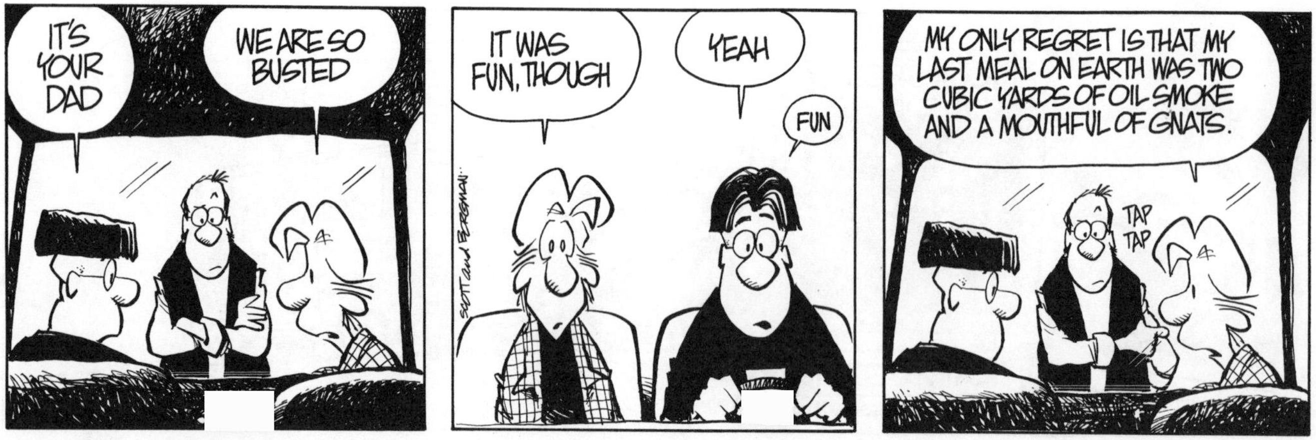
IT'S YOUR DAD
WE ARE SO BUSTED
IT WAS FUN, THOUGH
YEAH
FUN
SCOTT and BORGMAN
MY ONLY REGRET IS THAT MY LAST MEAL ON EARTH WAS TWO CUBIC YARDS OF OIL SMOKE AND A MOUTHFUL OF GNATS.
TAP TAP

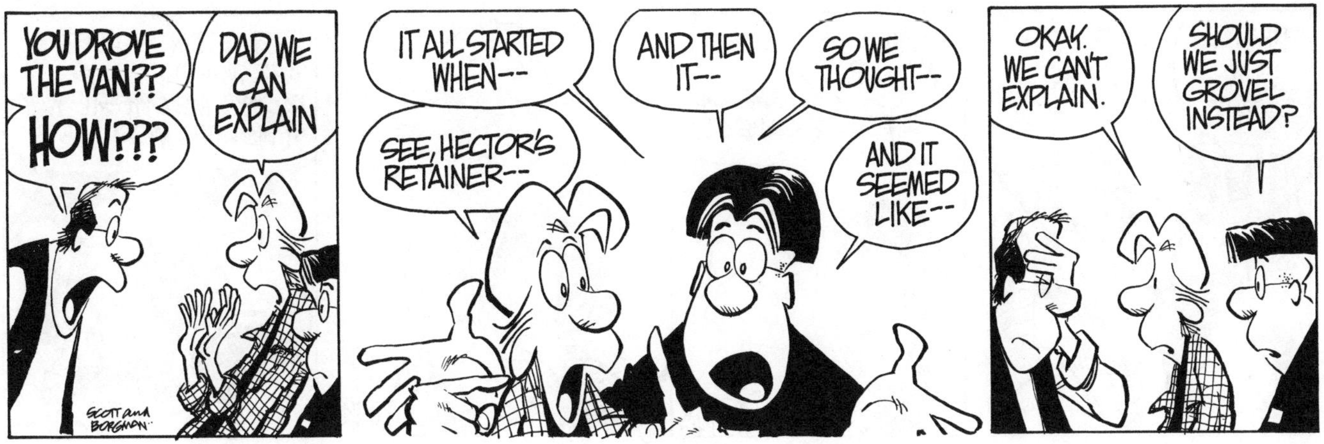
YOU DROVE THE VAN?? HOW???
DAD, WE CAN EXPLAIN
IT ALL STARTED WHEN--
SEE, HECTOR'S RETAINER--
AND THEN IT--
SO WE THOUGHT--
AND IT SEEMED LIKE--
OKAY. WE CAN'T EXPLAIN.
SHOULD WE JUST GROVEL INSTEAD?
SCOTT and BORGMAN

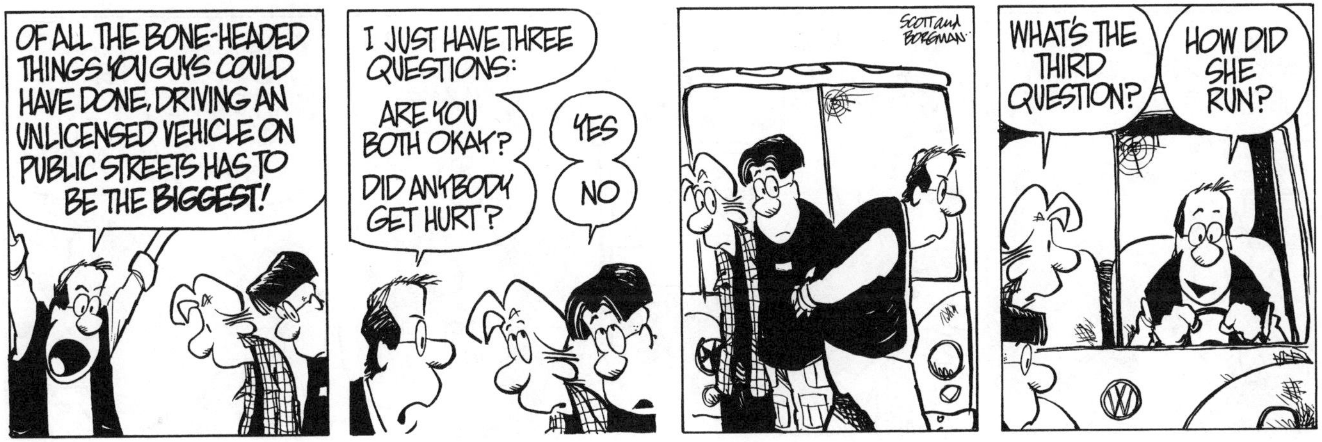
OF ALL THE BONE-HEADED THINGS YOU GUYS COULD HAVE DONE, DRIVING AN UNLICENSED VEHICLE ON PUBLIC STREETS HAS TO BE THE BIGGEST!
I JUST HAVE THREE QUESTIONS:
ARE YOU BOTH OKAY?
YES
DID ANYBODY GET HURT?
NO
SCOTT and BORGMAN
WHAT'S THE THIRD QUESTION?
HOW DID SHE RUN?

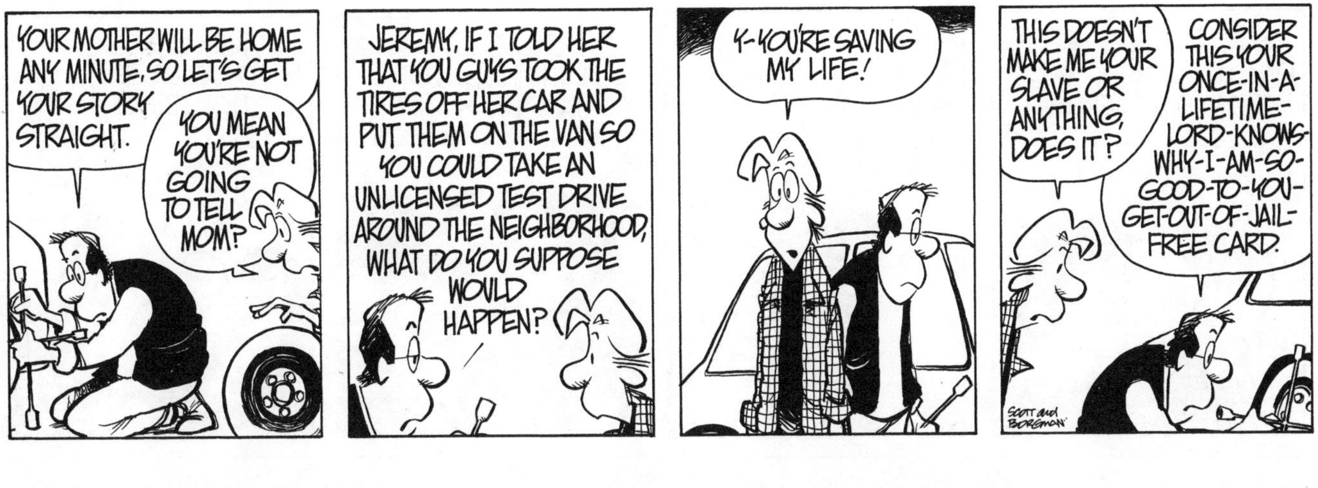
YOUR MOTHER WILL BE HOME ANY MINUTE, SO LET'S GET YOUR STORY STRAIGHT.
YOU MEAN YOU'RE NOT GOING TO TELL MOM?
JEREMY, IF I TOLD HER THAT YOU GUYS TOOK THE TIRES OFF HER CAR AND PUT THEM ON THE VAN SO YOU COULD TAKE AN UNLICENSED TEST DRIVE AROUND THE NEIGHBORHOOD, WHAT DO YOU SUPPOSE WOULD HAPPEN?
Y-YOU'RE SAVING MY LIFE!
THIS DOESN'T MAKE ME YOUR SLAVE OR ANYTHING, DOES IT?
CONSIDER THIS YOUR ONCE-IN-A-LIFETIME-LORD-KNOWS-WHY-I-AM-SO-GOOD-TO-YOU-GET-OUT-OF-JAIL-FREE CARD.
SCOTT and BORGMAN

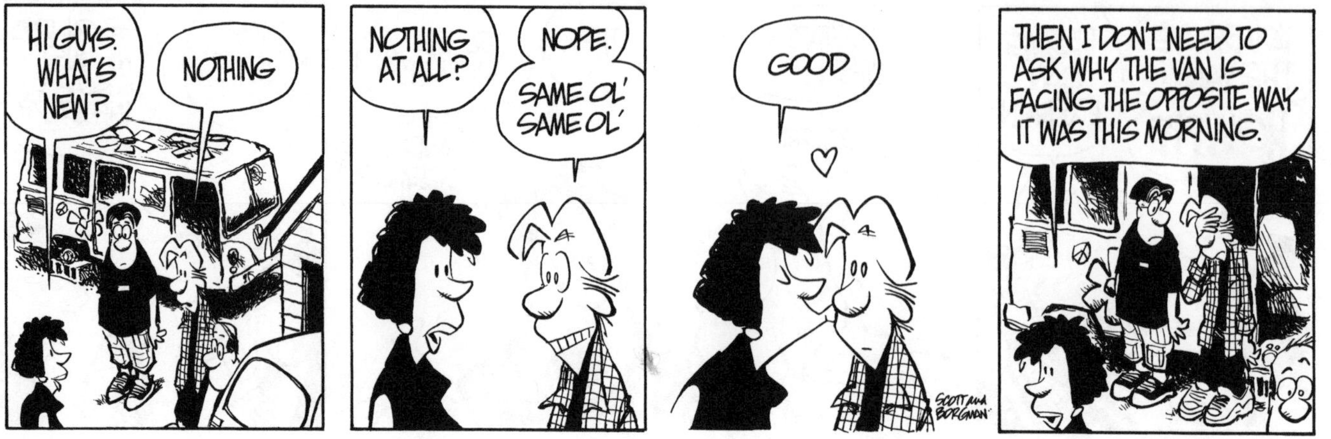
HI GUYS. WHAT'S NEW?
NOTHING
NOTHING AT ALL?
NOPE.
SAME OL' SAME OL'
GOOD
THEN I DON'T NEED TO ASK WHY THE VAN IS FACING THE OPPOSITE WAY IT WAS THIS MORNING.

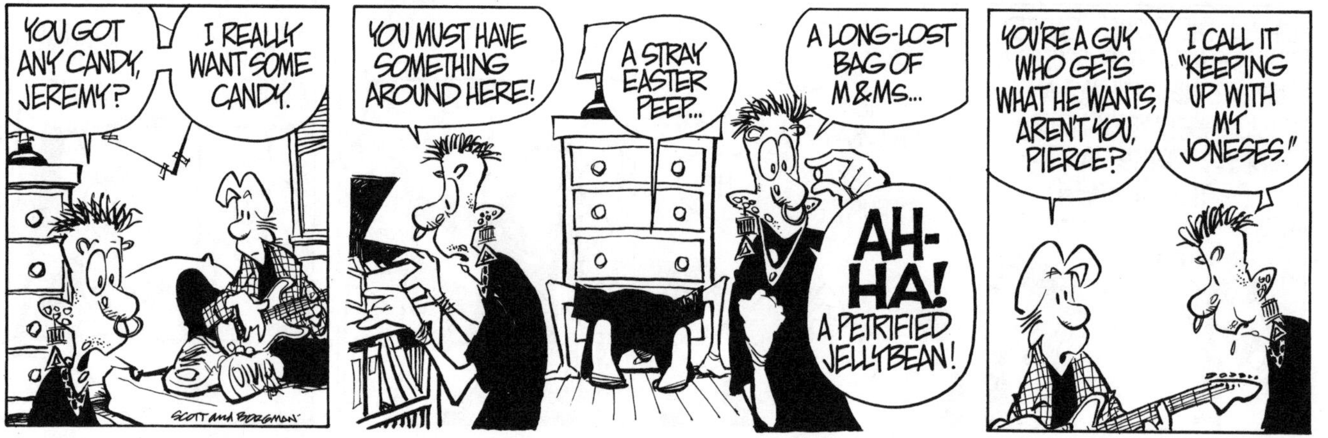
YOU GOT ANY CANDY, JEREMY?
I REALLY WANT SOME CANDY.
YOU MUST HAVE SOMETHING AROUND HERE!
A STRAY EASTER PEEP...
A LONG-LOST BAG OF M&MS...
AH-HA!
A PETRIFIED JELLYBEAN!
YOU'RE A GUY WHO GETS WHAT HE WANTS, AREN'T YOU, PIERCE?
I CALL IT "KEEPING UP WITH MY JONESES."

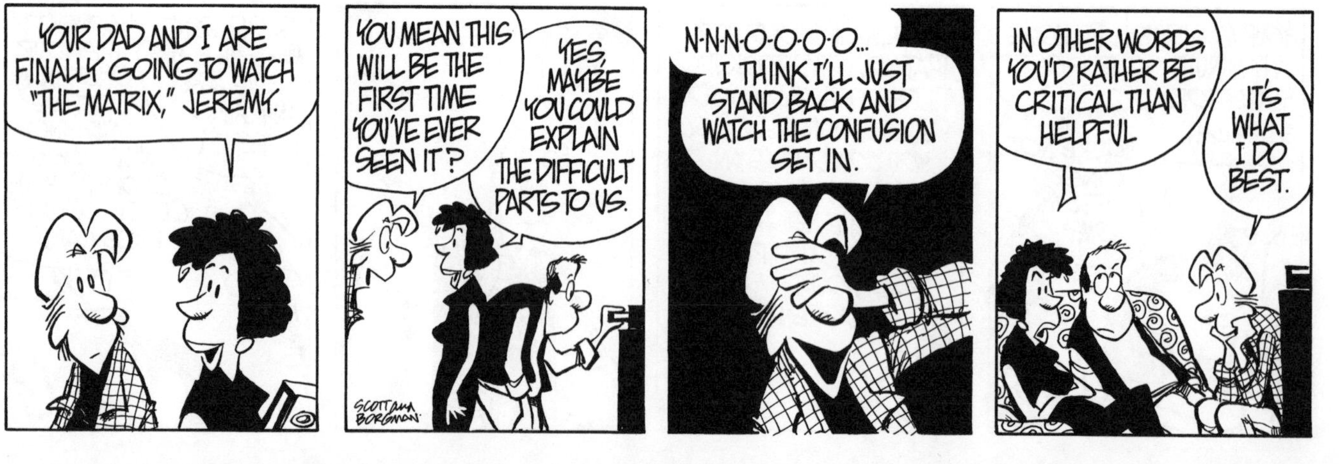
YOUR DAD AND I ARE FINALLY GOING TO WATCH "THE MATRIX," JEREMY.
YOU MEAN THIS WILL BE THE FIRST TIME YOU'VE EVER SEEN IT?
YES, MAYBE YOU COULD EXPLAIN THE DIFFICULT PARTS TO US.
N-N-N-O-O-O-O... I THINK I'LL JUST STAND BACK AND WATCH THE CONFUSION SET IN.
IN OTHER WORDS, YOU'D RATHER BE CRITICAL THAN HELPFUL
IT'S WHAT I DO BEST.

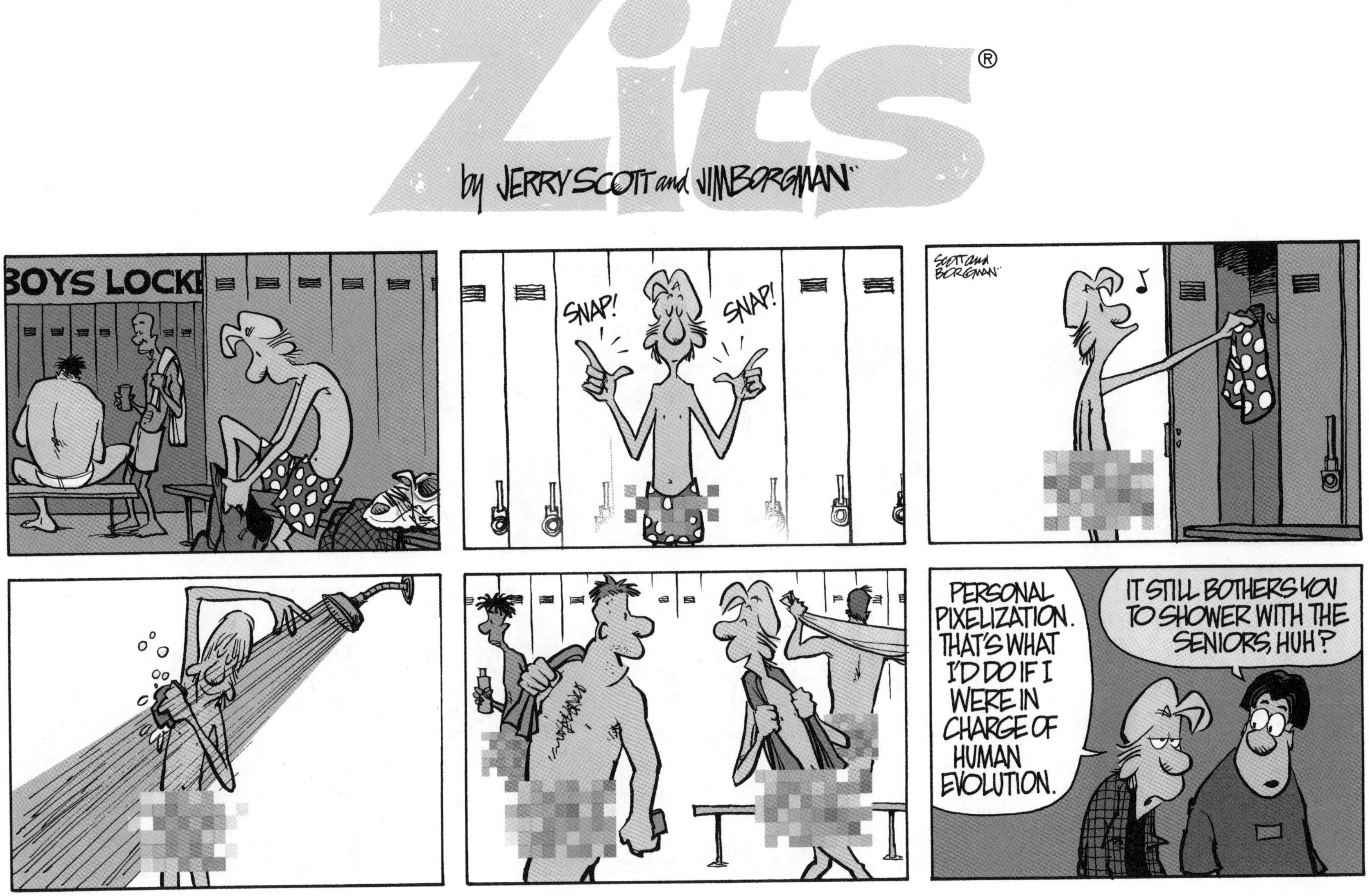
Zits®
by JERRY SCOTT and JIM BORGMAN
BOYS LOCK
SNAP!
SNAP!
SCOTT and BORGMAN
PERSONAL PIXELIZATION. THAT'S WHAT I'D DO IF I WERE IN CHARGE OF HUMAN EVOLUTION.
IT STILL BOTHERS YOU TO SHOWER WITH THE SENIORS, HUH?

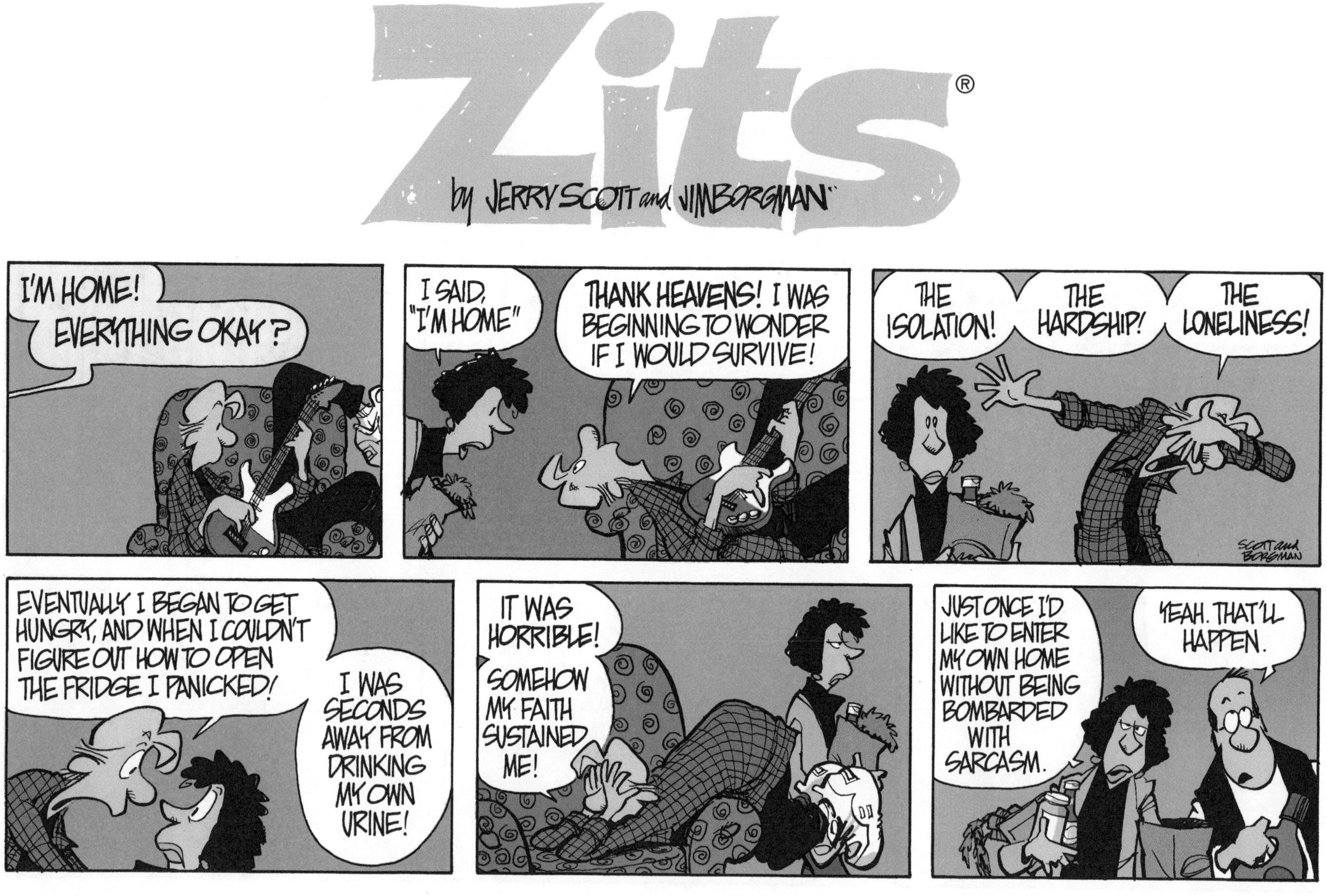
Zits®
by JERRY SCOTT and JIM BORGMAN
I'M HOME! EVERYTHING OKAY?
I SAID, "I'M HOME"
THANK HEAVENS! I WAS BEGINNING TO WONDER IF I WOULD SURVIVE!
THE ISOLATION!
THE HARDSHIP!
THE LONELINESS!
SCOTT and BORGMAN
EVENTUALLY I BEGAN TO GET HUNGRY, AND WHEN I COULDN'T FIGURE OUT HOW TO OPEN THE FRIDGE I PANICKED!
I WAS SECONDS AWAY FROM DRINKING MY OWN URINE!
IT WAS HORRIBLE!
SOMEHOW MY FAITH SUSTAINED ME!
JUST ONCE I'D LIKE TO ENTER MY OWN HOME WITHOUT BEING BOMBARDED WITH SARCASM.
YEAH. THAT'LL HAPPEN.

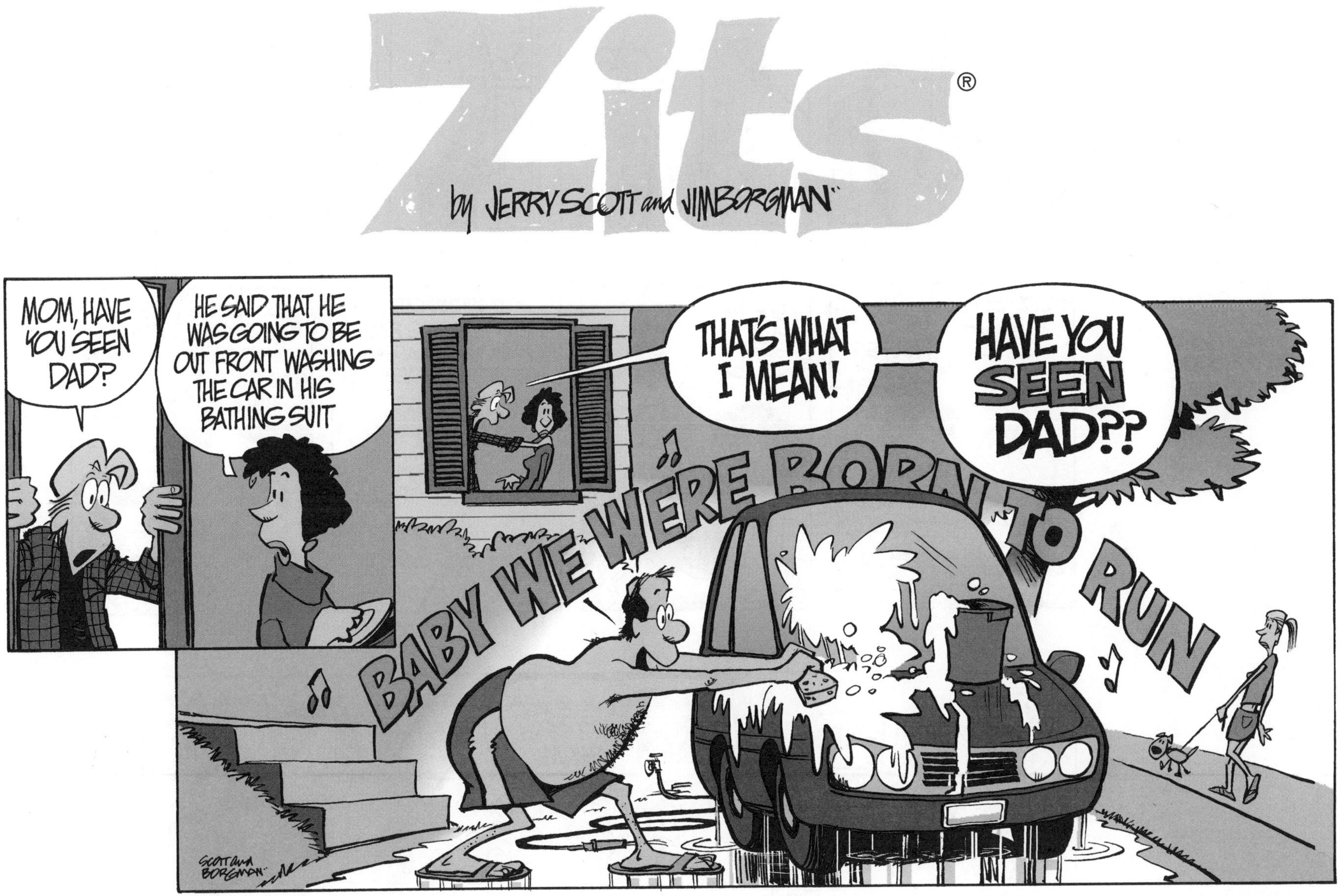
Zits®
by JERRY SCOTT and JIM BORGMAN
MOM, HAVE YOU SEEN DAD?
HE SAID THAT HE WAS GOING TO BE OUT FRONT WASHING THE CAR IN HIS BATHING SUIT
THAT'S WHAT I MEAN!
HAVE YOU SEEN DAD??
BABY WE WERE BORN TO RUN
SCOTT and BORGMAN

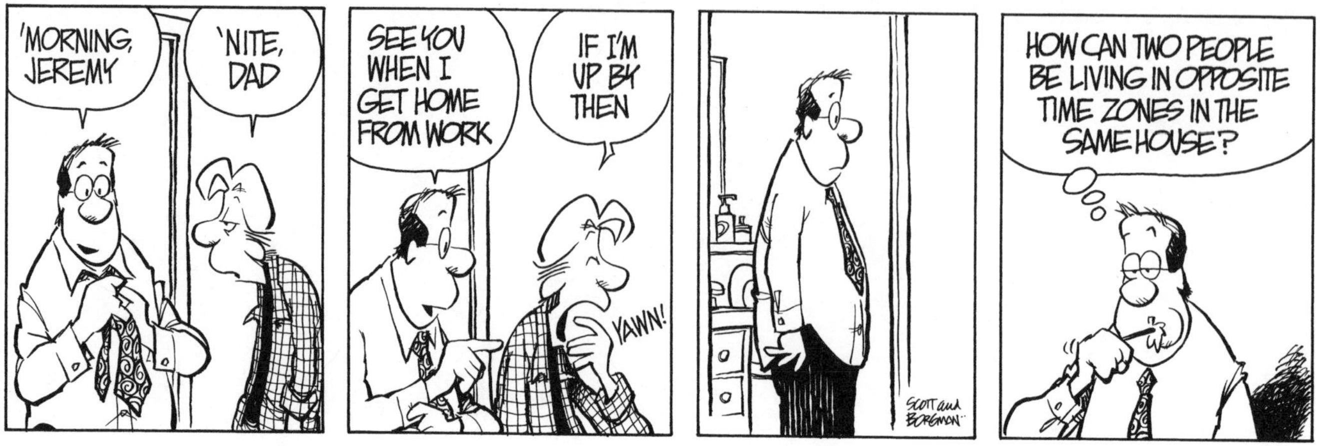
'MORNING, JEREMY
'NITE, DAD
SEE YOU WHEN I GET HOME FROM WORK
IF I'M UP BY THEN
YAWN!
HOW CAN TWO PEOPLE BE LIVING IN OPPOSITE TIME ZONES IN THE SAME HOUSE?

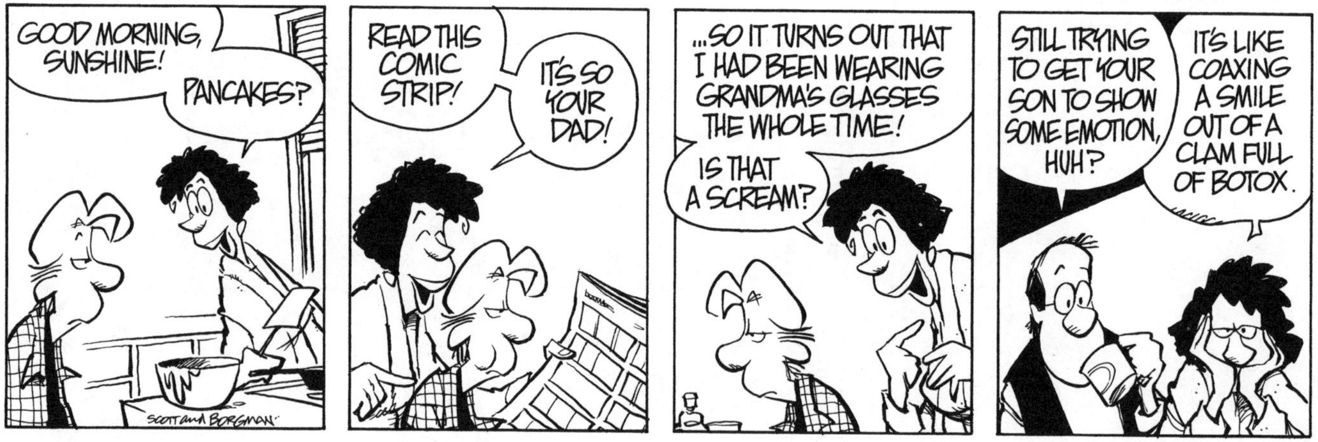
GOOD MORNING, SUNSHINE!
PANCAKES?
READ THIS COMIC STRIP!
IT'S SO YOUR DAD!
...SO IT TURNS OUT THAT I HAD BEEN WEARING GRANDMA'S GLASSES THE WHOLE TIME!
IS THAT A SCREAM?
STILL TRYING TO GET YOUR SON TO SHOW SOME EMOTION, HUH?
IT'S LIKE COAXING A SMILE OUT OF A CLAM FULL OF BOTOX.

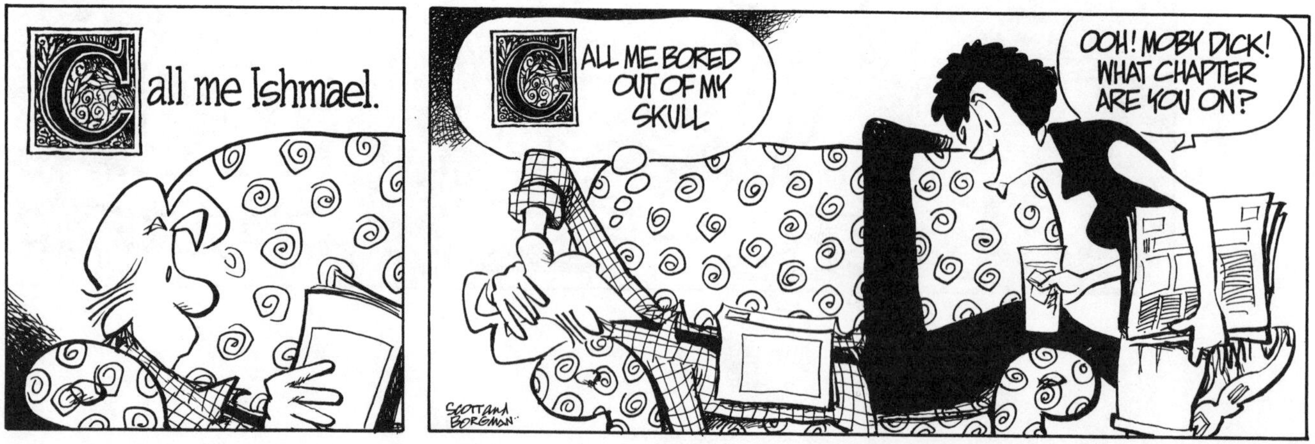
Call me Ishmael.
CALL ME BORED OUT OF MY SKULL
OOH! MOBY DICK! WHAT CHAPTER ARE YOU ON?

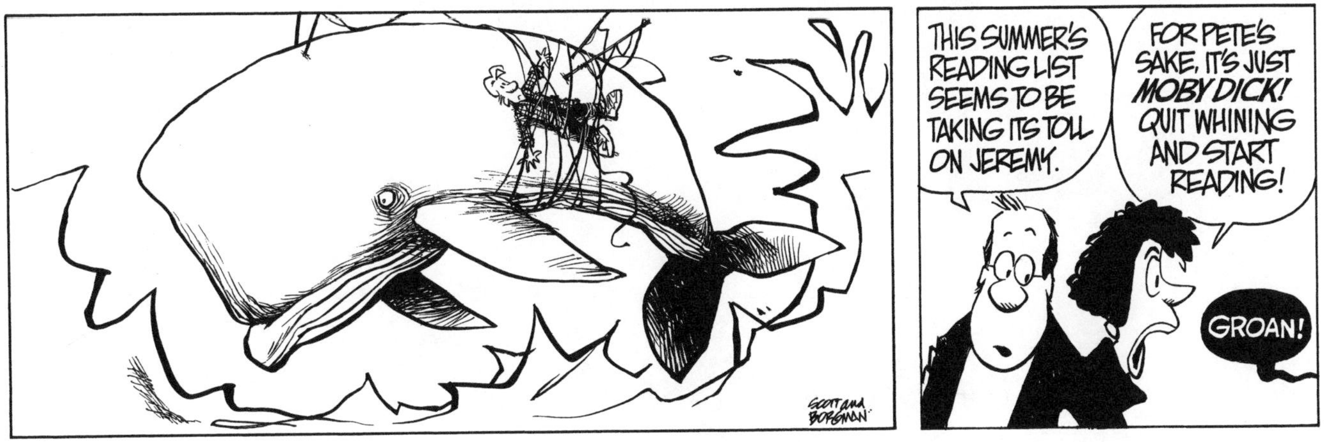
SCOTT and BORGMAN
THIS SUMMER'S READING LIST SEEMS TO BE TAKING ITS TOLL ON JEREMY.
FOR PETE'S SAKE, IT'S JUST **MOBY DICK!** QUIT WHINING AND START READING!
GROAN!

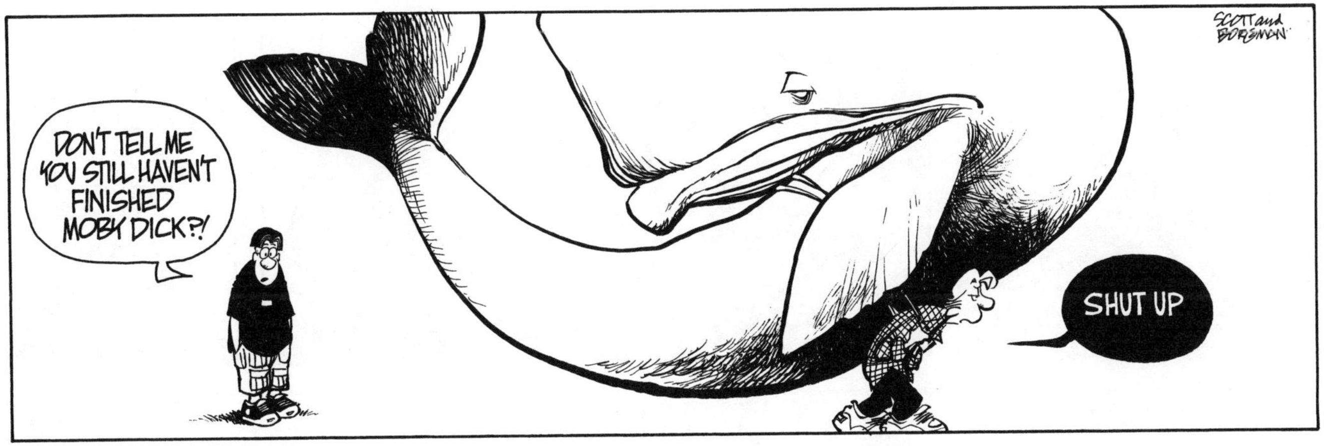
SCOTT and BORGMAN
DON'T TELL ME YOU STILL HAVEN'T FINISHED MOBY DICK?!
SHUT UP

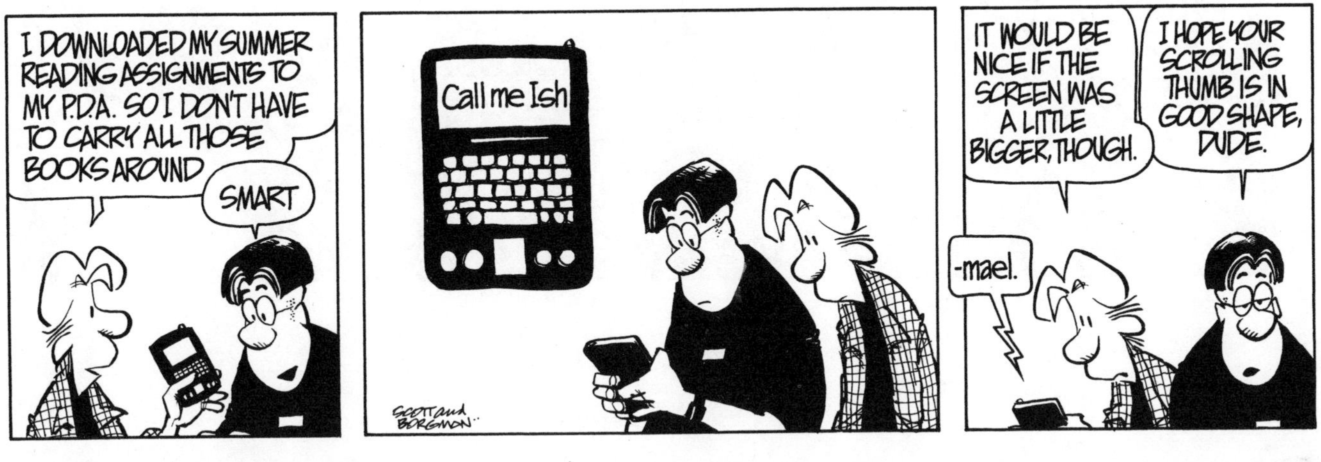
I DOWNLOADED MY SUMMER READING ASSIGNMENTS TO MY P.D.A. SO I DON'T HAVE TO CARRY ALL THOSE BOOKS AROUND
SMART
Call me Ish
SCOTT and BORGMAN
IT WOULD BE NICE IF THE SCREEN WAS A LITTLE BIGGER, THOUGH.
I HOPE YOUR SCROLLING THUMB IS IN GOOD SHAPE, DUDE.
-mael.

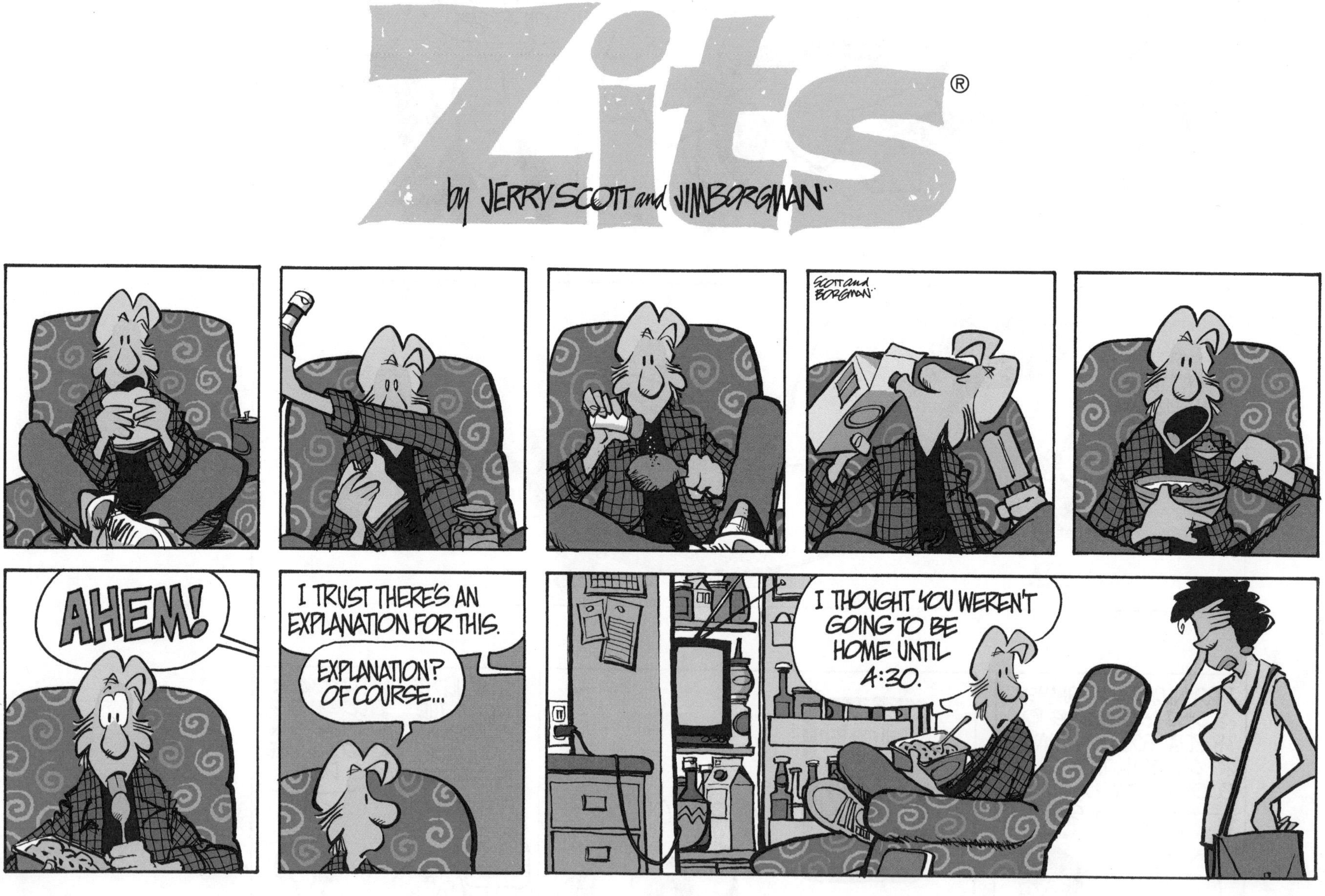
Zits®
by JERRY SCOTT and JIM BORGMAN
SCOTT and BORGMAN
AHEM!
I TRUST THERE'S AN EXPLANATION FOR THIS.
EXPLANATION? OF COURSE...
I THOUGHT YOU WEREN'T GOING TO BE HOME UNTIL 4:30.

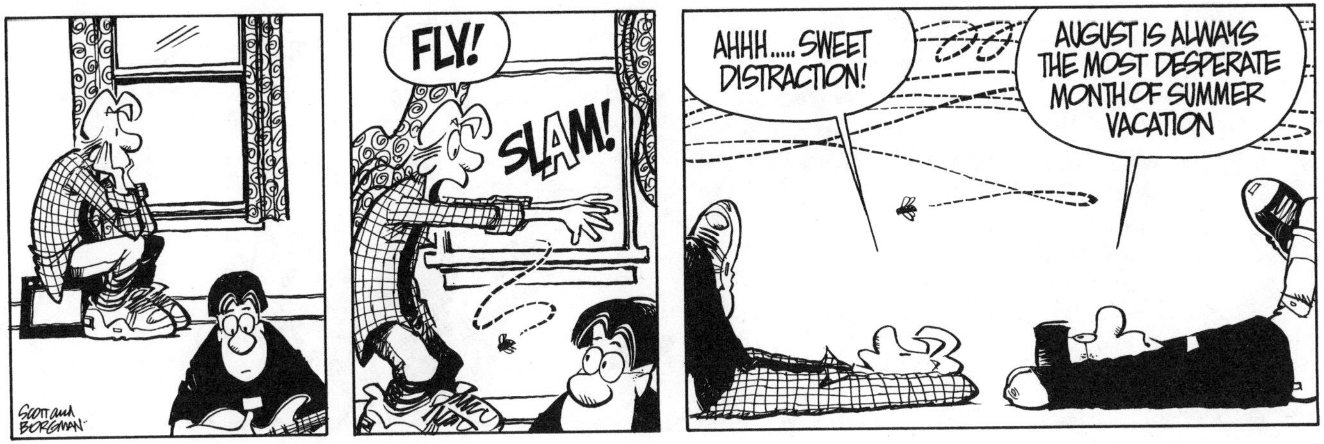
FLY!
SLAM!
AHHH..... SWEET DISTRACTION!
AUGUST IS ALWAYS THE MOST DESPERATE MONTH OF SUMMER VACATION
SCOTT AND BORGMAN

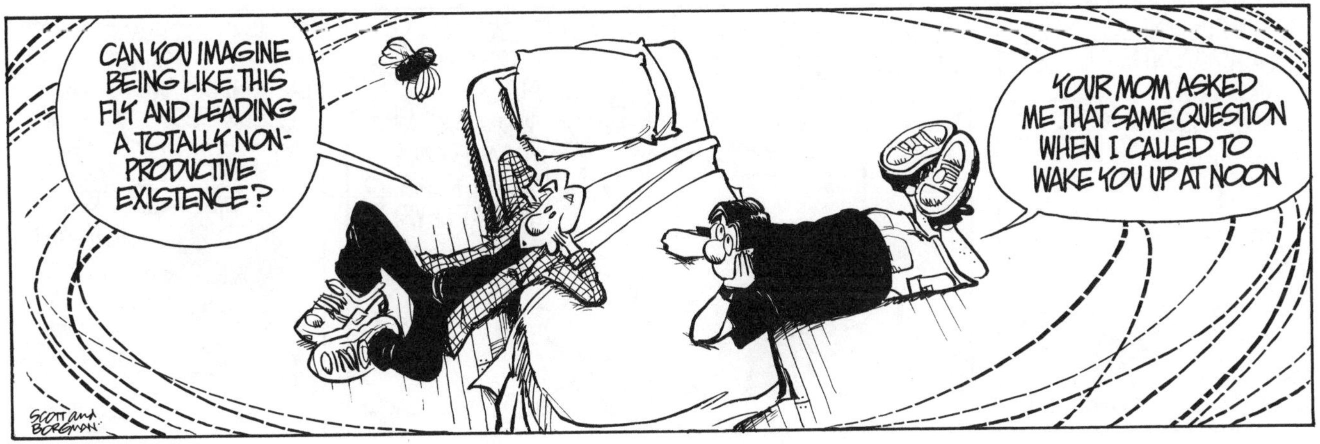
CAN YOU IMAGINE BEING LIKE THIS FLY AND LEADING A TOTALLY NON-PRODUCTIVE EXISTENCE?
YOUR MOM ASKED ME THAT SAME QUESTION WHEN I CALLED TO WAKE YOU UP AT NOON
SCOTT AND BORGMAN

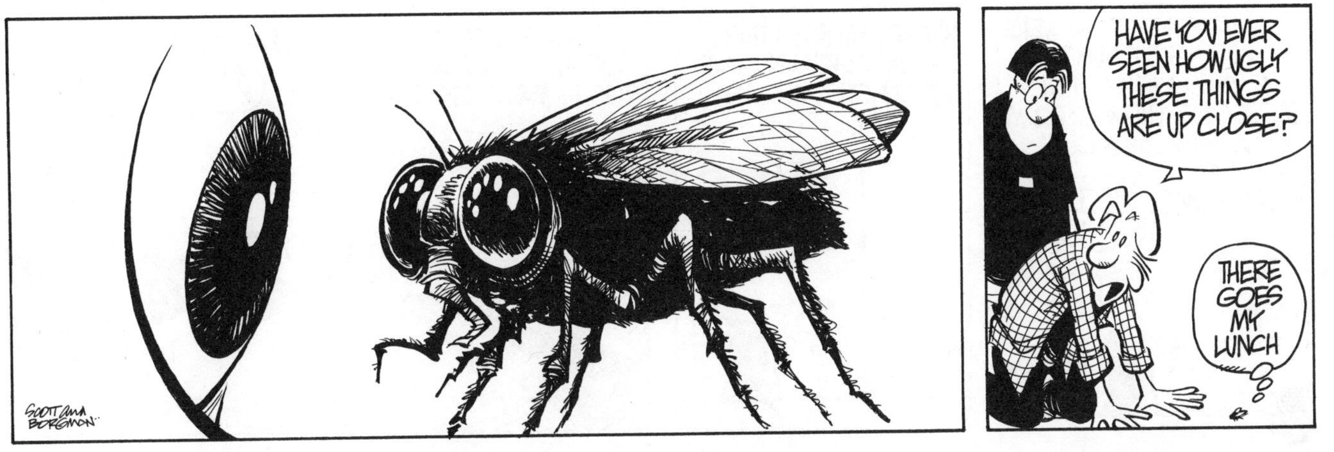
HAVE YOU EVER SEEN HOW UGLY THESE THINGS ARE UP CLOSE?
THERE GOES MY LUNCH
SCOTT AND BORGMAN

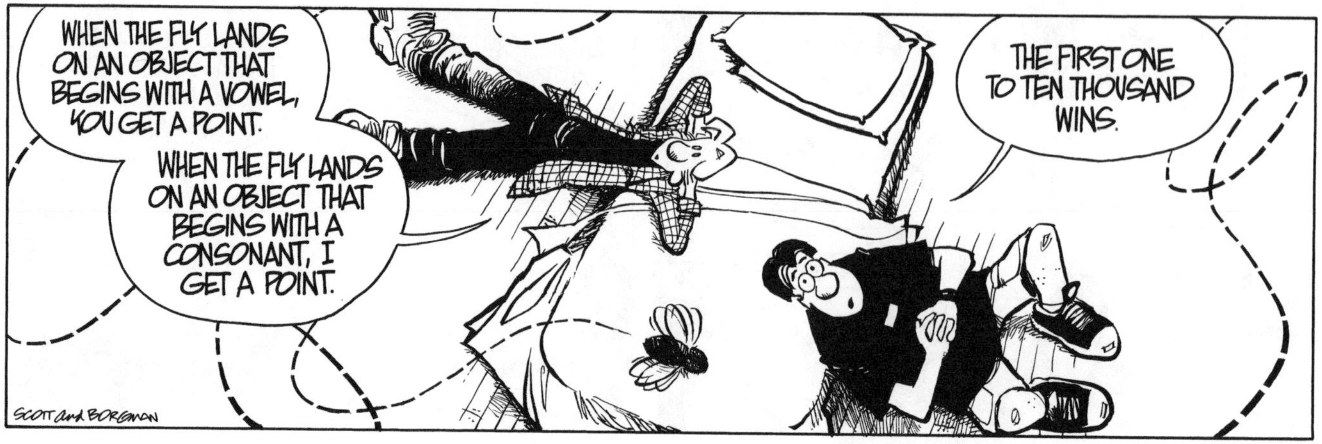
WHEN THE FLY LANDS ON AN OBJECT THAT BEGINS WITH A VOWEL, YOU GET A POINT.
WHEN THE FLY LANDS ON AN OBJECT THAT BEGINS WITH A CONSONANT, I GET A POINT.
THE FIRST ONE TO TEN THOUSAND WINS.
SCOTT and BORGMAN

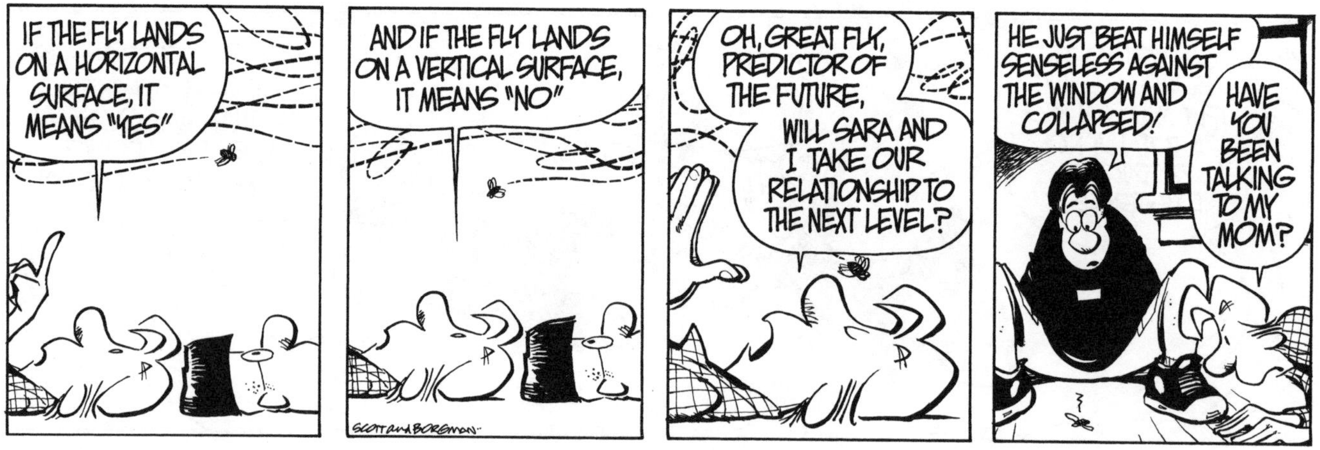
IF THE FLY LANDS ON A HORIZONTAL SURFACE, IT MEANS "YES"
AND IF THE FLY LANDS ON A VERTICAL SURFACE, IT MEANS "NO"
SCOTT and BORGMAN
OH, GREAT FLY, PREDICTOR OF THE FUTURE,
WILL SARA AND I TAKE OUR RELATIONSHIP TO THE NEXT LEVEL?
HE JUST BEAT HIMSELF SENSELESS AGAINST THE WINDOW AND COLLAPSED!
HAVE YOU BEEN TALKING TO MY MOM?

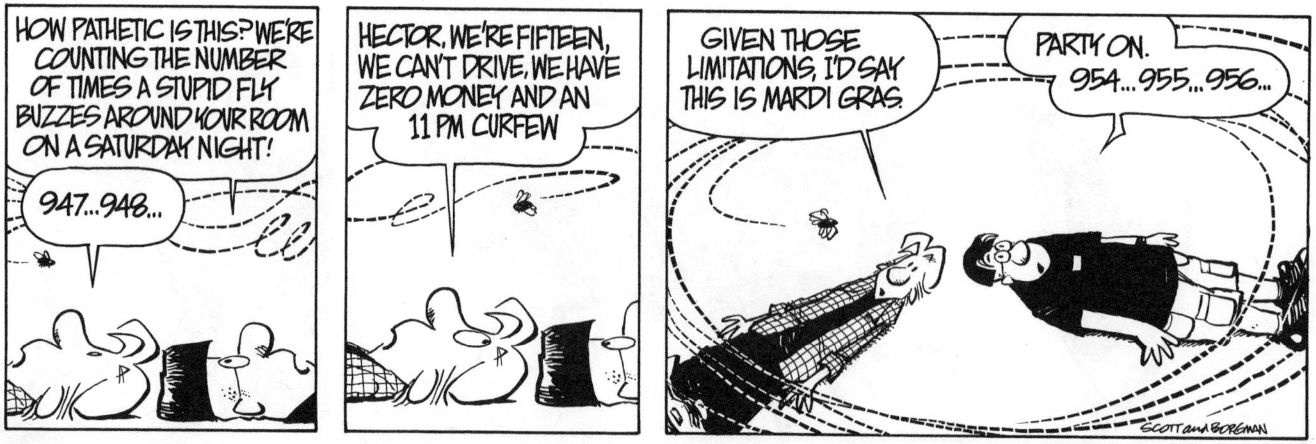
HOW PATHETIC IS THIS? WE'RE COUNTING THE NUMBER OF TIMES A STUPID FLY BUZZES AROUND YOUR ROOM ON A SATURDAY NIGHT!
947...948...
HECTOR, WE'RE FIFTEEN, WE CAN'T DRIVE, WE HAVE ZERO MONEY AND AN 11 PM CURFEW
GIVEN THOSE LIMITATIONS, I'D SAY THIS IS MARDI GRAS.
PARTY ON.
954...955...956...
SCOTT and BORGMAN

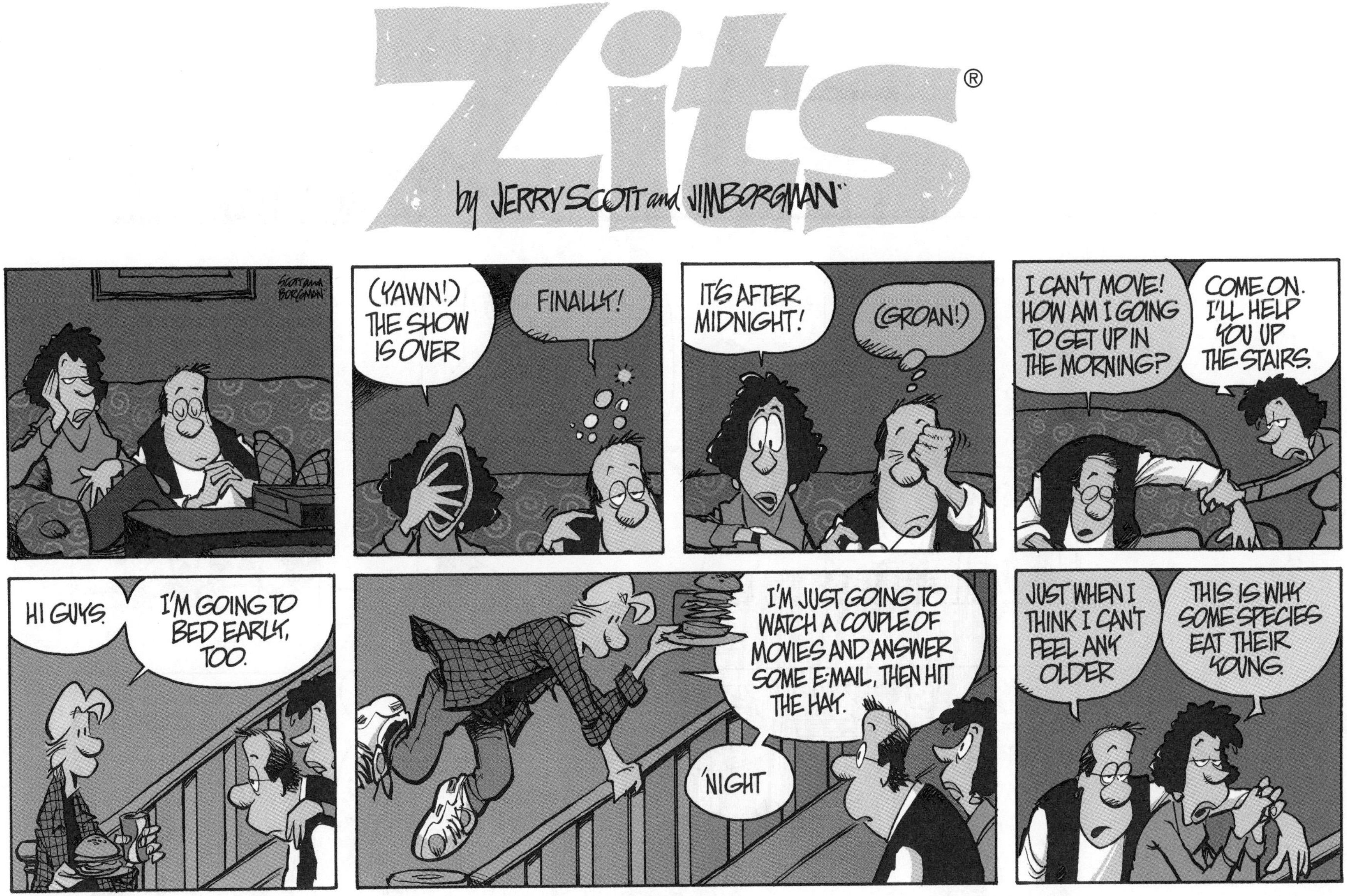
Zits®
by JERRY SCOTT and JIM BORGMAN
SCOTT and BORGMAN
(YAWN!) THE SHOW IS OVER
FINALLY!
IT'S AFTER MIDNIGHT!
(GROAN!)
I CAN'T MOVE! HOW AM I GOING TO GET UP IN THE MORNING?
COME ON. I'LL HELP YOU UP THE STAIRS.
HI GUYS.
I'M GOING TO BED EARLY, TOO.
I'M JUST GOING TO WATCH A COUPLE OF MOVIES AND ANSWER SOME E-MAIL, THEN HIT THE HAY.
'NIGHT
JUST WHEN I THINK I CAN'T FEEL ANY OLDER
THIS IS WHY SOME SPECIES EAT THEIR YOUNG.

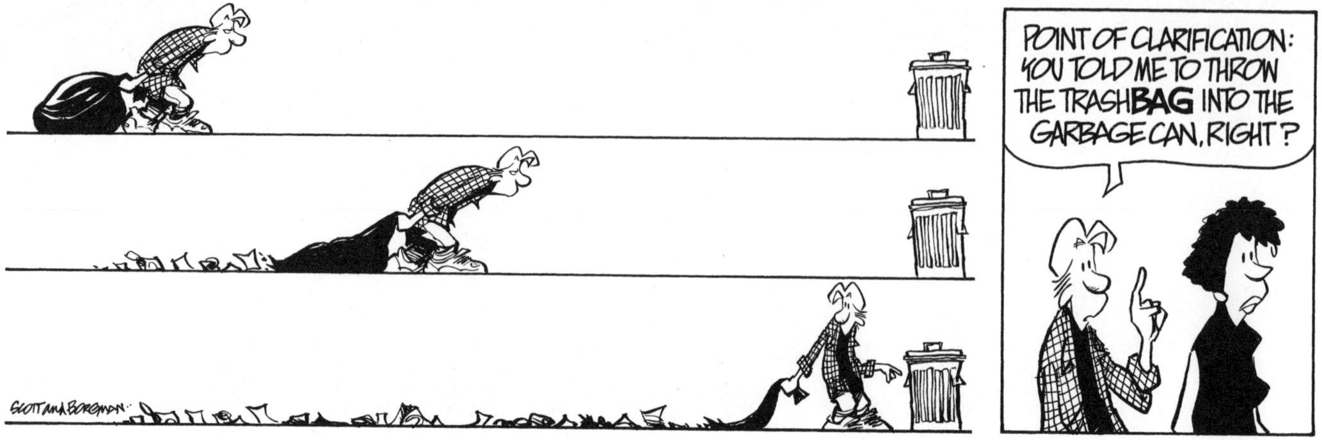
SCOTT and BORGMAN
POINT OF CLARIFICATION: YOU TOLD ME TO THROW THE TRASH**BAG** INTO THE GARBAGE CAN, RIGHT?

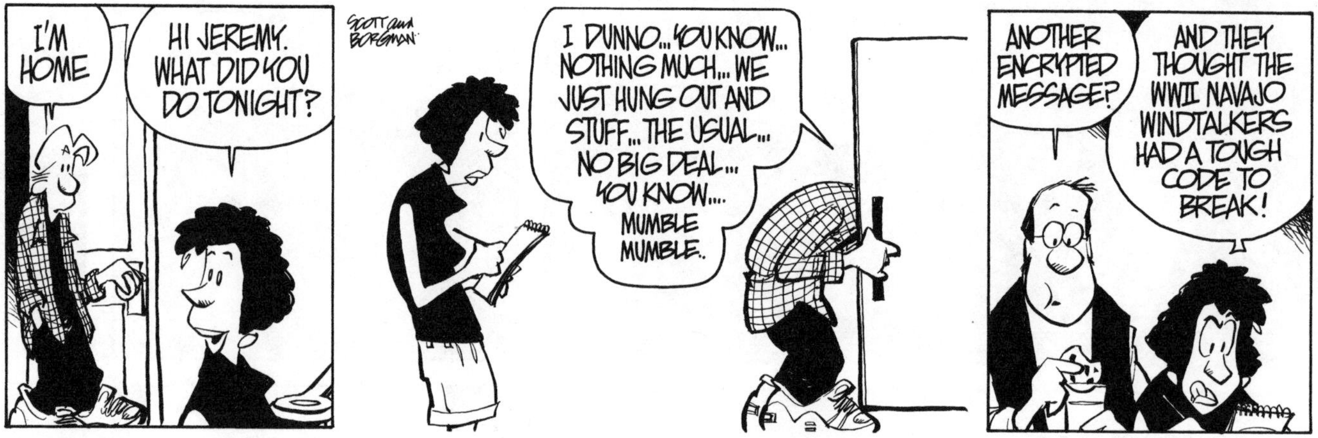
I'M HOME
HI JEREMY. WHAT DID YOU DO TONIGHT?
SCOTT and BORGMAN
I DUNNO... YOU KNOW... NOTHING MUCH... WE JUST HUNG OUT AND STUFF... THE USUAL... NO BIG DEAL... YOU KNOW.... MUMBLE MUMBLE..
ANOTHER ENCRYPTED MESSAGE?
AND THEY THOUGHT THE WWII NAVAJO WINDTALKERS HAD A TOUGH CODE TO BREAK!

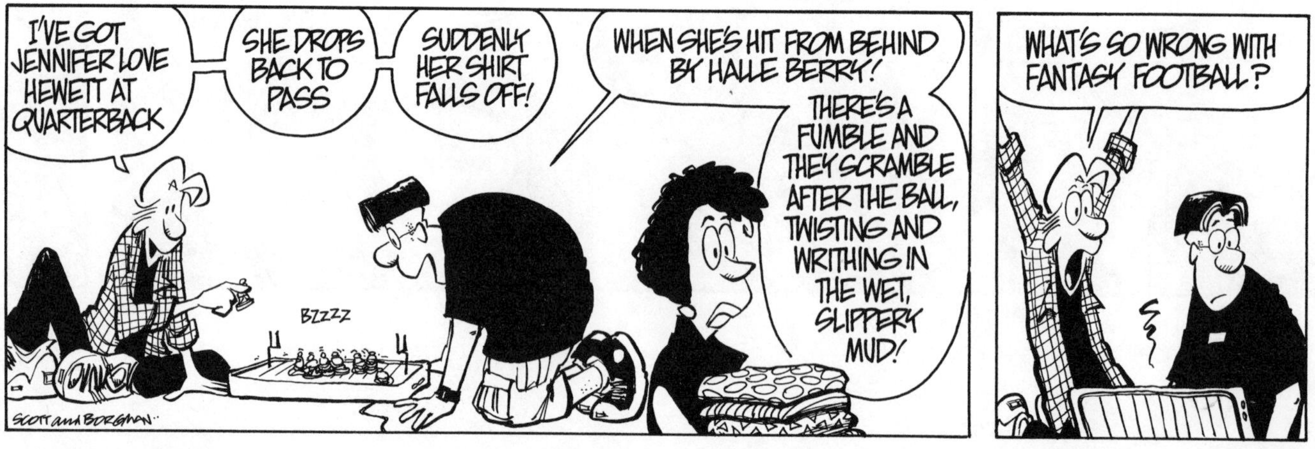
I'VE GOT JENNIFER LOVE HEWETT AT QUARTERBACK
SHE DROPS BACK TO PASS
SUDDENLY HER SHIRT FALLS OFF!
WHEN SHE'S HIT FROM BEHIND BY HALLE BERRY!
THERE'S A FUMBLE AND THEY SCRAMBLE AFTER THE BALL, TWISTING AND WRITHING IN THE WET, SLIPPERY MUD!
BZZZZ
SCOTT and BORGMAN
WHAT'S SO WRONG WITH FANTASY FOOTBALL?

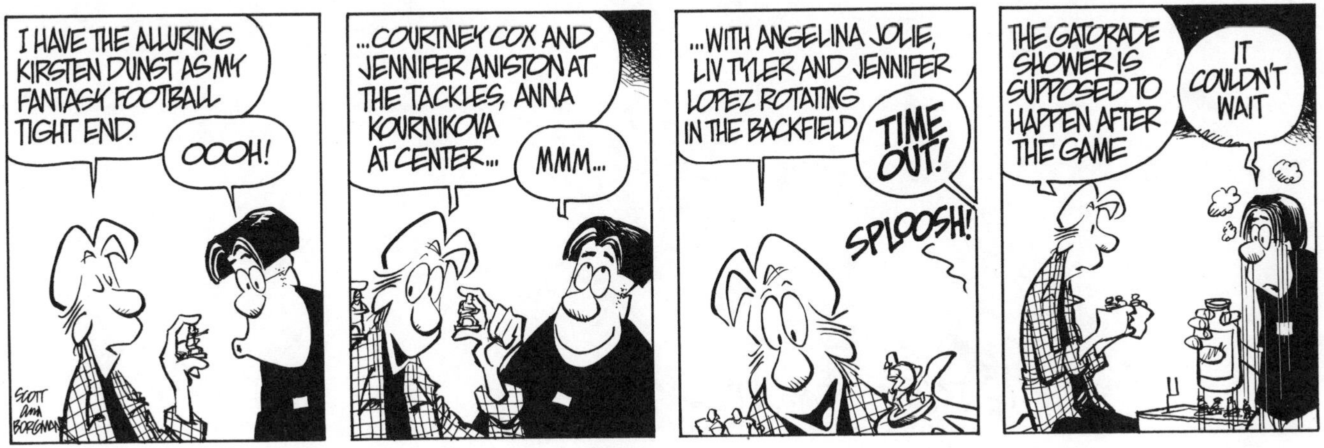
I HAVE THE ALLURING KIRSTEN DUNST AS MY FANTASY FOOTBALL TIGHT END.
OOOH!
...COURTNEY COX AND JENNIFER ANISTON AT THE TACKLES, ANNA KOURNIKOVA AT CENTER...
MMM...
...WITH ANGELINA JOLIE, LIV TYLER AND JENNIFER LOPEZ ROTATING IN THE BACKFIELD
TIME OUT!
SPLOOSH!
THE GATORADE SHOWER IS SUPPOSED TO HAPPEN AFTER THE GAME
IT COULDN'T WAIT

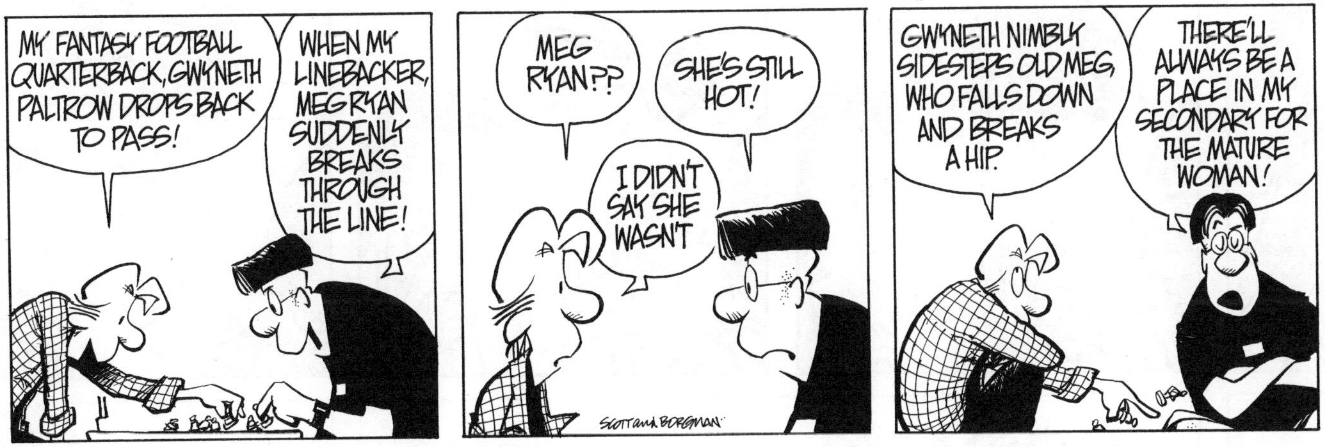
MY FANTASY FOOTBALL QUARTERBACK, GWYNETH PALTROW DROPS BACK TO PASS!
WHEN MY LINEBACKER, MEG RYAN SUDDENLY BREAKS THROUGH THE LINE!
MEG RYAN??
SHE'S STILL HOT!
I DIDN'T SAY SHE WASN'T
GWYNETH NIMBLY SIDESTEPS OLD MEG, WHO FALLS DOWN AND BREAKS A HIP.
THERE'LL ALWAYS BE A PLACE IN MY SECONDARY FOR THE MATURE WOMAN!

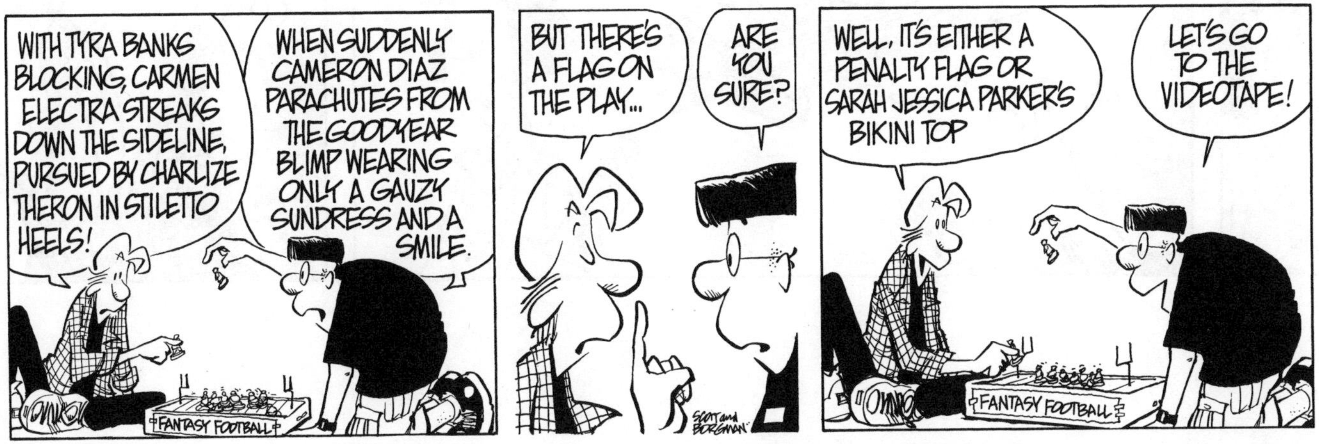
WITH TYRA BANKS BLOCKING, CARMEN ELECTRA STREAKS DOWN THE SIDELINE, PURSUED BY CHARLIZE THERON IN STILETTO HEELS!
WHEN SUDDENLY CAMERON DIAZ PARACHUTES FROM THE GOODYEAR BLIMP WEARING ONLY A GAUZY SUNDRESS AND A SMILE.
FANTASY FOOTBALL
BUT THERE'S A FLAG ON THE PLAY...
ARE YOU SURE?
WELL, IT'S EITHER A PENALTY FLAG OR SARAH JESSICA PARKER'S BIKINI TOP
LET'S GO TO THE VIDEOTAPE!
FANTASY FOOTBALL

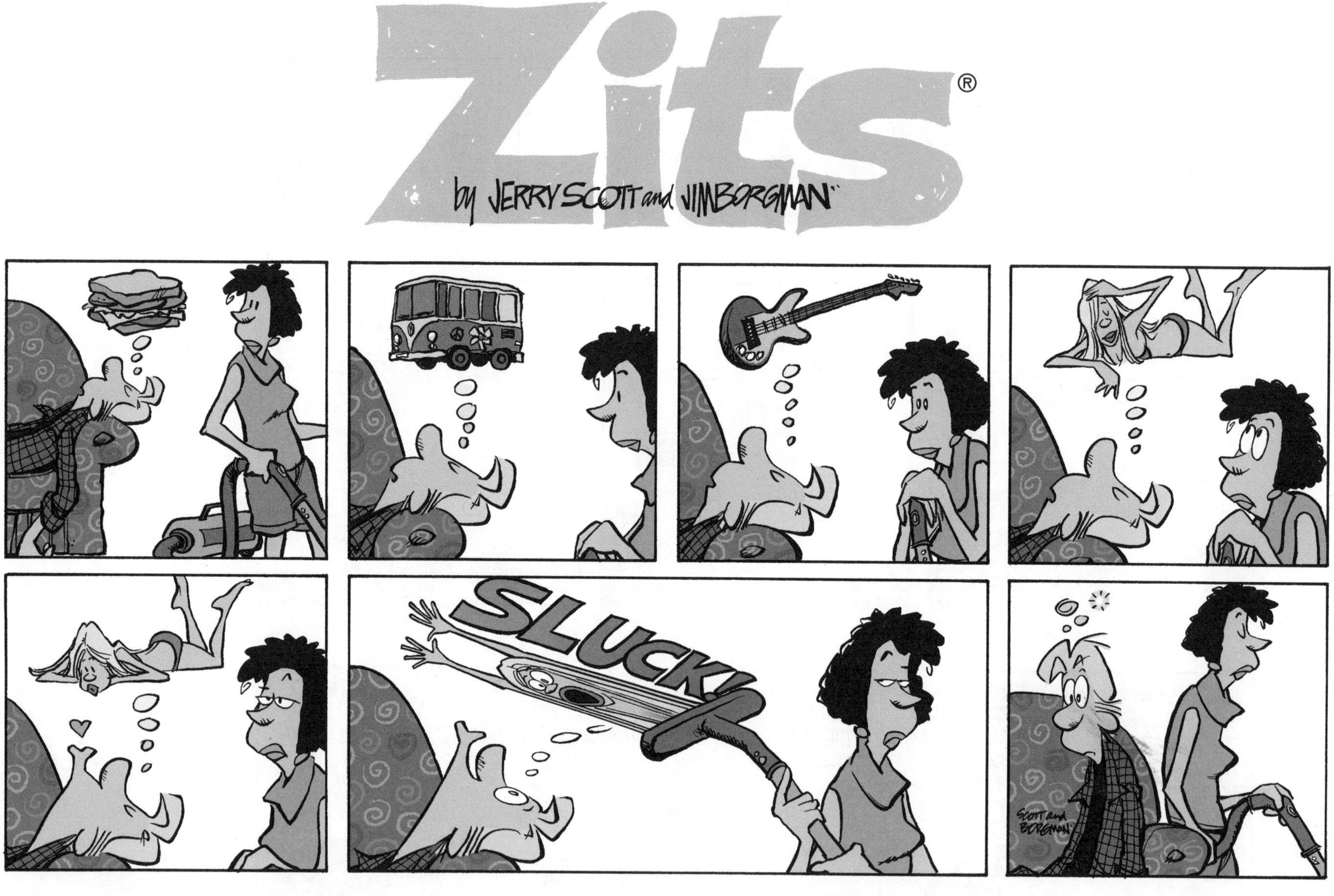
Zits®
by JERRY SCOTT and JIM BORGMAN
SLUCK!
SCOTT AND BORGMAN

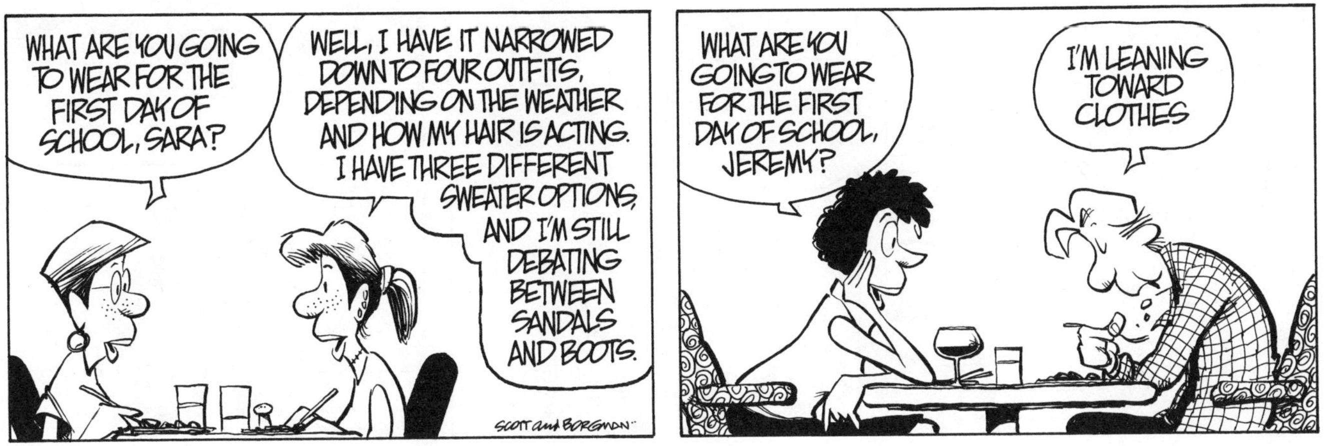
WHAT ARE YOU GOING TO WEAR FOR THE FIRST DAY OF SCHOOL, SARA?
WELL, I HAVE IT NARROWED DOWN TO FOUR OUTFITS, DEPENDING ON THE WEATHER AND HOW MY HAIR IS ACTING. I HAVE THREE DIFFERENT SWEATER OPTIONS, AND I'M STILL DEBATING BETWEEN SANDALS AND BOOTS.
SCOTT AND BORGMAN
WHAT ARE YOU GOING TO WEAR FOR THE FIRST DAY OF SCHOOL, JEREMY?
I'M LEANING TOWARD CLOTHES

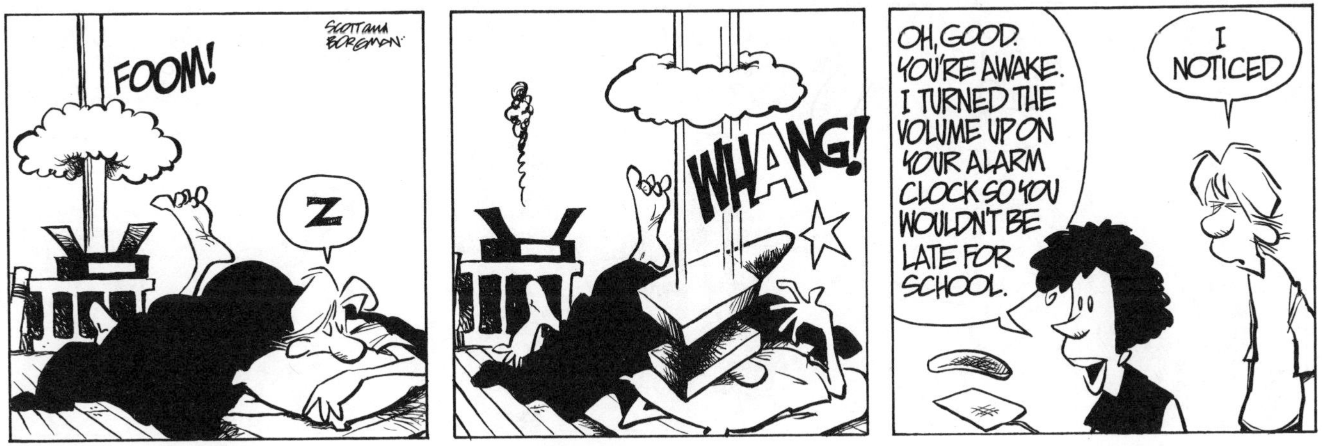
SCOTT AND BORGMAN
FOOM!
Z
WHANG!
OH, GOOD. YOU'RE AWAKE. I TURNED THE VOLUME UP ON YOUR ALARM CLOCK SO YOU WOULDN'T BE LATE FOR SCHOOL.
I NOTICED

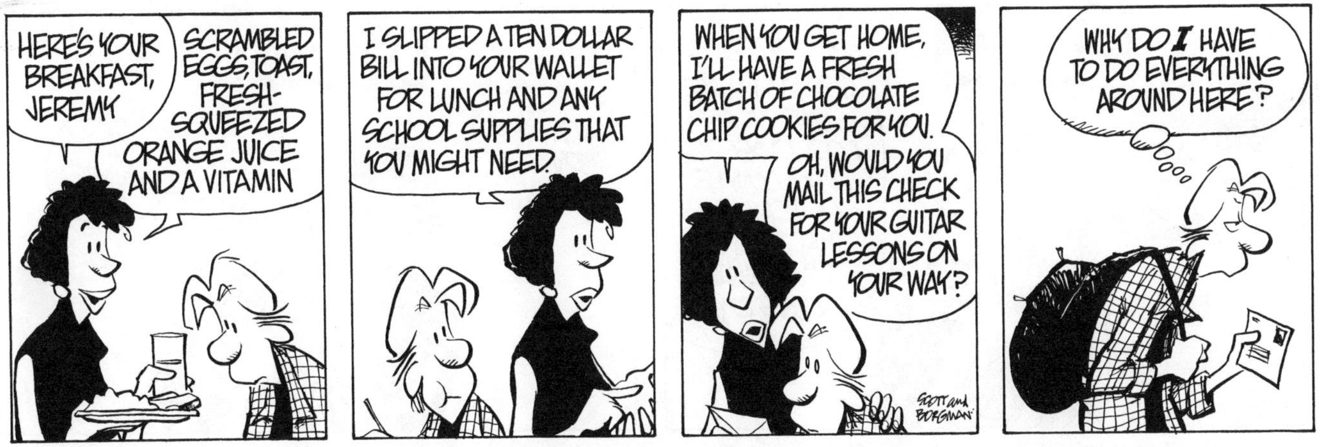
HERE'S YOUR BREAKFAST, JEREMY
SCRAMBLED EGGS, TOAST, FRESH-SQUEEZED ORANGE JUICE AND A VITAMIN
I SLIPPED A TEN DOLLAR BILL INTO YOUR WALLET FOR LUNCH AND ANY SCHOOL SUPPLIES THAT YOU MIGHT NEED.
WHEN YOU GET HOME, I'LL HAVE A FRESH BATCH OF CHOCOLATE CHIP COOKIES FOR YOU.
OH, WOULD YOU MAIL THIS CHECK FOR YOUR GUITAR LESSONS ON YOUR WAY?
SCOTT AND BORGMAN
WHY DO I HAVE TO DO EVERYTHING AROUND HERE?

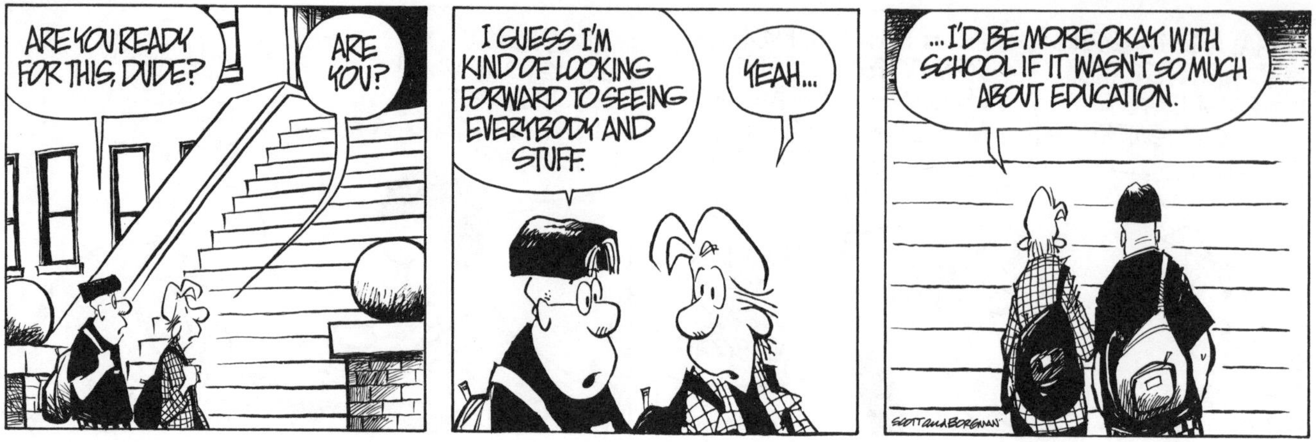
ARE YOU READY FOR THIS, DUDE?
ARE YOU?
I GUESS I'M KIND OF LOOKING FORWARD TO SEEING EVERYBODY AND STUFF.
YEAH...
...I'D BE MORE OKAY WITH SCHOOL IF IT WASN'T SO MUCH ABOUT EDUCATION.
SCOTT and BORGMAN

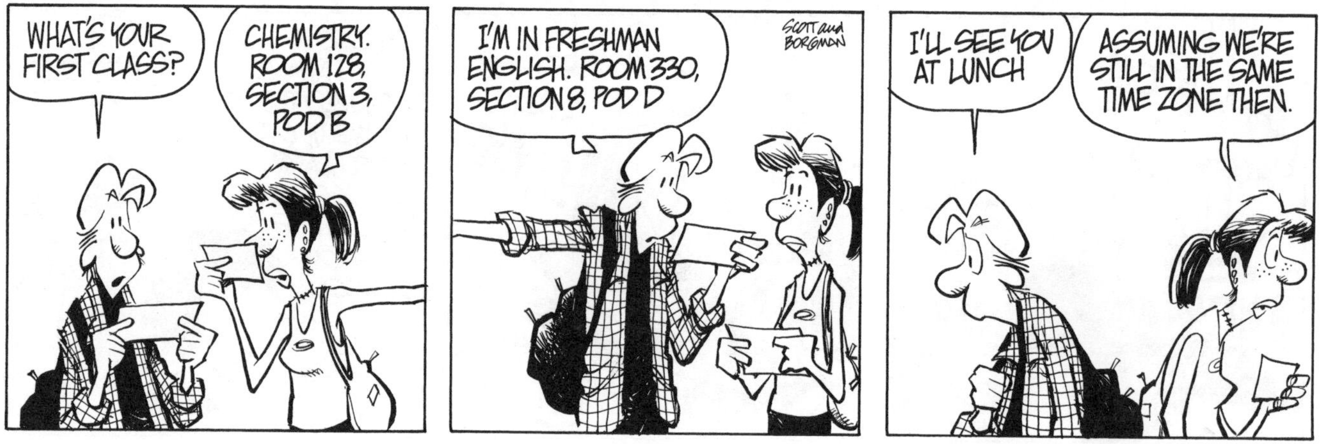
WHAT'S YOUR FIRST CLASS?
CHEMISTRY. ROOM 128, SECTION 3, POD B
I'M IN FRESHMAN ENGLISH. ROOM 330, SECTION 8, POD D
SCOTT and BORGMAN
I'LL SEE YOU AT LUNCH
ASSUMING WE'RE STILL IN THE SAME TIME ZONE THEN.

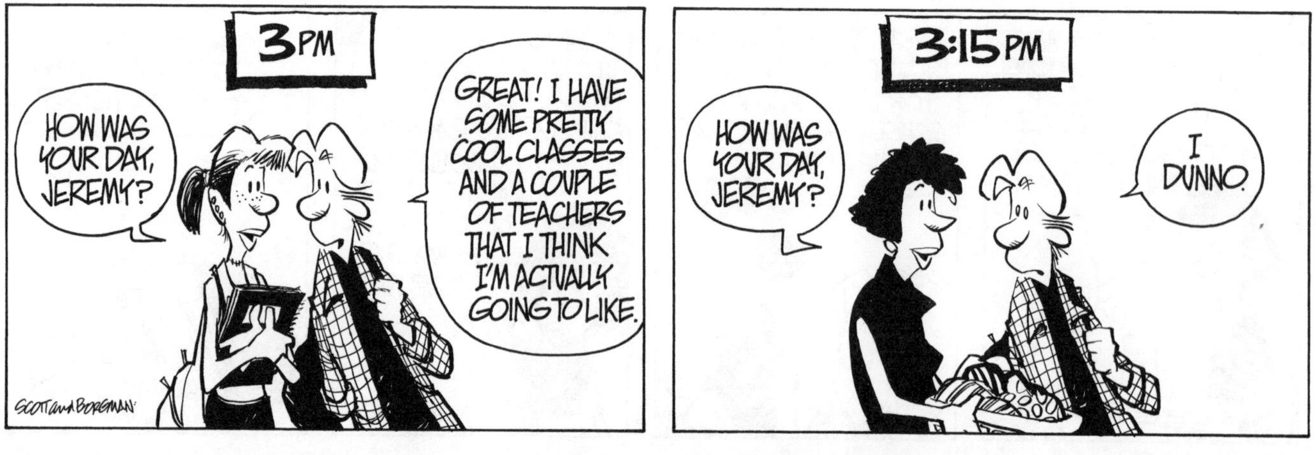
3PM
HOW WAS YOUR DAY, JEREMY?
GREAT! I HAVE SOME PRETTY COOL CLASSES AND A COUPLE OF TEACHERS THAT I THINK I'M ACTUALLY GOING TO LIKE.
SCOTT and BORGMAN
3:15PM
HOW WAS YOUR DAY, JEREMY?
I DUNNO.

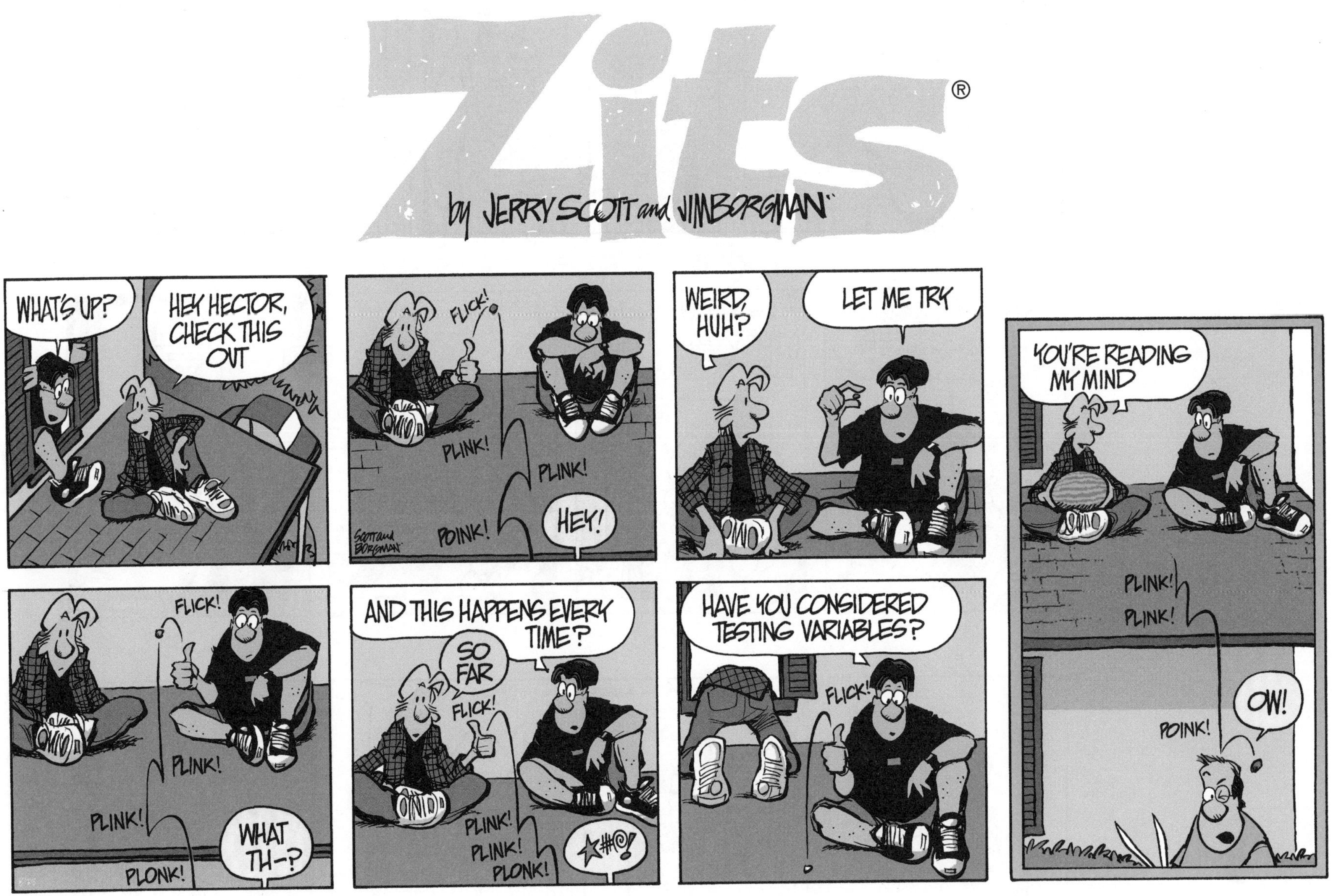
Zits®
by JERRY SCOTT and JIM BORGMAN
WHAT'S UP?
HEY HECTOR, CHECK THIS OUT
FLICK!
PLINK!
PLINK!
POINK!
HEY!
WEIRD, HUH?
LET ME TRY
FLICK!
PLINK!
PLINK!
PLONK!
WHAT TH-?
AND THIS HAPPENS EVERY TIME?
SO FAR
FLICK!
PLINK!
PLINK!
PLONK!
★#@!
HAVE YOU CONSIDERED TESTING VARIABLES?
FLICK!
YOU'RE READING MY MIND
PLINK!
PLINK!
POINK!
OW!

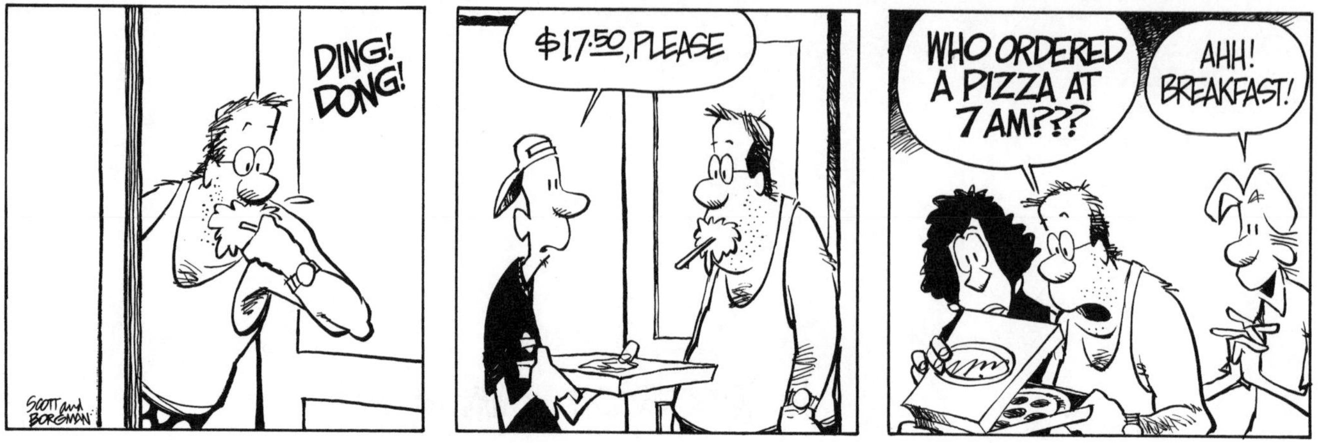
DING! DONG!
$17.50, PLEASE
WHO ORDERED A PIZZA AT 7 AM???
AHH! BREAKFAST!
SCOTT and BORGMAN

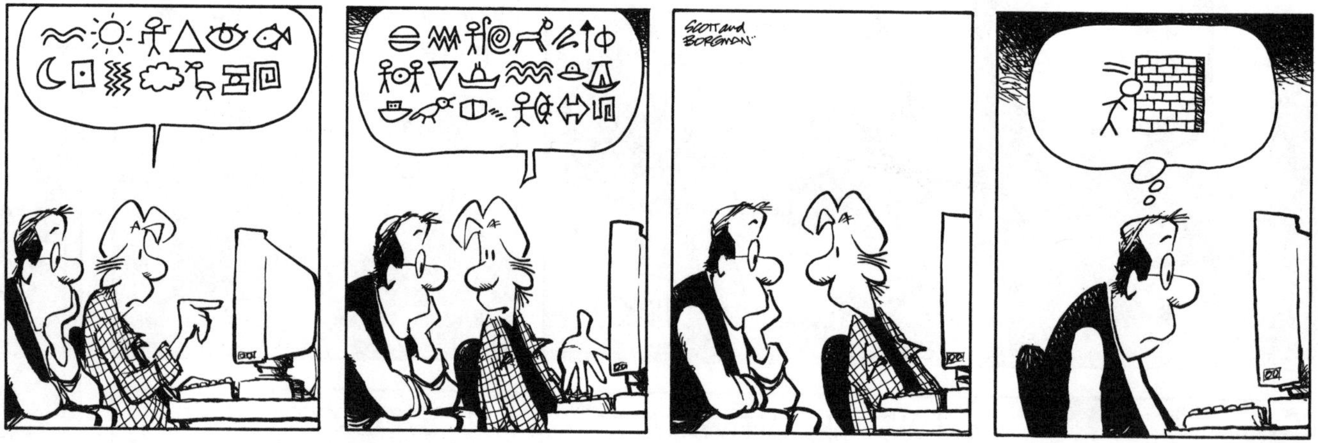
SCOTT and BORGMAN

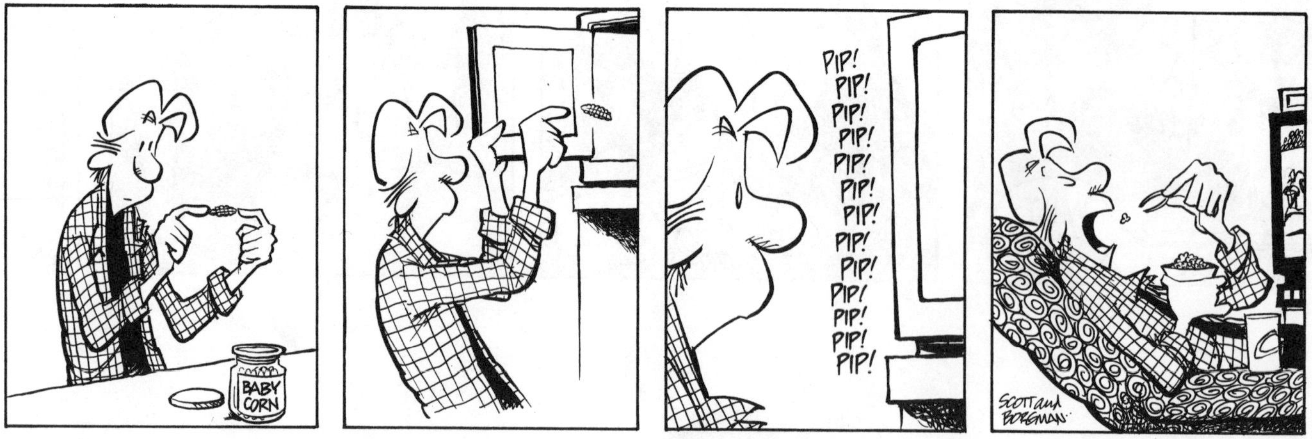
BABY CORN
PIP! PIP! PIP! PIP! PIP! PIP! PIP! PIP! PIP! PIP! PIP! PIP! PIP!
SCOTT and BORGMAN

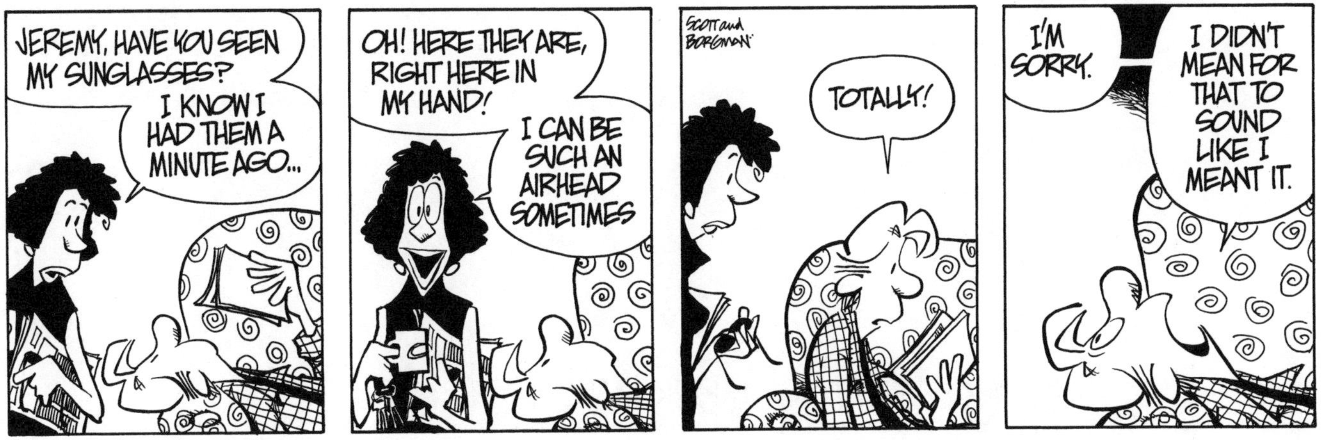
JEREMY, HAVE YOU SEEN MY SUNGLASSES?
I KNOW I HAD THEM A MINUTE AGO...
OH! HERE THEY ARE, RIGHT HERE IN MY HAND!
I CAN BE SUCH AN AIRHEAD SOMETIMES
SCOTT AND BORGMAN
TOTALLY!
I'M SORRY.
I DIDN'T MEAN FOR THAT TO SOUND LIKE I MEANT IT.

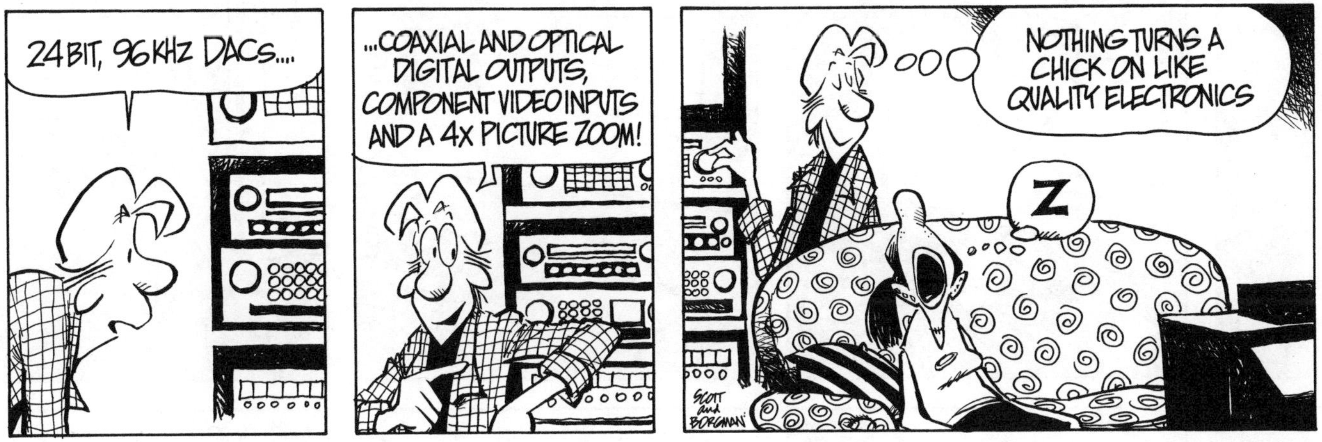
24 BIT, 96 KHz DACs....
...COAXIAL AND OPTICAL DIGITAL OUTPUTS, COMPONENT VIDEO INPUTS AND A 4X PICTURE ZOOM!
NOTHING TURNS A CHICK ON LIKE QUALITY ELECTRONICS
Z
SCOTT AND BORGMAN

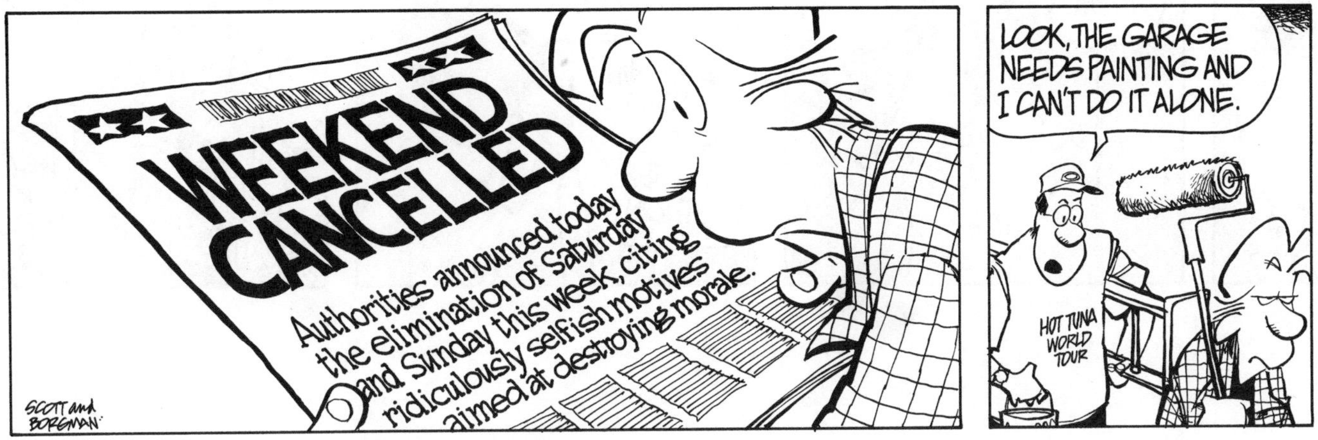
WEEKEND CANCELLED
Authorities announced today the elimination of Saturday and Sunday this week, citing ridiculously selfish motives aimed at destroying morale.
SCOTT AND BORGMAN
LOOK, THE GARAGE NEEDS PAINTING AND I CAN'T DO IT ALONE.
HOT TUNA WORLD TOUR

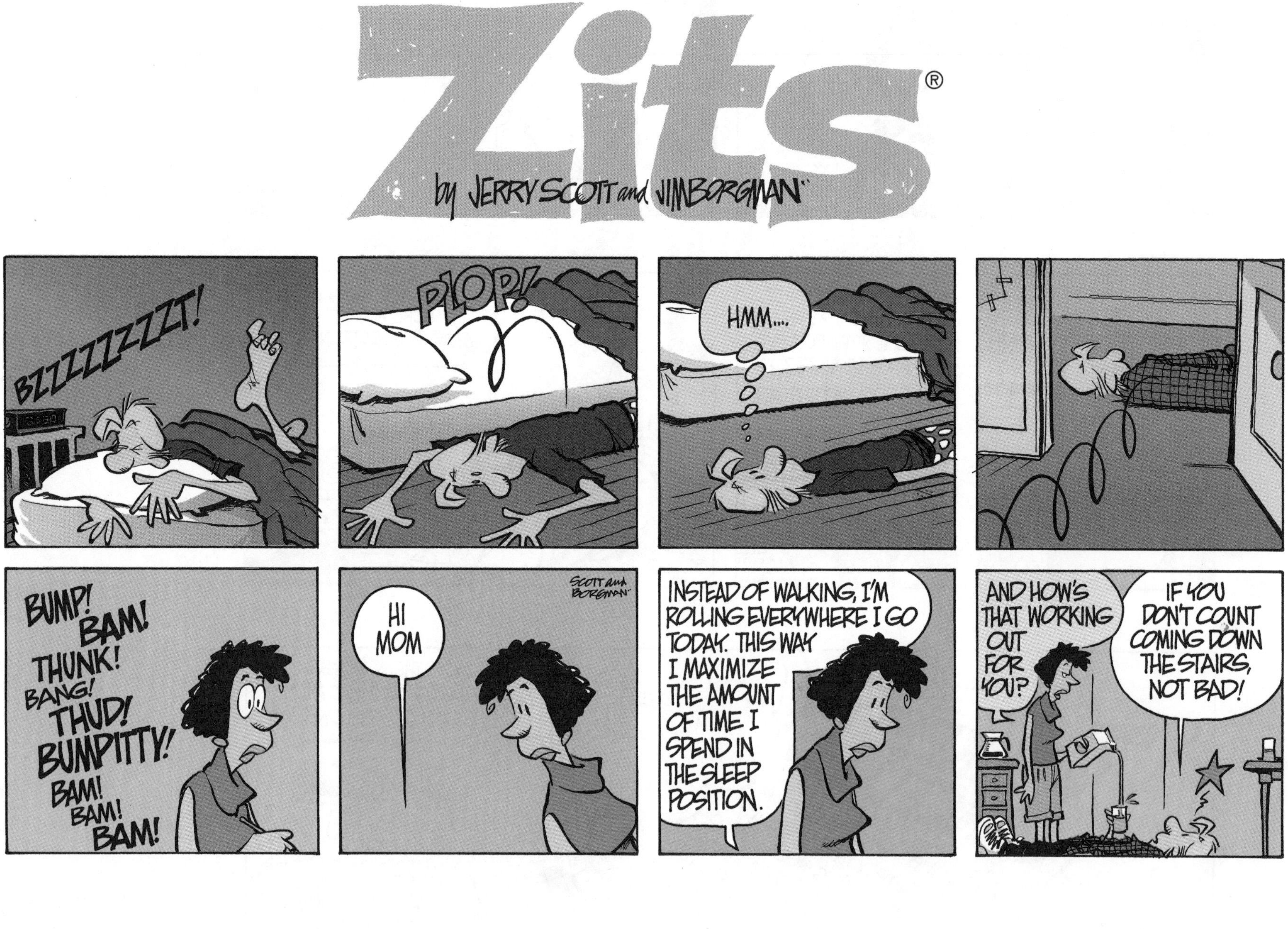
Zits®
by JERRY SCOTT and JIM BORGMAN
BZZZZZZZZZT!
PLOP!
HMM....
BUMP! BAM! THUNK! BANG! THUD! BUMPITTY! BAM! BAM! BAM!
SCOTT AND BORGMAN
HI MOM
INSTEAD OF WALKING, I'M ROLLING EVERYWHERE I GO TODAY. THIS WAY I MAXIMIZE THE AMOUNT OF TIME I SPEND IN THE SLEEP POSITION.
AND HOW'S THAT WORKING OUT FOR YOU?
IF YOU DON'T COUNT COMING DOWN THE STAIRS, NOT BAD!

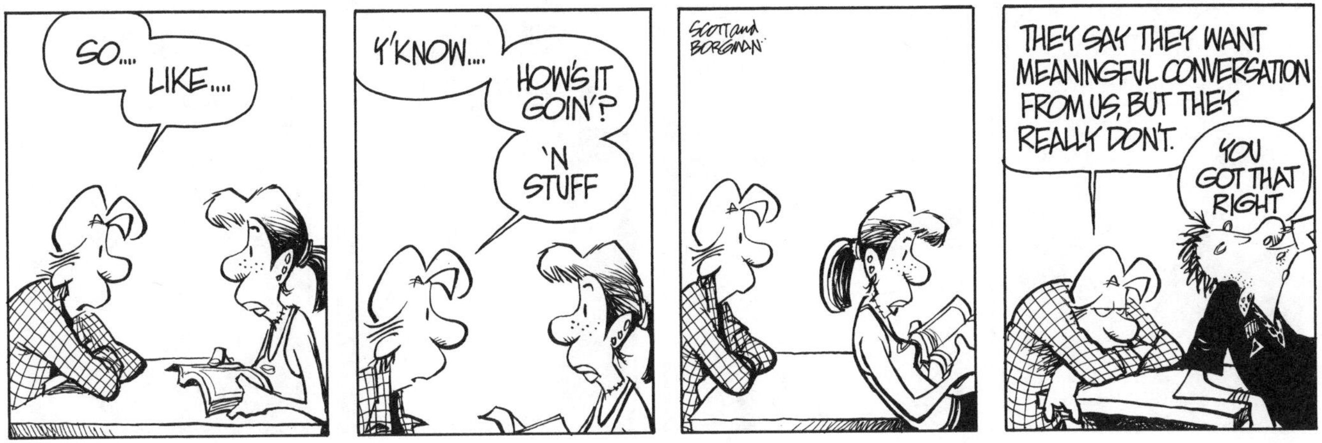
SO.... LIKE....
Y'KNOW....
HOW'S IT GOIN'?
'N STUFF
SCOTT and BORGMAN
THEY SAY THEY WANT MEANINGFUL CONVERSATION FROM US, BUT THEY REALLY DON'T.
YOU GOT THAT RIGHT

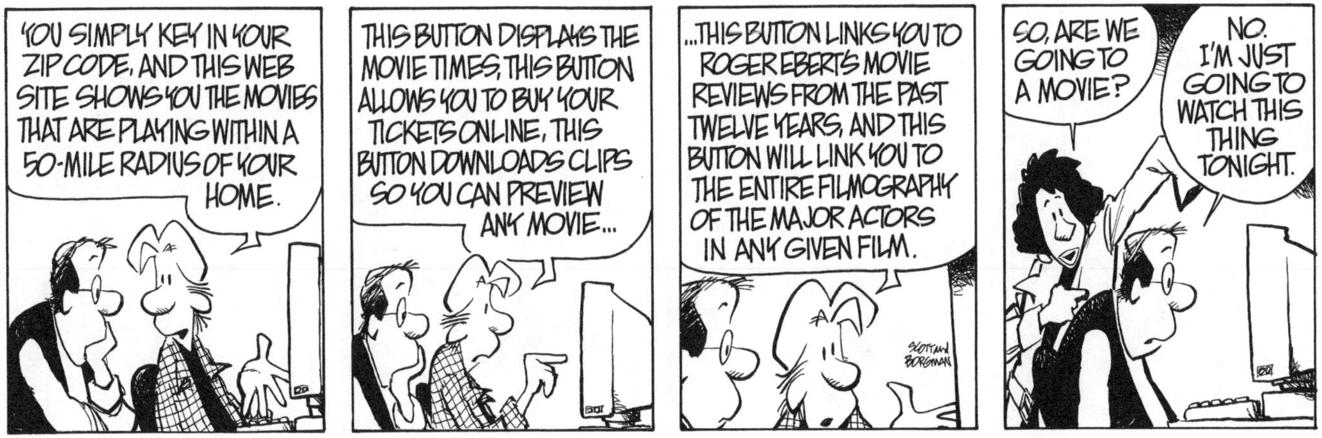
YOU SIMPLY KEY IN YOUR ZIP CODE, AND THIS WEB SITE SHOWS YOU THE MOVIES THAT ARE PLAYING WITHIN A 50-MILE RADIUS OF YOUR HOME.
THIS BUTTON DISPLAYS THE MOVIE TIMES, THIS BUTTON ALLOWS YOU TO BUY YOUR TICKETS ONLINE, THIS BUTTON DOWNLOADS CLIPS SO YOU CAN PREVIEW ANY MOVIE...
...THIS BUTTON LINKS YOU TO ROGER EBERT'S MOVIE REVIEWS FROM THE PAST TWELVE YEARS, AND THIS BUTTON WILL LINK YOU TO THE ENTIRE FILMOGRAPHY OF THE MAJOR ACTORS IN ANY GIVEN FILM.
SCOTT and BORGMAN
SO, ARE WE GOING TO A MOVIE?
NO. I'M JUST GOING TO WATCH THIS THING TONIGHT.

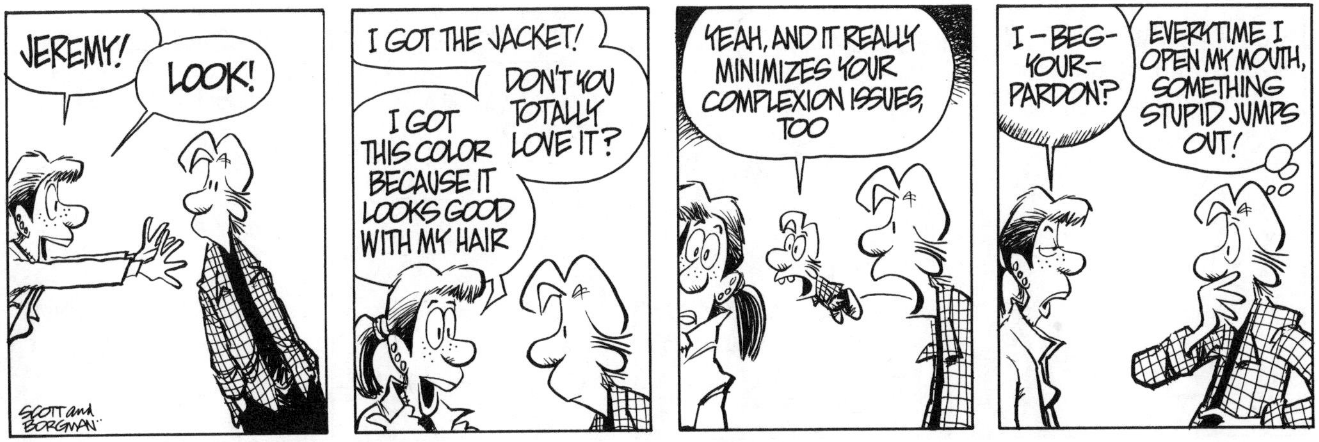
JEREMY!
LOOK!
SCOTT and BORGMAN
I GOT THE JACKET!
DON'T YOU TOTALLY LOVE IT?
I GOT THIS COLOR BECAUSE IT LOOKS GOOD WITH MY HAIR
YEAH, AND IT REALLY MINIMIZES YOUR COMPLEXION ISSUES, TOO
I-BEG-YOUR-PARDON?
EVERYTIME I OPEN MY MOUTH, SOMETHING STUPID JUMPS OUT!

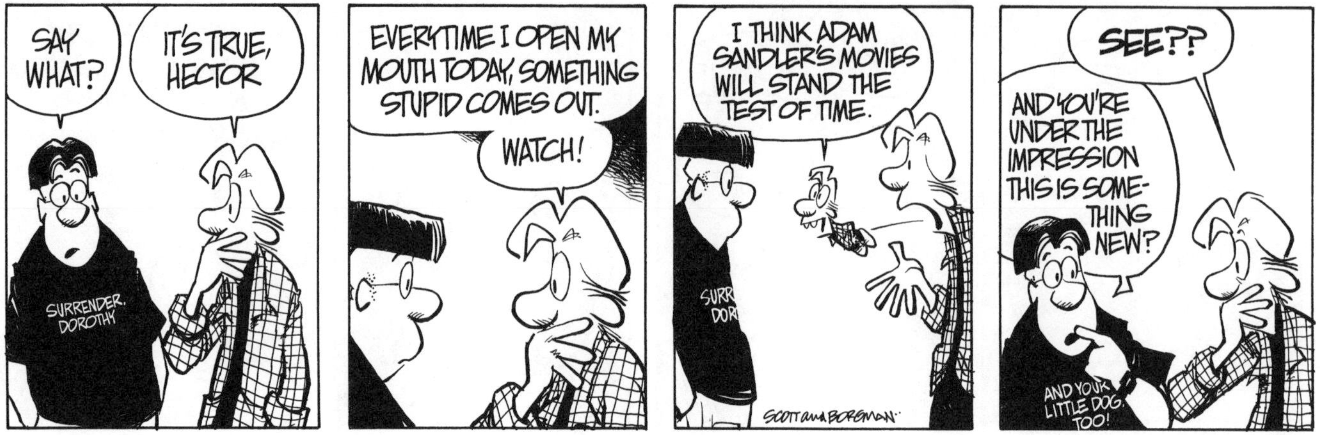
SAY WHAT?
IT'S TRUE, HECTOR
SURRENDER, DOROTHY
EVERYTIME I OPEN MY MOUTH TODAY, SOMETHING STUPID COMES OUT.
WATCH!
I THINK ADAM SANDLER'S MOVIES WILL STAND THE TEST OF TIME.
SCOTT and BORGMAN
SEE??
AND YOU'RE UNDER THE IMPRESSION THIS IS SOMETHING NEW?
AND YOUR LITTLE DOG, TOO!

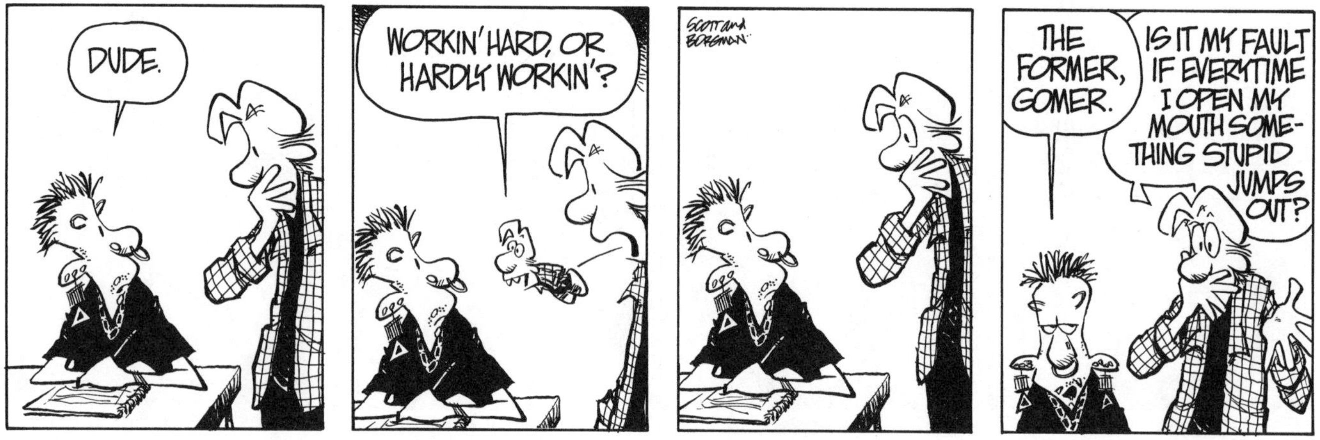
DUDE.
WORKIN' HARD, OR HARDLY WORKIN'?
SCOTT and BORGMAN
THE FORMER, GOMER.
IS IT MY FAULT IF EVERYTIME I OPEN MY MOUTH SOMETHING STUPID JUMPS OUT?

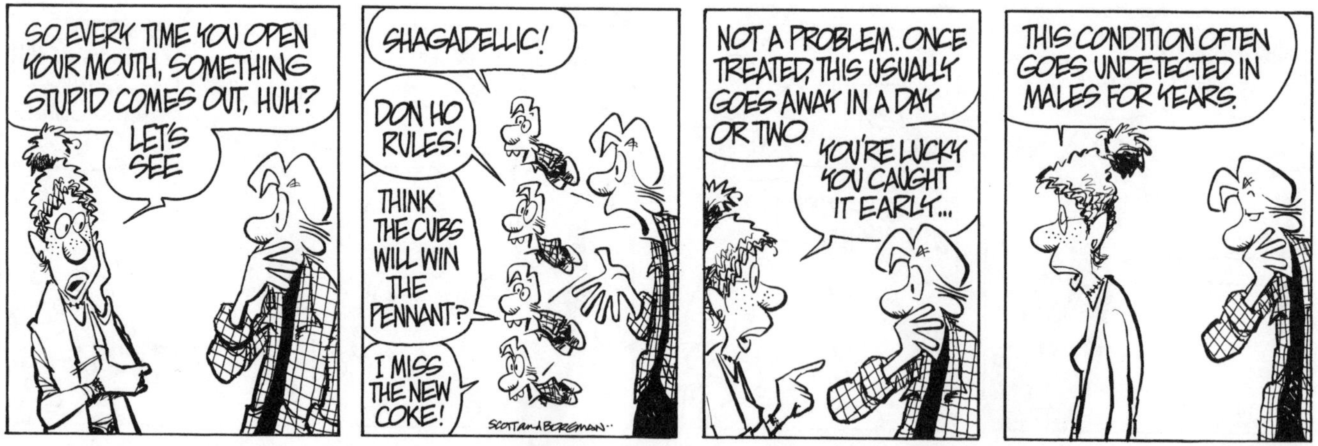
SO EVERY TIME YOU OPEN YOUR MOUTH, SOMETHING STUPID COMES OUT, HUH?
LET'S SEE
SHAGADELLIC!
DON HO RULES!
THINK THE CUBS WILL WIN THE PENNANT?
I MISS THE NEW COKE!
SCOTT and BORGMAN
NOT A PROBLEM. ONCE TREATED, THIS USUALLY GOES AWAY IN A DAY OR TWO.
YOU'RE LUCKY YOU CAUGHT IT EARLY...
THIS CONDITION OFTEN GOES UNDETECTED IN MALES FOR YEARS.

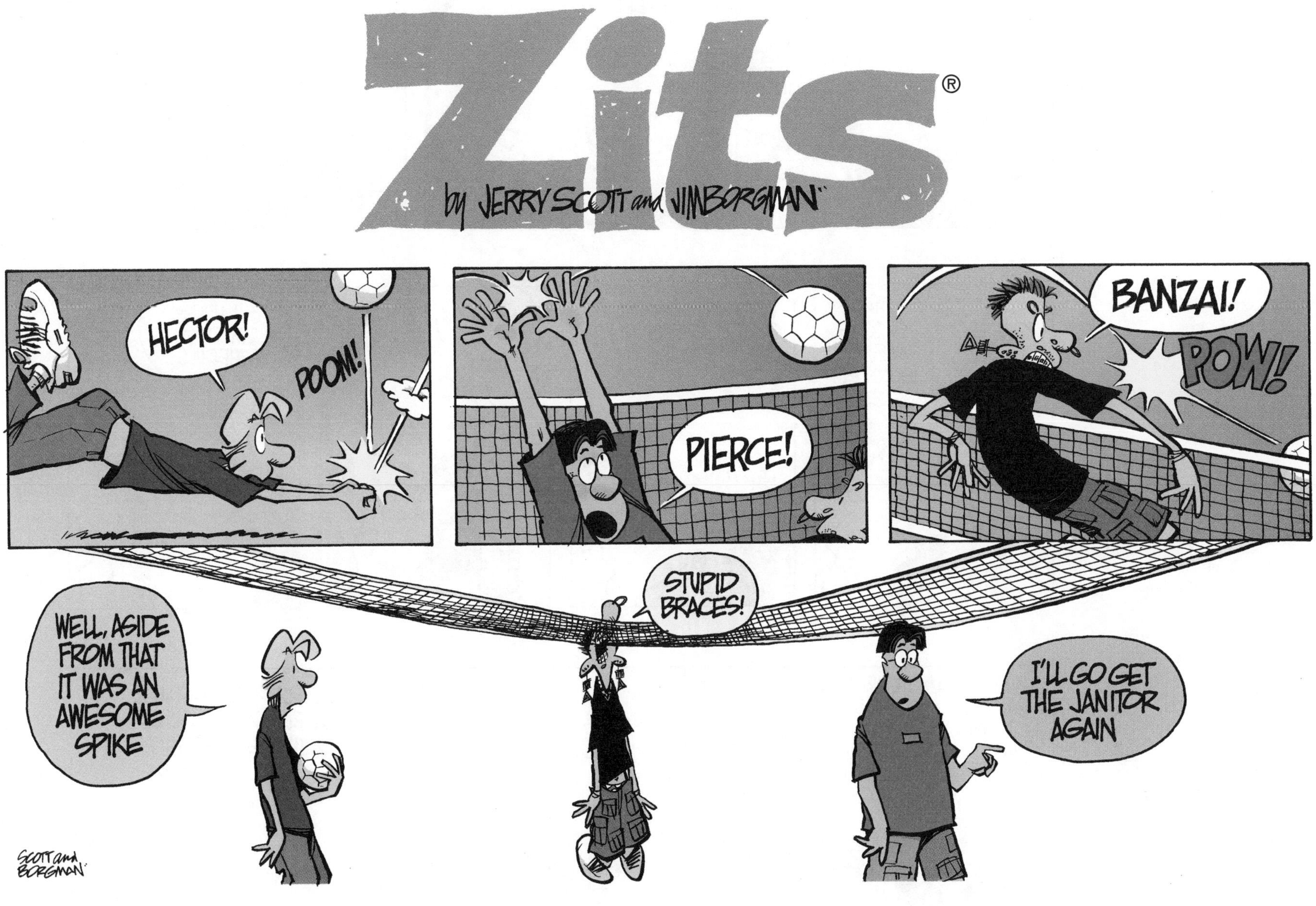
Zits®
by JERRY SCOTT and JIM BORGMAN
HECTOR!
POOM!
PIERCE!
BANZAI!
POW!
STUPID BRACES!
WELL, ASIDE FROM THAT IT WAS AN AWESOME SPIKE
I'LL GO GET THE JANITOR AGAIN
SCOTT and BORGMAN

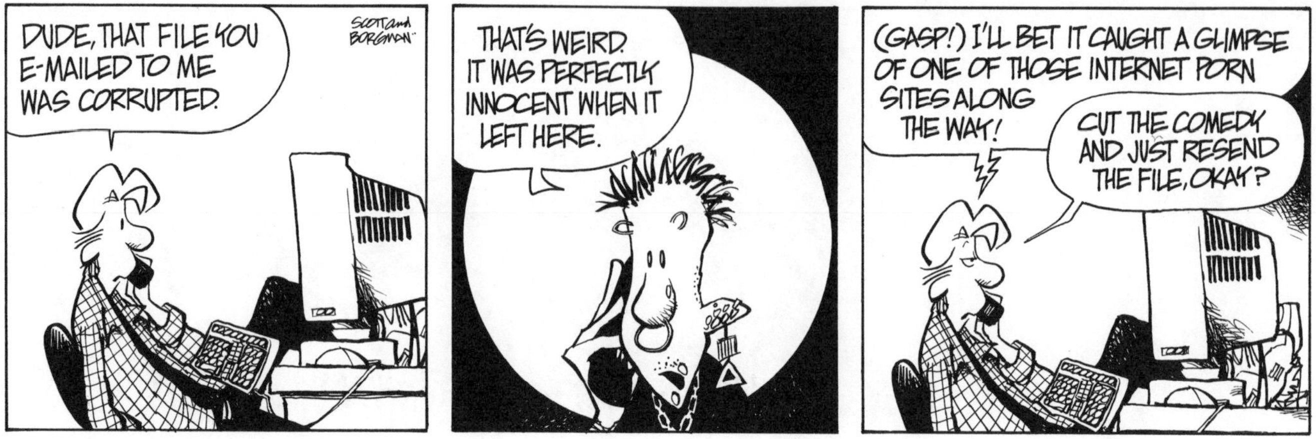

DUDE, THAT FILE YOU E-MAILED TO ME WAS CORRUPTED.
SCOTT and BORGMAN
THAT'S WEIRD. IT WAS PERFECTLY INNOCENT WHEN IT LEFT HERE.
(GASP!) I'LL BET IT CAUGHT A GLIMPSE OF ONE OF THOSE INTERNET PORN SITES ALONG THE WAY!
CUT THE COMEDY AND JUST RESEND THE FILE, OKAY?

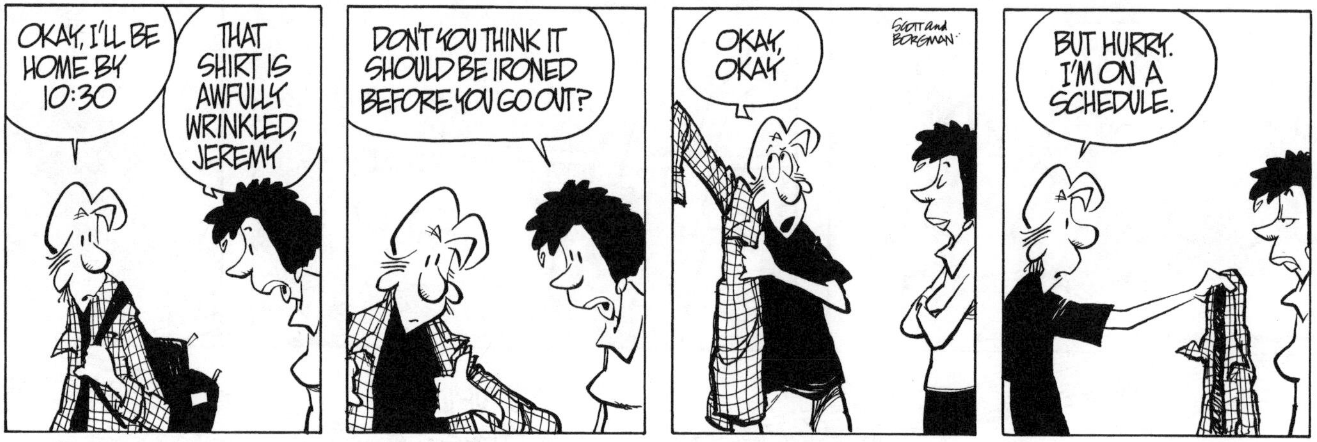

OKAY, I'LL BE HOME BY 10:30
THAT SHIRT IS AWFULLY WRINKLED, JEREMY
DON'T YOU THINK IT SHOULD BE IRONED BEFORE YOU GO OUT?
OKAY, OKAY
SCOTT and BORGMAN
BUT HURRY. I'M ON A SCHEDULE.

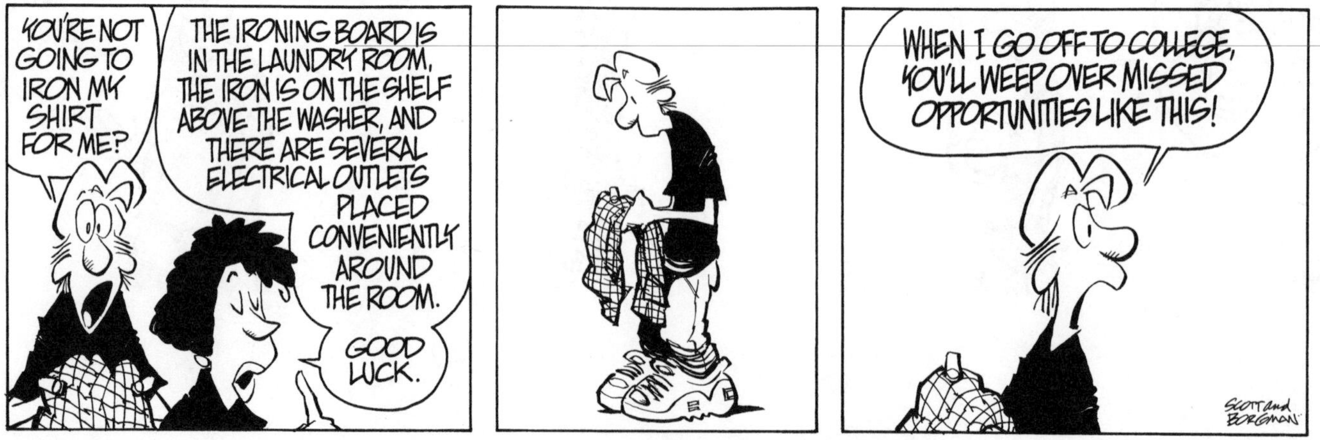

YOU'RE NOT GOING TO IRON MY SHIRT FOR ME?
THE IRONING BOARD IS IN THE LAUNDRY ROOM, THE IRON IS ON THE SHELF ABOVE THE WASHER, AND THERE ARE SEVERAL ELECTRICAL OUTLETS PLACED CONVENIENTLY AROUND THE ROOM.
GOOD LUCK.
WHEN I GO OFF TO COLLEGE, YOU'LL WEEP OVER MISSED OPPORTUNITIES LIKE THIS!
SCOTT and BORGMAN

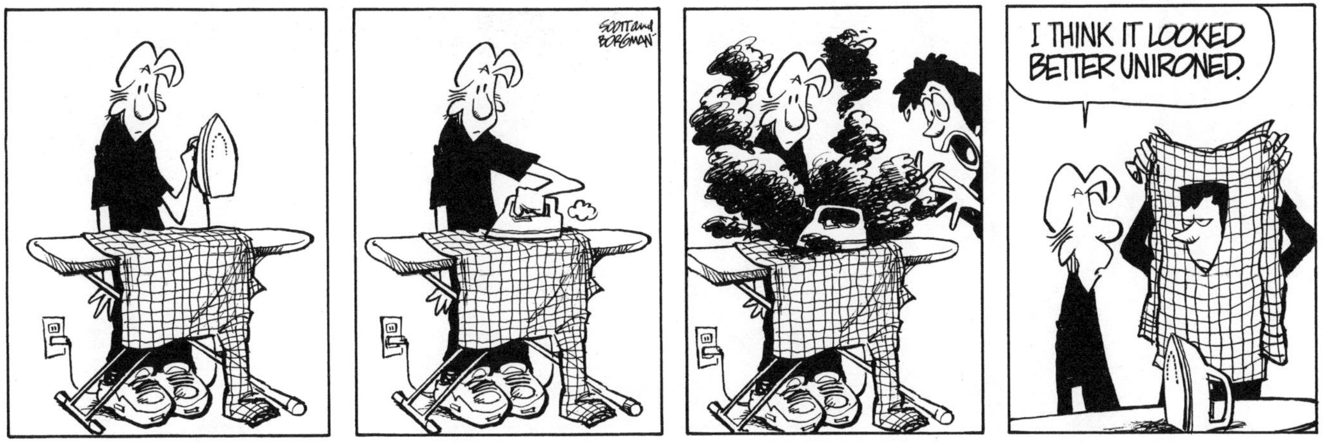
SCOTT and BORGMAN
I THINK IT LOOKED BETTER UNIRONED.

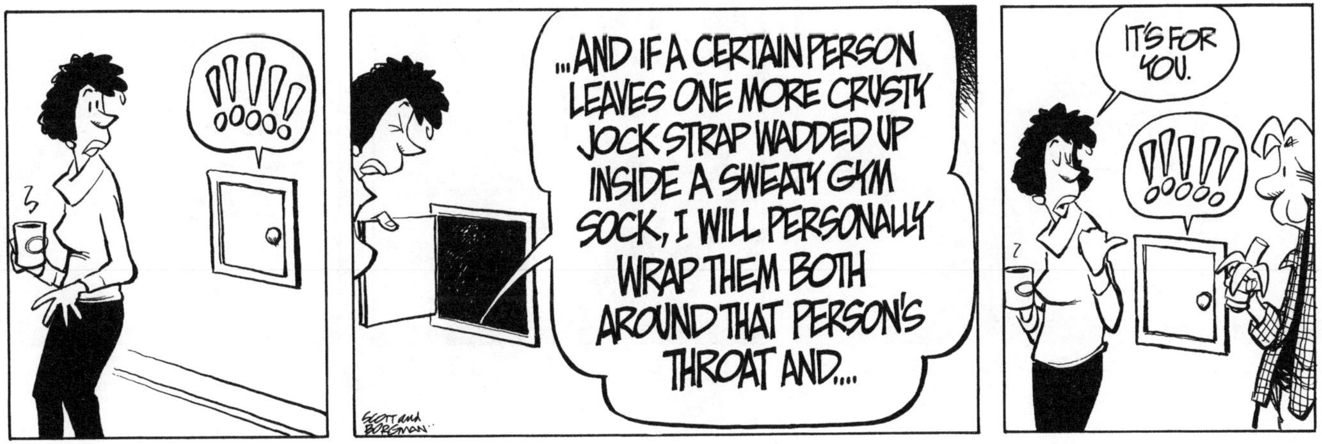
!!!!! ooooo
...AND IF A CERTAIN PERSON LEAVES ONE MORE CRUSTY JOCK STRAP WADDED UP INSIDE A SWEATY GYM SOCK, I WILL PERSONALLY WRAP THEM BOTH AROUND THAT PERSON'S THROAT AND....
SCOTT and BORGMAN
IT'S FOR YOU.
!!!!! ooooo

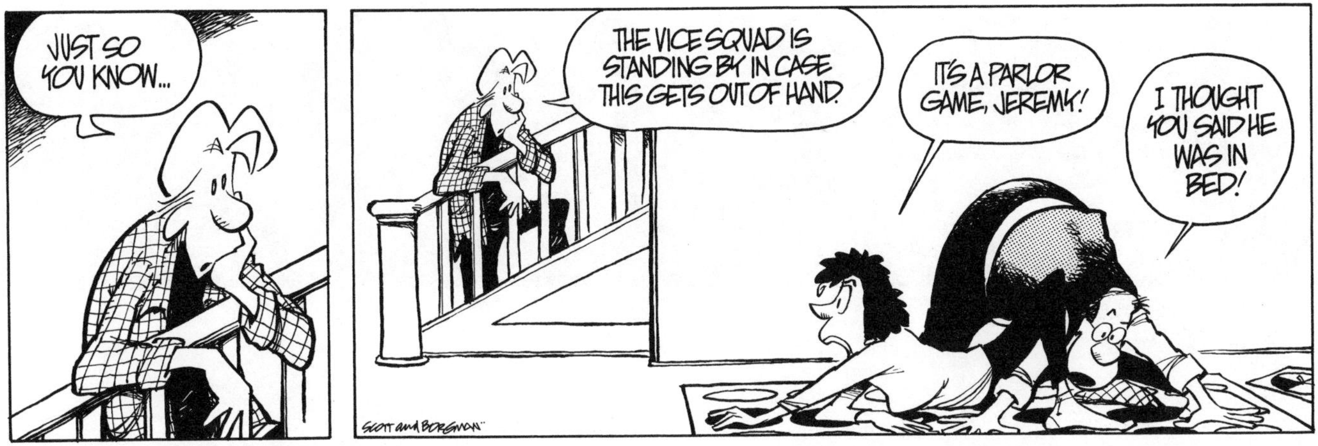
JUST SO YOU KNOW...
THE VICE SQUAD IS STANDING BY IN CASE THIS GETS OUT OF HAND.
IT'S A PARLOR GAME, JEREMY!
I THOUGHT YOU SAID HE WAS IN BED!
SCOTT and BORGMAN

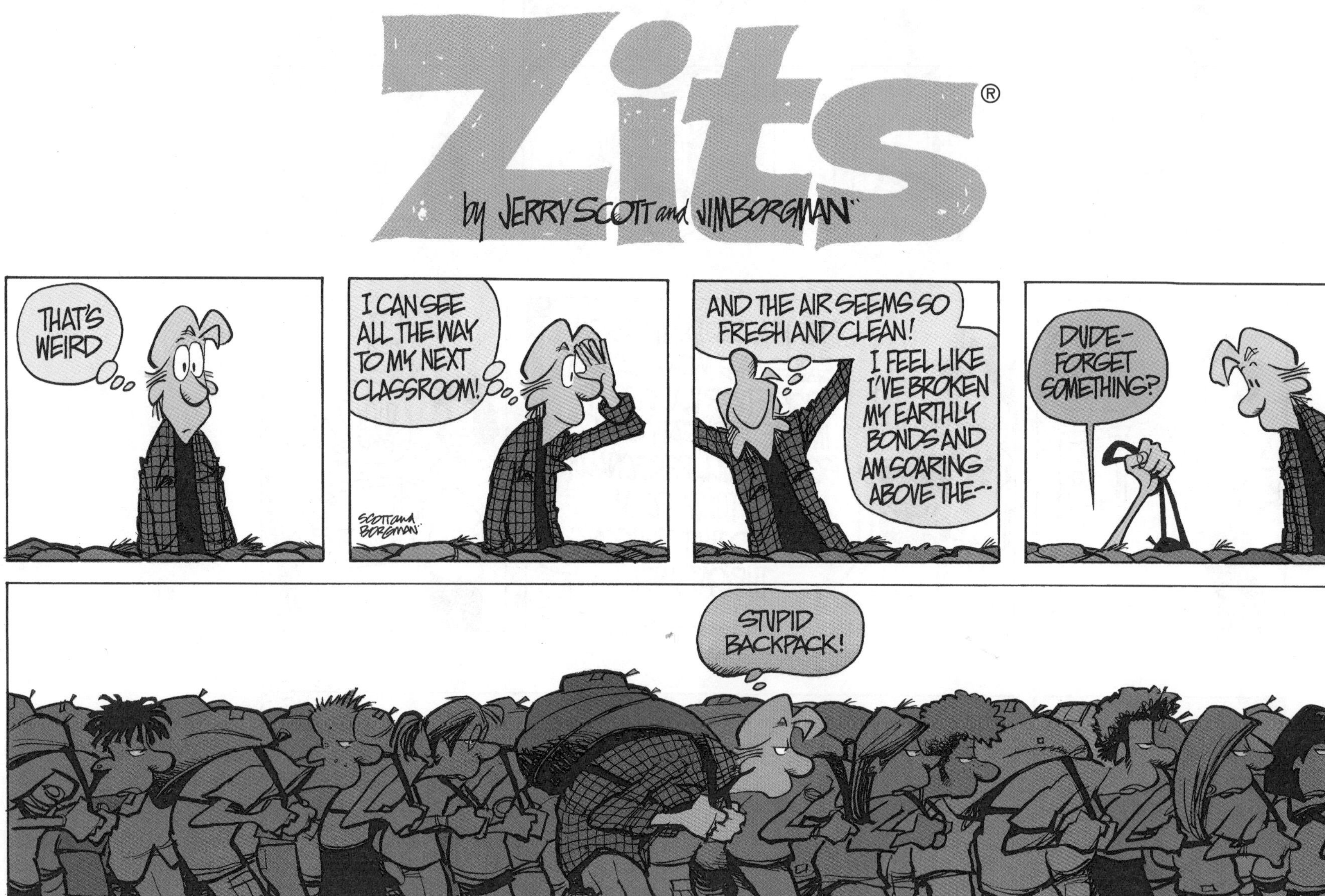
Zits®
by JERRY SCOTT and JIM BORGMAN
THAT'S WEIRD
I CAN SEE ALL THE WAY TO MY NEXT CLASSROOM!
SCOTT and BORGMAN
AND THE AIR SEEMS SO FRESH AND CLEAN!
I FEEL LIKE I'VE BROKEN MY EARTHLY BONDS AND AM SOARING ABOVE THE--
DUDE- FORGET SOMETHING?
STUPID BACKPACK!

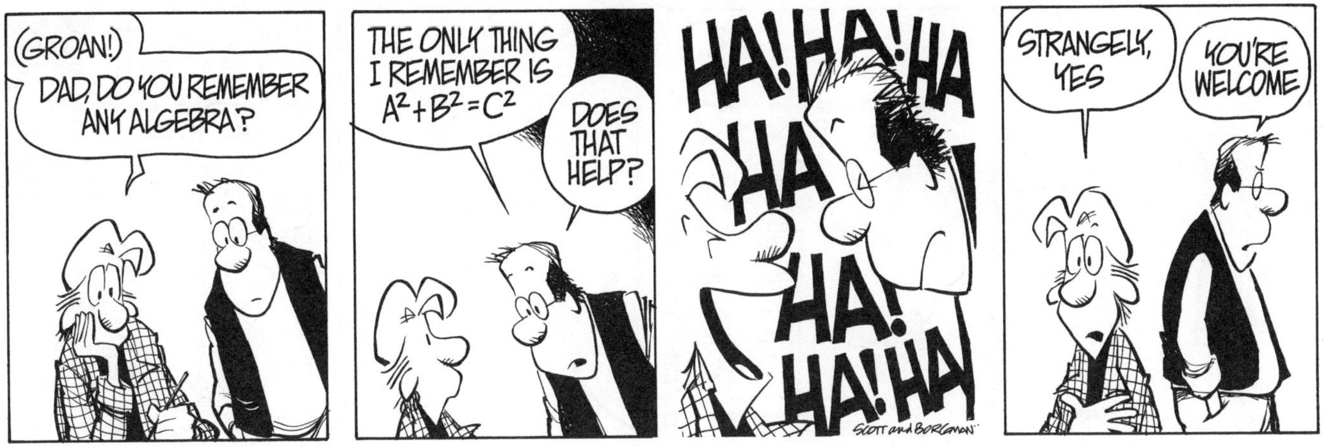
(GROAN!)
DAD, DO YOU REMEMBER ANY ALGEBRA?
THE ONLY THING I REMEMBER IS $A^2+B^2=C^2$
DOES THAT HELP?
HA! HA! HA HA HA! HA! HA!
STRANGELY, YES
YOU'RE WELCOME

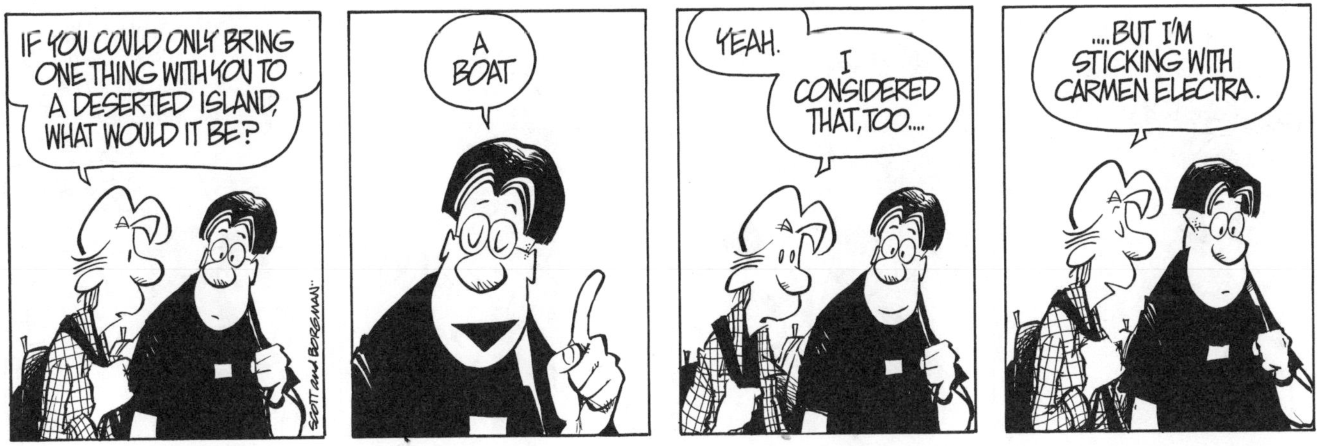
IF YOU COULD ONLY BRING ONE THING WITH YOU TO A DESERTED ISLAND, WHAT WOULD IT BE?
A BOAT
YEAH.
I CONSIDERED THAT, TOO....
....BUT I'M STICKING WITH CARMEN ELECTRA.

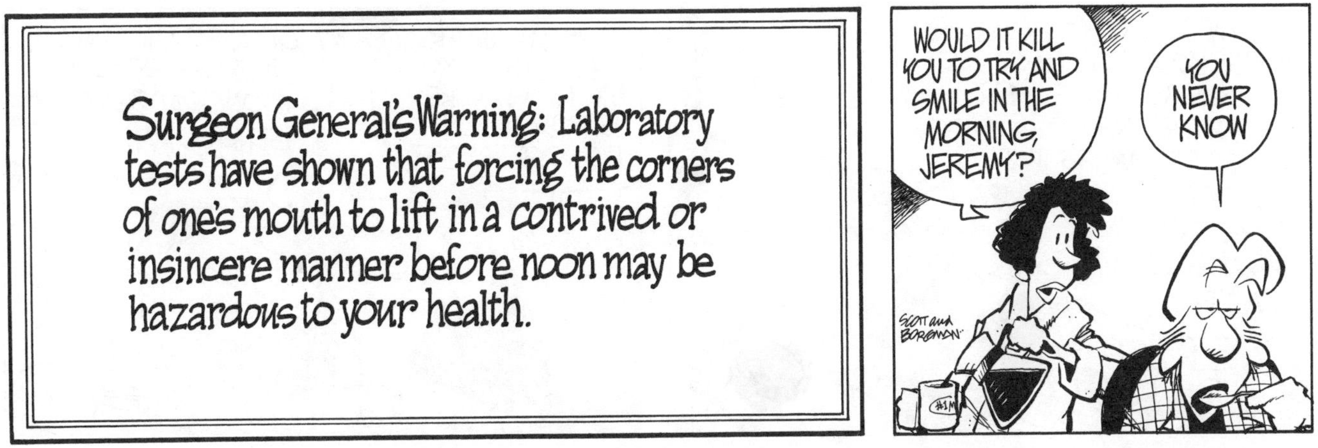
Surgeon General's Warning: Laboratory tests have shown that forcing the corners of one's mouth to lift in a contrived or insincere manner before noon may be hazardous to your health.
WOULD IT KILL YOU TO TRY AND SMILE IN THE MORNING, JEREMY?
YOU NEVER KNOW

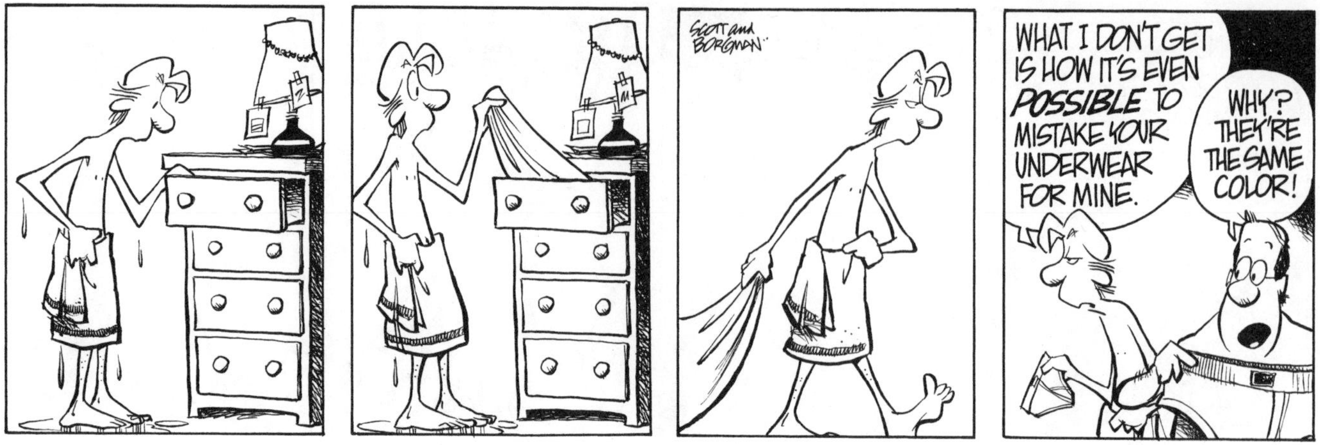
SCOTT and BORGMAN
WHAT I DON'T GET IS HOW IT'S EVEN POSSIBLE TO MISTAKE YOUR UNDERWEAR FOR MINE.
WHY? THEY'RE THE SAME COLOR!

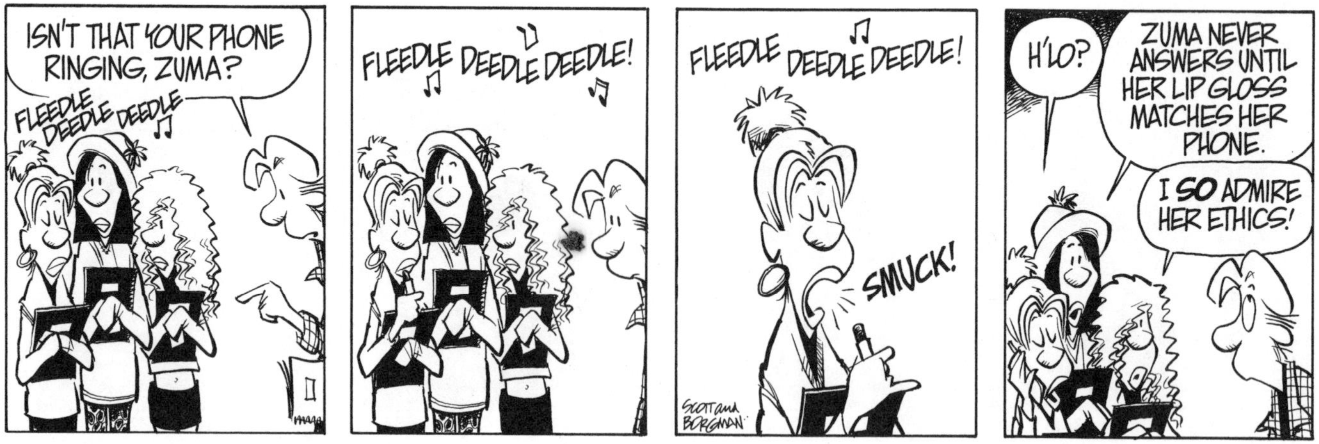
ISN'T THAT YOUR PHONE RINGING, ZUMA?
FLEEDLE DEEDLE DEEDLE
FLEEDLE DEEDLE DEEDLE!
FLEEDLE DEEDLE DEEDLE!
SMUCK!
SCOTT and BORGMAN
H'LO?
ZUMA NEVER ANSWERS UNTIL HER LIP GLOSS MATCHES HER PHONE.
I SO ADMIRE HER ETHICS!

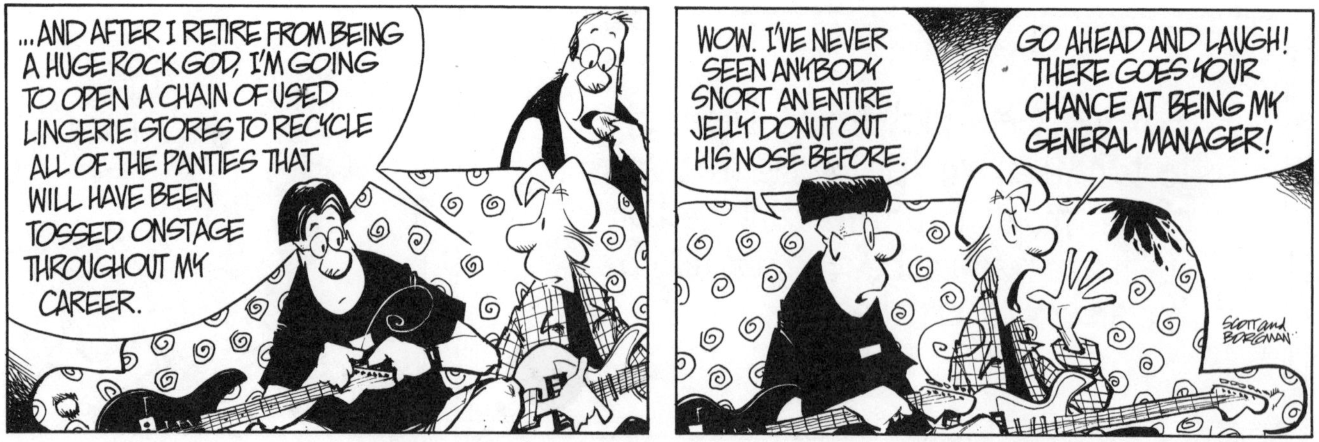
...AND AFTER I RETIRE FROM BEING A HUGE ROCK GOD, I'M GOING TO OPEN A CHAIN OF USED LINGERIE STORES TO RECYCLE ALL OF THE PANTIES THAT WILL HAVE BEEN TOSSED ONSTAGE THROUGHOUT MY CAREER.
WOW. I'VE NEVER SEEN ANYBODY SNORT AN ENTIRE JELLY DONUT OUT HIS NOSE BEFORE.
GO AHEAD AND LAUGH! THERE GOES YOUR CHANCE AT BEING MY GENERAL MANAGER!
SCOTT and BORGMAN

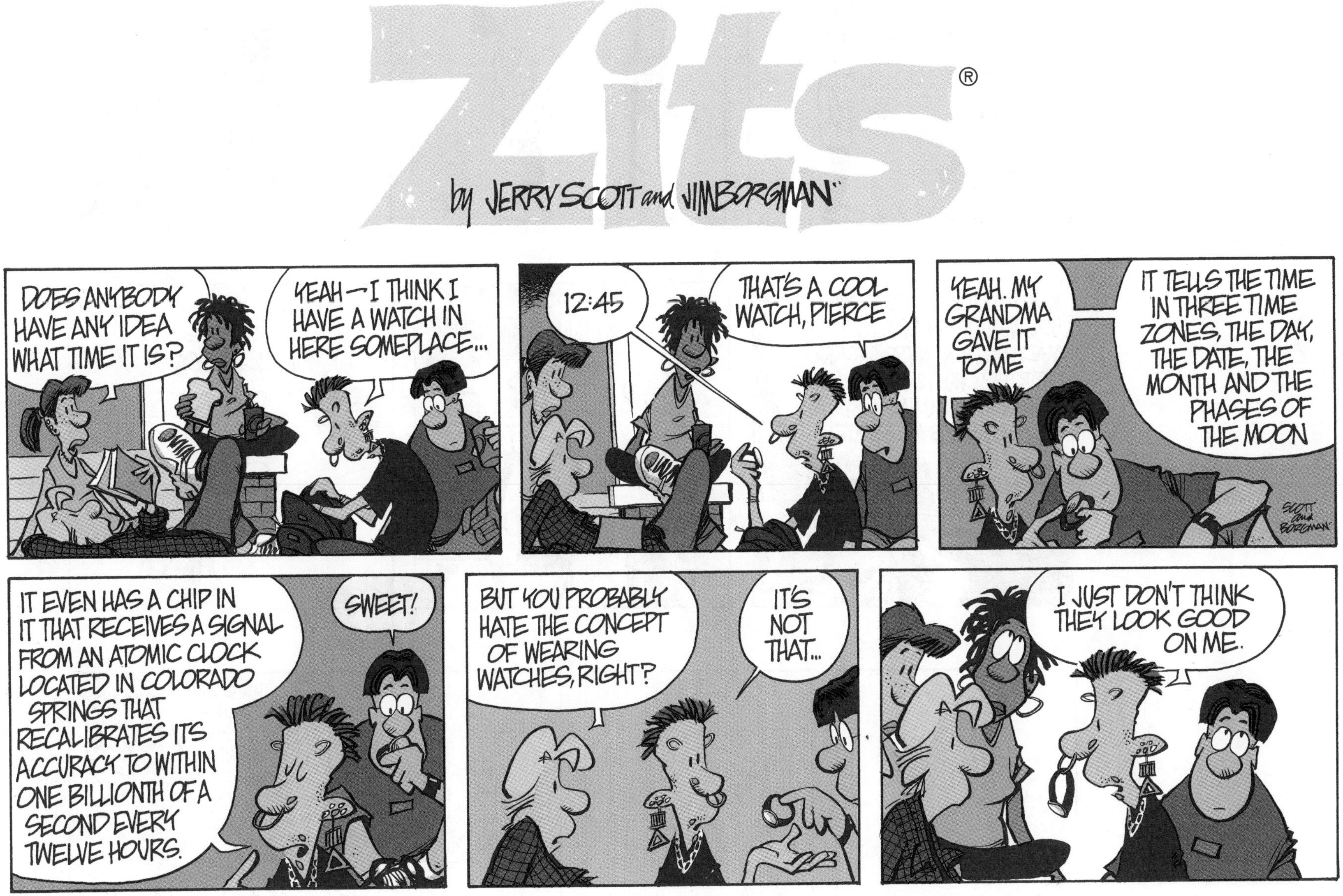
Zits®
by JERRY SCOTT and JIM BORGMAN
DOES ANYBODY HAVE ANY IDEA WHAT TIME IT IS?
YEAH—I THINK I HAVE A WATCH IN HERE SOMEPLACE...
12:45
THAT'S A COOL WATCH, PIERCE
YEAH. MY GRANDMA GAVE IT TO ME
IT TELLS THE TIME IN THREE TIME ZONES, THE DAY, THE DATE, THE MONTH AND THE PHASES OF THE MOON
SCOTT and BORGMAN
IT EVEN HAS A CHIP IN IT THAT RECEIVES A SIGNAL FROM AN ATOMIC CLOCK LOCATED IN COLORADO SPRINGS THAT RECALIBRATES ITS ACCURACY TO WITHIN ONE BILLIONTH OF A SECOND EVERY TWELVE HOURS.
SWEET!
BUT YOU PROBABLY HATE THE CONCEPT OF WEARING WATCHES, RIGHT?
IT'S NOT THAT...
I JUST DON'T THINK THEY LOOK GOOD ON ME.

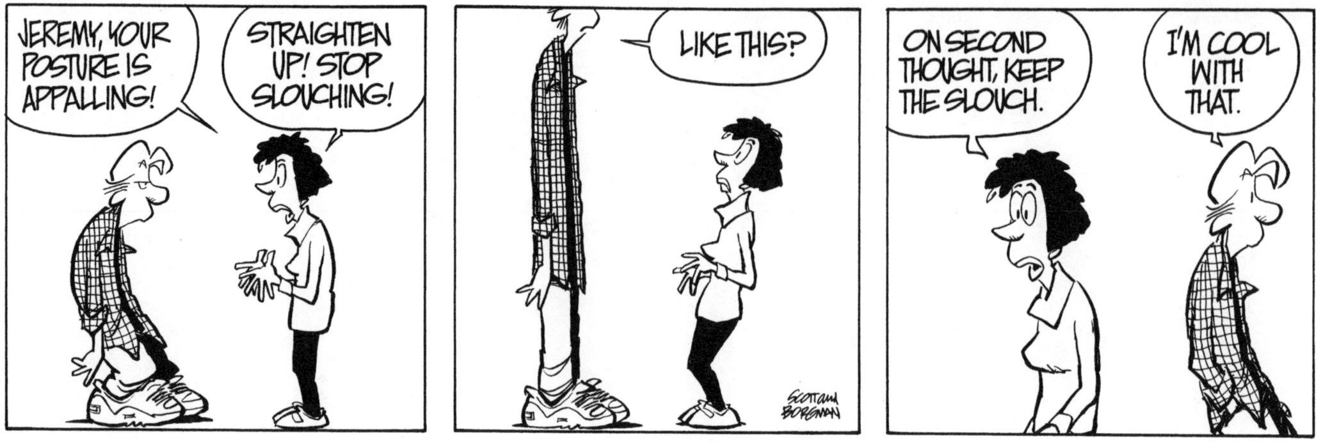
JEREMY, YOUR POSTURE IS APPALLING!
STRAIGHTEN UP! STOP SLOUCHING!
LIKE THIS?
ON SECOND THOUGHT, KEEP THE SLOUCH.
I'M COOL WITH THAT.
SCOTT and BORGMAN

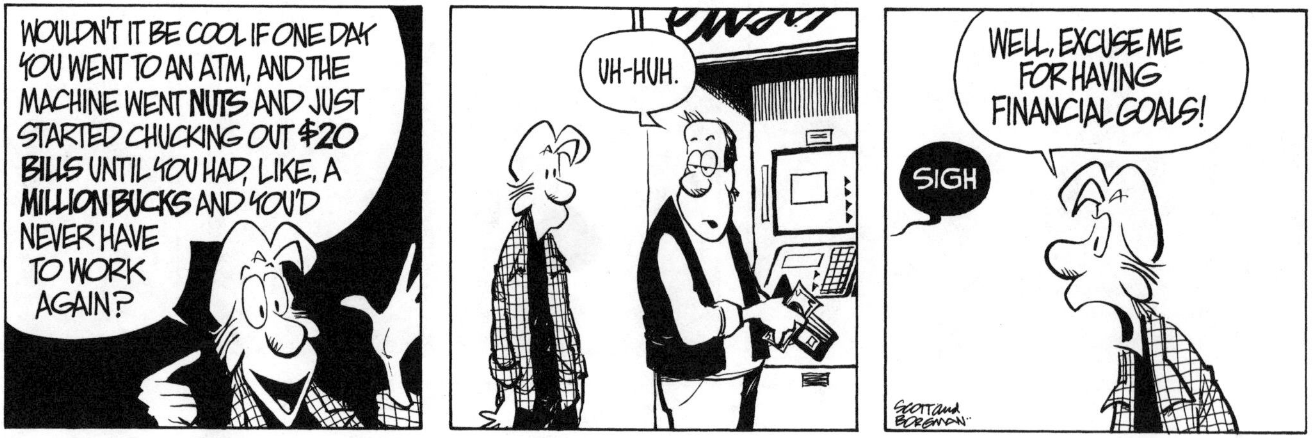
WOULDN'T IT BE COOL IF ONE DAY YOU WENT TO AN ATM, AND THE MACHINE WENT NUTS AND JUST STARTED CHUCKING OUT $20 BILLS UNTIL YOU HAD, LIKE, A MILLION BUCKS AND YOU'D NEVER HAVE TO WORK AGAIN?
UH-HUH.
SIGH
WELL, EXCUSE ME FOR HAVING FINANCIAL GOALS!
SCOTT and BORGMAN

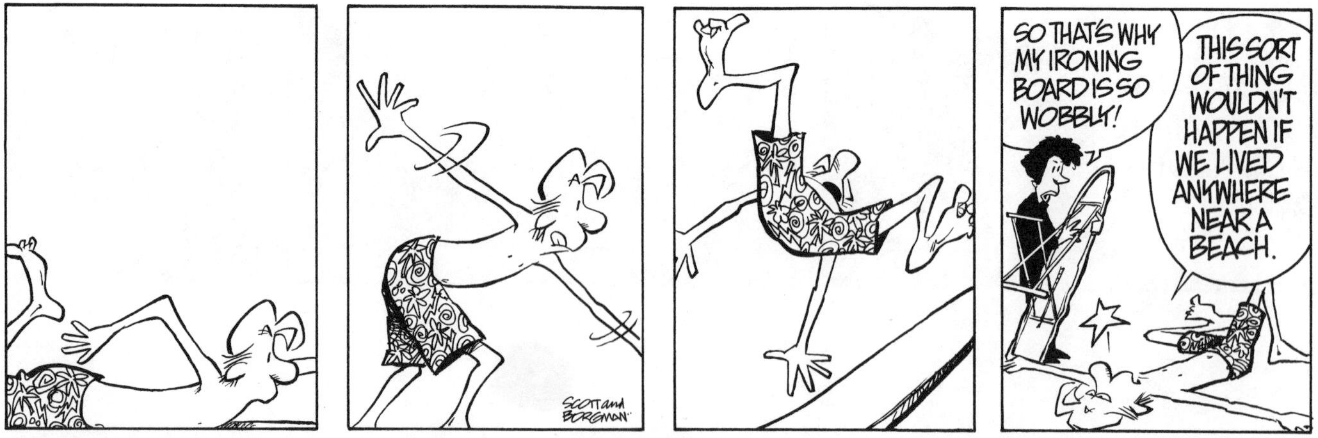
SCOTT and BORGMAN
SO THAT'S WHY MY IRONING BOARD IS SO WOBBLY!
THIS SORT OF THING WOULDN'T HAPPEN IF WE LIVED ANYWHERE NEAR A BEACH.

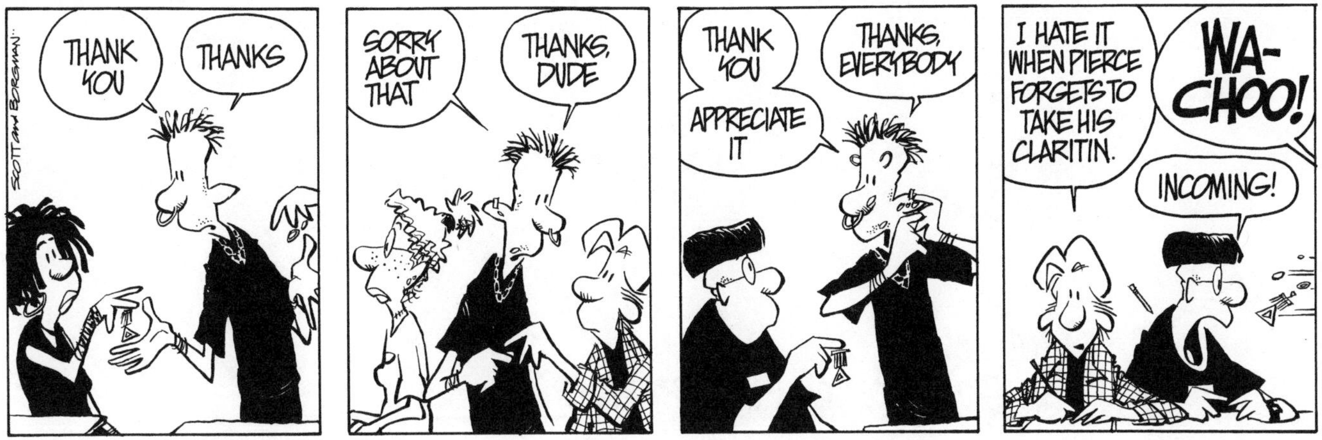
THANK YOU
THANKS
SORRY ABOUT THAT
THANKS, DUDE
THANK YOU
APPRECIATE IT
THANKS, EVERYBODY
I HATE IT WHEN PIERCE FORGETS TO TAKE HIS CLARITIN.
WA-CHOO!
INCOMING!

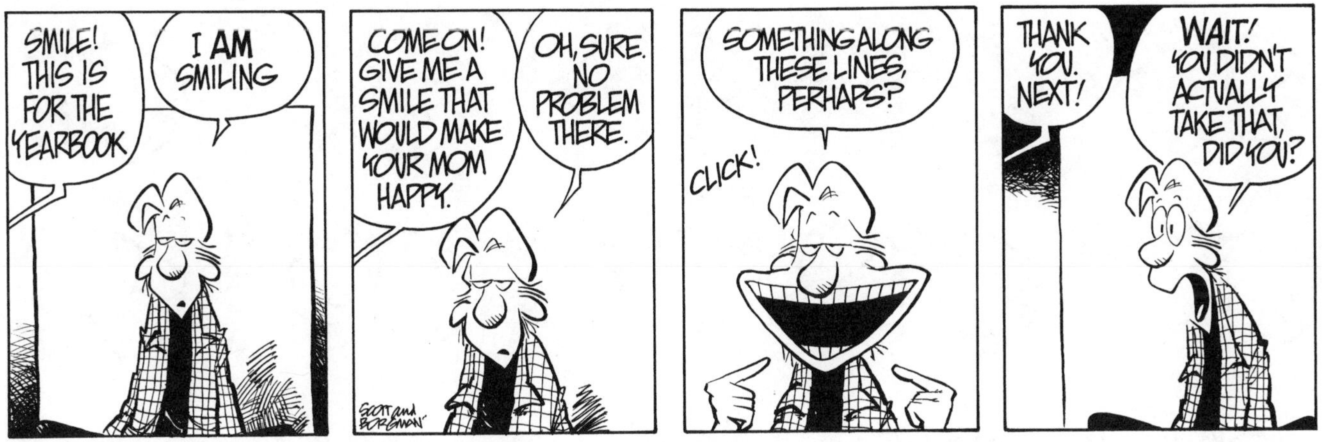
SMILE! THIS IS FOR THE YEARBOOK
I AM SMILING
COME ON! GIVE ME A SMILE THAT WOULD MAKE YOUR MOM HAPPY.
OH, SURE. NO PROBLEM THERE.
SOMETHING ALONG THESE LINES, PERHAPS?
CLICK!
THANK YOU. NEXT!
WAIT! YOU DIDN'T ACTUALLY TAKE THAT, DID YOU?

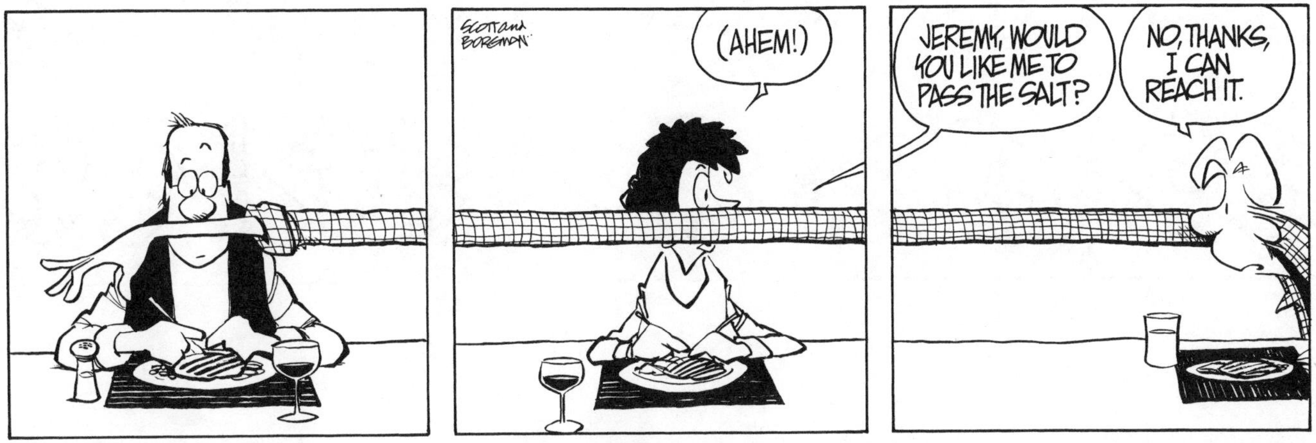
(AHEM!)
JEREMY, WOULD YOU LIKE ME TO PASS THE SALT?
NO, THANKS, I CAN REACH IT.

Zits®

by JERRY SCOTT and JIM BORGMAN

How Is Your Teenager Feeling Today?
A PARENT'S GUIDE TO THE FACIAL EXPRESSIONS OF THE SPECIES
SCOTT AND BORGMAN
MELLOW
BUMMED
STOKED
FUNKY
DUMPED
FRIED
RATTLED
BORED
TORQUED
SNARKY
SPACY
AMPED
WOUNDED
SURLY
CHEESED
CRUSHED
QUEASY
TIRED
HORNY
WHATEVER

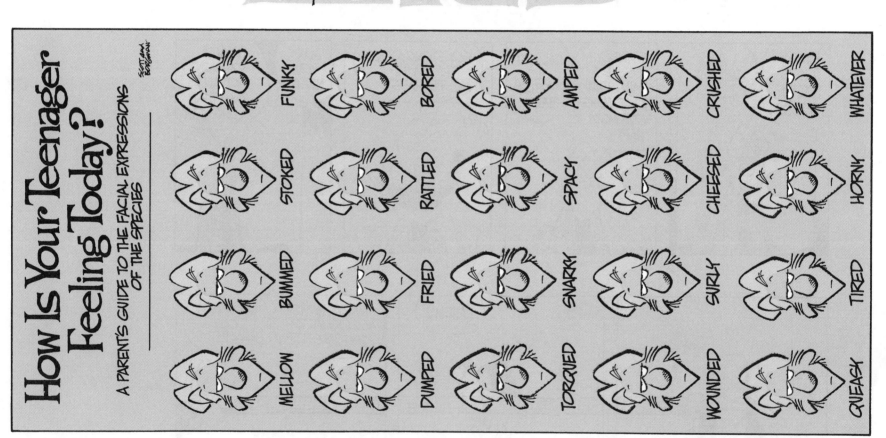

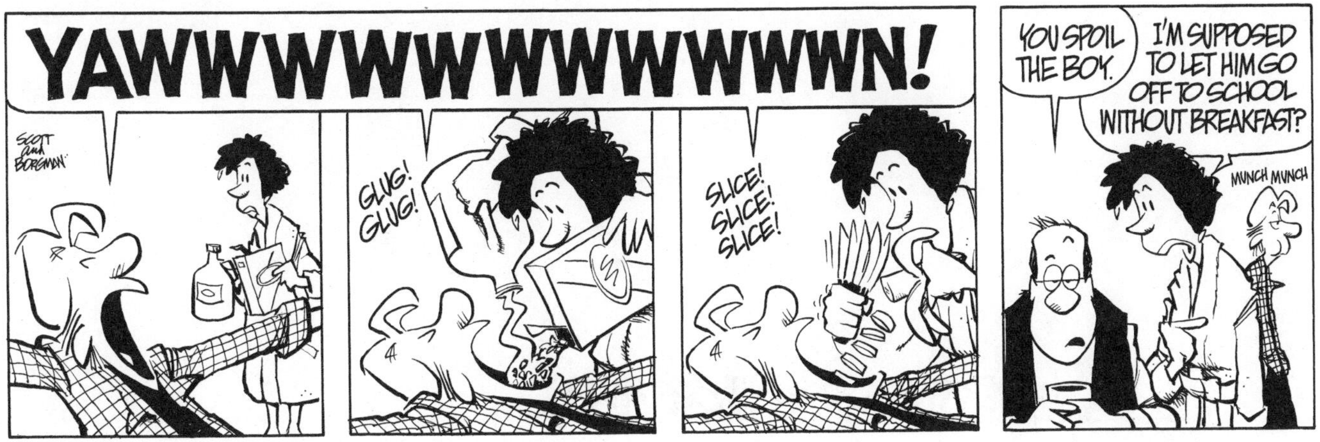
YAWWWWWWWWWWWWN!
GLUG! GLUG!
SLICE! SLICE! SLICE!
YOU SPOIL THE BOY.
I'M SUPPOSED TO LET HIM GO OFF TO SCHOOL WITHOUT BREAKFAST?
MUNCH MUNCH

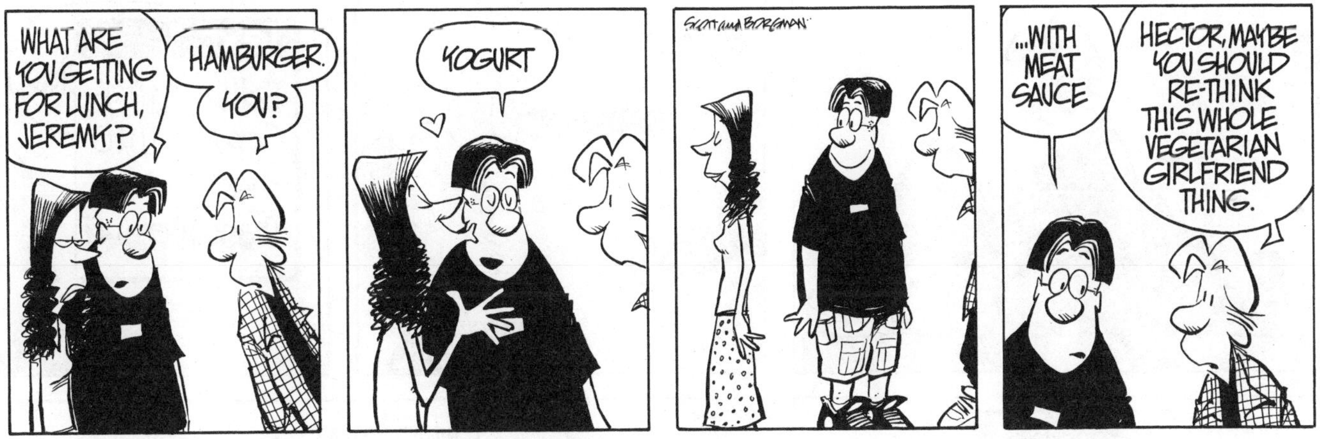
WHAT ARE YOU GETTING FOR LUNCH, JEREMY?
HAMBURGER.
YOU?
YOGURT
...WITH MEAT SAUCE
HECTOR, MAYBE YOU SHOULD RE-THINK THIS WHOLE VEGETARIAN GIRLFRIEND THING.

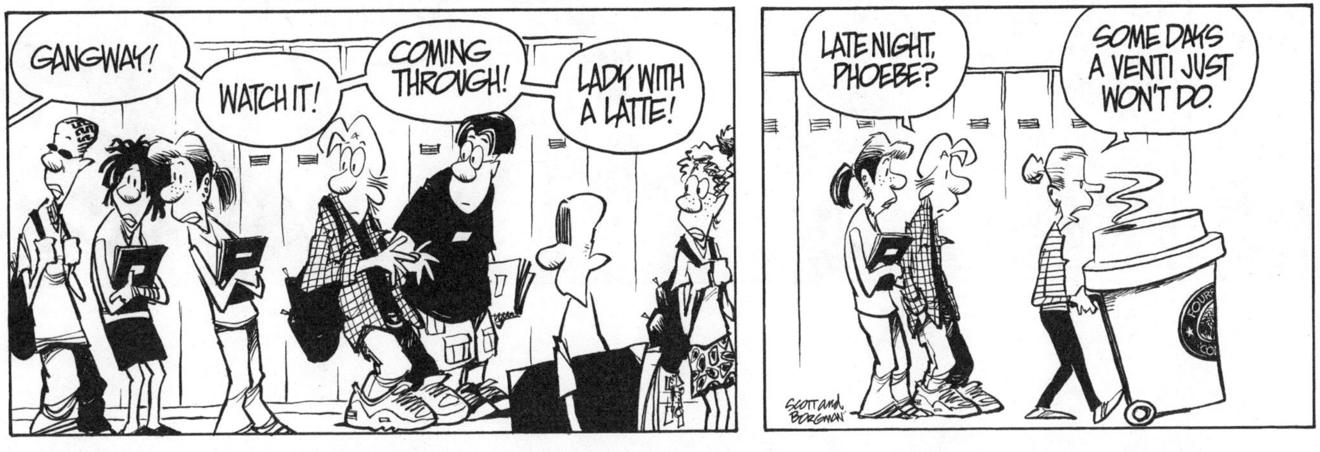
GANGWAY!
WATCH IT!
COMING THROUGH!
LADY WITH A LATTE!
LATE NIGHT, PHOEBE?
SOME DAYS A VENTI JUST WON'T DO.

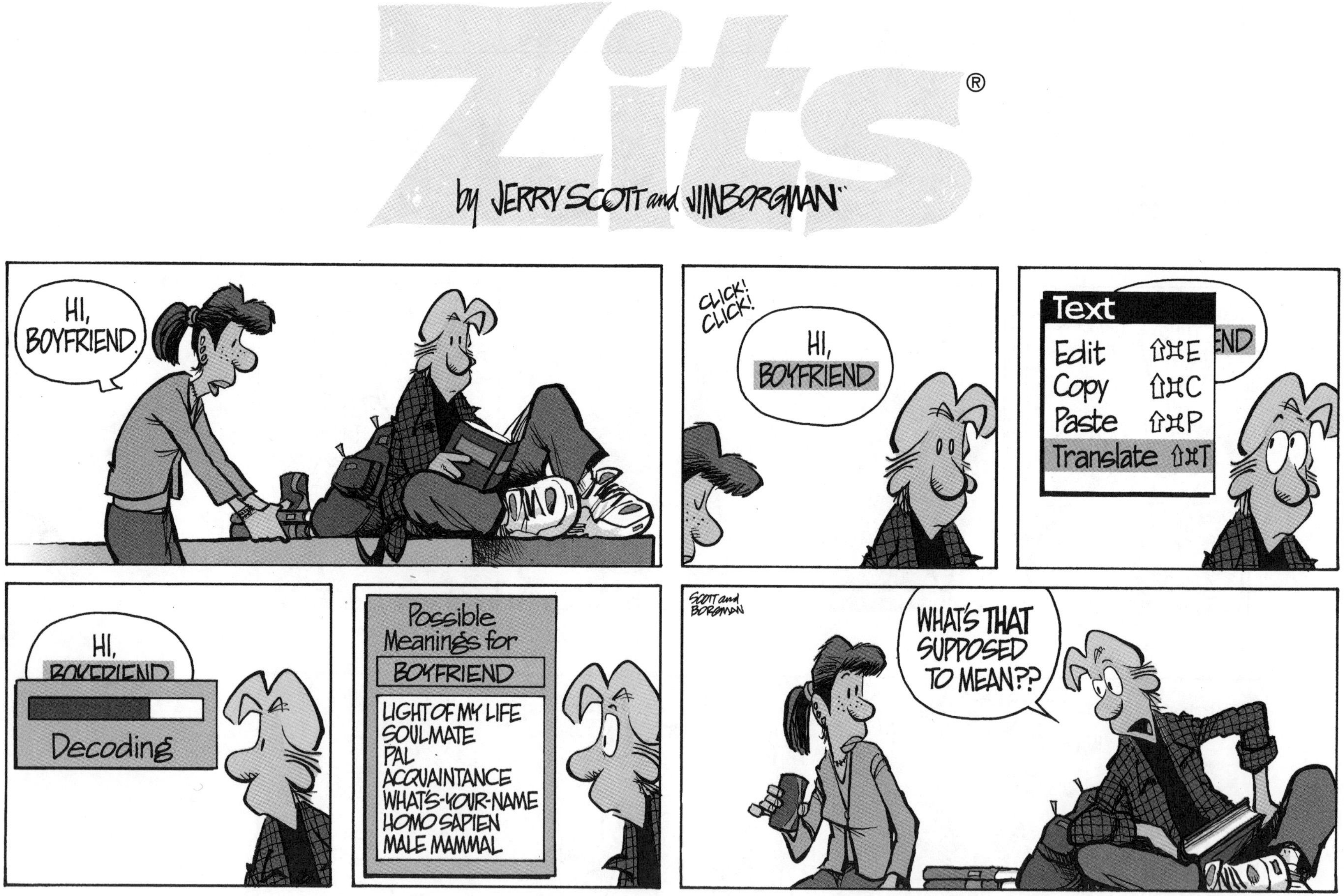
Zits®
by JERRY SCOTT and JIM BORGMAN
HI, BOYFRIEND.
CLICK! CLICK!
HI, BOYFRIEND
Text
Edit ⇧⌘E
Copy ⇧⌘C
Paste ⇧⌘P
Translate ⇧⌘T
HI,
Decoding
Possible Meanings for
BOYFRIEND
LIGHT OF MY LIFE
SOULMATE
PAL
ACQUAINTANCE
WHAT'S-YOUR-NAME
HOMO SAPIEN
MALE MAMMAL
SCOTT and BORGMAN
WHAT'S THAT SUPPOSED TO MEAN??

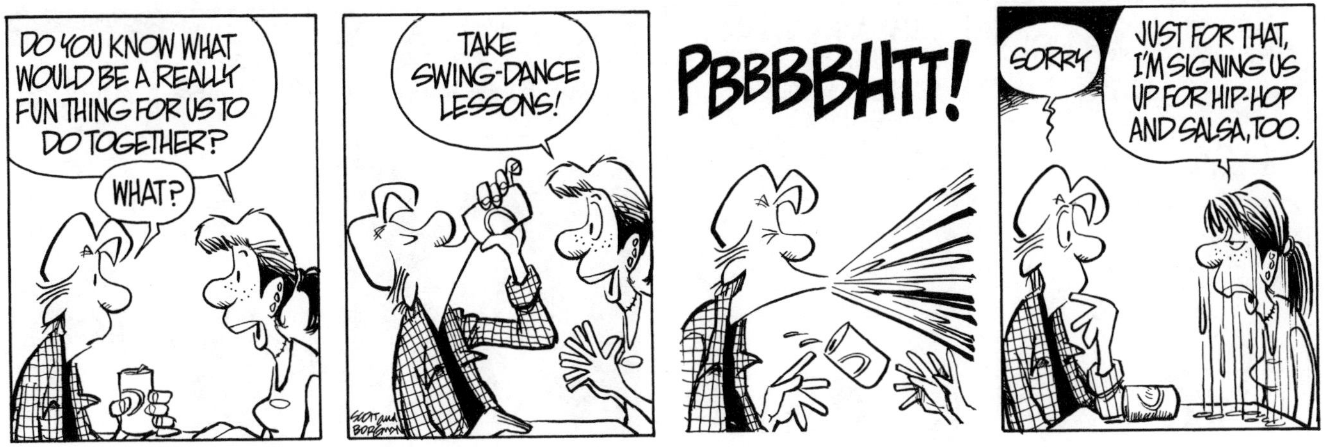
DO YOU KNOW WHAT WOULD BE A REALLY FUN THING FOR US TO DO TOGETHER?
WHAT?
TAKE SWING-DANCE LESSONS!
PBBBBHTT!
SORRY
JUST FOR THAT, I'M SIGNING US UP FOR HIP-HOP AND SALSA, TOO.

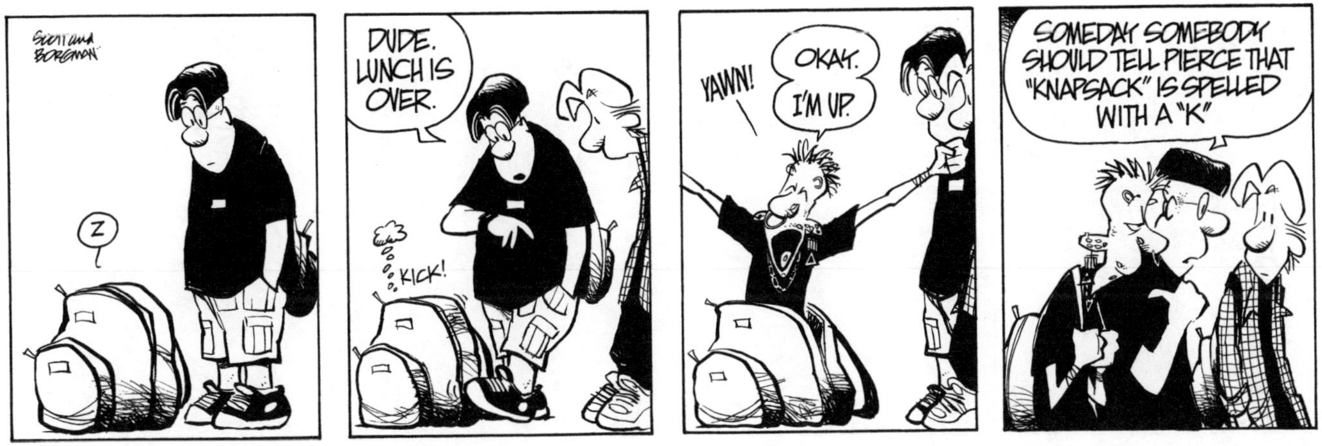
Z
DUDE. LUNCH IS OVER.
KICK!
YAWN!
OKAY. I'M UP.
SOMEDAY SOMEBODY SHOULD TELL PIERCE THAT "KNAPSACK" IS SPELLED WITH A "K"

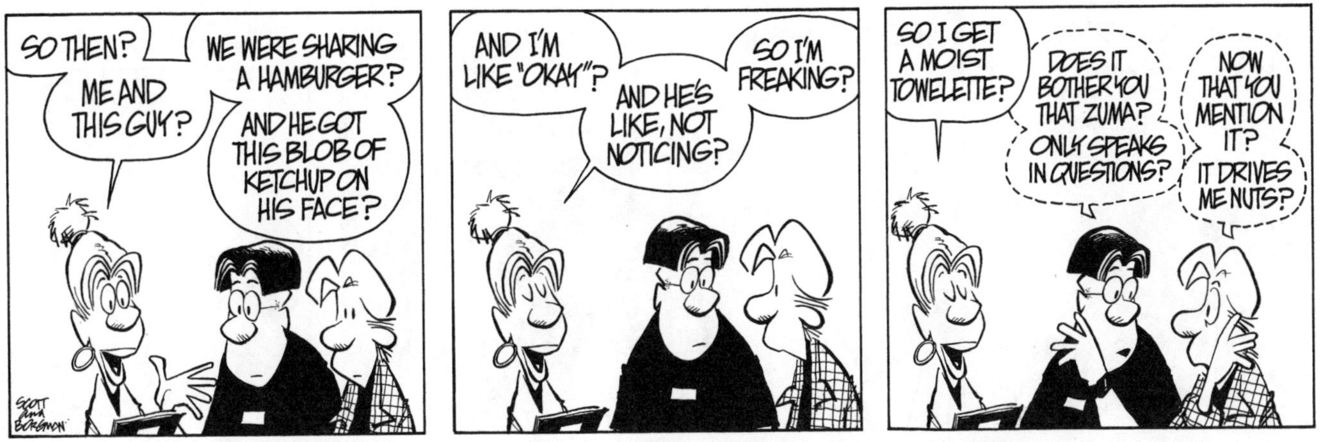
SO THEN?
ME AND THIS GUY?
WE WERE SHARING A HAMBURGER?
AND HE GOT THIS BLOB OF KETCHUP ON HIS FACE?
AND I'M LIKE "OKAY"?
AND HE'S LIKE, NOT NOTICING?
SO I'M FREAKING?
SO I GET A MOIST TOWELETTE?
DOES IT BOTHER YOU THAT ZUMA?
ONLY SPEAKS IN QUESTIONS?
NOW THAT YOU MENTION IT?
IT DRIVES ME NUTS?

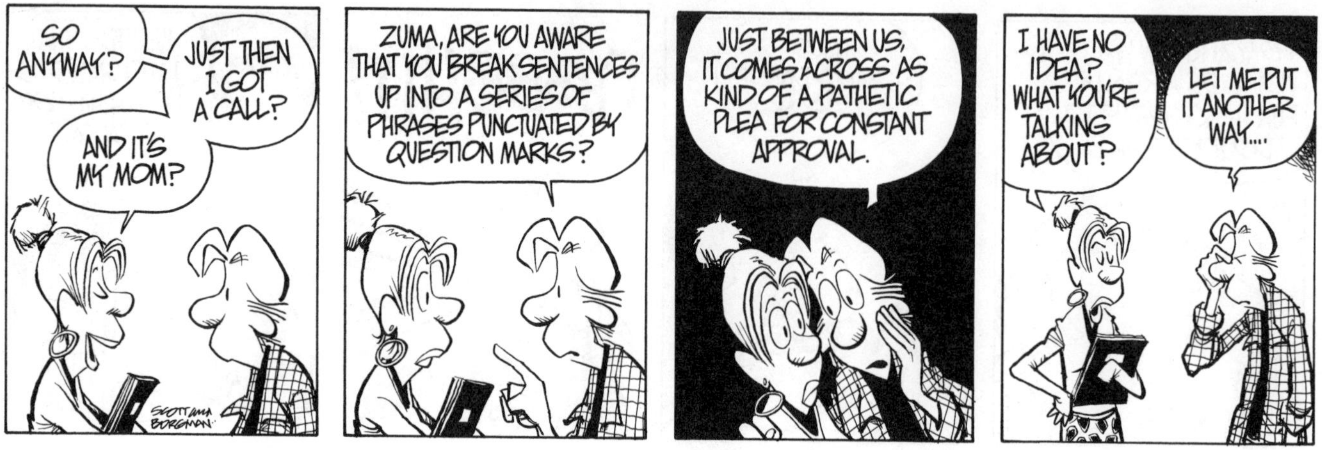
SO ANYWAY?
JUST THEN I GOT A CALL?
AND IT'S MY MOM?
ZUMA, ARE YOU AWARE THAT YOU BREAK SENTENCES UP INTO A SERIES OF PHRASES PUNCTUATED BY QUESTION MARKS?
JUST BETWEEN US, IT COMES ACROSS AS KIND OF A PATHETIC PLEA FOR CONSTANT APPROVAL.
I HAVE NO IDEA? WHAT YOU'RE TALKING ABOUT?
LET ME PUT IT ANOTHER WAY....

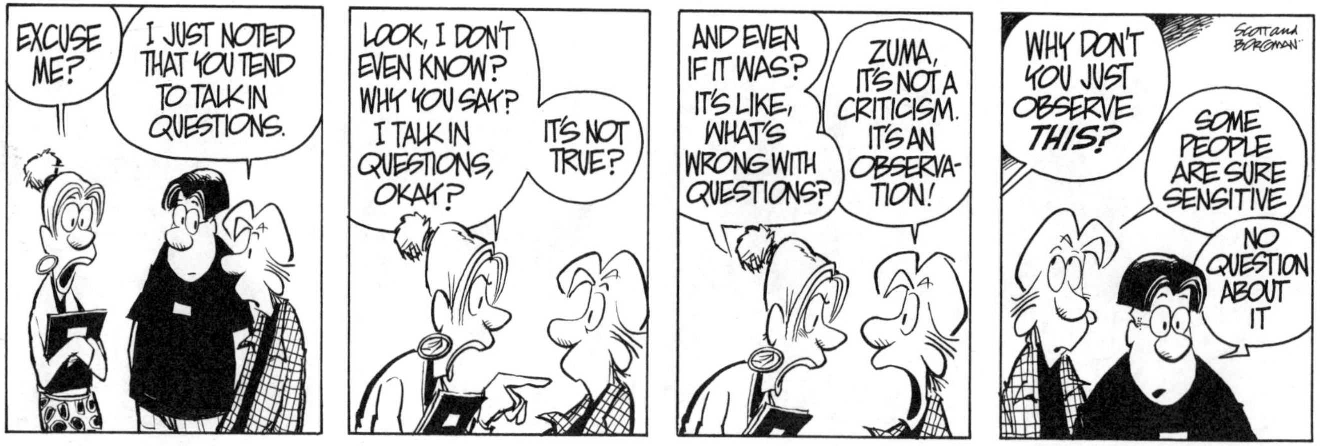
EXCUSE ME?
I JUST NOTED THAT YOU TEND TO TALK IN QUESTIONS.
LOOK, I DON'T EVEN KNOW? WHY YOU SAY? I TALK IN QUESTIONS, OKAY?
IT'S NOT TRUE?
AND EVEN IF IT WAS? IT'S LIKE, WHAT'S WRONG WITH QUESTIONS?
ZUMA, IT'S NOT A CRITICISM. IT'S AN OBSERVA-TION!
WHY DON'T YOU JUST OBSERVE *THIS?*
SOME PEOPLE ARE SURE SENSITIVE
NO QUESTION ABOUT IT

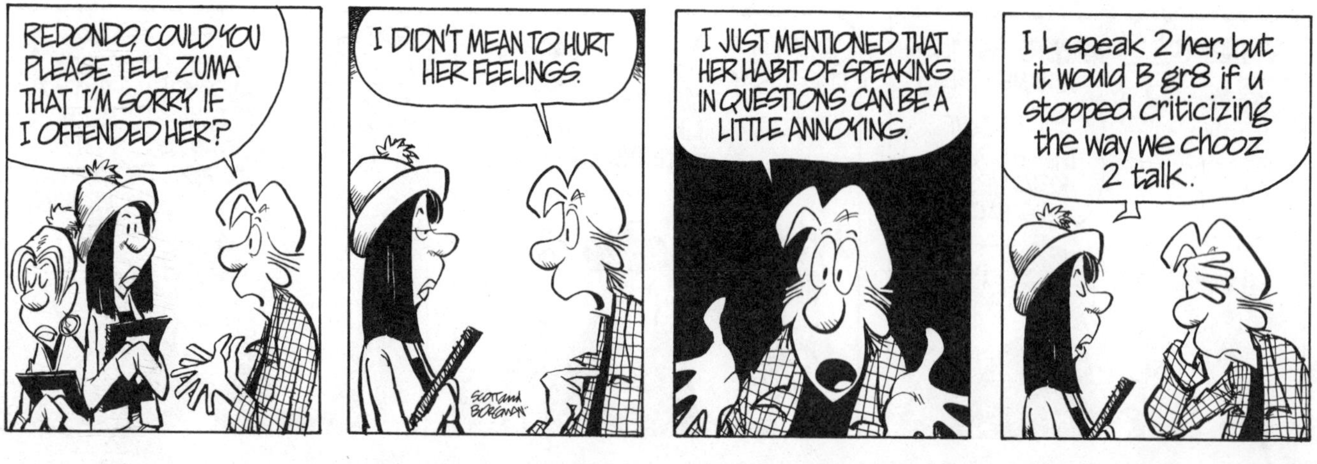
REDONDO, COULD YOU PLEASE TELL ZUMA THAT I'M SORRY IF I OFFENDED HER?
I DIDN'T MEAN TO HURT HER FEELINGS.
I JUST MENTIONED THAT HER HABIT OF SPEAKING IN QUESTIONS CAN BE A LITTLE ANNOYING.
I L speak 2 her; but it would B gr8 if u stopped criticizing the way we chooz 2 talk.

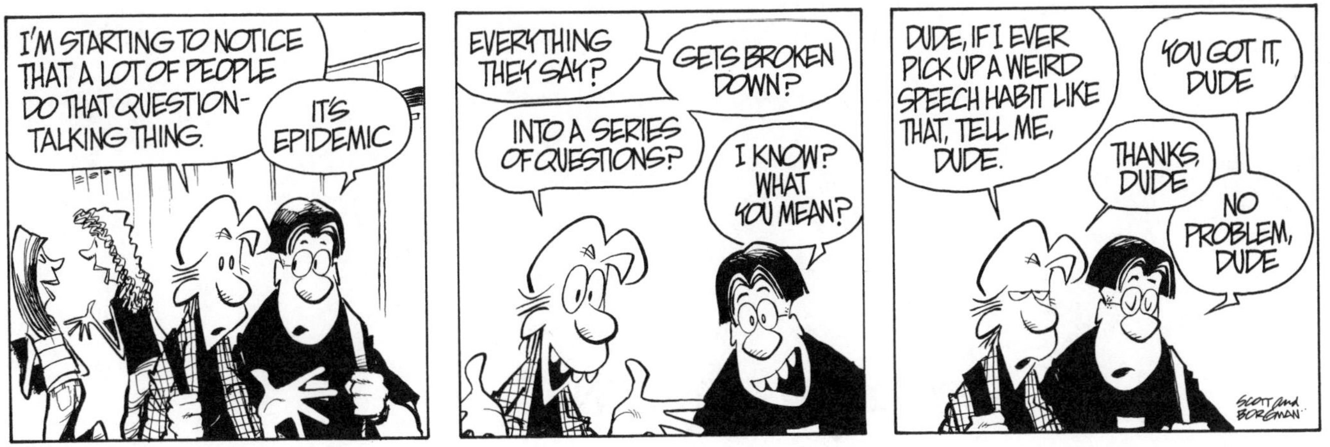
I'M STARTING TO NOTICE THAT A LOT OF PEOPLE DO THAT QUESTION-TALKING THING.
IT'S EPIDEMIC
EVERYTHING THEY SAY?
GETS BROKEN DOWN?
INTO A SERIES OF QUESTIONS?
I KNOW? WHAT YOU MEAN?
DUDE, IF I EVER PICK UP A WEIRD SPEECH HABIT LIKE THAT, TELL ME, DUDE.
YOU GOT IT, DUDE
THANKS, DUDE
NO PROBLEM, DUDE
SCOTT AND BORGMAN

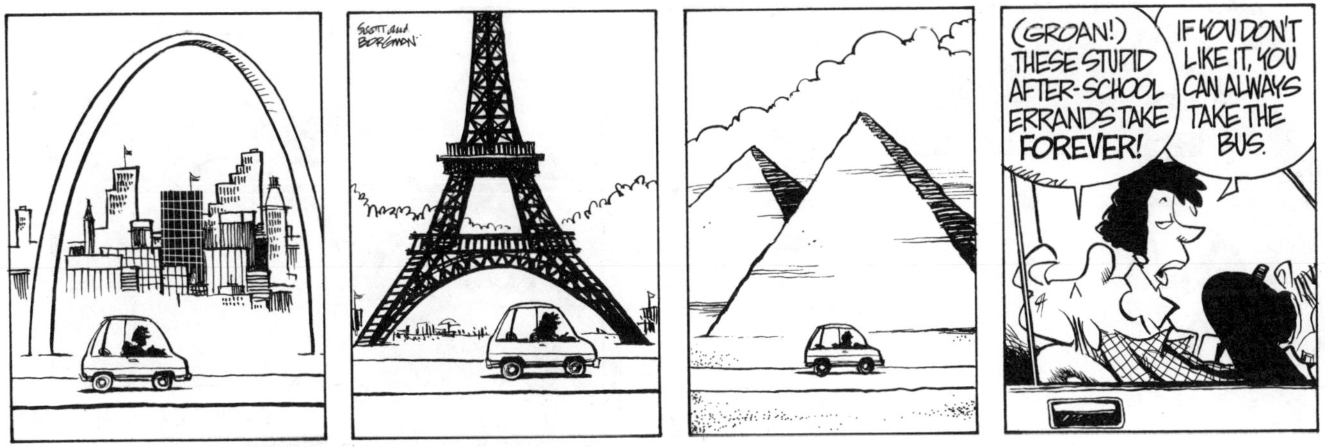
SCOTT AND BORGMAN
(GROAN!) THESE STUPID AFTER-SCHOOL ERRANDS TAKE **FOREVER!**
IF YOU DON'T LIKE IT, YOU CAN ALWAYS TAKE THE BUS.

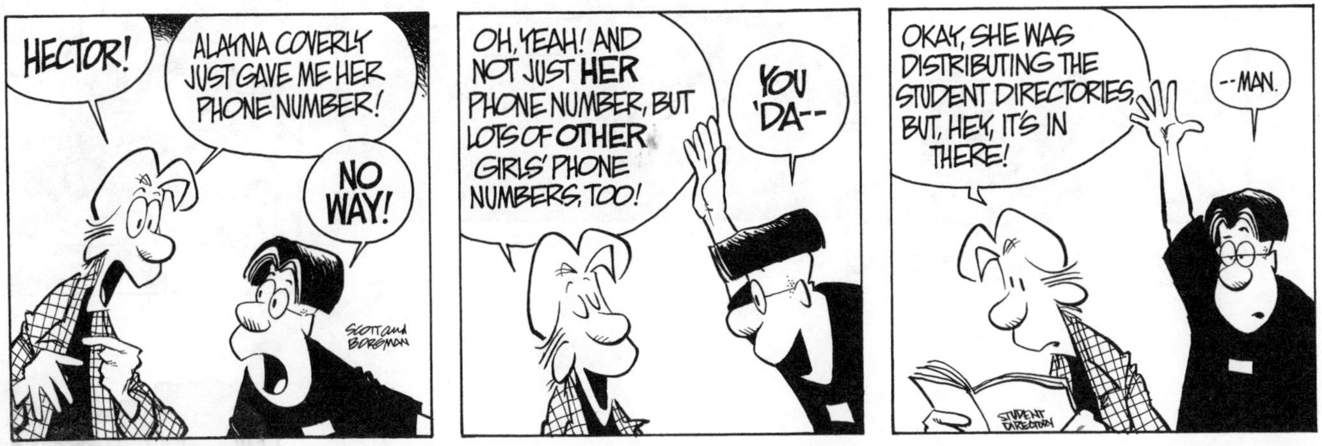
HECTOR!
ALAYNA COVERLY JUST GAVE ME HER PHONE NUMBER!
NO WAY!
SCOTT AND BORGMAN
OH, YEAH! AND NOT JUST **HER** PHONE NUMBER, BUT LOTS OF **OTHER** GIRLS' PHONE NUMBERS, TOO!
YOU 'DA--
OKAY, SHE WAS DISTRIBUTING THE STUDENT DIRECTORIES, BUT, HEY, IT'S IN THERE!
--MAN.
STUDENT DIRECTORY

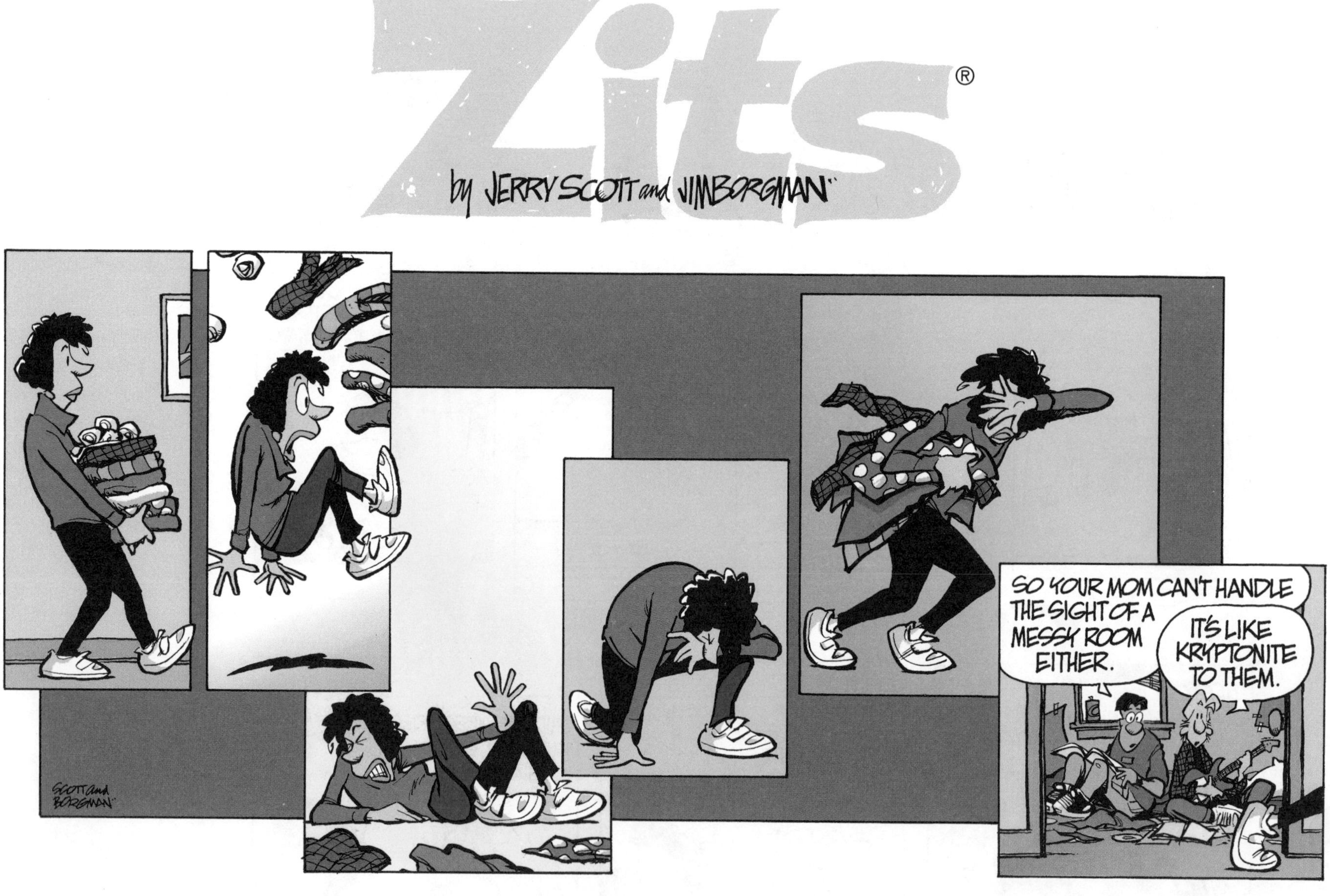
Zits®
by JERRY SCOTT and JIM BORGMAN
SCOTT and BORGMAN
SO YOUR MOM CAN'T HANDLE THE SIGHT OF A MESSY ROOM EITHER.
IT'S LIKE KRYPTONITE TO THEM.

Zits®

by JERRY SCOTT and JIM BORGMAN

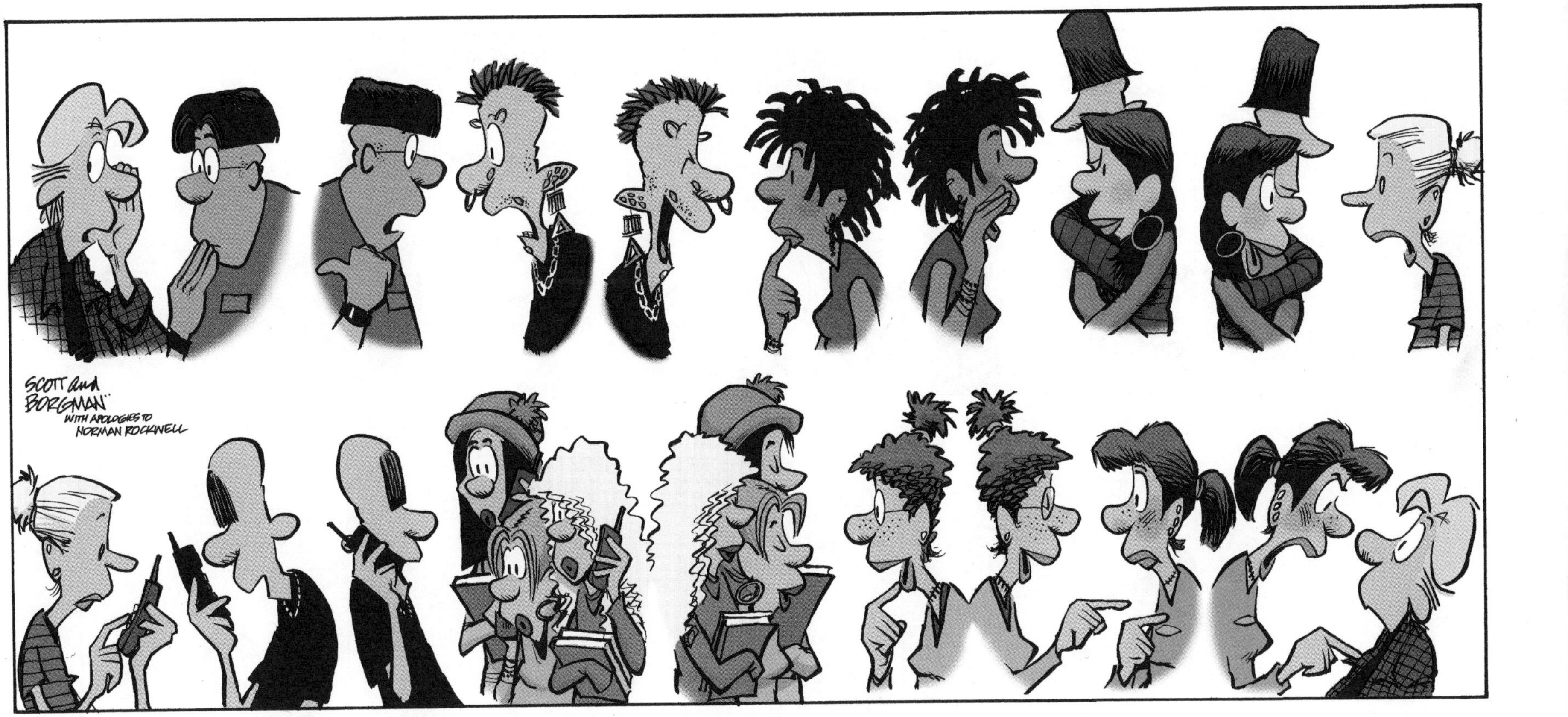

SCOTT and BORGMAN
WITH APOLOGIES TO NORMAN ROCKWELL

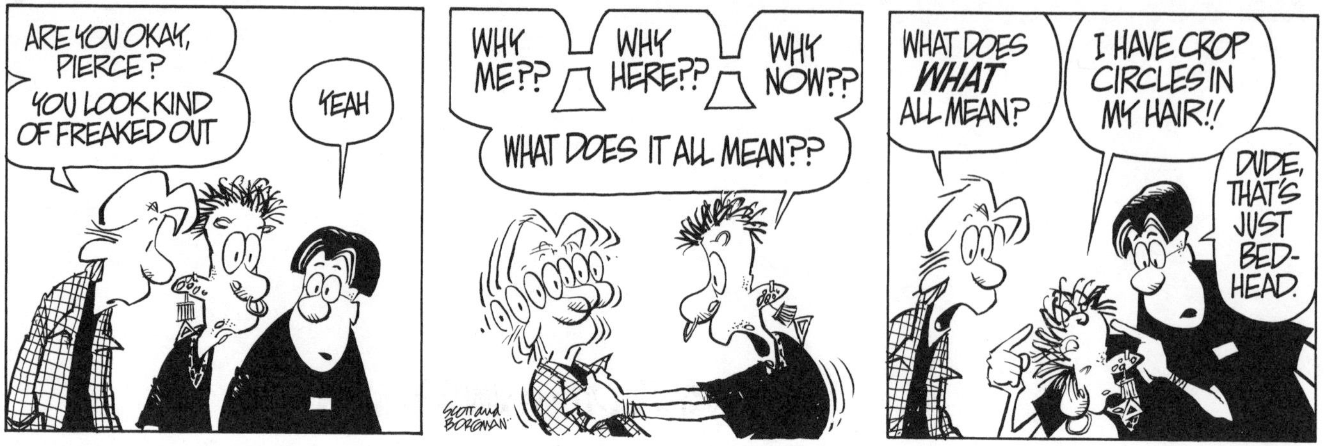
ARE YOU OKAY, PIERCE? YOU LOOK KIND OF FREAKED OUT
YEAH
WHY ME??
WHY HERE??
WHY NOW??
WHAT DOES IT ALL MEAN??
SCOTT and BORGMAN
WHAT DOES WHAT ALL MEAN?
I HAVE CROP CIRCLES IN MY HAIR!!
DUDE, THAT'S JUST BED-HEAD.

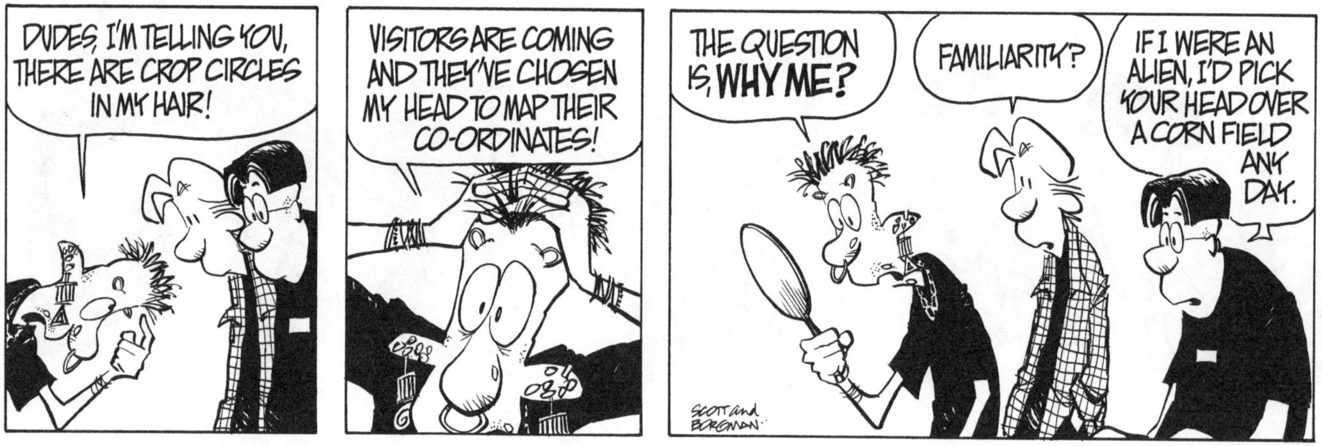
DUDES, I'M TELLING YOU, THERE ARE CROP CIRCLES IN MY HAIR!
VISITORS ARE COMING AND THEY'VE CHOSEN MY HEAD TO MAP THEIR CO-ORDINATES!
THE QUESTION IS, WHY ME?
FAMILIARITY?
IF I WERE AN ALIEN, I'D PICK YOUR HEAD OVER A CORN FIELD ANY DAY.
SCOTT and BORGMAN

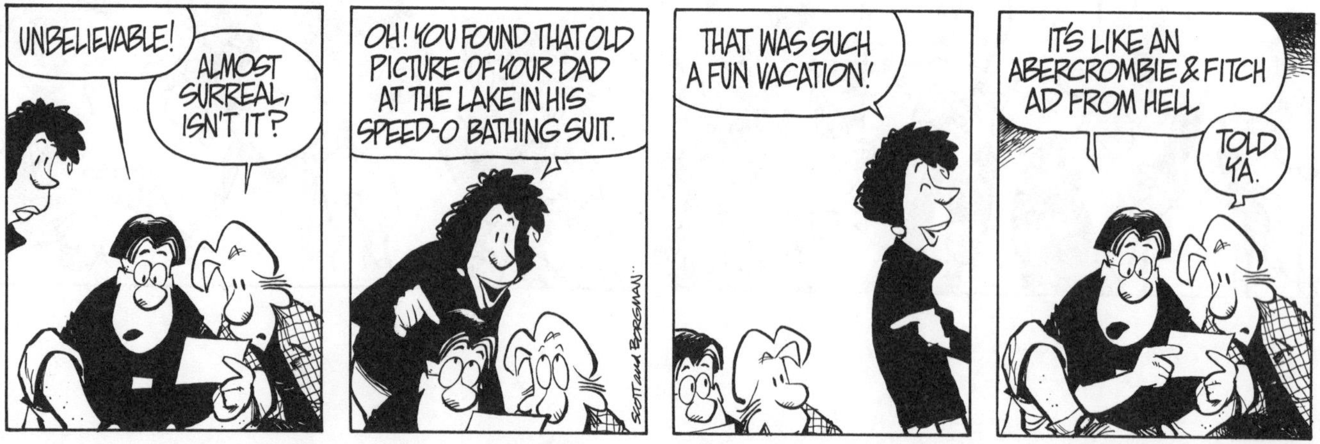
UNBELIEVABLE!
ALMOST SURREAL, ISN'T IT?
OH! YOU FOUND THAT OLD PICTURE OF YOUR DAD AT THE LAKE IN HIS SPEED-O BATHING SUIT.
SCOTT and BORGMAN
THAT WAS SUCH A FUN VACATION!
IT'S LIKE AN ABERCROMBIE & FITCH AD FROM HELL
TOLD YA.

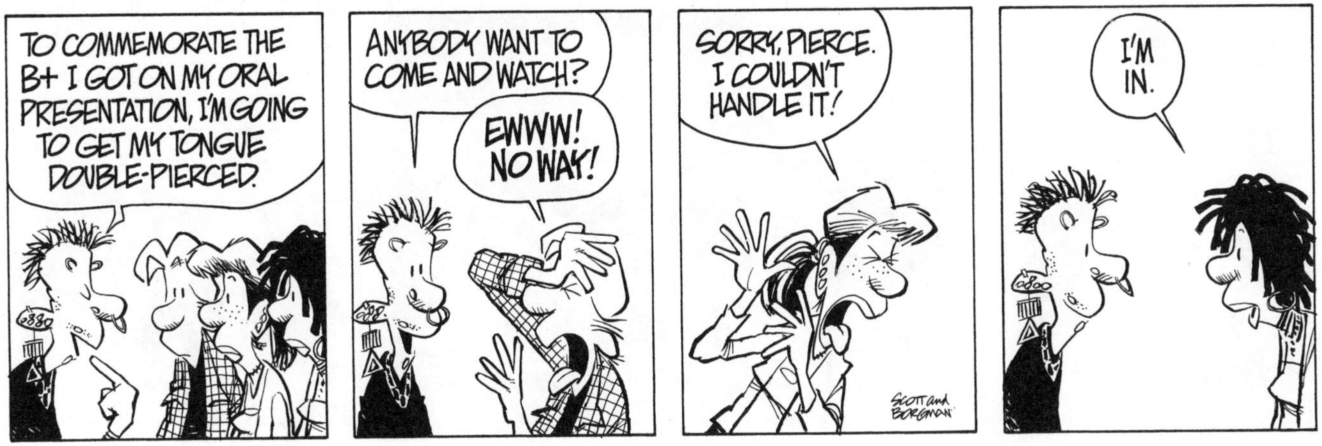
TO COMMEMORATE THE B+ I GOT ON MY ORAL PRESENTATION, I'M GOING TO GET MY TONGUE DOUBLE-PIERCED.
ANYBODY WANT TO COME AND WATCH?
EWWW! NO WAY!
SORRY, PIERCE. I COULDN'T HANDLE IT!
I'M IN.

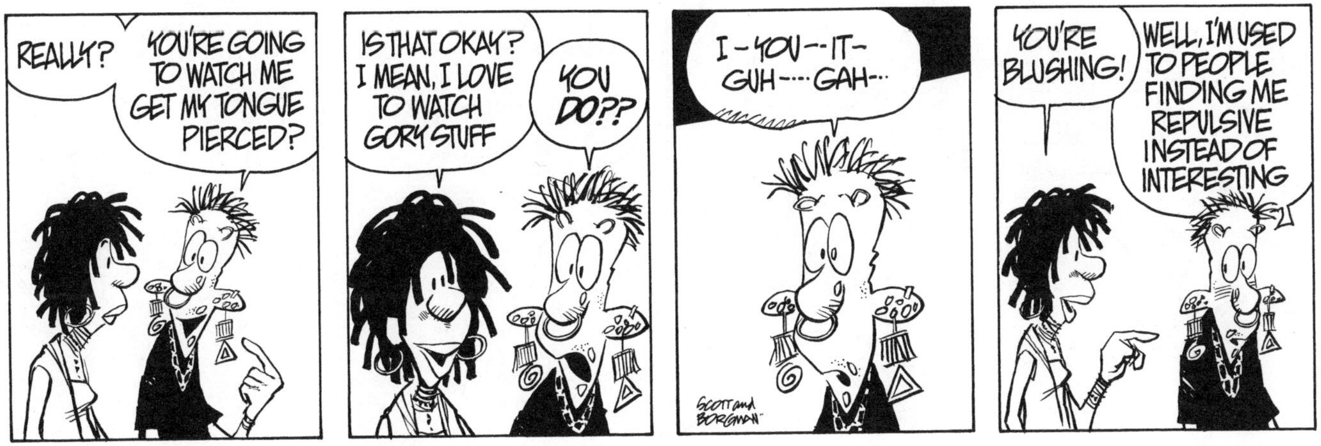
REALLY?
YOU'RE GOING TO WATCH ME GET MY TONGUE PIERCED?
IS THAT OKAY? I MEAN, I LOVE TO WATCH GORY STUFF
YOU DO??
I - YOU -- IT - GUH ---- GAH --
YOU'RE BLUSHING!
WELL, I'M USED TO PEOPLE FINDING ME REPULSIVE INSTEAD OF INTERESTING

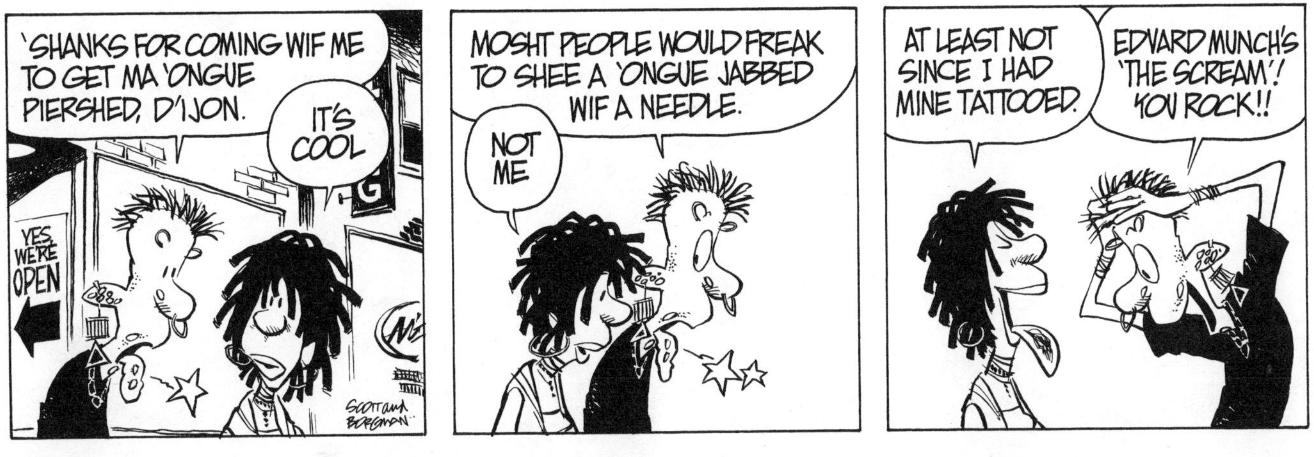
'SHANKS FOR COMING WIF ME TO GET MA 'ONGUE PIERSHED, D'IJON.
IT'S COOL
YES, WE'RE OPEN
G
MOSHT PEOPLE WOULD FREAK TO SHEE A 'ONGUE JABBED WIF A NEEDLE.
NOT ME
AT LEAST NOT SINCE I HAD MINE TATTOOED.
EDVARD MUNCH'S 'THE SCREAM'! YOU ROCK!!

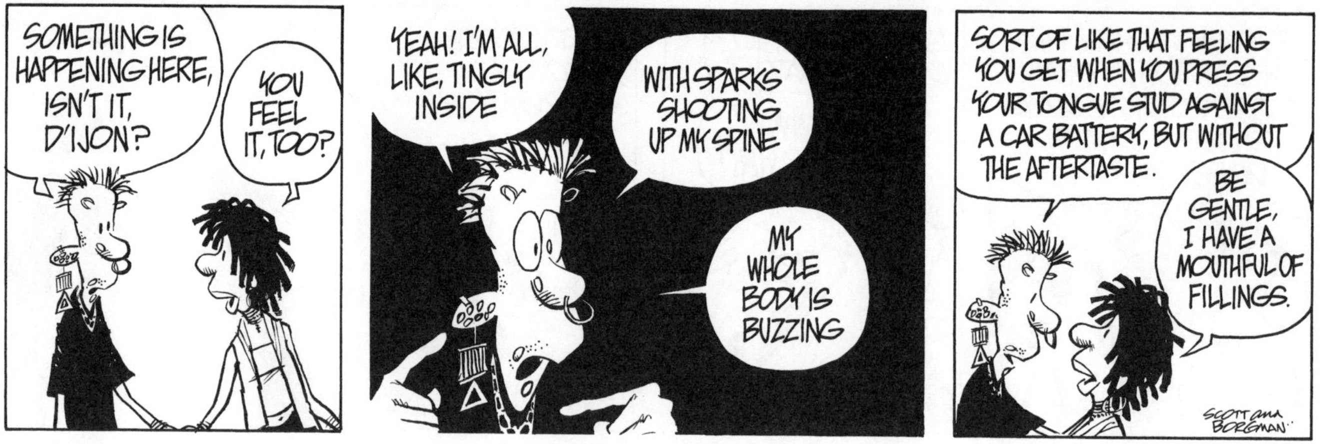
SOMETHING IS HAPPENING HERE, ISN'T IT, D'IJON?
YOU FEEL IT, TOO?
YEAH! I'M ALL, LIKE, TINGLY INSIDE
WITH SPARKS SHOOTING UP MY SPINE
MY WHOLE BODY IS BUZZING
SORT OF LIKE THAT FEELING YOU GET WHEN YOU PRESS YOUR TONGUE STUD AGAINST A CAR BATTERY, BUT WITHOUT THE AFTERTASTE.
BE GENTLE, I HAVE A MOUTHFUL OF FILLINGS.
SCOTT and BORGMAN

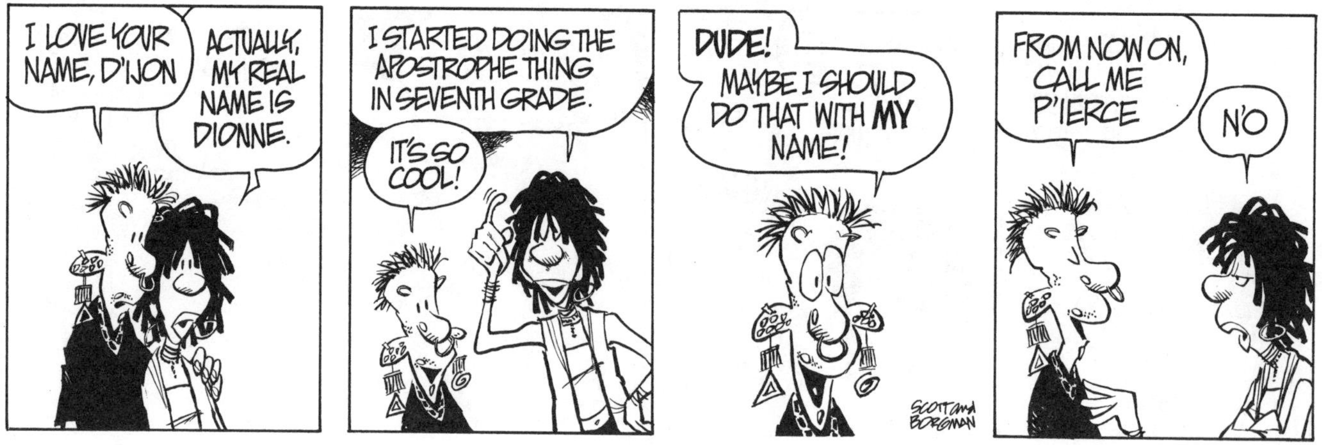
I LOVE YOUR NAME, D'IJON
ACTUALLY, MY REAL NAME IS DIONNE.
I STARTED DOING THE APOSTROPHE THING IN SEVENTH GRADE.
IT'S SO COOL!
DUDE! MAYBE I SHOULD DO THAT WITH MY NAME!
SCOTT and BORGMAN
FROM NOW ON, CALL ME P'IERCE
N'O

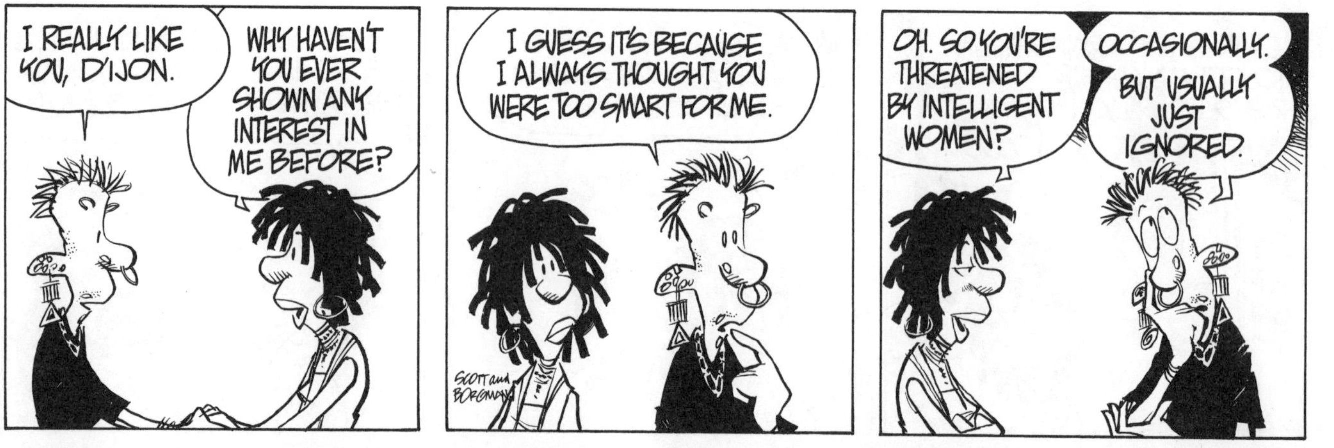
I REALLY LIKE YOU, D'IJON.
WHY HAVEN'T YOU EVER SHOWN ANY INTEREST IN ME BEFORE?
I GUESS IT'S BECAUSE I ALWAYS THOUGHT YOU WERE TOO SMART FOR ME.
SCOTT and BORGMAN
OH. SO YOU'RE THREATENED BY INTELLIGENT WOMEN?
OCCASIONALLY.
BUT USUALLY JUST IGNORED.

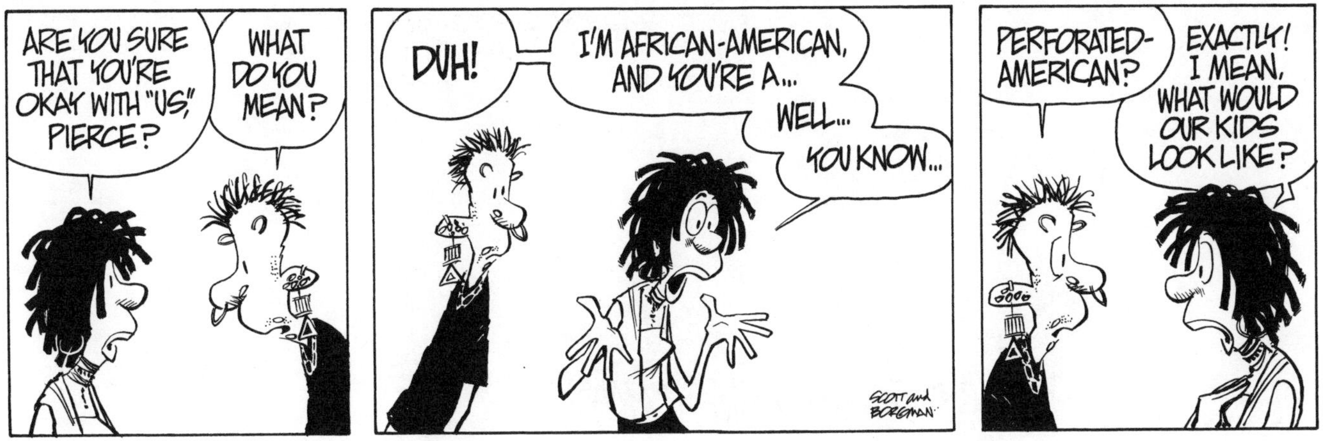
ARE YOU SURE THAT YOU'RE OKAY WITH "US," PIERCE?
WHAT DO YOU MEAN?
DUH!
I'M AFRICAN-AMERICAN, AND YOU'RE A...
WELL...
YOU KNOW...
PERFORATED-AMERICAN?
EXACTLY! I MEAN, WHAT WOULD OUR KIDS LOOK LIKE?
SCOTT and BORGMAN

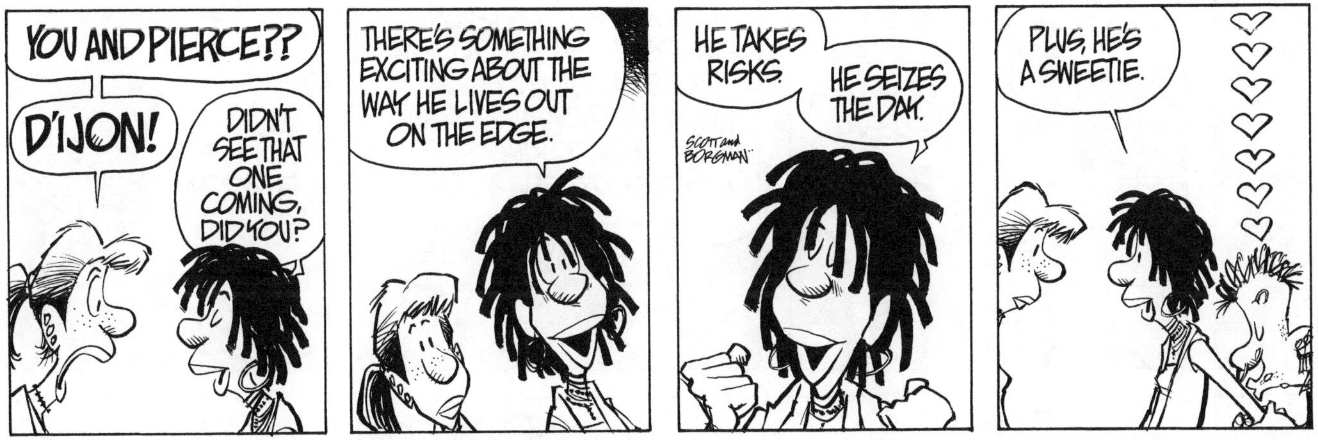
YOU AND PIERCE??
D'IJON!
DIDN'T SEE THAT ONE COMING, DID YOU?
THERE'S SOMETHING EXCITING ABOUT THE WAY HE LIVES OUT ON THE EDGE.
HE TAKES RISKS.
HE SEIZES THE DAY.
SCOTT and BORGMAN
PLUS, HE'S A SWEETIE.

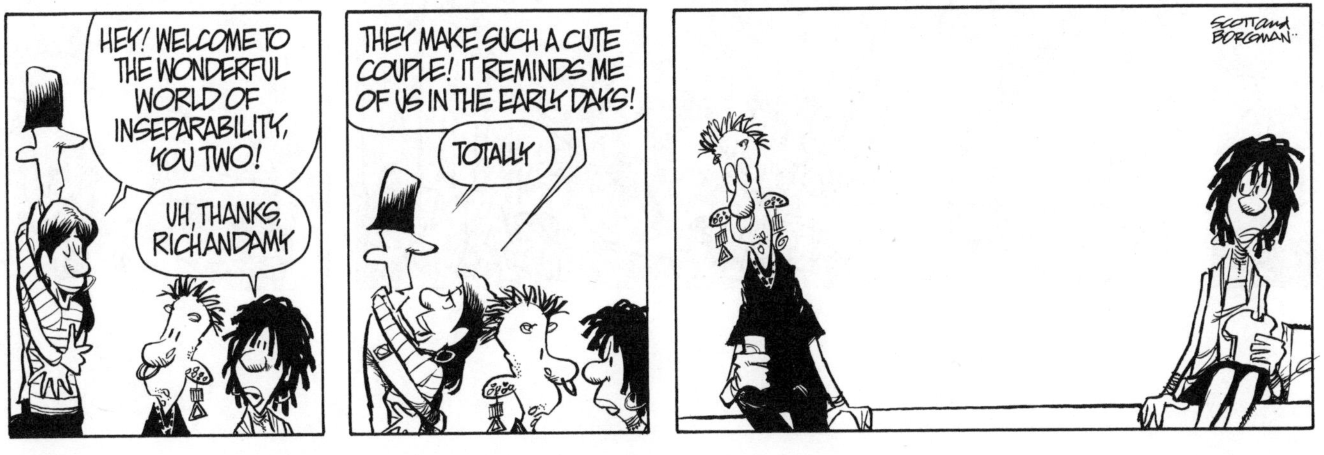
HEY! WELCOME TO THE WONDERFUL WORLD OF INSEPARABILITY, YOU TWO!
UH, THANKS, RICHANDAMY
THEY MAKE SUCH A CUTE COUPLE! IT REMINDS ME OF US IN THE EARLY DAYS!
TOTALLY
SCOTT and BORGMAN

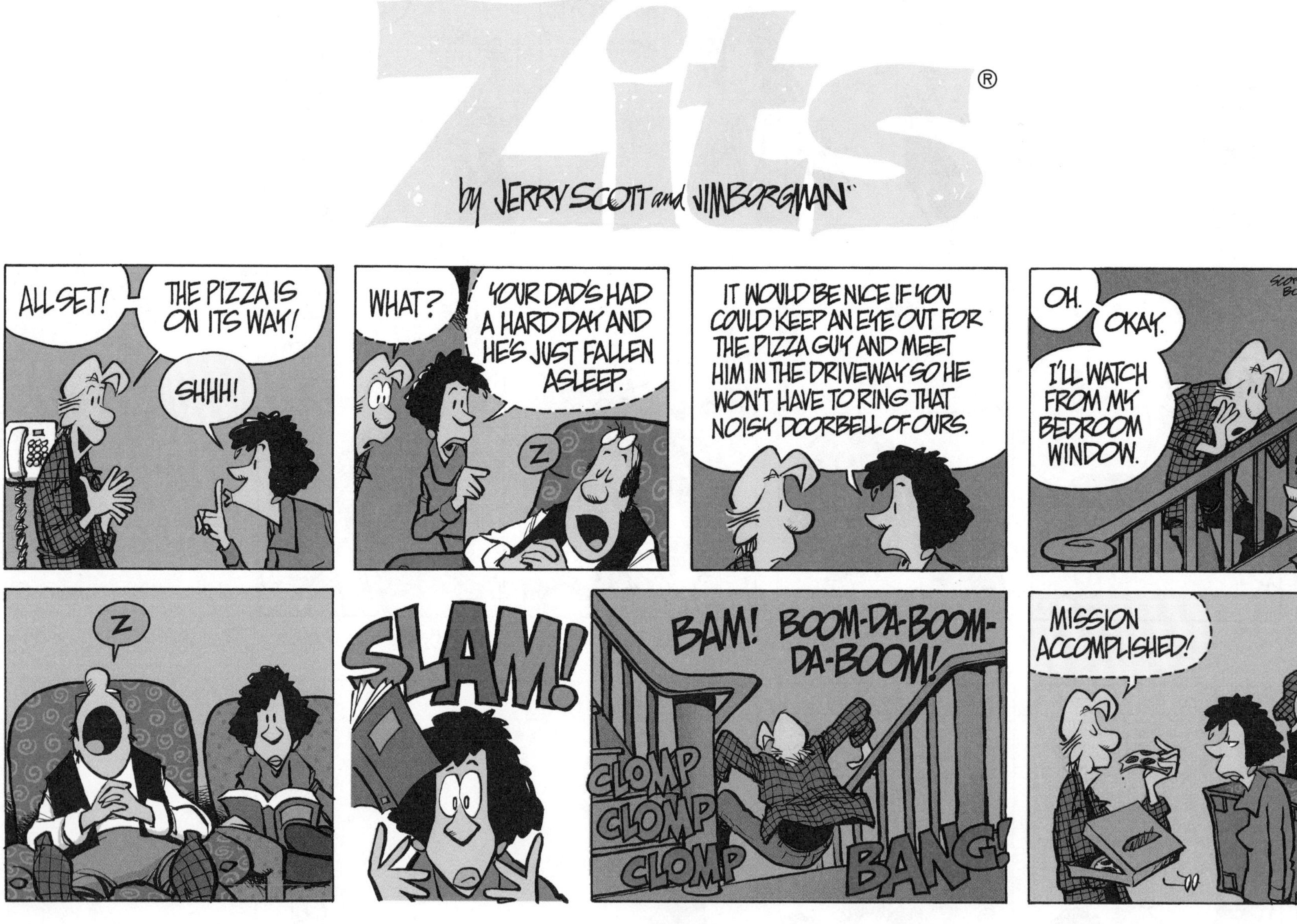
Zits®
by JERRY SCOTT and JIM BORGMAN
ALL SET!
THE PIZZA IS ON ITS WAY!
SHHH!
WHAT?
YOUR DAD'S HAD A HARD DAY AND HE'S JUST FALLEN ASLEEP.
Z
IT WOULD BE NICE IF YOU COULD KEEP AN EYE OUT FOR THE PIZZA GUY AND MEET HIM IN THE DRIVEWAY SO HE WON'T HAVE TO RING THAT NOISY DOORBELL OF OURS.
OH.
OKAY.
I'LL WATCH FROM MY BEDROOM WINDOW.
Z
SLAM!
BAM!
BOOM-DA-BOOM-DA-BOOM!
CLOMP
CLOMP
CLOMP
BANG!
MISSION ACCOMPLISHED!

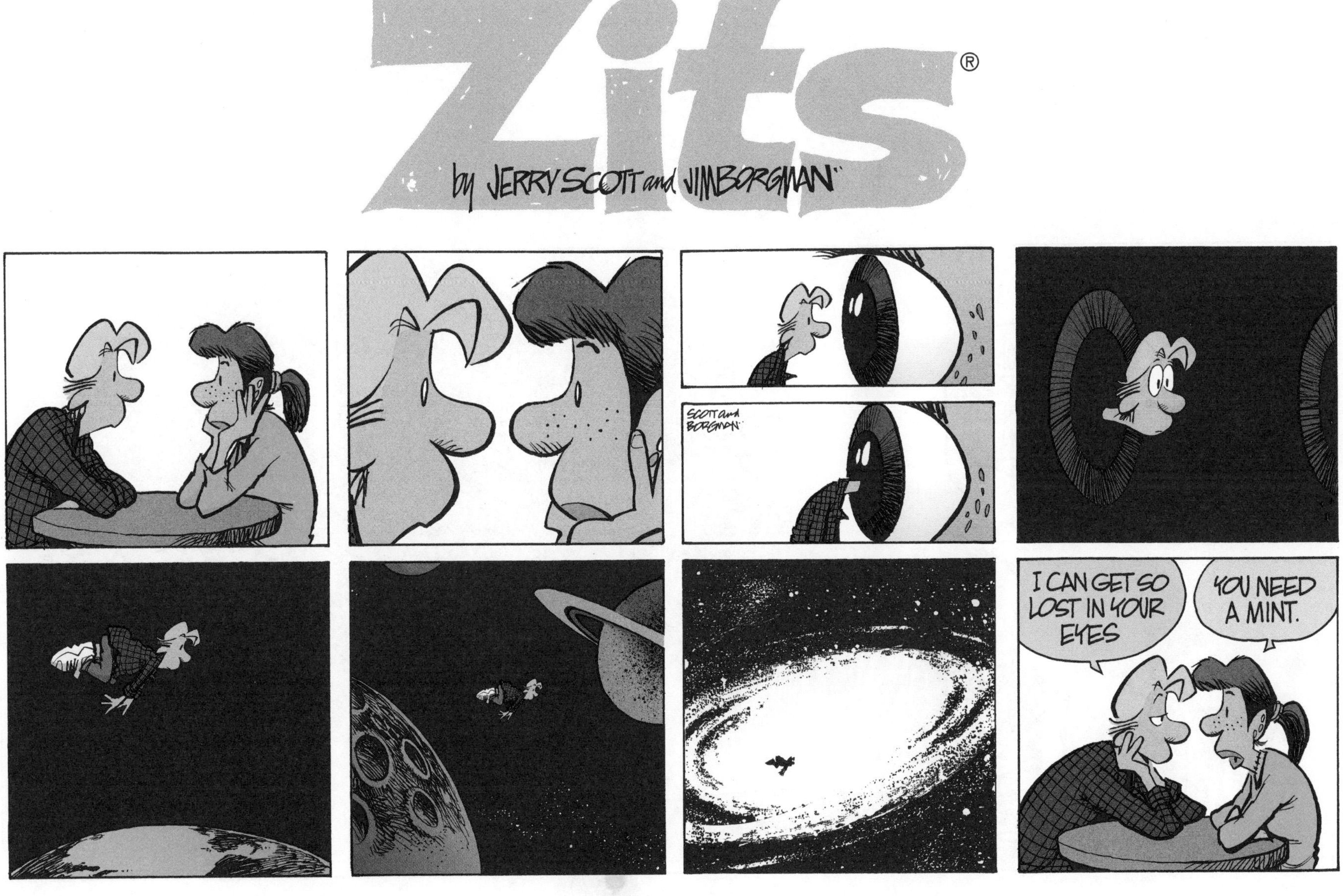
Zits®
by JERRY SCOTT and JIM BORGMAN
SCOTT and BORGMAN
I CAN GET SO LOST IN YOUR EYES
YOU NEED A MINT.

Zits®

by JERRY SCOTT and JIM BORGMAN

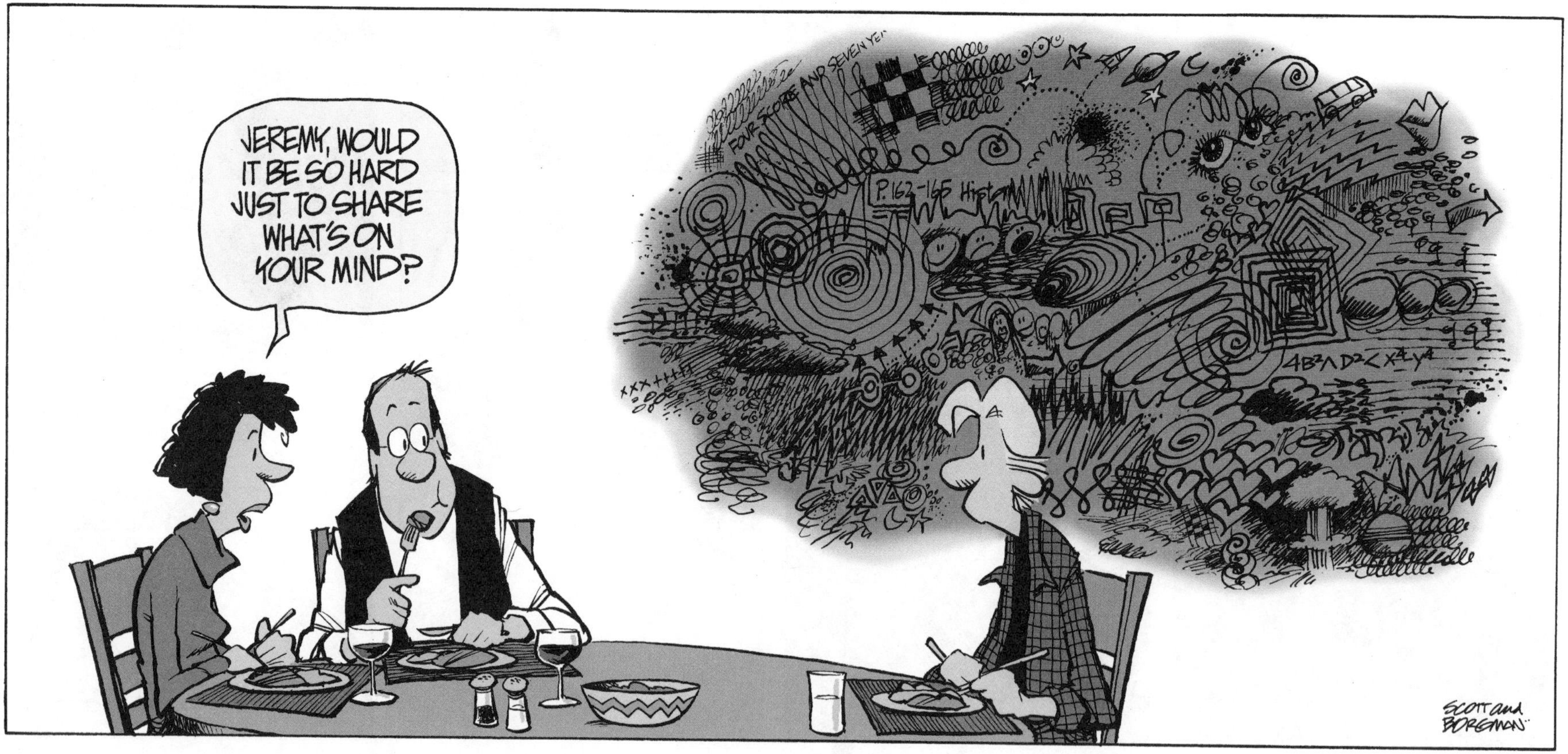
JEREMY, WOULD IT BE SO HARD JUST TO SHARE WHAT'S ON YOUR MIND?
SCOTT and BORGMAN

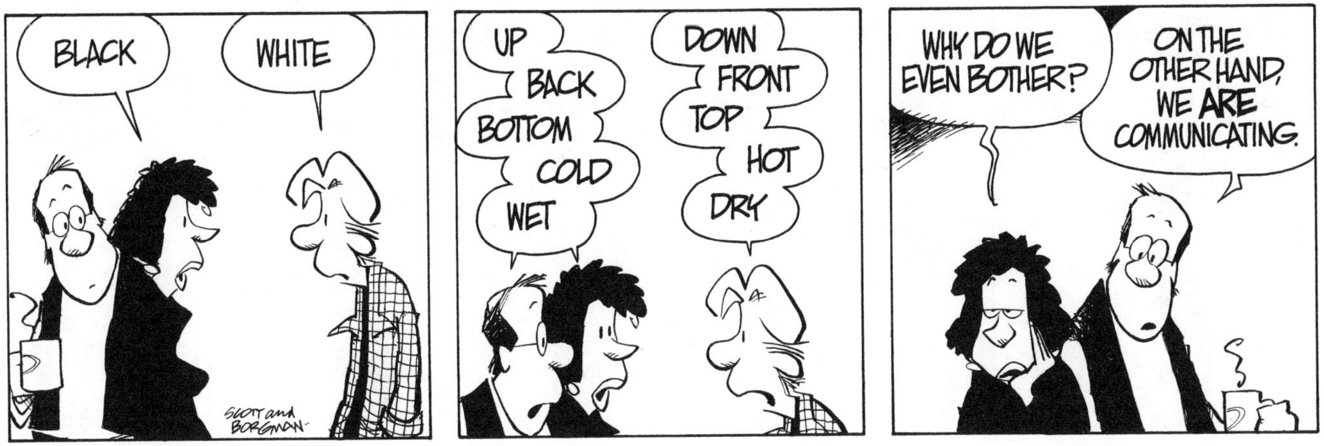
BLACK
WHITE
UP
BACK
BOTTOM
COLD
WET
DOWN
FRONT
TOP
HOT
DRY
WHY DO WE EVEN BOTHER?
ON THE OTHER HAND, WE **ARE** COMMUNICATING.

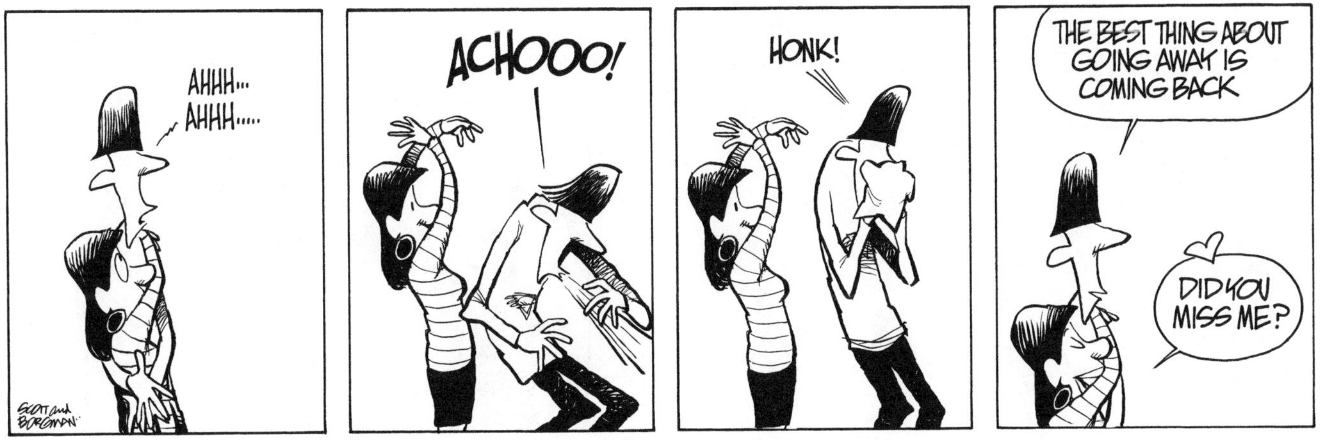
AHHH... AHHH.....
ACHOOO!
HONK!
THE BEST THING ABOUT GOING AWAY IS COMING BACK
DID YOU MISS ME?

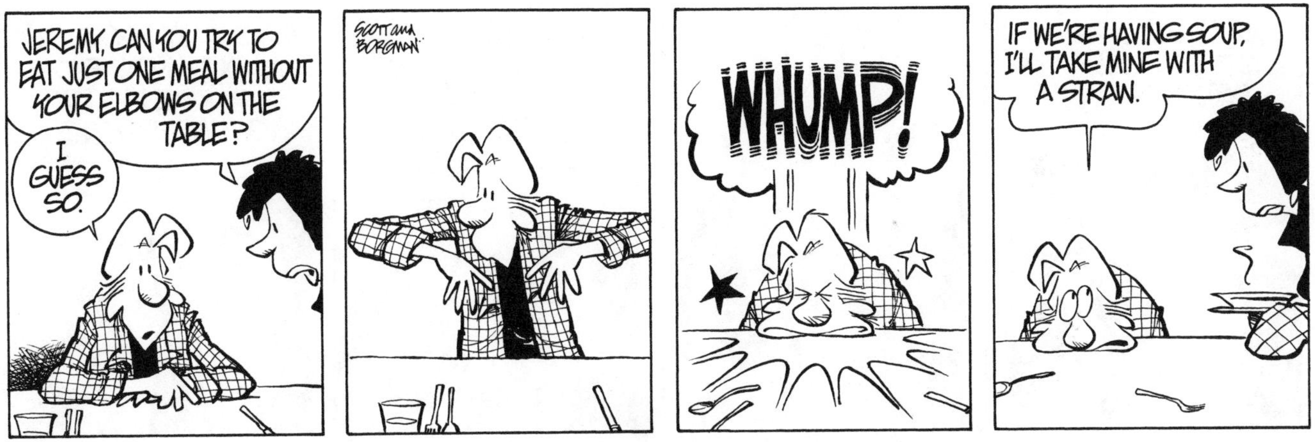
JEREMY, CAN YOU TRY TO EAT JUST ONE MEAL WITHOUT YOUR ELBOWS ON THE TABLE?
I GUESS SO.
WHUMP!
IF WE'RE HAVING SOUP, I'LL TAKE MINE WITH A STRAW.

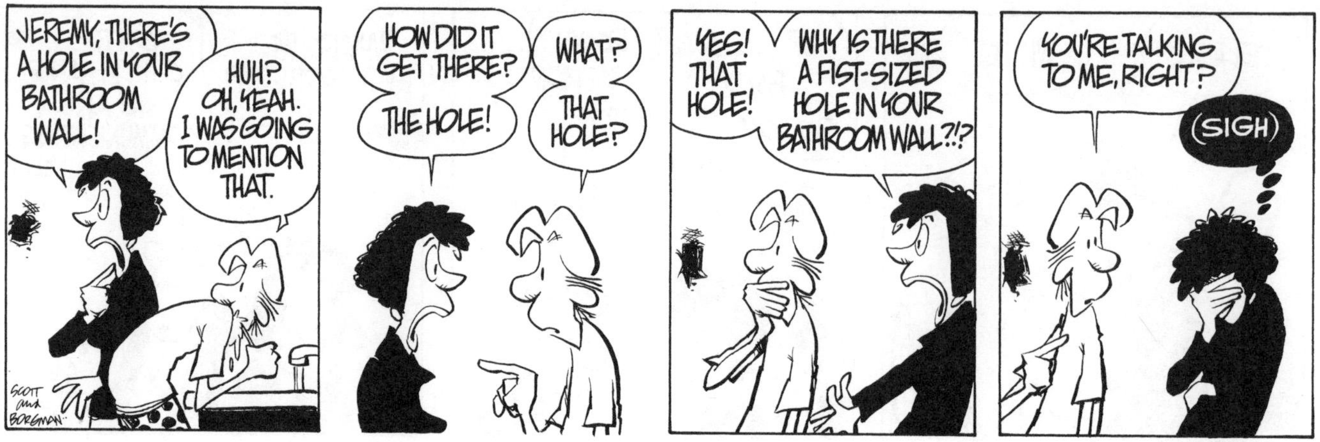
JEREMY, THERE'S A HOLE IN YOUR BATHROOM WALL!
HUH? OH, YEAH. I WAS GOING TO MENTION THAT.
SCOTT and BORGMAN
HOW DID IT GET THERE?
THE HOLE!
WHAT?
THAT HOLE?
YES! THAT HOLE!
WHY IS THERE A FIST-SIZED HOLE IN YOUR BATHROOM WALL?!?
YOU'RE TALKING TO ME, RIGHT?
(SIGH)

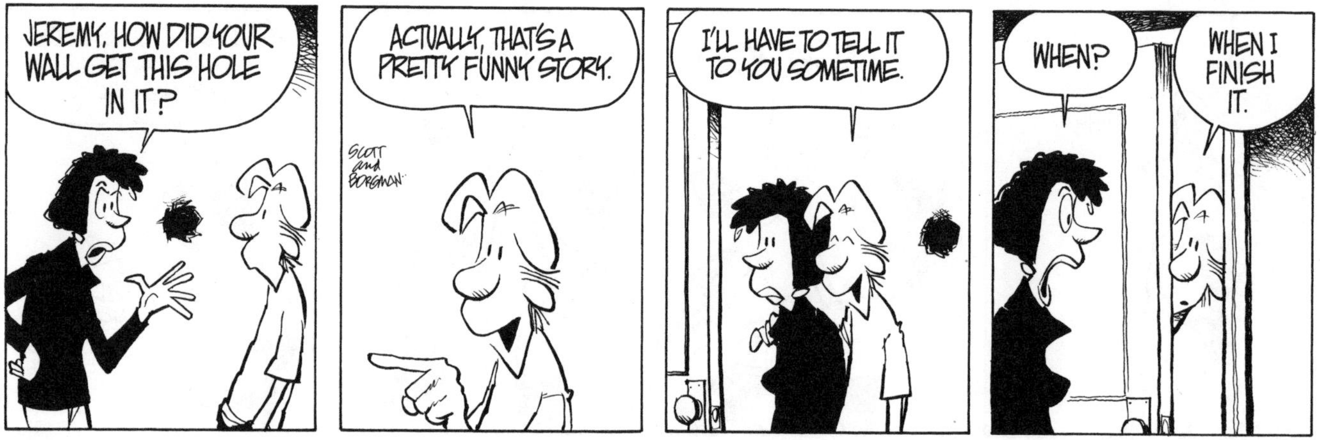
JEREMY, HOW DID YOUR WALL GET THIS HOLE IN IT?
ACTUALLY, THAT'S A PRETTY FUNNY STORY.
SCOTT and BORGMAN
I'LL HAVE TO TELL IT TO YOU SOMETIME.
WHEN?
WHEN I FINISH IT.

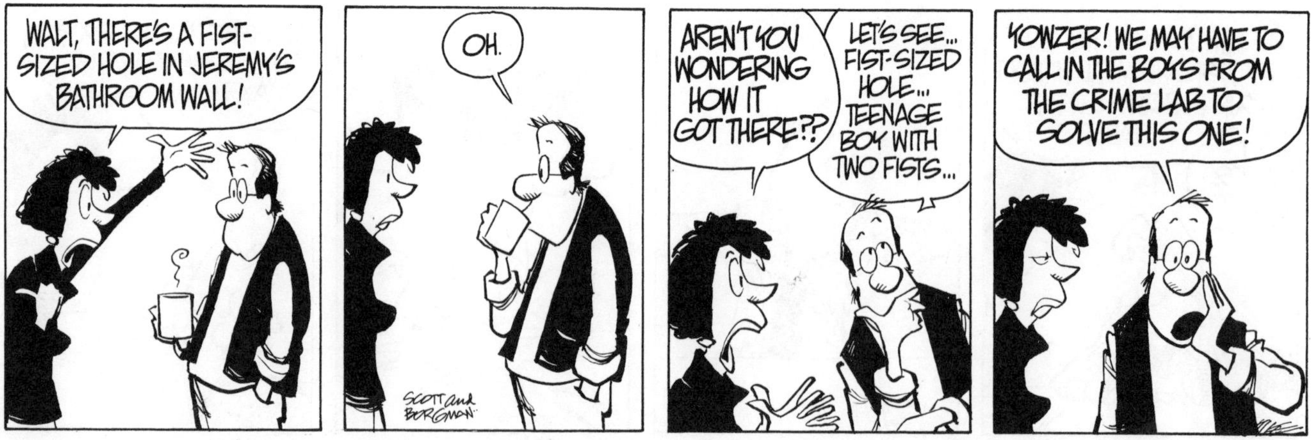
WALT, THERE'S A FIST-SIZED HOLE IN JEREMY'S BATHROOM WALL!
OH.
SCOTT and BORGMAN
AREN'T YOU WONDERING HOW IT GOT THERE??
LET'S SEE... FIST-SIZED HOLE... TEENAGE BOY WITH TWO FISTS...
YOWZER! WE MAY HAVE TO CALL IN THE BOYS FROM THE CRIME LAB TO SOLVE THIS ONE!

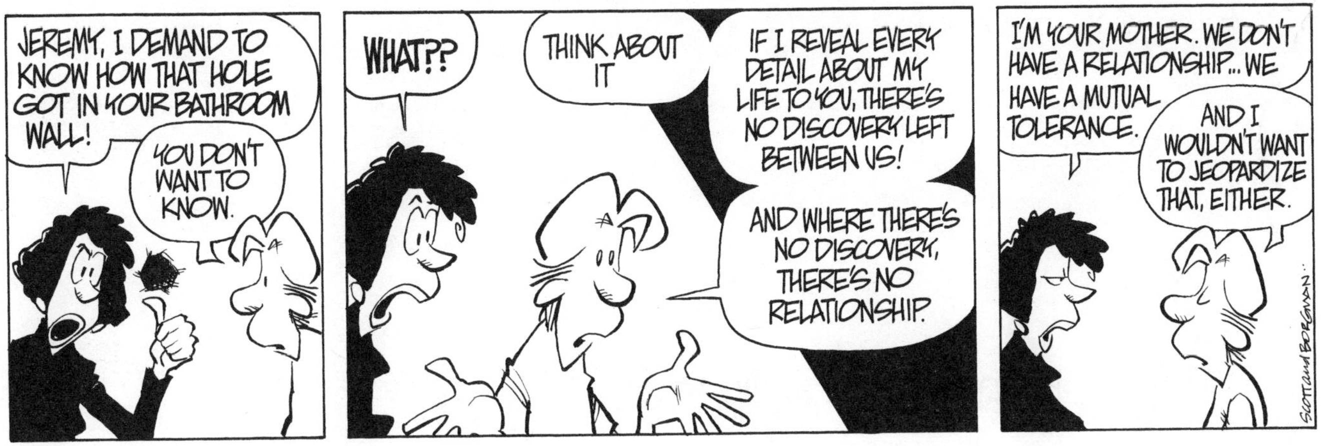
JEREMY, I DEMAND TO KNOW HOW THAT HOLE GOT IN YOUR BATHROOM WALL!
YOU DON'T WANT TO KNOW.
WHAT??
THINK ABOUT IT
IF I REVEAL EVERY DETAIL ABOUT MY LIFE TO YOU, THERE'S NO DISCOVERY LEFT BETWEEN US!
AND WHERE THERE'S NO DISCOVERY, THERE'S NO RELATIONSHIP.
I'M YOUR MOTHER. WE DON'T HAVE A RELATIONSHIP... WE HAVE A MUTUAL TOLERANCE.
AND I WOULDN'T WANT TO JEOPARDIZE THAT, EITHER.
SCOTT and BORGMAN

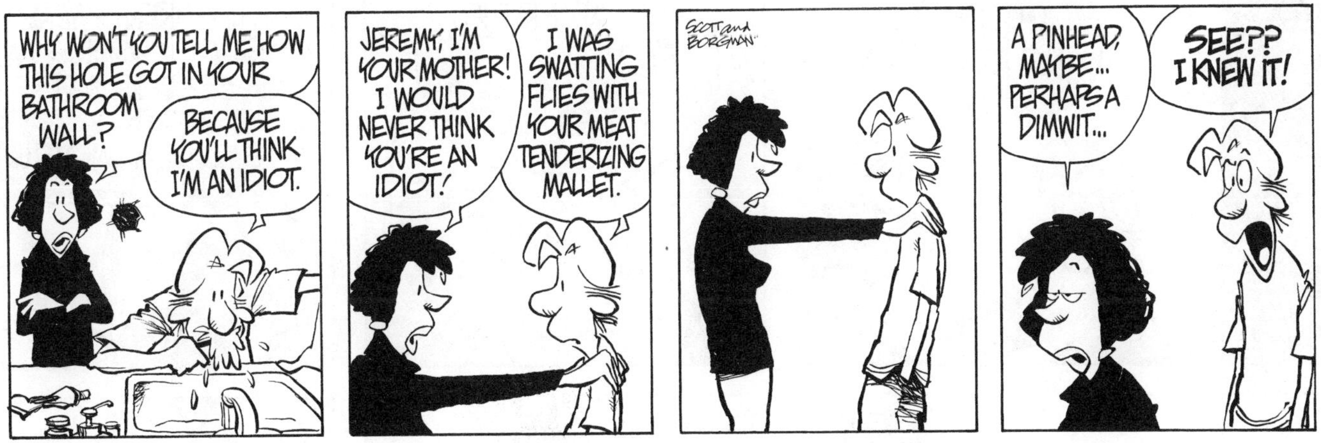
WHY WON'T YOU TELL ME HOW THIS HOLE GOT IN YOUR BATHROOM WALL?
BECAUSE YOU'LL THINK I'M AN IDIOT.
JEREMY, I'M YOUR MOTHER! I WOULD NEVER THINK YOU'RE AN IDIOT!
I WAS SWATTING FLIES WITH YOUR MEAT TENDERIZING MALLET.
SCOTT and BORGMAN
A PINHEAD, MAYBE... PERHAPS A DIMWIT...
SEE?? I KNEW IT!

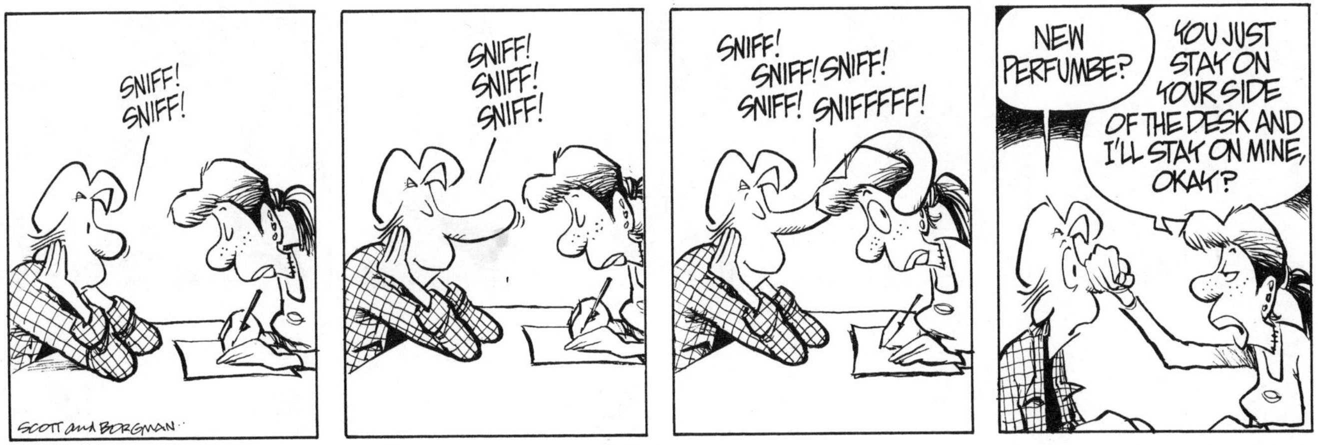
SNIFF! SNIFF!
SNIFF! SNIFF! SNIFF!
SNIFF! SNIFF! SNIFF! SNIFF! SNIFFFFF!
NEW PERFUMBE?
YOU JUST STAY ON YOUR SIDE OF THE DESK AND I'LL STAY ON MINE, OKAY?
SCOTT and BORGMAN

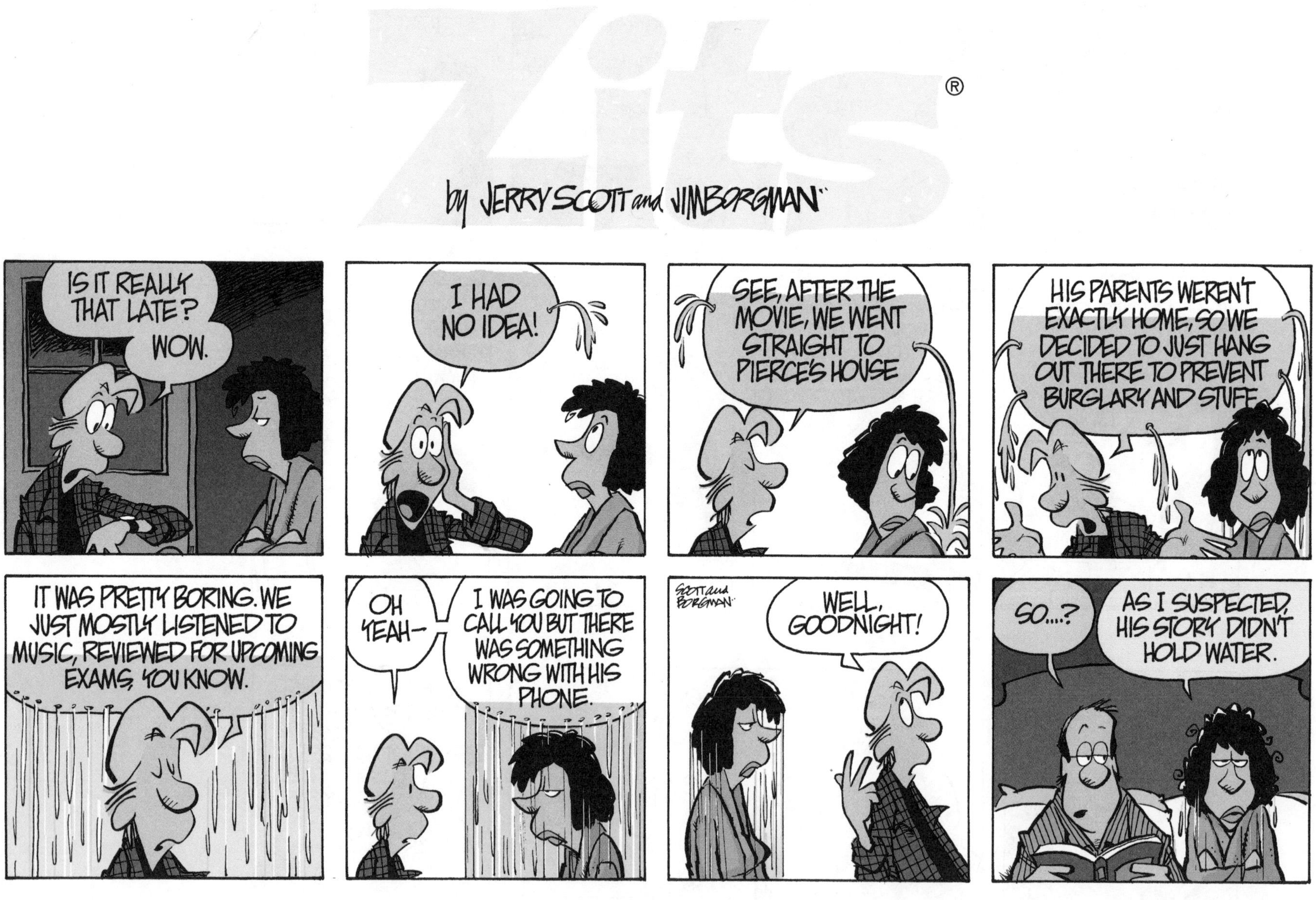
Zits®
by JERRY SCOTT and JIM BORGMAN
IS IT REALLY THAT LATE?
WOW.
I HAD NO IDEA!
SEE, AFTER THE MOVIE, WE WENT STRAIGHT TO PIERCE'S HOUSE
HIS PARENTS WEREN'T EXACTLY HOME, SO WE DECIDED TO JUST HANG OUT THERE TO PREVENT BURGLARY AND STUFF.
IT WAS PRETTY BORING. WE JUST MOSTLY LISTENED TO MUSIC, REVIEWED FOR UPCOMING EXAMS, YOU KNOW.
OH YEAH—
I WAS GOING TO CALL YOU BUT THERE WAS SOMETHING WRONG WITH HIS PHONE.
SCOTT and BORGMAN
WELL, GOODNIGHT!
SO....?
AS I SUSPECTED, HIS STORY DIDN'T HOLD WATER.

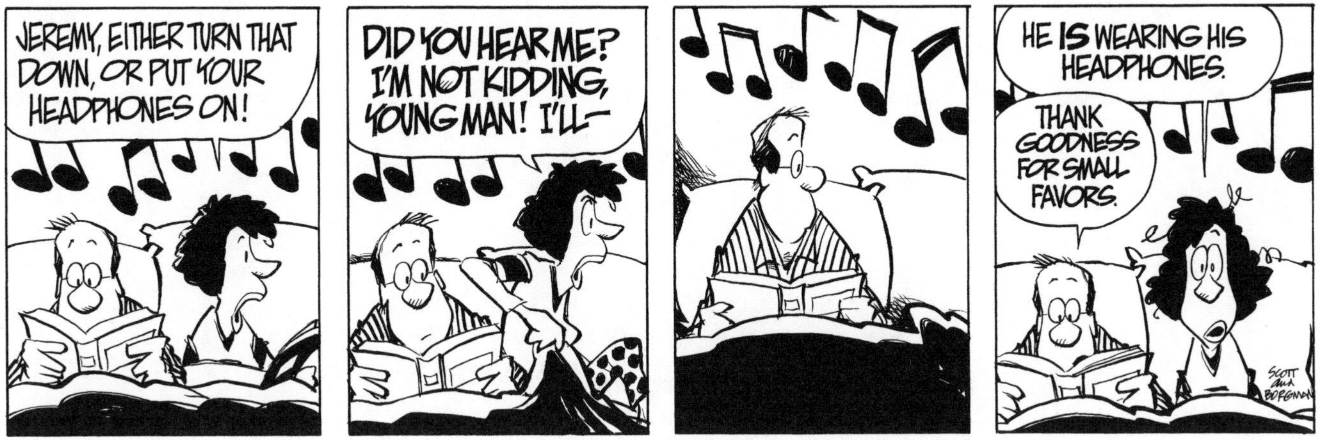
JEREMY, EITHER TURN THAT DOWN, OR PUT YOUR HEADPHONES ON!
DID YOU HEAR ME? I'M NOT KIDDING, YOUNG MAN! I'LL—
HE **IS** WEARING HIS HEADPHONES.
THANK GOODNESS FOR SMALL FAVORS.
SCOTT AND BORGMAN

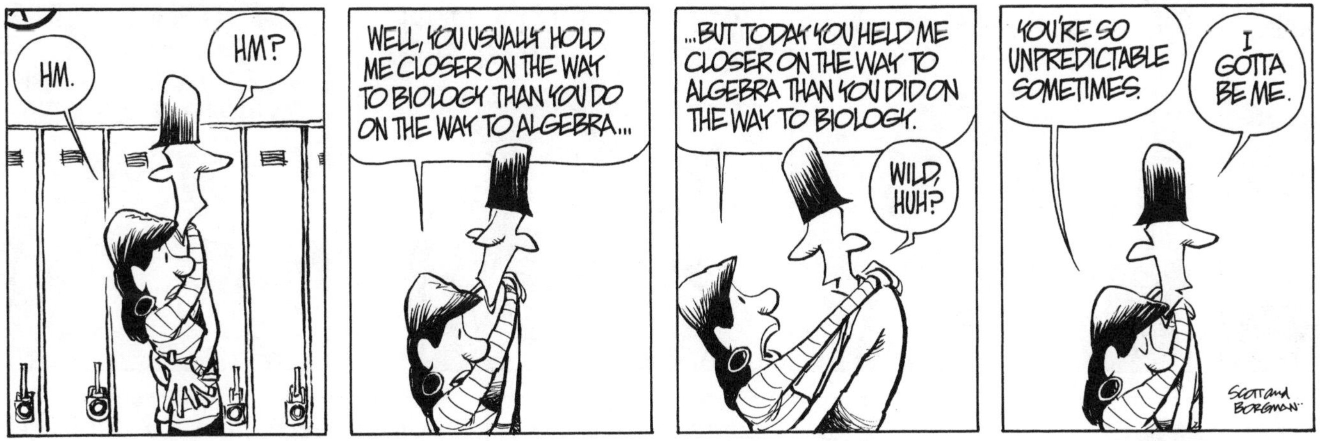
HM.
HM?
WELL, YOU USUALLY HOLD ME CLOSER ON THE WAY TO BIOLOGY THAN YOU DO ON THE WAY TO ALGEBRA...
...BUT TODAY YOU HELD ME CLOSER ON THE WAY TO ALGEBRA THAN YOU DID ON THE WAY TO BIOLOGY.
WILD, HUH?
YOU'RE SO UNPREDICTABLE SOMETIMES.
I GOTTA BE ME.
SCOTT AND BORGMAN

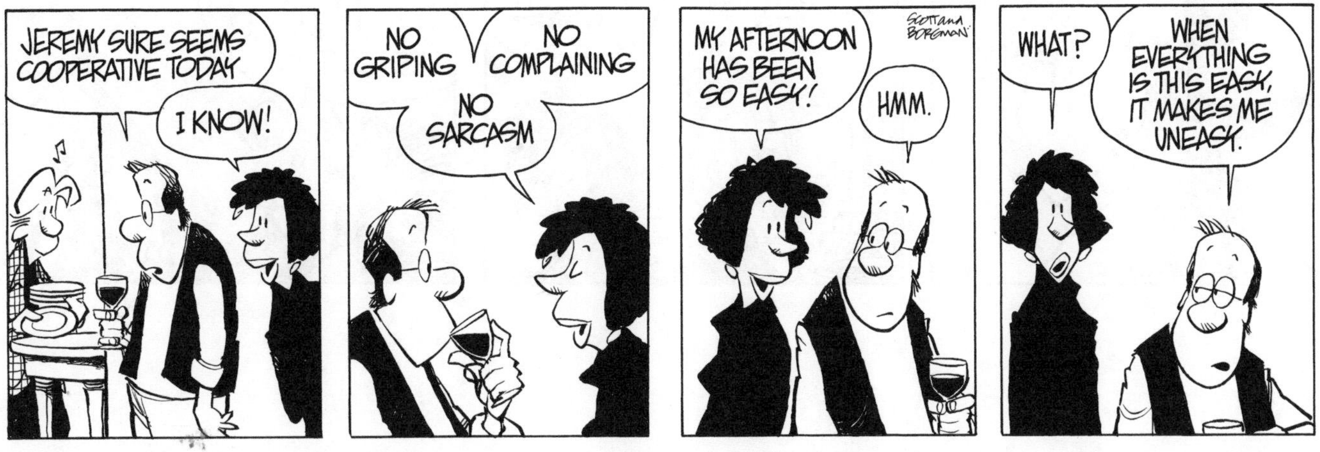
JEREMY SURE SEEMS COOPERATIVE TODAY
I KNOW!
NO GRIPING
NO COMPLAINING
NO SARCASM
MY AFTERNOON HAS BEEN SO EASY!
HMM.
SCOTT AND BORGMAN
WHAT?
WHEN EVERYTHING IS THIS EASY, IT MAKES ME UNEASY.

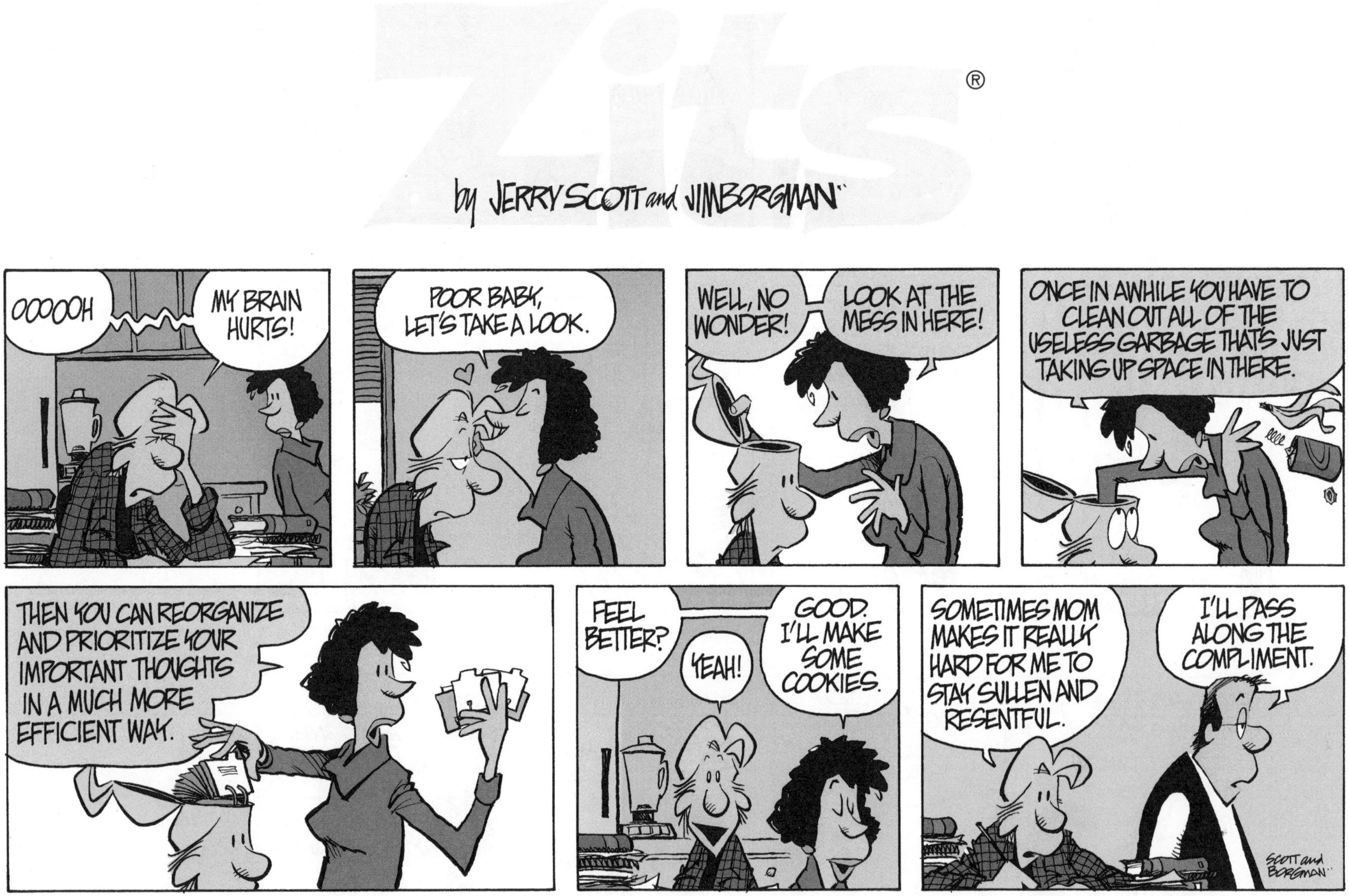
Zits®
by JERRY SCOTT and JIM BORGMAN
OOOOOH
MY BRAIN HURTS!
POOR BABY, LET'S TAKE A LOOK.
WELL, NO WONDER!
LOOK AT THE MESS IN HERE!
ONCE IN AWHILE YOU HAVE TO CLEAN OUT ALL OF THE USELESS GARBAGE THAT'S JUST TAKING UP SPACE IN THERE.
THEN YOU CAN REORGANIZE AND PRIORITIZE YOUR IMPORTANT THOUGHTS IN A MUCH MORE EFFICIENT WAY.
FEEL BETTER?
YEAH!
GOOD. I'LL MAKE SOME COOKIES.
SOMETIMES MOM MAKES IT REALLY HARD FOR ME TO STAY SULLEN AND RESENTFUL.
I'LL PASS ALONG THE COMPLIMENT.
SCOTT and BORGMAN

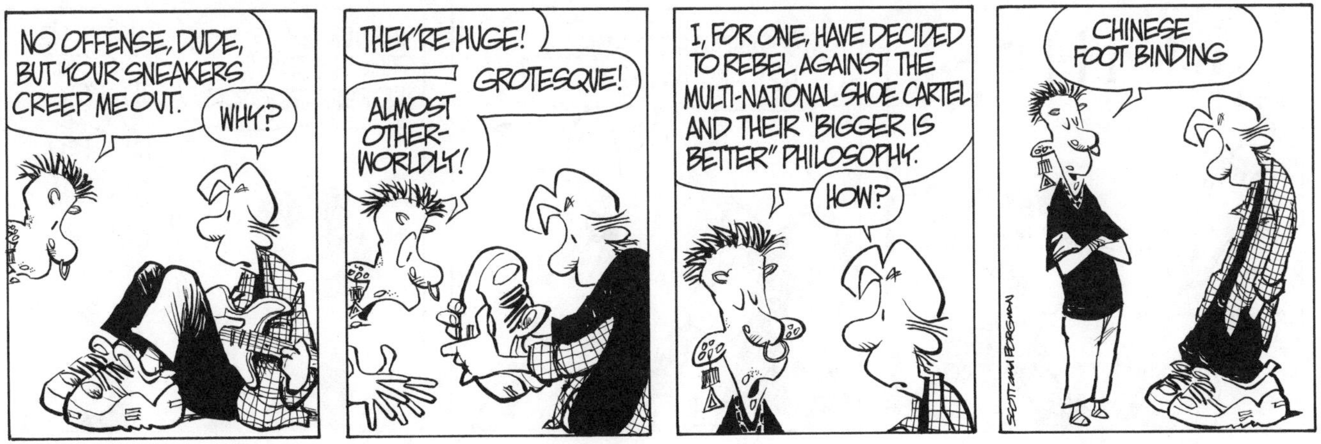
NO OFFENSE, DUDE, BUT YOUR SNEAKERS CREEP ME OUT.
WHY?
THEY'RE HUGE!
GROTESQUE!
ALMOST OTHER-WORLDLY!
I, FOR ONE, HAVE DECIDED TO REBEL AGAINST THE MULTI-NATIONAL SHOE CARTEL AND THEIR "BIGGER IS BETTER" PHILOSOPHY.
HOW?
CHINESE FOOT BINDING
SCOTT and BORGMAN

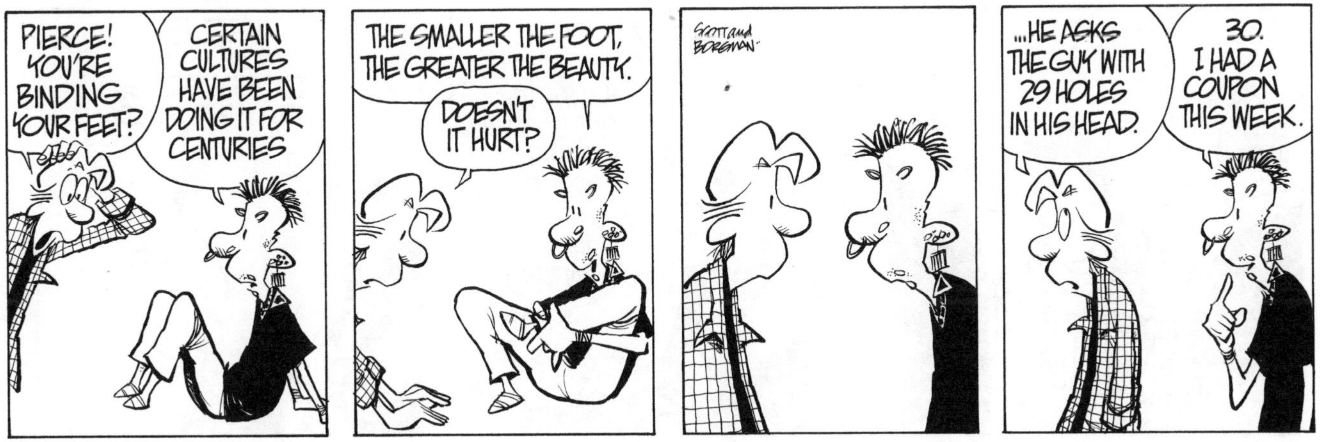
PIERCE! YOU'RE BINDING YOUR FEET?
CERTAIN CULTURES HAVE BEEN DOING IT FOR CENTURIES
THE SMALLER THE FOOT, THE GREATER THE BEAUTY.
DOESN'T IT HURT?
SCOTT and BORGMAN
...HE ASKS THE GUY WITH 29 HOLES IN HIS HEAD.
30. I HAD A COUPON THIS WEEK.

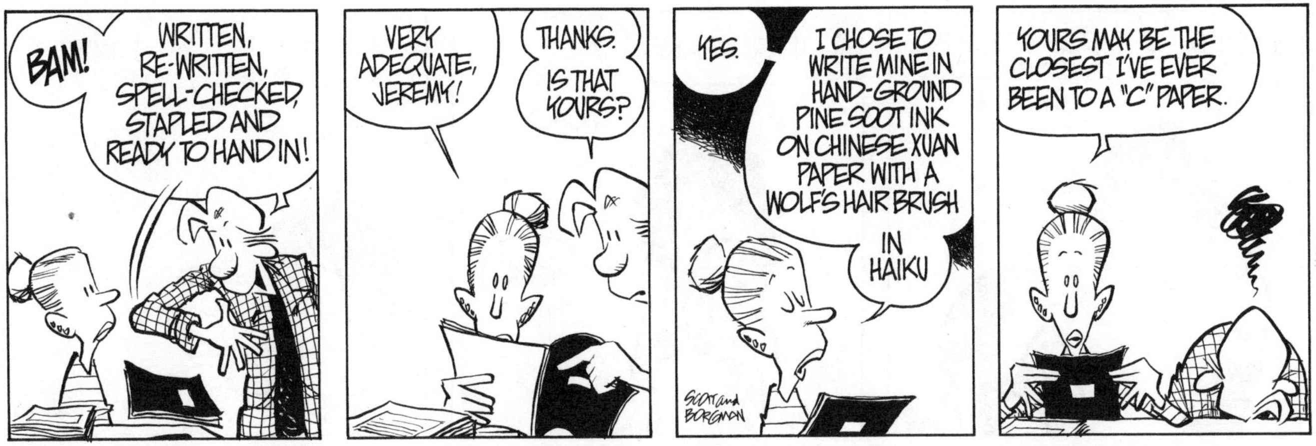
BAM!
WRITTEN, RE-WRITTEN, SPELL-CHECKED, STAPLED AND READY TO HAND IN!
VERY ADEQUATE, JEREMY!
THANKS.
IS THAT YOURS?
YES.
I CHOSE TO WRITE MINE IN HAND-GROUND PINE SOOT INK ON CHINESE XUAN PAPER WITH A WOLF'S HAIR BRUSH
IN HAIKU
SCOTT and BORGMAN
YOURS MAY BE THE CLOSEST I'VE EVER BEEN TO A "C" PAPER.

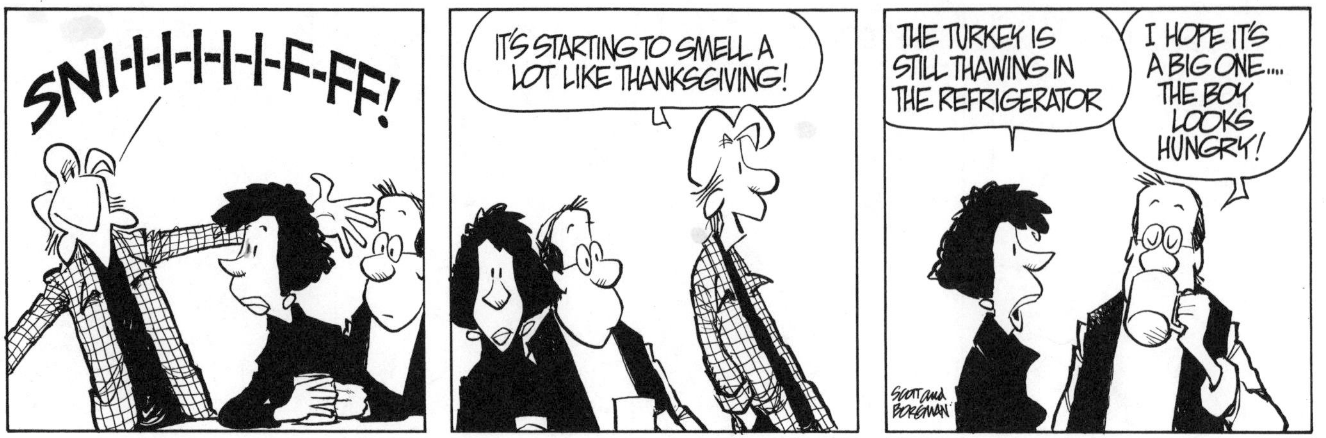
SNI-I-I-I-I-I-F-FF!
IT'S STARTING TO SMELL A LOT LIKE THANKSGIVING!
THE TURKEY IS STILL THAWING IN THE REFRIGERATOR
I HOPE IT'S A BIG ONE.... THE BOY LOOKS HUNGRY!
SCOTT and BORGMAN

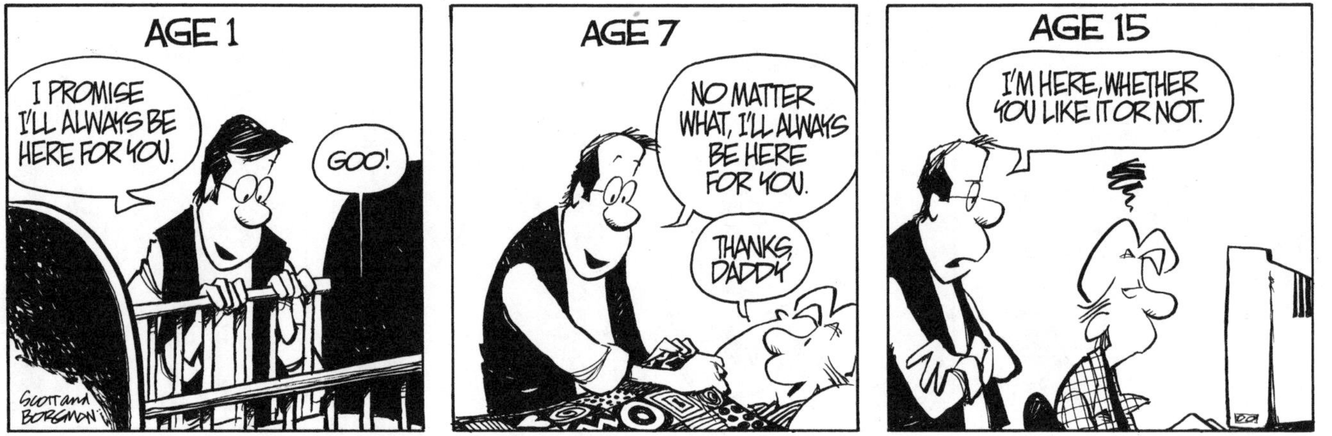
AGE 1
I PROMISE I'LL ALWAYS BE HERE FOR YOU.
GOO!
SCOTT and BORGMAN
AGE 7
NO MATTER WHAT, I'LL ALWAYS BE HERE FOR YOU.
THANKS, DADDY
AGE 15
I'M HERE, WHETHER YOU LIKE IT OR NOT.

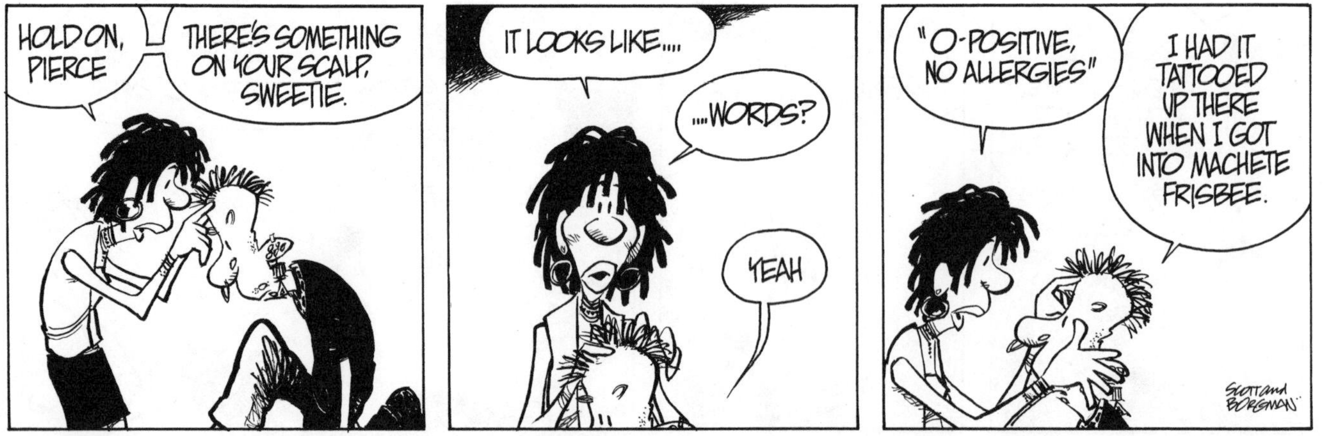
HOLD ON, PIERCE
THERE'S SOMETHING ON YOUR SCALP, SWEETIE.
IT LOOKS LIKE....
....WORDS?
YEAH
"O-POSITIVE, NO ALLERGIES"
I HAD IT TATTOOED UP THERE WHEN I GOT INTO MACHETE FRISBEE.
SCOTT and BORGMAN

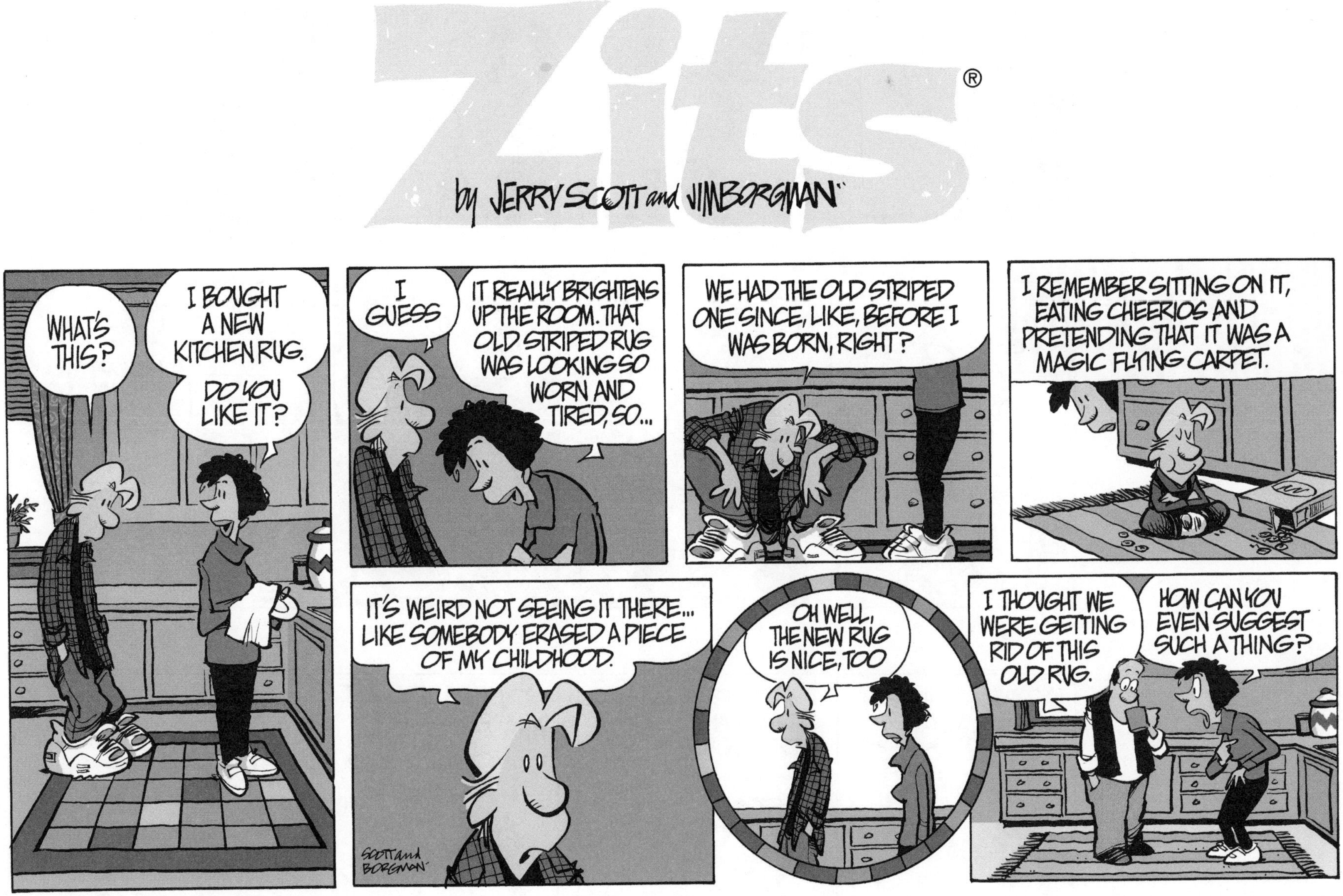
Zits
by JERRY SCOTT and JIM BORGMAN
WHAT'S THIS?
I BOUGHT A NEW KITCHEN RUG.
DO YOU LIKE IT?
I GUESS
IT REALLY BRIGHTENS UP THE ROOM. THAT OLD STRIPED RUG WAS LOOKING SO WORN AND TIRED, SO...
WE HAD THE OLD STRIPED ONE SINCE, LIKE, BEFORE I WAS BORN, RIGHT?
I REMEMBER SITTING ON IT, EATING CHEERIOS AND PRETENDING THAT IT WAS A MAGIC FLYING CARPET.
IT'S WEIRD NOT SEEING IT THERE... LIKE SOMEBODY ERASED A PIECE OF MY CHILDHOOD.
SCOTT and BORGMAN
OH WELL, THE NEW RUG IS NICE, TOO
I THOUGHT WE WERE GETTING RID OF THIS OLD RUG.
HOW CAN YOU EVEN SUGGEST SUCH A THING?

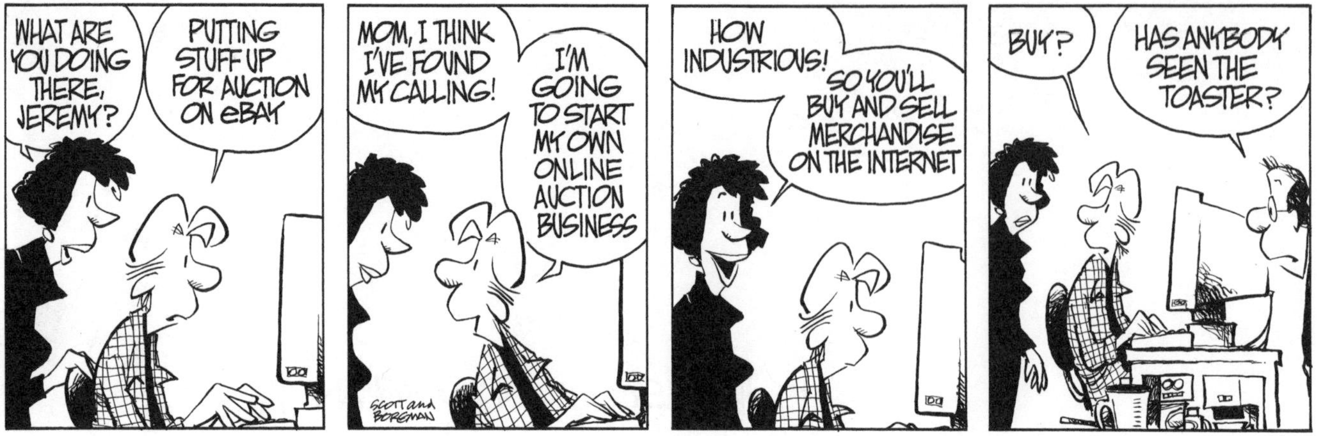
WHAT ARE YOU DOING THERE, JEREMY?
PUTTING STUFF UP FOR AUCTION ON eBAY
MOM, I THINK I'VE FOUND MY CALLING!
I'M GOING TO START MY OWN ONLINE AUCTION BUSINESS
HOW INDUSTRIOUS!
SO YOU'LL BUY AND SELL MERCHANDISE ON THE INTERNET
BUY?
HAS ANYBODY SEEN THE TOASTER?
SCOTT and BORGMAN

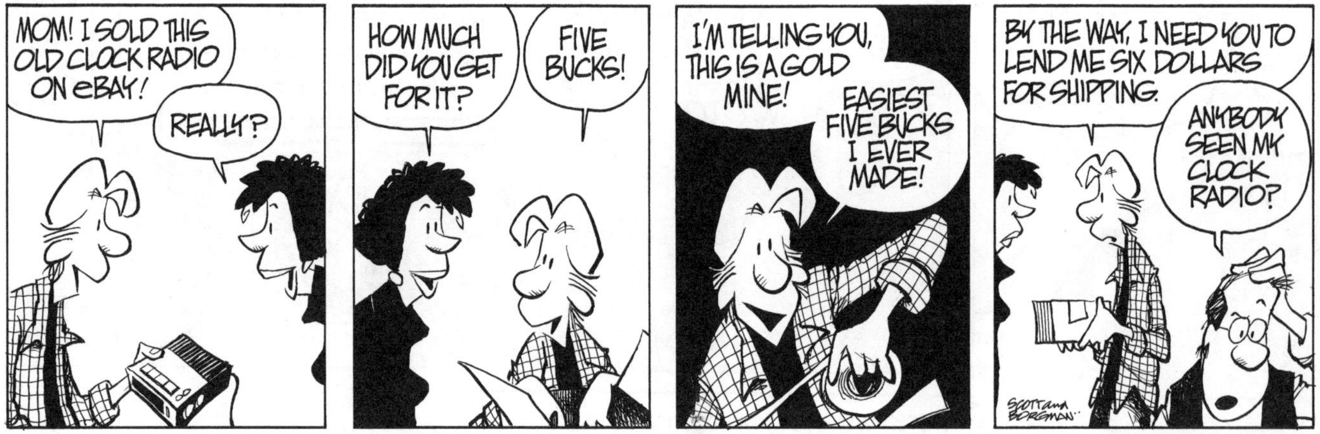
MOM! I SOLD THIS OLD CLOCK RADIO ON eBAY!
REALLY?
HOW MUCH DID YOU GET FOR IT?
FIVE BUCKS!
I'M TELLING YOU, THIS IS A GOLD MINE!
EASIEST FIVE BUCKS I EVER MADE!
BY THE WAY, I NEED YOU TO LEND ME SIX DOLLARS FOR SHIPPING.
ANYBODY SEEN MY CLOCK RADIO?
SCOTT and BORGMAN

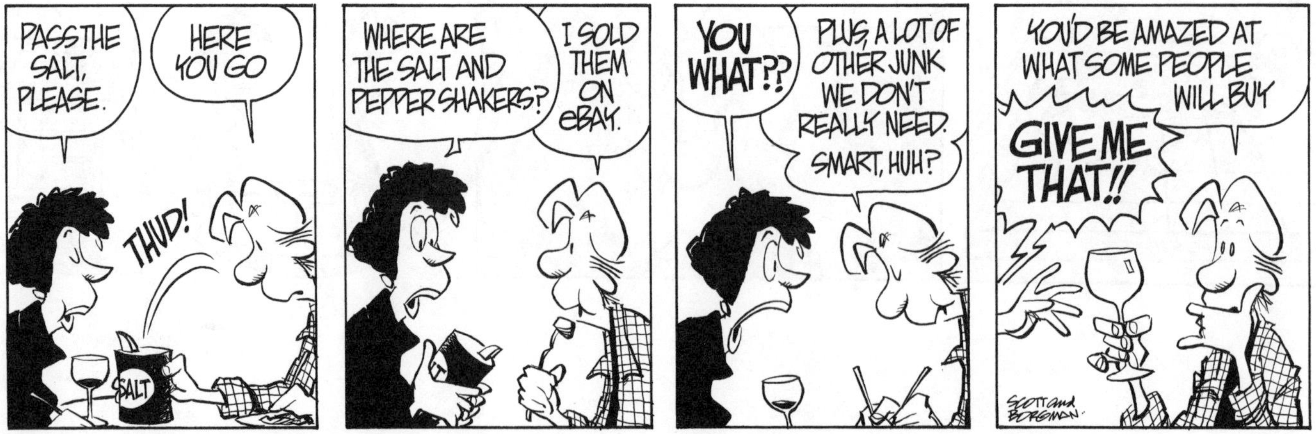
PASS THE SALT, PLEASE.
HERE YOU GO
THUD!
SALT
WHERE ARE THE SALT AND PEPPER SHAKERS?
I SOLD THEM ON eBAY.
YOU WHAT??
PLUS, A LOT OF OTHER JUNK WE DON'T REALLY NEED.
SMART, HUH?
YOU'D BE AMAZED AT WHAT SOME PEOPLE WILL BUY
GIVE ME THAT!!
SCOTT and BORGMAN

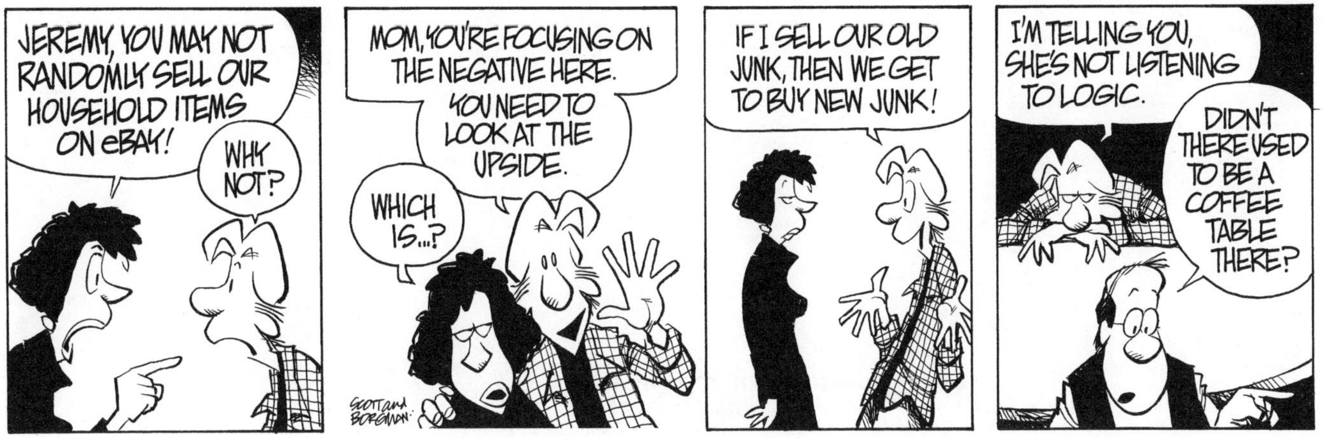
JEREMY, YOU MAY NOT RANDOMLY SELL OUR HOUSEHOLD ITEMS ON eBAY!
WHY NOT?
MOM, YOU'RE FOCUSING ON THE NEGATIVE HERE.
YOU NEED TO LOOK AT THE UPSIDE.
WHICH IS...?
SCOTT and BORGMAN
IF I SELL OUR OLD JUNK, THEN WE GET TO BUY NEW JUNK!
I'M TELLING YOU, SHE'S NOT LISTENING TO LOGIC.
DIDN'T THERE USED TO BE A COFFEE TABLE THERE?

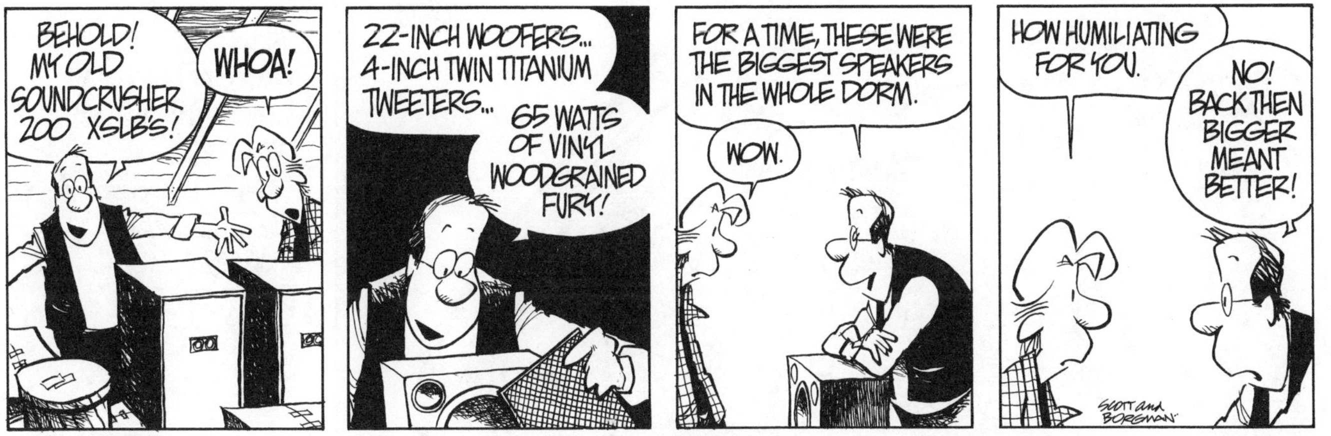
BEHOLD! MY OLD SOUNDCRUSHER 200 XSLB'S!
WHOA!
22-INCH WOOFERS... 4-INCH TWIN TITANIUM TWEETERS...
65 WATTS OF VINYL WOODGRAINED FURY!
FOR A TIME, THESE WERE THE BIGGEST SPEAKERS IN THE WHOLE DORM.
WOW.
HOW HUMILIATING FOR YOU.
NO! BACK THEN BIGGER MEANT BETTER!
SCOTT and BORGMAN

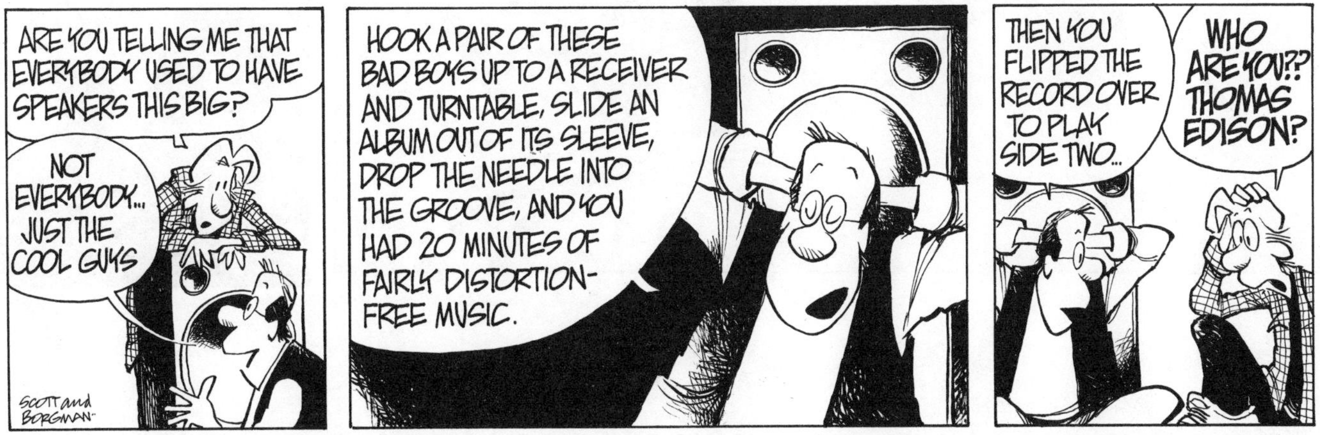
ARE YOU TELLING ME THAT EVERYBODY USED TO HAVE SPEAKERS THIS BIG?
NOT EVERYBODY... JUST THE COOL GUYS
SCOTT and BORGMAN
HOOK A PAIR OF THESE BAD BOYS UP TO A RECEIVER AND TURNTABLE, SLIDE AN ALBUM OUT OF ITS SLEEVE, DROP THE NEEDLE INTO THE GROOVE, AND YOU HAD 20 MINUTES OF FAIRLY DISTORTION-FREE MUSIC.
THEN YOU FLIPPED THE RECORD OVER TO PLAY SIDE TWO...
WHO ARE YOU?? THOMAS EDISON?

Zits®

by JERRY SCOTT and JIM BORGMAN

SCOTT and BORGMAN
THERE ARE NO WORDS TO EXPRESS THE LIMITLESS DEPTH OF PITY I FEEL FOR THE IGNORANCE BEFORE ME, ASTONISHING IN ITS STARK FRANKNESS, PREDICTABLE AS THE SUNRISE, EVER-EXPANDING AS THE UNIVERSE ITSELF, AND FORTUNATELY—OH! SO FORTUNATELY!—NEITHER GENETIC NOR CONTAGIOUS
ALL I DID WAS EXPLAIN WHICH PEDAL WAS THE GAS AND WHICH WAS THE BRAKE, JEREMY! DON'T GIVE ME THAT LOOK!
WHAT LOOK?

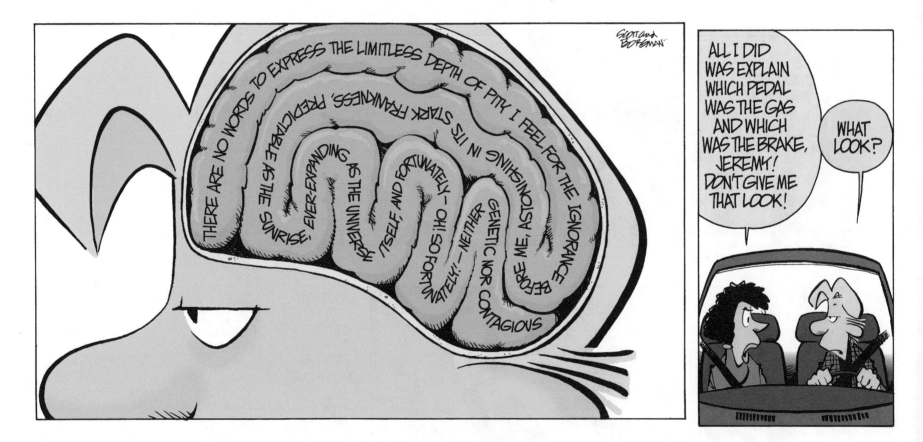

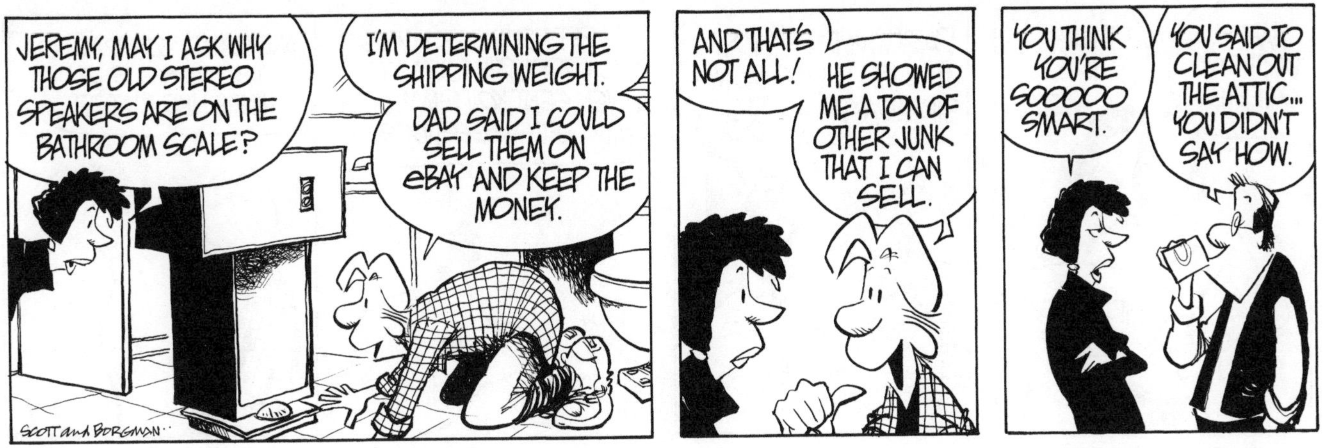
JEREMY, MAY I ASK WHY THOSE OLD STEREO SPEAKERS ARE ON THE BATHROOM SCALE?
I'M DETERMINING THE SHIPPING WEIGHT.
DAD SAID I COULD SELL THEM ON eBAY AND KEEP THE MONEY.
SCOTT and BORGMAN
AND THAT'S NOT ALL!
HE SHOWED ME A TON OF OTHER JUNK THAT I CAN SELL.
YOU THINK YOU'RE SOOOOO SMART.
YOU SAID TO CLEAN OUT THE ATTIC... YOU DIDN'T SAY HOW.

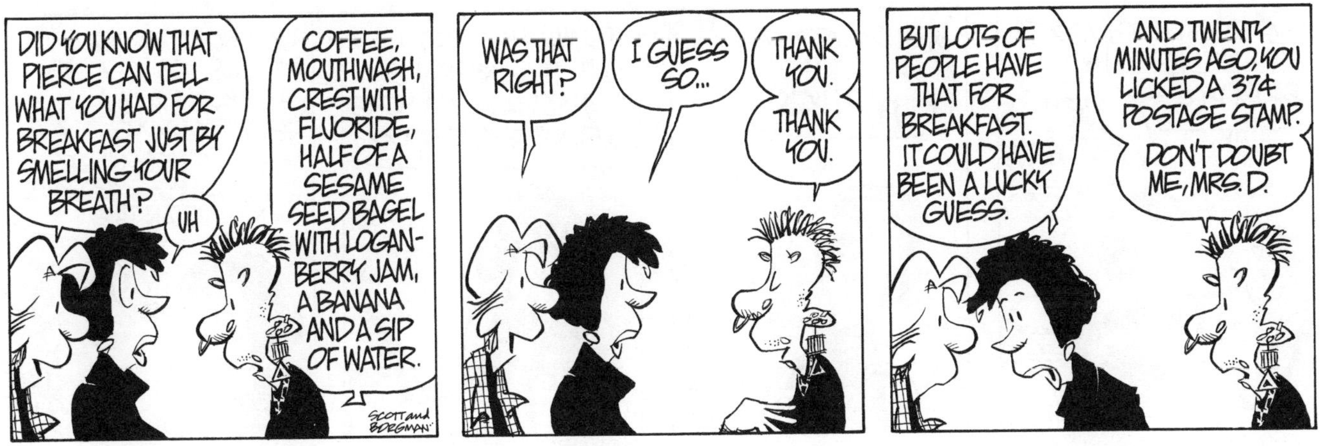
DID YOU KNOW THAT PIERCE CAN TELL WHAT YOU HAD FOR BREAKFAST JUST BY SMELLING YOUR BREATH?
UH
COFFEE, MOUTHWASH, CREST WITH FLUORIDE, HALF OF A SESAME SEED BAGEL WITH LOGAN-BERRY JAM, A BANANA AND A SIP OF WATER.
SCOTT and BORGMAN
WAS THAT RIGHT?
I GUESS SO...
THANK YOU.
THANK YOU.
BUT LOTS OF PEOPLE HAVE THAT FOR BREAKFAST. IT COULD HAVE BEEN A LUCKY GUESS.
AND TWENTY MINUTES AGO, YOU LICKED A 37¢ POSTAGE STAMP.
DON'T DOUBT ME, MRS. D.

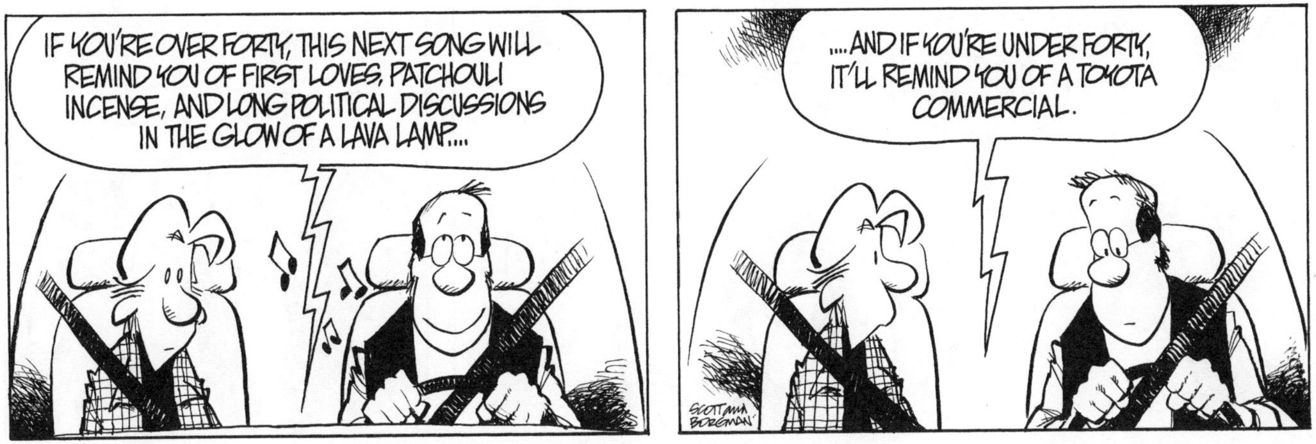
IF YOU'RE OVER FORTY, THIS NEXT SONG WILL REMIND YOU OF FIRST LOVES, PATCHOULI INCENSE, AND LONG POLITICAL DISCUSSIONS IN THE GLOW OF A LAVA LAMP....
....AND IF YOU'RE UNDER FORTY, IT'LL REMIND YOU OF A TOYOTA COMMERCIAL.
SCOTT and BORGMAN

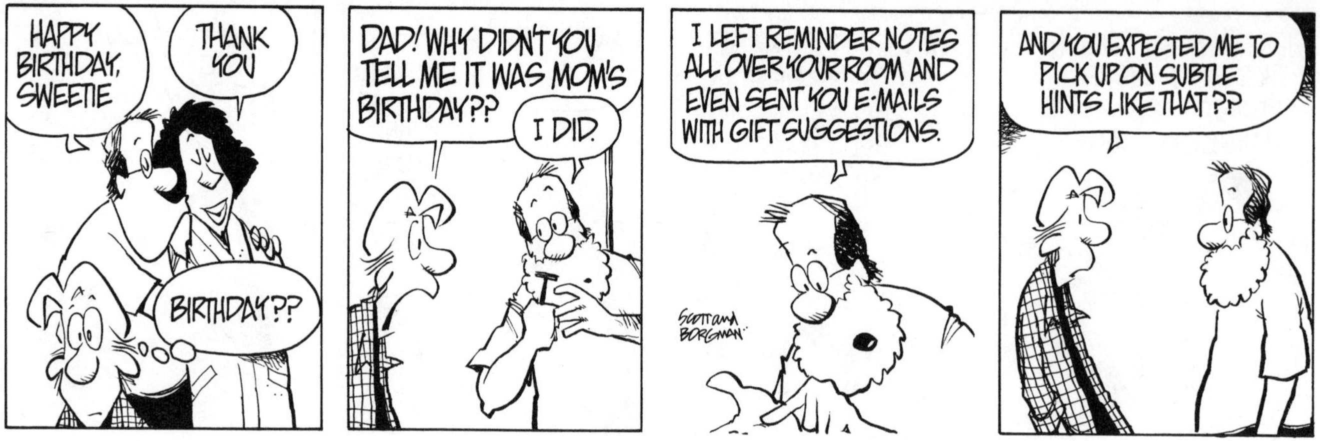
HAPPY BIRTHDAY, SWEETIE
THANK YOU
BIRTHDAY??
DAD! WHY DIDN'T YOU TELL ME IT WAS MOM'S BIRTHDAY??
I DID.
I LEFT REMINDER NOTES ALL OVER YOUR ROOM AND EVEN SENT YOU E-MAILS WITH GIFT SUGGESTIONS.
SCOTT and BORGMAN
AND YOU EXPECTED ME TO PICK UP ON SUBTLE HINTS LIKE THAT??

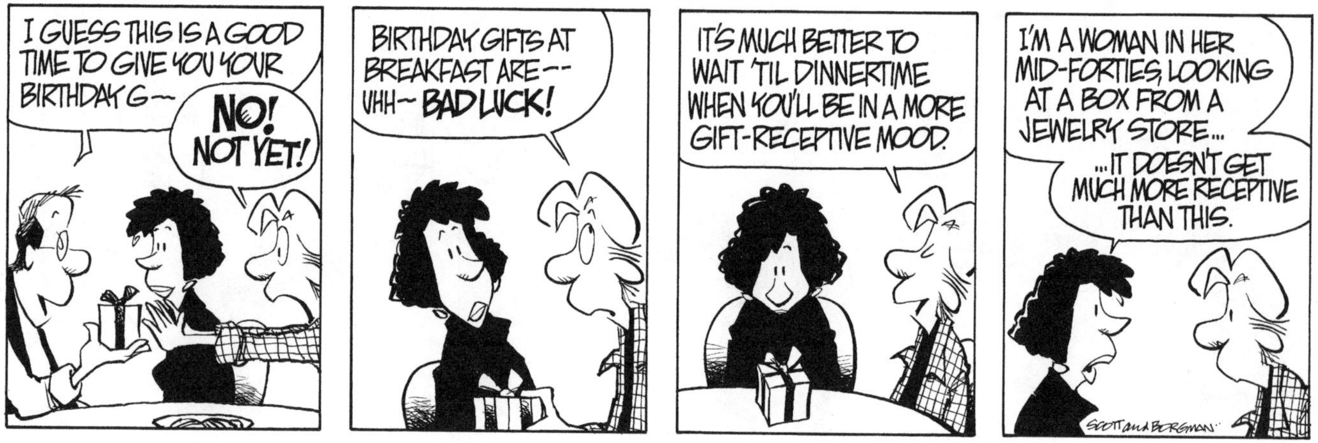
I GUESS THIS IS A GOOD TIME TO GIVE YOU YOUR BIRTHDAY G~
NO! NOT YET!
BIRTHDAY GIFTS AT BREAKFAST ARE-- UHH~ BAD LUCK!
IT'S MUCH BETTER TO WAIT 'TIL DINNERTIME WHEN YOU'LL BE IN A MORE GIFT-RECEPTIVE MOOD.
I'M A WOMAN IN HER MID-FORTIES, LOOKING AT A BOX FROM A JEWELRY STORE...
...IT DOESN'T GET MUCH MORE RECEPTIVE THAN THIS.
SCOTT and BORGMAN

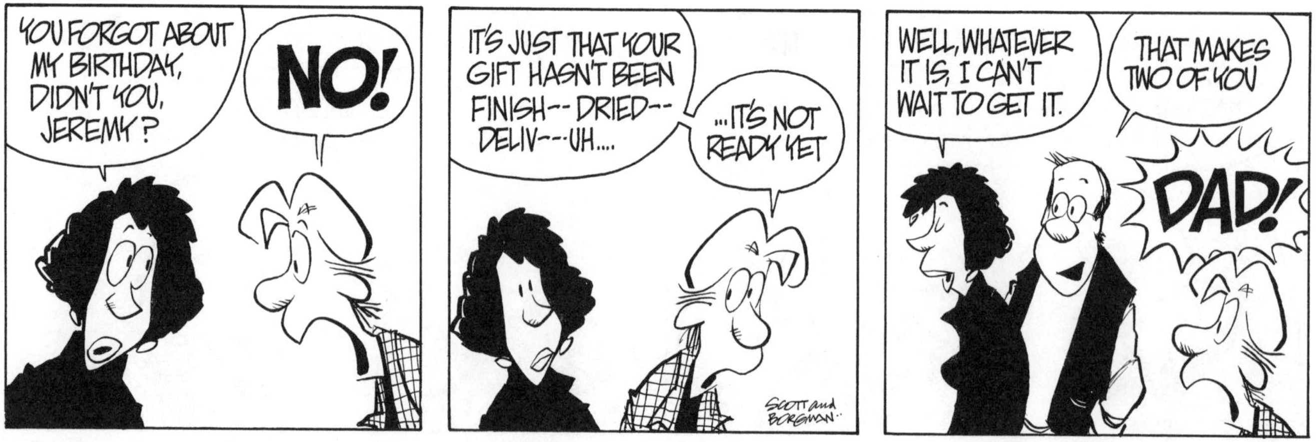
YOU FORGOT ABOUT MY BIRTHDAY, DIDN'T YOU, JEREMY?
NO!
IT'S JUST THAT YOUR GIFT HASN'T BEEN FINISH-- DRIED-- DELIV---UH....
...IT'S NOT READY YET
SCOTT and BORGMAN
WELL, WHATEVER IT IS, I CAN'T WAIT TO GET IT.
THAT MAKES TWO OF YOU
DAD!

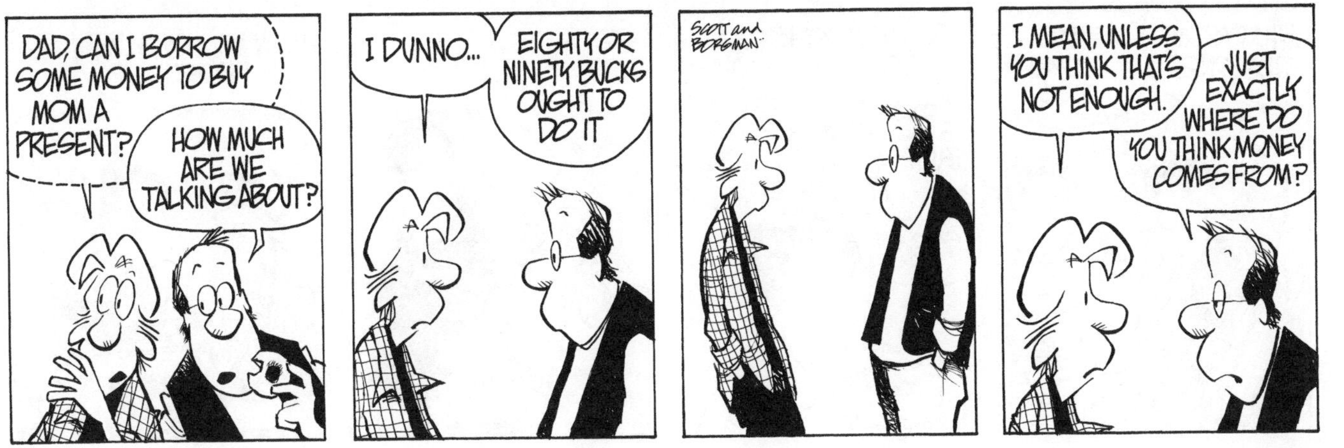
DAD, CAN I BORROW SOME MONEY TO BUY MOM A PRESENT?
HOW MUCH ARE WE TALKING ABOUT?
I DUNNO...
EIGHTY OR NINETY BUCKS OUGHT TO DO IT
SCOTT and BORGMAN
I MEAN, UNLESS YOU THINK THAT'S NOT ENOUGH.
JUST EXACTLY WHERE DO YOU THINK MONEY COMES FROM?

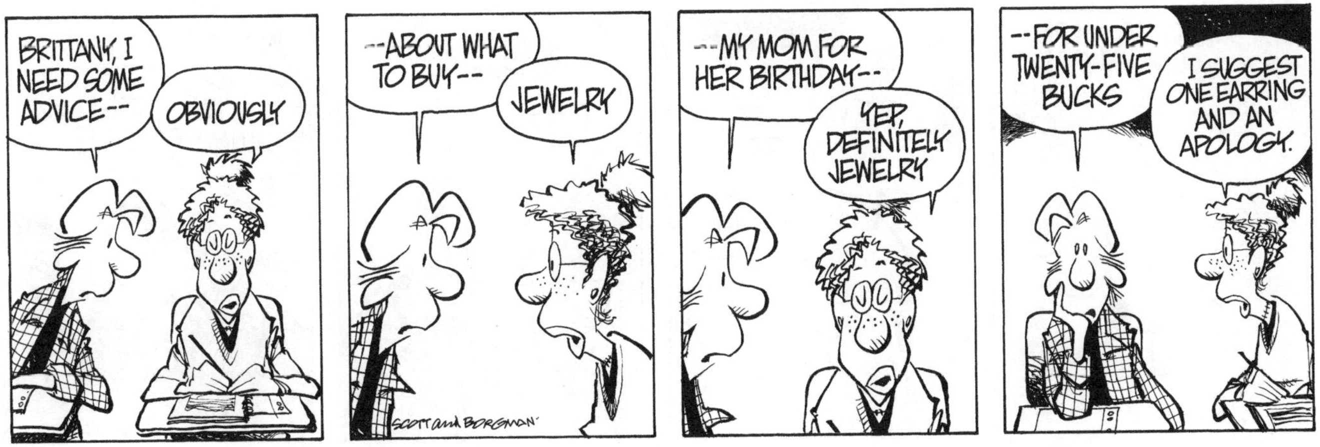
BRITTANY, I NEED SOME ADVICE--
OBVIOUSLY
--ABOUT WHAT TO BUY--
JEWELRY
SCOTT and BORGMAN
--MY MOM FOR HER BIRTHDAY--
YEP, DEFINITELY JEWELRY
--FOR UNDER TWENTY-FIVE BUCKS
I SUGGEST ONE EARRING AND AN APOLOGY.

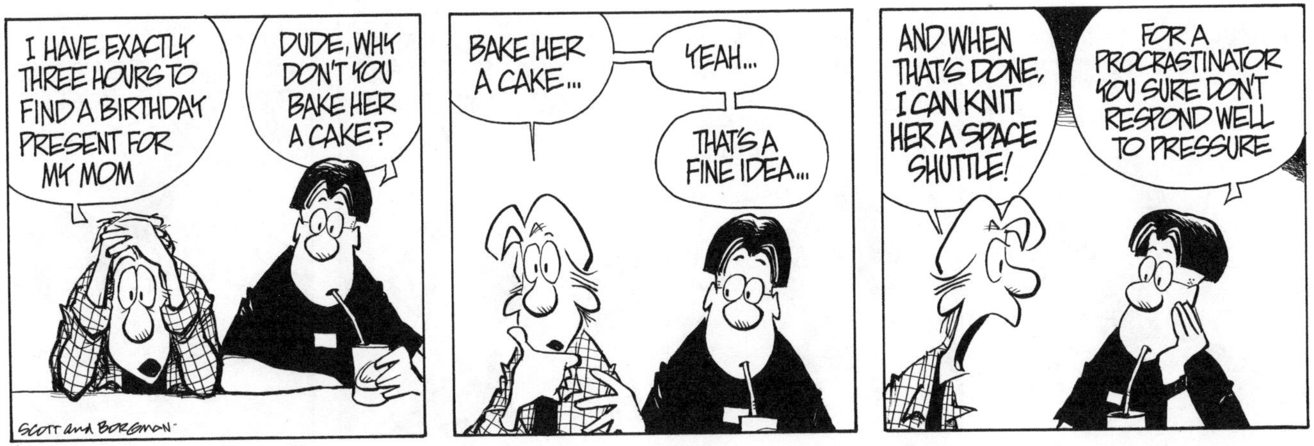
I HAVE EXACTLY THREE HOURS TO FIND A BIRTHDAY PRESENT FOR MY MOM
DUDE, WHY DON'T YOU BAKE HER A CAKE?
SCOTT and BORGMAN
BAKE HER A CAKE...
YEAH...
THAT'S A FINE IDEA...
AND WHEN THAT'S DONE, I CAN KNIT HER A SPACE SHUTTLE!
FOR A PROCRASTINATOR YOU SURE DON'T RESPOND WELL TO PRESSURE

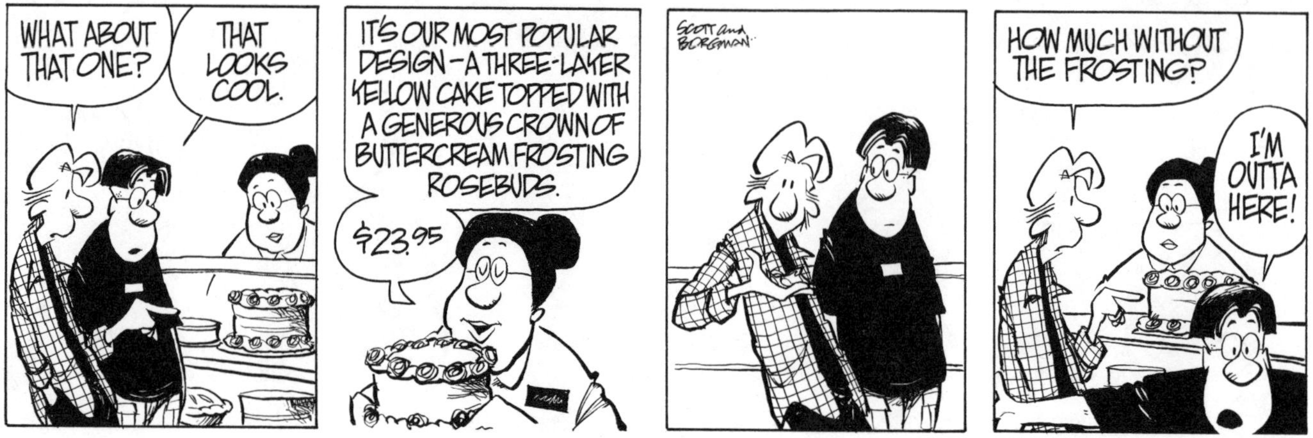

WHAT ABOUT THAT ONE?
THAT LOOKS COOL.
IT'S OUR MOST POPULAR DESIGN–A THREE-LAYER YELLOW CAKE TOPPED WITH A GENEROUS CROWN OF BUTTERCREAM FROSTING ROSEBUDS.
$23.95
SCOTT and BORGMAN
HOW MUCH WITHOUT THE FROSTING?
I'M OUTTA HERE!

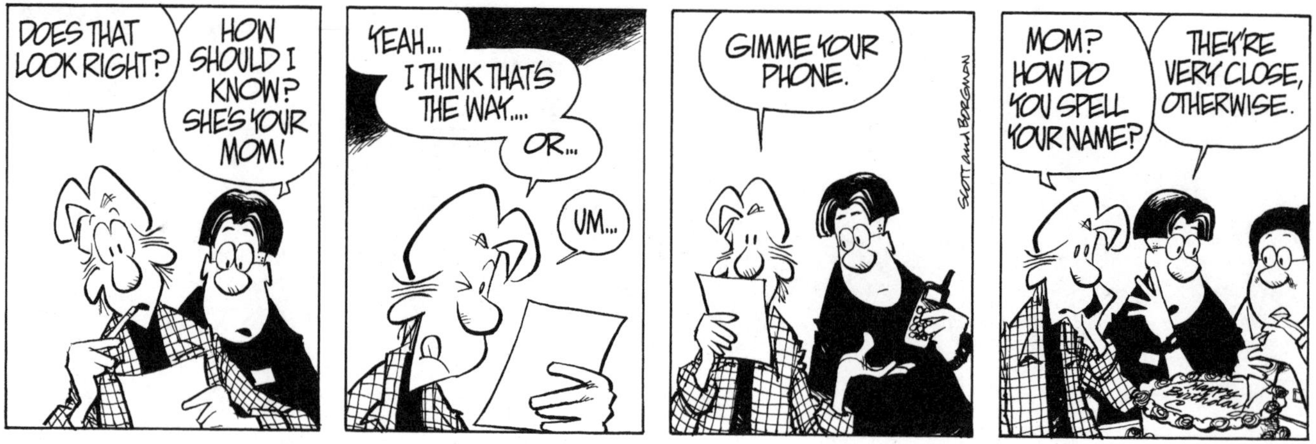

DOES THAT LOOK RIGHT?
HOW SHOULD I KNOW? SHE'S YOUR MOM!
YEAH... I THINK THAT'S THE WAY....
OR...
UM...
GIMME YOUR PHONE.
SCOTT and BORGMAN
MOM? HOW DO YOU SPELL YOUR NAME?
THEY'RE VERY CLOSE, OTHERWISE.

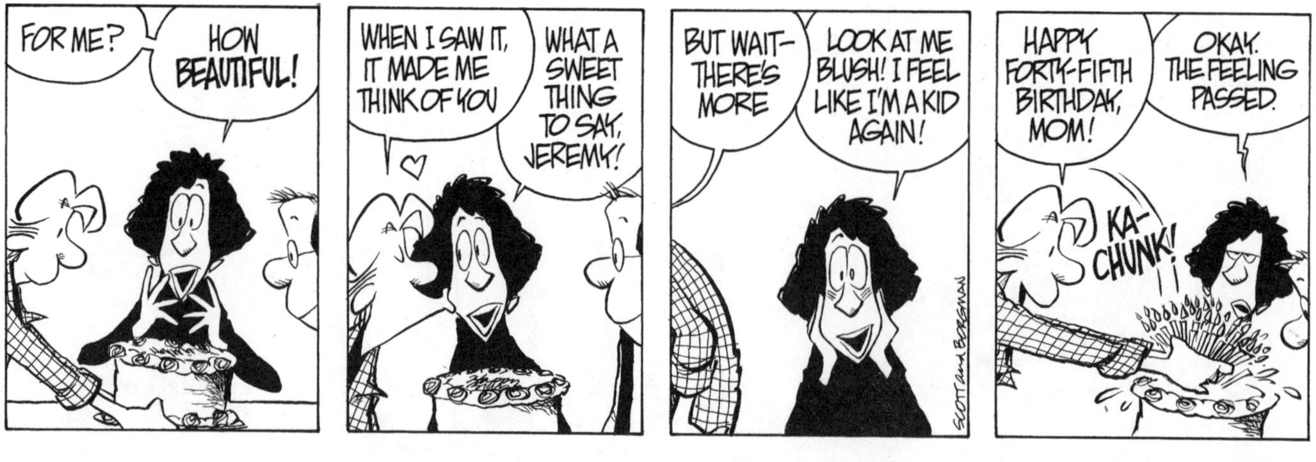

FOR ME?
HOW **BEAUTIFUL!**
WHEN I SAW IT, IT MADE ME THINK OF YOU
WHAT A SWEET THING TO SAY, JEREMY!
BUT WAIT– THERE'S MORE
LOOK AT ME BLUSH! I FEEL LIKE I'M A KID AGAIN!
SCOTT and BORGMAN
HAPPY FORTY-FIFTH BIRTHDAY, MOM!
OKAY. THE FEELING PASSED.
KA-CHUNK!

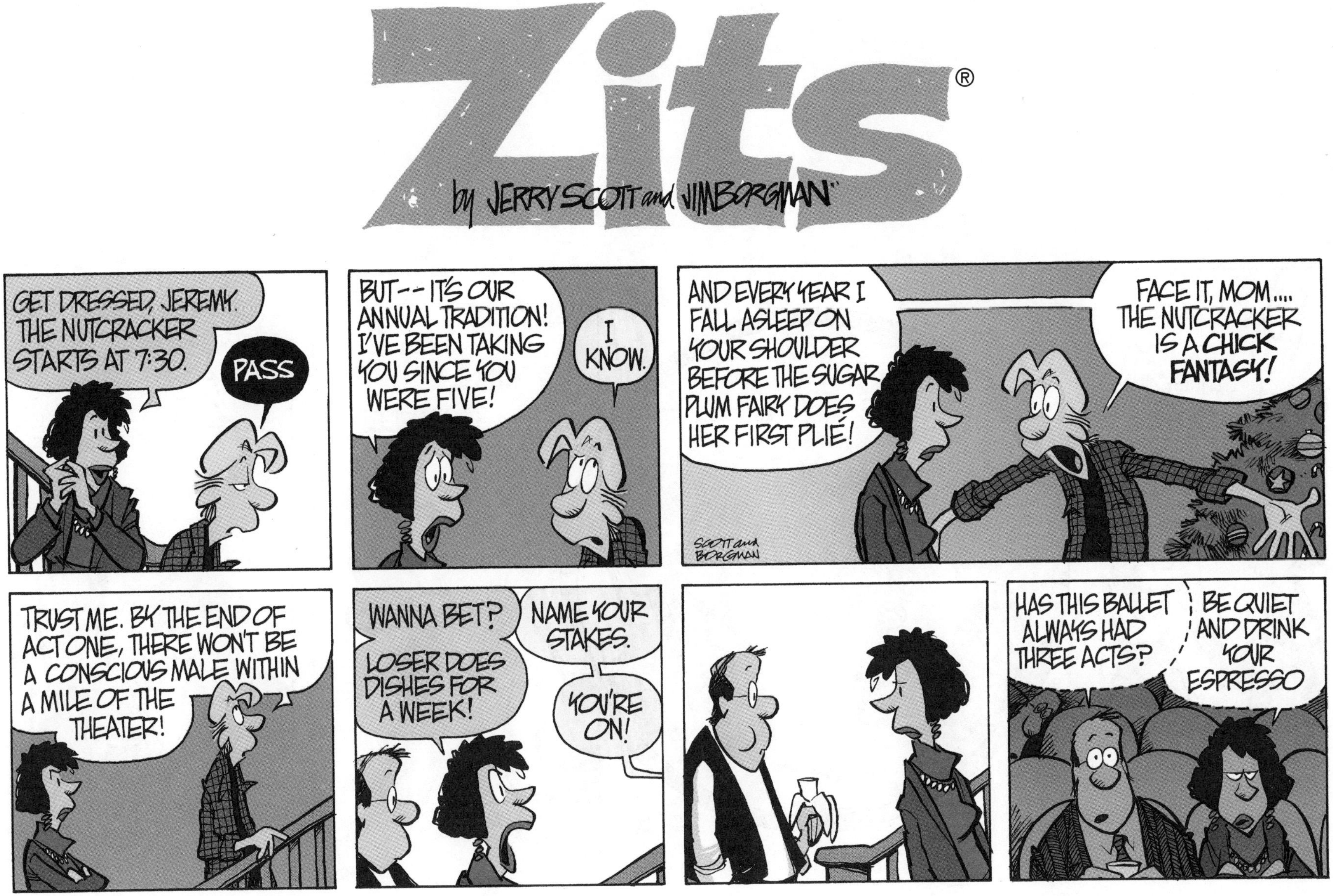
Zits®
by JERRY SCOTT and JIM BORGMAN
GET DRESSED, JEREMY. THE NUTCRACKER STARTS AT 7:30.
PASS
BUT-- IT'S OUR ANNUAL TRADITION! I'VE BEEN TAKING YOU SINCE YOU WERE FIVE!
I KNOW.
AND EVERY YEAR I FALL ASLEEP ON YOUR SHOULDER BEFORE THE SUGAR PLUM FAIRY DOES HER FIRST PLIÉ!
FACE IT, MOM.... THE NUTCRACKER IS A CHICK FANTASY!
SCOTT and BORGMAN
TRUST ME. BY THE END OF ACT ONE, THERE WON'T BE A CONSCIOUS MALE WITHIN A MILE OF THE THEATER!
WANNA BET?
NAME YOUR STAKES.
LOSER DOES DISHES FOR A WEEK!
YOU'RE ON!
HAS THIS BALLET ALWAYS HAD THREE ACTS?
BE QUIET AND DRINK YOUR ESPRESSO

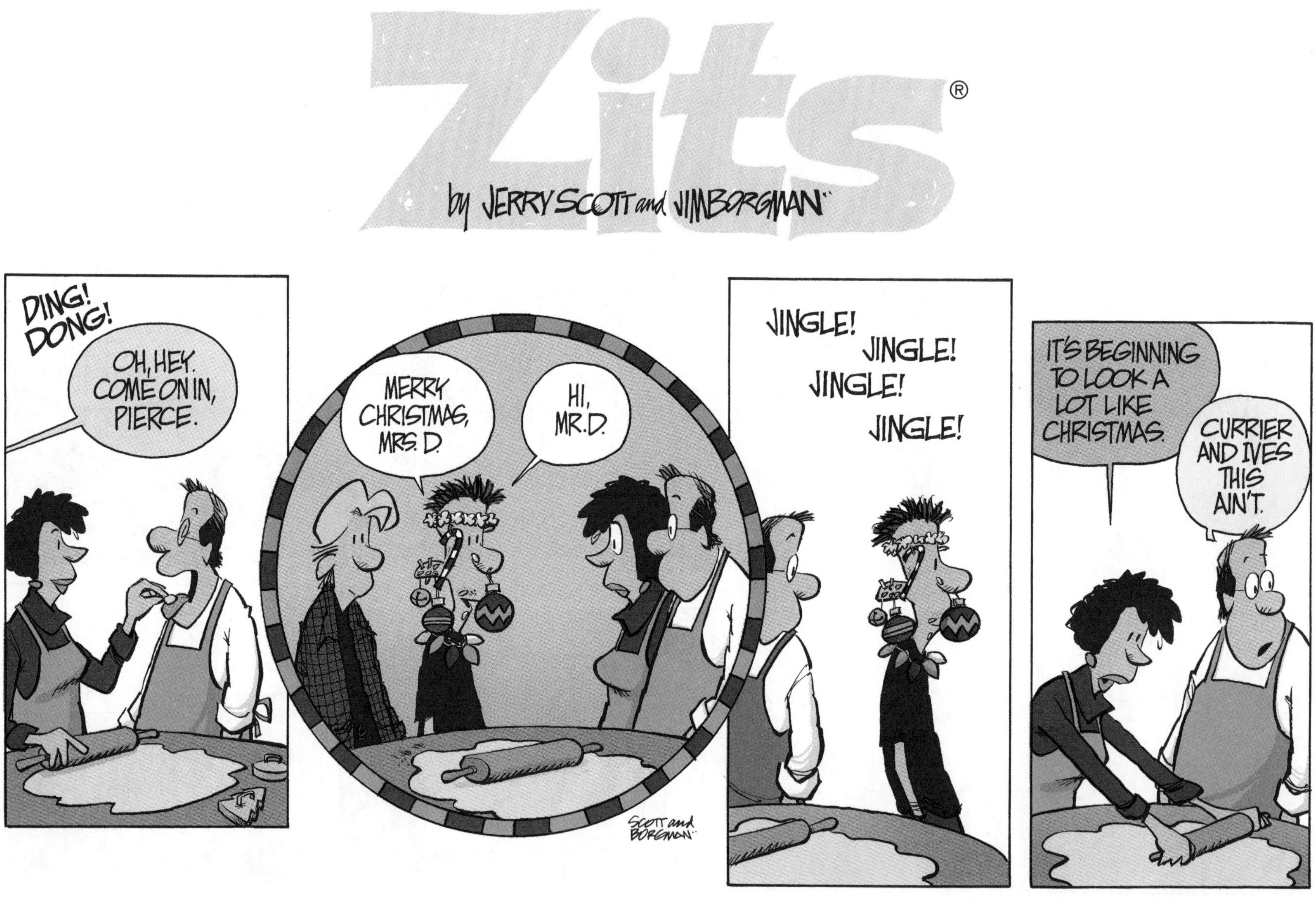
Zits®
by JERRY SCOTT and JIM BORGMAN
DING! DONG!
OH, HEY. COME ON IN, PIERCE.
MERRY CHRISTMAS, MRS. D.
HI, MR. D.
JINGLE! JINGLE! JINGLE! JINGLE!
IT'S BEGINNING TO LOOK A LOT LIKE CHRISTMAS.
CURRIER AND IVES THIS AIN'T.

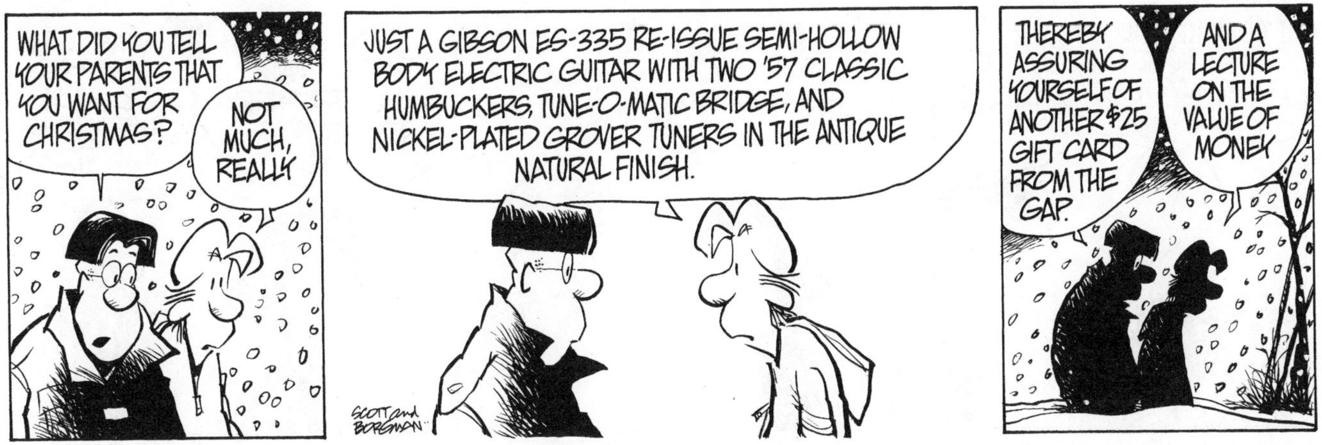
WHAT DID YOU TELL YOUR PARENTS THAT YOU WANT FOR CHRISTMAS?
NOT MUCH, REALLY
JUST A GIBSON ES-335 RE-ISSUE SEMI-HOLLOW BODY ELECTRIC GUITAR WITH TWO '57 CLASSIC HUMBUCKERS, TUNE-O-MATIC BRIDGE, AND NICKEL-PLATED GROVER TUNERS IN THE ANTIQUE NATURAL FINISH.
SCOTT and BORGMAN
THEREBY ASSURING YOURSELF OF ANOTHER $25 GIFT CARD FROM THE GAP.
AND A LECTURE ON THE VALUE OF MONEY

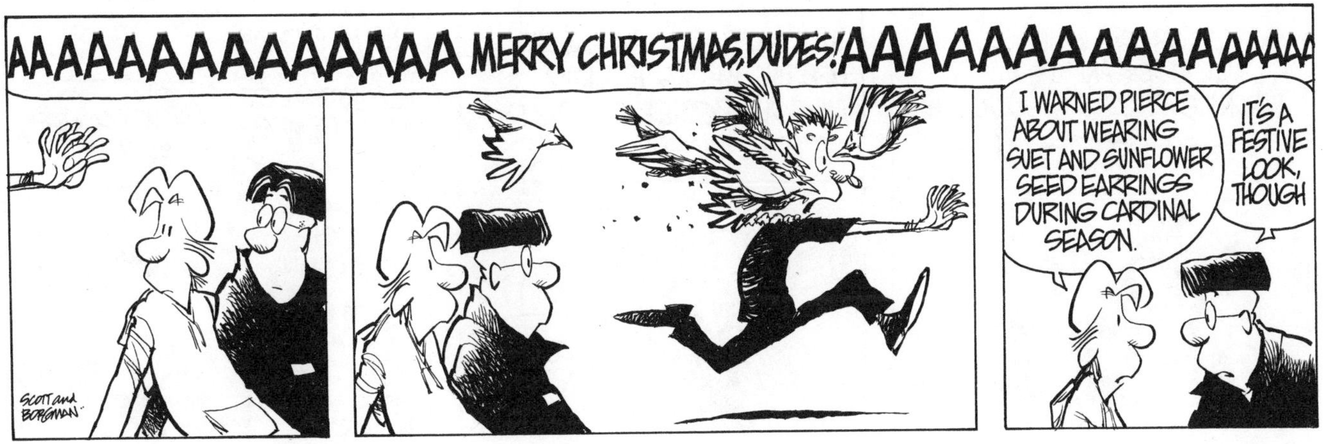
AAAAAAAAAAAAAA MERRY CHRISTMAS, DUDES! AAAAAAAAAAAAAAAA
SCOTT and BORGMAN
I WARNED PIERCE ABOUT WEARING SUET AND SUNFLOWER SEED EARRINGS DURING CARDINAL SEASON.
IT'S A FESTIVE LOOK, THOUGH

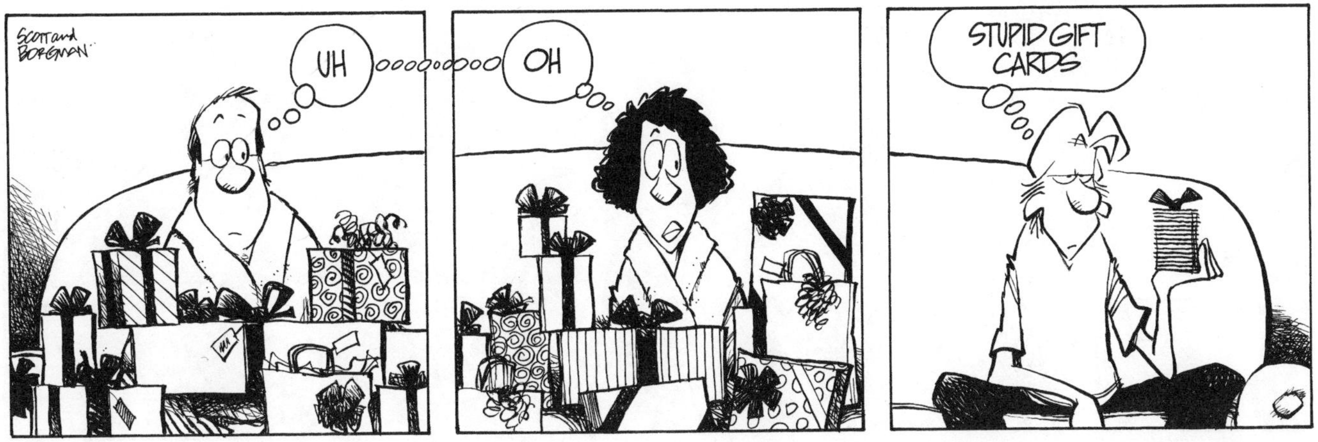
SCOTT and BORGMAN
UH
OH
STUPID GIFT CARDS

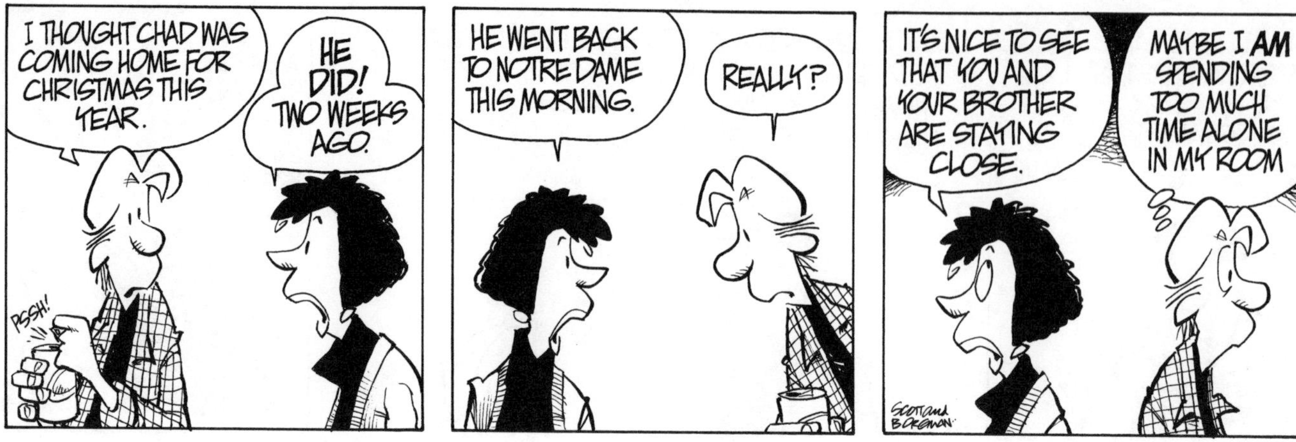
I THOUGHT CHAD WAS COMING HOME FOR CHRISTMAS THIS YEAR.
PSSH!
HE DID! TWO WEEKS AGO.
HE WENT BACK TO NOTRE DAME THIS MORNING.
REALLY?
IT'S NICE TO SEE THAT YOU AND YOUR BROTHER ARE STAYING CLOSE.
MAYBE I AM SPENDING TOO MUCH TIME ALONE IN MY ROOM

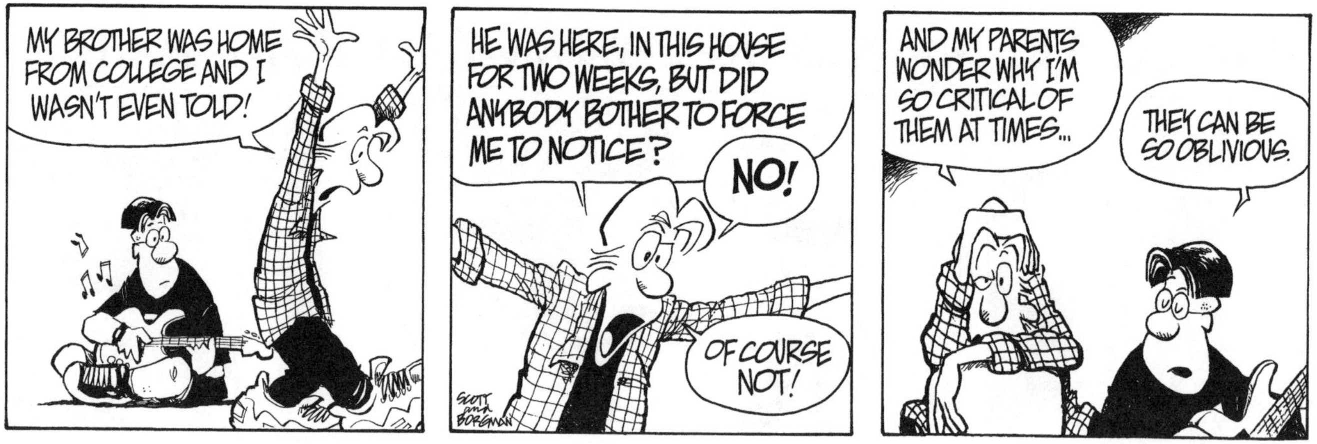
MY BROTHER WAS HOME FROM COLLEGE AND I WASN'T EVEN TOLD!
HE WAS HERE, IN THIS HOUSE FOR TWO WEEKS, BUT DID ANYBODY BOTHER TO FORCE ME TO NOTICE?
NO!
OF COURSE NOT!
AND MY PARENTS WONDER WHY I'M SO CRITICAL OF THEM AT TIMES...
THEY CAN BE SO OBLIVIOUS.

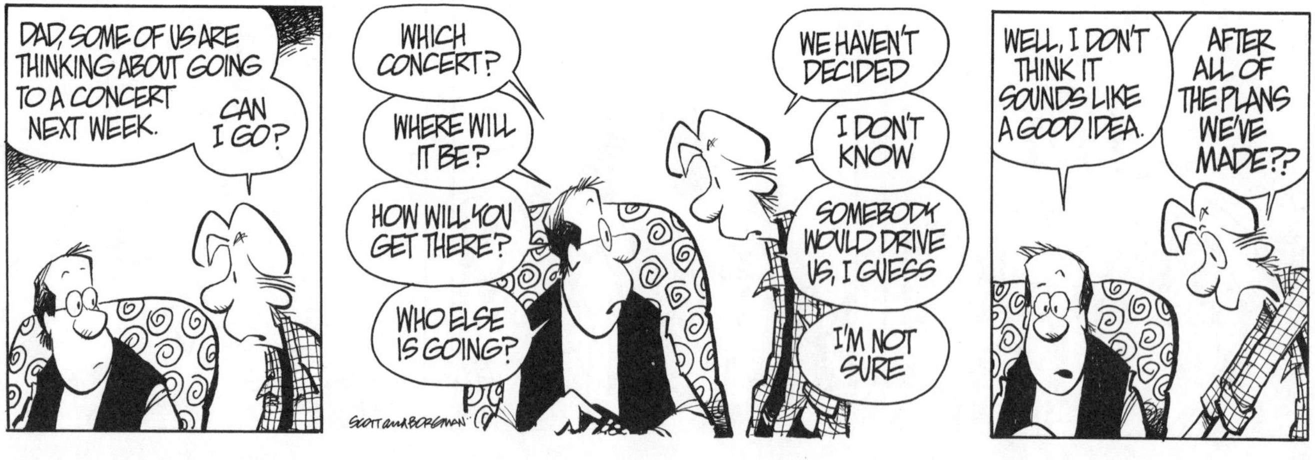
DAD, SOME OF US ARE THINKING ABOUT GOING TO A CONCERT NEXT WEEK.
CAN I GO?
WHICH CONCERT?
WE HAVEN'T DECIDED
WHERE WILL IT BE?
I DON'T KNOW
HOW WILL YOU GET THERE?
SOMEBODY WOULD DRIVE US, I GUESS
WHO ELSE IS GOING?
I'M NOT SURE
WELL, I DON'T THINK IT SOUNDS LIKE A GOOD IDEA.
AFTER ALL OF THE PLANS WE'VE MADE??

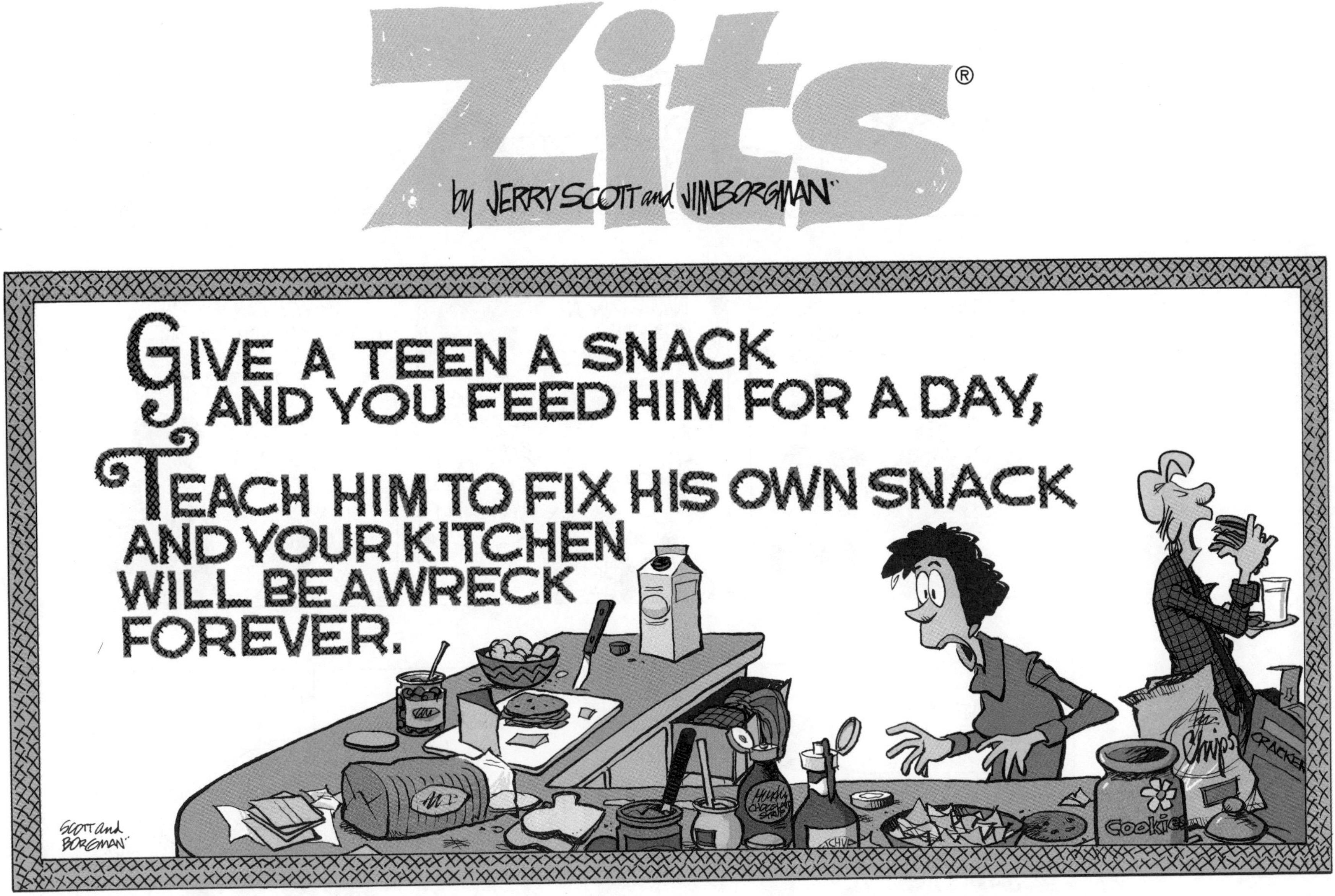
Zits®
by JERRY SCOTT and JIM BORGMAN
GIVE A TEEN A SNACK AND YOU FEED HIM FOR A DAY,
TEACH HIM TO FIX HIS OWN SNACK AND YOUR KITCHEN WILL BE A WRECK FOREVER.
Chips
CRACKERS
Cookies
SCOTT and BORGMAN

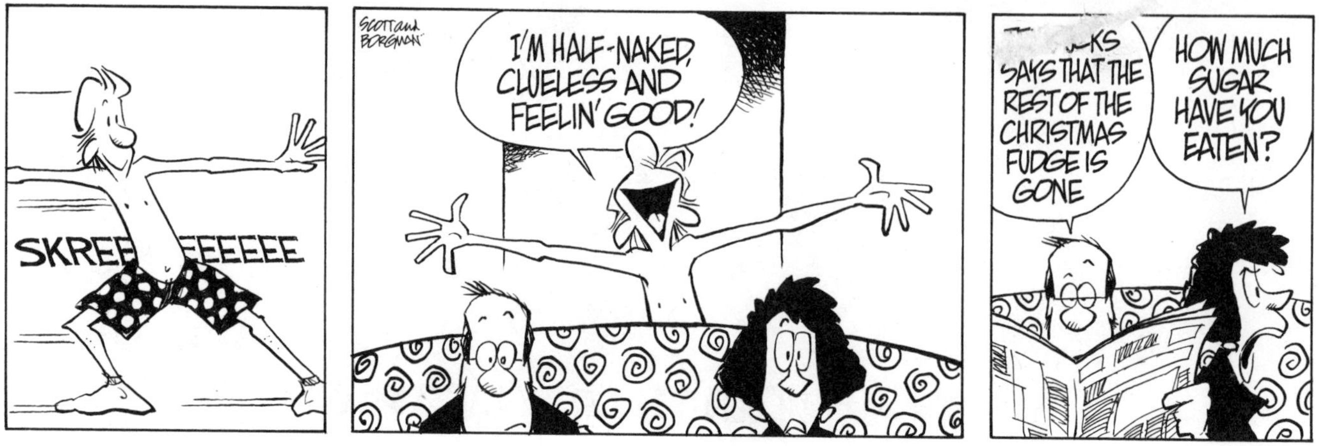
SKREEEEEEEEE
SCOTT and BORGMAN
I'M HALF-NAKED, CLUELESS AND FEELIN' GOOD!
SAYS THAT THE REST OF THE CHRISTMAS FUDGE IS GONE
HOW MUCH SUGAR HAVE YOU EATEN?

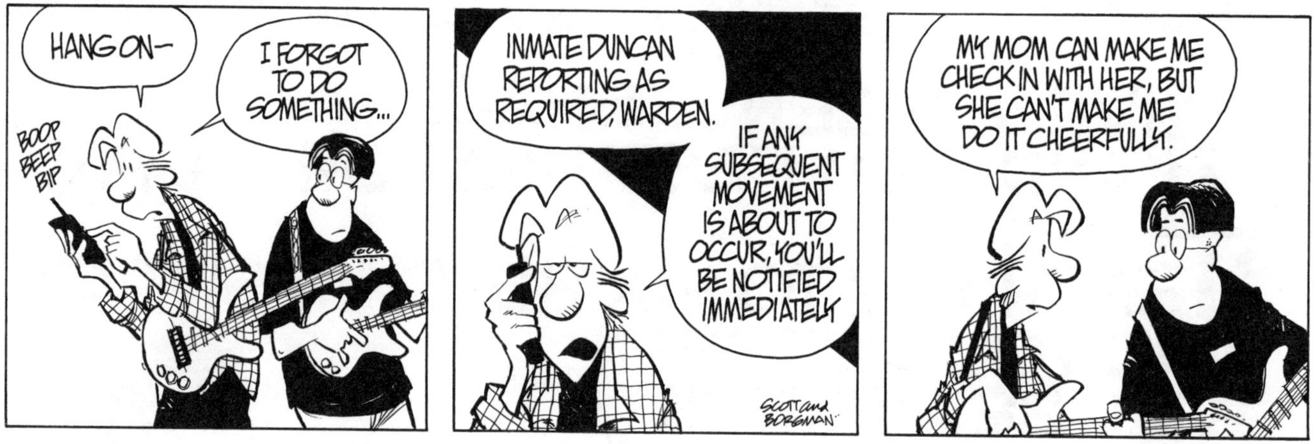
HANG ON-
I FORGOT TO DO SOMETHING...
BOOP BEEP BIP
INMATE DUNCAN REPORTING AS REQUIRED, WARDEN.
IF ANY SUBSEQUENT MOVEMENT IS ABOUT TO OCCUR, YOU'LL BE NOTIFIED IMMEDIATELY.
SCOTT and BORGMAN
MY MOM CAN MAKE ME CHECK IN WITH HER, BUT SHE CAN'T MAKE ME DO IT CHEERFULLY.

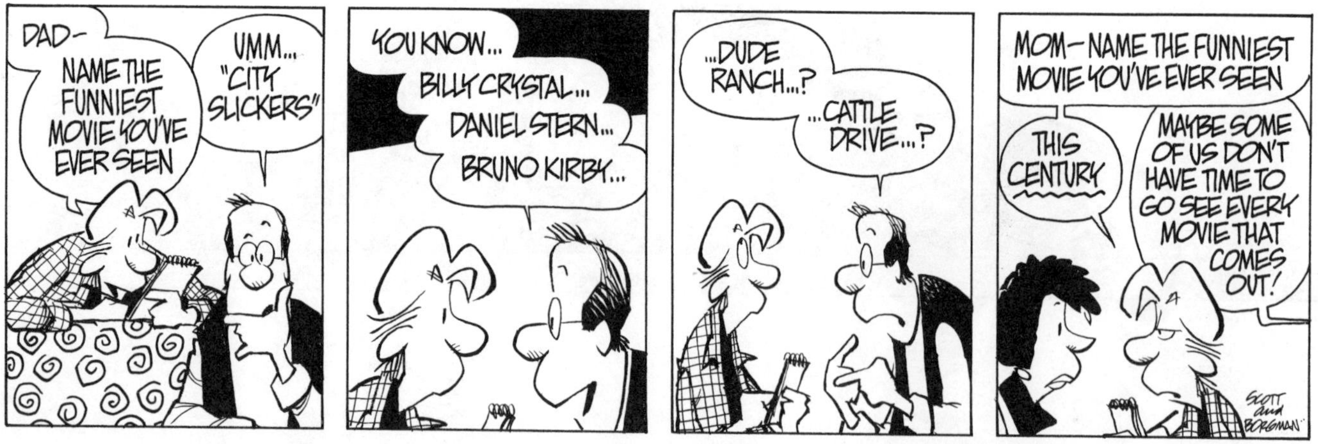
DAD-
NAME THE FUNNIEST MOVIE YOU'VE EVER SEEN
UMM... "CITY SLICKERS"
YOU KNOW...
BILLY CRYSTAL...
DANIEL STERN...
BRUNO KIRBY...
...DUDE RANCH...?
...CATTLE DRIVE...?
MOM– NAME THE FUNNIEST MOVIE YOU'VE EVER SEEN
THIS CENTURY
MAYBE SOME OF US DON'T HAVE TIME TO GO SEE EVERY MOVIE THAT COMES OUT!
SCOTT and BORGMAN

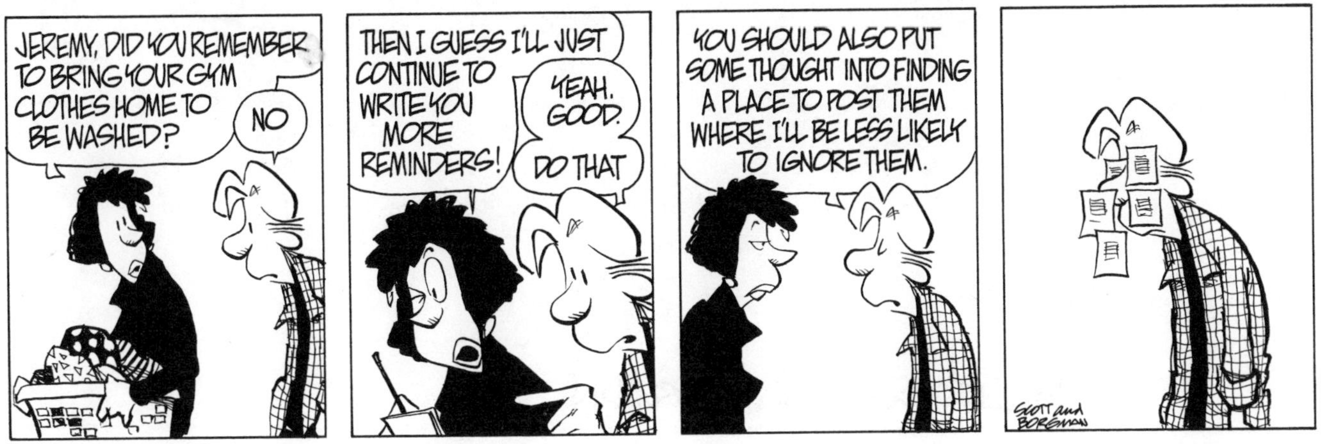
JEREMY, DID YOU REMEMBER TO BRING YOUR GYM CLOTHES HOME TO BE WASHED?
NO
THEN I GUESS I'LL JUST CONTINUE TO WRITE YOU MORE REMINDERS!
YEAH. GOOD.
DO THAT
YOU SHOULD ALSO PUT SOME THOUGHT INTO FINDING A PLACE TO POST THEM WHERE I'LL BE LESS LIKELY TO IGNORE THEM.
SCOTT AND BORGMAN

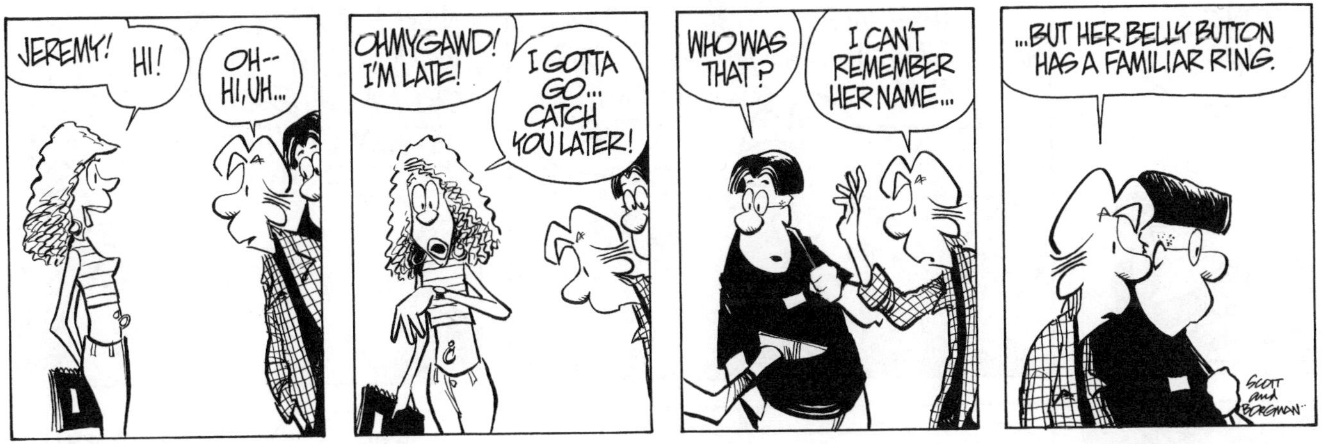
JEREMY!
HI!
OH-- HI, UH...
OHMYGAWD! I'M LATE!
I GOTTA GO... CATCH YOU LATER!
WHO WAS THAT?
I CAN'T REMEMBER HER NAME...
...BUT HER BELLY BUTTON HAS A FAMILIAR RING.
SCOTT AND BORGMAN

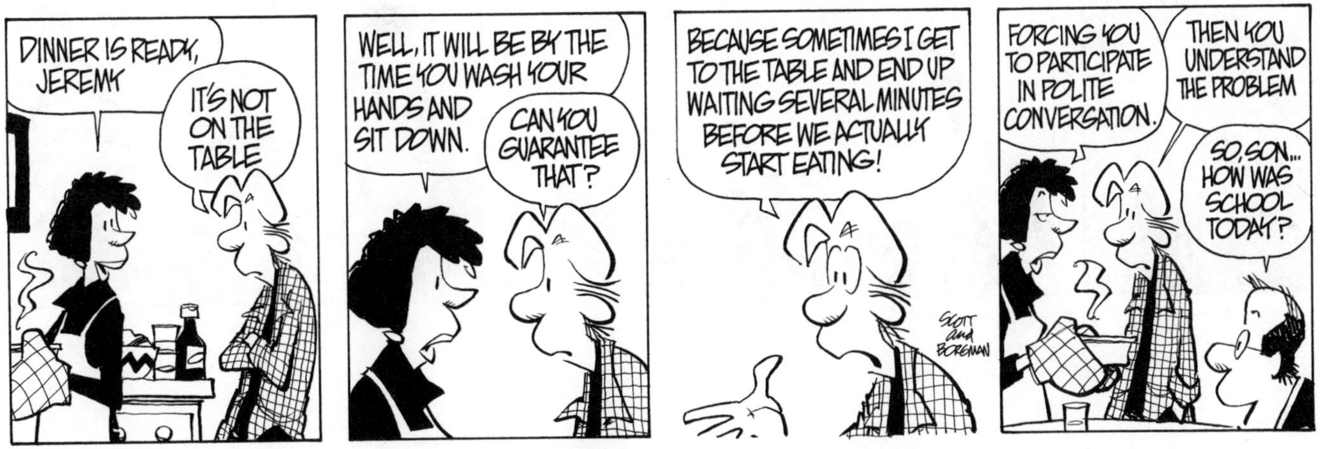
DINNER IS READY, JEREMY
IT'S NOT ON THE TABLE
WELL, IT WILL BE BY THE TIME YOU WASH YOUR HANDS AND SIT DOWN.
CAN YOU GUARANTEE THAT?
BECAUSE SOMETIMES I GET TO THE TABLE AND END UP WAITING SEVERAL MINUTES BEFORE WE ACTUALLY START EATING!
SCOTT AND BORGMAN
FORCING YOU TO PARTICIPATE IN POLITE CONVERSATION.
THEN YOU UNDERSTAND THE PROBLEM
SO, SON... HOW WAS SCHOOL TODAY?

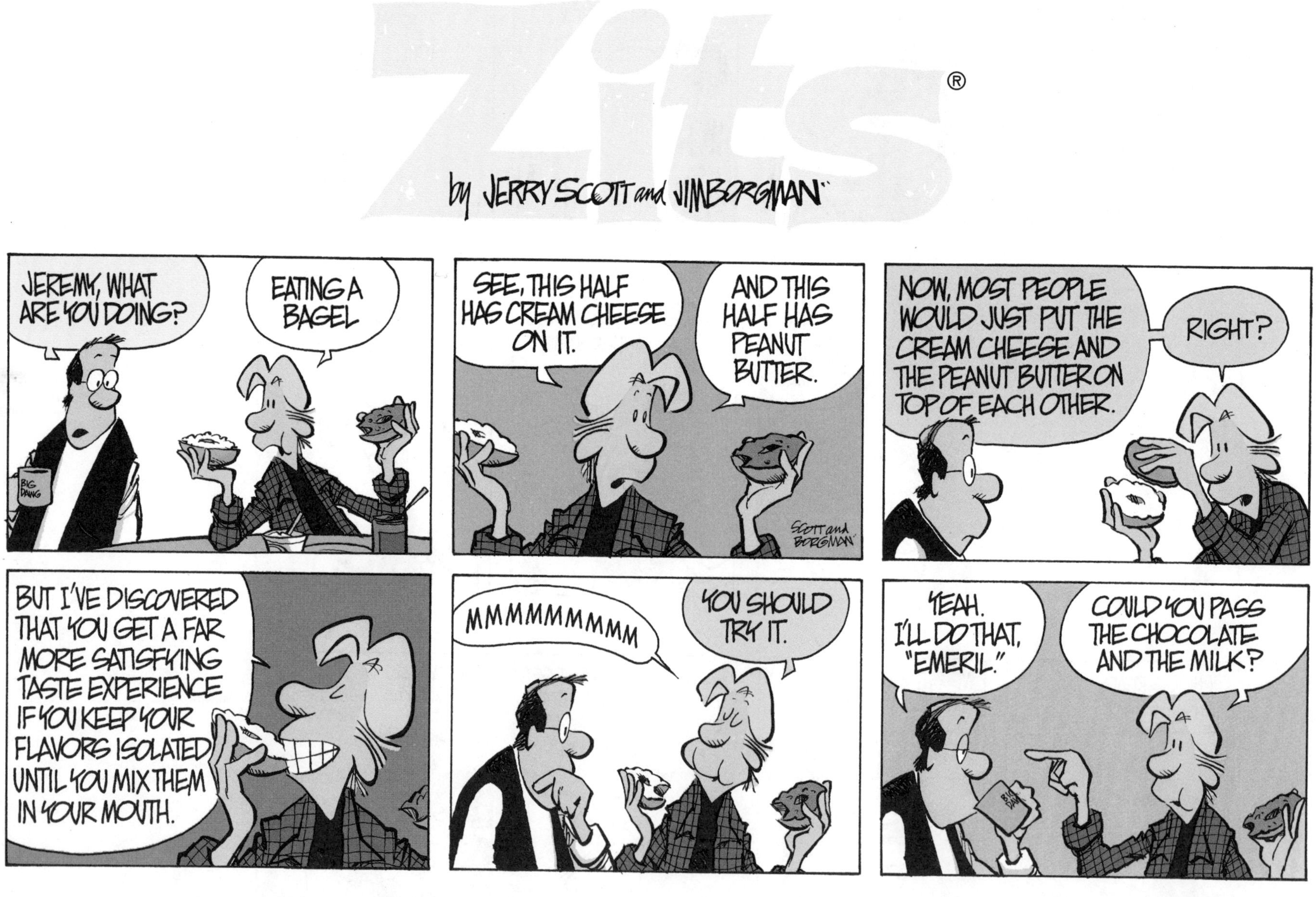
Zits®
by JERRY SCOTT and JIM BORGMAN
JEREMY, WHAT ARE YOU DOING?
EATING A BAGEL
BIG DAWG
SEE, THIS HALF HAS CREAM CHEESE ON IT.
AND THIS HALF HAS PEANUT BUTTER.
SCOTT and BORGMAN
NOW, MOST PEOPLE WOULD JUST PUT THE CREAM CHEESE AND THE PEANUT BUTTER ON TOP OF EACH OTHER.
RIGHT?
BUT I'VE DISCOVERED THAT YOU GET A FAR MORE SATISFYING TASTE EXPERIENCE IF YOU KEEP YOUR FLAVORS ISOLATED UNTIL YOU MIX THEM IN YOUR MOUTH.
MMMMMMMMMM
YOU SHOULD TRY IT.
YEAH. I'LL DO THAT, "EMERIL."
COULD YOU PASS THE CHOCOLATE AND THE MILK?

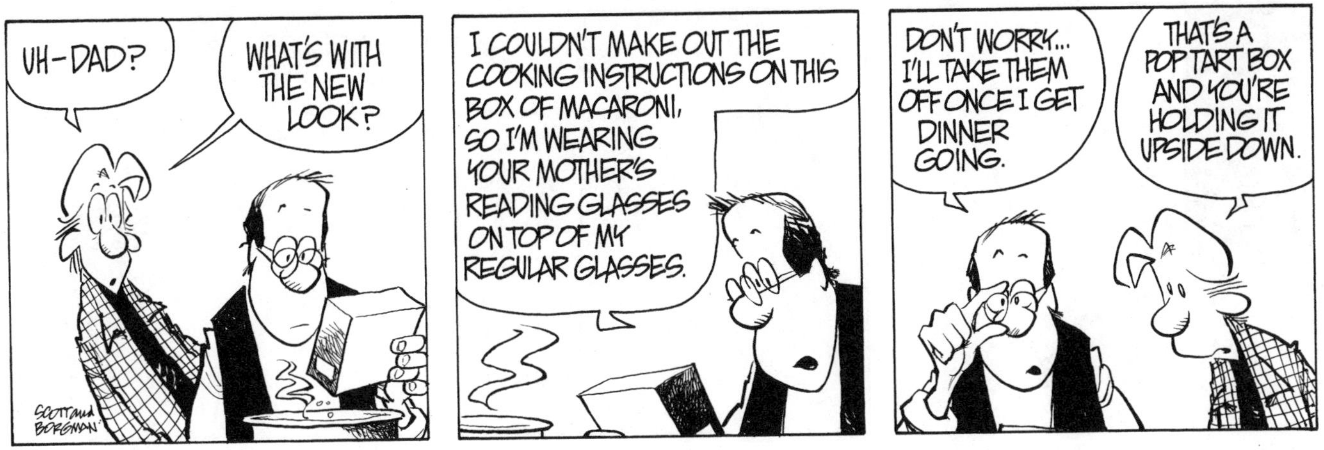
UH-DAD?
WHAT'S WITH THE NEW LOOK?
I COULDN'T MAKE OUT THE COOKING INSTRUCTIONS ON THIS BOX OF MACARONI, SO I'M WEARING YOUR MOTHER'S READING GLASSES ON TOP OF MY REGULAR GLASSES.
DON'T WORRY... I'LL TAKE THEM OFF ONCE I GET DINNER GOING.
THAT'S A POP TART BOX AND YOU'RE HOLDING IT UPSIDE DOWN.
SCOTT AND BORGMAN

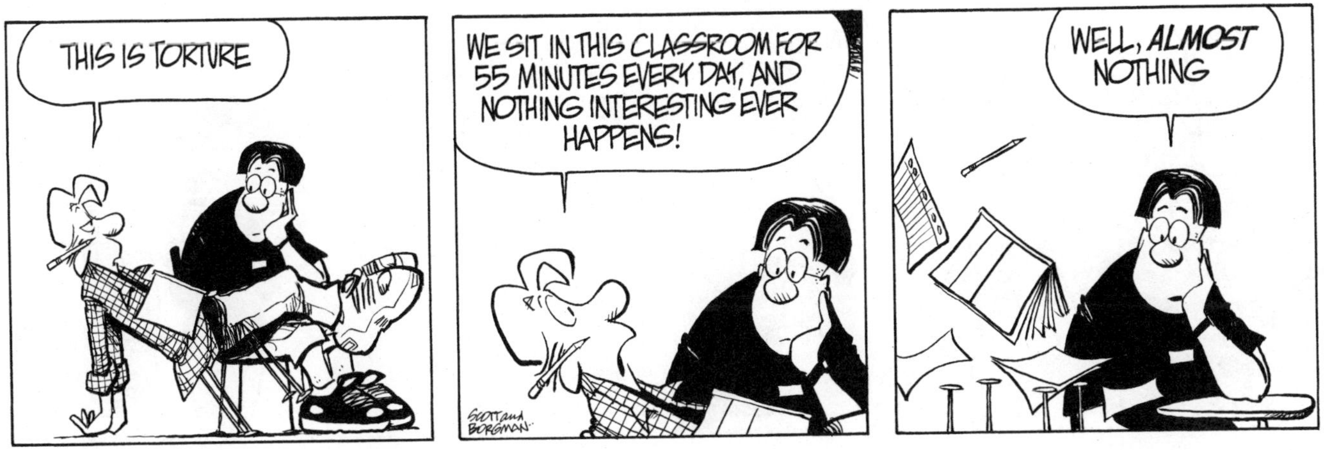
THIS IS TORTURE
WE SIT IN THIS CLASSROOM FOR 55 MINUTES EVERY DAY, AND NOTHING INTERESTING EVER HAPPENS!
WELL, ***ALMOST*** NOTHING
SCOTT AND BORGMAN

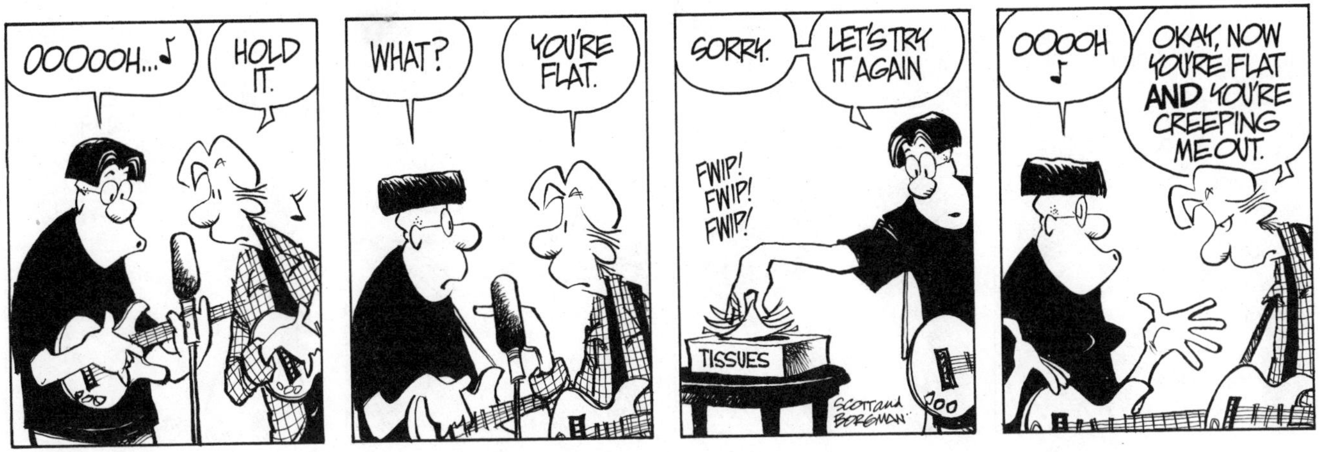
OOOOOH...
HOLD IT.
WHAT?
YOU'RE FLAT.
SORRY.
LET'S TRY IT AGAIN
FWIP! FWIP! FWIP!
TISSUES
OOOOH
OKAY, NOW YOU'RE FLAT **AND** YOU'RE CREEPING ME OUT.
SCOTT AND BORGMAN

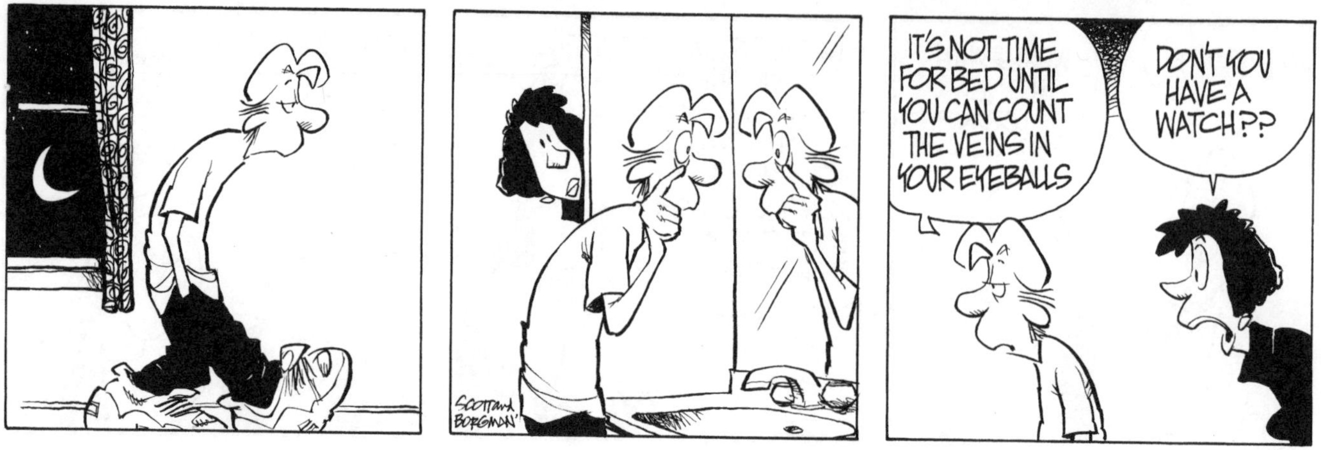
SCOTT and BORGMAN
IT'S NOT TIME FOR BED UNTIL YOU CAN COUNT THE VEINS IN YOUR EYEBALLS
DON'T YOU HAVE A WATCH??

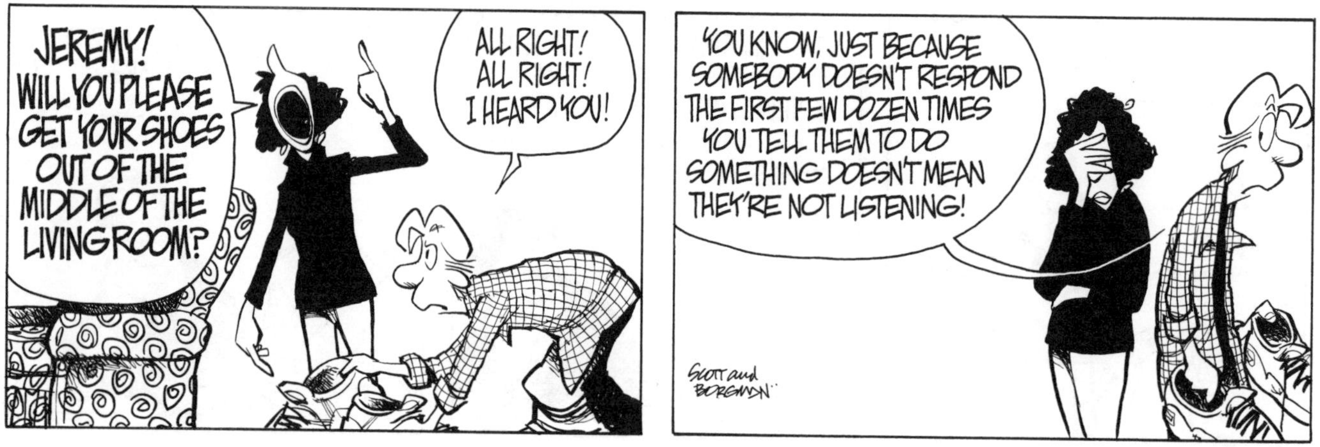
JEREMY! WILL YOU PLEASE GET YOUR SHOES OUT OF THE MIDDLE OF THE LIVING ROOM?
ALL RIGHT! ALL RIGHT! I HEARD YOU!
YOU KNOW, JUST BECAUSE SOMEBODY DOESN'T RESPOND THE FIRST FEW DOZEN TIMES YOU TELL THEM TO DO SOMETHING DOESN'T MEAN THEY'RE NOT LISTENING!
SCOTT and BORGMAN

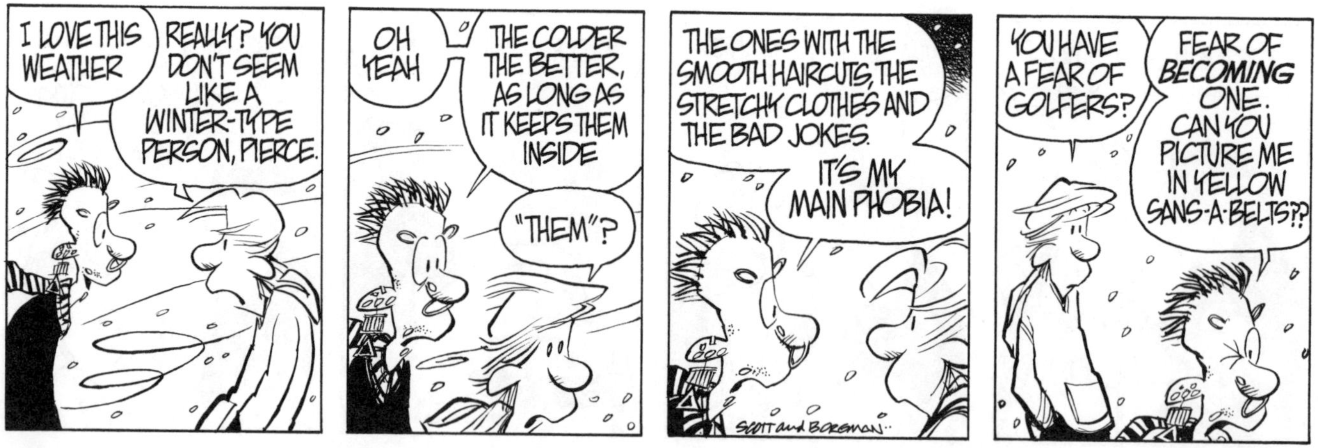
I LOVE THIS WEATHER
REALLY? YOU DON'T SEEM LIKE A WINTER-TYPE PERSON, PIERCE.
OH YEAH
THE COLDER THE BETTER, AS LONG AS IT KEEPS THEM INSIDE
"THEM"?
THE ONES WITH THE SMOOTH HAIRCUTS, THE STRETCHY CLOTHES AND THE BAD JOKES.
IT'S MY MAIN PHOBIA!
SCOTT and BORGMAN
YOU HAVE A FEAR OF GOLFERS?
FEAR OF *BECOMING* ONE. CAN YOU PICTURE ME IN YELLOW SANS-A-BELTS??

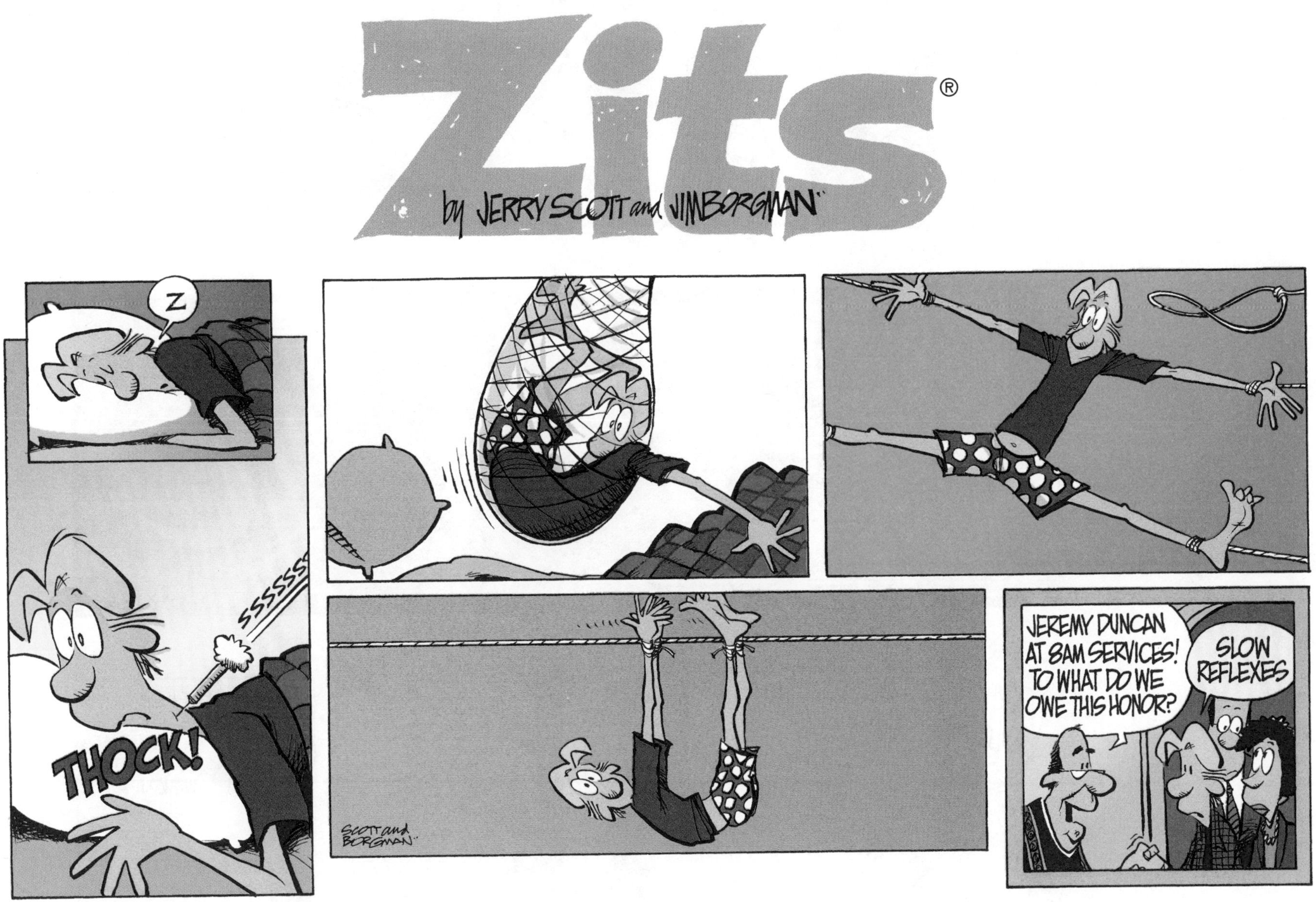
Zits®
by JERRY SCOTT and JIM BORGMAN
Z
SSSSSS
THOCK!
SCOTT and BORGMAN
JEREMY DUNCAN AT 8AM SERVICES! TO WHAT DO WE OWE THIS HONOR?
SLOW REFLEXES

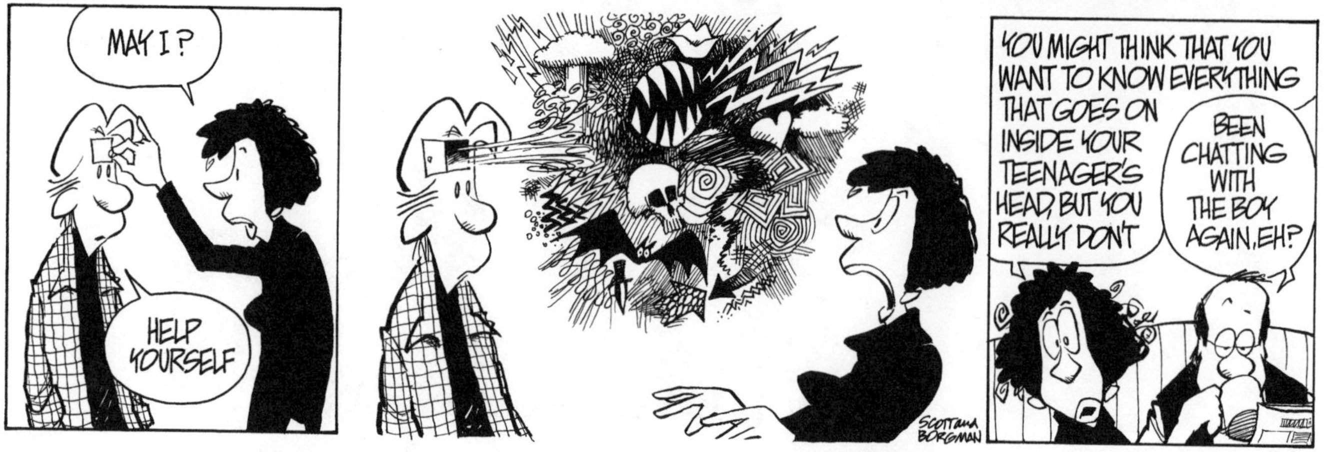
MAY I?
HELP YOURSELF
YOU MIGHT THINK THAT YOU WANT TO KNOW EVERYTHING THAT GOES ON INSIDE YOUR TEENAGER'S HEAD, BUT YOU REALLY DON'T
BEEN CHATTING WITH THE BOY AGAIN, EH?
SCOTT AND BORGMAN

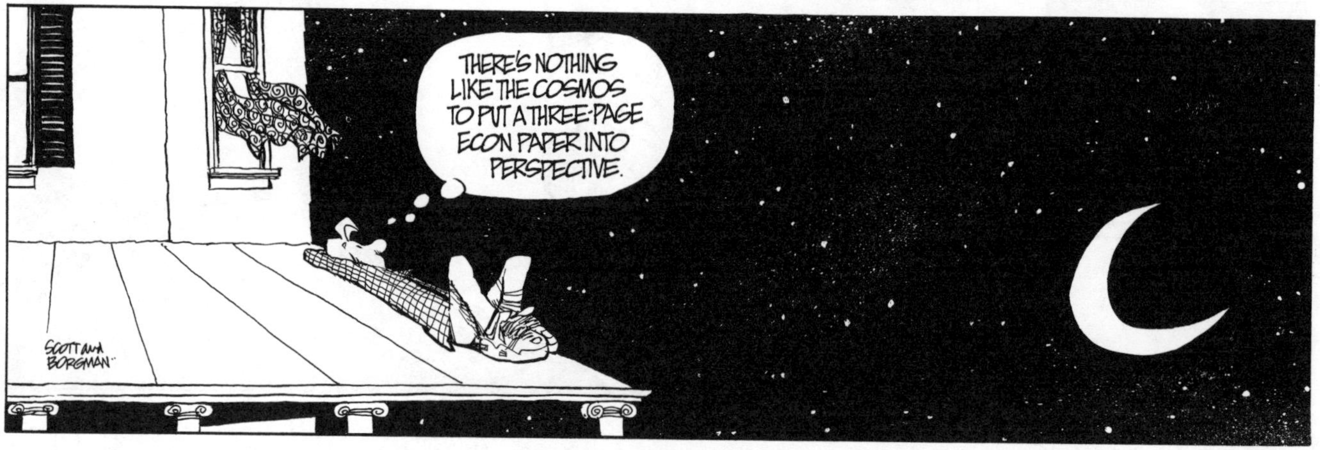
THERE'S NOTHING LIKE THE COSMOS TO PUT A THREE-PAGE ECON PAPER INTO PERSPECTIVE.
SCOTT AND BORGMAN

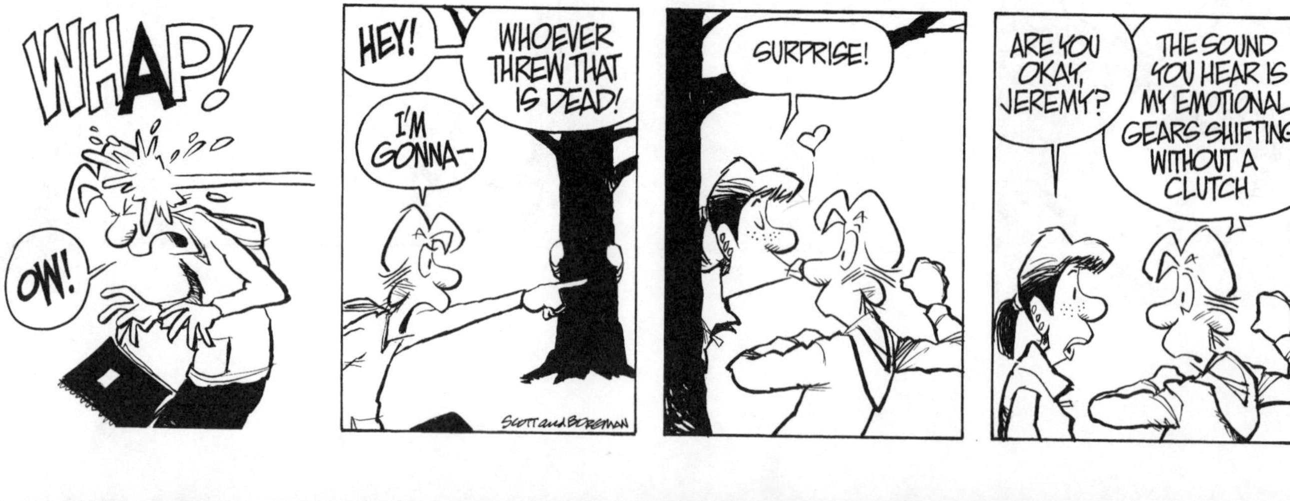
WHAP!
OW!
HEY!
WHOEVER THREW THAT IS DEAD!
I'M GONNA-
SCOTT AND BORGMAN
SURPRISE!
ARE YOU OKAY, JEREMY?
THE SOUND YOU HEAR IS MY EMOTIONAL GEARS SHIFTING WITHOUT A CLUTCH

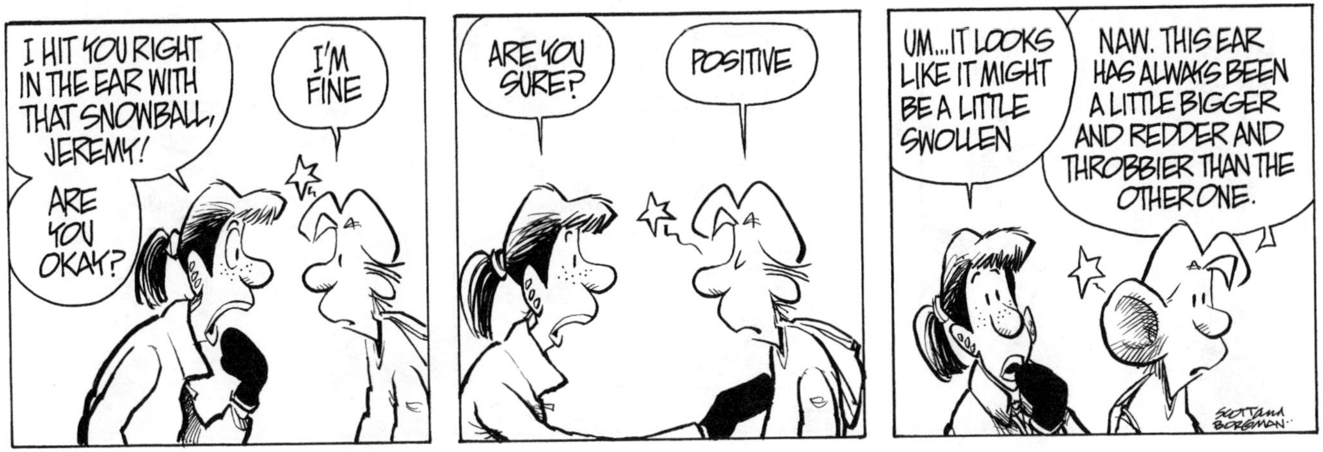
I HIT YOU RIGHT IN THE EAR WITH THAT SNOWBALL, JEREMY!
ARE YOU OKAY?
I'M FINE
ARE YOU SURE?
POSITIVE
UM...IT LOOKS LIKE IT MIGHT BE A LITTLE SWOLLEN
NAW. THIS EAR HAS ALWAYS BEEN A LITTLE BIGGER AND REDDER AND THROBBIER THAN THE OTHER ONE.

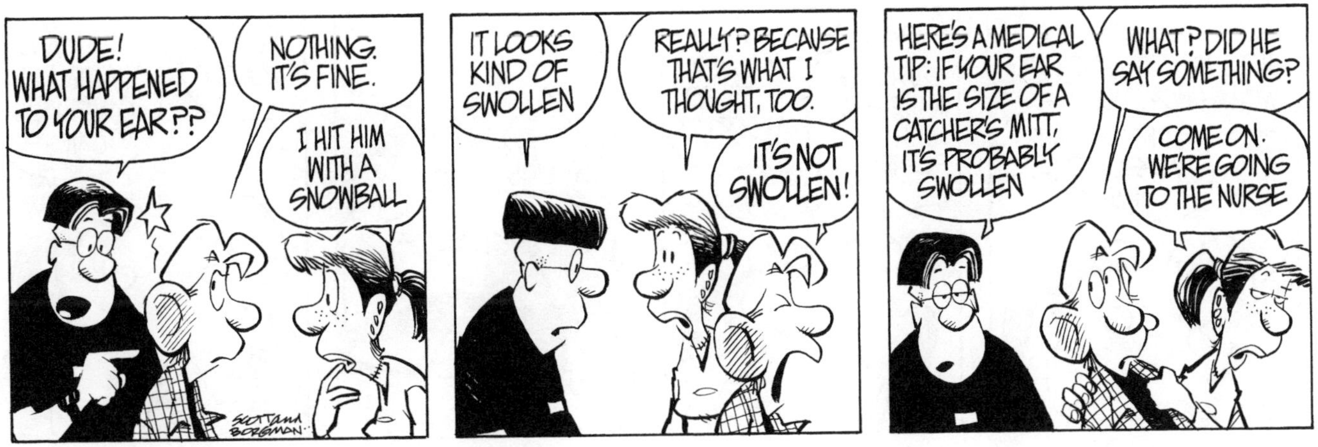
DUDE! WHAT HAPPENED TO YOUR EAR??
NOTHING. IT'S FINE.
I HIT HIM WITH A SNOWBALL
IT LOOKS KIND OF SWOLLEN
REALLY? BECAUSE THAT'S WHAT I THOUGHT, TOO.
IT'S NOT SWOLLEN!
HERE'S A MEDICAL TIP: IF YOUR EAR IS THE SIZE OF A CATCHER'S MITT, IT'S PROBABLY SWOLLEN
WHAT? DID HE SAY SOMETHING?
COME ON. WE'RE GOING TO THE NURSE

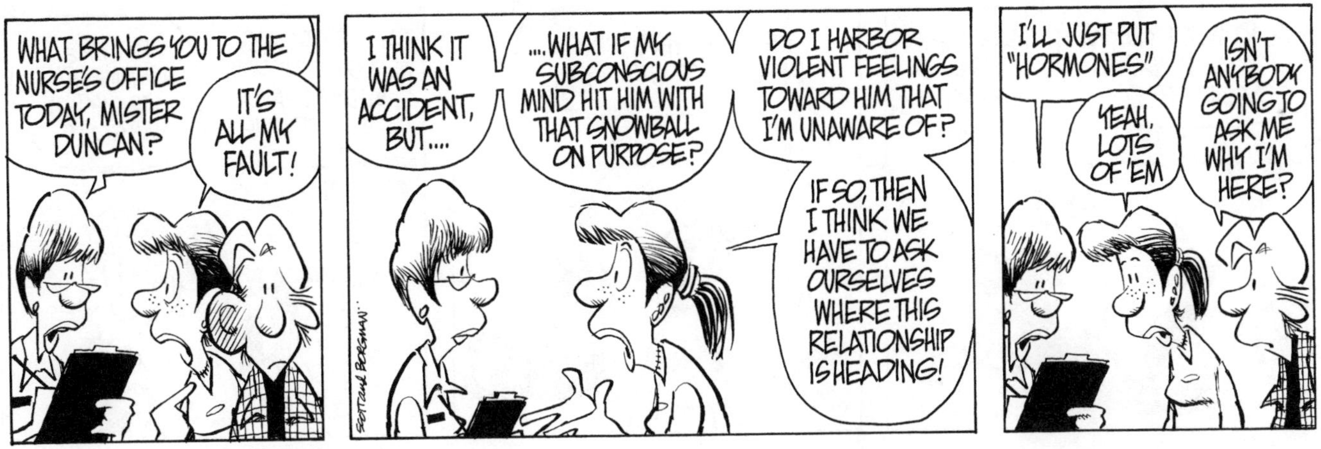
WHAT BRINGS YOU TO THE NURSE'S OFFICE TODAY, MISTER DUNCAN?
IT'S ALL MY FAULT!
I THINK IT WAS AN ACCIDENT, BUT....
....WHAT IF MY SUBCONSCIOUS MIND HIT HIM WITH THAT SNOWBALL ON PURPOSE?
DO I HARBOR VIOLENT FEELINGS TOWARD HIM THAT I'M UNAWARE OF?
IF SO, THEN I THINK WE HAVE TO ASK OURSELVES WHERE THIS RELATIONSHIP IS HEADING!
I'LL JUST PUT "HORMONES"
YEAH, LOTS OF 'EM
ISN'T ANYBODY GOING TO ASK ME WHY I'M HERE?

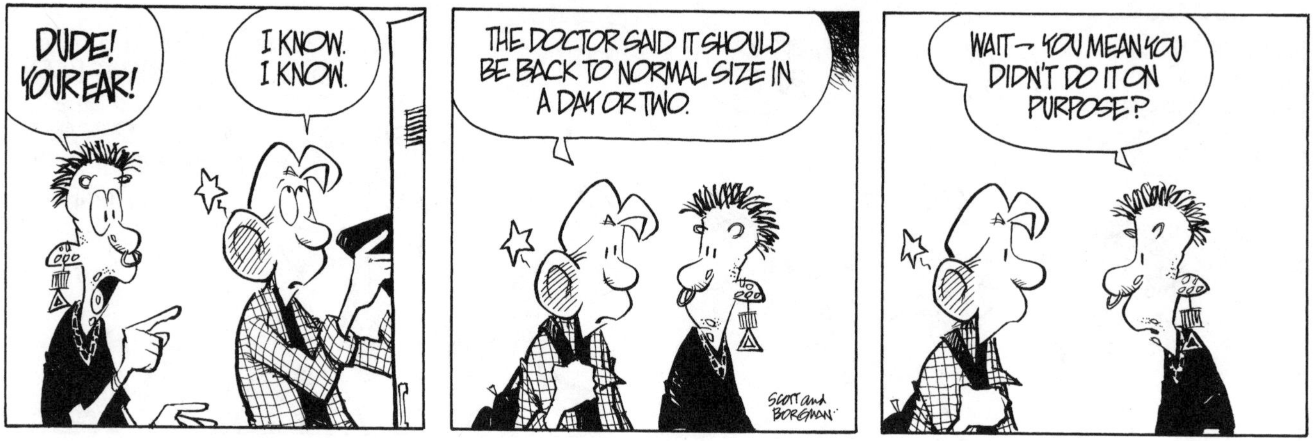
DUDE! YOUR EAR!
I KNOW. I KNOW.
THE DOCTOR SAID IT SHOULD BE BACK TO NORMAL SIZE IN A DAY OR TWO.
SCOTT and BORGMAN
WAIT – YOU MEAN YOU DIDN'T DO IT ON PURPOSE?

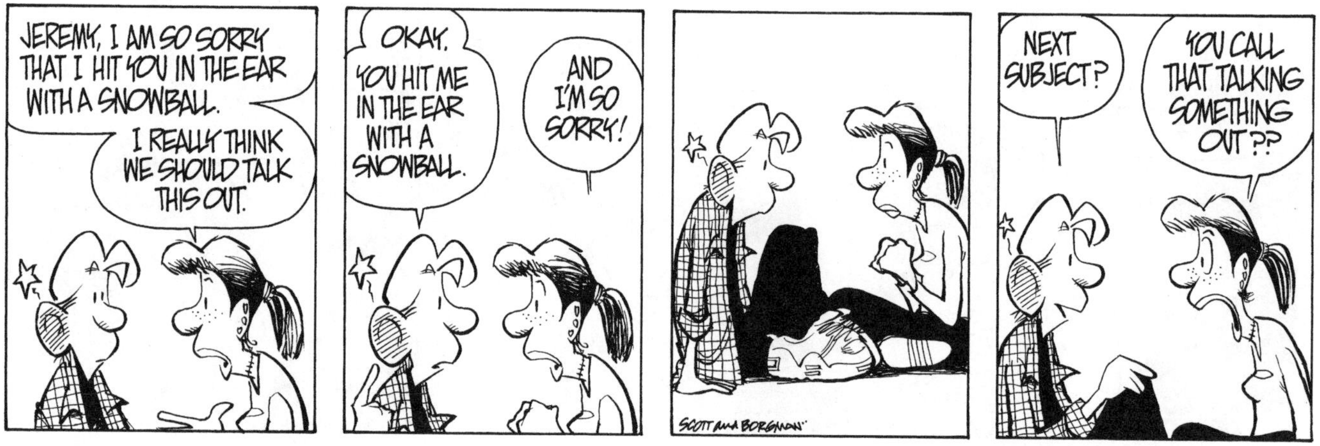
JEREMY, I AM SO SORRY THAT I HIT YOU IN THE EAR WITH A SNOWBALL.
I REALLY THINK WE SHOULD TALK THIS OUT.
OKAY.
YOU HIT ME IN THE EAR WITH A SNOWBALL.
AND I'M SO SORRY!
SCOTT and BORGMAN
NEXT SUBJECT?
YOU CALL THAT TALKING SOMETHING OUT??

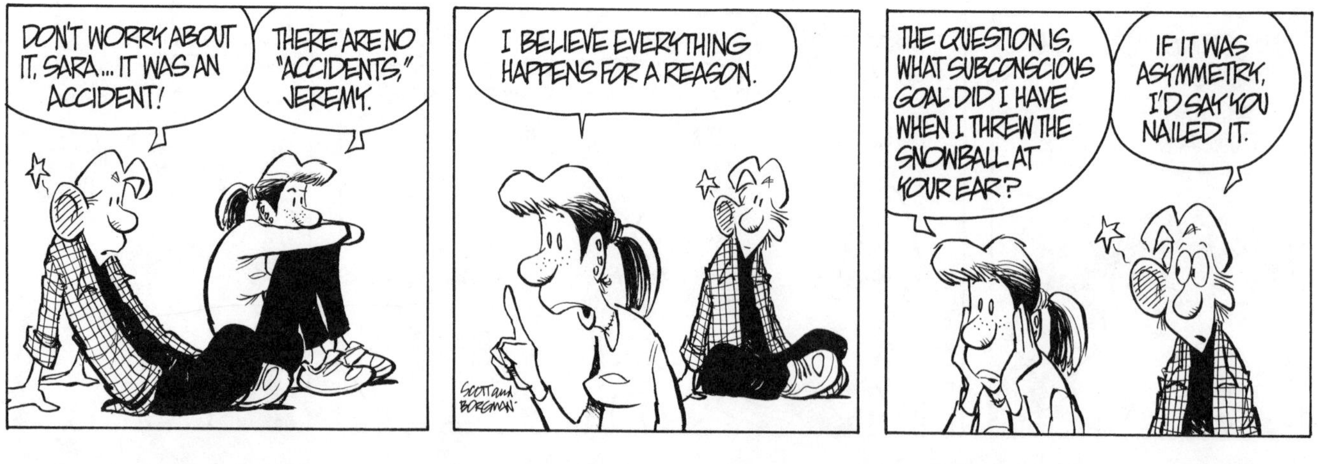
DON'T WORRY ABOUT IT, SARA... IT WAS AN ACCIDENT!
THERE ARE NO "ACCIDENTS," JEREMY.
I BELIEVE EVERYTHING HAPPENS FOR A REASON.
SCOTT and BORGMAN
THE QUESTION IS, WHAT SUBCONSCIOUS GOAL DID I HAVE WHEN I THREW THE SNOWBALL AT YOUR EAR?
IF IT WAS ASYMMETRY, I'D SAY YOU NAILED IT.

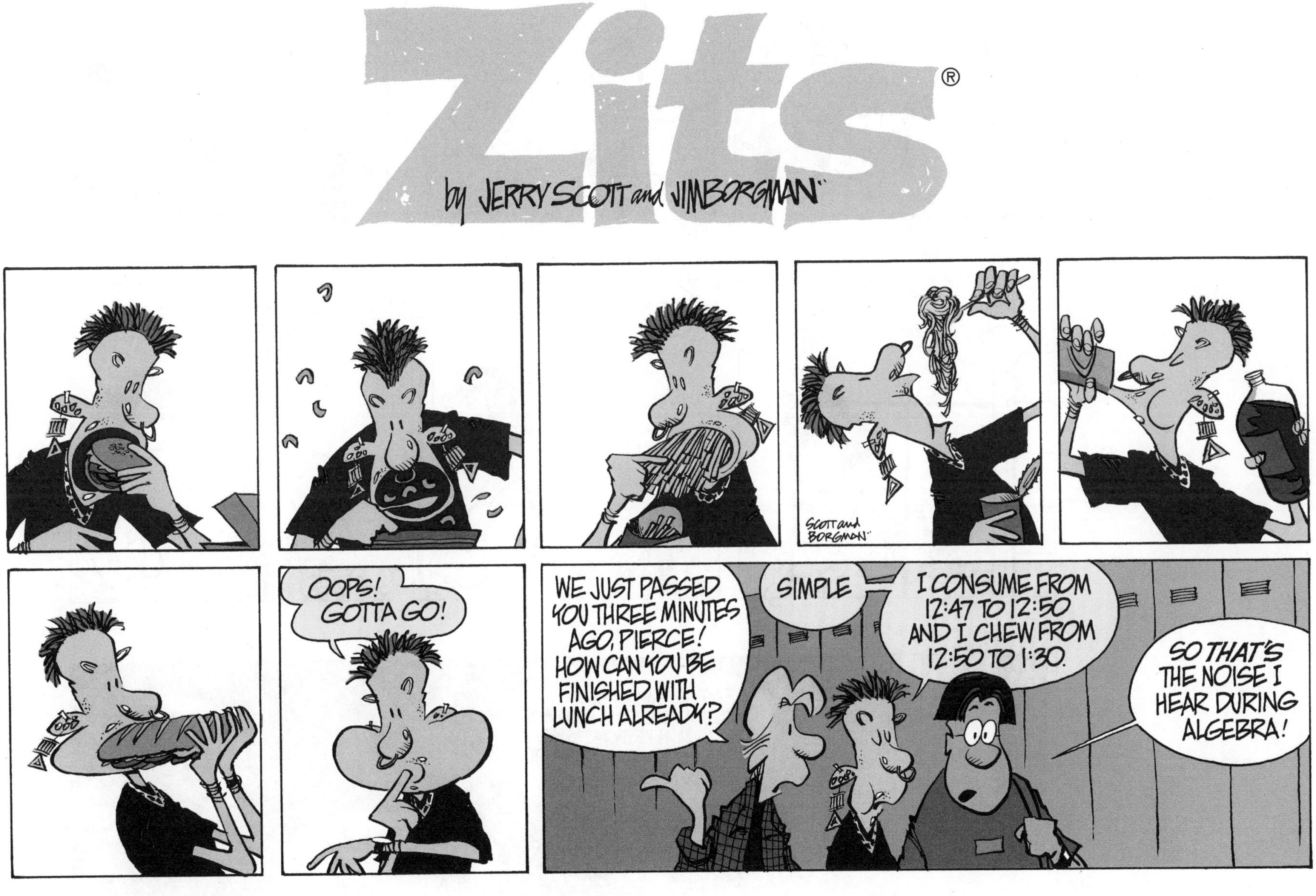
Zits®
by JERRY SCOTT and JIM BORGMAN
SCOTT and BORGMAN
OOPS! GOTTA GO!
WE JUST PASSED YOU THREE MINUTES AGO, PIERCE! HOW CAN YOU BE FINISHED WITH LUNCH ALREADY?
SIMPLE
I CONSUME FROM 12:47 TO 12:50 AND I CHEW FROM 12:50 TO 1:30.
SO THAT'S THE NOISE I HEAR DURING ALGEBRA!

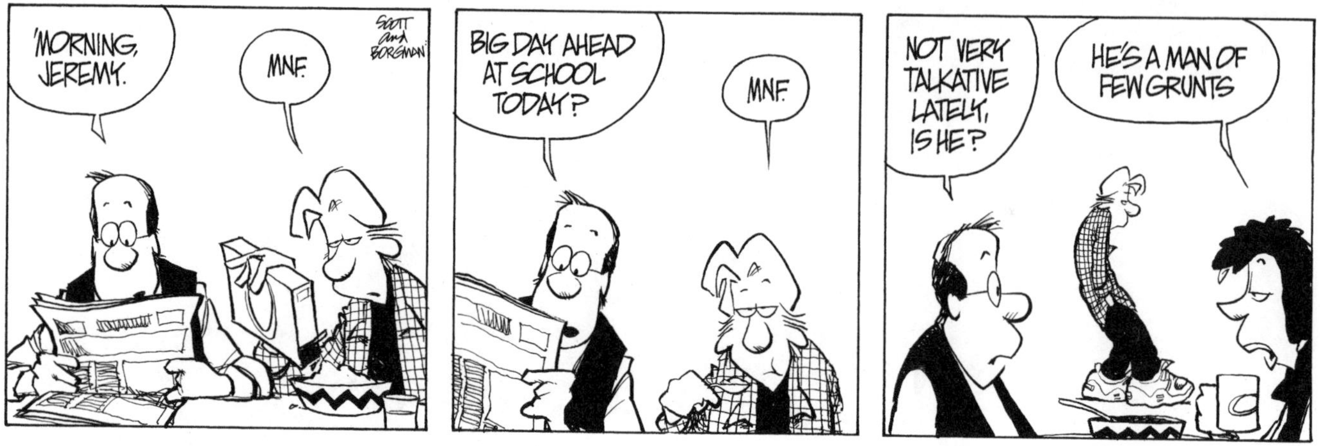
'MORNING, JEREMY.
MNF.
SCOTT AND BORGMAN
BIG DAY AHEAD AT SCHOOL TODAY?
MNF.
NOT VERY TALKATIVE LATELY, IS HE?
HE'S A MAN OF FEW GRUNTS

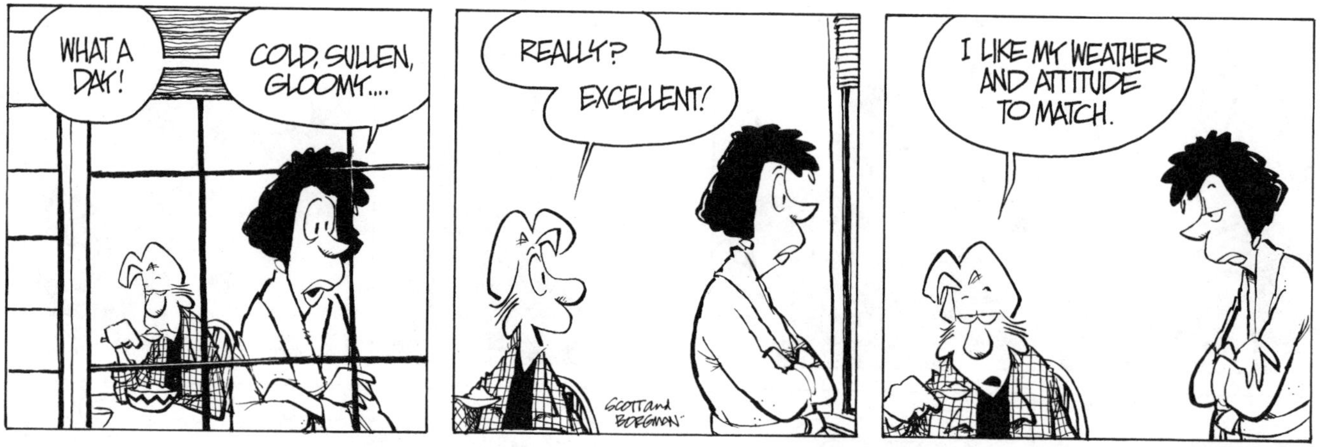
WHAT A DAY!
COLD, SULLEN, GLOOMY....
REALLY?
EXCELLENT!
SCOTT AND BORGMAN
I LIKE MY WEATHER AND ATTITUDE TO MATCH.

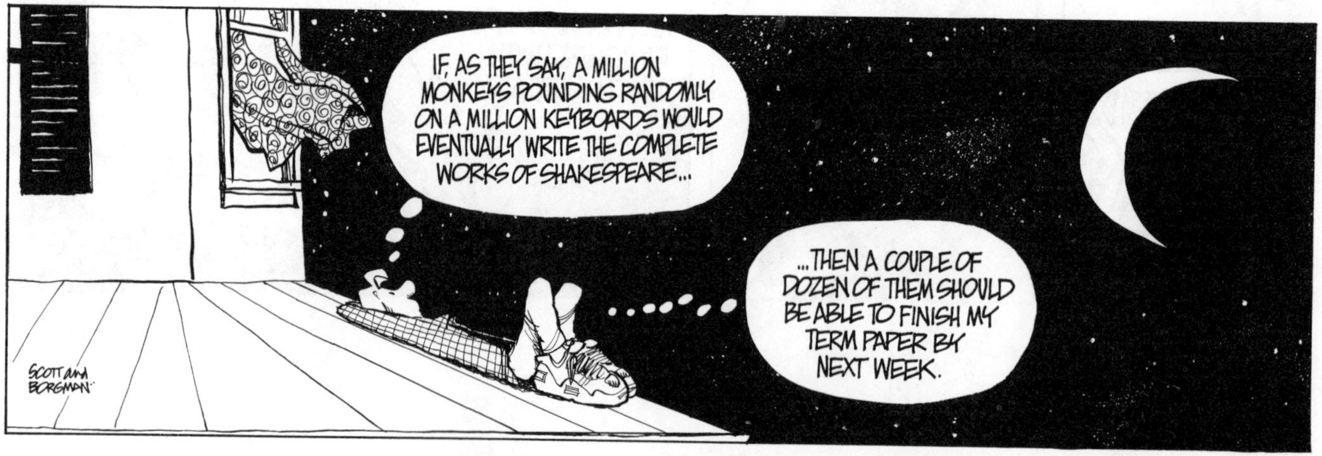
IF, AS THEY SAY, A MILLION MONKEYS POUNDING RANDOMLY ON A MILLION KEYBOARDS WOULD EVENTUALLY WRITE THE COMPLETE WORKS OF SHAKESPEARE...
...THEN A COUPLE OF DOZEN OF THEM SHOULD BE ABLE TO FINISH MY TERM PAPER BY NEXT WEEK.
SCOTT AND BORGMAN

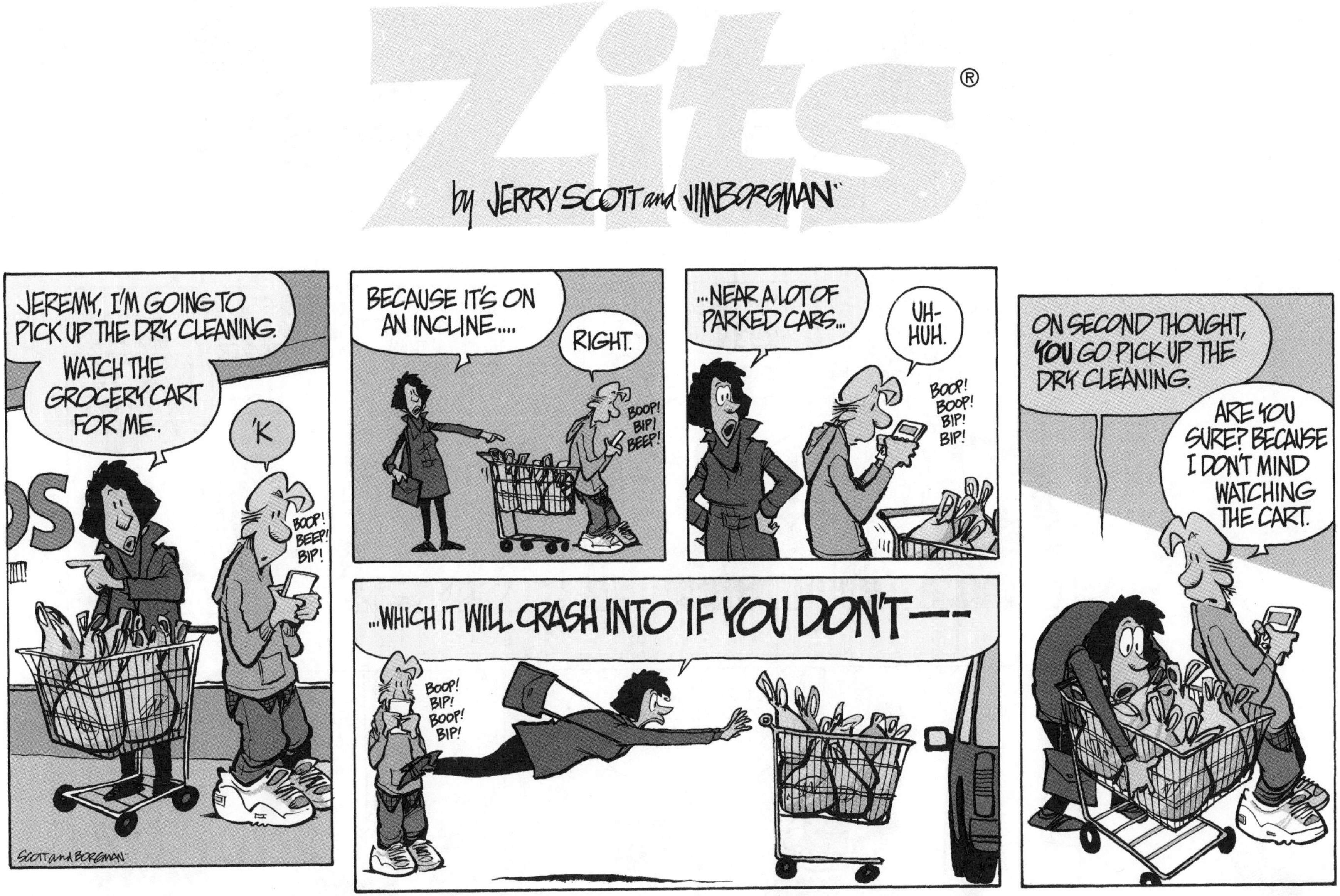
Zits®
by JERRY SCOTT and JIM BORGMAN
JEREMY, I'M GOING TO PICK UP THE DRY CLEANING.
WATCH THE GROCERY CART FOR ME.
'K
BOOP! BEEP! BIP!
SCOTT and BORGMAN
BECAUSE IT'S ON AN INCLINE....
RIGHT.
BOOP! BIP! BEEP!
...NEAR A LOT OF PARKED CARS...
UH-HUH.
BOOP! BOOP! BIP! BIP!
...WHICH IT WILL CRASH INTO IF YOU DON'T---
BOOP! BIP! BOOP! BIP!
ON SECOND THOUGHT, YOU GO PICK UP THE DRY CLEANING.
ARE YOU SURE? BECAUSE I DON'T MIND WATCHING THE CART.

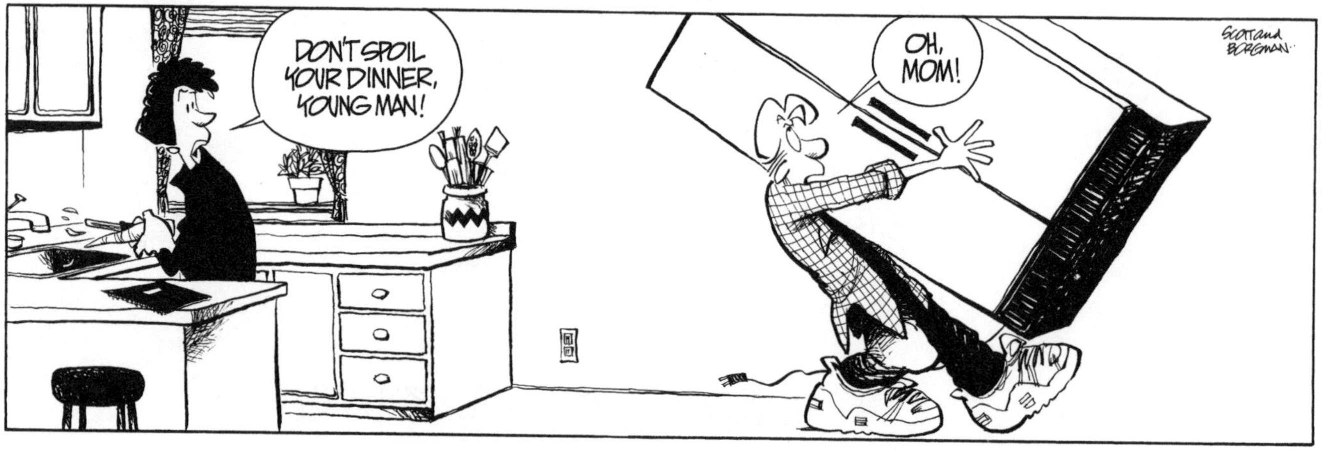
DON'T SPOIL YOUR DINNER, YOUNG MAN!
OH, MOM!

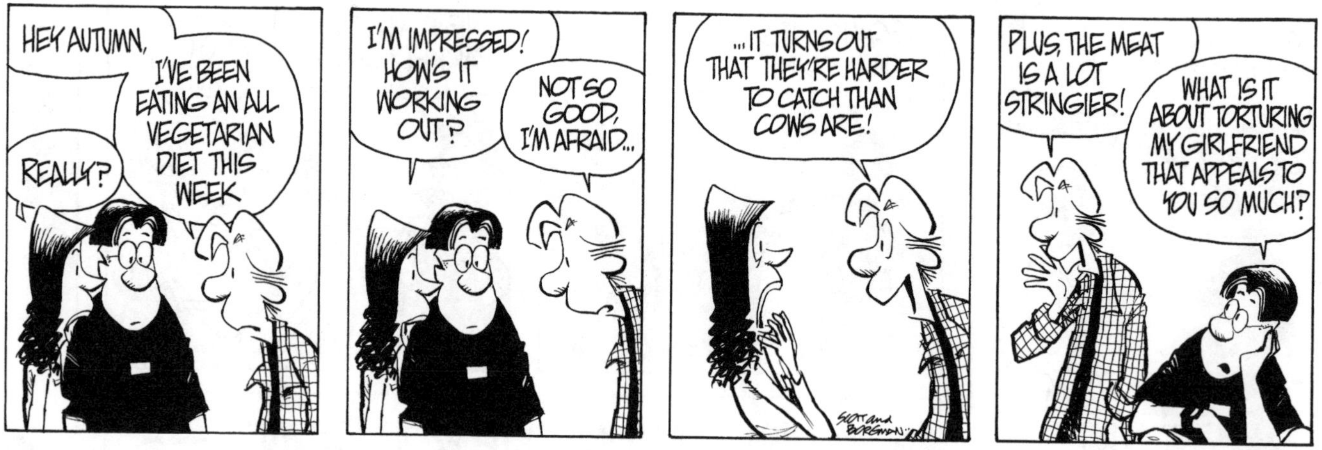
HEY AUTUMN,
I'VE BEEN EATING AN ALL VEGETARIAN DIET THIS WEEK
REALLY?
I'M IMPRESSED! HOW'S IT WORKING OUT?
NOT SO GOOD, I'M AFRAID...
...IT TURNS OUT THAT THEY'RE HARDER TO CATCH THAN COWS ARE!
PLUS, THE MEAT IS A LOT STRINGIER!
WHAT IS IT ABOUT TORTURING MY GIRLFRIEND THAT APPEALS TO YOU SO MUCH?

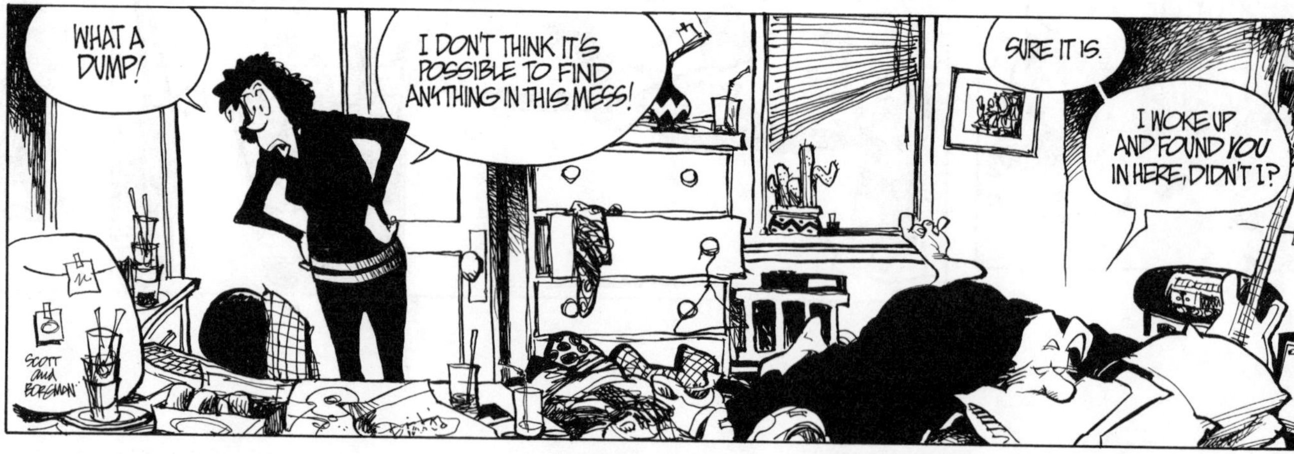
WHAT A DUMP!
I DON'T THINK IT'S POSSIBLE TO FIND ANYTHING IN THIS MESS!
SURE IT IS.
I WOKE UP AND FOUND **YOU** IN HERE, DIDN'T I?

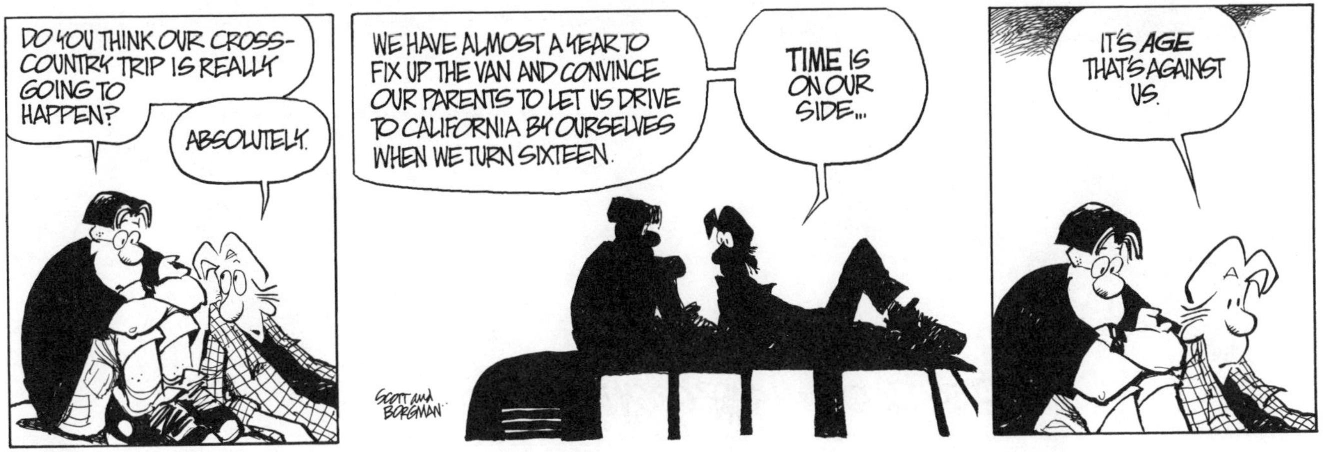
DO YOU THINK OUR CROSS-COUNTRY TRIP IS REALLY GOING TO HAPPEN?
ABSOLUTELY.
WE HAVE ALMOST A YEAR TO FIX UP THE VAN AND CONVINCE OUR PARENTS TO LET US DRIVE TO CALIFORNIA BY OURSELVES WHEN WE TURN SIXTEEN.
TIME IS ON OUR SIDE...
SCOTT and BORGMAN
IT'S AGE THAT'S AGAINST US.

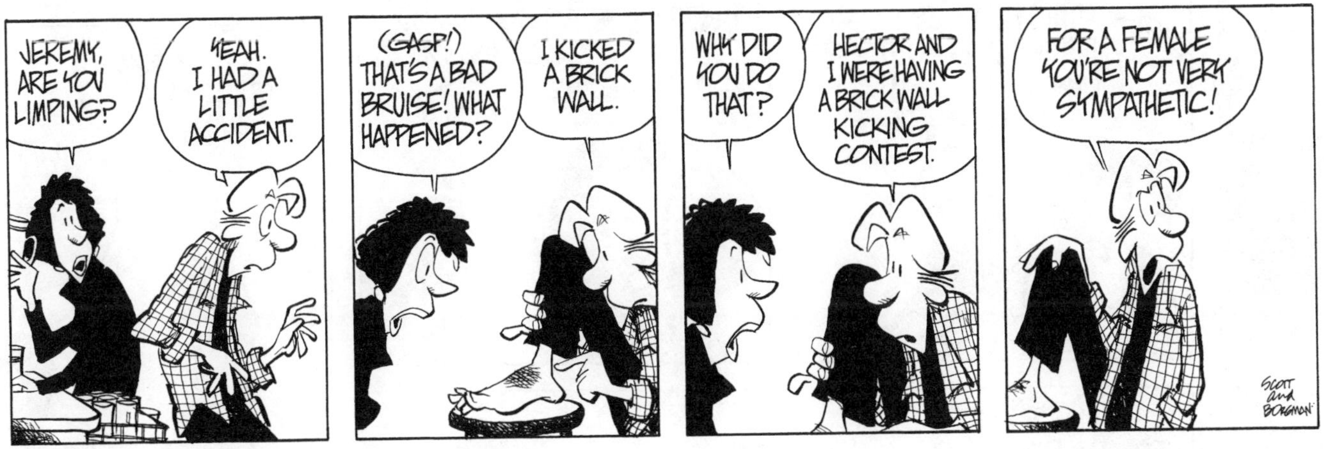
JEREMY, ARE YOU LIMPING?
YEAH. I HAD A LITTLE ACCIDENT.
(GASP!) THAT'S A BAD BRUISE! WHAT HAPPENED?
I KICKED A BRICK WALL.
WHY DID YOU DO THAT?
HECTOR AND I WERE HAVING A BRICK WALL KICKING CONTEST.
FOR A FEMALE YOU'RE NOT VERY SYMPATHETIC!
SCOTT and BORGMAN

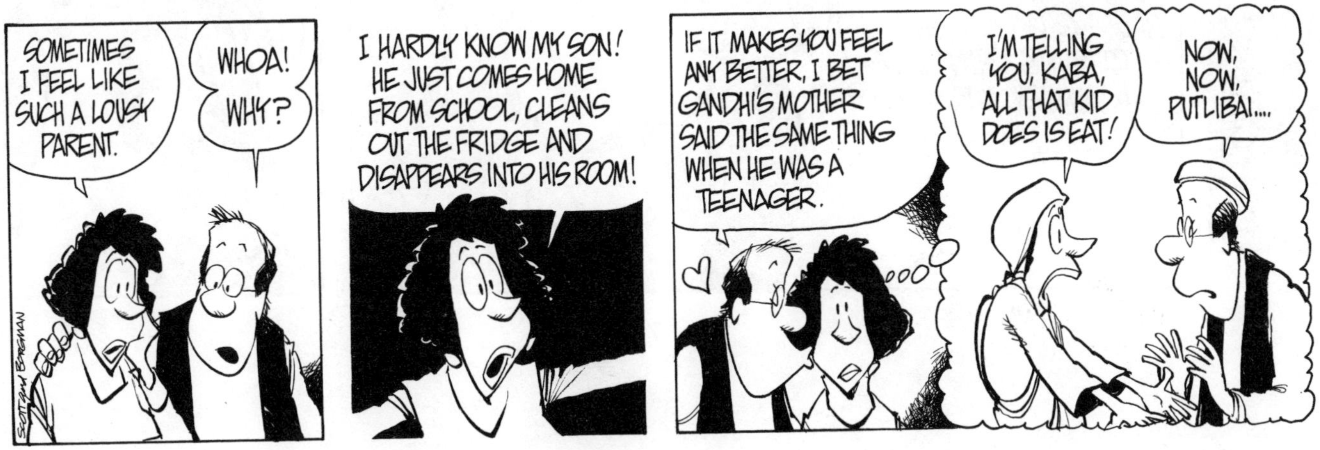
SOMETIMES I FEEL LIKE SUCH A LOUSY PARENT.
WHOA! WHY?
SCOTT and BORGMAN
I HARDLY KNOW MY SON! HE JUST COMES HOME FROM SCHOOL, CLEANS OUT THE FRIDGE AND DISAPPEARS INTO HIS ROOM!
IF IT MAKES YOU FEEL ANY BETTER, I BET GANDHI'S MOTHER SAID THE SAME THING WHEN HE WAS A TEENAGER.
I'M TELLING YOU, KABA, ALL THAT KID DOES IS EAT!
NOW, NOW, PUTLIBAI....

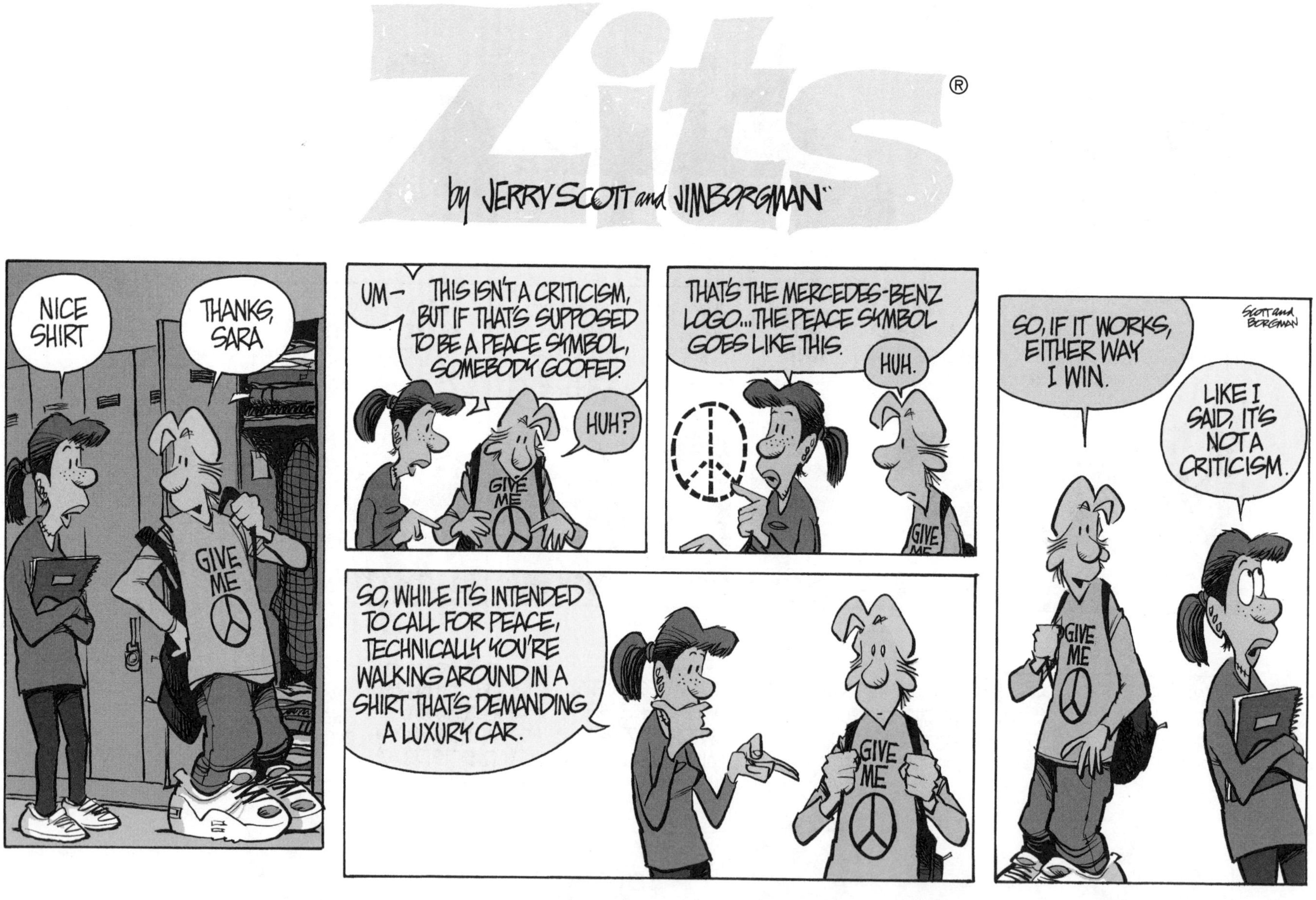

Zits®
by JERRY SCOTT and JIM BORGMAN
NICE SHIRT
THANKS, SARA
GIVE ME
UM–
THIS ISN'T A CRITICISM, BUT IF THAT'S SUPPOSED TO BE A PEACE SYMBOL, SOMEBODY GOOFED.
HUH?
GIVE ME
THAT'S THE MERCEDES-BENZ LOGO... THE PEACE SYMBOL GOES LIKE THIS.
HUH.
SO, WHILE IT'S INTENDED TO CALL FOR PEACE, TECHNICALLY YOU'RE WALKING AROUND IN A SHIRT THAT'S DEMANDING A LUXURY CAR.
GIVE ME
SCOTT and BORGMAN
SO, IF IT WORKS, EITHER WAY I WIN.
LIKE I SAID, IT'S NOT A CRITICISM.
GIVE ME

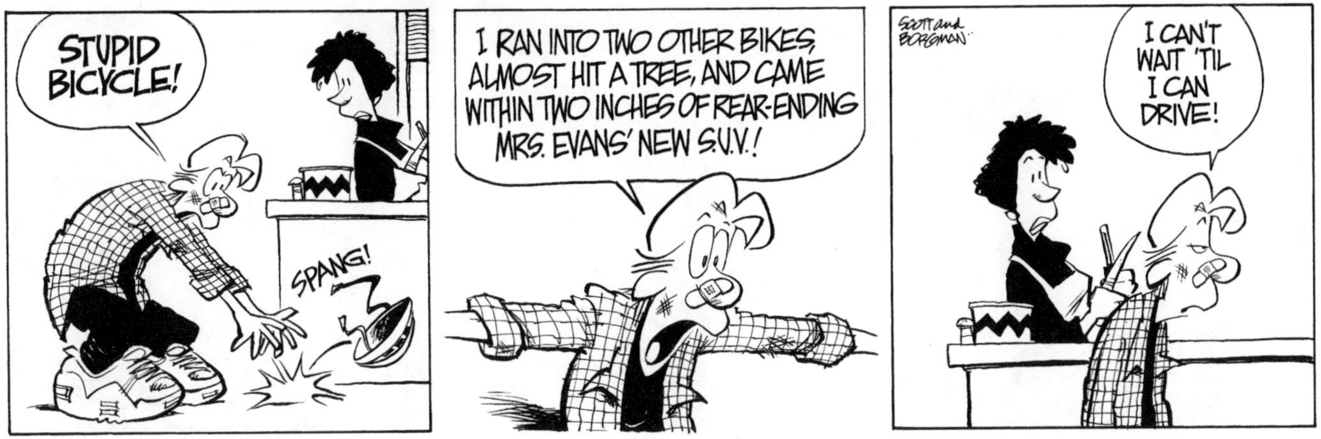
STUPID BICYCLE!
SPANG!
I RAN INTO TWO OTHER BIKES, ALMOST HIT A TREE, AND CAME WITHIN TWO INCHES OF REAR-ENDING MRS. EVANS' NEW S.U.V.!
SCOTT and BORGMAN
I CAN'T WAIT 'TIL I CAN DRIVE!

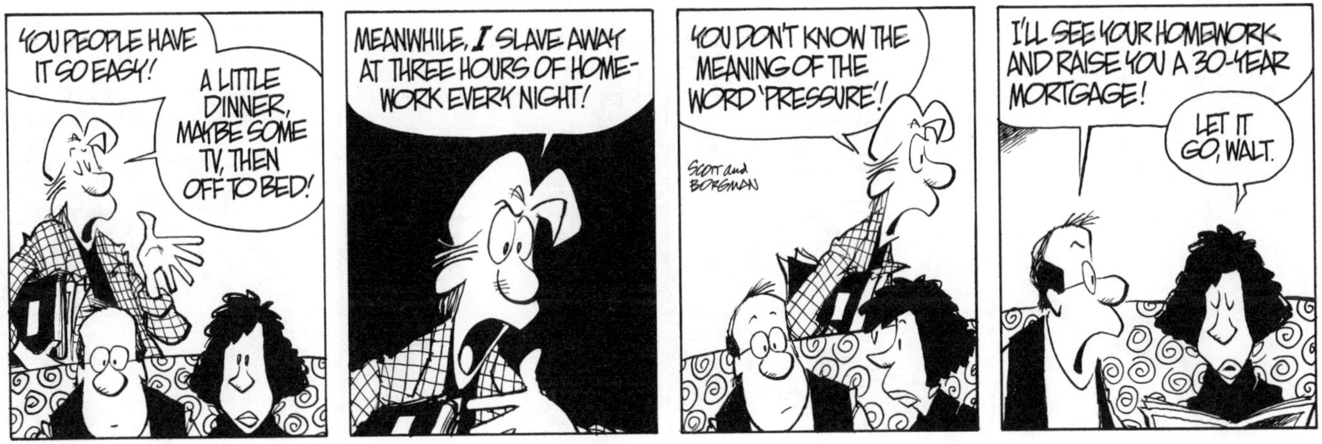
YOU PEOPLE HAVE IT SO EASY!
A LITTLE DINNER, MAYBE SOME TV, THEN OFF TO BED!
MEANWHILE, I SLAVE AWAY AT THREE HOURS OF HOMEWORK EVERY NIGHT!
YOU DON'T KNOW THE MEANING OF THE WORD 'PRESSURE'!
SCOTT and BORGMAN
I'LL SEE YOUR HOMEWORK AND RAISE YOU A 30-YEAR MORTGAGE!
LET IT GO, WALT.

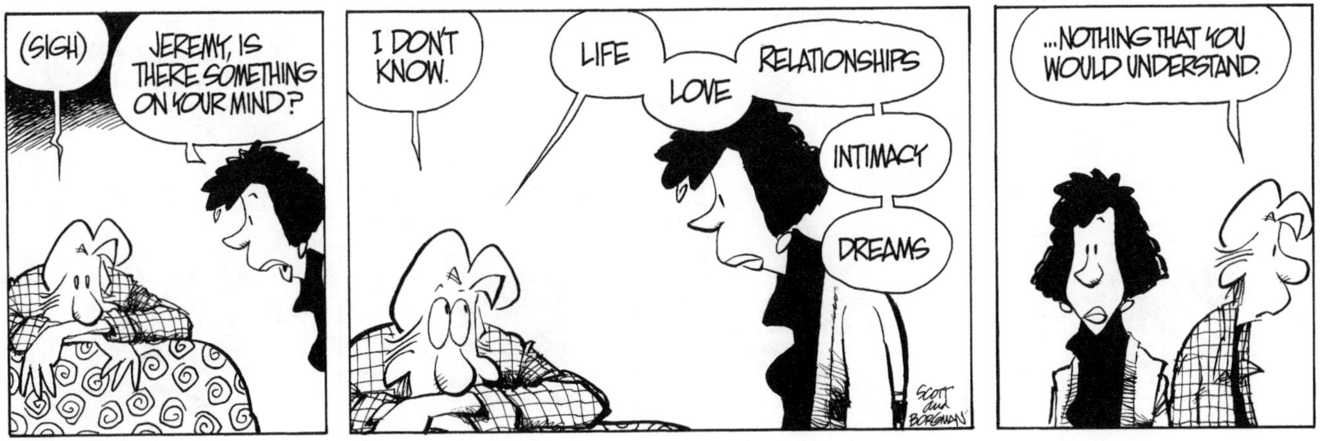
(SIGH)
JEREMY, IS THERE SOMETHING ON YOUR MIND?
I DON'T KNOW.
LIFE
LOVE
RELATIONSHIPS
INTIMACY
DREAMS
SCOTT and BORGMAN
...NOTHING THAT YOU WOULD UNDERSTAND.

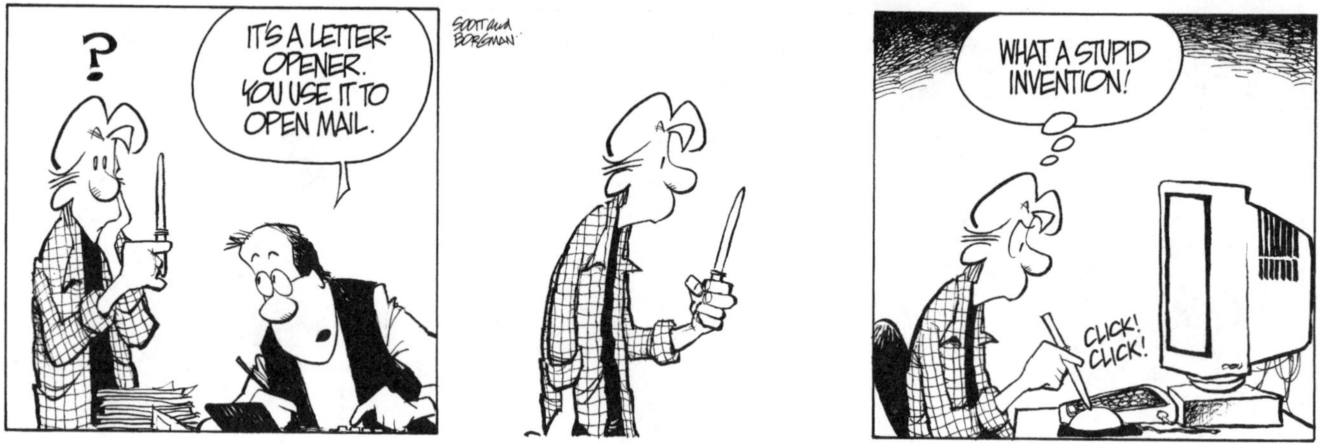
SCOTT and BORGMAN
?
IT'S A LETTER-OPENER. YOU USE IT TO OPEN MAIL.
WHAT A STUPID INVENTION!
CLICK! CLICK!

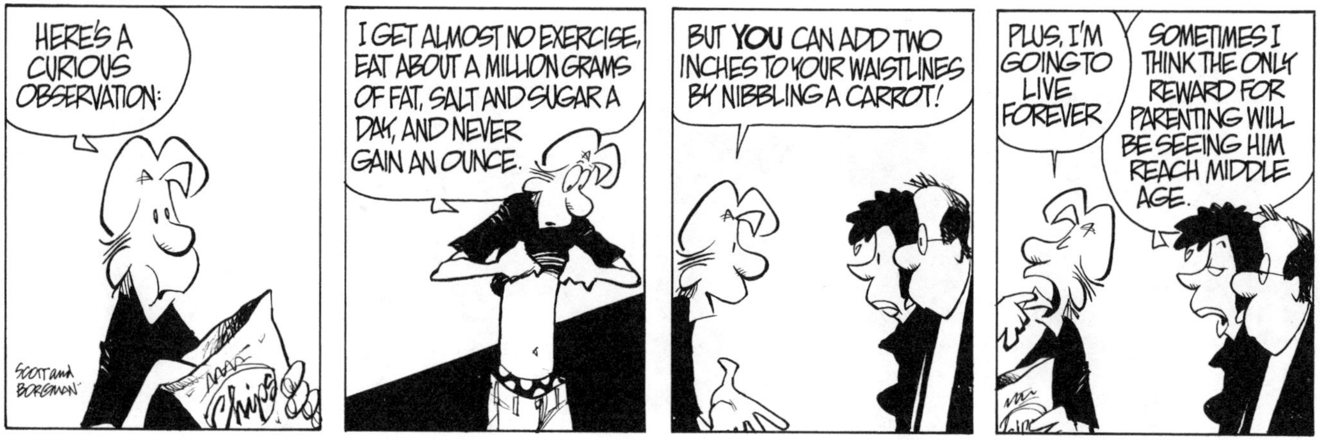
HERE'S A CURIOUS OBSERVATION:
SCOTT and BORGMAN
I GET ALMOST NO EXERCISE, EAT ABOUT A MILLION GRAMS OF FAT, SALT AND SUGAR A DAY, AND NEVER GAIN AN OUNCE.
BUT **YOU** CAN ADD TWO INCHES TO YOUR WAISTLINES BY NIBBLING A CARROT!
PLUS, I'M GOING TO LIVE FOREVER
SOMETIMES I THINK THE ONLY REWARD FOR PARENTING WILL BE SEEING HIM REACH MIDDLE AGE.

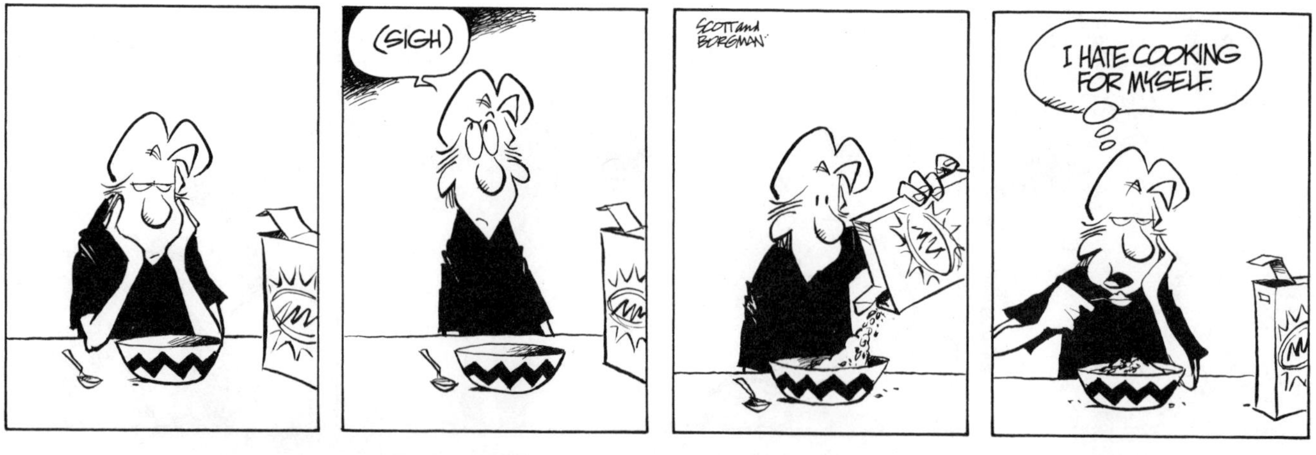
(SIGH)
SCOTT and BORGMAN
I HATE COOKING FOR MYSELF.

Zits®

by JERRY SCOTT and JIM BORGMAN

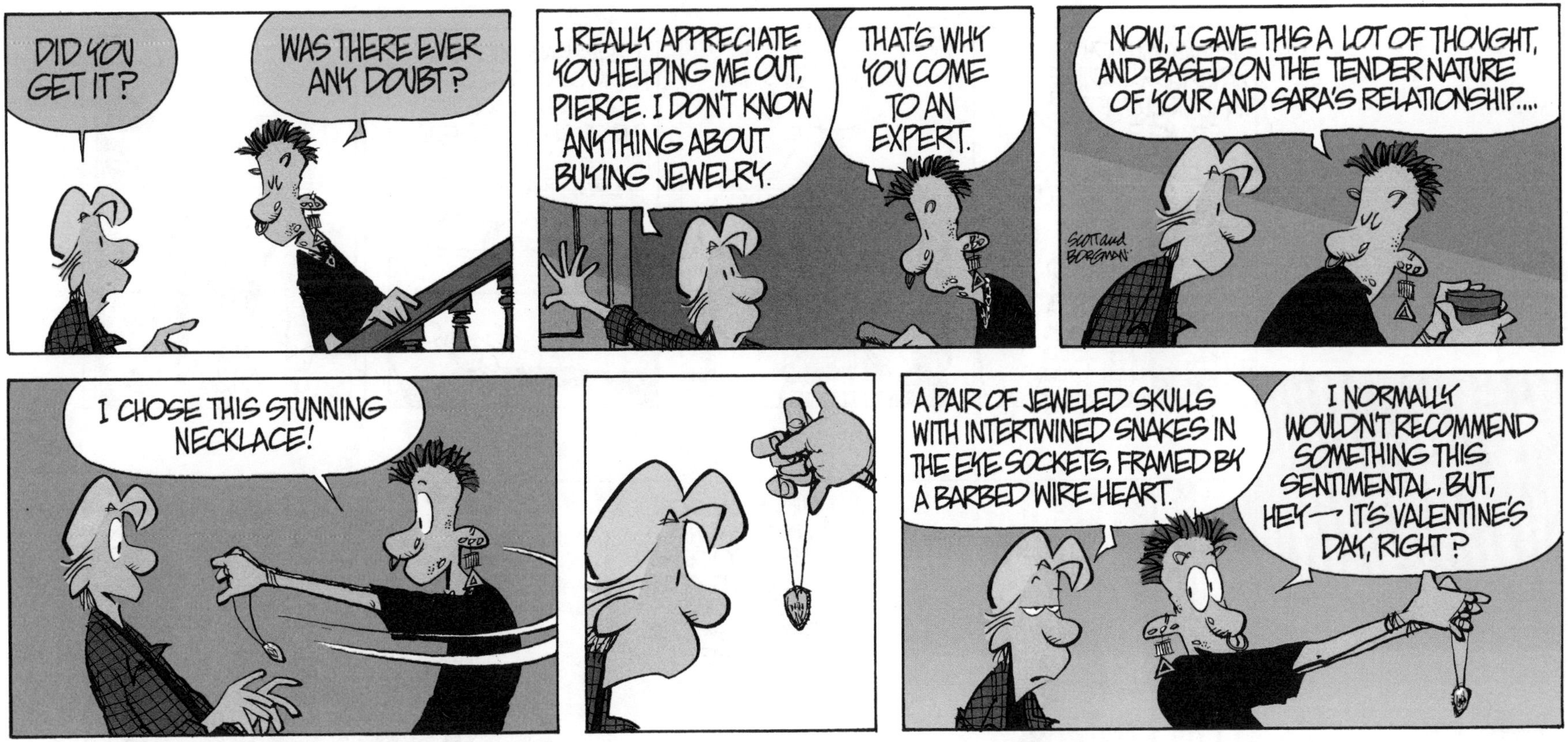
DID YOU GET IT?
WAS THERE EVER ANY DOUBT?
I REALLY APPRECIATE YOU HELPING ME OUT, PIERCE. I DON'T KNOW ANYTHING ABOUT BUYING JEWELRY.
THAT'S WHY YOU COME TO AN EXPERT.
NOW, I GAVE THIS A LOT OF THOUGHT, AND BASED ON THE TENDER NATURE OF YOUR AND SARA'S RELATIONSHIP....
SCOTT and BORGMAN
I CHOSE THIS STUNNING NECKLACE!
A PAIR OF JEWELED SKULLS WITH INTERTWINED SNAKES IN THE EYE SOCKETS, FRAMED BY A BARBED WIRE HEART.
I NORMALLY WOULDN'T RECOMMEND SOMETHING THIS SENTIMENTAL, BUT, HEY→ IT'S VALENTINE'S DAY, RIGHT?

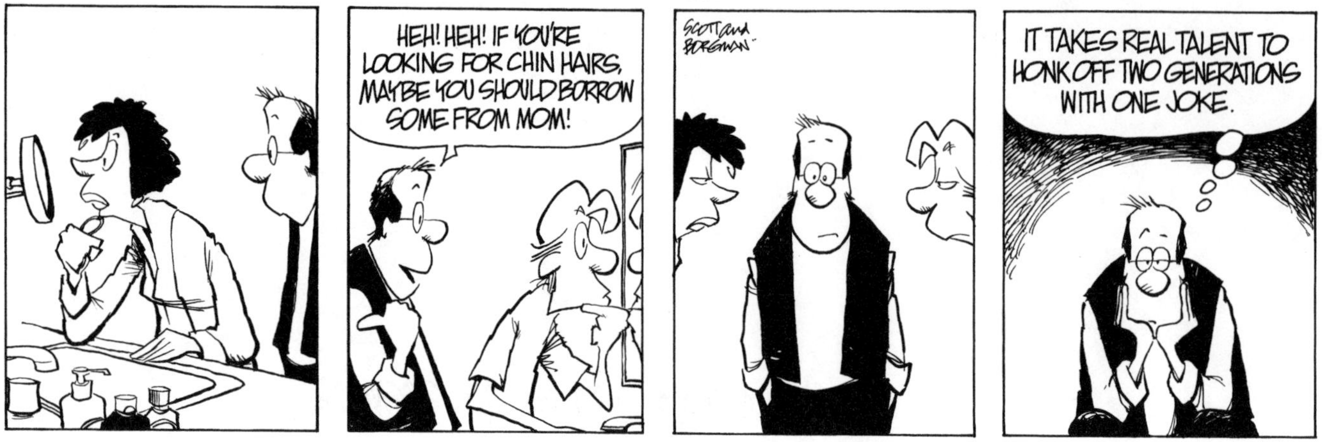
HEH! HEH! IF YOU'RE LOOKING FOR CHIN HAIRS, MAYBE YOU SHOULD BORROW SOME FROM MOM!
IT TAKES REAL TALENT TO HONK OFF TWO GENERATIONS WITH ONE JOKE.

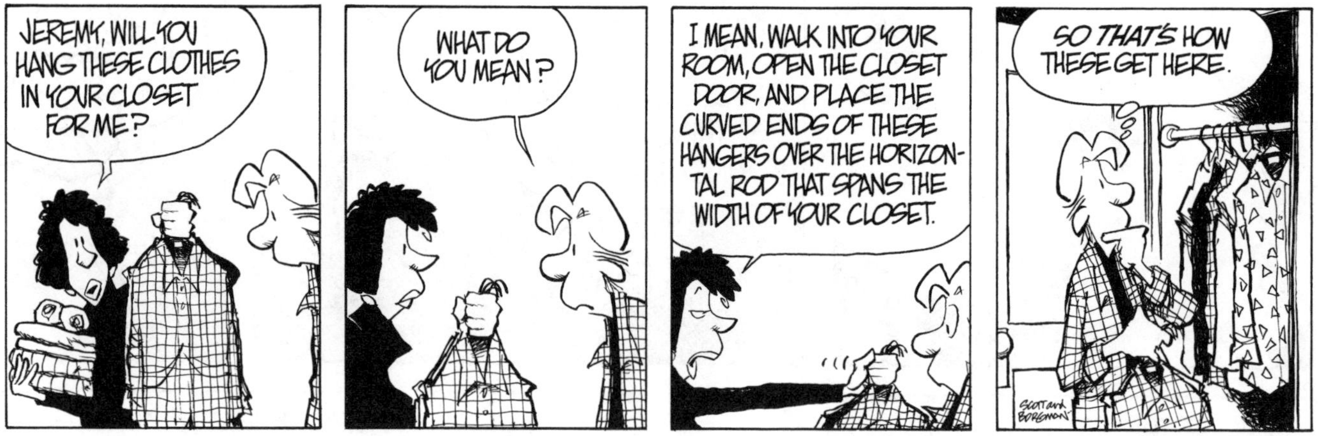
JEREMY, WILL YOU HANG THESE CLOTHES IN YOUR CLOSET FOR ME?
WHAT DO YOU MEAN?
I MEAN, WALK INTO YOUR ROOM, OPEN THE CLOSET DOOR, AND PLACE THE CURVED ENDS OF THESE HANGERS OVER THE HORIZONTAL ROD THAT SPANS THE WIDTH OF YOUR CLOSET.
SO *THAT'S* HOW THESE GET HERE.

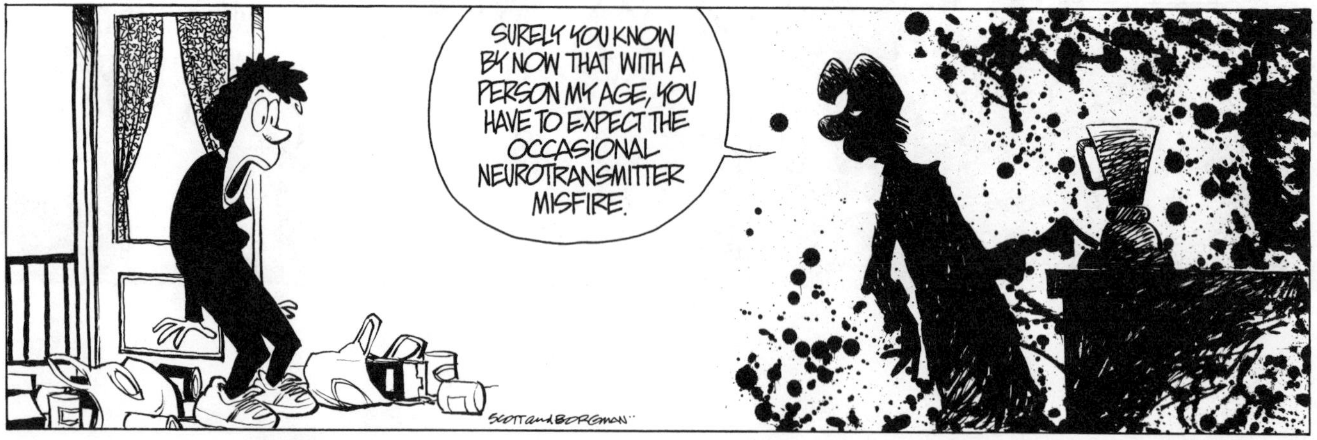
SURELY YOU KNOW BY NOW THAT WITH A PERSON MY AGE, YOU HAVE TO EXPECT THE OCCASIONAL NEUROTRANSMITTER MISFIRE.

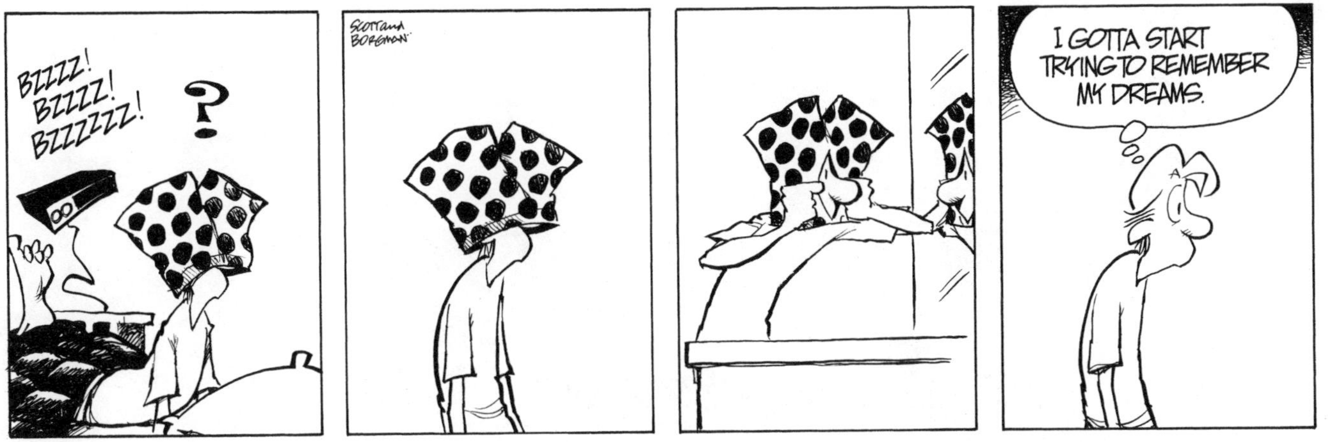
BZZZZ! BZZZZ! BZZZZZZ!
?
I GOTTA START TRYING TO REMEMBER MY DREAMS.

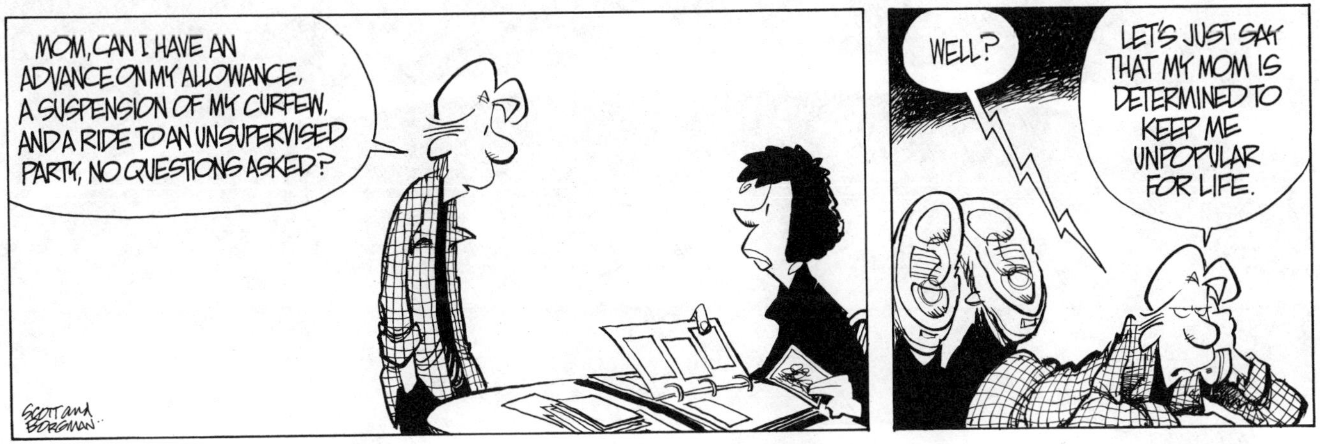
MOM, CAN I HAVE AN ADVANCE ON MY ALLOWANCE, A SUSPENSION OF MY CURFEW, AND A RIDE TO AN UNSUPERVISED PARTY, NO QUESTIONS ASKED?
WELL?
LET'S JUST SAY THAT MY MOM IS DETERMINED TO KEEP ME UNPOPULAR FOR LIFE.

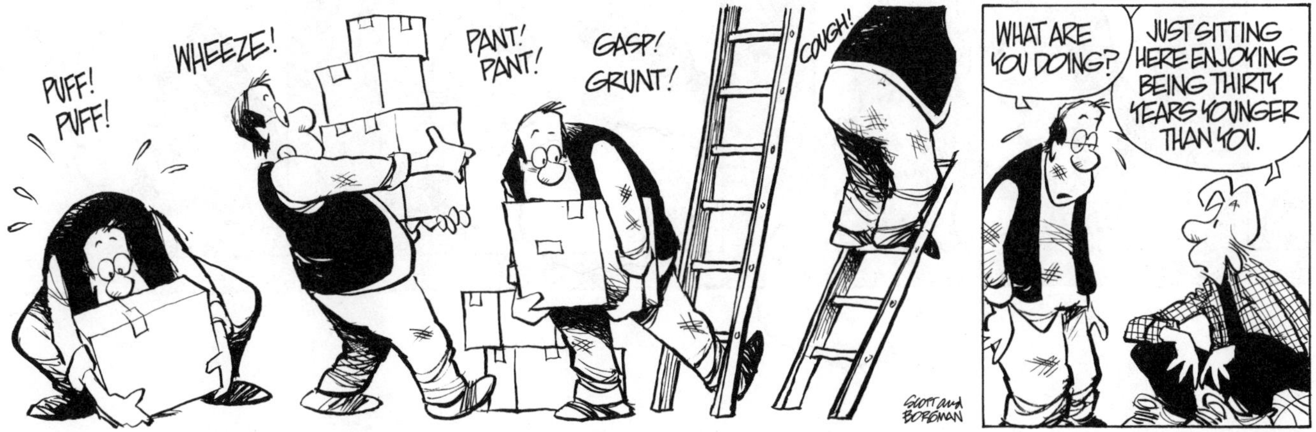
PUFF! PUFF!
WHEEZE!
PANT! PANT!
GASP! GRUNT!
COUGH!
WHAT ARE YOU DOING?
JUST SITTING HERE ENJOYING BEING THIRTY YEARS YOUNGER THAN YOU.

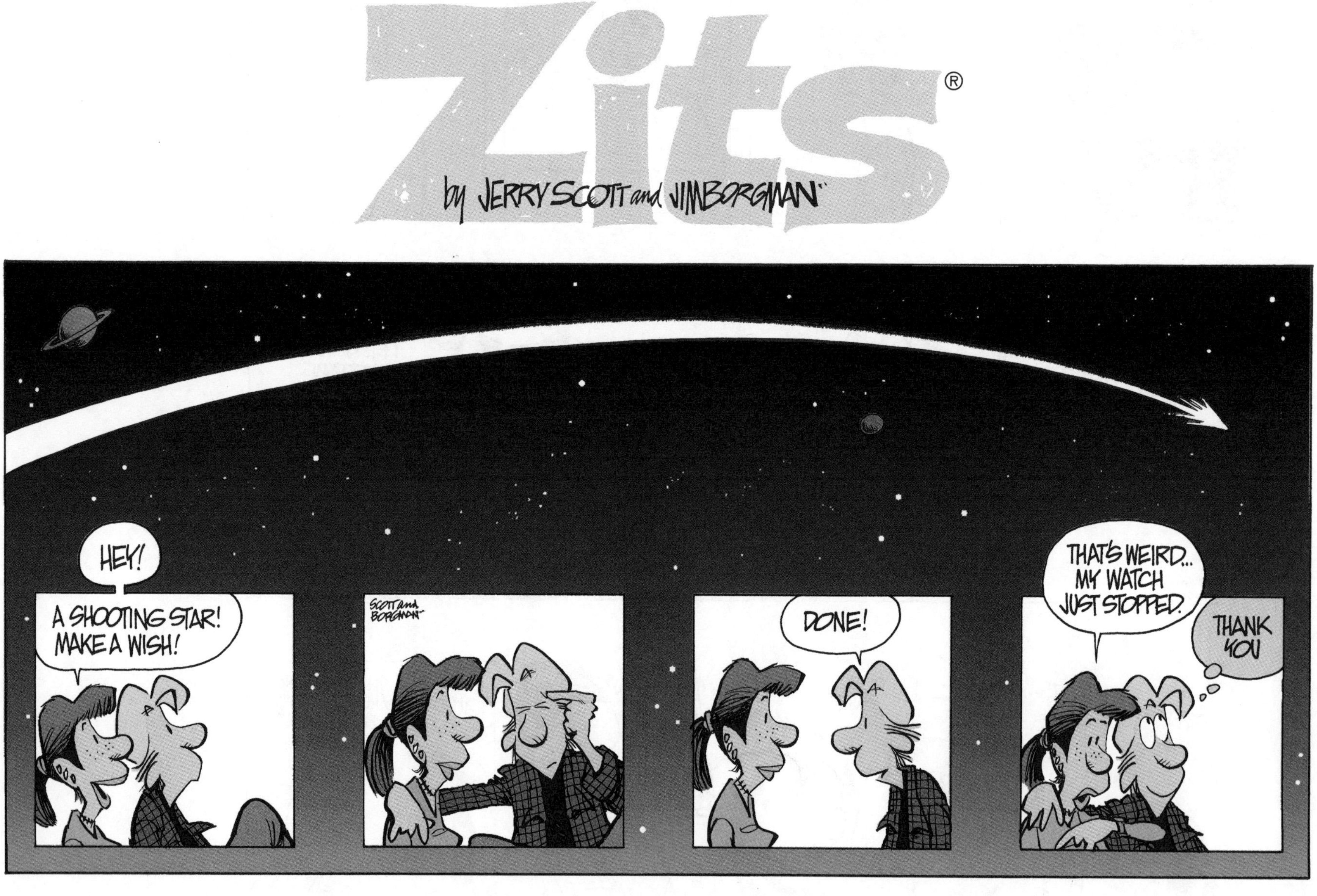
Zits®
by JERRY SCOTT and JIM BORGMAN
HEY!
A SHOOTING STAR! MAKE A WISH!
SCOTT and BORGMAN
DONE!
THAT'S WEIRD... MY WATCH JUST STOPPED.
THANK YOU

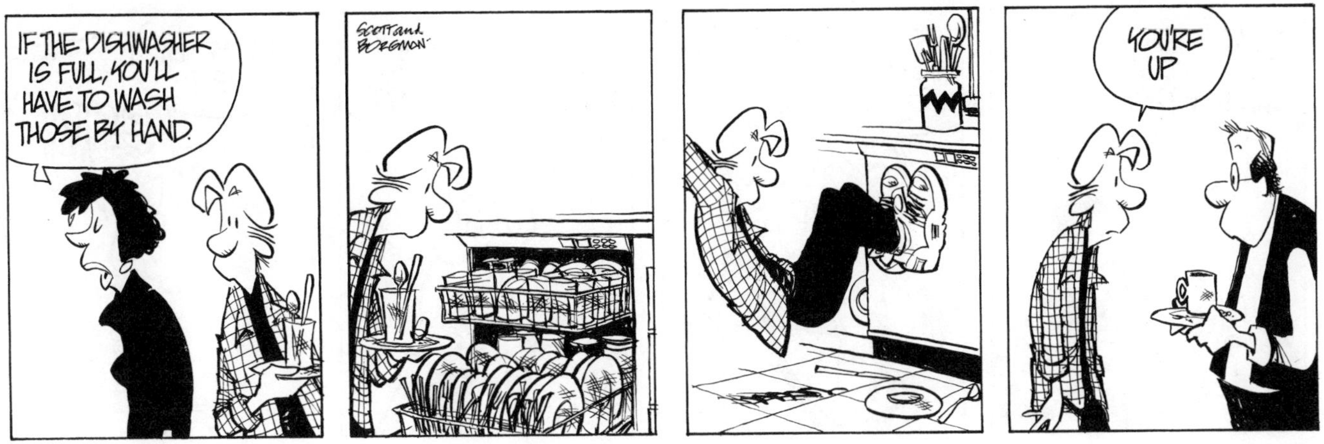
IF THE DISHWASHER IS FULL, YOU'LL HAVE TO WASH THOSE BY HAND.
YOU'RE UP

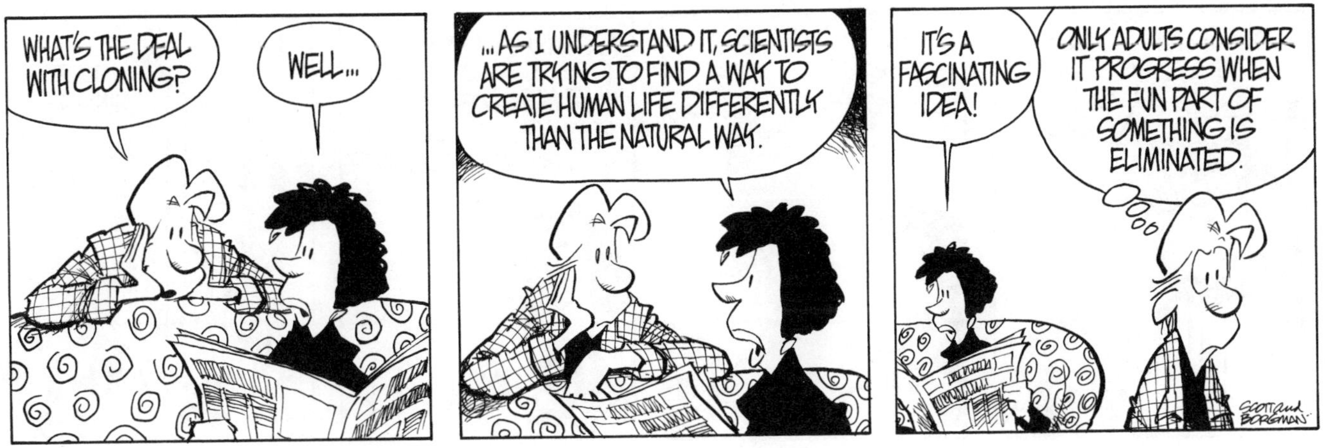
WHAT'S THE DEAL WITH CLONING?
WELL...
...AS I UNDERSTAND IT, SCIENTISTS ARE TRYING TO FIND A WAY TO CREATE HUMAN LIFE DIFFERENTLY THAN THE NATURAL WAY.
IT'S A FASCINATING IDEA!
ONLY ADULTS CONSIDER IT PROGRESS WHEN THE FUN PART OF SOMETHING IS ELIMINATED.

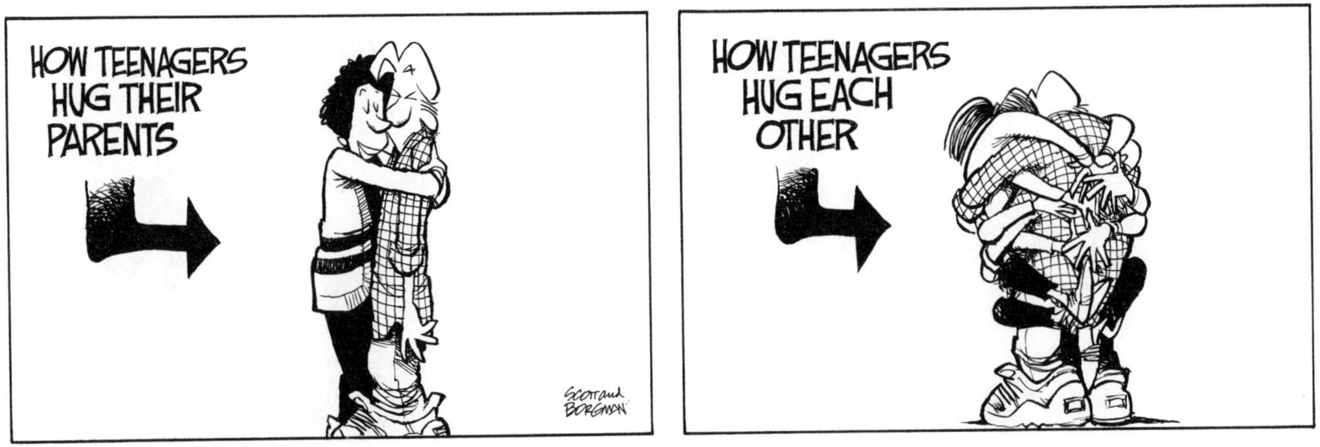
HOW TEENAGERS HUG THEIR PARENTS
HOW TEENAGERS HUG EACH OTHER

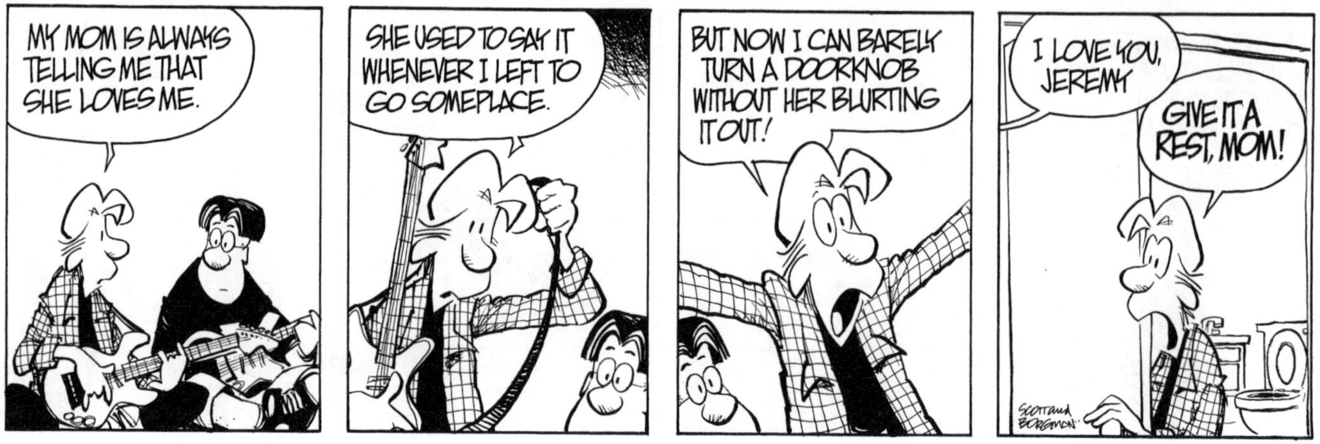
MY MOM IS ALWAYS TELLING ME THAT SHE LOVES ME.
SHE USED TO SAY IT WHENEVER I LEFT TO GO SOMEPLACE.
BUT NOW I CAN BARELY TURN A DOORKNOB WITHOUT HER BLURTING IT OUT!
I LOVE YOU, JEREMY
GIVE IT A REST, MOM!
SCOTT and BORGMAN

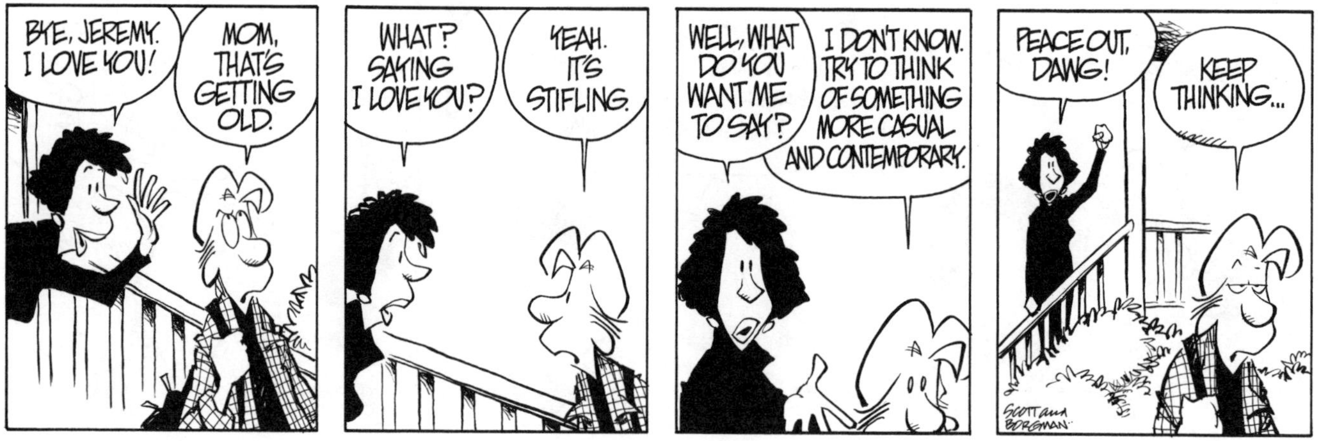
BYE, JEREMY. I LOVE YOU!
MOM, THAT'S GETTING OLD.
WHAT? SAYING I LOVE YOU?
YEAH. IT'S STIFLING.
WELL, WHAT DO YOU WANT ME TO SAY?
I DON'T KNOW. TRY TO THINK OF SOMETHING MORE CASUAL AND CONTEMPORARY.
PEACE OUT, DAWG!
KEEP THINKING...
SCOTT and BORGMAN

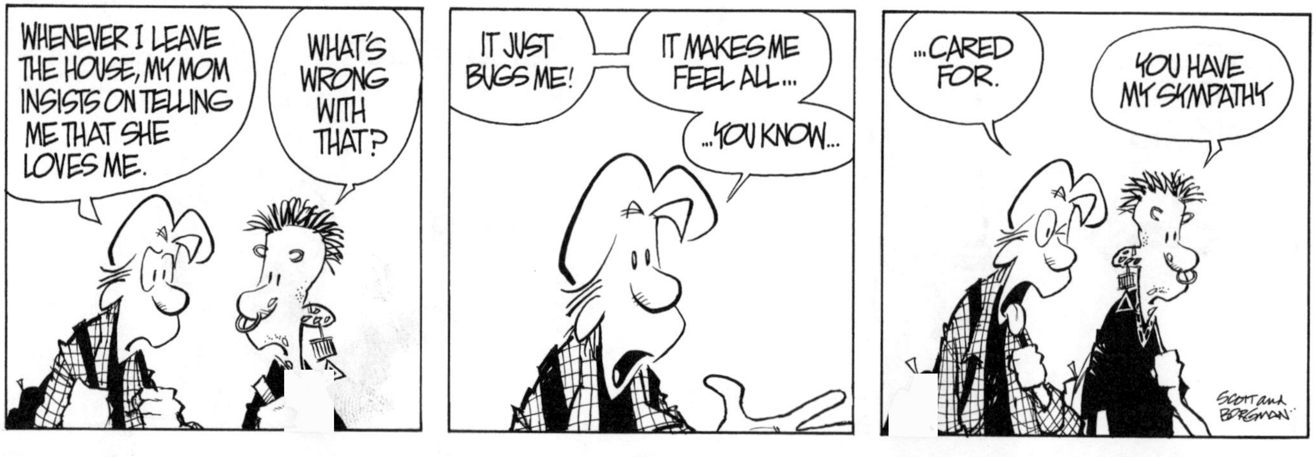
WHENEVER I LEAVE THE HOUSE, MY MOM INSISTS ON TELLING ME THAT SHE LOVES ME.
WHAT'S WRONG WITH THAT?
IT JUST BUGS ME!
IT MAKES ME FEEL ALL...
...YOU KNOW...
...CARED FOR.
YOU HAVE MY SYMPATHY
SCOTT and BORGMAN

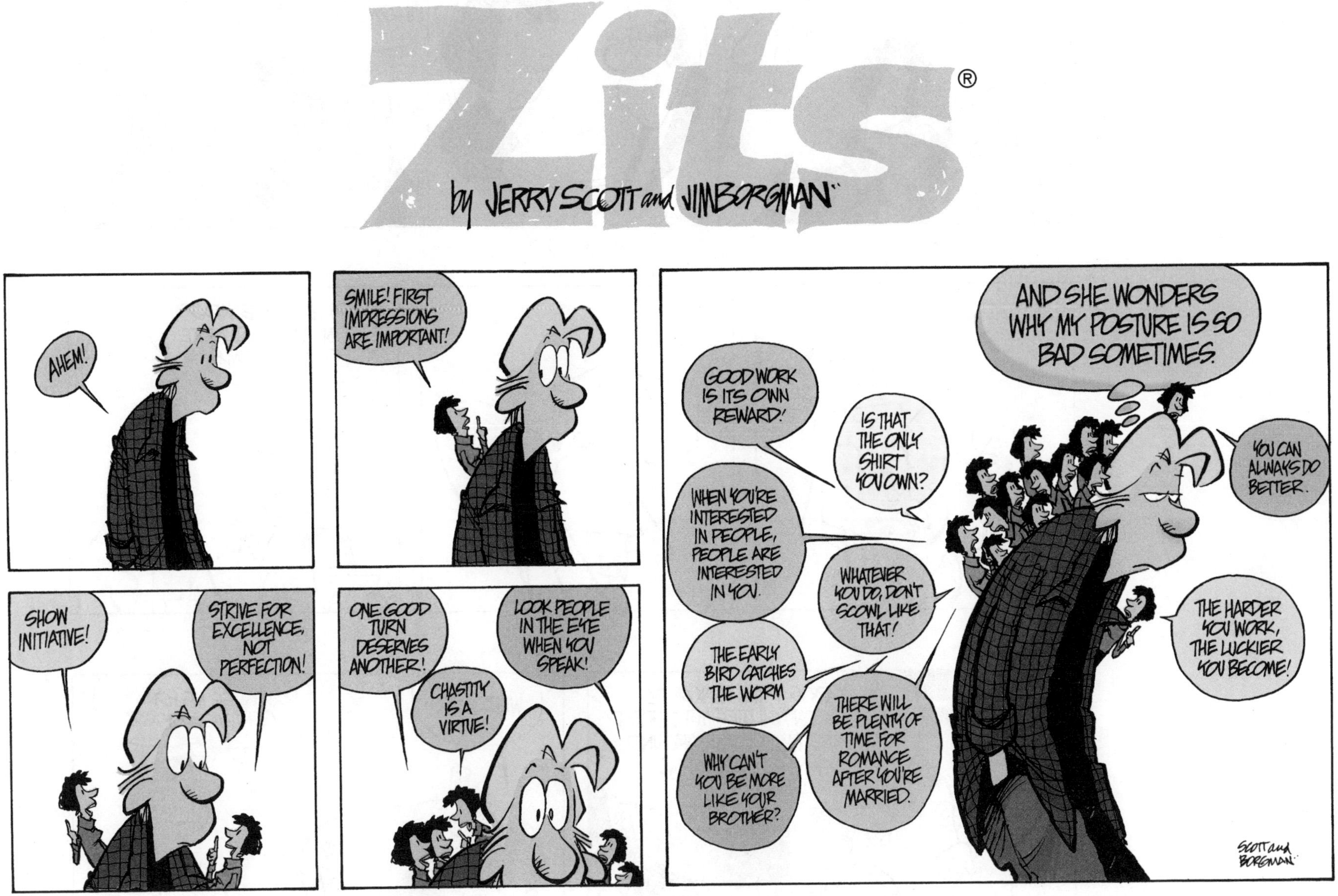
Zits®
by JERRY SCOTT and JIM BORGMAN
AHEM!
SMILE! FIRST IMPRESSIONS ARE IMPORTANT!
SHOW INITIATIVE!
STRIVE FOR EXCELLENCE, NOT PERFECTION!
ONE GOOD TURN DESERVES ANOTHER!
CHASTITY IS A VIRTUE!
LOOK PEOPLE IN THE EYE WHEN YOU SPEAK!
AND SHE WONDERS WHY MY POSTURE IS SO BAD SOMETIMES.
GOOD WORK IS ITS OWN REWARD!
IS THAT THE ONLY SHIRT YOU OWN?
YOU CAN ALWAYS DO BETTER.
WHEN YOU'RE INTERESTED IN PEOPLE, PEOPLE ARE INTERESTED IN YOU.
WHATEVER YOU DO, DON'T SCOWL LIKE THAT!
THE HARDER YOU WORK, THE LUCKIER YOU BECOME!
THE EARLY BIRD CATCHES THE WORM
THERE WILL BE PLENTY OF TIME FOR ROMANCE AFTER YOU'RE MARRIED.
WHY CAN'T YOU BE MORE LIKE YOUR BROTHER?
SCOTT and BORGMAN

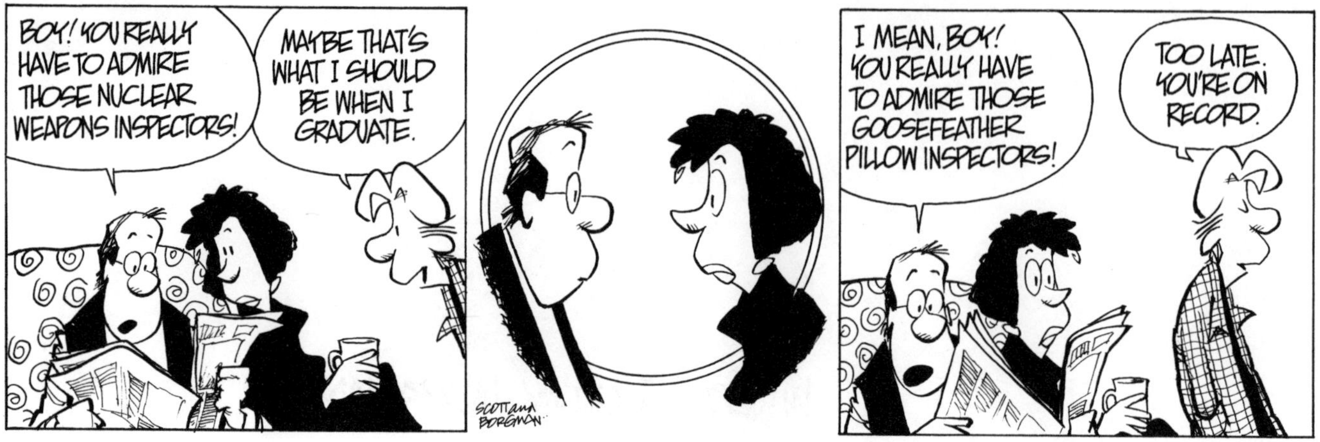
BOY! YOU REALLY HAVE TO ADMIRE THOSE NUCLEAR WEAPONS INSPECTORS!
MAYBE THAT'S WHAT I SHOULD BE WHEN I GRADUATE.
I MEAN, BOY! YOU REALLY HAVE TO ADMIRE THOSE GOOSEFEATHER PILLOW INSPECTORS!
TOO LATE. YOU'RE ON RECORD.

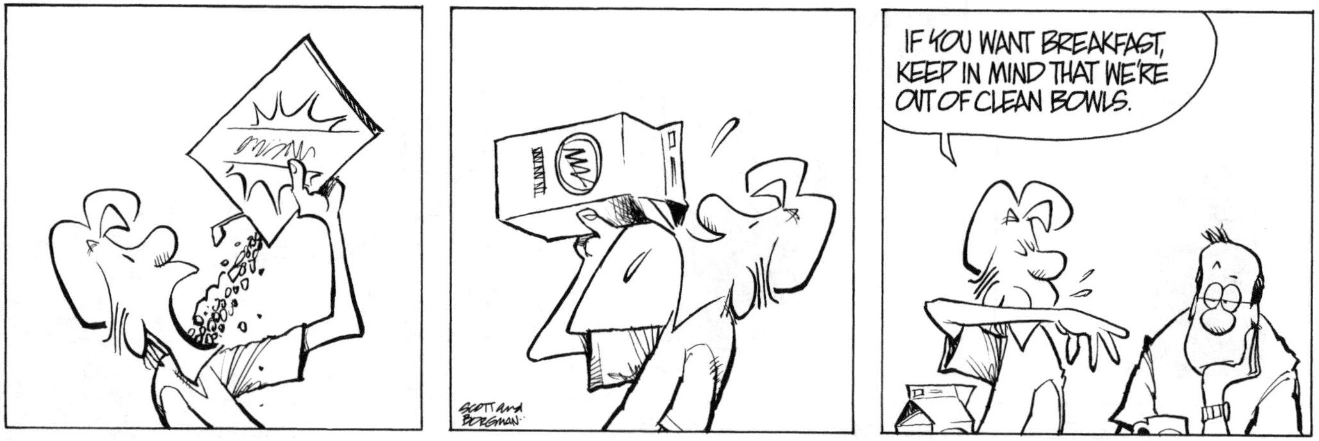
IF YOU WANT BREAKFAST, KEEP IN MIND THAT WE'RE OUT OF CLEAN BOWLS.

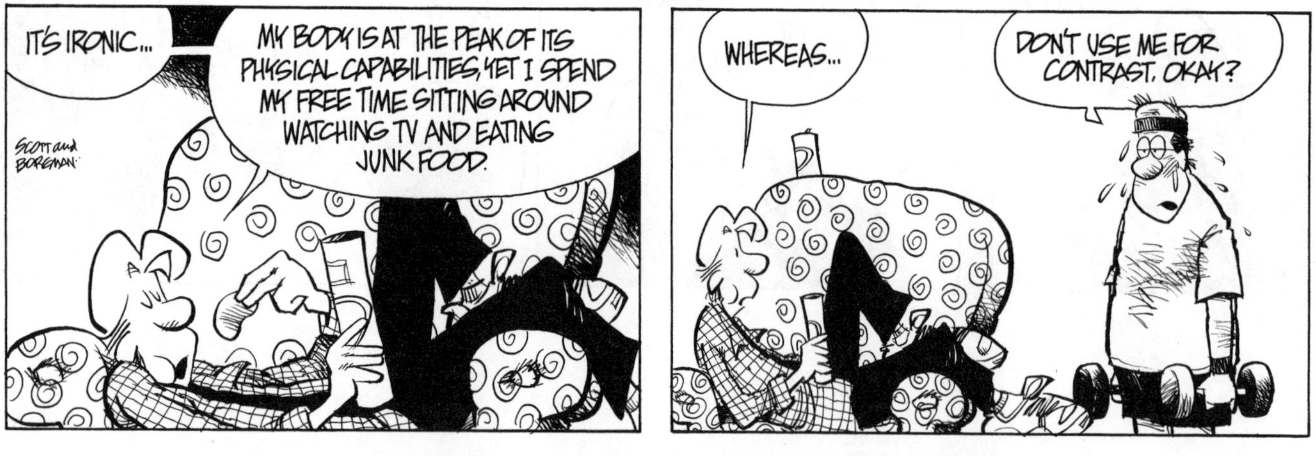
IT'S IRONIC...
MY BODY IS AT THE PEAK OF ITS PHYSICAL CAPABILITIES, YET I SPEND MY FREE TIME SITTING AROUND WATCHING TV AND EATING JUNK FOOD.
WHEREAS...
DON'T USE ME FOR CONTRAST, OKAY?

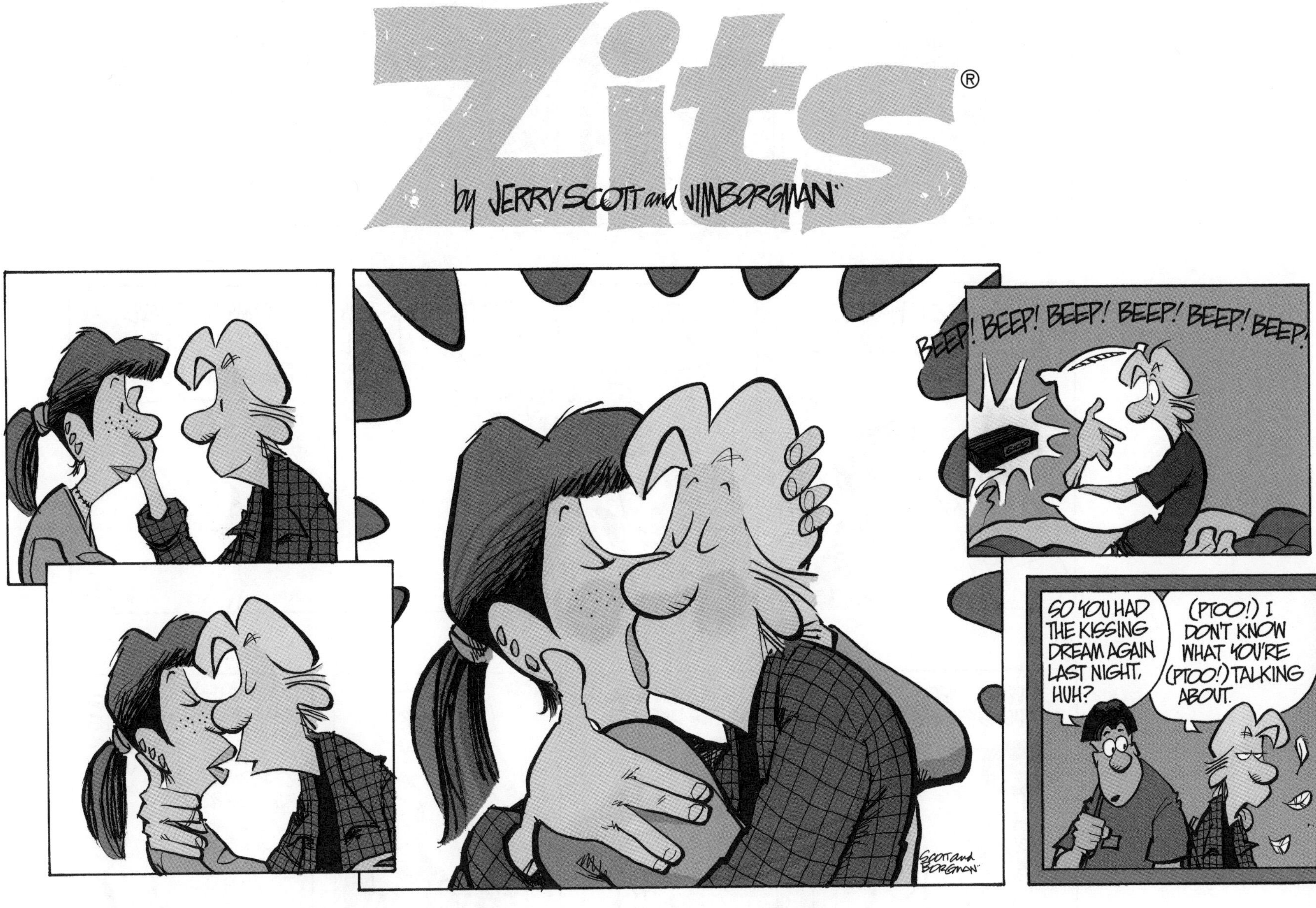
Zits®
by JERRY SCOTT and JIM BORGMAN
BEEP! BEEP! BEEP! BEEP! BEEP! BEEP!
SO YOU HAD THE KISSING DREAM AGAIN LAST NIGHT, HUH?
(PTOO!) I DON'T KNOW WHAT YOU'RE (PTOO!) TALKING ABOUT.
SCOTT and BORGMAN

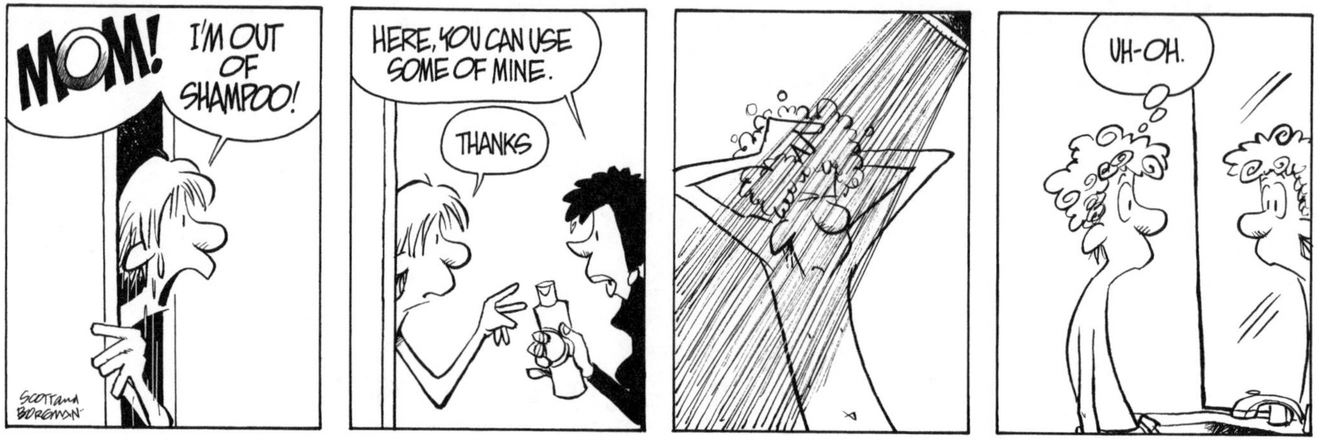
MOM! I'M OUT OF SHAMPOO!
HERE, YOU CAN USE SOME OF MINE.
THANKS
UH-OH.

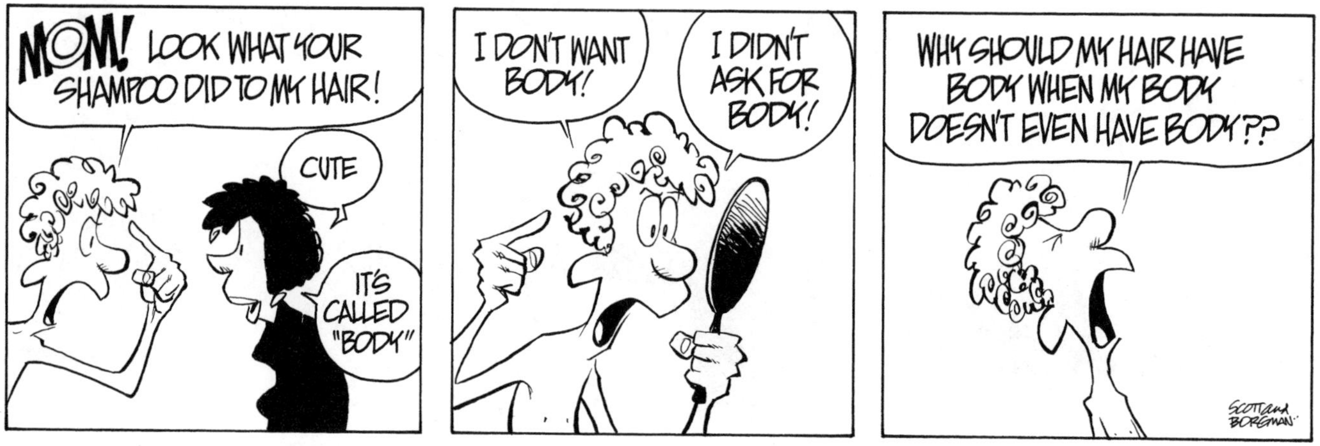
MOM! LOOK WHAT YOUR SHAMPOO DID TO MY HAIR!
CUTE
IT'S CALLED "BODY"
I DON'T WANT BODY!
I DIDN'T ASK FOR BODY!
WHY SHOULD MY HAIR HAVE BODY WHEN MY BODY DOESN'T EVEN HAVE BODY??

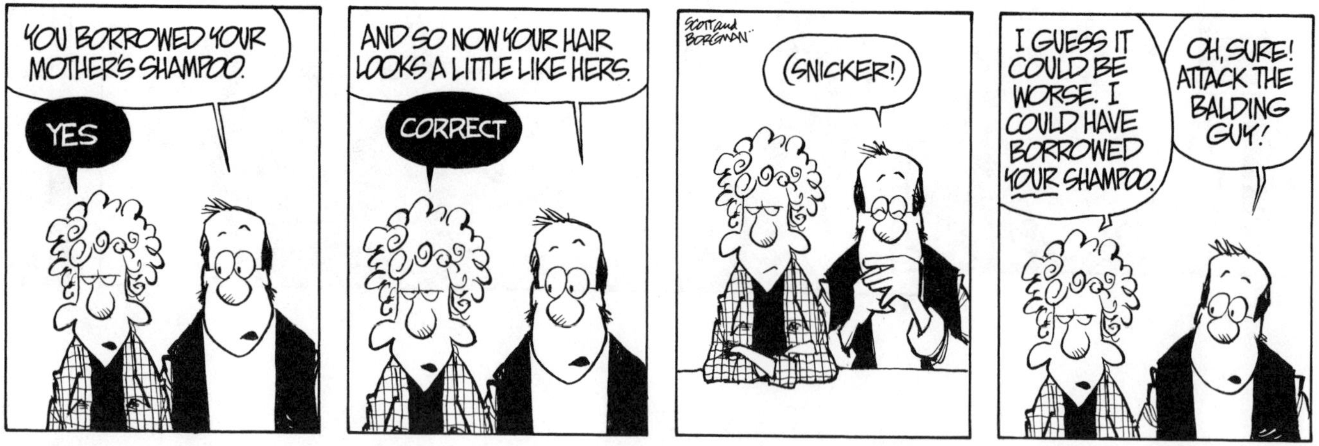
YOU BORROWED YOUR MOTHER'S SHAMPOO.
YES
AND SO NOW YOUR HAIR LOOKS A LITTLE LIKE HERS.
CORRECT
(SNICKER!)
I GUESS IT COULD BE WORSE. I COULD HAVE BORROWED YOUR SHAMPOO.
OH, SURE! ATTACK THE BALDING GUY!

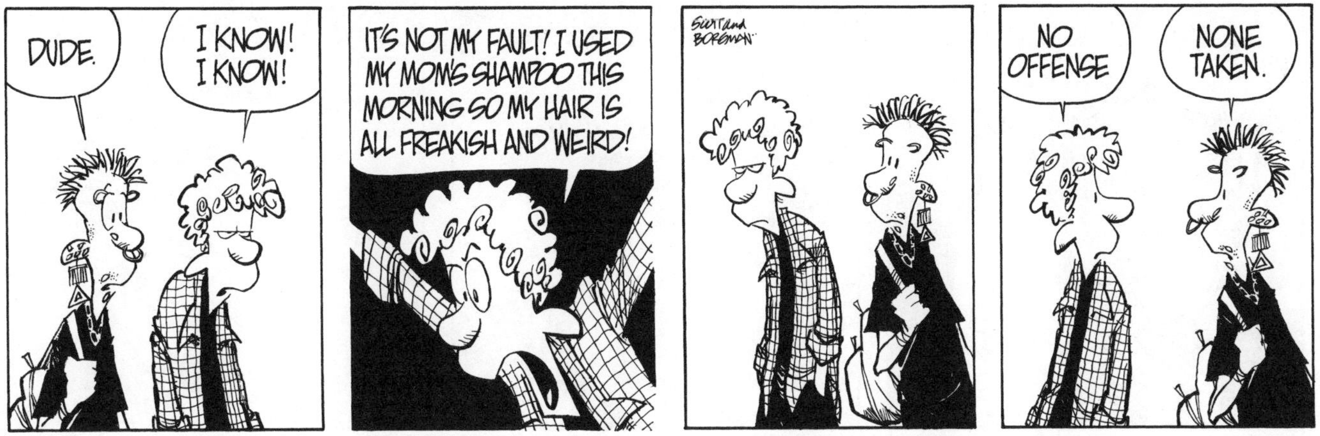
DUDE.
I KNOW! I KNOW!
IT'S NOT MY FAULT! I USED MY MOM'S SHAMPOO THIS MORNING SO MY HAIR IS ALL FREAKISH AND WEIRD!
SCOTT and BORGMAN
NO OFFENSE
NONE TAKEN.

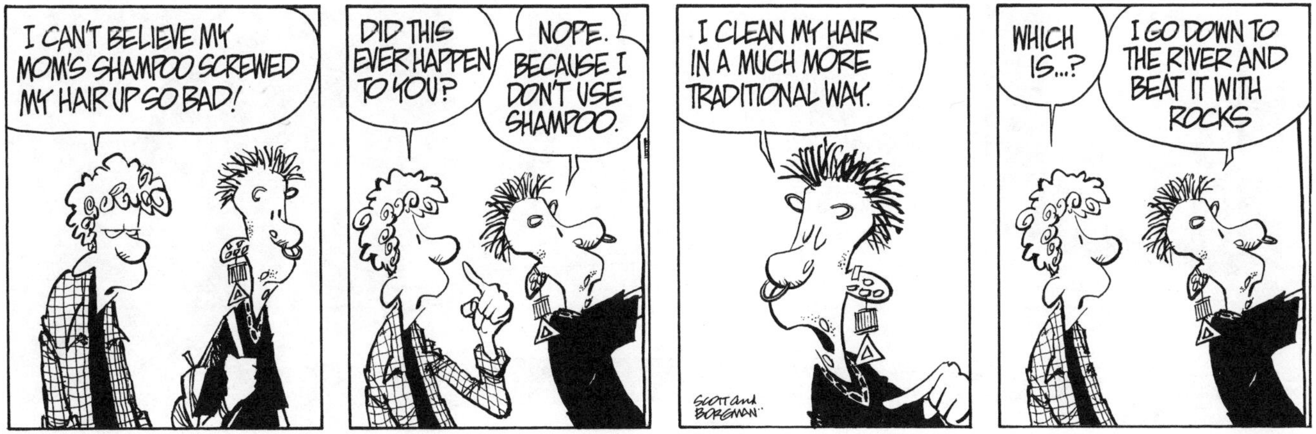
I CAN'T BELIEVE MY MOM'S SHAMPOO SCREWED MY HAIR UP SO BAD!
DID THIS EVER HAPPEN TO YOU?
NOPE. BECAUSE I DON'T USE SHAMPOO.
I CLEAN MY HAIR IN A MUCH MORE TRADITIONAL WAY.
SCOTT and BORGMAN
WHICH IS...?
I GO DOWN TO THE RIVER AND BEAT IT WITH ROCKS

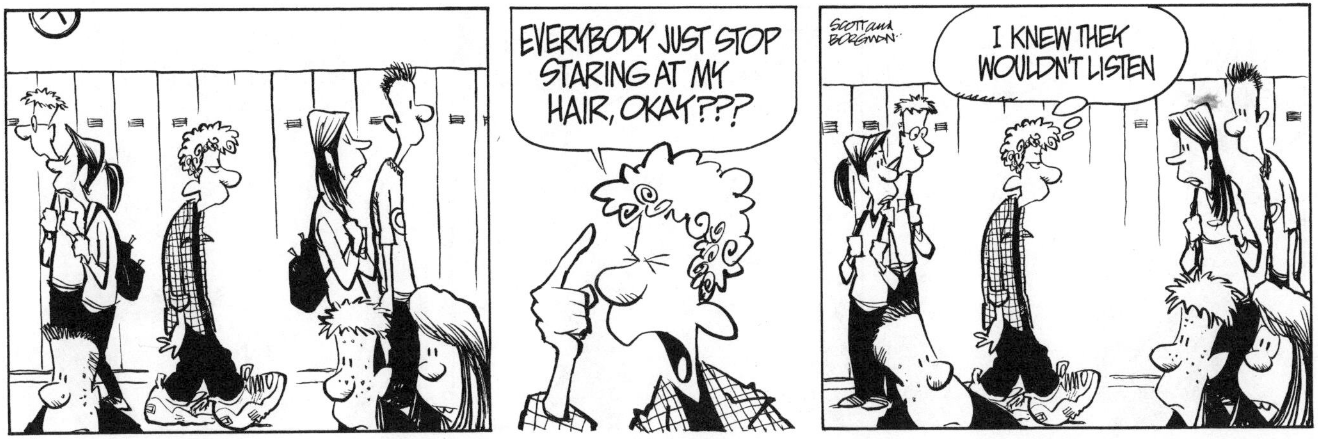
EVERYBODY JUST STOP STARING AT MY HAIR, OKAY???
SCOTT and BORGMAN
I KNEW THEY WOULDN'T LISTEN

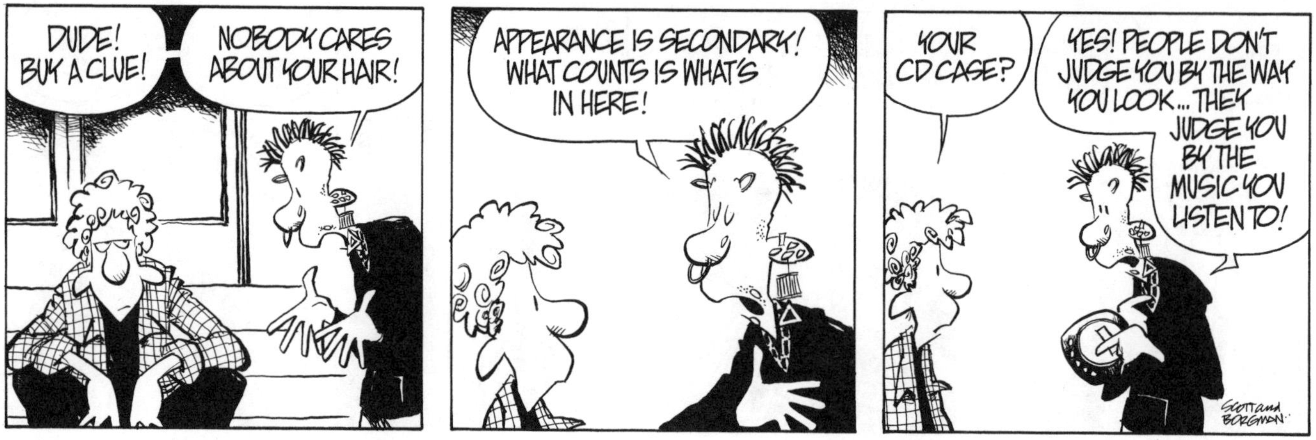
DUDE! BUY A CLUE!
NOBODY CARES ABOUT YOUR HAIR!
APPEARANCE IS SECONDARY! WHAT COUNTS IS WHAT'S IN HERE!
YOUR CD CASE?
YES! PEOPLE DON'T JUDGE YOU BY THE WAY YOU LOOK... THEY JUDGE YOU BY THE MUSIC YOU LISTEN TO!
SCOTT AND BORGMAN

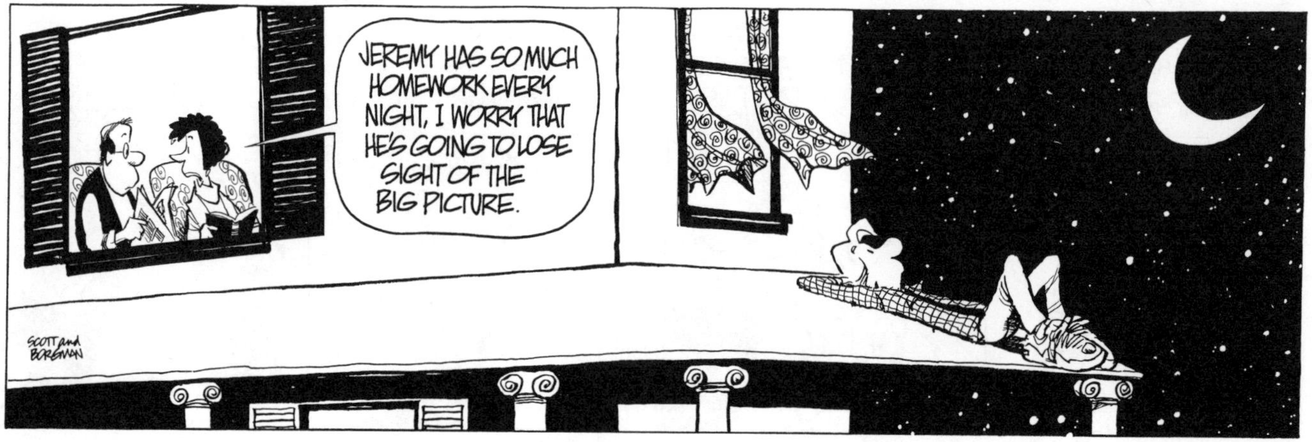
JEREMY HAS SO MUCH HOMEWORK EVERY NIGHT, I WORRY THAT HE'S GOING TO LOSE SIGHT OF THE BIG PICTURE.
SCOTT AND BORGMAN

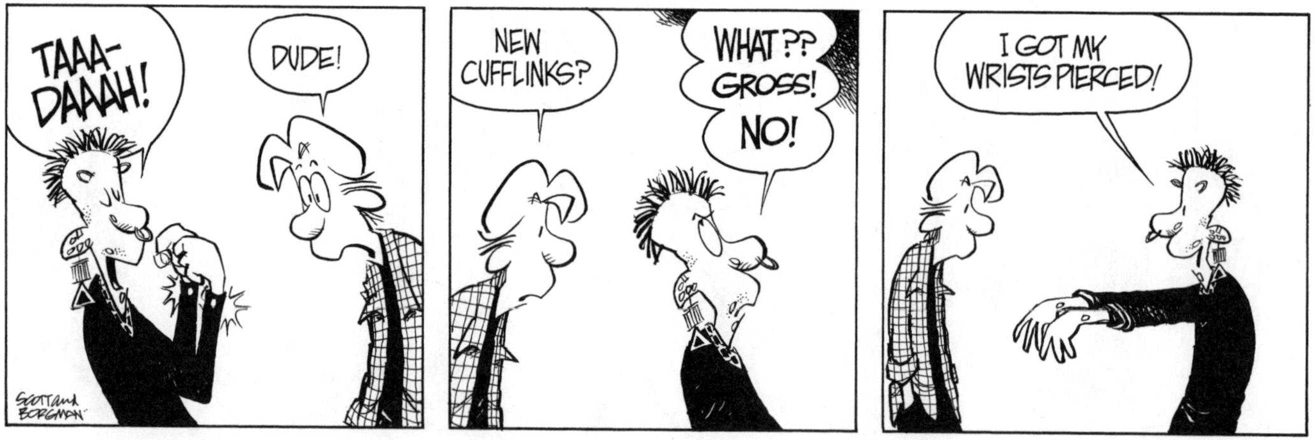
TAAA-DAAAH!
DUDE!
NEW CUFFLINKS?
WHAT?? GROSS! NO!
I GOT MY WRISTS PIERCED!
SCOTT AND BORGMAN

Zits®

by JERRY SCOTT and JIM BORGMAN

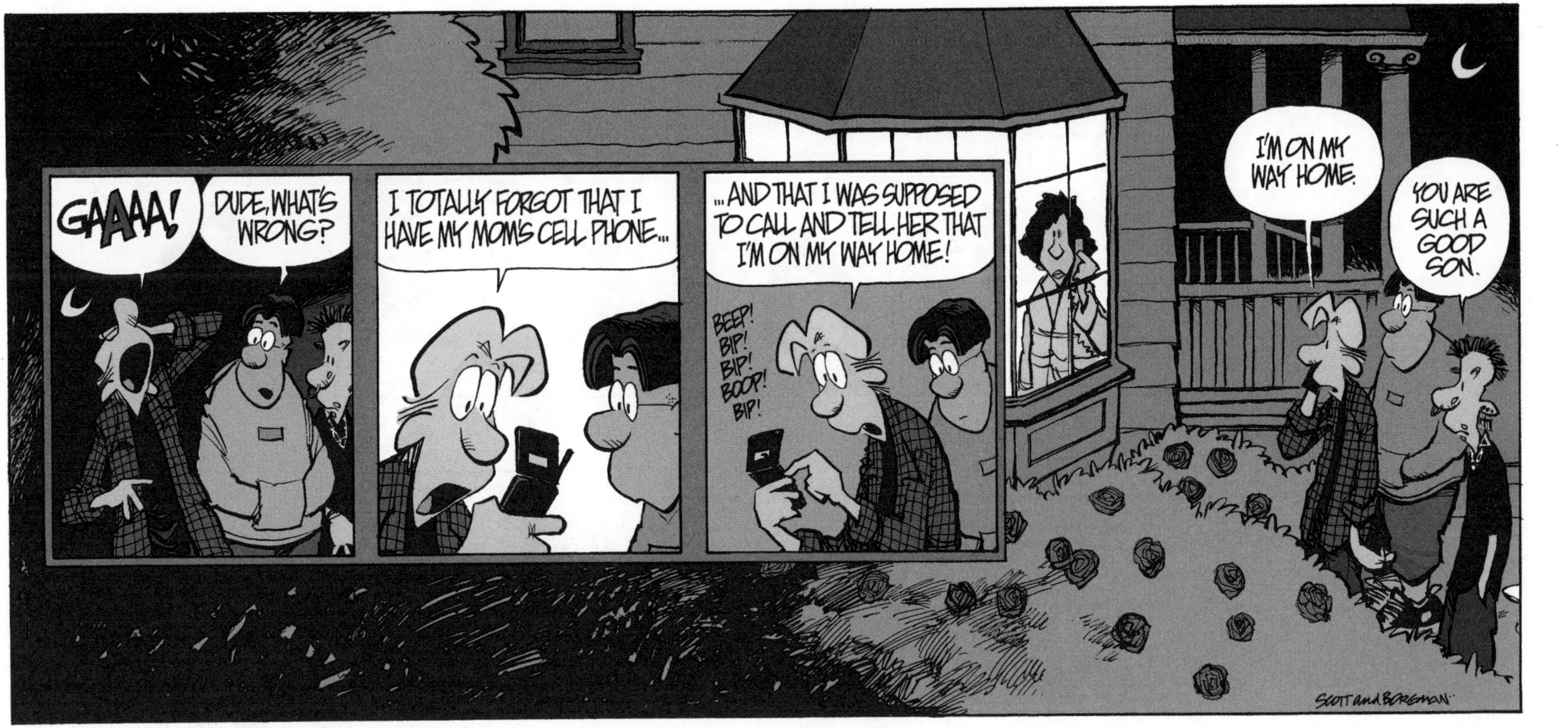
GAAAA!
DUDE, WHAT'S WRONG?
I TOTALLY FORGOT THAT I HAVE MY MOM'S CELL PHONE...
...AND THAT I WAS SUPPOSED TO CALL AND TELL HER THAT I'M ON MY WAY HOME!
BEEP! BIP! BIP! BOOP! BIP!
I'M ON MY WAY HOME.
YOU ARE SUCH A GOOD SON.
SCOTT and BORGMAN

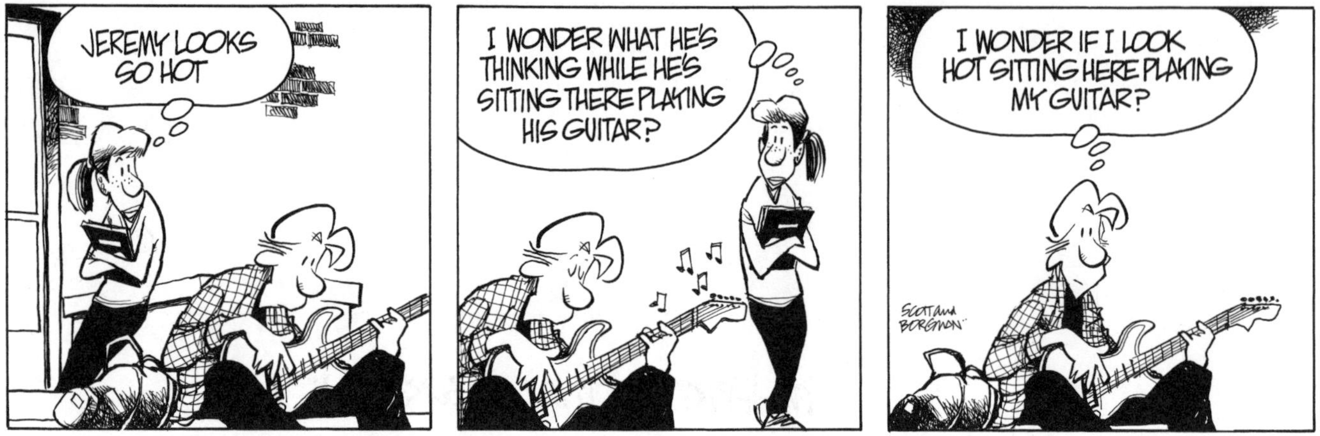
JEREMY LOOKS SO HOT
I WONDER WHAT HE'S THINKING WHILE HE'S SITTING THERE PLAYING HIS GUITAR?
I WONDER IF I LOOK HOT SITTING HERE PLAYING MY GUITAR?

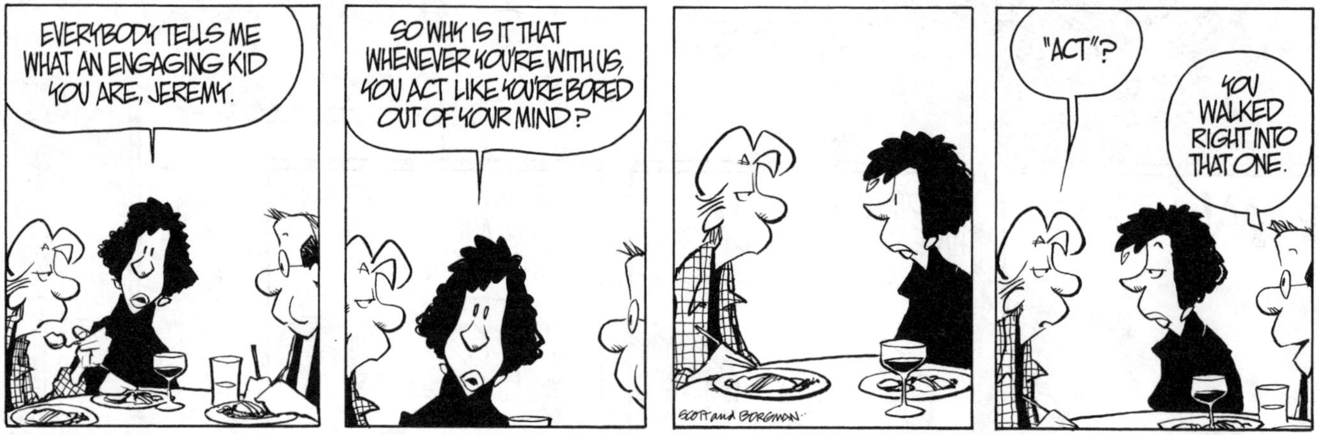
EVERYBODY TELLS ME WHAT AN ENGAGING KID YOU ARE, JEREMY.
SO WHY IS IT THAT WHENEVER YOU'RE WITH US, YOU ACT LIKE YOU'RE BORED OUT OF YOUR MIND?
"ACT"?
YOU WALKED RIGHT INTO THAT ONE.

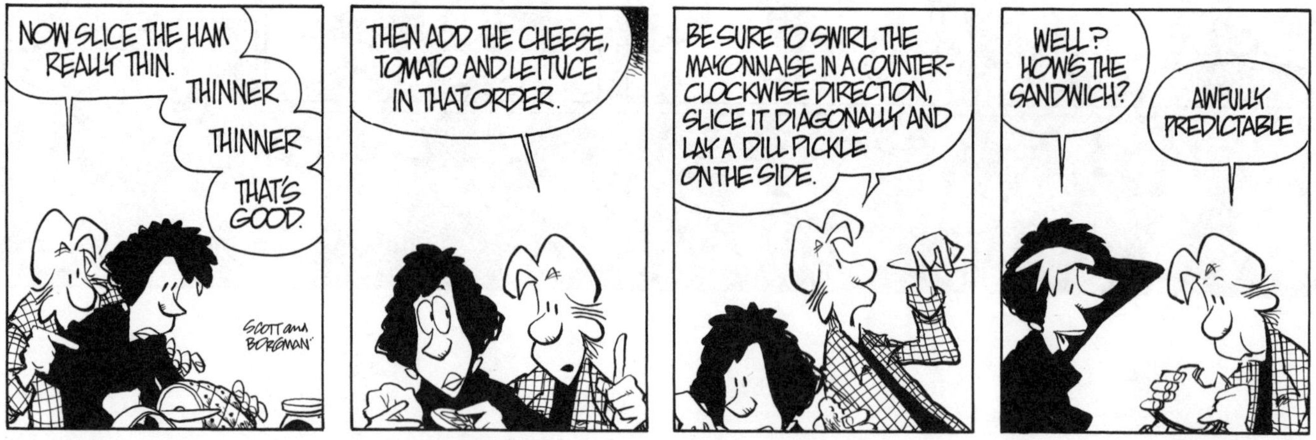
NOW SLICE THE HAM REALLY THIN.
THINNER
THINNER
THAT'S GOOD.
THEN ADD THE CHEESE, TOMATO AND LETTUCE IN THAT ORDER.
BE SURE TO SWIRL THE MAYONNAISE IN A COUNTER-CLOCKWISE DIRECTION, SLICE IT DIAGONALLY AND LAY A DILL PICKLE ON THE SIDE.
WELL? HOW'S THE SANDWICH?
AWFULLY PREDICTABLE

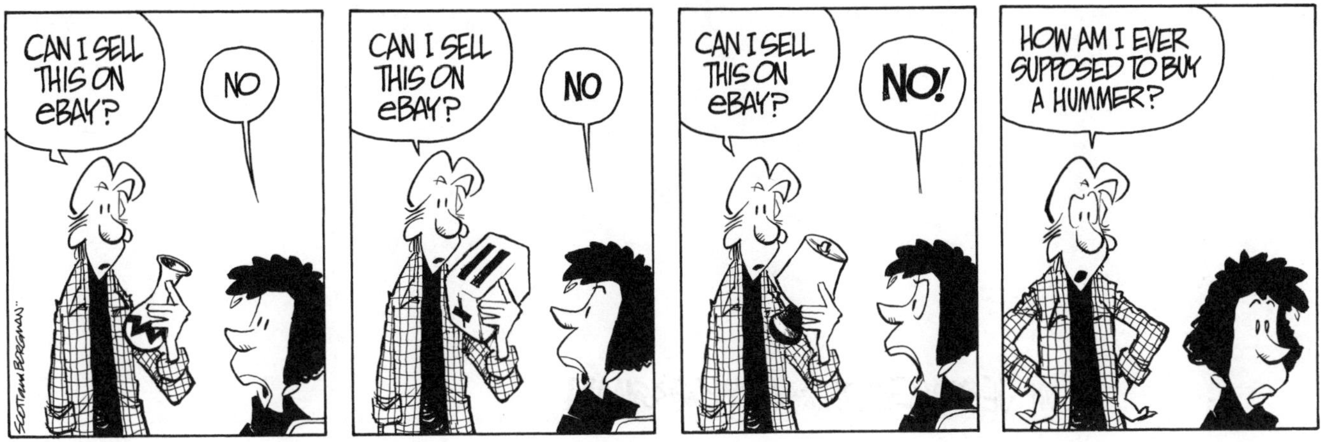
CAN I SELL THIS ON eBAY?
NO
CAN I SELL THIS ON eBAY?
NO
CAN I SELL THIS ON eBAY?
NO!
HOW AM I EVER SUPPOSED TO BUY A HUMMER?

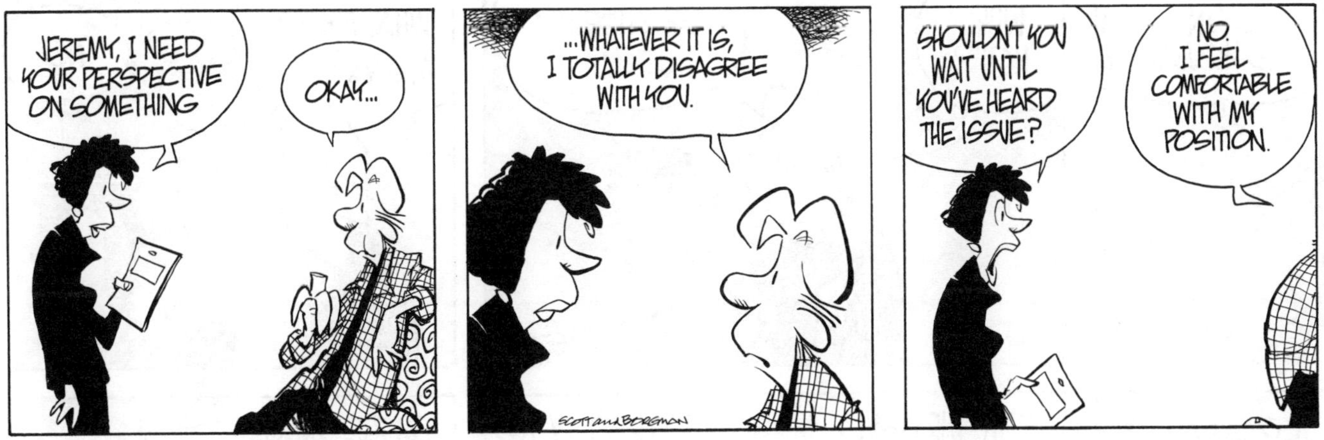
JEREMY, I NEED YOUR PERSPECTIVE ON SOMETHING
OKAY...
...WHATEVER IT IS, I TOTALLY DISAGREE WITH YOU.
SCOTT and BORGMAN
SHOULDN'T YOU WAIT UNTIL YOU'VE HEARD THE ISSUE?
NO. I FEEL COMFORTABLE WITH MY POSITION.

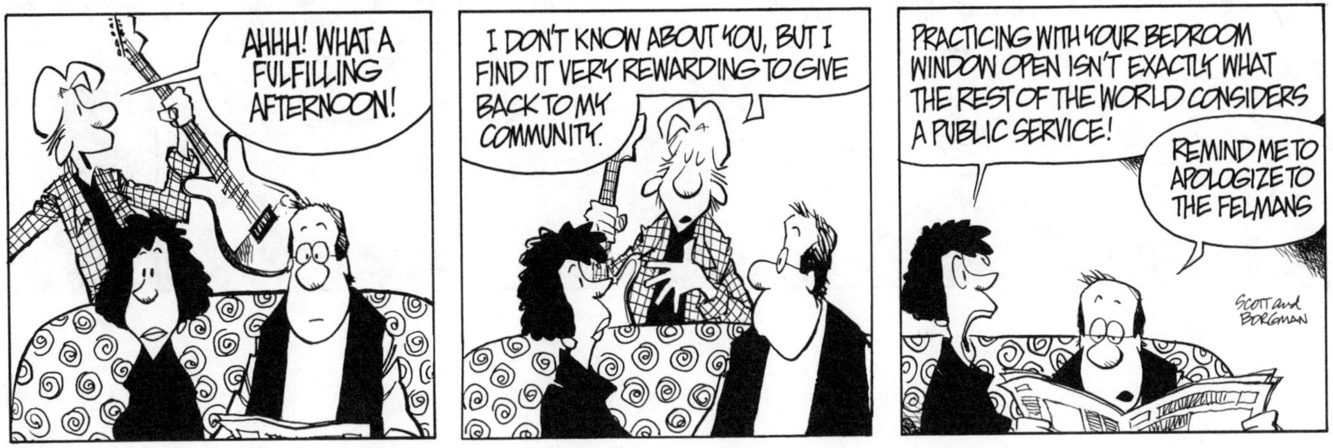
AHHH! WHAT A FULFILLING AFTERNOON!
I DON'T KNOW ABOUT YOU, BUT I FIND IT VERY REWARDING TO GIVE BACK TO MY COMMUNITY.
PRACTICING WITH YOUR BEDROOM WINDOW OPEN ISN'T EXACTLY WHAT THE REST OF THE WORLD CONSIDERS A PUBLIC SERVICE!
REMIND ME TO APOLOGIZE TO THE FELMANS
SCOTT and BORGMAN

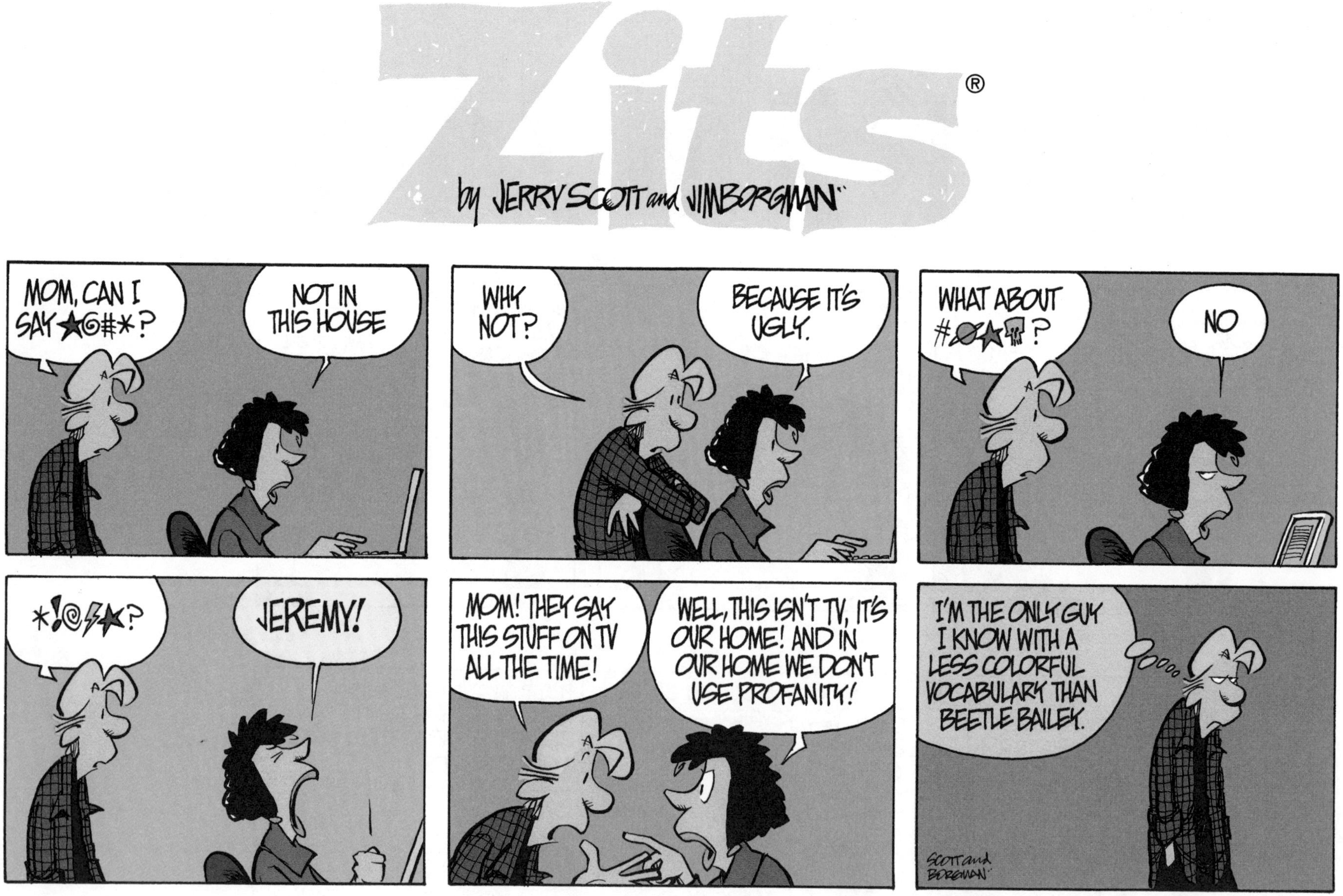
Zits®
by JERRY SCOTT and JIM BORGMAN
MOM, CAN I SAY ★@#*?
NOT IN THIS HOUSE
WHY NOT?
BECAUSE IT'S UGLY.
WHAT ABOUT #★?
NO
*!@★?
JEREMY!
MOM! THEY SAY THIS STUFF ON TV ALL THE TIME!
WELL, THIS ISN'T TV, IT'S OUR HOME! AND IN OUR HOME WE DON'T USE PROFANITY!
I'M THE ONLY GUY I KNOW WITH A LESS COLORFUL VOCABULARY THAN BEETLE BAILEY.
SCOTT and BORGMAN

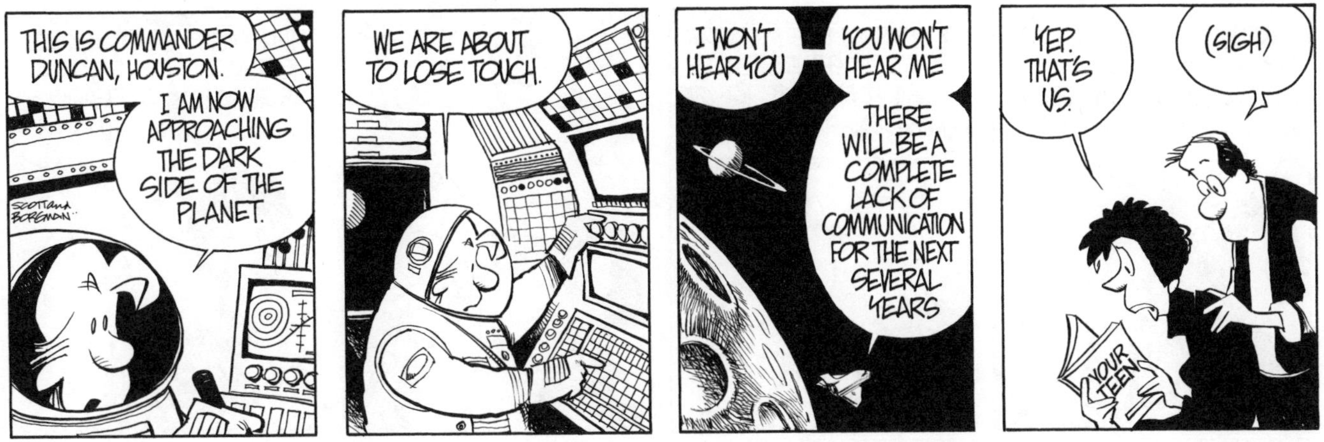
THIS IS COMMANDER DUNCAN, HOUSTON.
I AM NOW APPROACHING THE DARK SIDE OF THE PLANET.
SCOTT and BORGMAN
WE ARE ABOUT TO LOSE TOUCH.
I WON'T HEAR YOU
YOU WON'T HEAR ME
THERE WILL BE A COMPLETE LACK OF COMMUNICATION FOR THE NEXT SEVERAL YEARS
YEP. THAT'S US.
(SIGH)
YOUR TEEN

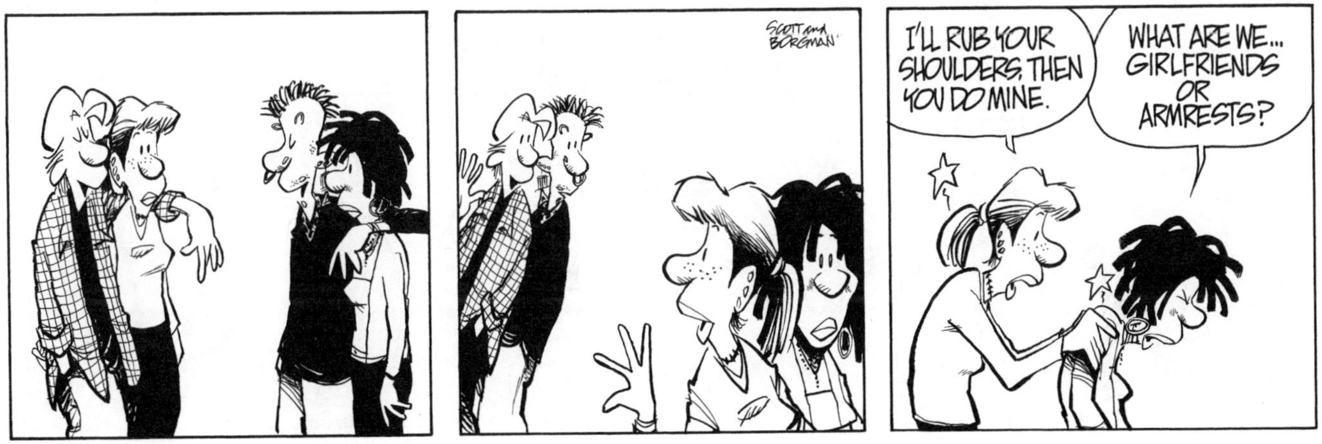
SCOTT and BORGMAN
I'LL RUB YOUR SHOULDERS, THEN YOU DO MINE.
WHAT ARE WE... GIRLFRIENDS OR ARMRESTS?

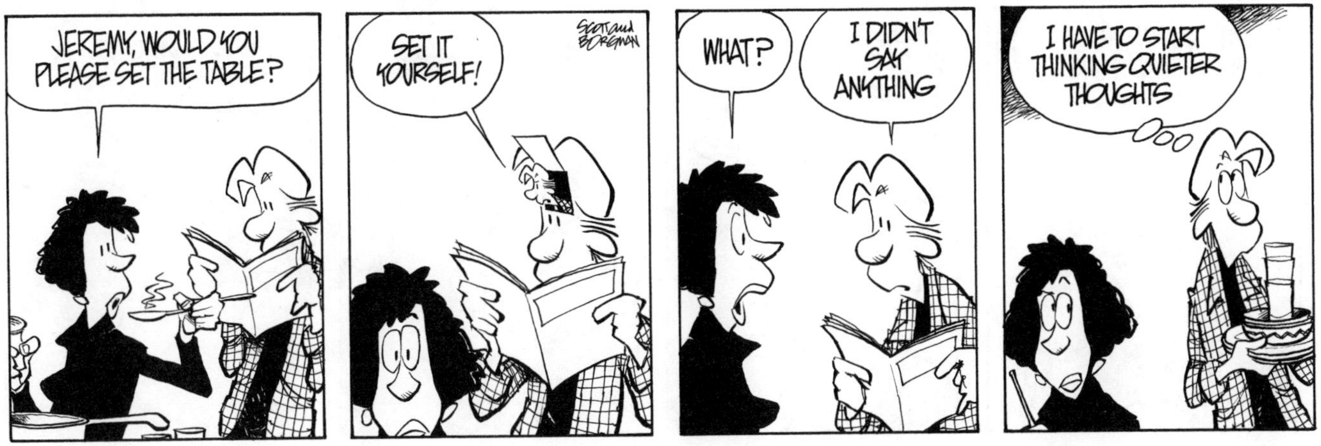
JEREMY, WOULD YOU PLEASE SET THE TABLE?
SET IT YOURSELF!
SCOTT and BORGMAN
WHAT?
I DIDN'T SAY ANYTHING
I HAVE TO START THINKING QUIETER THOUGHTS

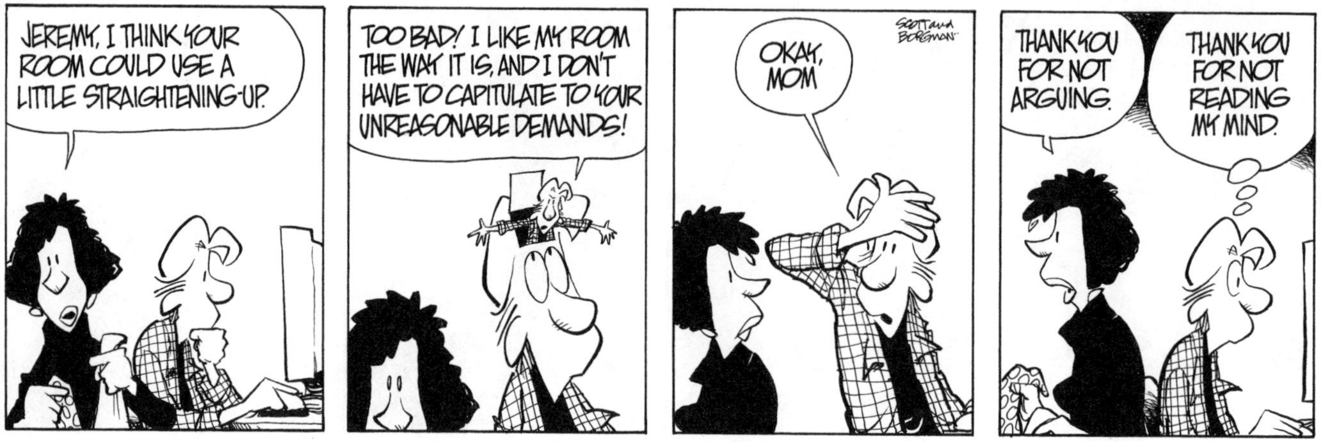
JEREMY, I THINK YOUR ROOM COULD USE A LITTLE STRAIGHTENING-UP.
TOO BAD! I LIKE MY ROOM THE WAY IT IS, AND I DON'T HAVE TO CAPITULATE TO YOUR UNREASONABLE DEMANDS!
OKAY, MOM
THANK YOU FOR NOT ARGUING.
THANK YOU FOR NOT READING MY MIND.

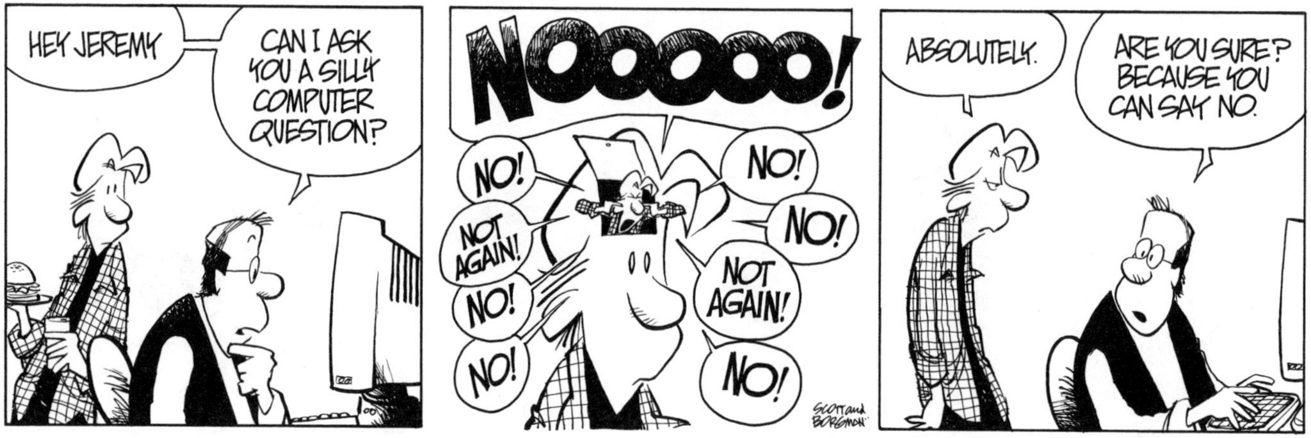
HEY JEREMY
CAN I ASK YOU A SILLY COMPUTER QUESTION?
NOOOOO!
NO!
NO!
NOT AGAIN!
NO!
NOT AGAIN!
NO!
NO!
NO!
ABSOLUTELY.
ARE YOU SURE? BECAUSE YOU CAN SAY NO.

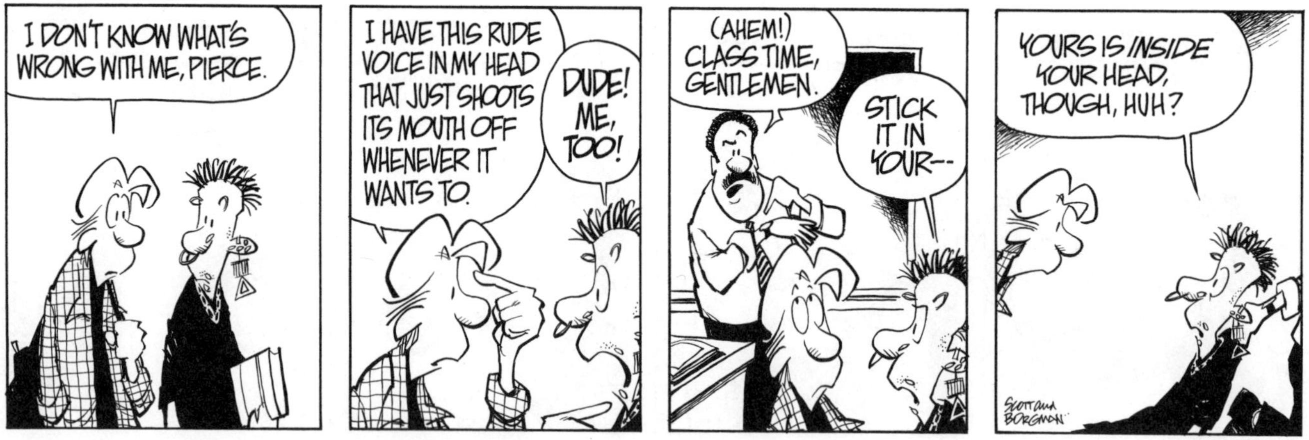
I DON'T KNOW WHAT'S WRONG WITH ME, PIERCE.
I HAVE THIS RUDE VOICE IN MY HEAD THAT JUST SHOOTS ITS MOUTH OFF WHENEVER IT WANTS TO.
DUDE! ME, TOO!
(AHEM!) CLASS TIME, GENTLEMEN.
STICK IT IN YOUR--
YOURS IS INSIDE YOUR HEAD, THOUGH, HUH?

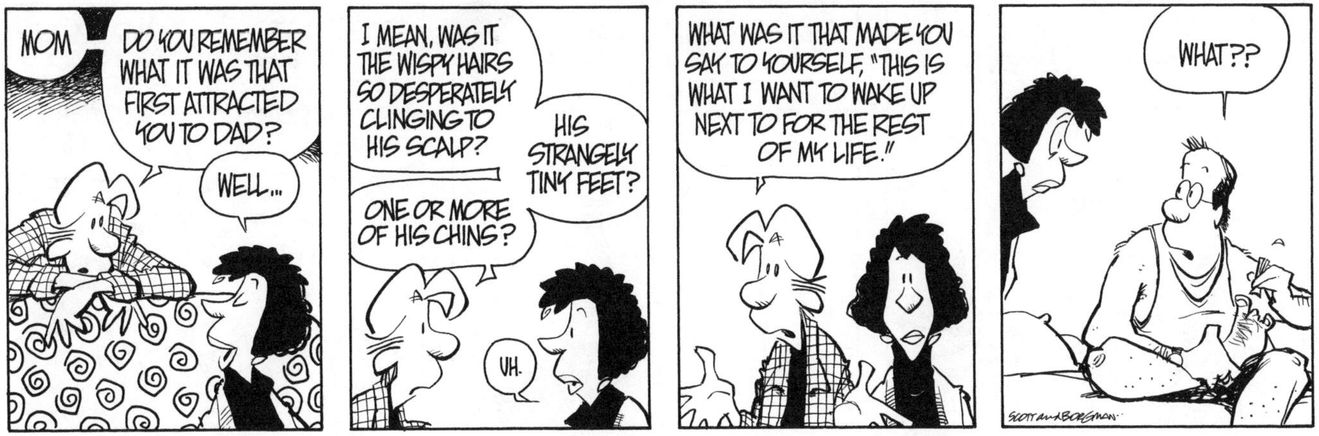
MOM
DO YOU REMEMBER WHAT IT WAS THAT FIRST ATTRACTED YOU TO DAD?
WELL...
I MEAN, WAS IT THE WISPY HAIRS SO DESPERATELY CLINGING TO HIS SCALP?
HIS STRANGELY TINY FEET?
ONE OR MORE OF HIS CHINS?
UH.
WHAT WAS IT THAT MADE YOU SAY TO YOURSELF, "THIS IS WHAT I WANT TO WAKE UP NEXT TO FOR THE REST OF MY LIFE."
WHAT??

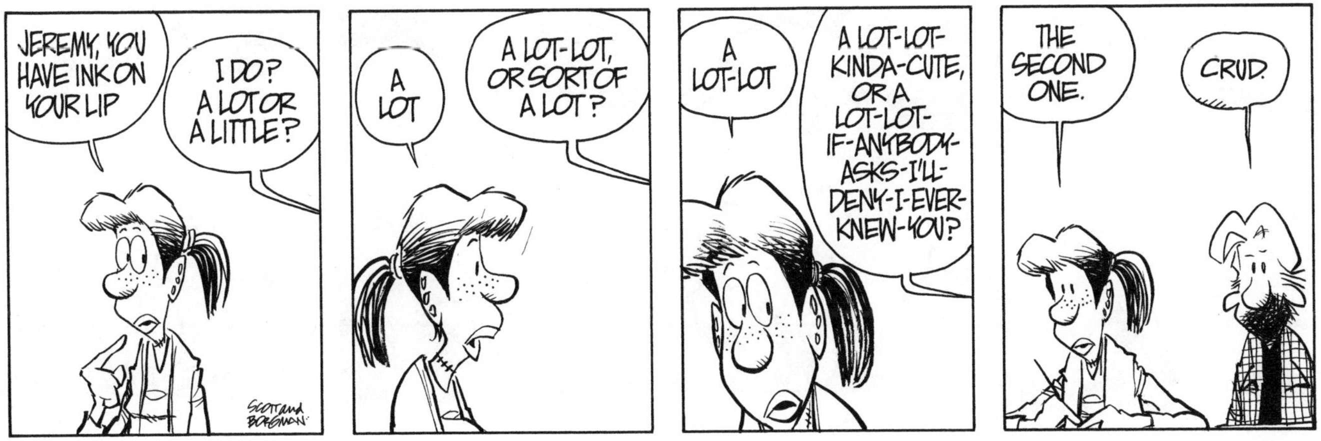
JEREMY, YOU HAVE INK ON YOUR LIP
I DO? A LOT OR A LITTLE?
A LOT
A LOT-LOT, OR SORT OF A LOT?
A LOT-LOT
A LOT-LOT-KINDA-CUTE, OR A LOT-LOT-IF-ANYBODY-ASKS-I'LL-DENY-I-EVER-KNEW-YOU?
THE SECOND ONE.
CRUD.

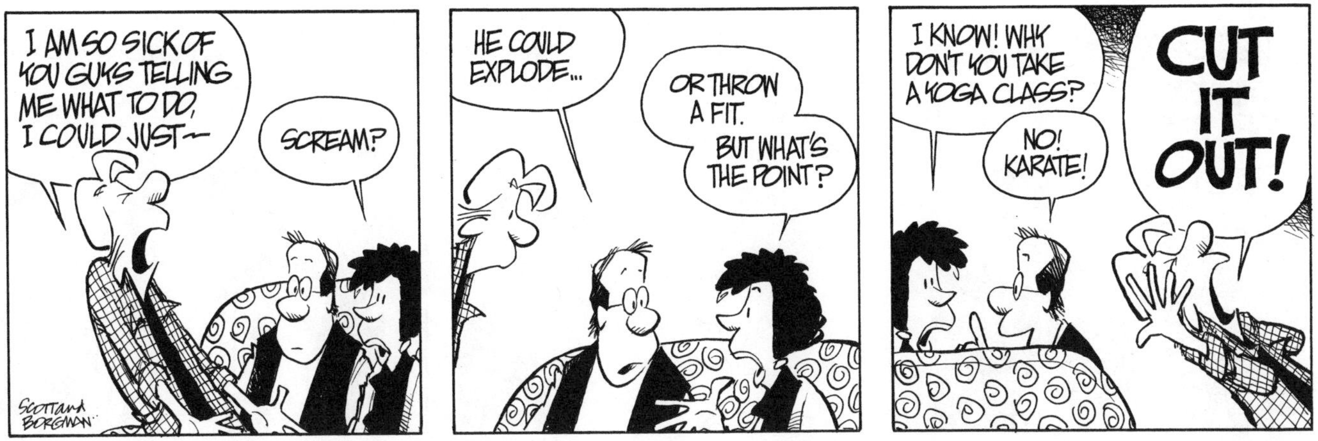
I AM SO SICK OF YOU GUYS TELLING ME WHAT TO DO, I COULD JUST--
SCREAM?
HE COULD EXPLODE...
OR THROW A FIT.
BUT WHAT'S THE POINT?
I KNOW! WHY DON'T YOU TAKE A YOGA CLASS?
NO! KARATE!
CUT IT OUT!

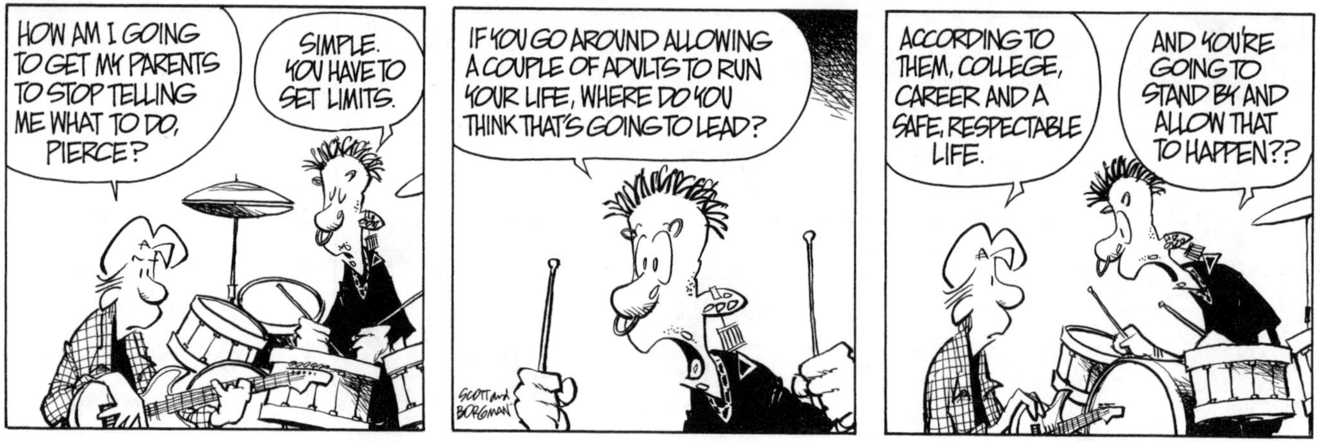
HOW AM I GOING TO GET MY PARENTS TO STOP TELLING ME WHAT TO DO, PIERCE?
SIMPLE. YOU HAVE TO SET LIMITS.
IF YOU GO AROUND ALLOWING A COUPLE OF ADULTS TO RUN YOUR LIFE, WHERE DO YOU THINK THAT'S GOING TO LEAD?
ACCORDING TO THEM, COLLEGE, CAREER AND A SAFE, RESPECTABLE LIFE.
AND YOU'RE GOING TO STAND BY AND ALLOW THAT TO HAPPEN??

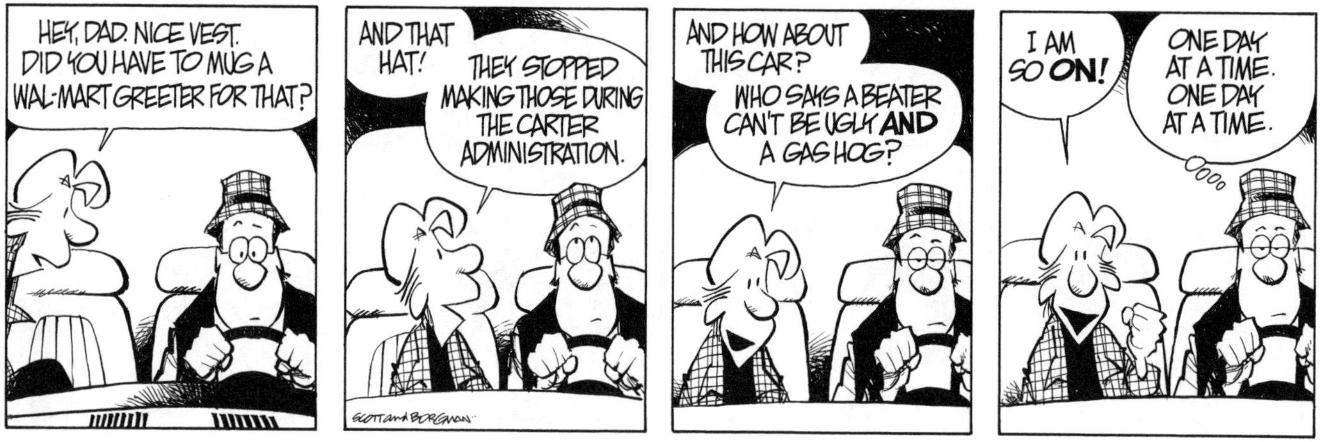
HEY, DAD. NICE VEST. DID YOU HAVE TO MUG A WAL-MART GREETER FOR THAT?
AND THAT HAT!
THEY STOPPED MAKING THOSE DURING THE CARTER ADMINISTRATION.
AND HOW ABOUT THIS CAR?
WHO SAYS A BEATER CAN'T BE UGLY **AND** A GAS HOG?
I AM SO **ON**!
ONE DAY AT A TIME. ONE DAY AT A TIME.

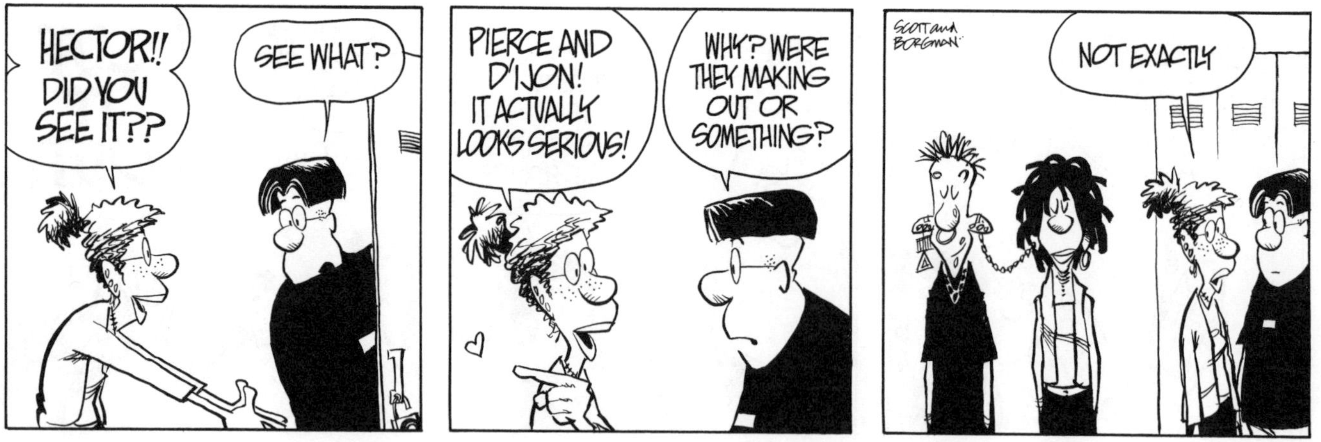
HECTOR!! DID YOU SEE IT??
SEE WHAT?
PIERCE AND D'JON! IT ACTUALLY LOOKS SERIOUS!
WHY? WERE THEY MAKING OUT OR SOMETHING?
NOT EXACTLY

Zits®

by JERRY SCOTT and JIM BORGMAN

(SIGH)
AH, SPRINGTIME!
WHEN A YOUNG MAN'S FANCY TURNS TO THOUGHTS OF LOVE.
SCOTT and BORGMAN
AS OPPOSED TO WHAT?

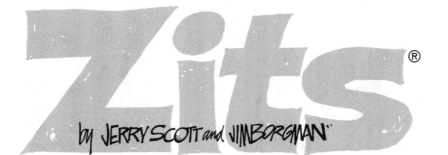

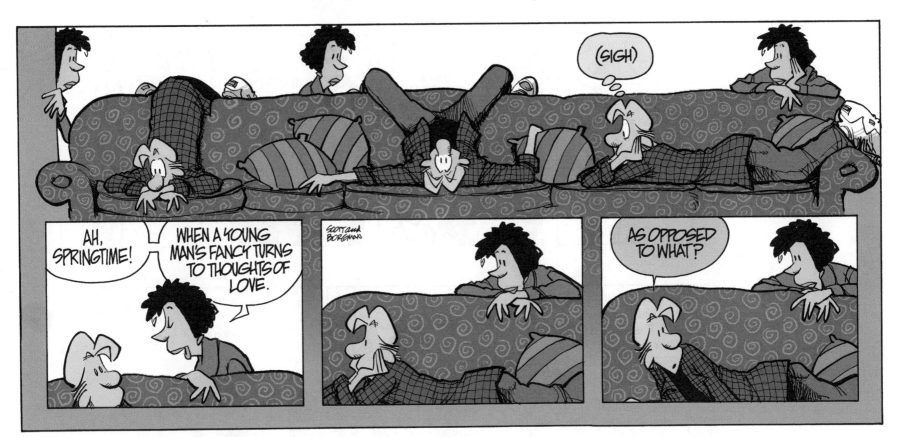

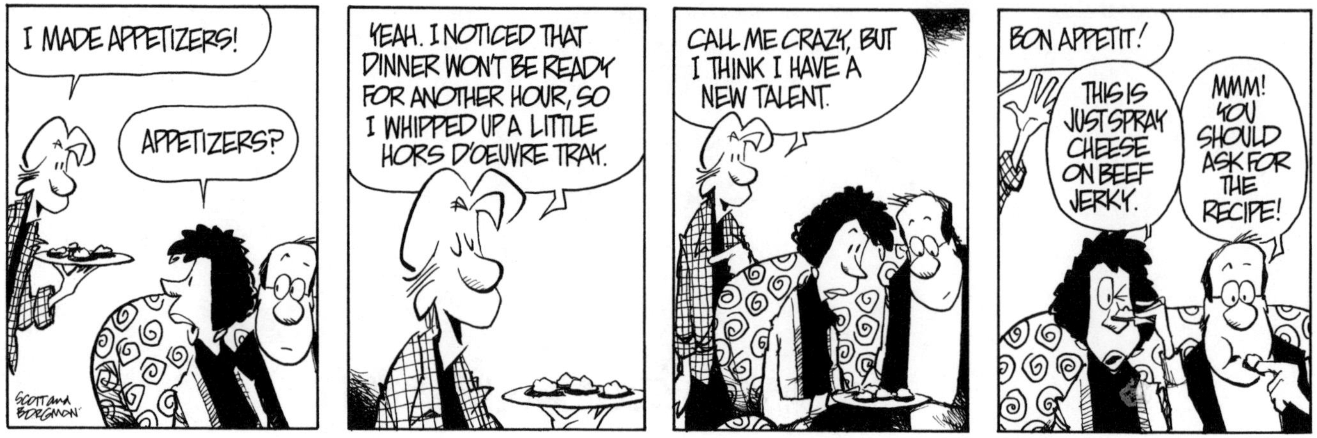
I MADE APPETIZERS!
APPETIZERS?
YEAH. I NOTICED THAT DINNER WON'T BE READY FOR ANOTHER HOUR, SO I WHIPPED UP A LITTLE HORS D'OEUVRE TRAY.
CALL ME CRAZY, BUT I THINK I HAVE A NEW TALENT.
BON APPETIT!
THIS IS JUST SPRAY CHEESE ON BEEF JERKY.
MMM! YOU SHOULD ASK FOR THE RECIPE!
SCOTT AND BORGMAN

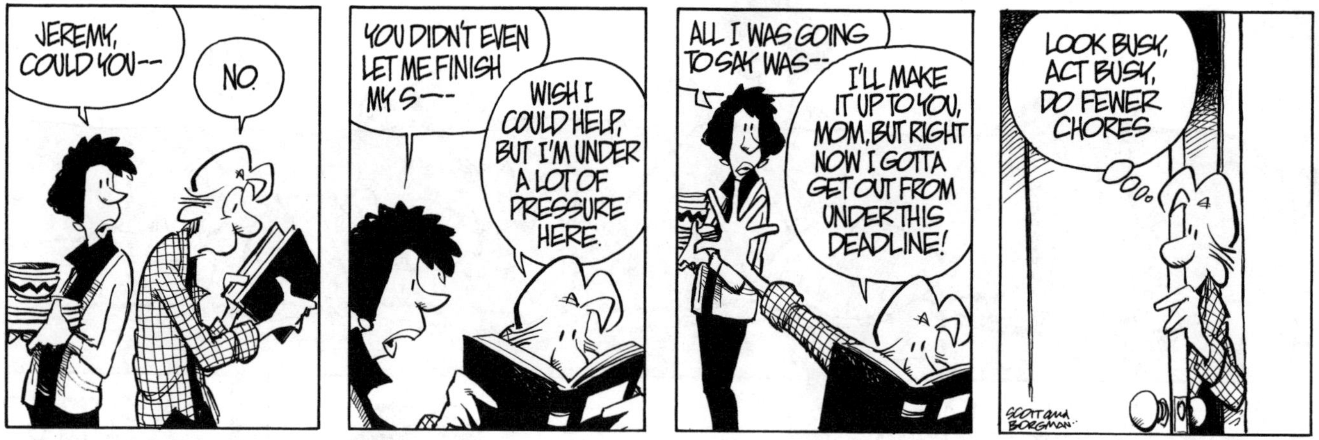
JEREMY, COULD YOU--
NO.
YOU DIDN'T EVEN LET ME FINISH MY S---
WISH I COULD HELP, BUT I'M UNDER A LOT OF PRESSURE HERE.
ALL I WAS GOING TO SAY WAS--
I'LL MAKE IT UP TO YOU, MOM, BUT RIGHT NOW I GOTTA GET OUT FROM UNDER THIS DEADLINE!
LOOK BUSY, ACT BUSY, DO FEWER CHORES
SCOTT AND BORGMAN

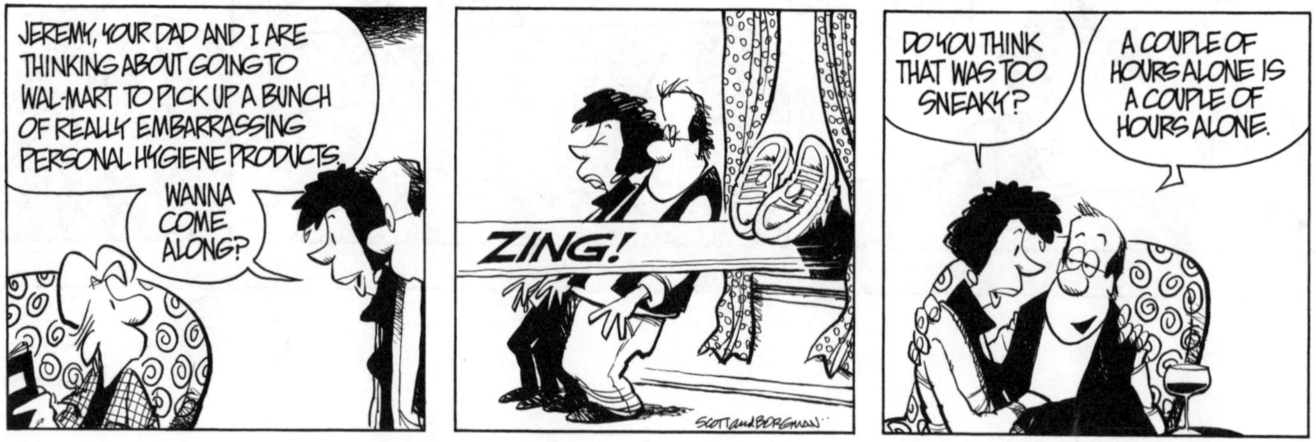
JEREMY, YOUR DAD AND I ARE THINKING ABOUT GOING TO WAL-MART TO PICK UP A BUNCH OF REALLY EMBARRASSING PERSONAL HYGIENE PRODUCTS.
WANNA COME ALONG?
ZING!
SCOTT AND BORGMAN
DO YOU THINK THAT WAS TOO SNEAKY?
A COUPLE OF HOURS ALONE IS A COUPLE OF HOURS ALONE.

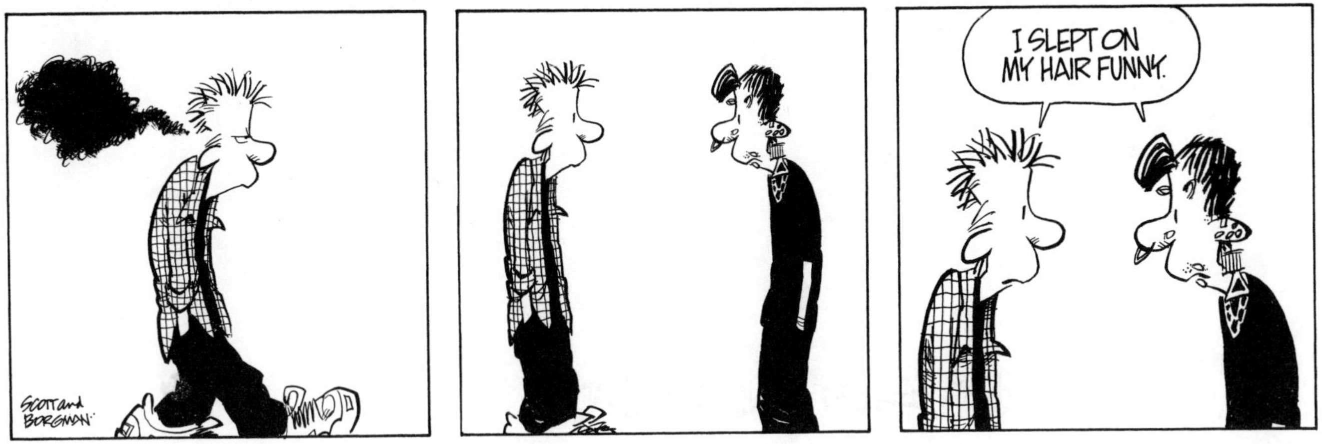
SCOTT and BORGMAN
I SLEPT ON MY HAIR FUNNY.

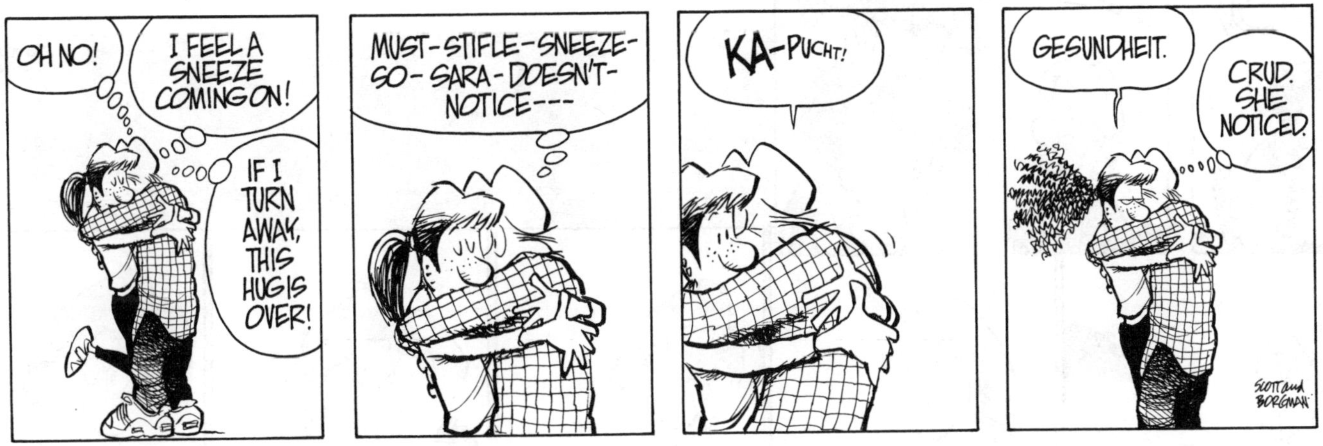
OH NO!
I FEEL A SNEEZE COMING ON!
IF I TURN AWAY, THIS HUG IS OVER!
MUST-STIFLE-SNEEZE-SO-SARA-DOESN'T-NOTICE---
KA-PUCHT!
GESUNDHEIT.
CRUD. SHE NOTICED.
SCOTT and BORGMAN

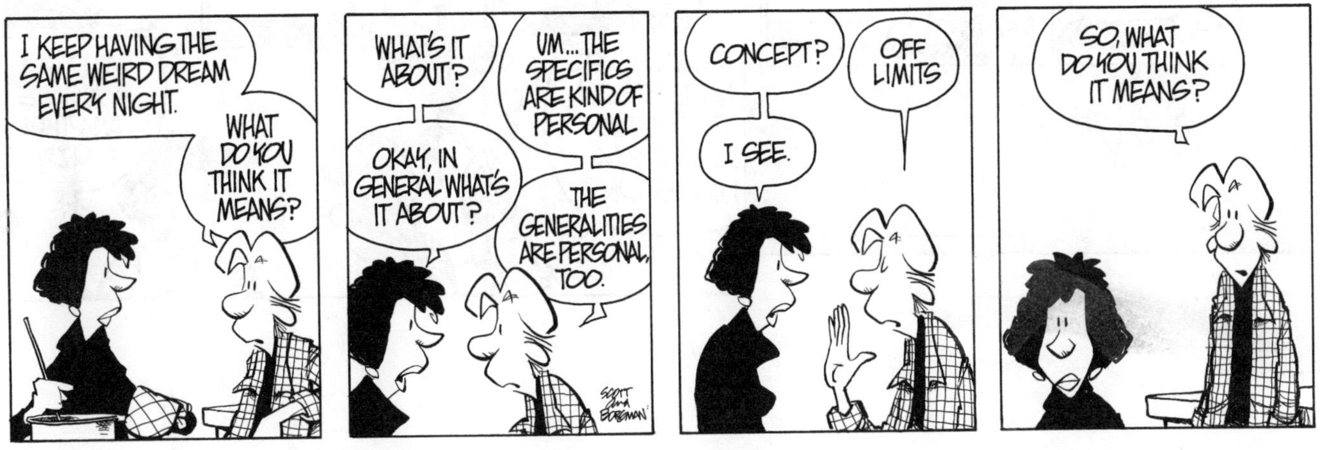
I KEEP HAVING THE SAME WEIRD DREAM EVERY NIGHT.
WHAT DO YOU THINK IT MEANS?
WHAT'S IT ABOUT?
UM... THE SPECIFICS ARE KIND OF PERSONAL
OKAY, IN GENERAL WHAT'S IT ABOUT?
THE GENERALITIES ARE PERSONAL, TOO.
SCOTT and BORGMAN
CONCEPT?
OFF LIMITS
I SEE.
SO, WHAT DO YOU THINK IT MEANS?

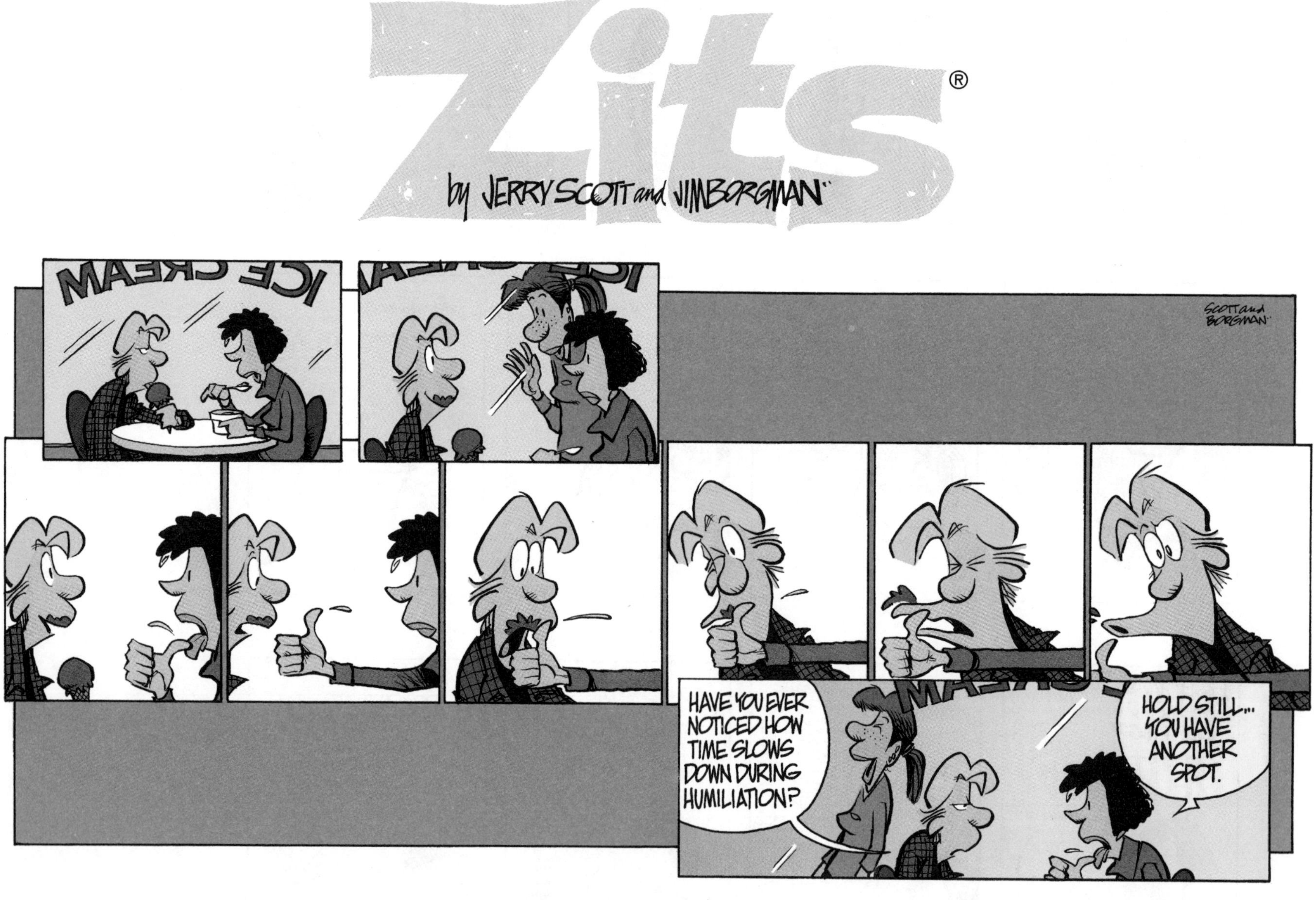
Zits®
by JERRY SCOTT and JIM BORGMAN
SCOTT and BORGMAN
HAVE YOU EVER NOTICED HOW TIME SLOWS DOWN DURING HUMILIATION?
HOLD STILL... YOU HAVE ANOTHER SPOT.

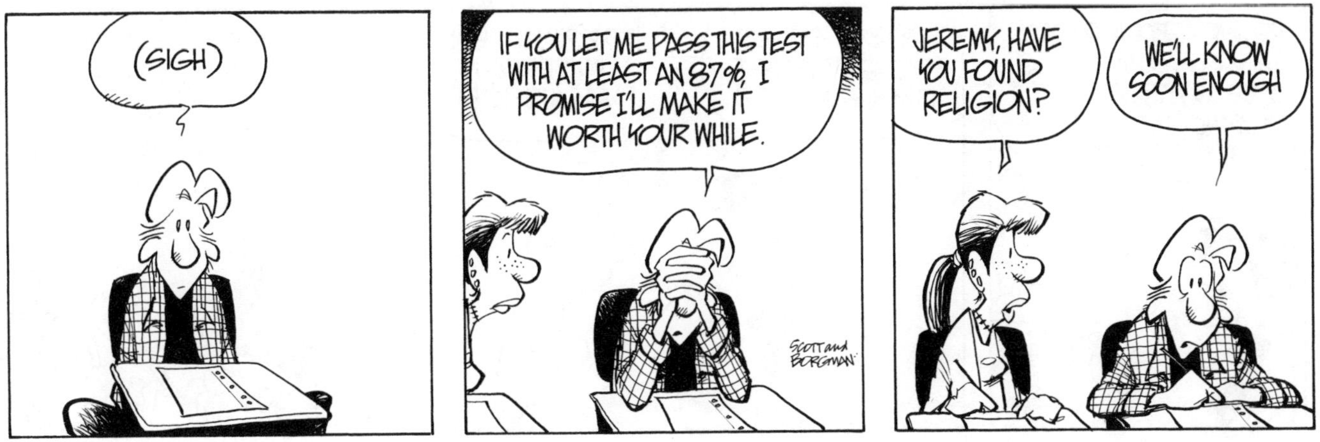

(SIGH)
IF YOU LET ME PASS THIS TEST WITH AT LEAST AN 87%, I PROMISE I'LL MAKE IT WORTH YOUR WHILE.
JEREMY, HAVE YOU FOUND RELIGION?
WE'LL KNOW SOON ENOUGH

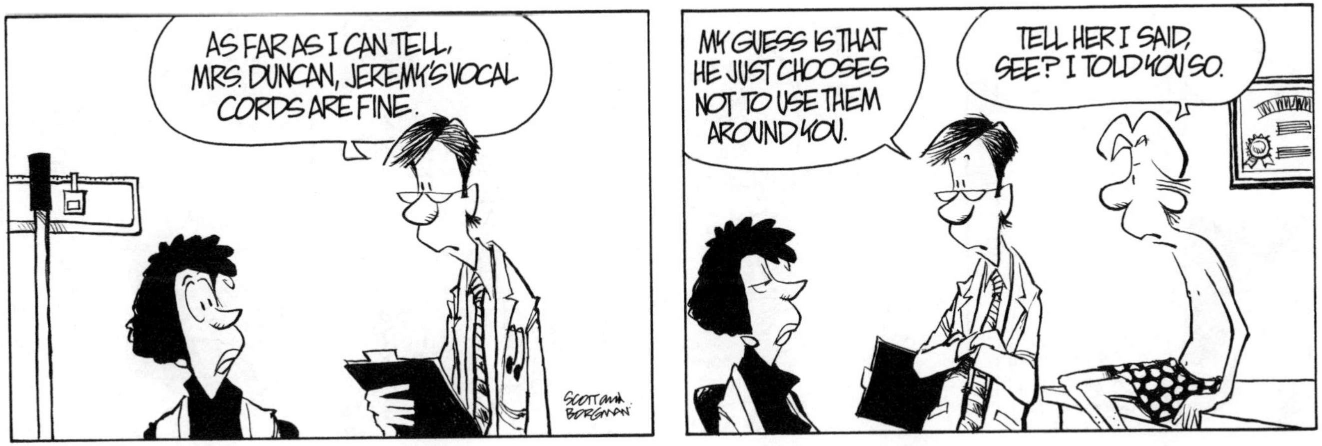

AS FAR AS I CAN TELL, MRS. DUNCAN, JEREMY'S VOCAL CORDS ARE FINE.
MY GUESS IS THAT HE JUST CHOOSES NOT TO USE THEM AROUND YOU.
TELL HER I SAID, SEE? I TOLD YOU SO.

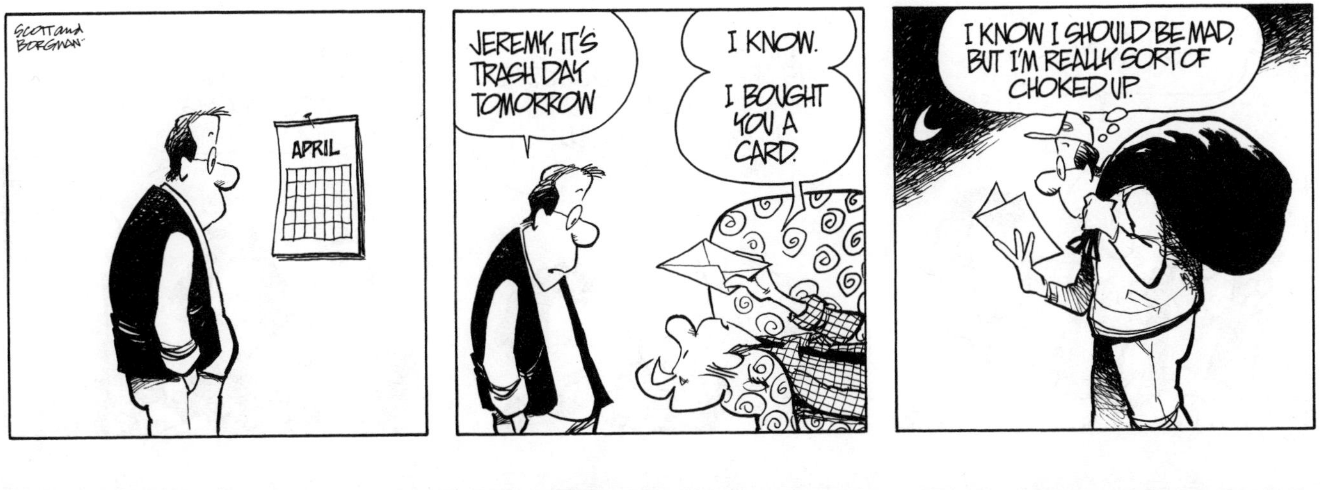

APRIL
JEREMY, IT'S TRASH DAY TOMORROW
I KNOW.
I BOUGHT YOU A CARD.
I KNOW I SHOULD BE MAD, BUT I'M REALLY SORT OF CHOKED UP.

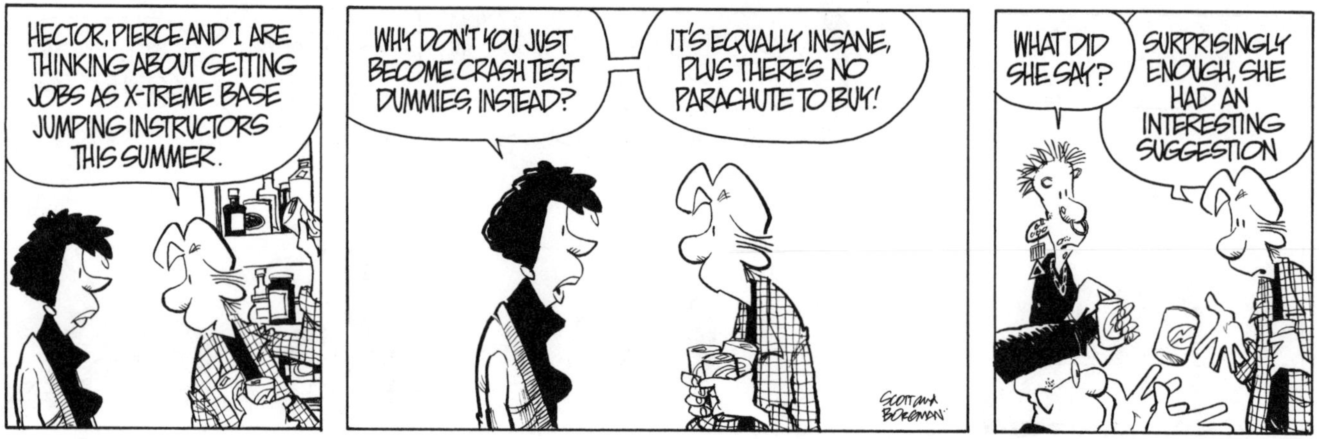
HECTOR, PIERCE AND I ARE THINKING ABOUT GETTING JOBS AS X-TREME BASE JUMPING INSTRUCTORS THIS SUMMER.
WHY DON'T YOU JUST BECOME CRASH TEST DUMMIES, INSTEAD?
IT'S EQUALLY INSANE, PLUS THERE'S NO PARACHUTE TO BUY!
SCOTT AND BORGMAN
WHAT DID SHE SAY?
SURPRISINGLY ENOUGH, SHE HAD AN INTERESTING SUGGESTION

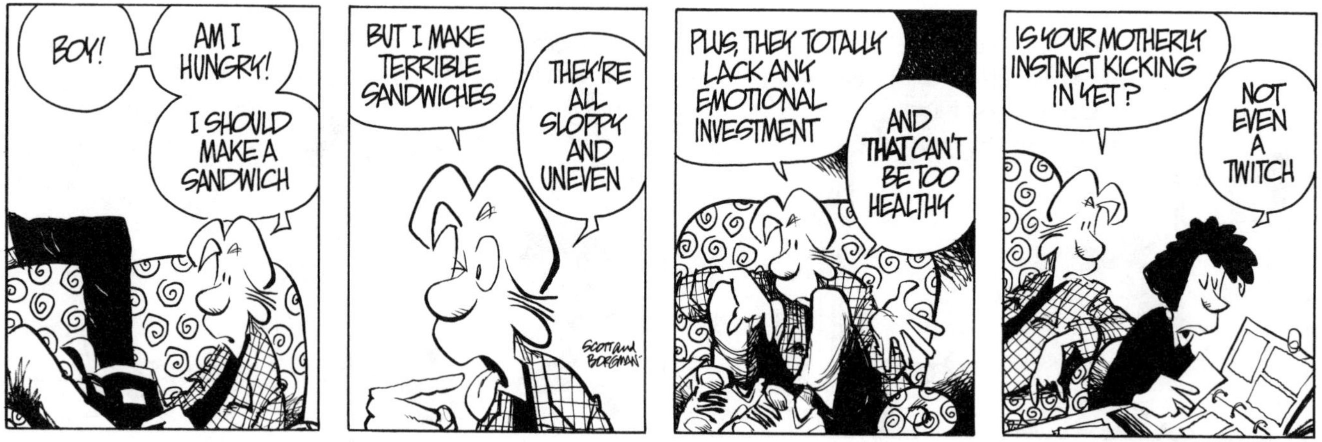
BOY!
AM I HUNGRY!
I SHOULD MAKE A SANDWICH
BUT I MAKE TERRIBLE SANDWICHES
THEY'RE ALL SLOPPY AND UNEVEN
SCOTT AND BORGMAN
PLUS, THEY TOTALLY LACK ANY EMOTIONAL INVESTMENT
AND THAT CAN'T BE TOO HEALTHY
IS YOUR MOTHERLY INSTINCT KICKING IN YET?
NOT EVEN A TWITCH

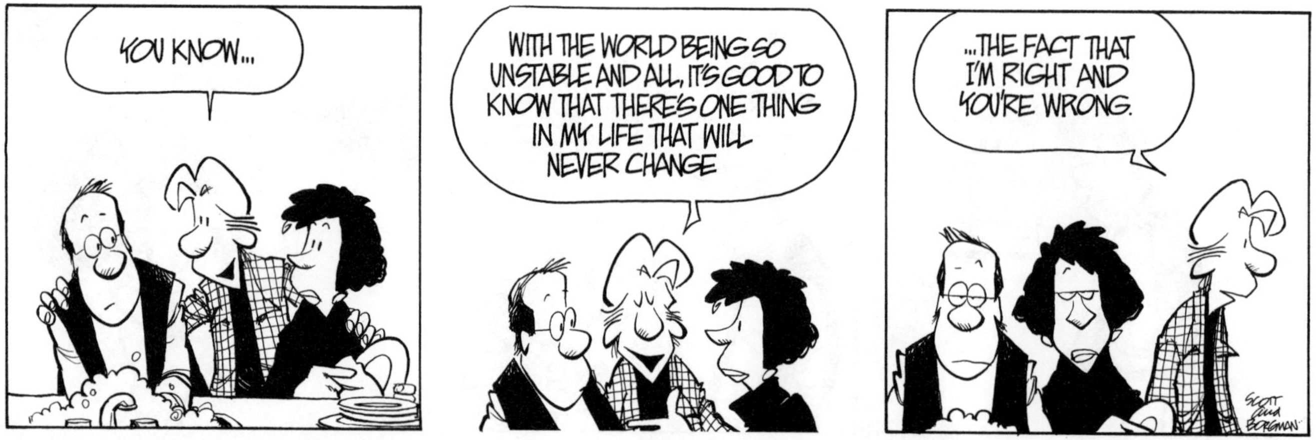
YOU KNOW...
WITH THE WORLD BEING SO UNSTABLE AND ALL, IT'S GOOD TO KNOW THAT THERE'S ONE THING IN MY LIFE THAT WILL NEVER CHANGE
...THE FACT THAT I'M RIGHT AND YOU'RE WRONG.
SCOTT AND BORGMAN

Zits®

by JERRY SCOTT and JIM BORGMAN

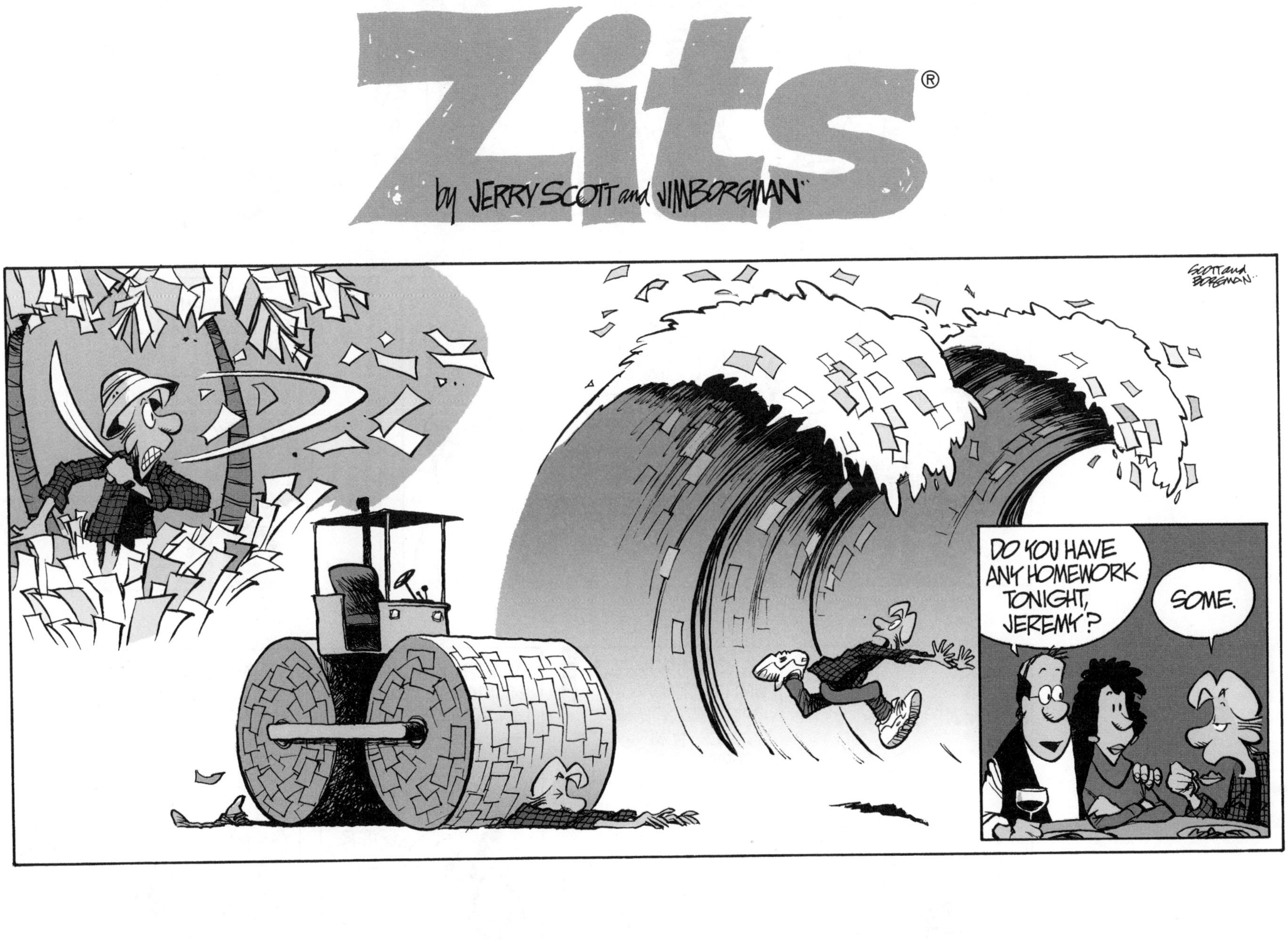
SCOTT and BORGMAN
DO YOU HAVE ANY HOMEWORK TONIGHT, JEREMY?
SOME.

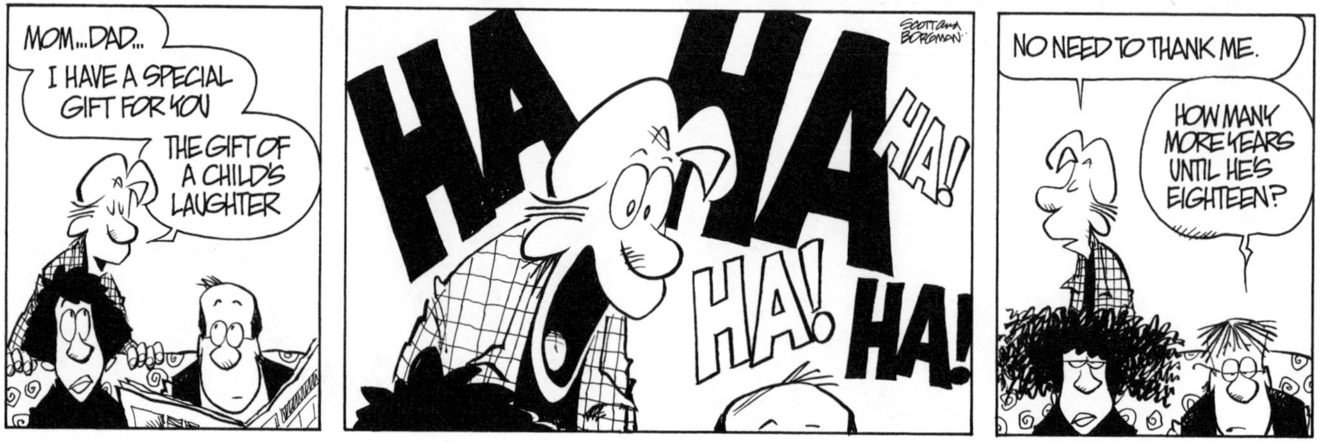
MOM...DAD...
I HAVE A SPECIAL GIFT FOR YOU
THE GIFT OF A CHILD'S LAUGHTER
SCOTT and BORGMAN
HA HA HA! HA! HA!
NO NEED TO THANK ME.
HOW MANY MORE YEARS UNTIL HE'S EIGHTEEN?

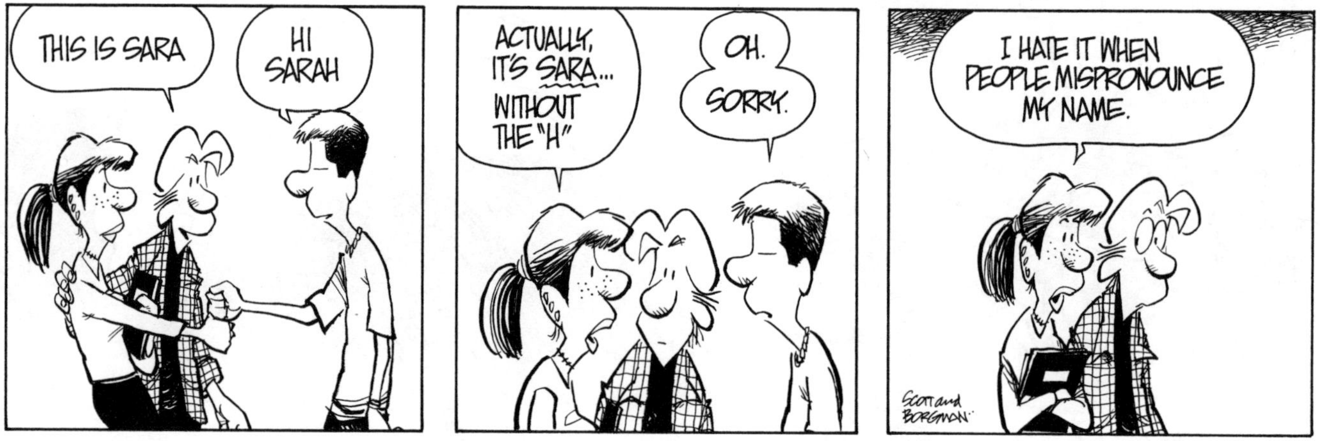
THIS IS SARA
HI SARAH
ACTUALLY, IT'S SARA... WITHOUT THE "H"
OH.
SORRY.
I HATE IT WHEN PEOPLE MISPRONOUNCE MY NAME.
SCOTT and BORGMAN

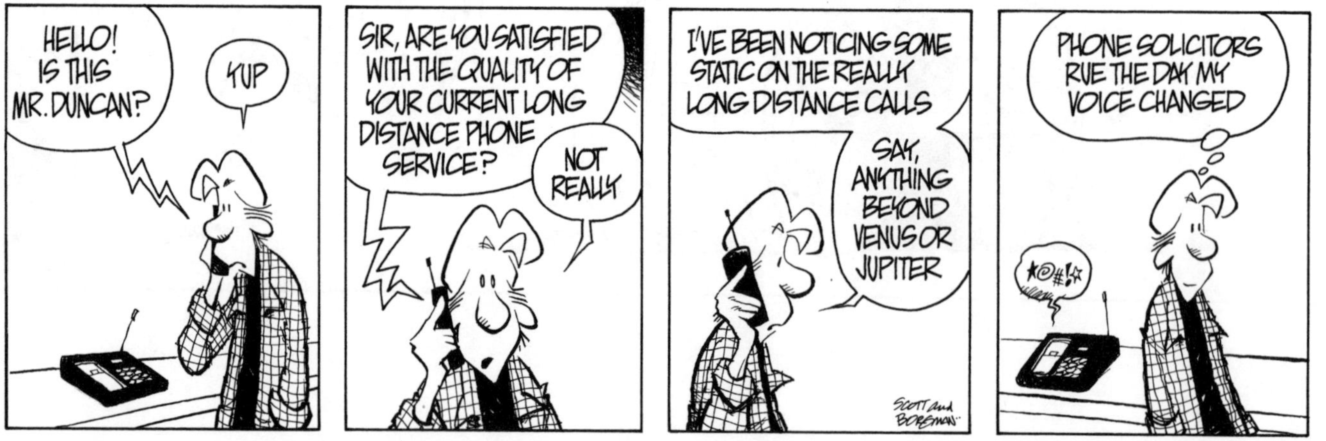
HELLO! IS THIS MR. DUNCAN?
YUP
SIR, ARE YOU SATISFIED WITH THE QUALITY OF YOUR CURRENT LONG DISTANCE PHONE SERVICE?
NOT REALLY
I'VE BEEN NOTICING SOME STATIC ON THE REALLY LONG DISTANCE CALLS
SAY, ANYTHING BEYOND VENUS OR JUPITER
SCOTT and BORGMAN
PHONE SOLICITORS RUE THE DAY MY VOICE CHANGED
★@#!☆

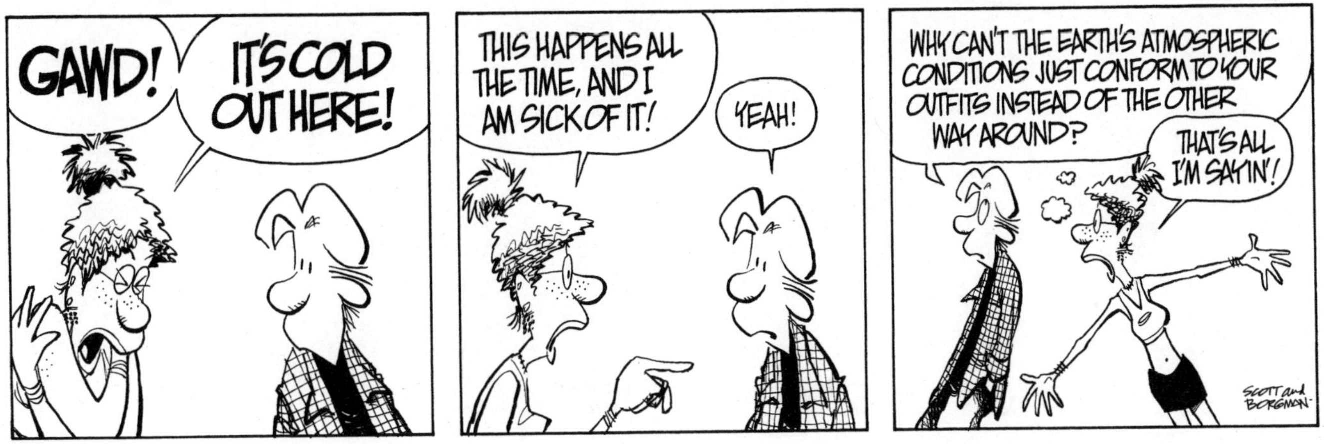
GAWD!
IT'S COLD OUT HERE!
THIS HAPPENS ALL THE TIME, AND I AM SICK OF IT!
YEAH!
WHY CAN'T THE EARTH'S ATMOSPHERIC CONDITIONS JUST CONFORM TO YOUR OUTFITS INSTEAD OF THE OTHER WAY AROUND?
THAT'S ALL I'M SAYIN'!
SCOTT and BORGMAN

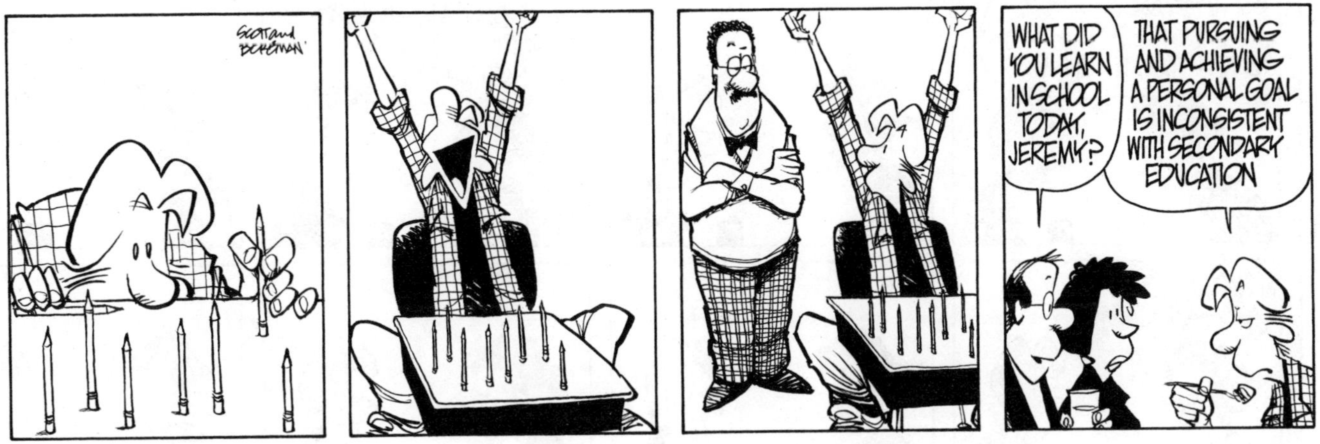
SCOTT and BORGMAN
WHAT DID YOU LEARN IN SCHOOL TODAY, JEREMY?
THAT PURSUING AND ACHIEVING A PERSONAL GOAL IS INCONSISTENT WITH SECONDARY EDUCATION

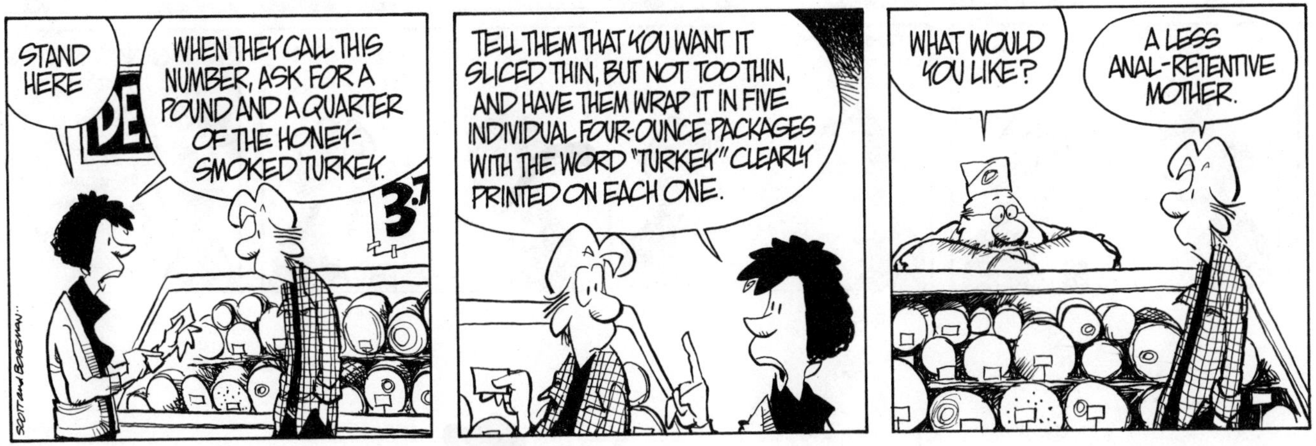
STAND HERE
WHEN THEY CALL THIS NUMBER, ASK FOR A POUND AND A QUARTER OF THE HONEY-SMOKED TURKEY.
SCOTT and BORGMAN
TELL THEM THAT YOU WANT IT SLICED THIN, BUT NOT TOO THIN, AND HAVE THEM WRAP IT IN FIVE INDIVIDUAL FOUR-OUNCE PACKAGES WITH THE WORD "TURKEY" CLEARLY PRINTED ON EACH ONE.
WHAT WOULD YOU LIKE?
A LESS ANAL-RETENTIVE MOTHER.

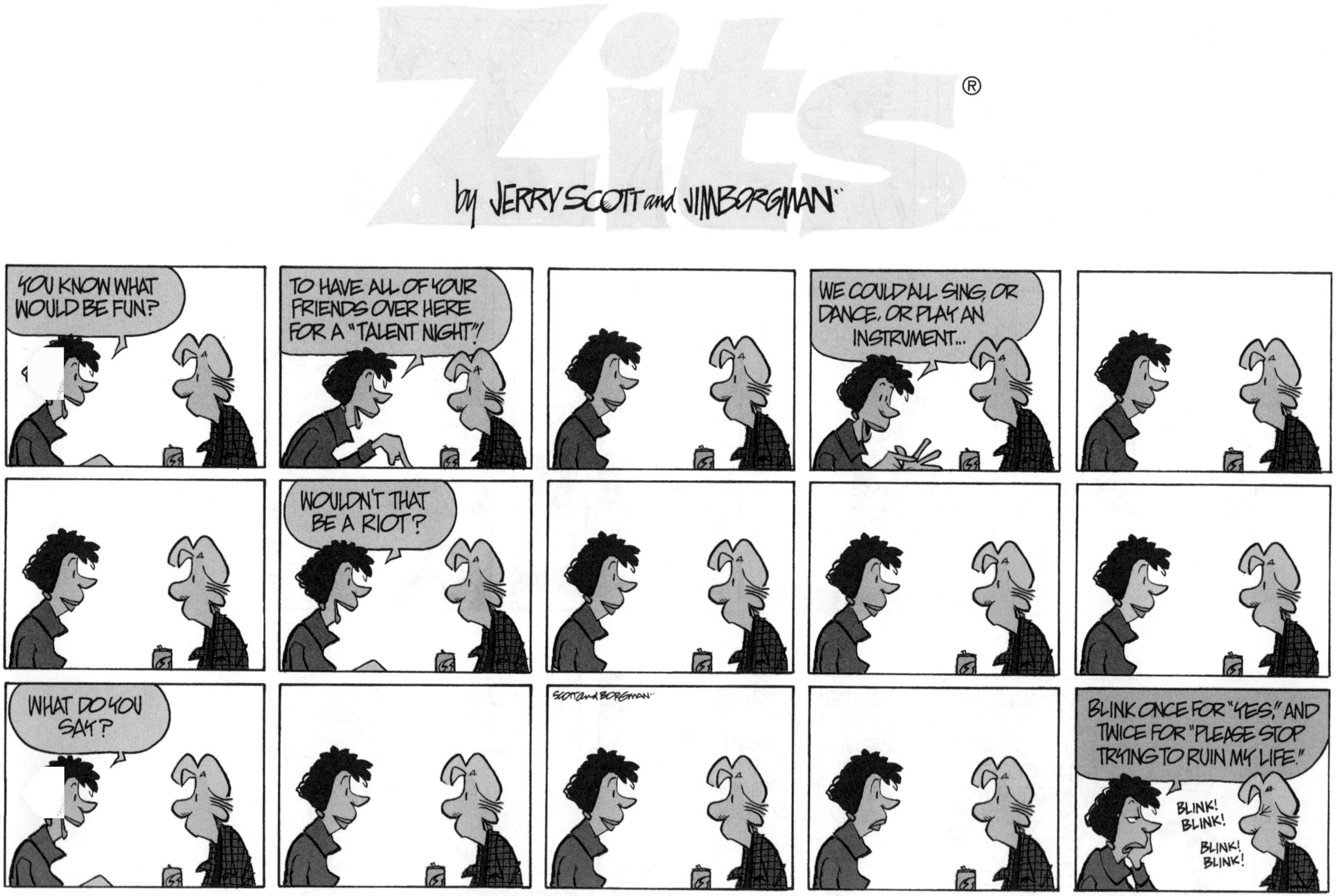
Zits®
by JERRY SCOTT and JIM BORGMAN
YOU KNOW WHAT WOULD BE FUN?
TO HAVE ALL OF YOUR FRIENDS OVER HERE FOR A "TALENT NIGHT"!
WE COULD ALL SING, OR DANCE, OR PLAY AN INSTRUMENT...
WOULDN'T THAT BE A RIOT?
WHAT DO YOU SAY?
SCOTT and BORGMAN
BLINK ONCE FOR "YES," AND TWICE FOR "PLEASE STOP TRYING TO RUIN MY LIFE."
BLINK! BLINK!
BLINK! BLINK!

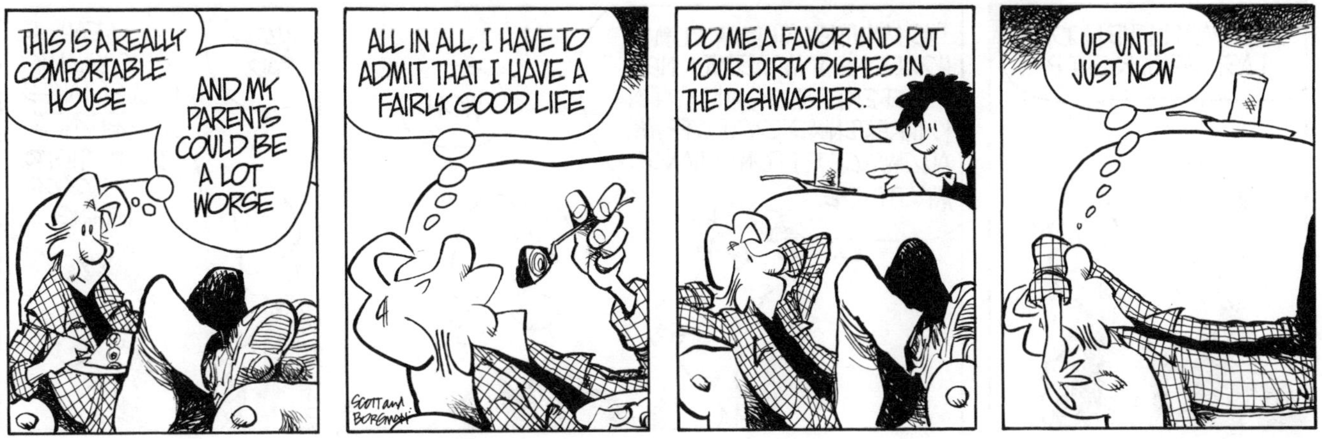
THIS IS A REALLY COMFORTABLE HOUSE
AND MY PARENTS COULD BE A LOT WORSE
ALL IN ALL, I HAVE TO ADMIT THAT I HAVE A FAIRLY GOOD LIFE
SCOTT and BORGMAN
DO ME A FAVOR AND PUT YOUR DIRTY DISHES IN THE DISHWASHER.
UP UNTIL JUST NOW

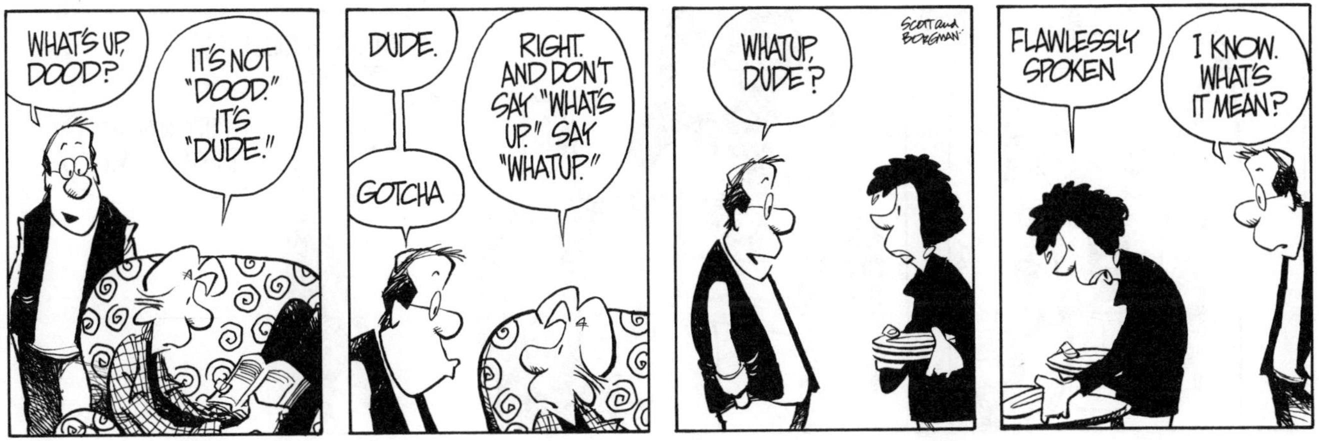
WHAT'S UP, DOOD?
IT'S NOT "DOOD." IT'S "DUDE."
DUDE.
GOTCHA
RIGHT. AND DON'T SAY "WHAT'S UP." SAY "WHATUP."
SCOTT and BORGMAN
WHATUP, DUDE?
FLAWLESSLY SPOKEN
I KNOW. WHAT'S IT MEAN?

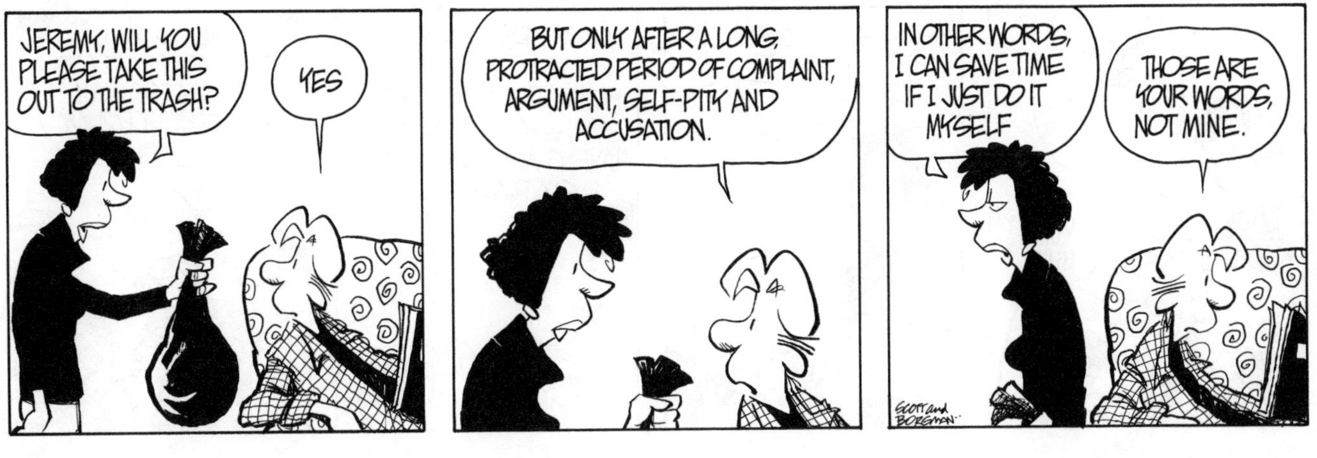
JEREMY, WILL YOU PLEASE TAKE THIS OUT TO THE TRASH?
YES
BUT ONLY AFTER A LONG, PROTRACTED PERIOD OF COMPLAINT, ARGUMENT, SELF-PITY AND ACCUSATION.
IN OTHER WORDS, I CAN SAVE TIME IF I JUST DO IT MYSELF
THOSE ARE YOUR WORDS, NOT MINE.
SCOTT and BORGMAN

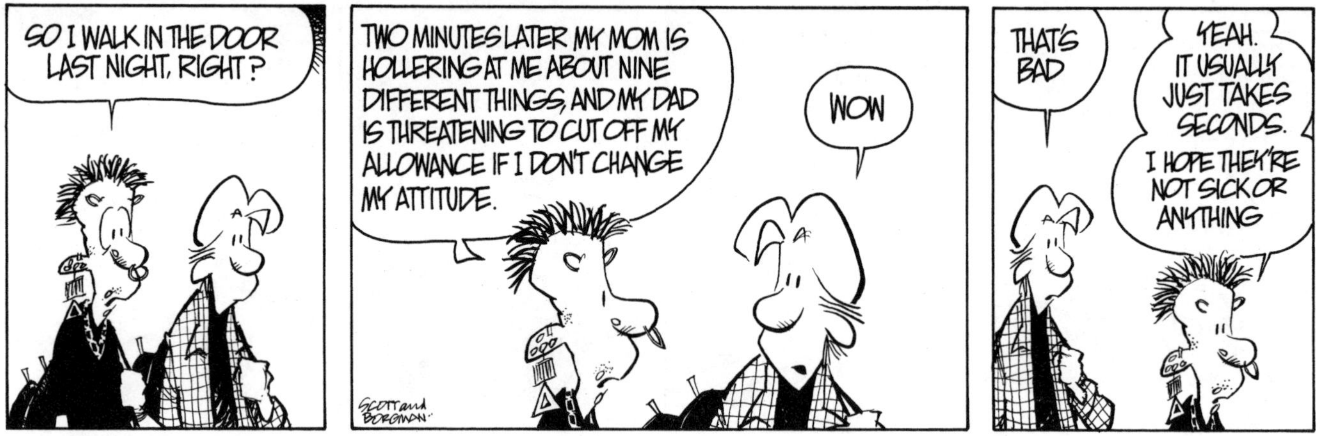
SO I WALK IN THE DOOR LAST NIGHT, RIGHT?
TWO MINUTES LATER MY MOM IS HOLLERING AT ME ABOUT NINE DIFFERENT THINGS, AND MY DAD IS THREATENING TO CUT OFF MY ALLOWANCE IF I DON'T CHANGE MY ATTITUDE.
WOW
THAT'S BAD
YEAH. IT USUALLY JUST TAKES SECONDS.
I HOPE THEY'RE NOT SICK OR ANYTHING
SCOTT and BORGMAN

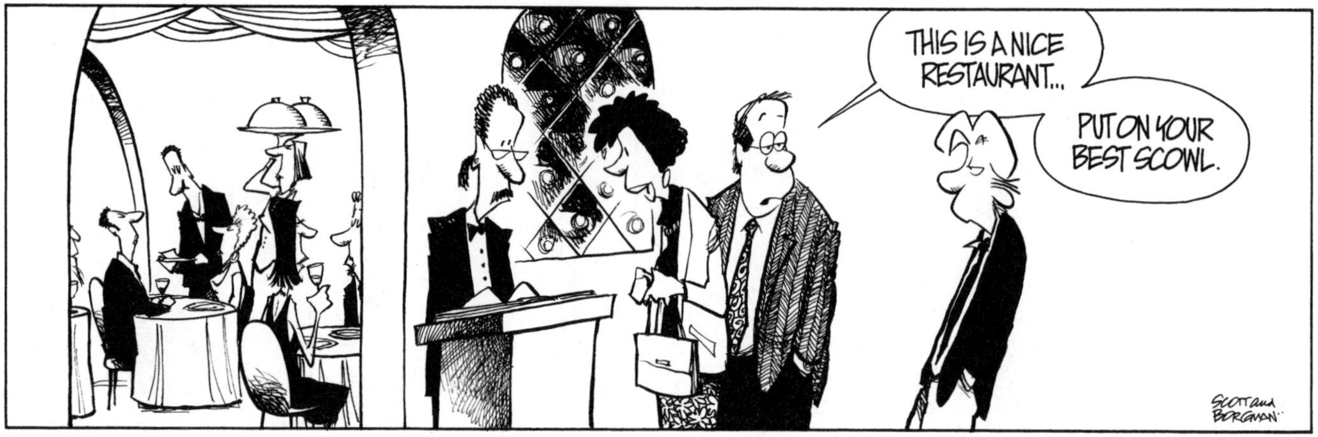
THIS IS A NICE RESTAURANT...
PUT ON YOUR BEST SCOWL.
SCOTT and BORGMAN

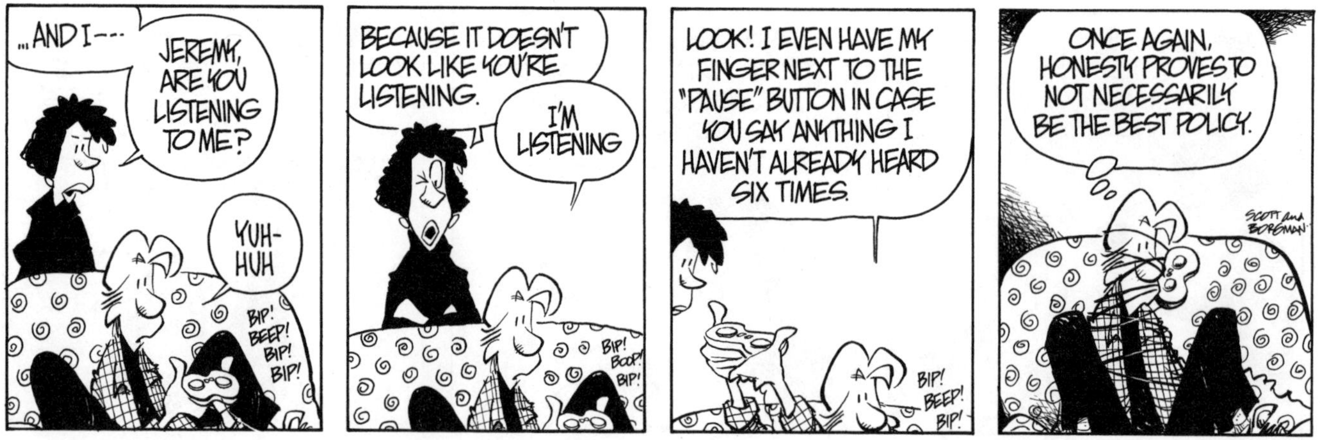
...AND I---
JEREMY, ARE YOU LISTENING TO ME?
YUH-HUH
BIP! BEEP! BIP! BIP!
BECAUSE IT DOESN'T LOOK LIKE YOU'RE LISTENING.
I'M LISTENING
BIP! BOOP! BIP!
LOOK! I EVEN HAVE MY FINGER NEXT TO THE "PAUSE" BUTTON IN CASE YOU SAY ANYTHING I HAVEN'T ALREADY HEARD SIX TIMES.
BIP! BEEP! BIP!
ONCE AGAIN, HONESTY PROVES TO NOT NECESSARILY BE THE BEST POLICY.
SCOTT and BORGMAN

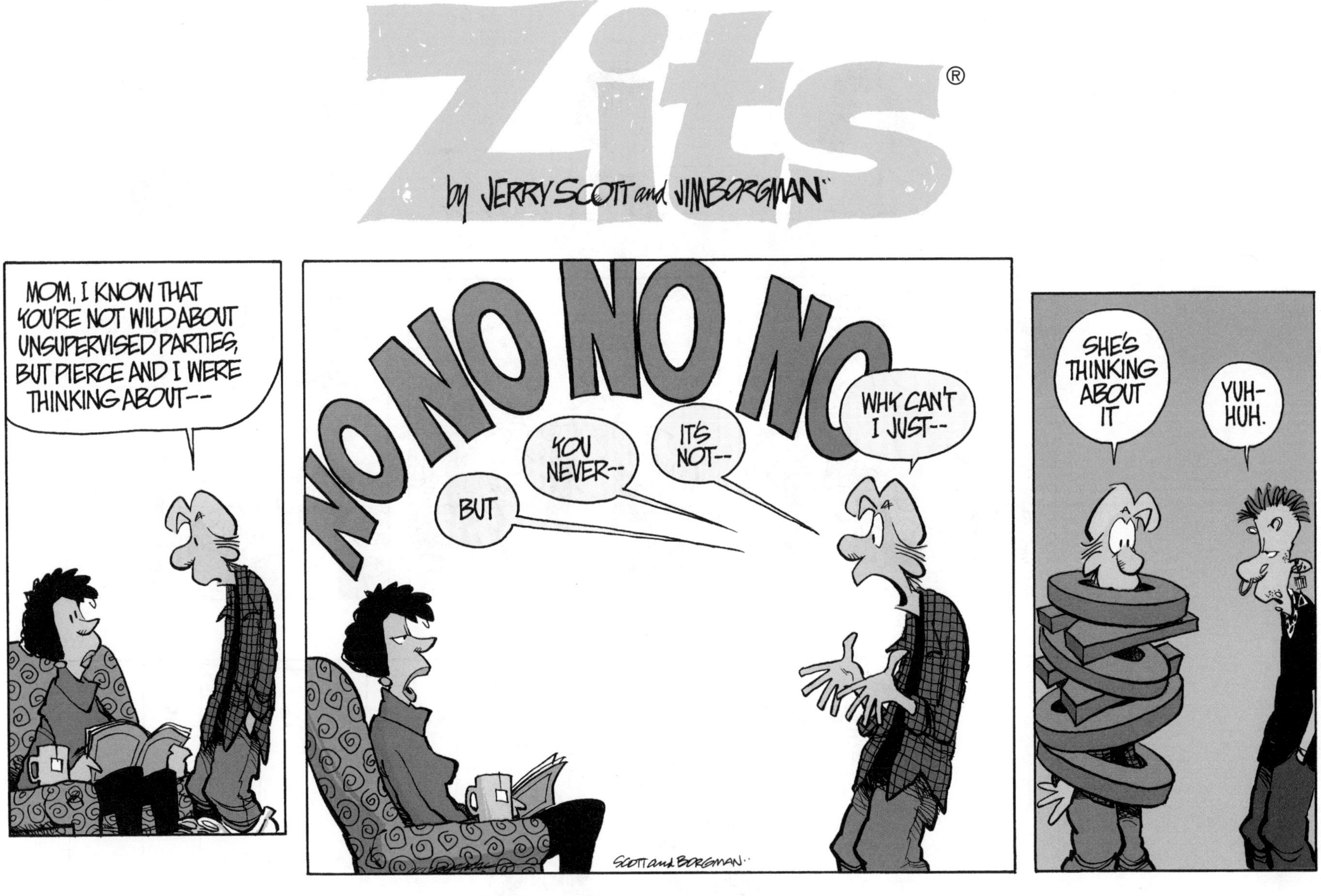
Zits®
by JERRY SCOTT and JIM BORGMAN
MOM, I KNOW THAT YOU'RE NOT WILD ABOUT UNSUPERVISED PARTIES, BUT PIERCE AND I WERE THINKING ABOUT--
NO NO NO NO NO
BUT
YOU NEVER--
IT'S NOT--
WHY CAN'T I JUST--
SCOTT and BORGMAN
SHE'S THINKING ABOUT IT
YUH-HUH.

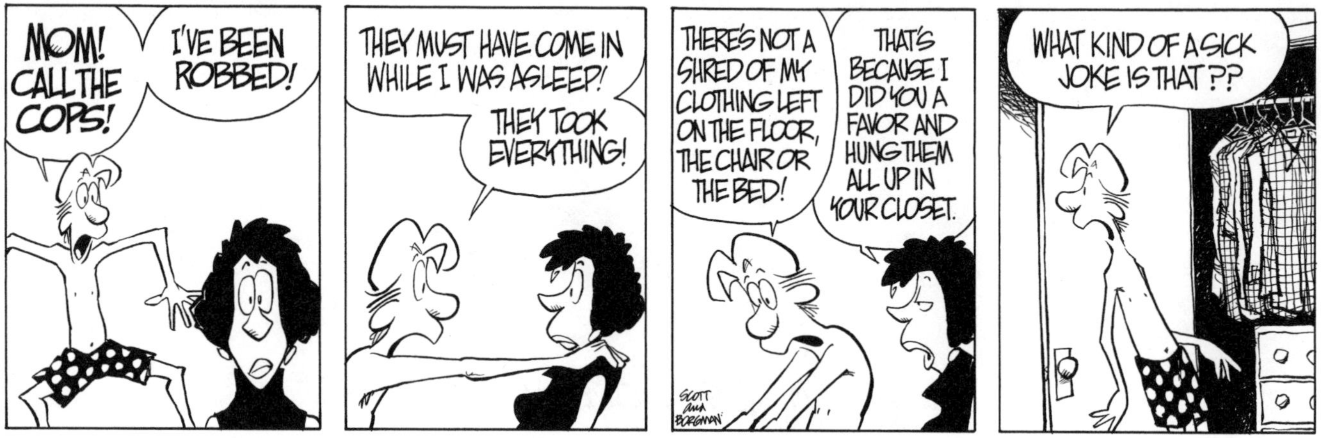
MOM! CALL THE COPS!
I'VE BEEN ROBBED!
THEY MUST HAVE COME IN WHILE I WAS ASLEEP!
THEY TOOK EVERYTHING!
THERE'S NOT A SHRED OF MY CLOTHING LEFT ON THE FLOOR, THE CHAIR OR THE BED!
THAT'S BECAUSE I DID YOU A FAVOR AND HUNG THEM ALL UP IN YOUR CLOSET.
WHAT KIND OF A SICK JOKE IS THAT??

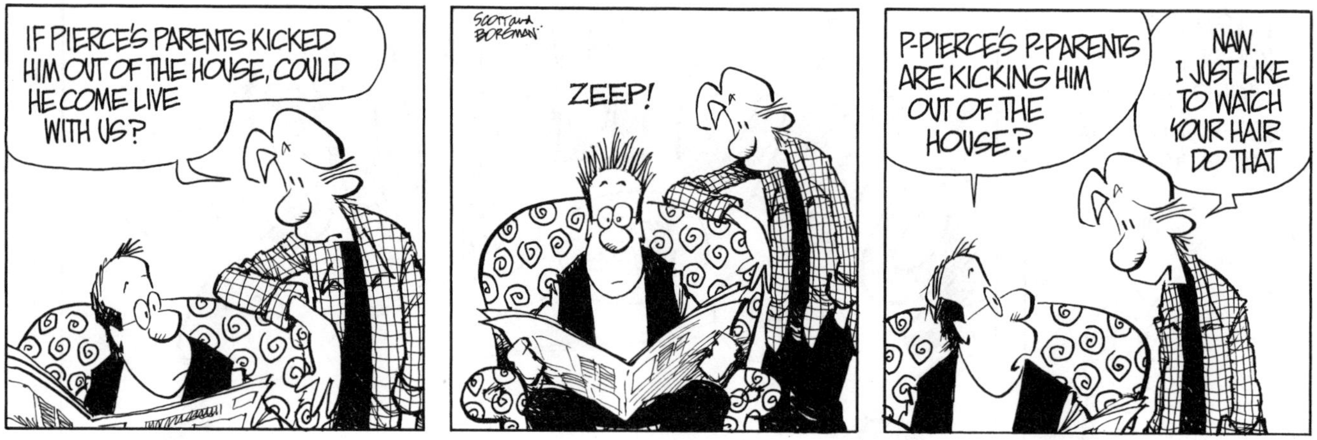
IF PIERCE'S PARENTS KICKED HIM OUT OF THE HOUSE, COULD HE COME LIVE WITH US?
ZEEP!
P-PIERCE'S P-PARENTS ARE KICKING HIM OUT OF THE HOUSE?
NAW. I JUST LIKE TO WATCH YOUR HAIR DO THAT

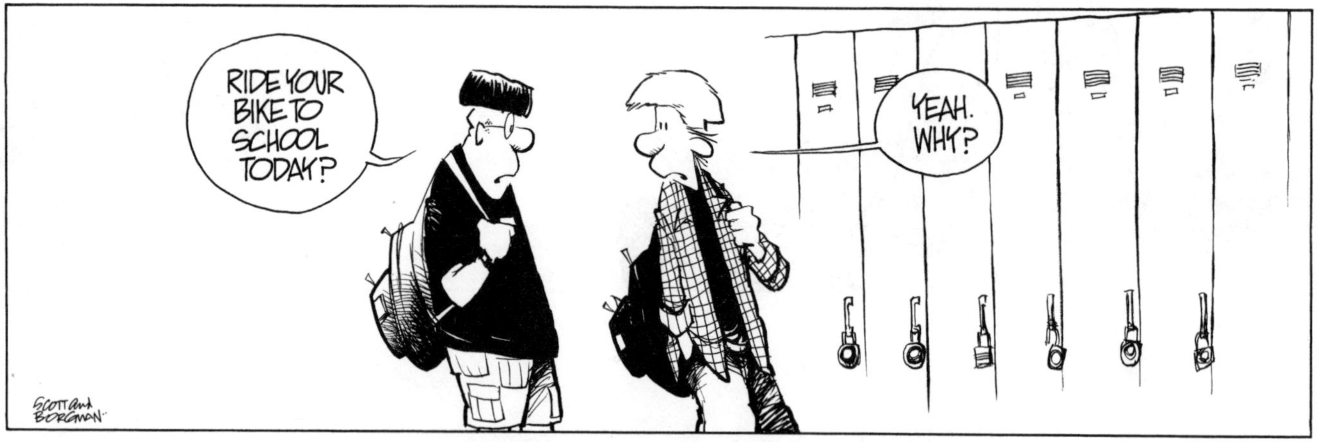
RIDE YOUR BIKE TO SCHOOL TODAY?
YEAH. WHY?

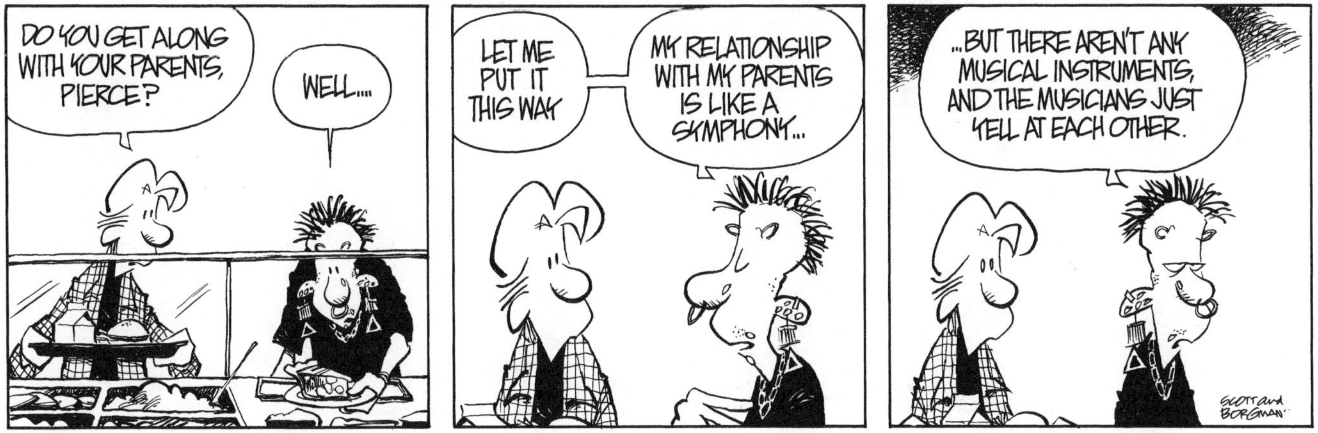
DO YOU GET ALONG WITH YOUR PARENTS, PIERCE?
WELL....
LET ME PUT IT THIS WAY
MY RELATIONSHIP WITH MY PARENTS IS LIKE A SYMPHONY...
...BUT THERE AREN'T ANY MUSICAL INSTRUMENTS, AND THE MUSICIANS JUST YELL AT EACH OTHER.
SCOTT and BORGMAN

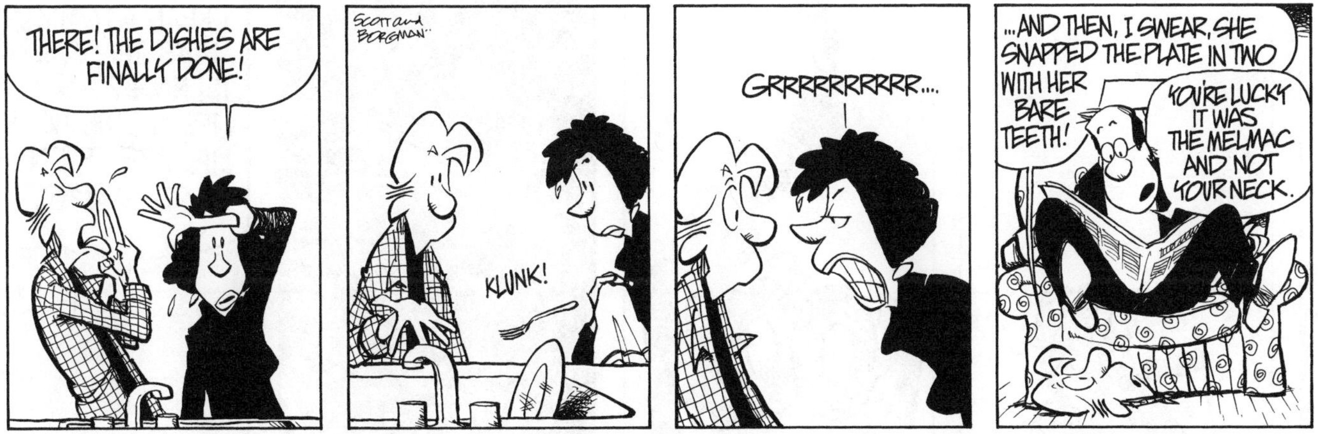
THERE! THE DISHES ARE FINALLY DONE!
SCOTT and BORGMAN
KLUNK!
GRRRRRRRRR....
...AND THEN, I SWEAR, SHE SNAPPED THE PLATE IN TWO WITH HER BARE TEETH!
YOU'RE LUCKY IT WAS THE MELMAC AND NOT YOUR NECK.

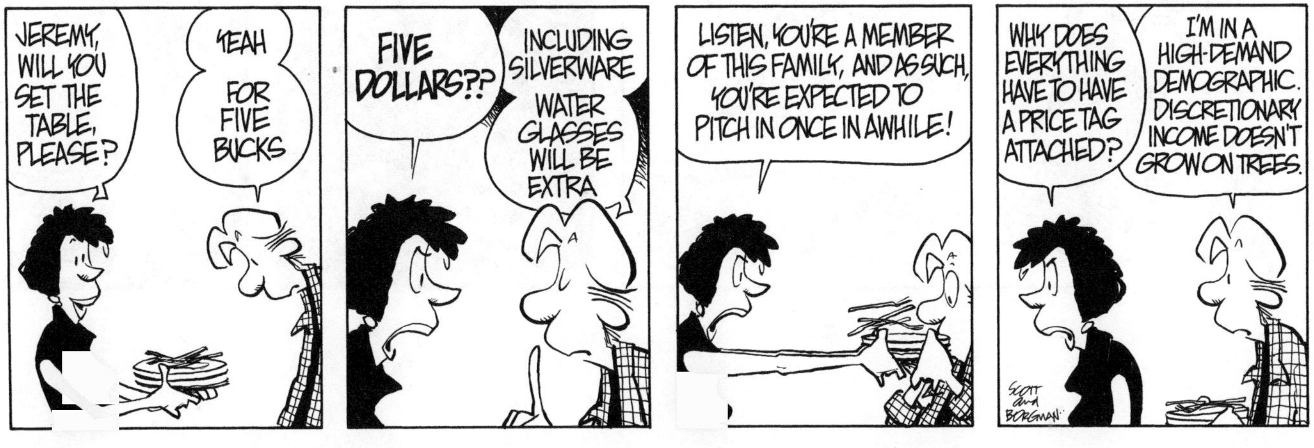
JEREMY, WILL YOU SET THE TABLE, PLEASE?
YEAH
FOR FIVE BUCKS
FIVE DOLLARS??
INCLUDING SILVERWARE
WATER GLASSES WILL BE EXTRA
LISTEN, YOU'RE A MEMBER OF THIS FAMILY, AND AS SUCH, YOU'RE EXPECTED TO PITCH IN ONCE IN AWHILE!
WHY DOES EVERYTHING HAVE TO HAVE A PRICE TAG ATTACHED?
I'M IN A HIGH-DEMAND DEMOGRAPHIC. DISCRETIONARY INCOME DOESN'T GROW ON TREES.
SCOTT and BORGMAN

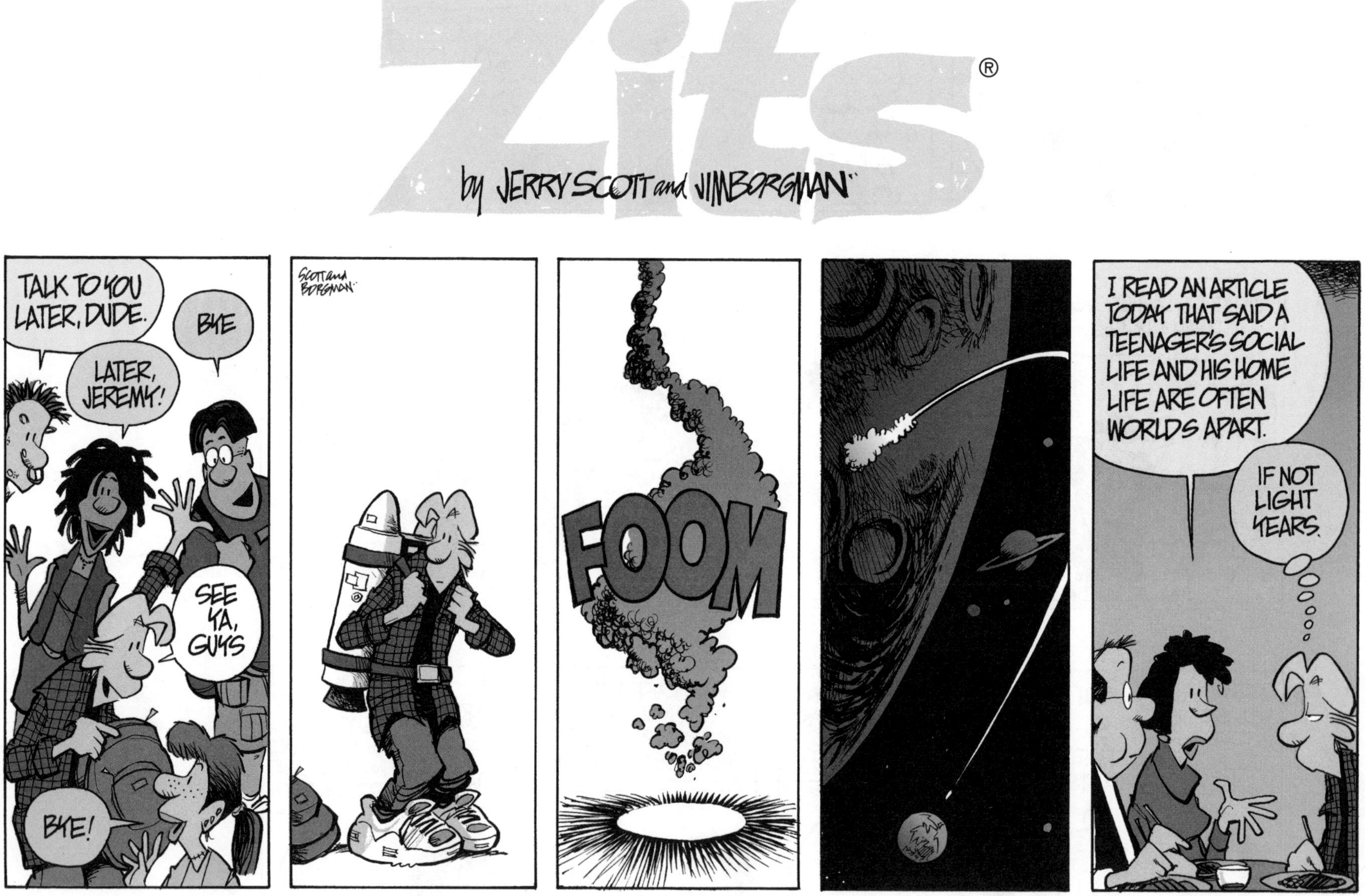
Zits®
by JERRY SCOTT and JIM BORGMAN
TALK TO YOU LATER, DUDE.
LATER, JEREMY!
BYE
SEE YA, GUYS
BYE!
SCOTT AND BORGMAN
FOOM
I READ AN ARTICLE TODAY THAT SAID A TEENAGER'S SOCIAL LIFE AND HIS HOME LIFE ARE OFTEN WORLDS APART.
IF NOT LIGHT YEARS.

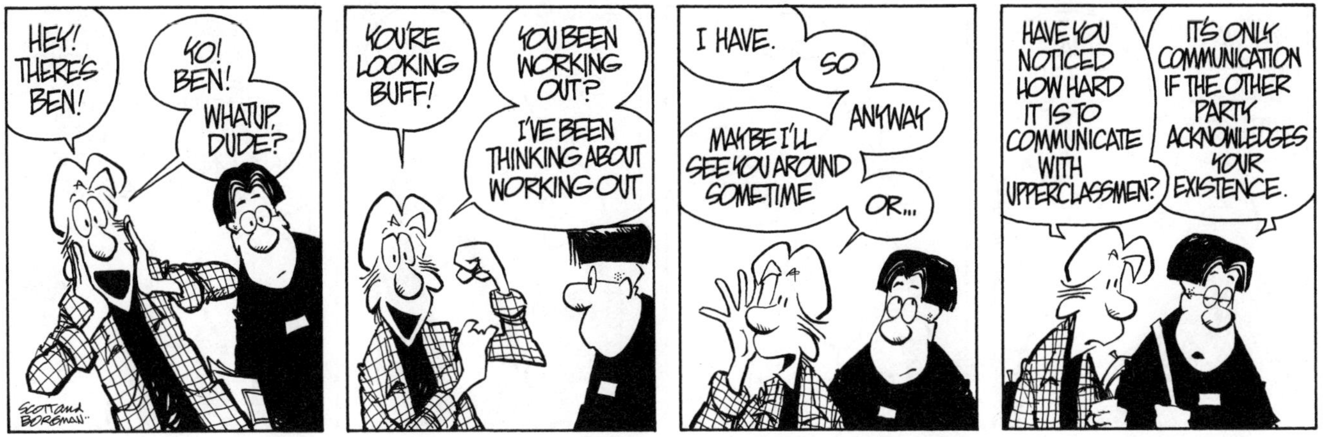
HEY! THERE'S BEN!
YO! BEN!
WHAT UP, DUDE?
SCOTT and BORGMAN
YOU'RE LOOKING BUFF!
YOU BEEN WORKING OUT?
I'VE BEEN THINKING ABOUT WORKING OUT
I HAVE.
SO
ANYWAY
MAYBE I'LL SEE YOU AROUND SOMETIME
OR...
HAVE YOU NOTICED HOW HARD IT IS TO COMMUNICATE WITH UPPERCLASSMEN?
IT'S ONLY COMMUNICATION IF THE OTHER PARTY ACKNOWLEDGES YOUR EXISTENCE.

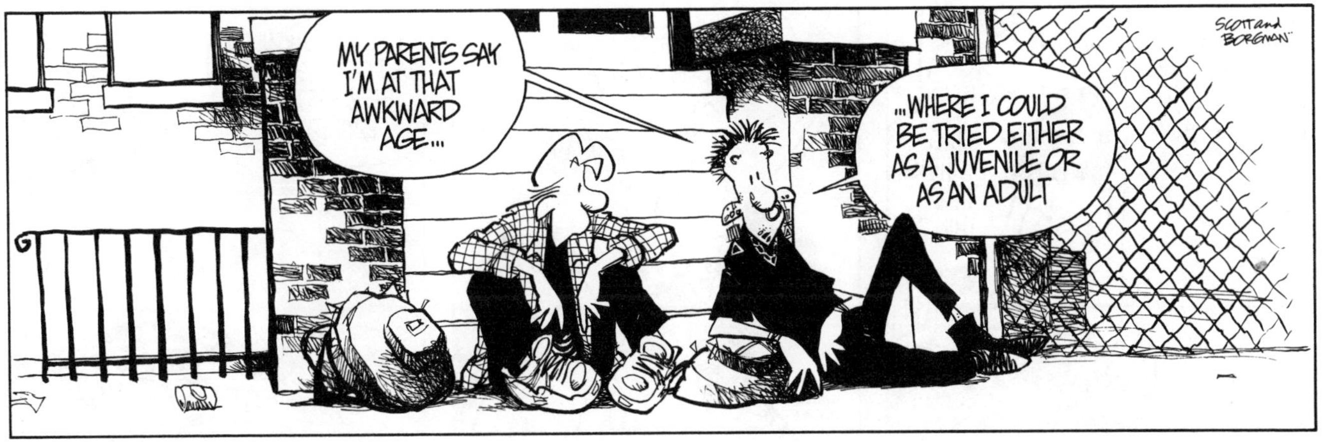
SCOTT and BORGMAN
MY PARENTS SAY I'M AT THAT AWKWARD AGE...
...WHERE I COULD BE TRIED EITHER AS A JUVENILE OR AS AN ADULT

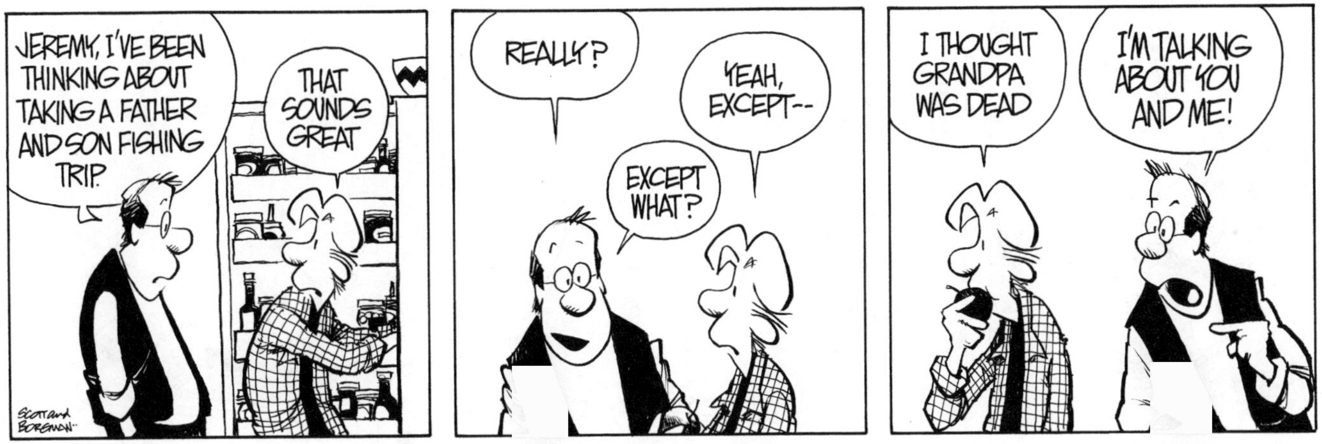
JEREMY, I'VE BEEN THINKING ABOUT TAKING A FATHER AND SON FISHING TRIP.
THAT SOUNDS GREAT
SCOTT and BORGMAN
REALLY?
YEAH, EXCEPT--
EXCEPT WHAT?
I THOUGHT GRANDPA WAS DEAD
I'M TALKING ABOUT YOU AND ME!

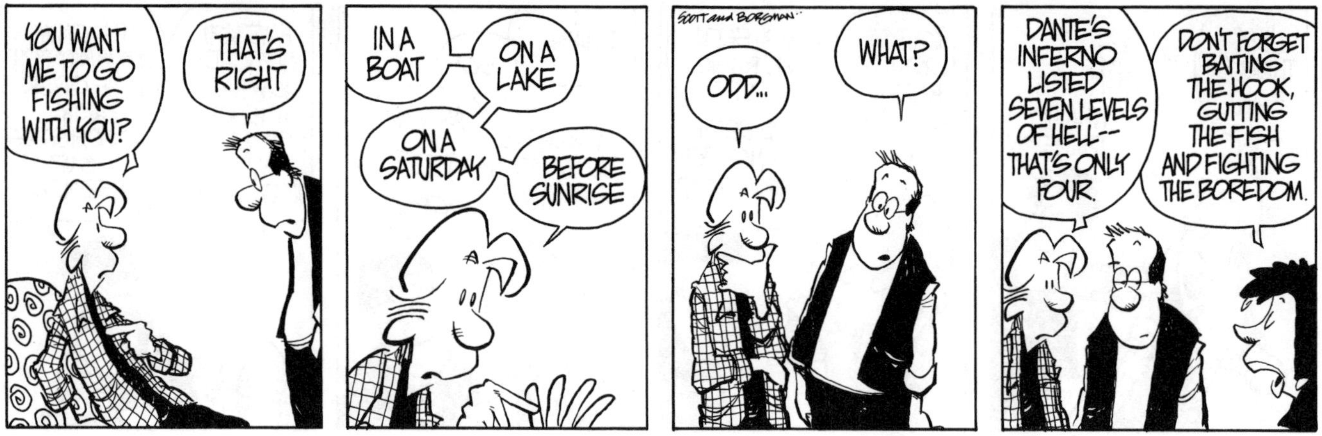
YOU WANT ME TO GO FISHING WITH YOU?
THAT'S RIGHT
IN A BOAT
ON A LAKE
ON A SATURDAY
BEFORE SUNRISE
ODD...
WHAT?
DANTE'S INFERNO LISTED SEVEN LEVELS OF HELL-- THAT'S ONLY FOUR.
DON'T FORGET BAITING THE HOOK, GUTTING THE FISH AND FIGHTING THE BOREDOM.

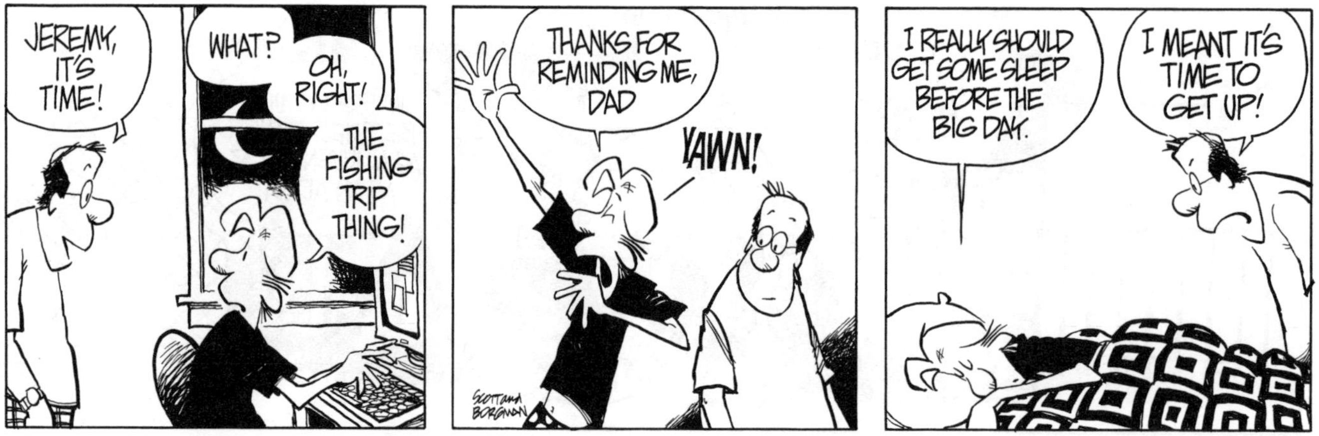
JEREMY, IT'S TIME!
WHAT?
OH, RIGHT!
THE FISHING TRIP THING!
THANKS FOR REMINDING ME, DAD
YAWN!
I REALLY SHOULD GET SOME SLEEP BEFORE THE BIG DAY.
I MEANT IT'S TIME TO GET UP!

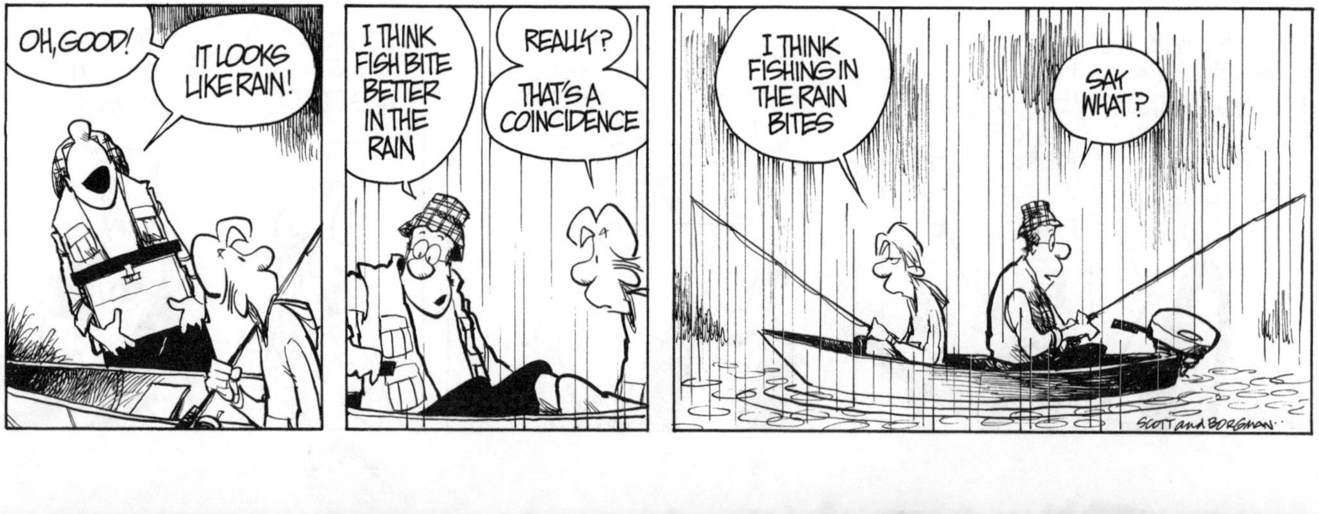
OH, GOOD!
IT LOOKS LIKE RAIN!
I THINK FISH BITE BETTER IN THE RAIN
REALLY?
THAT'S A COINCIDENCE
I THINK FISHING IN THE RAIN BITES
SAY WHAT?

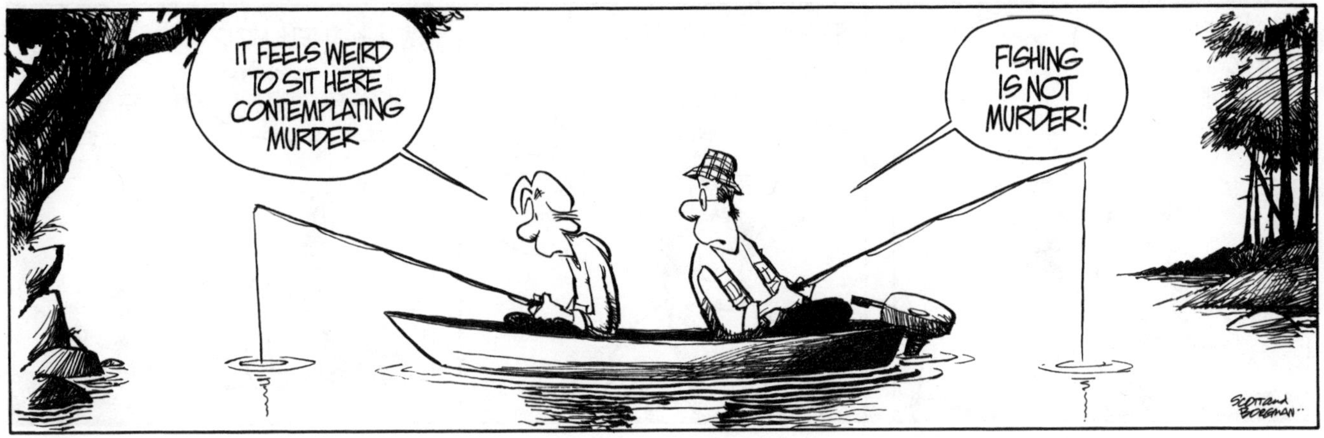
IT FEELS WEIRD TO SIT HERE CONTEMPLATING MURDER
FISHING IS NOT MURDER!

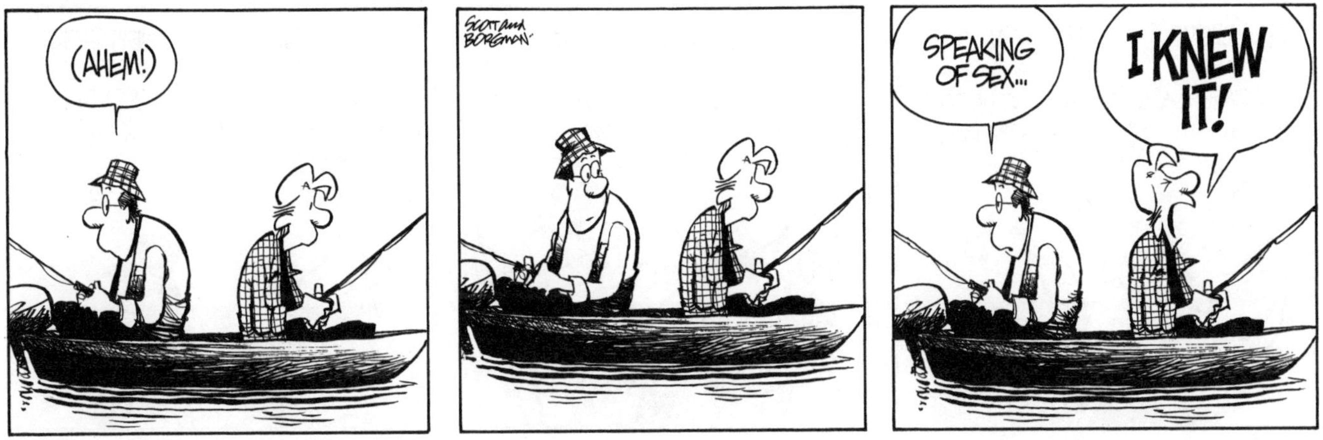
(AHEM!)
SPEAKING OF SEX...
I KNEW IT!

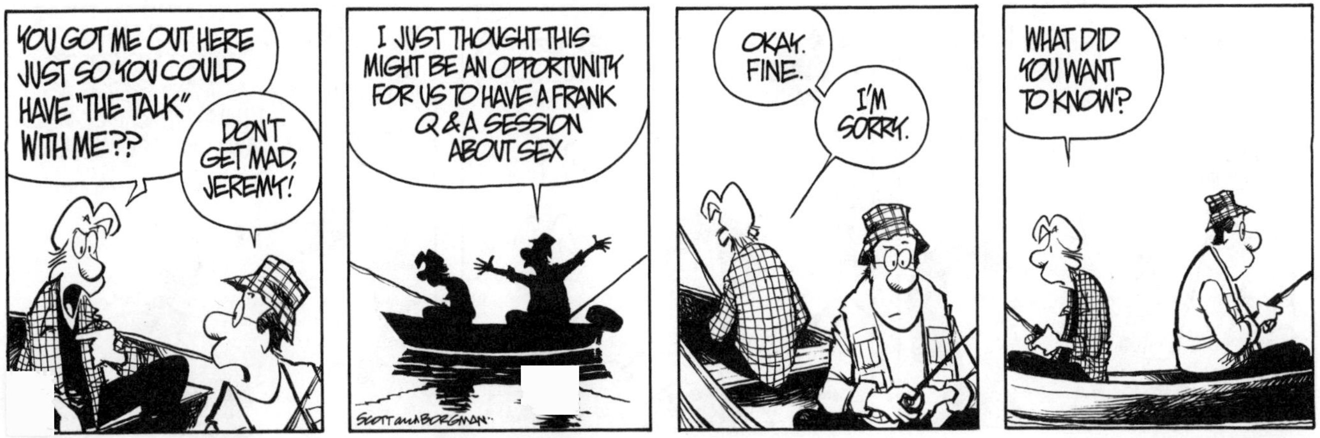
YOU GOT ME OUT HERE JUST SO YOU COULD HAVE "THE TALK" WITH ME??
DON'T GET MAD, JEREMY!
I JUST THOUGHT THIS MIGHT BE AN OPPORTUNITY FOR US TO HAVE A FRANK Q & A SESSION ABOUT SEX
OKAY. FINE.
I'M SORRY.
WHAT DID YOU WANT TO KNOW?

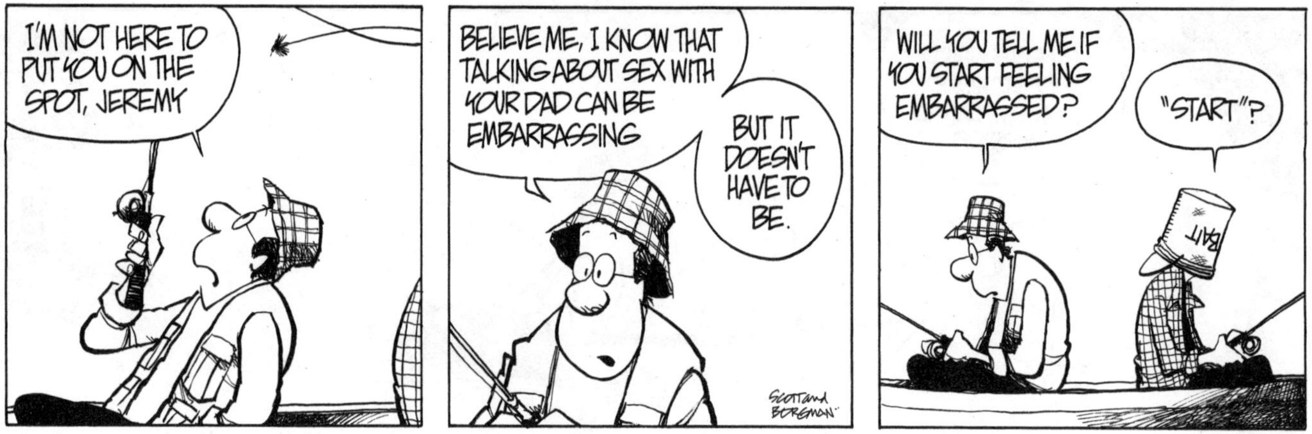
I'M NOT HERE TO PUT YOU ON THE SPOT, JEREMY
BELIEVE ME, I KNOW THAT TALKING ABOUT SEX WITH YOUR DAD CAN BE EMBARRASSING
BUT IT DOESN'T HAVE TO BE.
WILL YOU TELL ME IF YOU START FEELING EMBARRASSED?
"START"?
SCOTT and BORGMAN

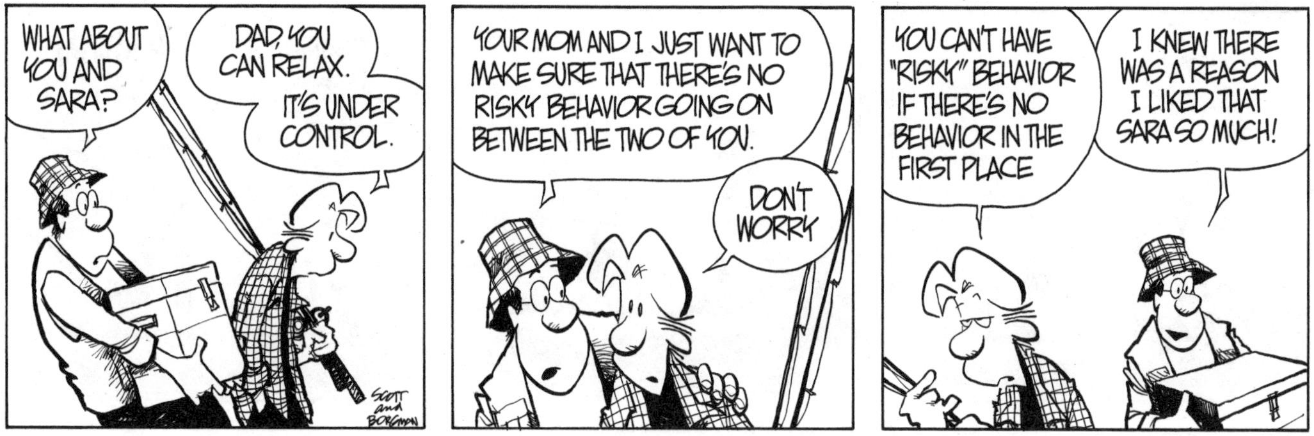
WHAT ABOUT YOU AND SARA?
DAD, YOU CAN RELAX.
IT'S UNDER CONTROL.
SCOTT and BORGMAN
YOUR MOM AND I JUST WANT TO MAKE SURE THAT THERE'S NO RISKY BEHAVIOR GOING ON BETWEEN THE TWO OF YOU.
DON'T WORRY
YOU CAN'T HAVE "RISKY" BEHAVIOR IF THERE'S NO BEHAVIOR IN THE FIRST PLACE
I KNEW THERE WAS A REASON I LIKED THAT SARA SO MUCH!

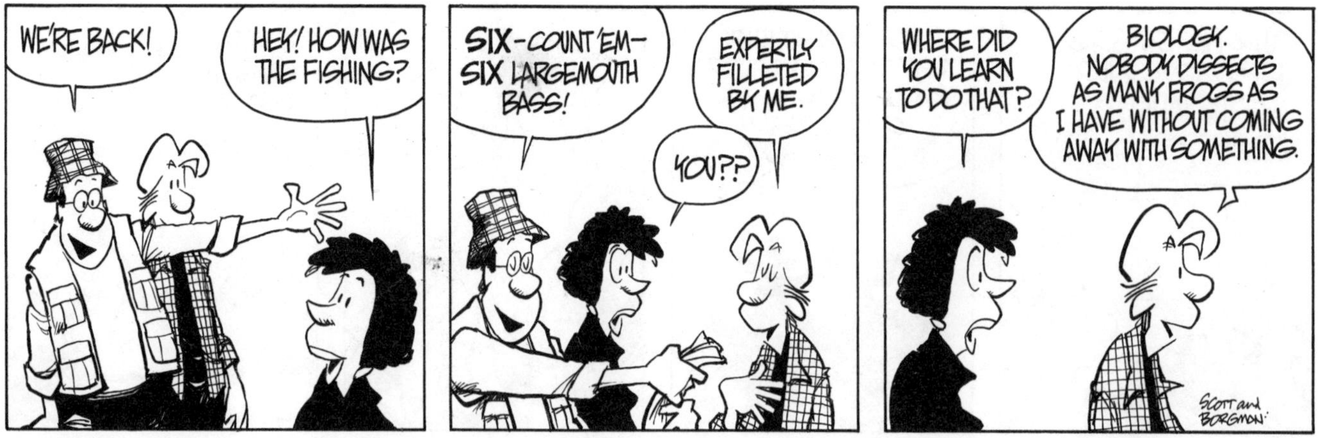
WE'RE BACK!
HEY! HOW WAS THE FISHING?
SIX-COUNT 'EM-SIX LARGEMOUTH BASS!
EXPERTLY FILLETED BY ME.
YOU??
WHERE DID YOU LEARN TO DO THAT?
BIOLOGY. NOBODY DISSECTS AS MANY FROGS AS I HAVE WITHOUT COMING AWAY WITH SOMETHING.
SCOTT and BORGMAN

Zits®

by JERRY SCOTT and JIM BORGMAN

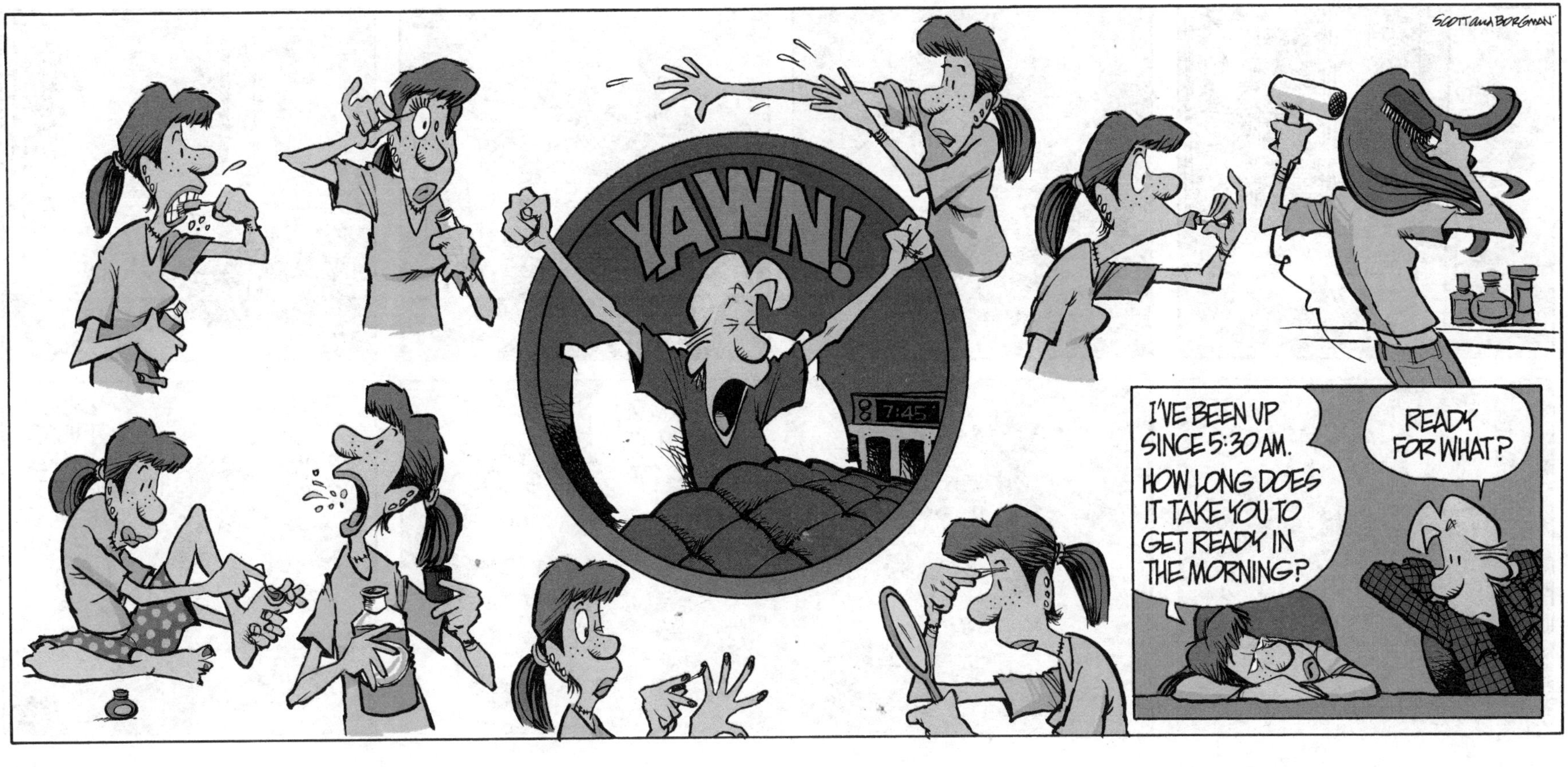
SCOTT and BORGMAN
YAWN!
7:45
I'VE BEEN UP SINCE 5:30 AM.
HOW LONG DOES IT TAKE YOU TO GET READY IN THE MORNING?
READY FOR WHAT?

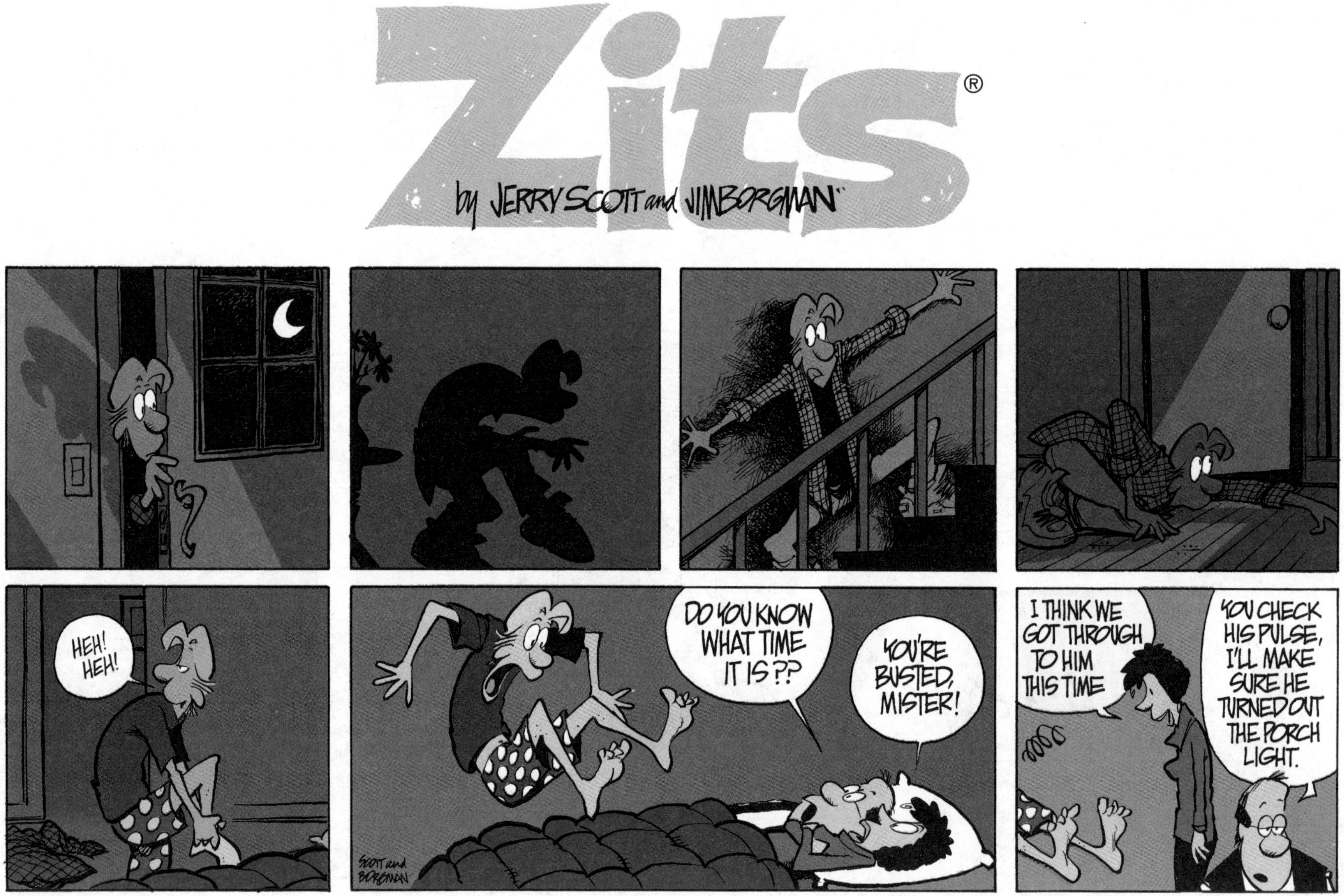

Zits®
by JERRY SCOTT and JIM BORGMAN
HEH! HEH!
DO YOU KNOW WHAT TIME IT IS??
YOU'RE BUSTED, MISTER!
SCOTT and BORGMAN
I THINK WE GOT THROUGH TO HIM THIS TIME
YOU CHECK HIS PULSE, I'LL MAKE SURE HE TURNED OUT THE PORCH LIGHT.

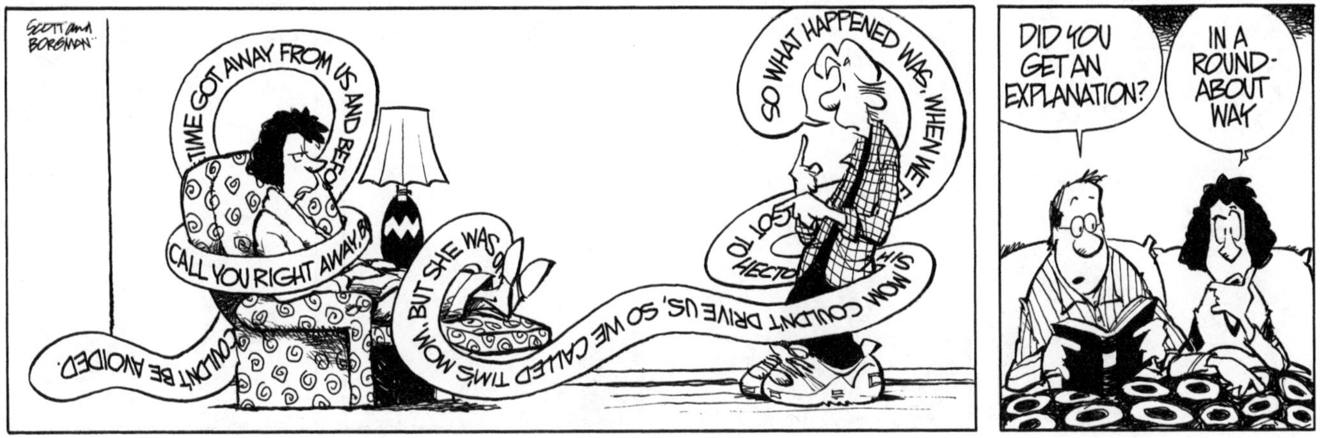
SCOTT AND BORGMAN
SO WHAT HAPPENED WAS, WHEN WE
GOT TO
HECTO
HIS MOM COULDN'T DRIVE US, SO WE CALLED TIM'S MOM, BUT SHE WAS
TIME GOT AWAY FROM US AND BEFO
CALL YOU RIGHT AWAY, B
COULDN'T BE AVOIDED.
DID YOU GET AN EXPLANATION?
IN A ROUND-ABOUT WAY

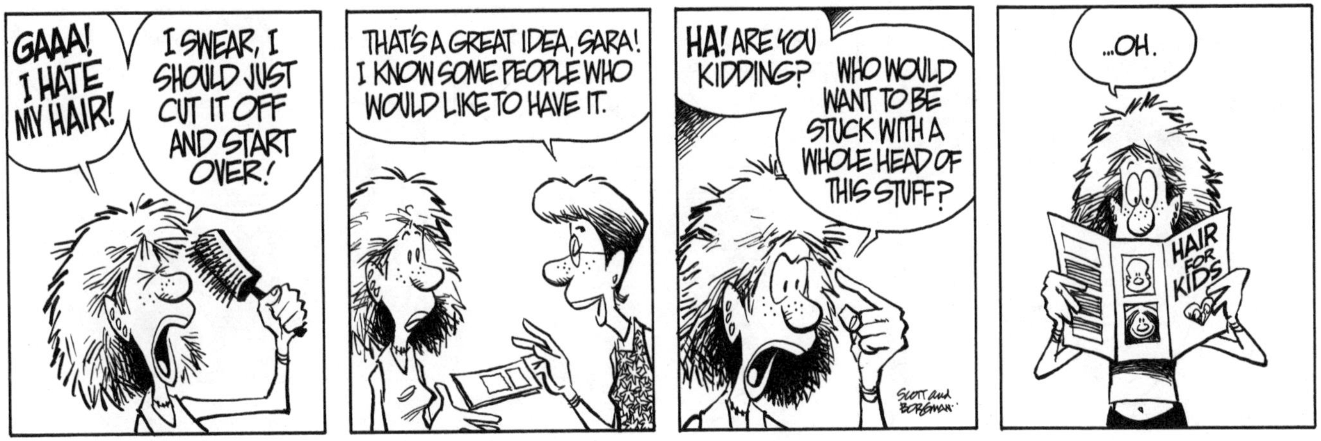
GAAA! I HATE MY HAIR!
I SWEAR, I SHOULD JUST CUT IT OFF AND START OVER!
THAT'S A GREAT IDEA, SARA! I KNOW SOME PEOPLE WHO WOULD LIKE TO HAVE IT.
HA! ARE YOU KIDDING?
WHO WOULD WANT TO BE STUCK WITH A WHOLE HEAD OF THIS STUFF?
SCOTT AND BORGMAN
...OH.
HAIR FOR KIDS

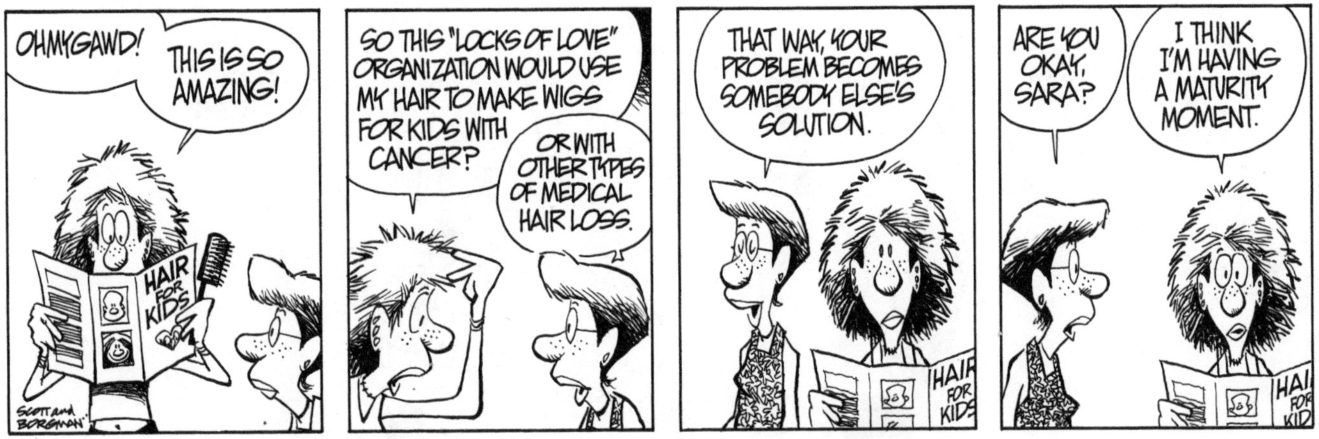
OHMYGAWD!
THIS IS SO AMAZING!
HAIR FOR KIDS
SCOTT AND BORGMAN
SO THIS "LOCKS OF LOVE" ORGANIZATION WOULD USE MY HAIR TO MAKE WIGS FOR KIDS WITH CANCER?
OR WITH OTHER TYPES OF MEDICAL HAIR LOSS.
THAT WAY, YOUR PROBLEM BECOMES SOMEBODY ELSE'S SOLUTION.
ARE YOU OKAY, SARA?
I THINK I'M HAVING A MATURITY MOMENT.

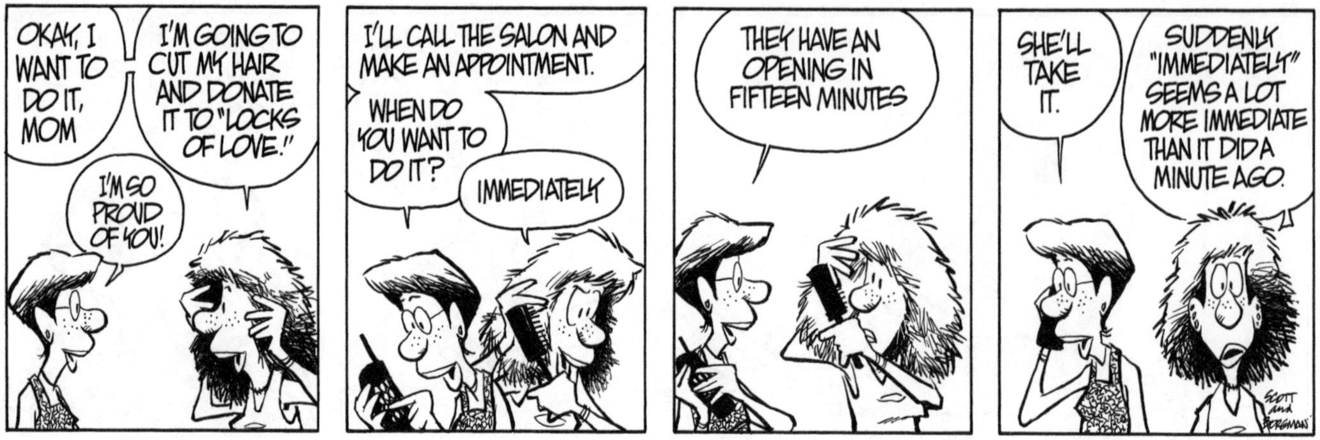
OKAY, I WANT TO DO IT, MOM
I'M GOING TO CUT MY HAIR AND DONATE IT TO "LOCKS OF LOVE."
I'M SO PROUD OF YOU!
I'LL CALL THE SALON AND MAKE AN APPOINTMENT.
WHEN DO YOU WANT TO DO IT?
IMMEDIATELY
THEY HAVE AN OPENING IN FIFTEEN MINUTES
SHE'LL TAKE IT.
SUDDENLY "IMMEDIATELY" SEEMS A LOT MORE IMMEDIATE THAN IT DID A MINUTE AGO.
SCOTT AND BORGMAN

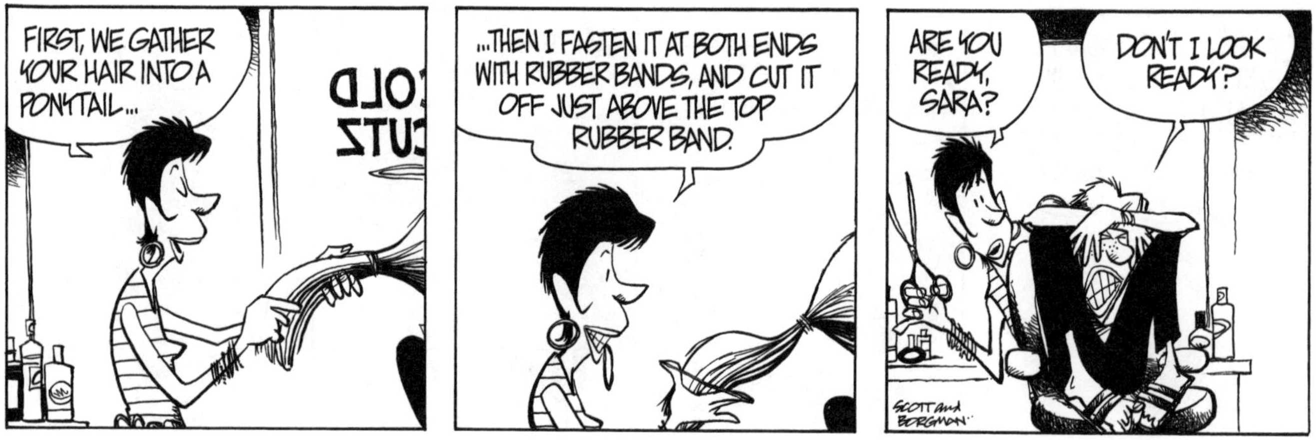
FIRST, WE GATHER YOUR HAIR INTO A PONYTAIL...
...THEN I FASTEN IT AT BOTH ENDS WITH RUBBER BANDS, AND CUT IT OFF JUST ABOVE THE TOP RUBBER BAND.
ARE YOU READY, SARA?
DON'T I LOOK READY?
SCOTT AND BORGMAN

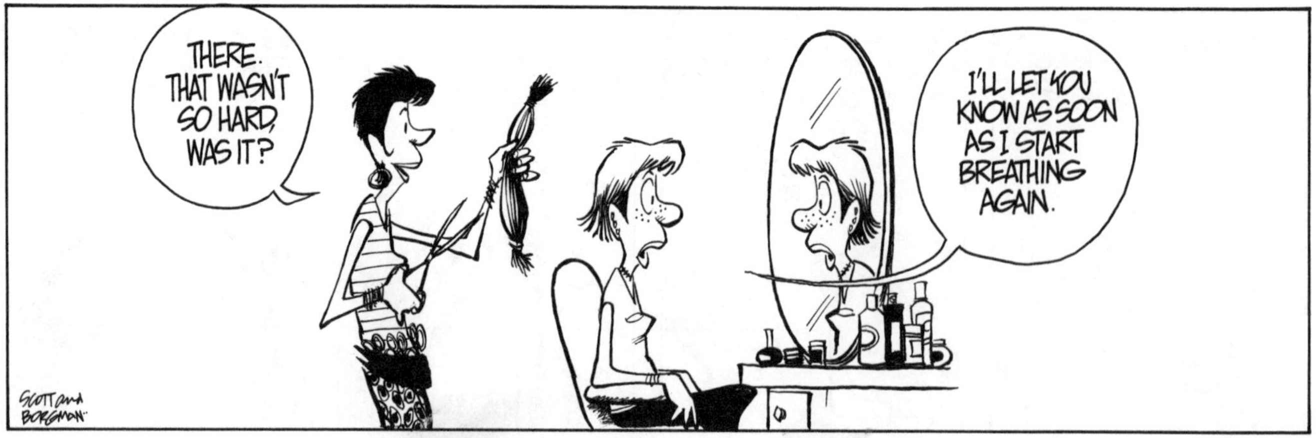
THERE. THAT WASN'T SO HARD, WAS IT?
I'LL LET YOU KNOW AS SOON AS I START BREATHING AGAIN.
SCOTT AND BORGMAN

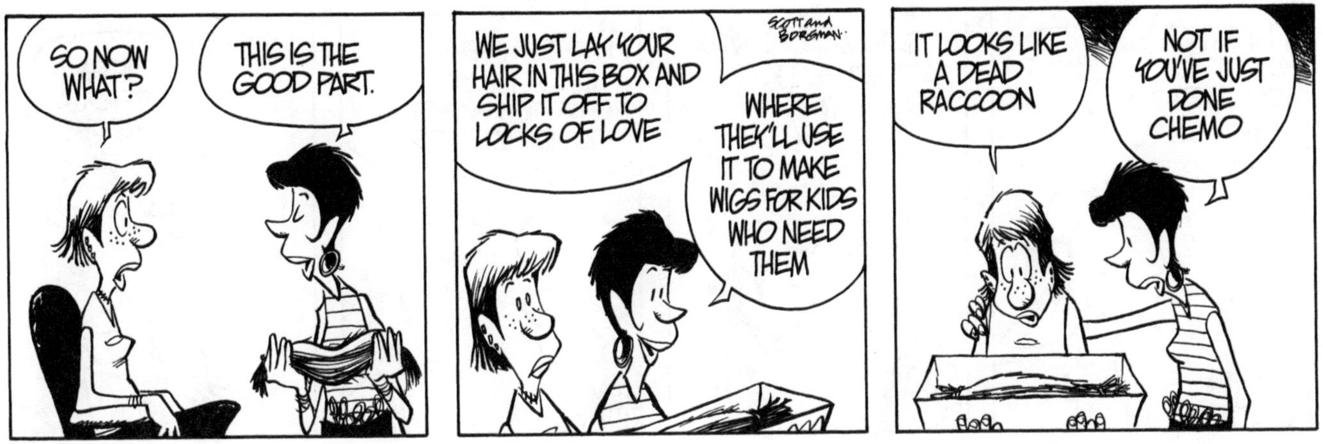
SO NOW WHAT?
THIS IS THE GOOD PART.
SCOTT AND BORGMAN
WE JUST LAY YOUR HAIR IN THIS BOX AND SHIP IT OFF TO LOCKS OF LOVE
WHERE THEY'LL USE IT TO MAKE WIGS FOR KIDS WHO NEED THEM
IT LOOKS LIKE A DEAD RACCOON
NOT IF YOU'VE JUST DONE CHEMO

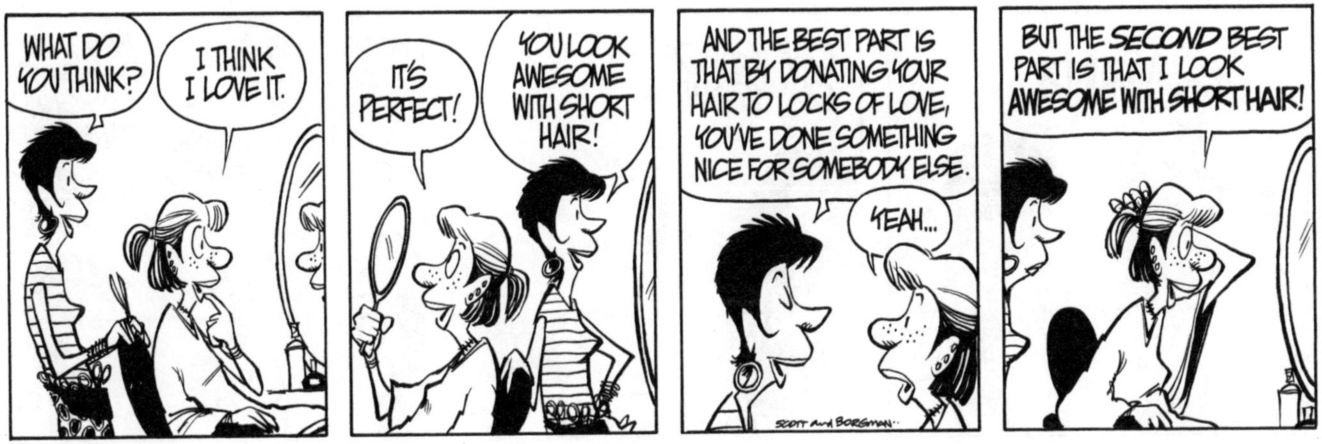
WHAT DO YOU THINK?
I THINK I LOVE IT.
IT'S PERFECT!
YOU LOOK AWESOME WITH SHORT HAIR!
AND THE BEST PART IS THAT BY DONATING YOUR HAIR TO LOCKS OF LOVE, YOU'VE DONE SOMETHING NICE FOR SOMEBODY ELSE.
YEAH...
SCOTT AND BORGMAN
BUT THE SECOND BEST PART IS THAT I LOOK AWESOME WITH SHORT HAIR!

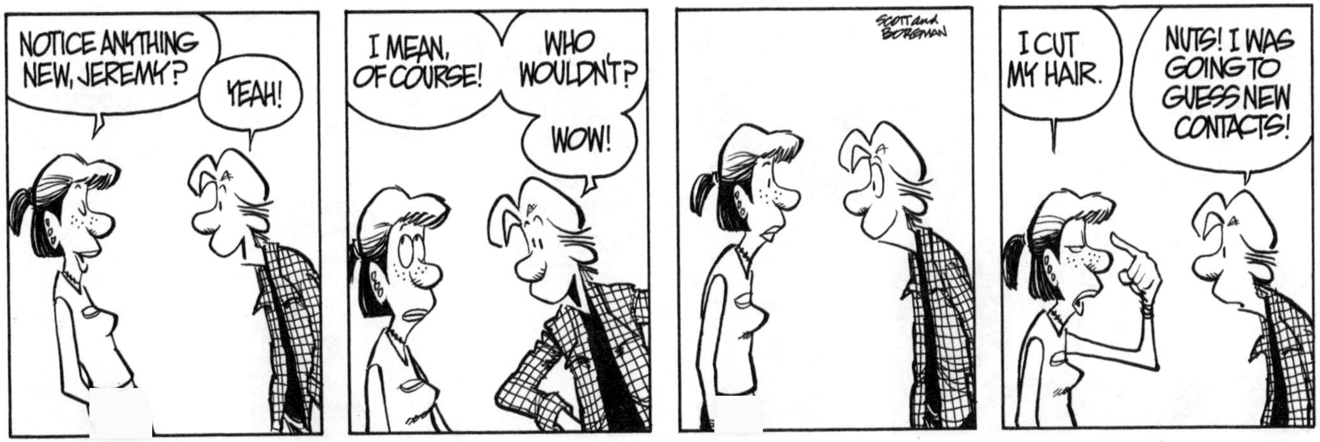
NOTICE ANYTHING NEW, JEREMY?
YEAH!
I MEAN, OF COURSE!
WHO WOULDN'T?
WOW!
SCOTT AND BORGMAN
I CUT MY HAIR.
NUTS! I WAS GOING TO GUESS NEW CONTACTS!

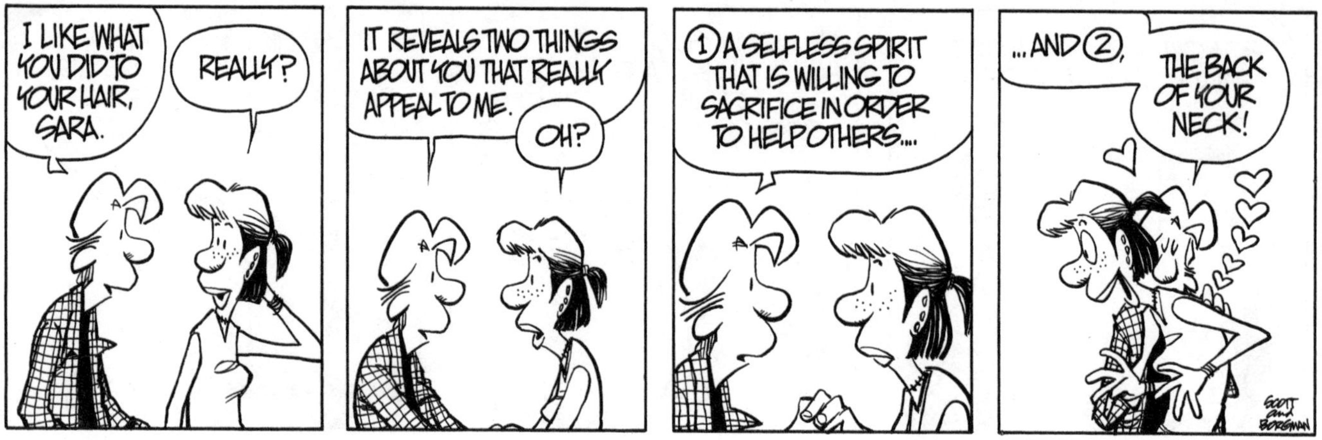
I LIKE WHAT YOU DID TO YOUR HAIR, SARA.
REALLY?
IT REVEALS TWO THINGS ABOUT YOU THAT REALLY APPEAL TO ME.
OH?
① A SELFLESS SPIRIT THAT IS WILLING TO SACRIFICE IN ORDER TO HELP OTHERS....
...AND ②,
THE BACK OF YOUR NECK!
SCOTT AND BORGMAN

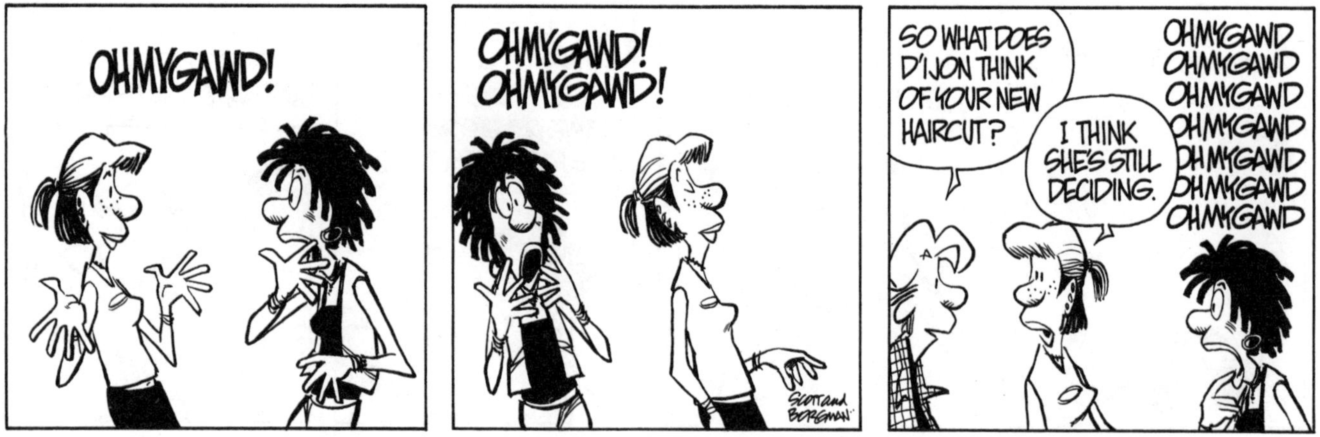
OHMYGAWD!
OHMYGAWD! OHMYGAWD!
SCOTT AND BORGMAN
SO WHAT DOES D'IJON THINK OF YOUR NEW HAIRCUT?
I THINK SHE'S STILL DECIDING.
OHMYGAWD OHMYGAWD OHMYGAWD OHMYGAWD OHMYGAWD OHMYGAWD OHMYGAWD

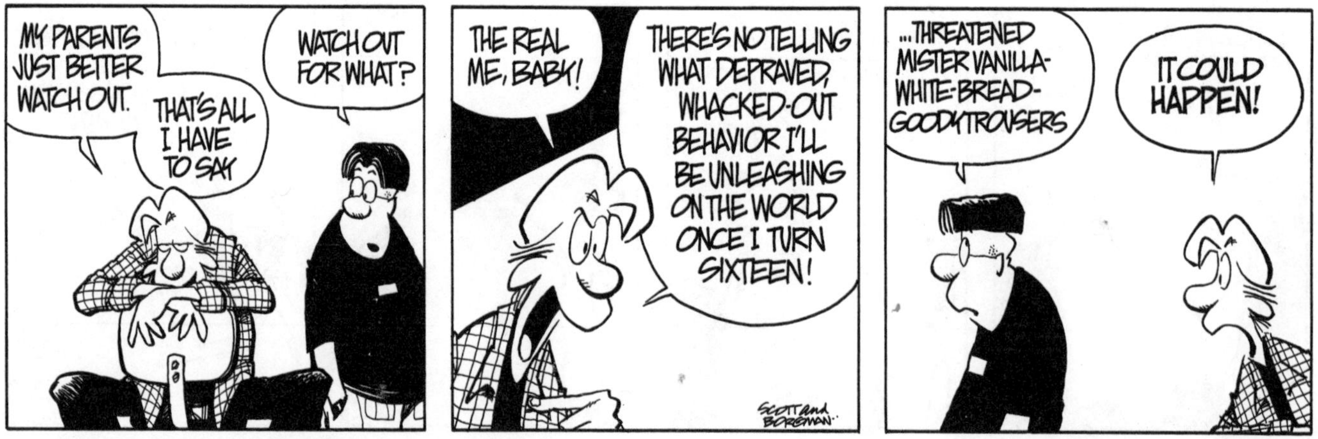
MY PARENTS JUST BETTER WATCH OUT.
THAT'S ALL I HAVE TO SAY
WATCH OUT FOR WHAT?
THE REAL ME, BABY!
THERE'S NO TELLING WHAT DEPRAVED, WHACKED-OUT BEHAVIOR I'LL BE UNLEASHING ON THE WORLD ONCE I TURN SIXTEEN!
SCOTT AND BORGMAN
...THREATENED MISTER VANILLA-WHITE-BREAD-GOODYTROUSERS
IT COULD HAPPEN!

Zits®

by JERRY SCOTT and JIM BORGMAN

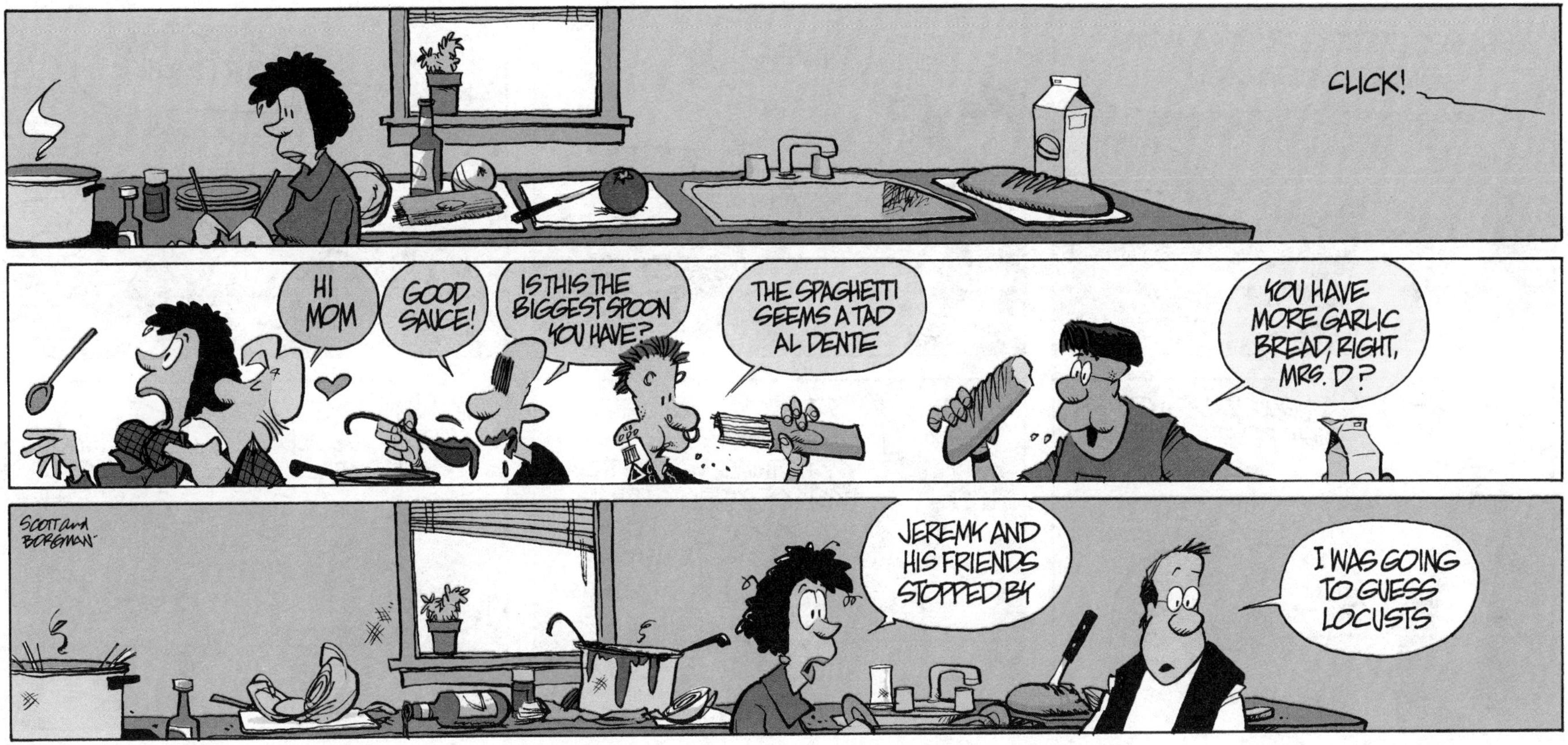

CLICK!
HI MOM
GOOD SAUCE!
IS THIS THE BIGGEST SPOON YOU HAVE?
THE SPAGHETTI SEEMS A TAD AL DENTE
YOU HAVE MORE GARLIC BREAD, RIGHT, MRS. D?
SCOTT and BORGMAN
JEREMY AND HIS FRIENDS STOPPED BY
I WAS GOING TO GUESS LOCUSTS

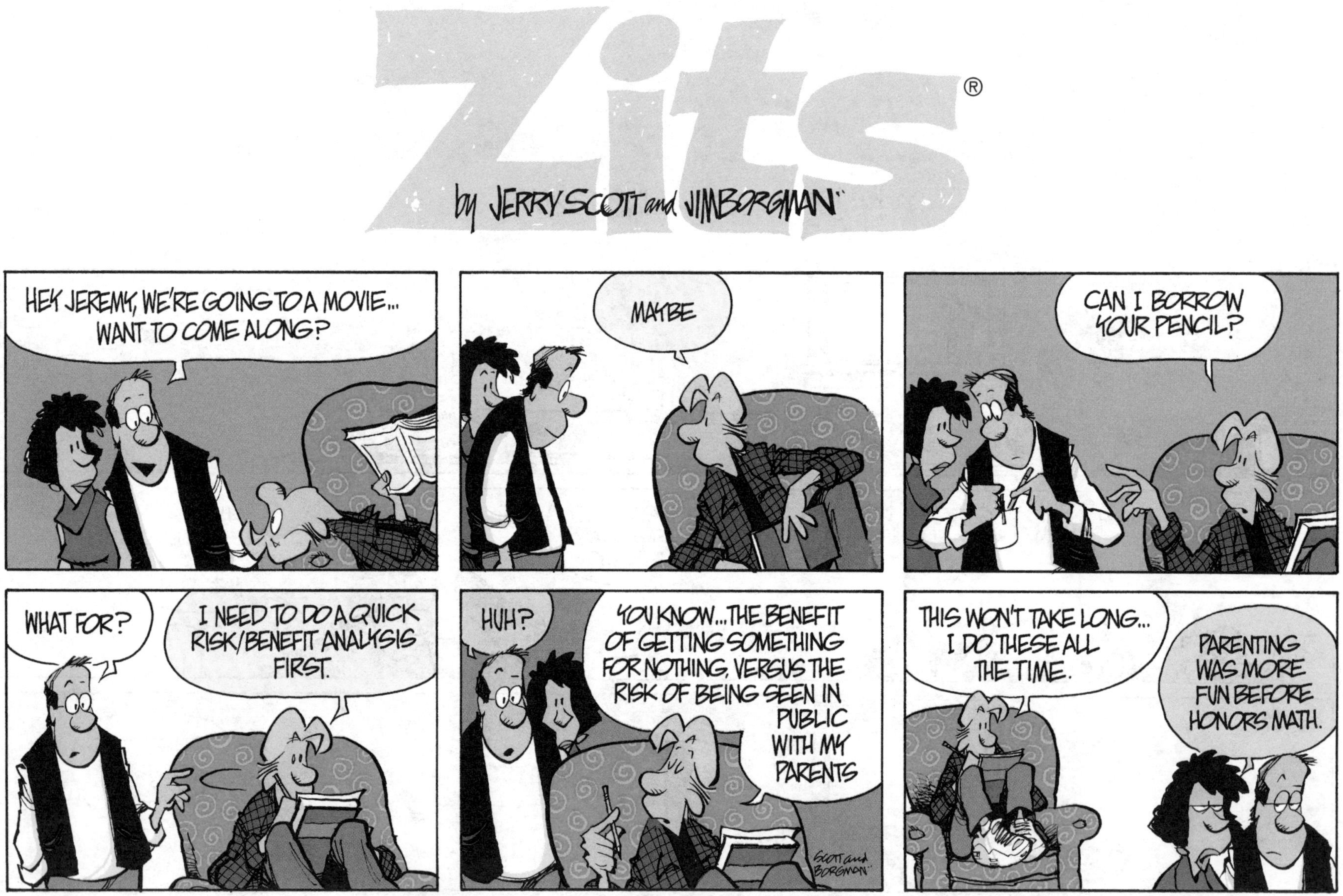
Zits®
by JERRY SCOTT and JIM BORGMAN
HEY JEREMY, WE'RE GOING TO A MOVIE... WANT TO COME ALONG?
MAYBE
CAN I BORROW YOUR PENCIL?
WHAT FOR?
I NEED TO DO A QUICK RISK/BENEFIT ANALYSIS FIRST.
HUH?
YOU KNOW...THE BENEFIT OF GETTING SOMETHING FOR NOTHING, VERSUS THE RISK OF BEING SEEN IN PUBLIC WITH MY PARENTS
SCOTT and BORGMAN
THIS WON'T TAKE LONG... I DO THESE ALL THE TIME.
PARENTING WAS MORE FUN BEFORE HONORS MATH.

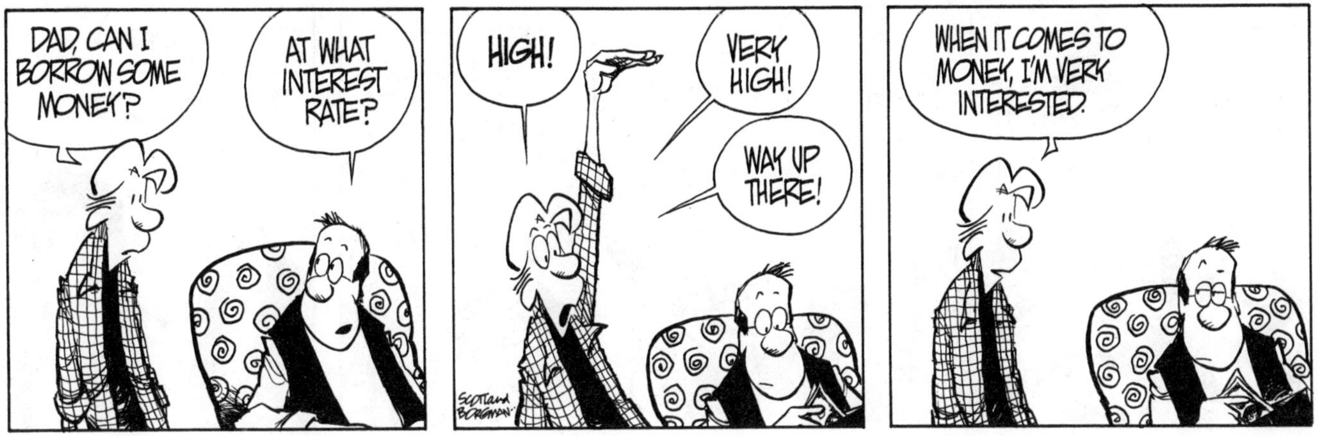
DAD, CAN I BORROW SOME MONEY?
AT WHAT INTEREST RATE?
HIGH!
VERY HIGH!
WAY UP THERE!
WHEN IT COMES TO MONEY, I'M VERY INTERESTED.
SCOTT AND BORGMAN

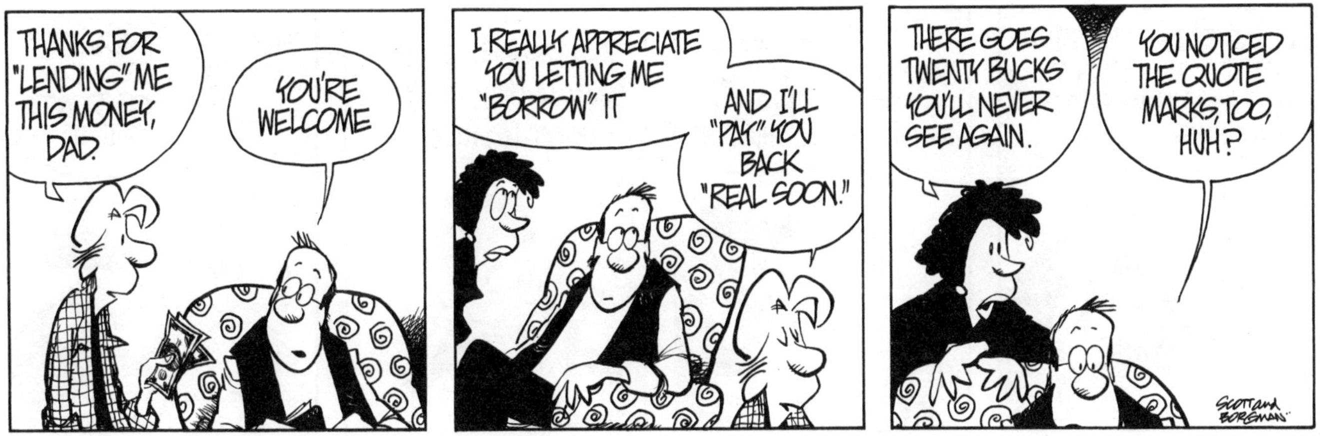
THANKS FOR "LENDING" ME THIS MONEY, DAD.
YOU'RE WELCOME
I REALLY APPRECIATE YOU LETTING ME "BORROW" IT
AND I'LL "PAY" YOU BACK "REAL SOON."
THERE GOES TWENTY BUCKS YOU'LL NEVER SEE AGAIN.
YOU NOTICED THE QUOTE MARKS, TOO, HUH?
SCOTT AND BORGMAN

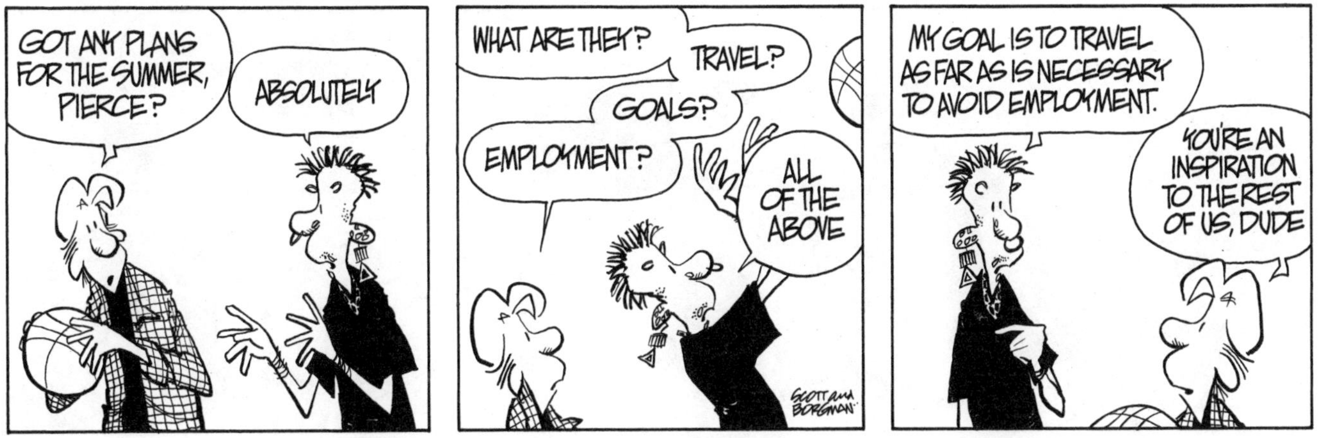
GOT ANY PLANS FOR THE SUMMER, PIERCE?
ABSOLUTELY
WHAT ARE THEY?
TRAVEL?
GOALS?
EMPLOYMENT?
ALL OF THE ABOVE
MY GOAL IS TO TRAVEL AS FAR AS IS NECESSARY TO AVOID EMPLOYMENT.
YOU'RE AN INSPIRATION TO THE REST OF US, DUDE
SCOTT AND BORGMAN

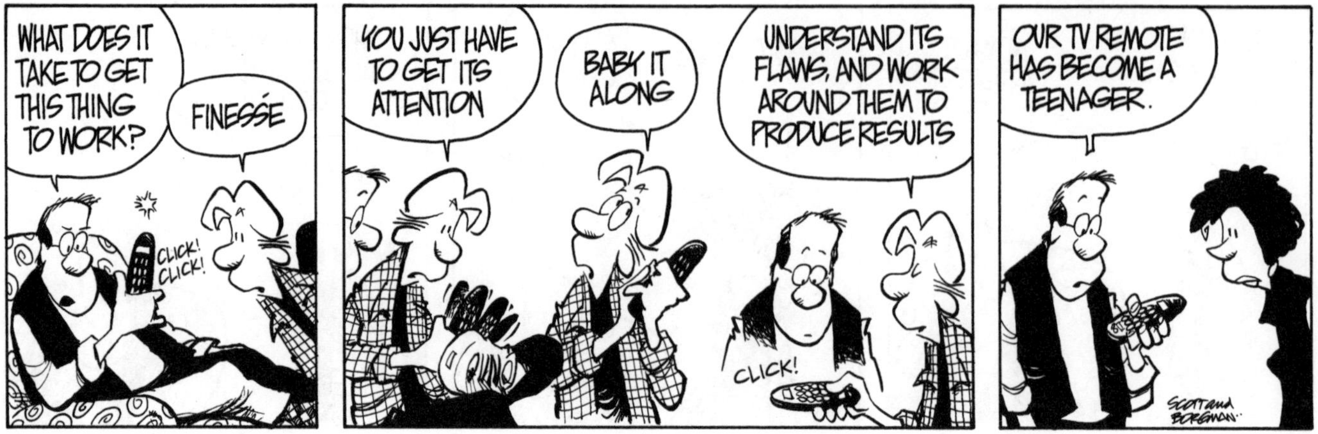
WHAT DOES IT TAKE TO GET THIS THING TO WORK?
FINESSE
CLICK! CLICK!
YOU JUST HAVE TO GET ITS ATTENTION
BABY IT ALONG
UNDERSTAND ITS FLAWS, AND WORK AROUND THEM TO PRODUCE RESULTS
CLICK!
OUR TV REMOTE HAS BECOME A TEENAGER.

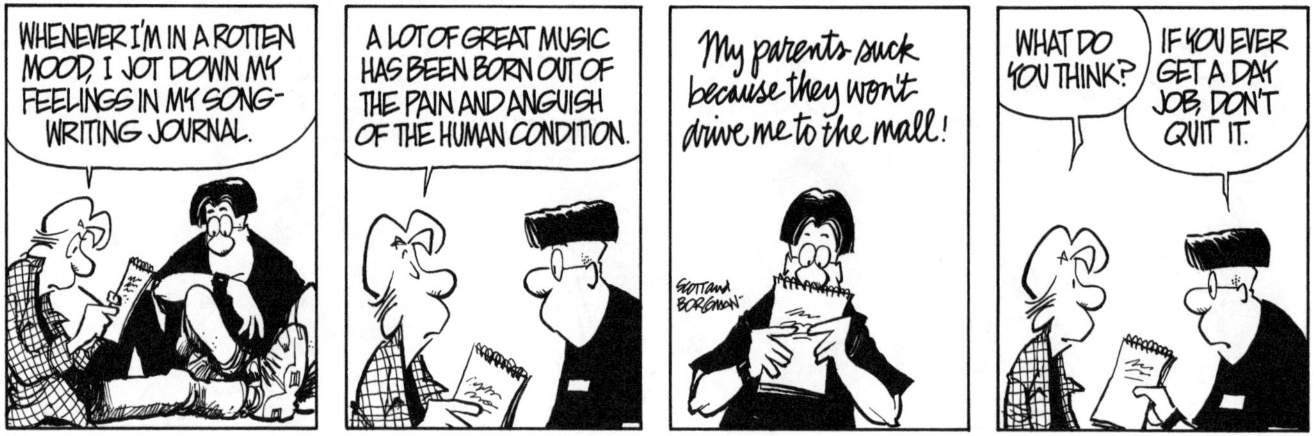
WHENEVER I'M IN A ROTTEN MOOD, I JOT DOWN MY FEELINGS IN MY SONG-WRITING JOURNAL.
A LOT OF GREAT MUSIC HAS BEEN BORN OUT OF THE PAIN AND ANGUISH OF THE HUMAN CONDITION.
My parents suck because they won't drive me to the mall!
WHAT DO YOU THINK?
IF YOU EVER GET A DAY JOB, DON'T QUIT IT.

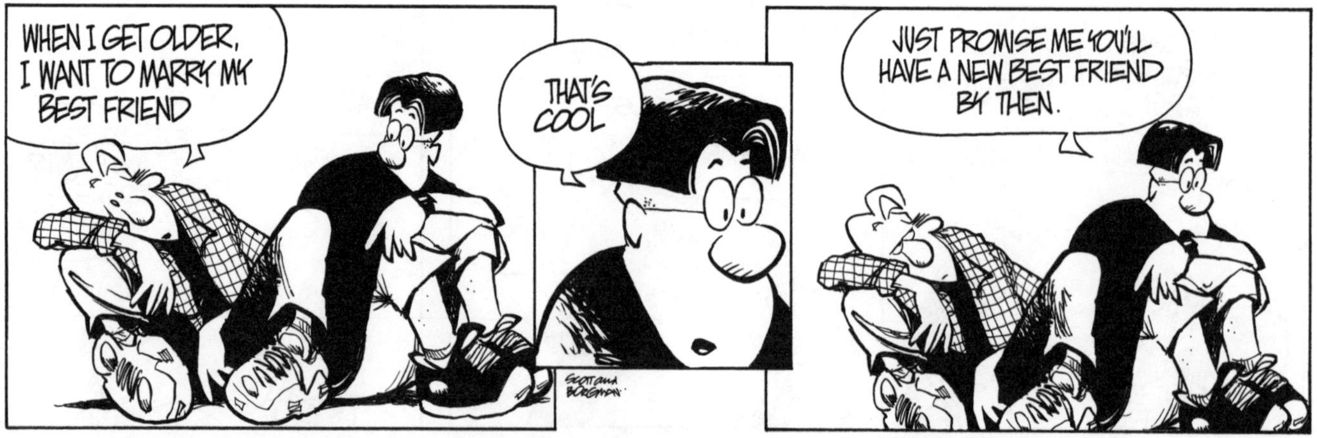
WHEN I GET OLDER, I WANT TO MARRY MY BEST FRIEND
THAT'S COOL
JUST PROMISE ME YOU'LL HAVE A NEW BEST FRIEND BY THEN.

Zits®

by JERRY SCOTT and JIM BORGMAN

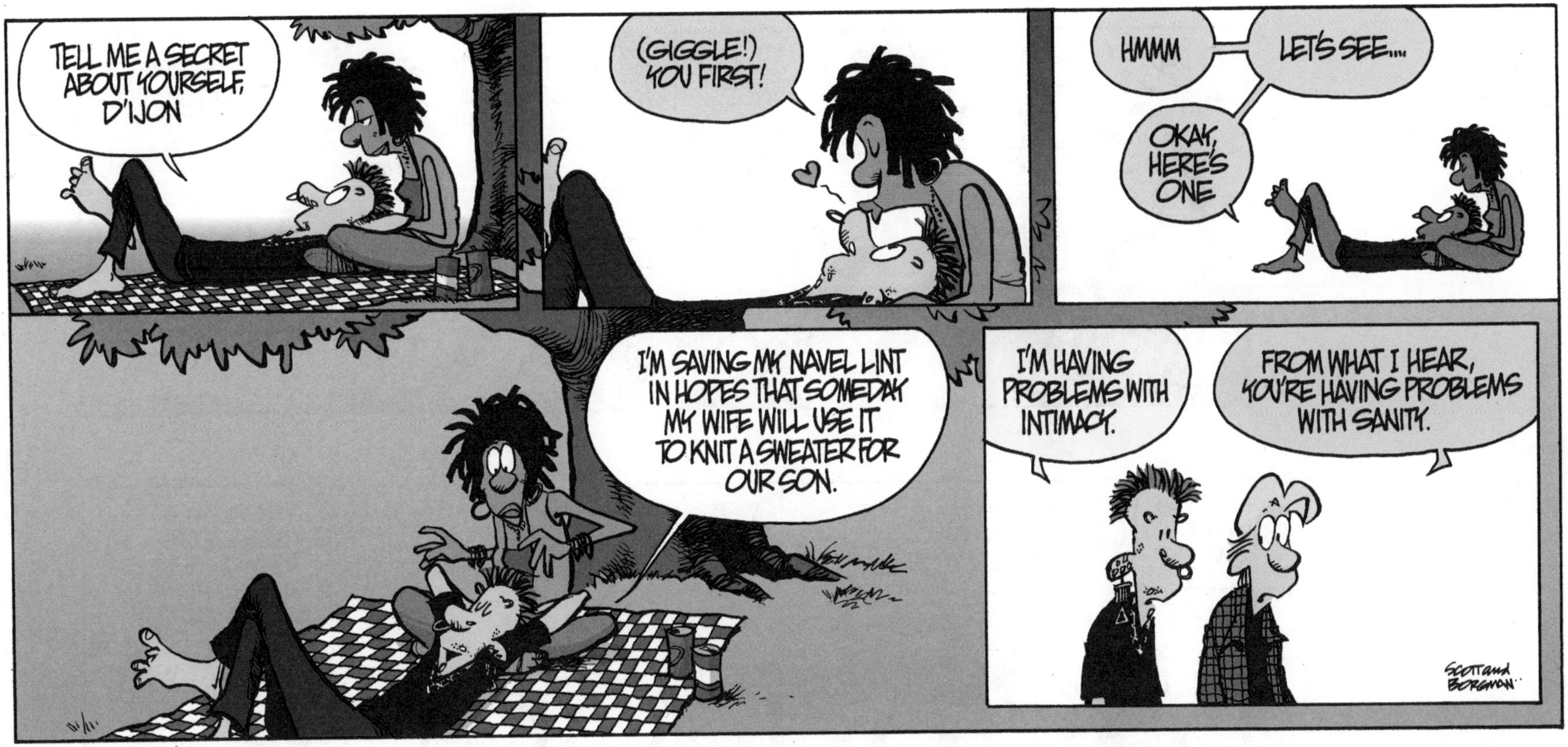

TELL ME A SECRET ABOUT YOURSELF, D'IJON
(GIGGLE!) YOU FIRST!
HMMM
LET'S SEE....
OKAY, HERE'S ONE
I'M SAVING MY NAVEL LINT IN HOPES THAT SOMEDAY MY WIFE WILL USE IT TO KNIT A SWEATER FOR OUR SON.
I'M HAVING PROBLEMS WITH INTIMACY.
FROM WHAT I HEAR, YOU'RE HAVING PROBLEMS WITH SANITY.
SCOTT and BORGMAN

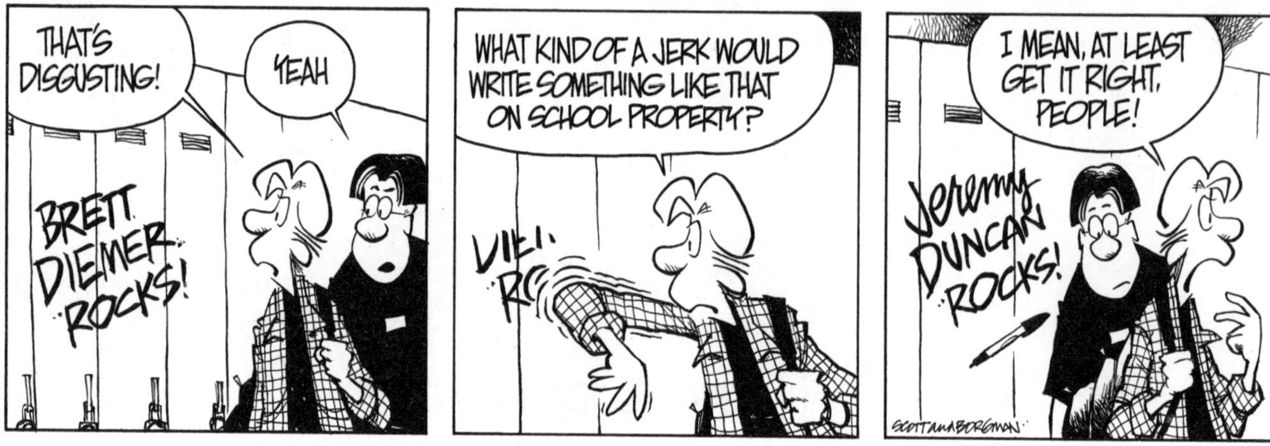
THAT'S DISGUSTING!
YEAH
BRETT DIEMER ROCKS!
WHAT KIND OF A JERK WOULD WRITE SOMETHING LIKE THAT ON SCHOOL PROPERTY?
I MEAN, AT LEAST GET IT RIGHT, PEOPLE!
Jeremy DUNCAN ROCKS!
SCOTT and BORGMAN

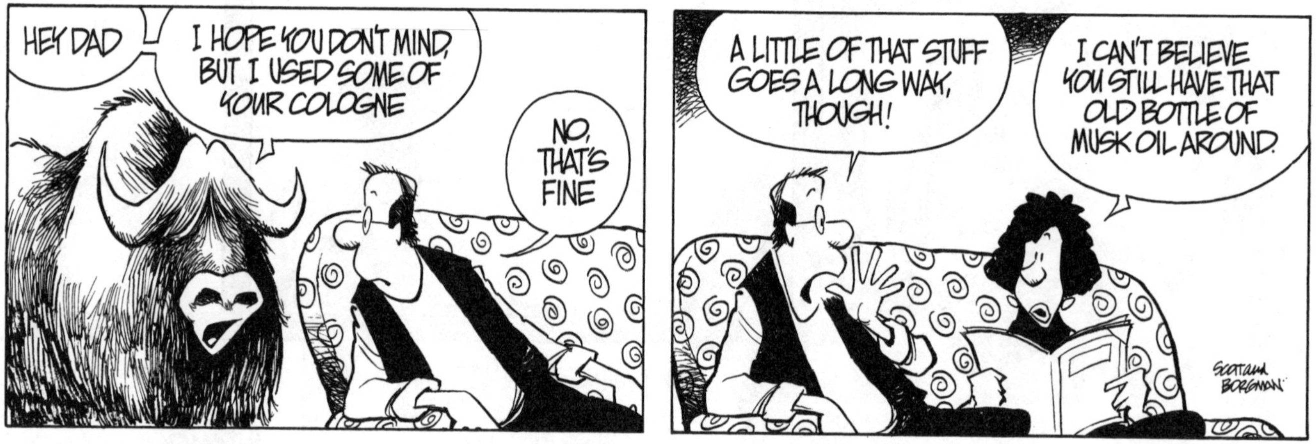
HEY DAD
I HOPE YOU DON'T MIND, BUT I USED SOME OF YOUR COLOGNE
NO, THAT'S FINE
A LITTLE OF THAT STUFF GOES A LONG WAY, THOUGH!
I CAN'T BELIEVE YOU STILL HAVE THAT OLD BOTTLE OF MUSK OIL AROUND.
SCOTT and BORGMAN

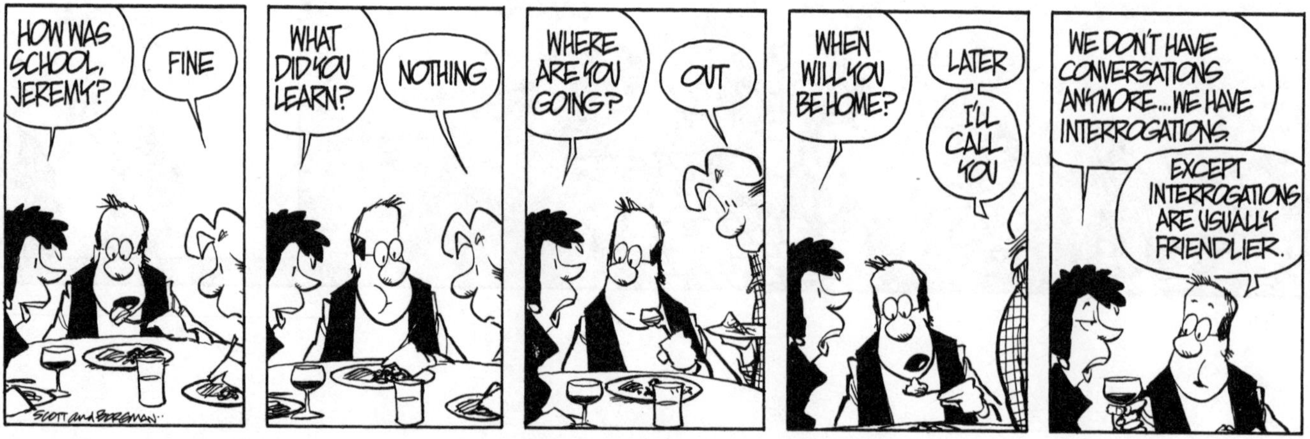
HOW WAS SCHOOL, JEREMY?
FINE
WHAT DID YOU LEARN?
NOTHING
WHERE ARE YOU GOING?
OUT
WHEN WILL YOU BE HOME?
LATER
I'LL CALL YOU
WE DON'T HAVE CONVERSATIONS ANYMORE... WE HAVE INTERROGATIONS.
EXCEPT INTERROGATIONS ARE USUALLY FRIENDLIER.
SCOTT and BORGMAN

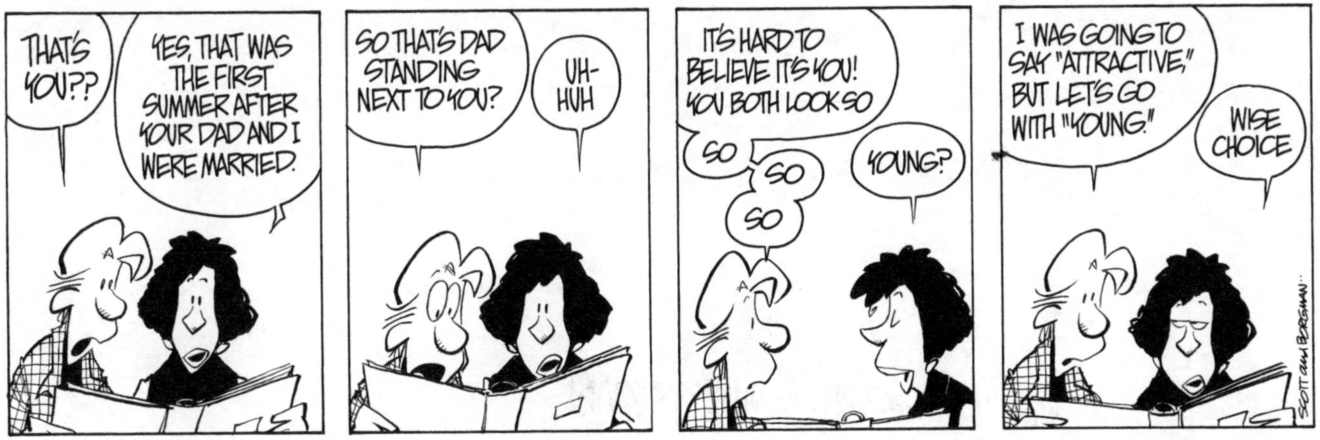
THAT'S YOU??
YES, THAT WAS THE FIRST SUMMER AFTER YOUR DAD AND I WERE MARRIED.
SO THAT'S DAD STANDING NEXT TO YOU?
UH-HUH
IT'S HARD TO BELIEVE IT'S YOU! YOU BOTH LOOK SO
SO
SO
SO
YOUNG?
I WAS GOING TO SAY "ATTRACTIVE," BUT LET'S GO WITH "YOUNG."
WISE CHOICE
SCOTT and BORGMAN

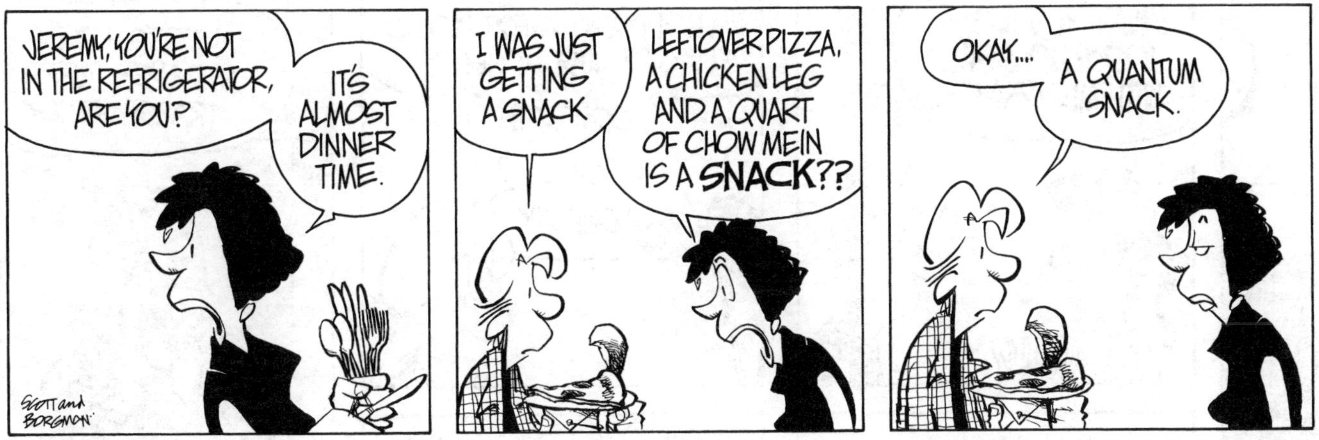
JEREMY, YOU'RE NOT IN THE REFRIGERATOR, ARE YOU?
IT'S ALMOST DINNER TIME.
SCOTT and BORGMAN
I WAS JUST GETTING A SNACK
LEFTOVER PIZZA, A CHICKEN LEG AND A QUART OF CHOW MEIN IS A SNACK??
OKAY....
A QUANTUM SNACK.

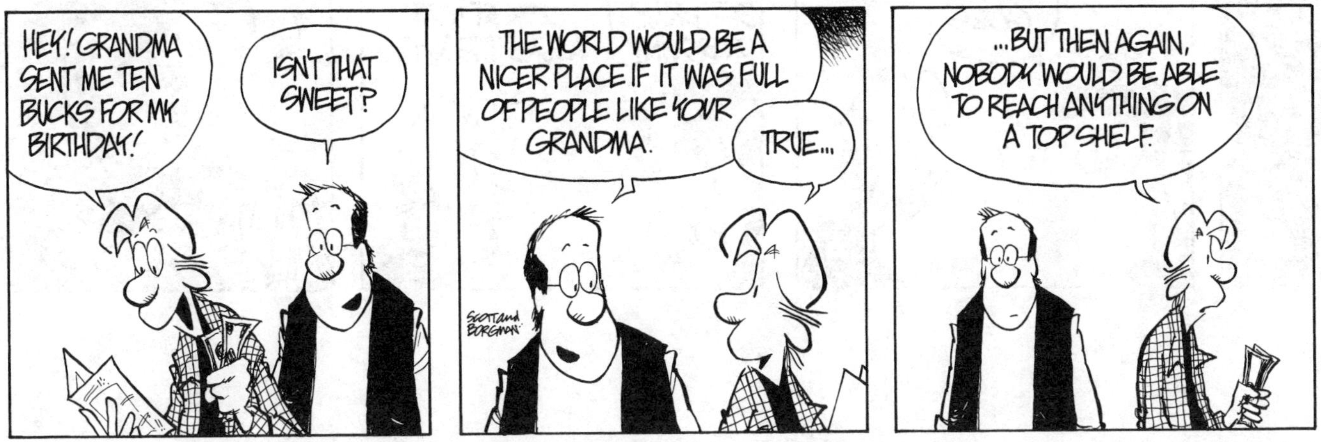
HEY! GRANDMA SENT ME TEN BUCKS FOR MY BIRTHDAY!
ISN'T THAT SWEET?
THE WORLD WOULD BE A NICER PLACE IF IT WAS FULL OF PEOPLE LIKE YOUR GRANDMA.
TRUE...
SCOTT and BORGMAN
...BUT THEN AGAIN, NOBODY WOULD BE ABLE TO REACH ANYTHING ON A TOP SHELF.

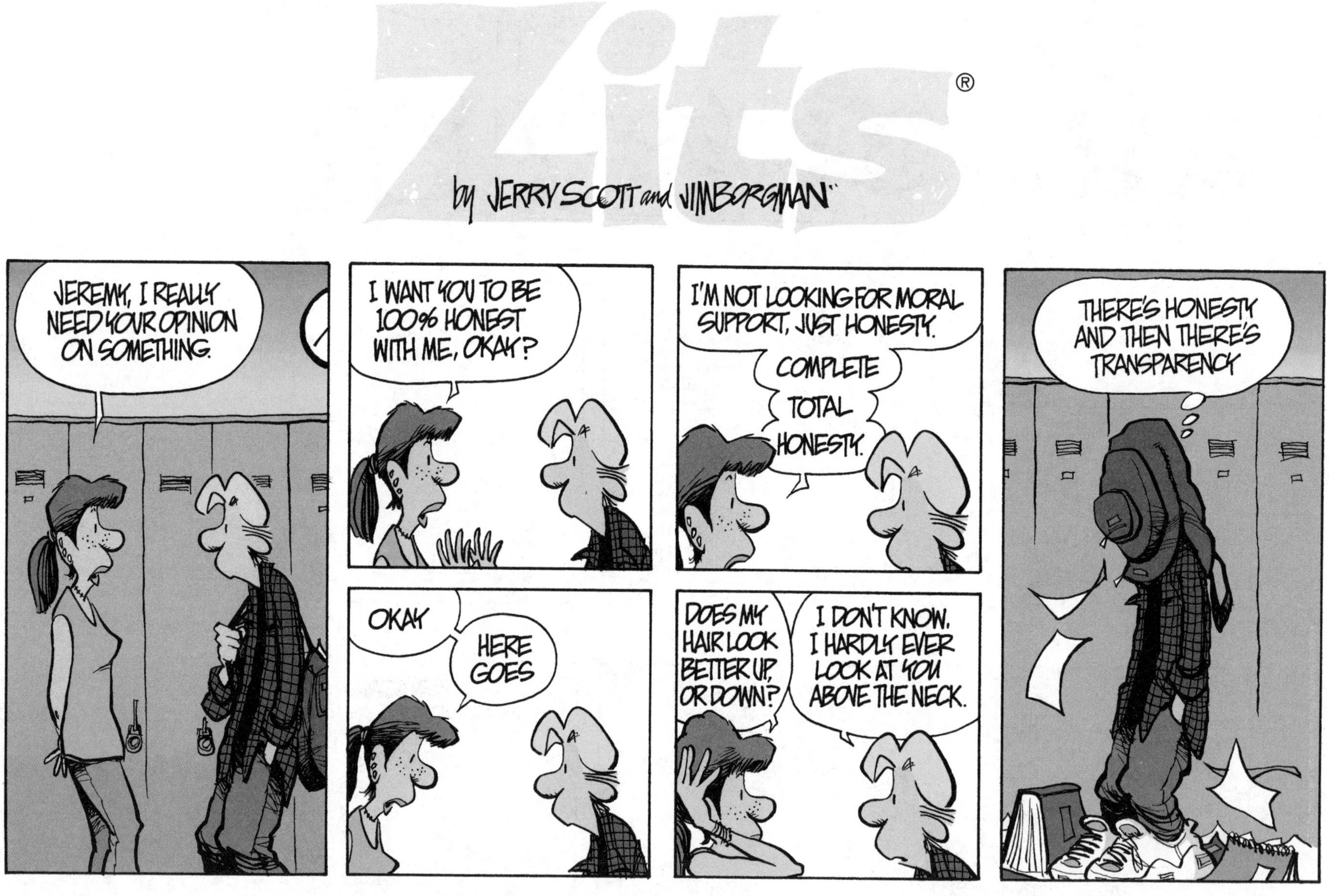
Zits®
by JERRY SCOTT and JIM BORGMAN
JEREMY, I REALLY NEED YOUR OPINION ON SOMETHING.
I WANT YOU TO BE 100% HONEST WITH ME, OKAY?
I'M NOT LOOKING FOR MORAL SUPPORT, JUST HONESTY.
COMPLETE TOTAL HONESTY.
OKAY
HERE GOES
DOES MY HAIR LOOK BETTER UP, OR DOWN?
I DON'T KNOW. I HARDLY EVER LOOK AT YOU ABOVE THE NECK.
THERE'S HONESTY AND THEN THERE'S TRANSPARENCY

JEREMY, I WANT YOU TO MOW THE LAWN TODAY.
TALK ABOUT YOUR DIRTY LOOKS!
I'M GONNA NEED THE SPRAY N' WASH
AND WHEN YOU FINISH MOWING THE LAWN, YOU CAN CLEAN OUT THE SHED.
VVVRUUUU
WOW! IT STARTED ON THE FIRST PULL!
I HAVE PLENTY OF GAS
AND THE MOWER SOUNDS GREAT
UMMMMMMMM
WHAT ELSE CAN GO WRONG???

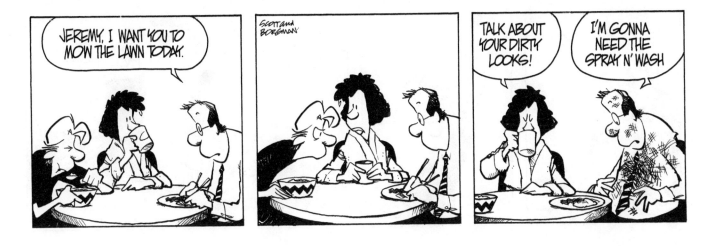

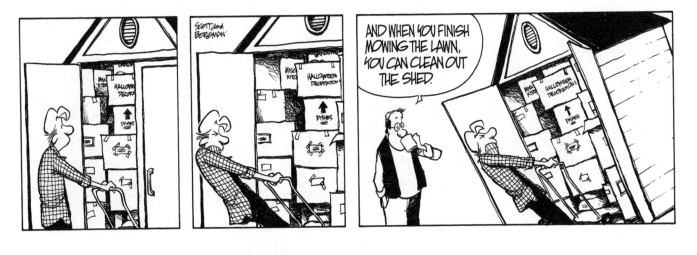

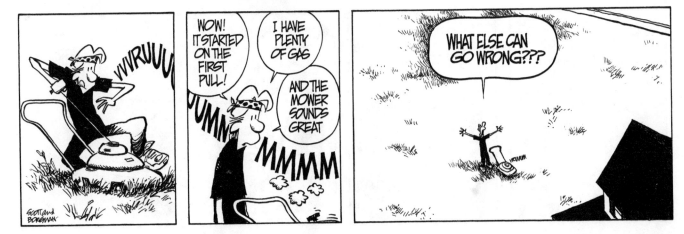

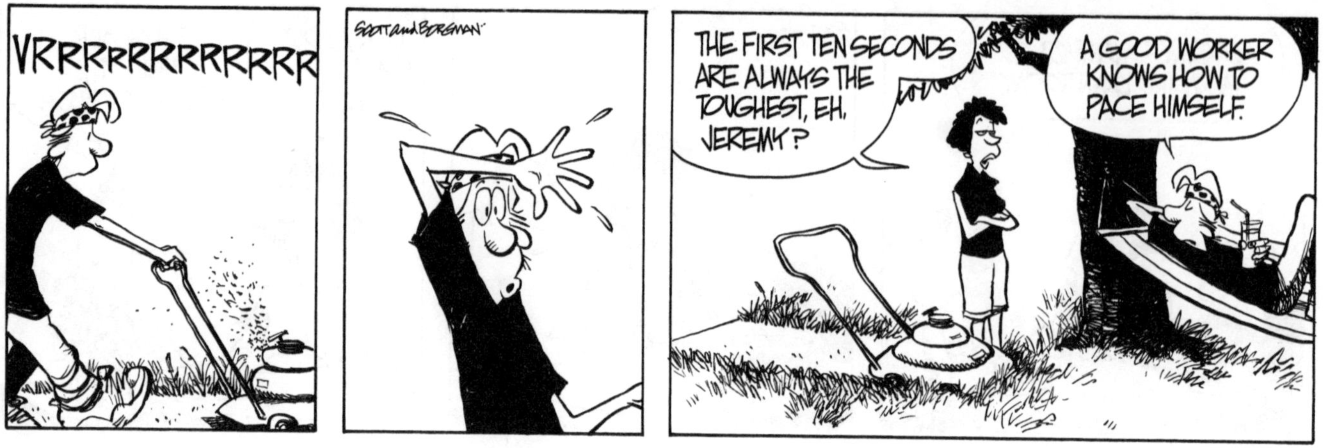
VRRRRRRRRRRRR
SCOTT and BORGMAN
THE FIRST TEN SECONDS ARE ALWAYS THE TOUGHEST, EH, JEREMY?
A GOOD WORKER KNOWS HOW TO PACE HIMSELF.

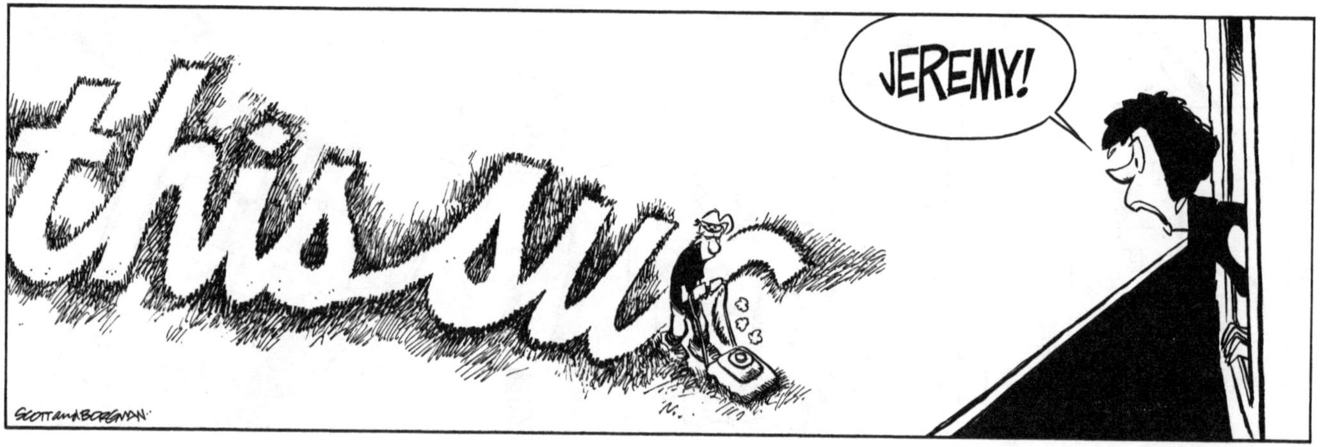
this su
JEREMY!
SCOTT and BORGMAN

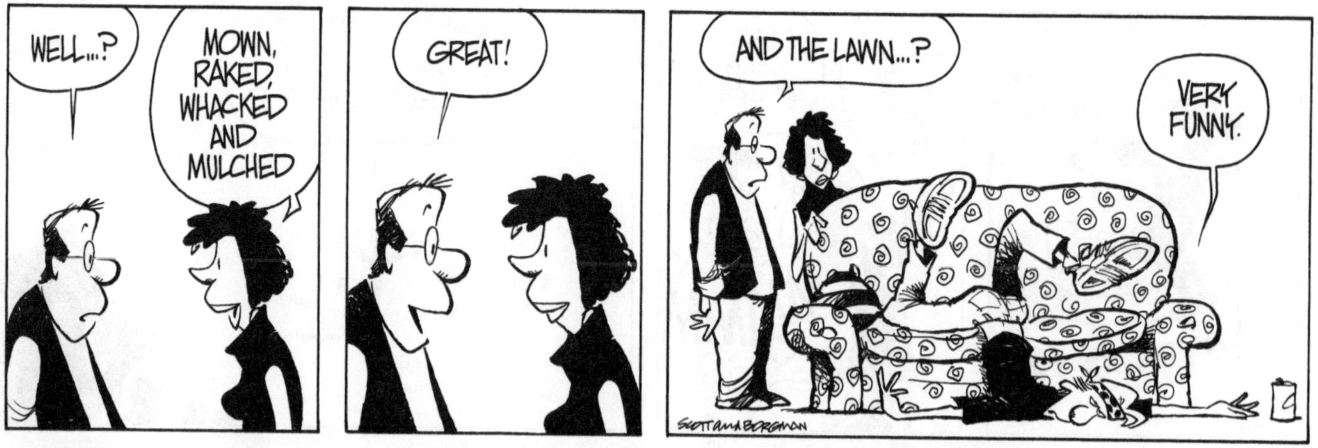
WELL...?
MOWN, RAKED, WHACKED AND MULCHED
GREAT!
AND THE LAWN...?
VERY FUNNY.
SCOTT and BORGMAN

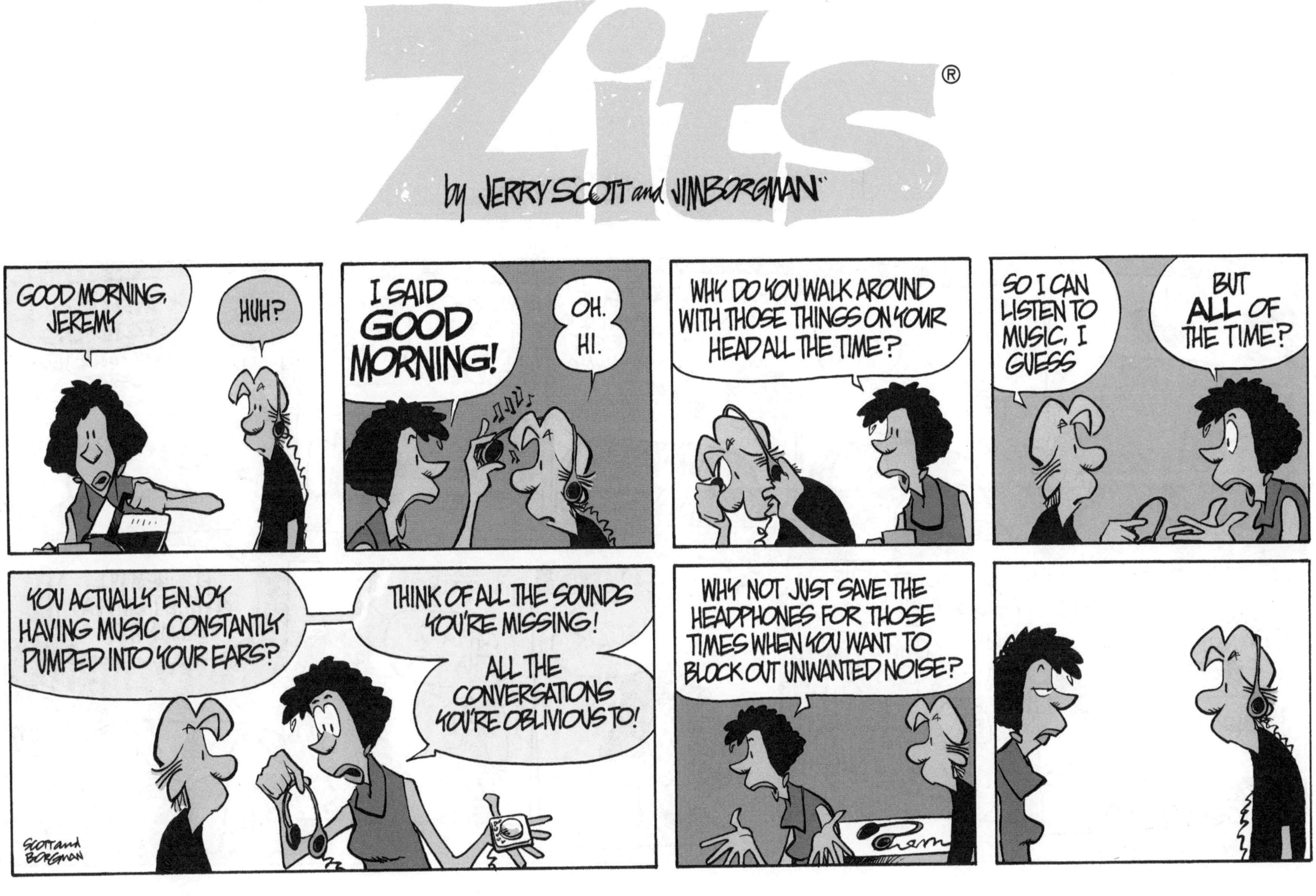
Zits®
by JERRY SCOTT and JIM BORGMAN
GOOD MORNING, JEREMY
HUH?
I SAID GOOD MORNING!
OH. HI.
WHY DO YOU WALK AROUND WITH THOSE THINGS ON YOUR HEAD ALL THE TIME?
SO I CAN LISTEN TO MUSIC, I GUESS
BUT ALL OF THE TIME?
YOU ACTUALLY ENJOY HAVING MUSIC CONSTANTLY PUMPED INTO YOUR EARS?
THINK OF ALL THE SOUNDS YOU'RE MISSING!
ALL THE CONVERSATIONS YOU'RE OBLIVIOUS TO!
SCOTT and BORGMAN
WHY NOT JUST SAVE THE HEADPHONES FOR THOSE TIMES WHEN YOU WANT TO BLOCK OUT UNWANTED NOISE?

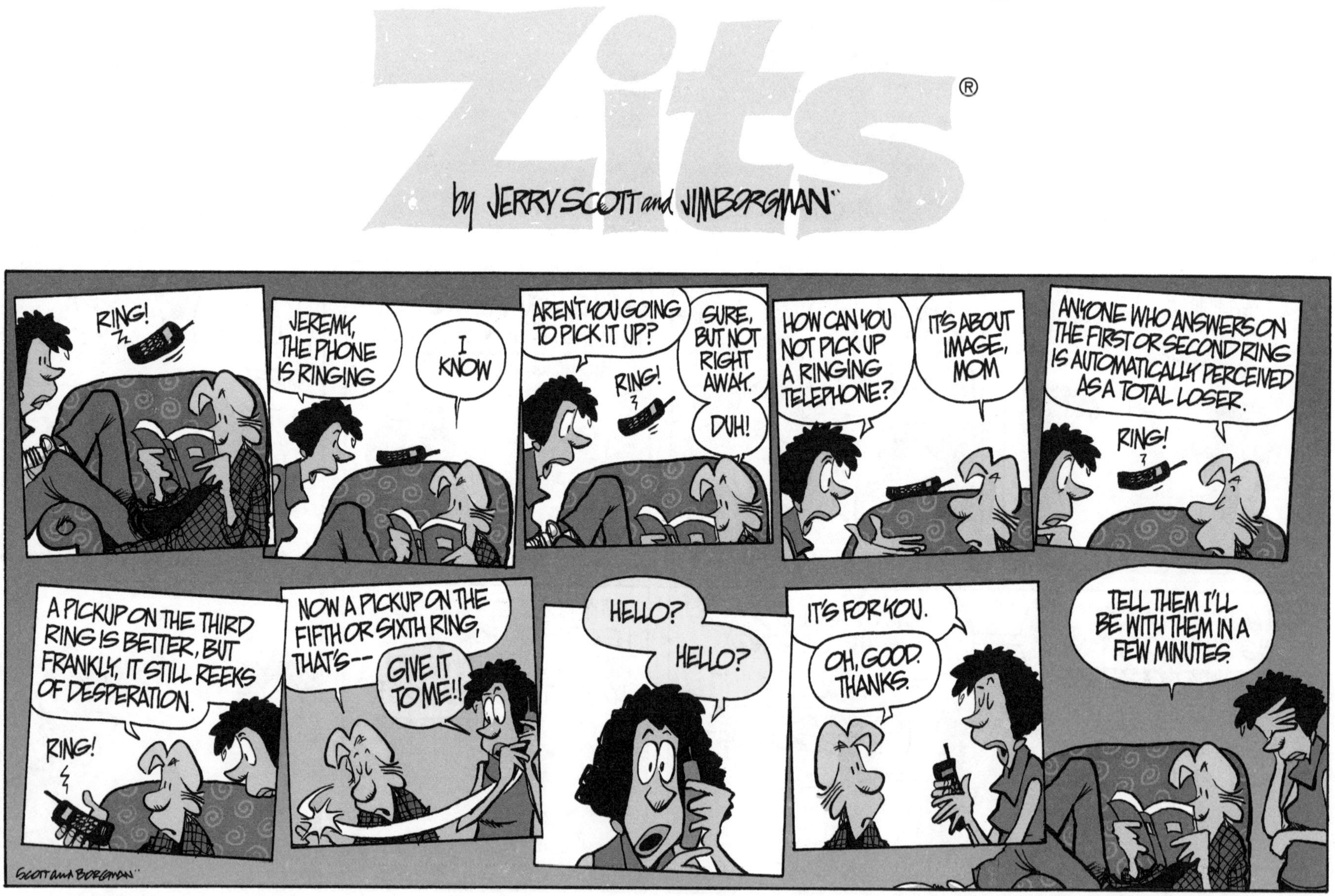
Zits®
by JERRY SCOTT and JIM BORGMAN
RING!
JEREMY, THE PHONE IS RINGING
I KNOW
AREN'T YOU GOING TO PICK IT UP?
RING!
SURE, BUT NOT RIGHT AWAY.
DUH!
HOW CAN YOU NOT PICK UP A RINGING TELEPHONE?
IT'S ABOUT IMAGE, MOM
ANYONE WHO ANSWERS ON THE FIRST OR SECOND RING IS AUTOMATICALLY PERCEIVED AS A TOTAL LOSER.
RING!
A PICKUP ON THE THIRD RING IS BETTER, BUT FRANKLY, IT STILL REEKS OF DESPERATION.
RING!
NOW A PICKUP ON THE FIFTH OR SIXTH RING, THAT'S--
GIVE IT TO ME!!
HELLO?
HELLO?
IT'S FOR YOU.
OH, GOOD. THANKS.
TELL THEM I'LL BE WITH THEM IN A FEW MINUTES.
SCOTT and BORGMAN

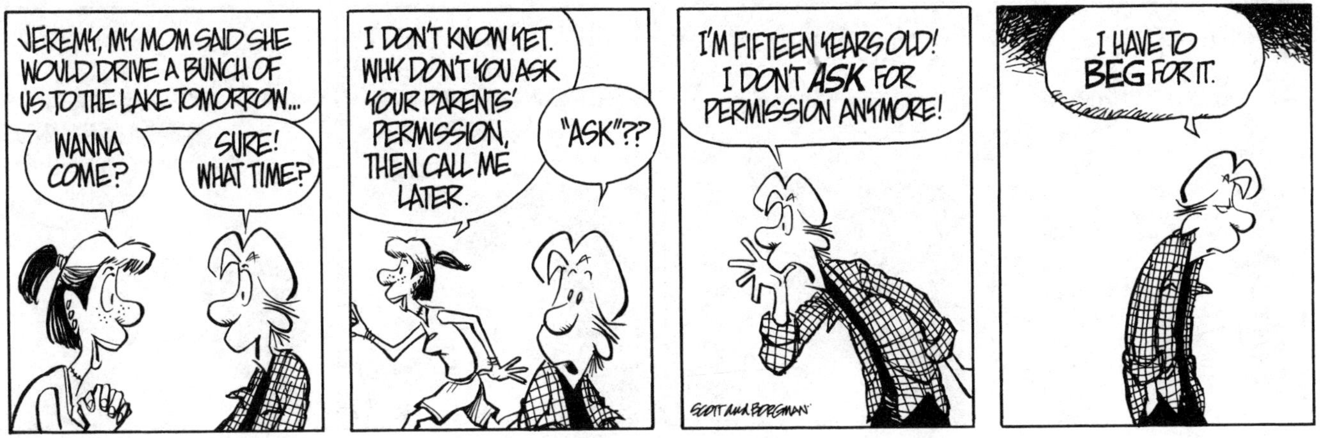
JEREMY, MY MOM SAID SHE WOULD DRIVE A BUNCH OF US TO THE LAKE TOMORROW...
WANNA COME?
SURE! WHAT TIME?
I DON'T KNOW YET. WHY DON'T YOU ASK YOUR PARENTS' PERMISSION, THEN CALL ME LATER.
"ASK"??
I'M FIFTEEN YEARS OLD! I DON'T ASK FOR PERMISSION ANYMORE!
SCOTT AND BORGMAN
I HAVE TO BEG FOR IT.

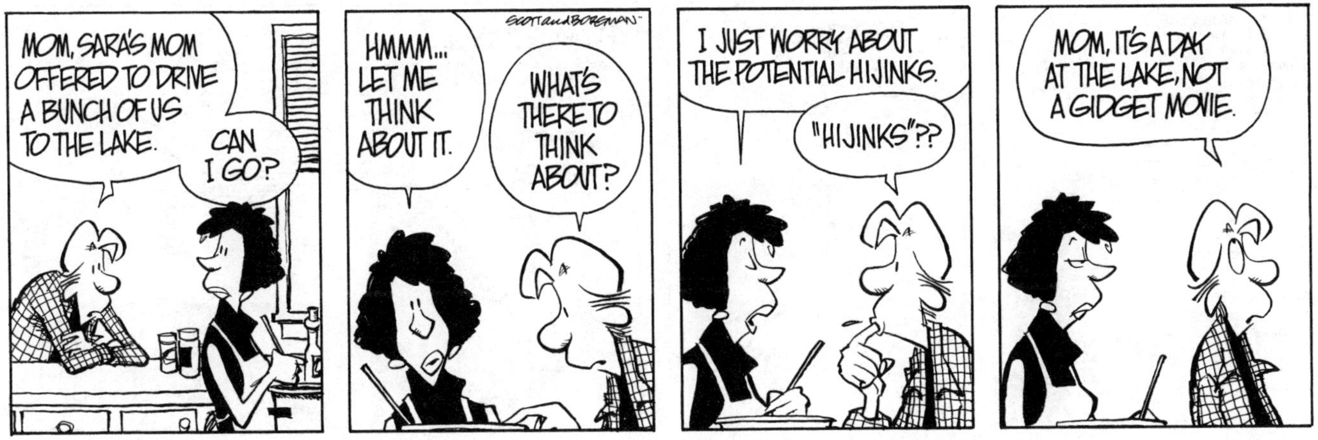
MOM, SARA'S MOM OFFERED TO DRIVE A BUNCH OF US TO THE LAKE.
CAN I GO?
SCOTT AND BORGMAN
HMMM... LET ME THINK ABOUT IT.
WHAT'S THERE TO THINK ABOUT?
I JUST WORRY ABOUT THE POTENTIAL HIJINKS.
"HIJINKS"??
MOM, IT'S A DAY AT THE LAKE, NOT A GIDGET MOVIE.

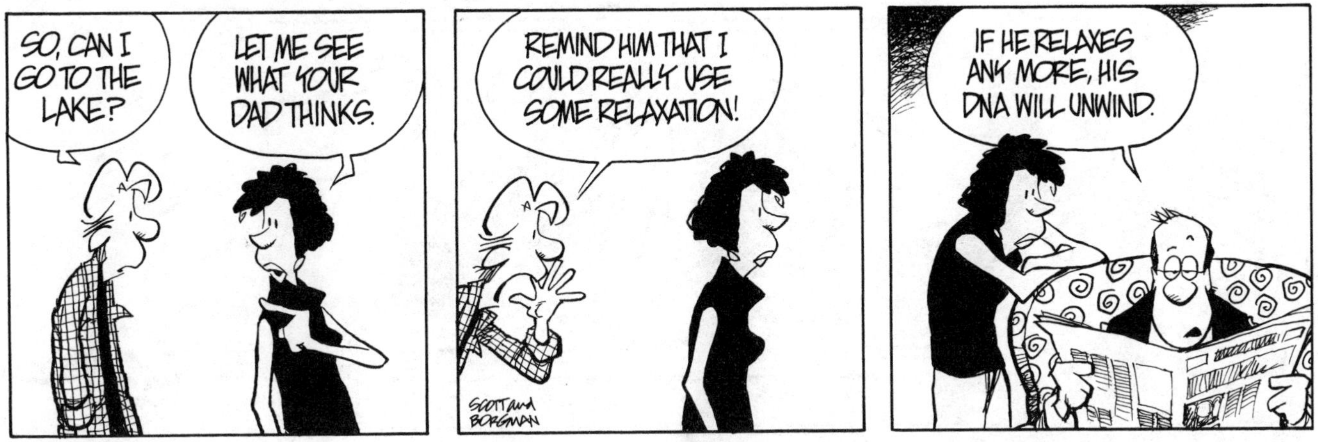
SO, CAN I GO TO THE LAKE?
LET ME SEE WHAT YOUR DAD THINKS.
REMIND HIM THAT I COULD REALLY USE SOME RELAXATION!
SCOTT AND BORGMAN
IF HE RELAXES ANY MORE, HIS DNA WILL UNWIND.

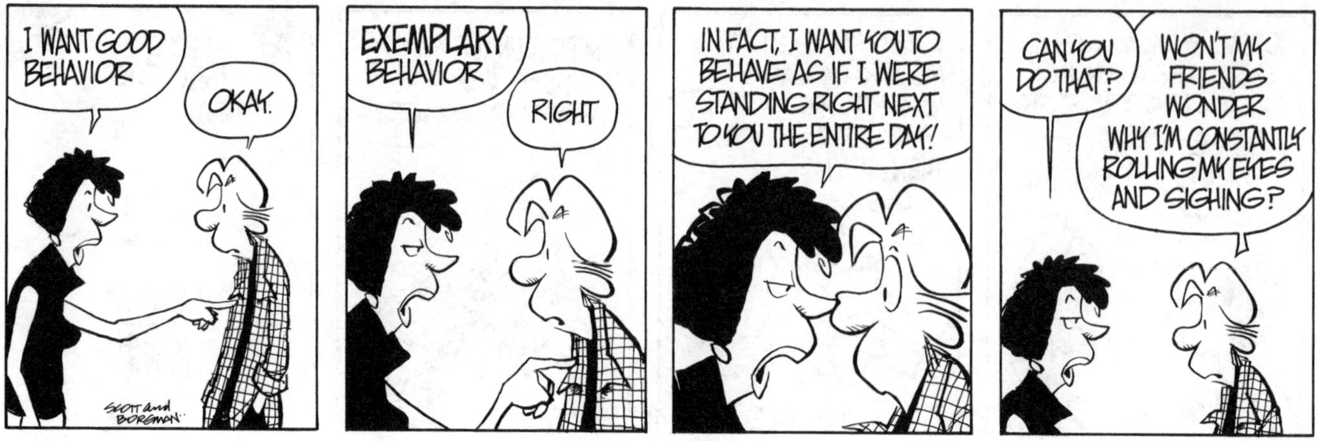
I WANT GOOD BEHAVIOR
OKAY.
EXEMPLARY BEHAVIOR
RIGHT
IN FACT, I WANT YOU TO BEHAVE AS IF I WERE STANDING RIGHT NEXT TO YOU THE ENTIRE DAY!
CAN YOU DO THAT?
WON'T MY FRIENDS WONDER WHY I'M CONSTANTLY ROLLING MY EYES AND SIGHING?
SCOTT and BORGMAN

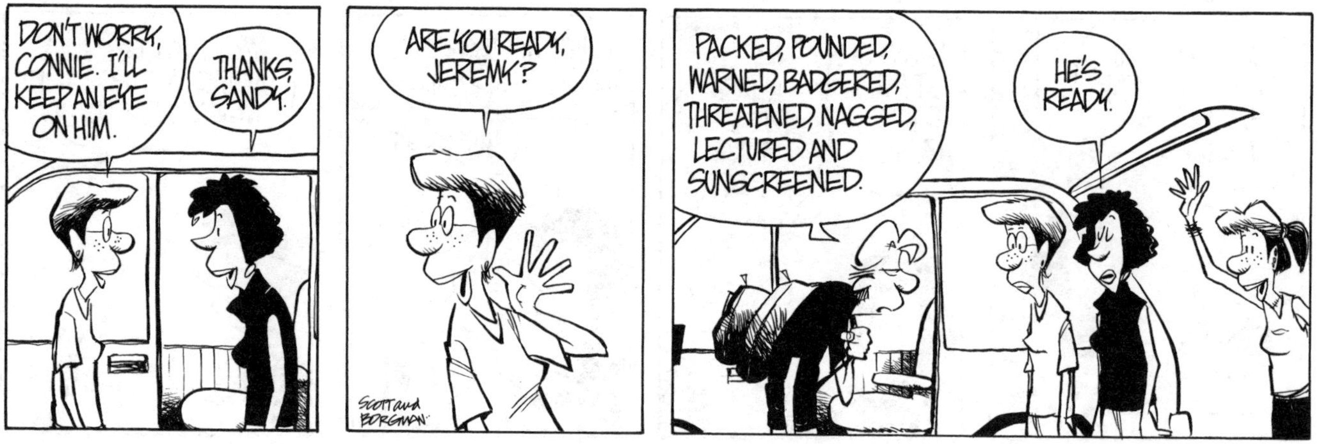
DON'T WORRY, CONNIE. I'LL KEEP AN EYE ON HIM.
THANKS, SANDY.
ARE YOU READY, JEREMY?
SCOTT and BORGMAN
PACKED, POUNDED, WARNED, BADGERED, THREATENED, NAGGED, LECTURED AND SUNSCREENED.
HE'S READY.

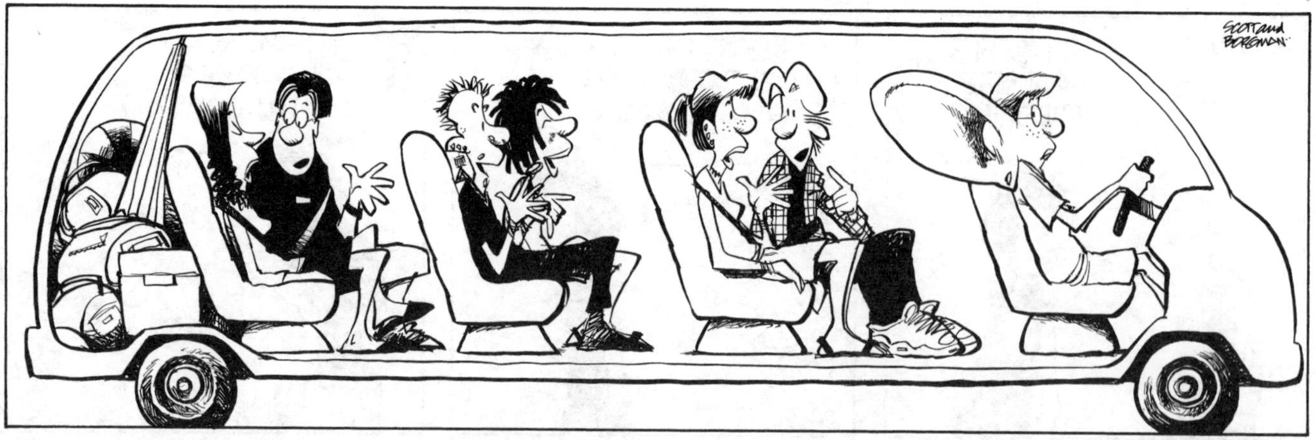
SCOTT and BORGMAN

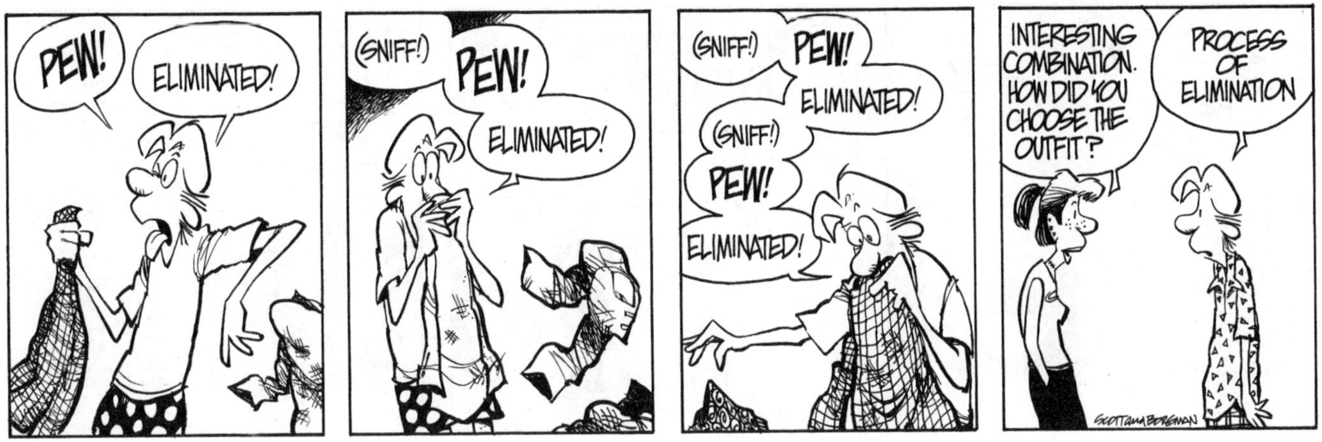
PEW!
ELIMINATED!
(SNIFF!)
PEW!
ELIMINATED!
(SNIFF!)
PEW!
ELIMINATED!
(SNIFF!)
PEW!
ELIMINATED!
INTERESTING COMBINATION. HOW DID YOU CHOOSE THE OUTFIT?
PROCESS OF ELIMINATION

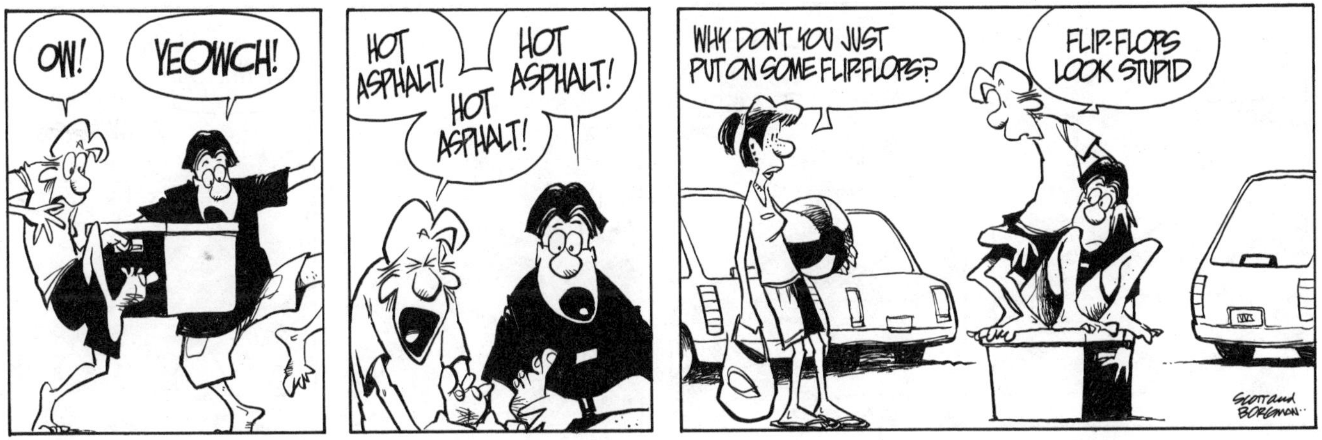
OW!
YEOWCH!
HOT ASPHALT!
HOT ASPHALT!
HOT ASPHALT!
WHY DON'T YOU JUST PUT ON SOME FLIP-FLOPS?
FLIP-FLOPS LOOK STUPID

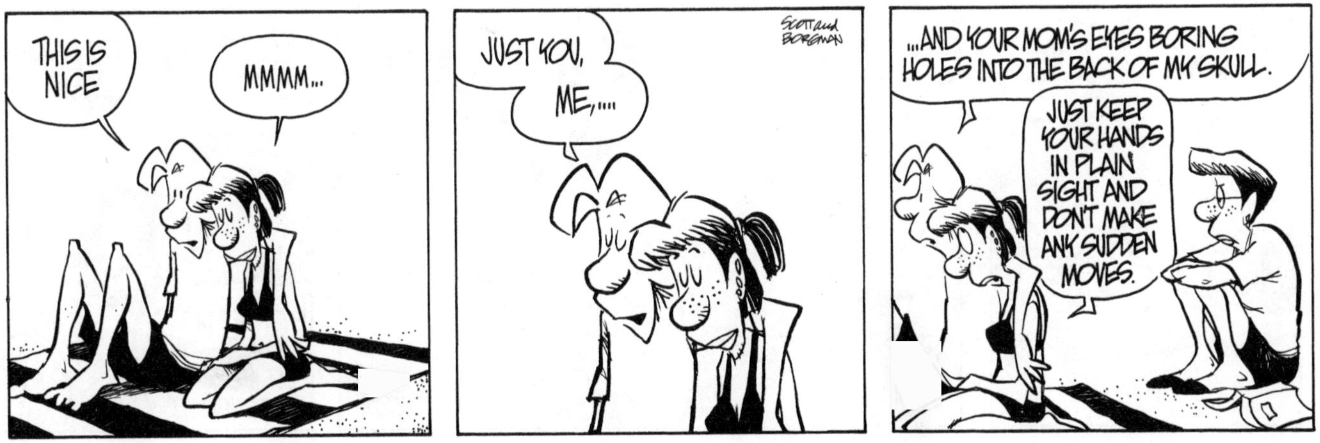
THIS IS NICE
MMMM...
JUST YOU,
ME,....
...AND YOUR MOM'S EYES BORING HOLES INTO THE BACK OF MY SKULL.
JUST KEEP YOUR HANDS IN PLAIN SIGHT AND DON'T MAKE ANY SUDDEN MOVES.

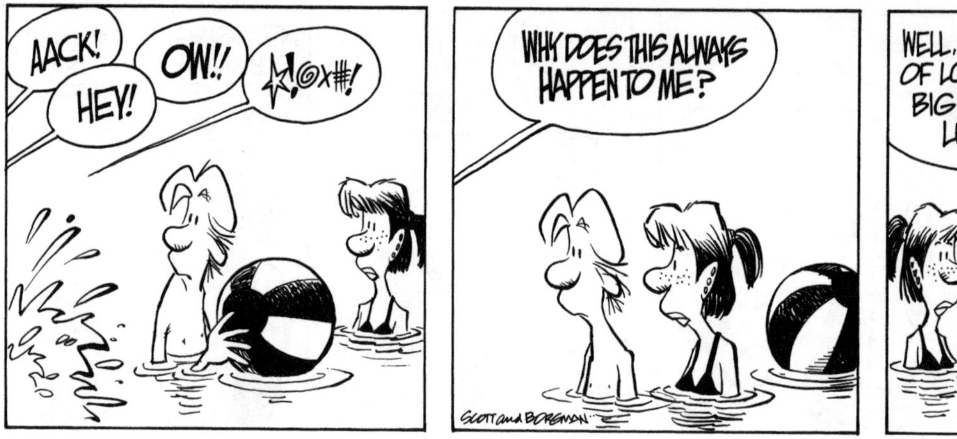
AACK!
HEY!
OW!!
WHY DOES THIS ALWAYS HAPPEN TO ME?
SCOTT and BORGMAN
WELL, YOU DO SORT OF LOOK LIKE ONE BIG FISHING LURE.
WHO ASKED YOU?

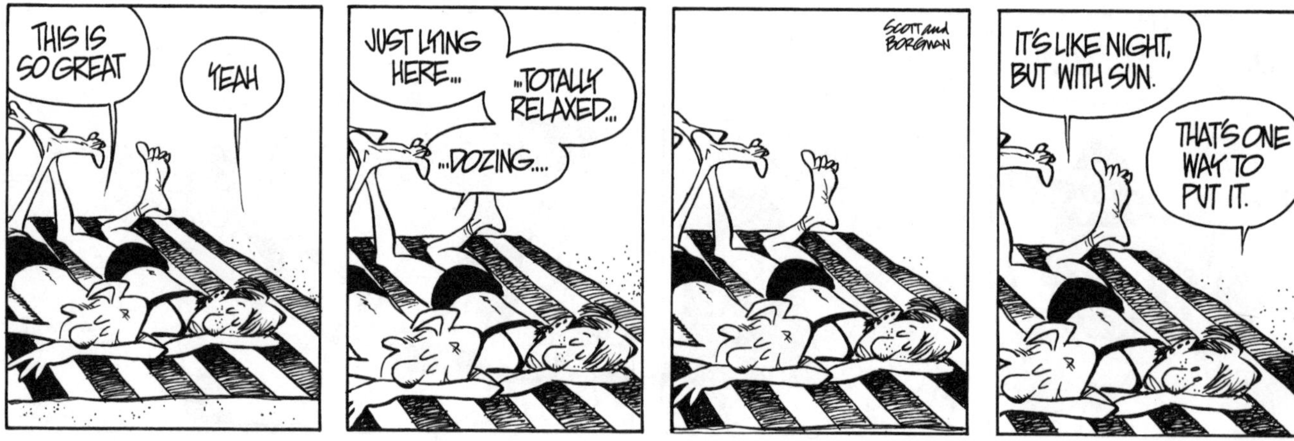
THIS IS SO GREAT
YEAH
JUST LYING HERE...
...TOTALLY RELAXED...
...DOZING....
SCOTT and BORGMAN
IT'S LIKE NIGHT, BUT WITH SUN.
THAT'S ONE WAY TO PUT IT.

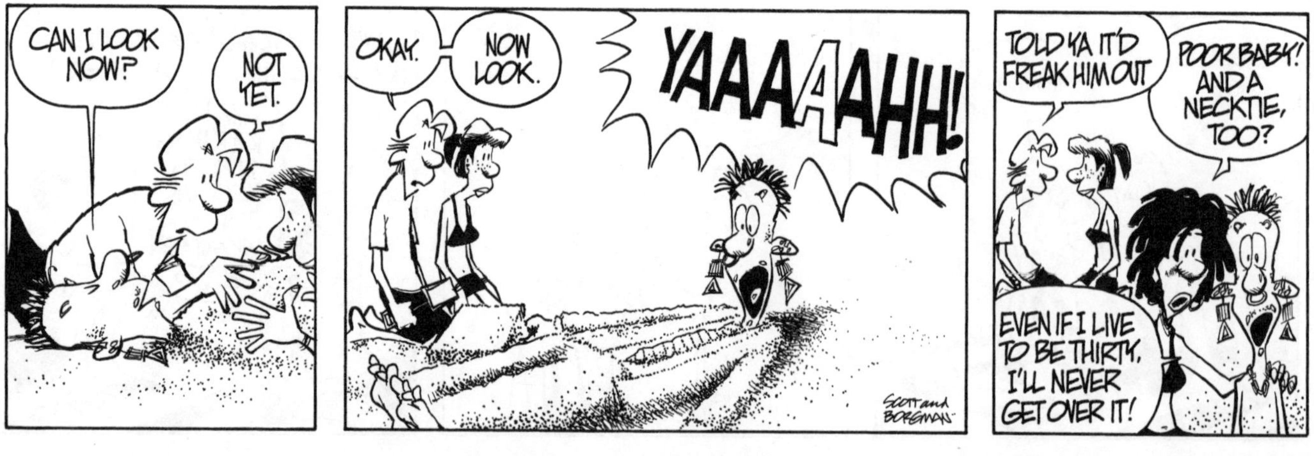
CAN I LOOK NOW?
NOT YET.
OKAY.
NOW LOOK.
YAAAAAHH!
SCOTT and BORGMAN
TOLD YA IT'D FREAK HIM OUT.
POOR BABY! AND A NECKTIE, TOO?
EVEN IF I LIVE TO BE THIRTY, I'LL NEVER GET OVER IT!

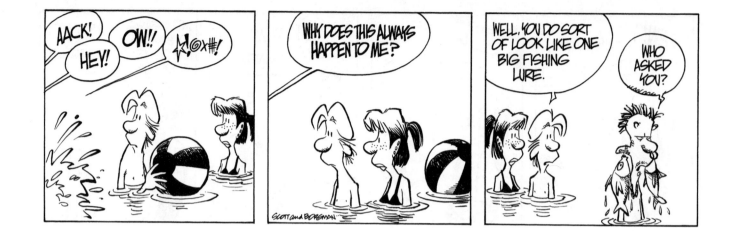

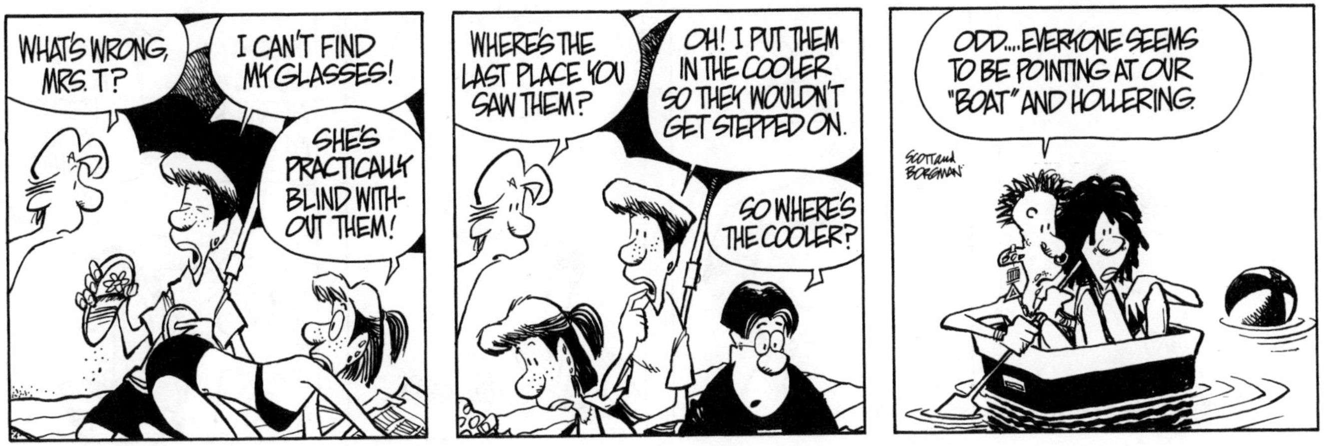
WHAT'S WRONG, MRS. T?
I CAN'T FIND MY GLASSES!
SHE'S PRACTICALLY BLIND WITH-OUT THEM!
WHERE'S THE LAST PLACE YOU SAW THEM?
OH! I PUT THEM IN THE COOLER SO THEY WOULDN'T GET STEPPED ON.
SO WHERE'S THE COOLER?
ODD.... EVERYONE SEEMS TO BE POINTING AT OUR "BOAT" AND HOLLERING.
SCOTT and BORGMAN

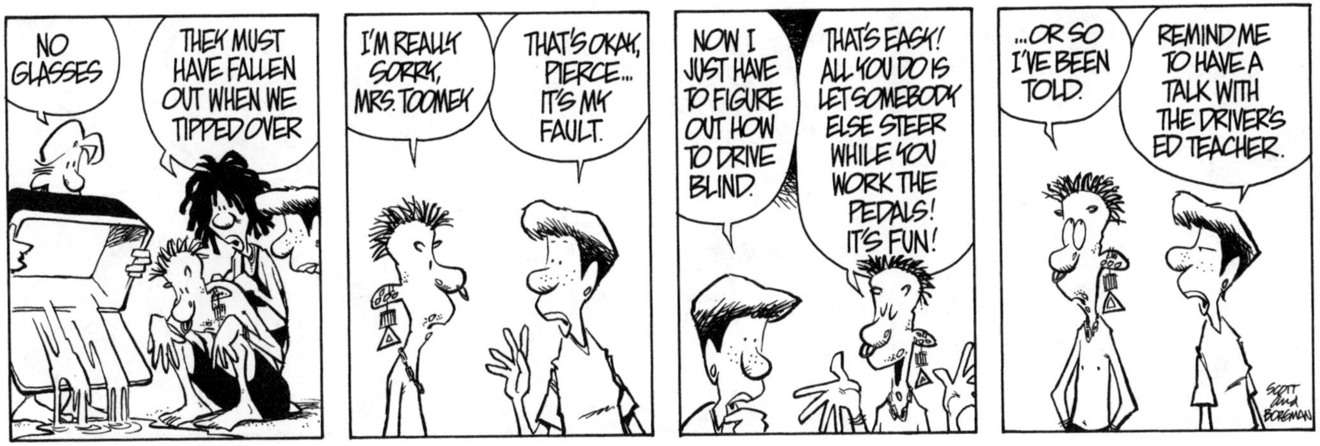
NO GLASSES
THEY MUST HAVE FALLEN OUT WHEN WE TIPPED OVER
I'M REALLY SORRY, MRS. TOOMEY
THAT'S OKAY, PIERCE... IT'S MY FAULT.
NOW I JUST HAVE TO FIGURE OUT HOW TO DRIVE BLIND.
THAT'S EASY! ALL YOU DO IS LET SOMEBODY ELSE STEER WHILE YOU WORK THE PEDALS! IT'S FUN!
...OR SO I'VE BEEN TOLD.
REMIND ME TO HAVE A TALK WITH THE DRIVER'S ED TEACHER.
SCOTT and BORGMAN

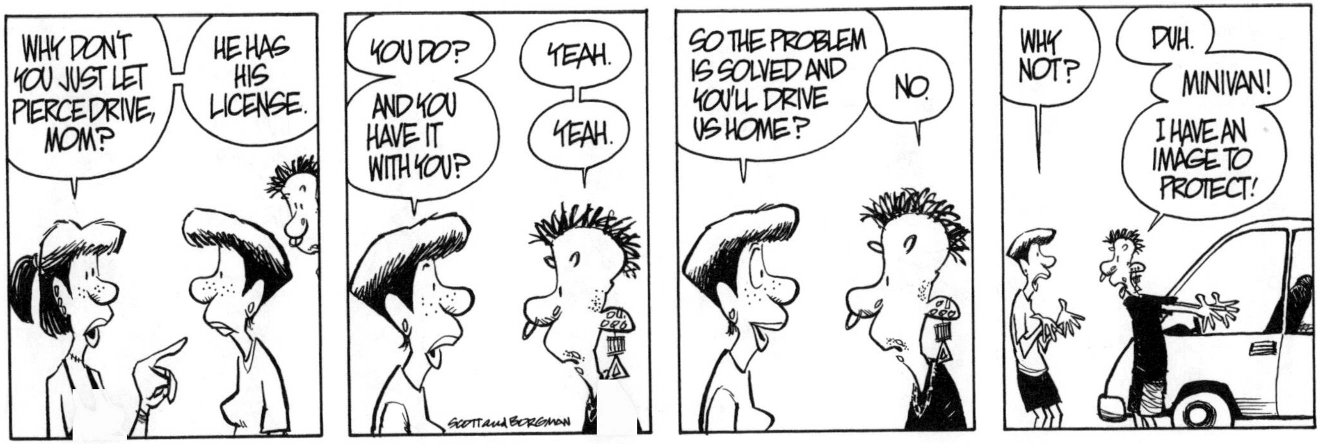
WHY DON'T YOU JUST LET PIERCE DRIVE, MOM?
HE HAS HIS LICENSE.
YOU DO?
YEAH.
AND YOU HAVE IT WITH YOU?
YEAH.
SCOTT and BORGMAN
SO THE PROBLEM IS SOLVED AND YOU'LL DRIVE US HOME?
NO.
WHY NOT?
DUH.
MINIVAN!
I HAVE AN IMAGE TO PROTECT!

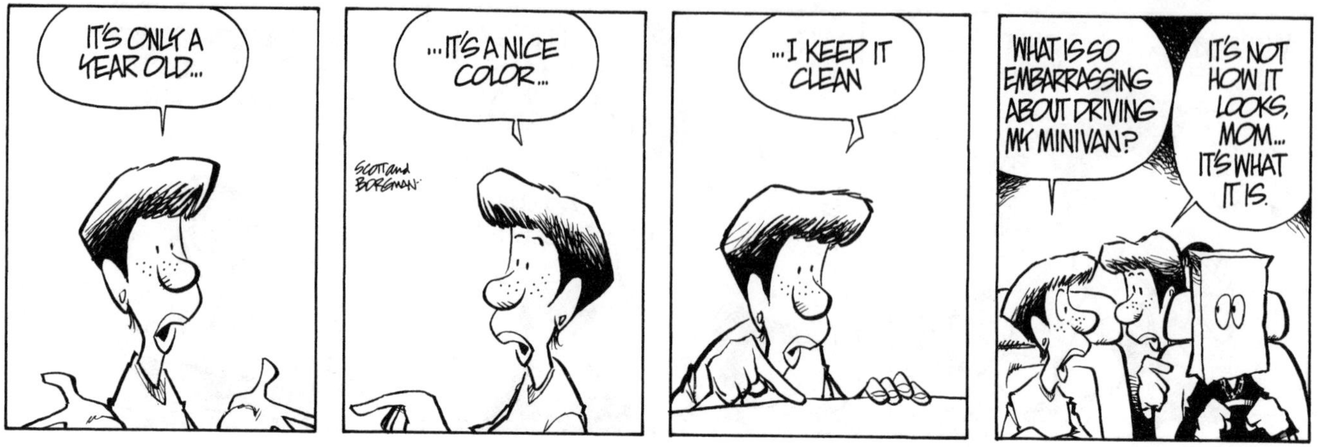
IT'S ONLY A YEAR OLD...
...IT'S A NICE COLOR...
SCOTT and BORGMAN
...I KEEP IT CLEAN
WHAT IS SO EMBARRASSING ABOUT DRIVING MY MINIVAN?
IT'S NOT HOW IT LOOKS, MOM... IT'S WHAT IT IS.

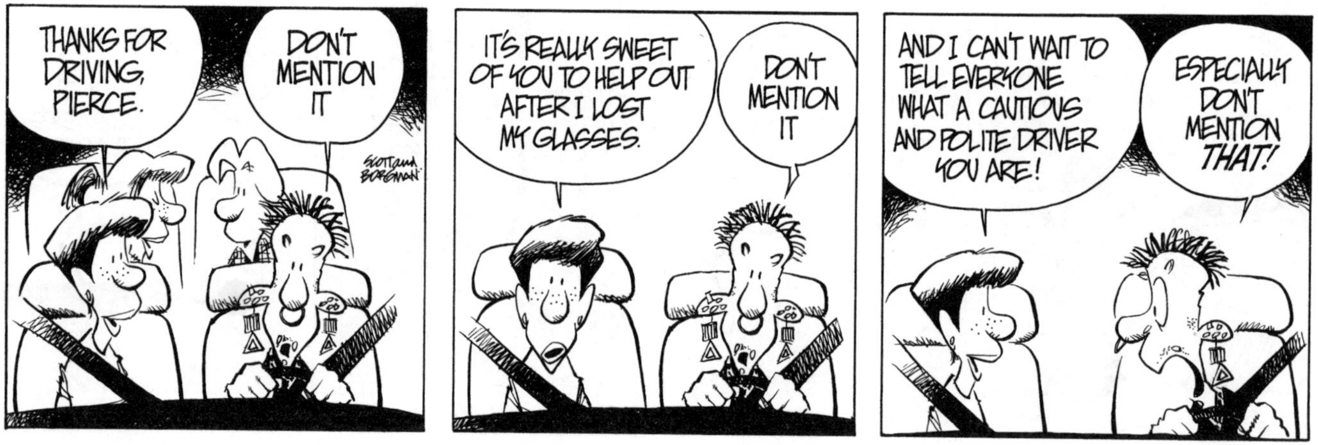
THANKS FOR DRIVING, PIERCE.
DON'T MENTION IT
SCOTT and BORGMAN
IT'S REALLY SWEET OF YOU TO HELP OUT AFTER I LOST MY GLASSES.
DON'T MENTION IT
AND I CAN'T WAIT TO TELL EVERYONE WHAT A CAUTIOUS AND POLITE DRIVER YOU ARE!
ESPECIALLY DON'T MENTION *THAT!*

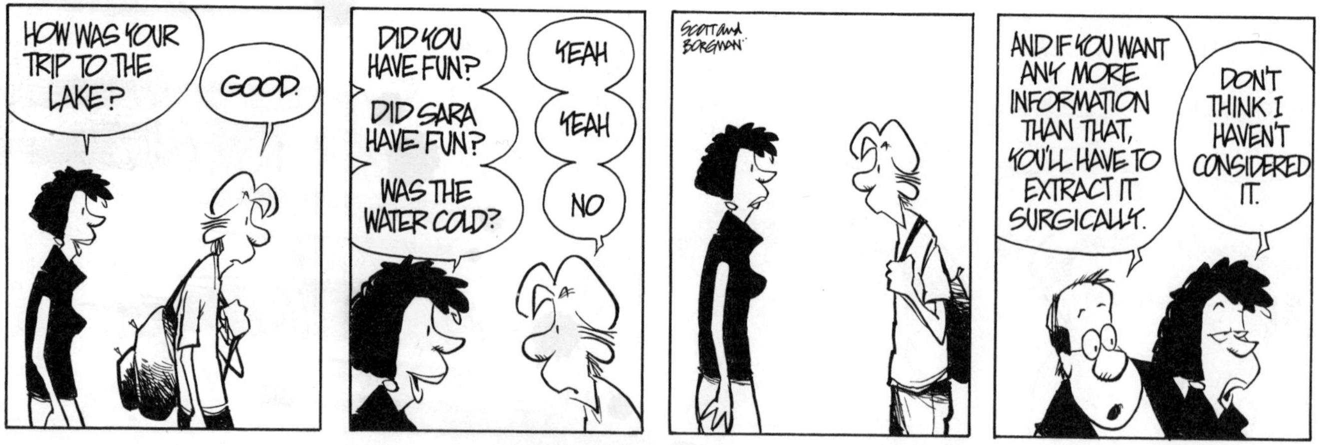
HOW WAS YOUR TRIP TO THE LAKE?
GOOD.
DID YOU HAVE FUN?
YEAH
DID SARA HAVE FUN?
YEAH
WAS THE WATER COLD?
NO
SCOTT and BORGMAN
AND IF YOU WANT ANY MORE INFORMATION THAN THAT, YOU'LL HAVE TO EXTRACT IT SURGICALLY.
DON'T THINK I HAVEN'T CONSIDERED IT.

Zits®

by JERRY SCOTT and JIM BORGMAN

THIS IS WHERE I COME TO GET AWAY FROM IT ALL
PARAMUS V.F.W. HALL
GINGIVITIS

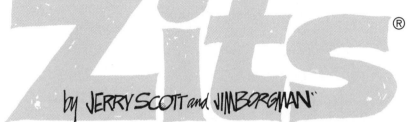

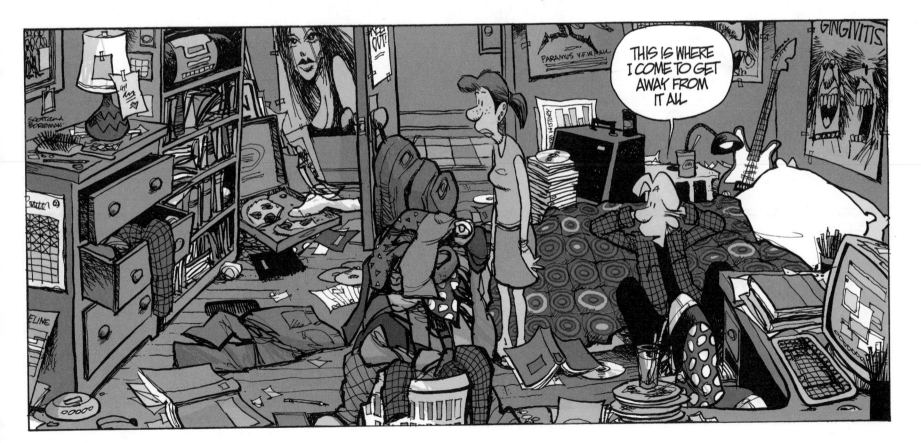

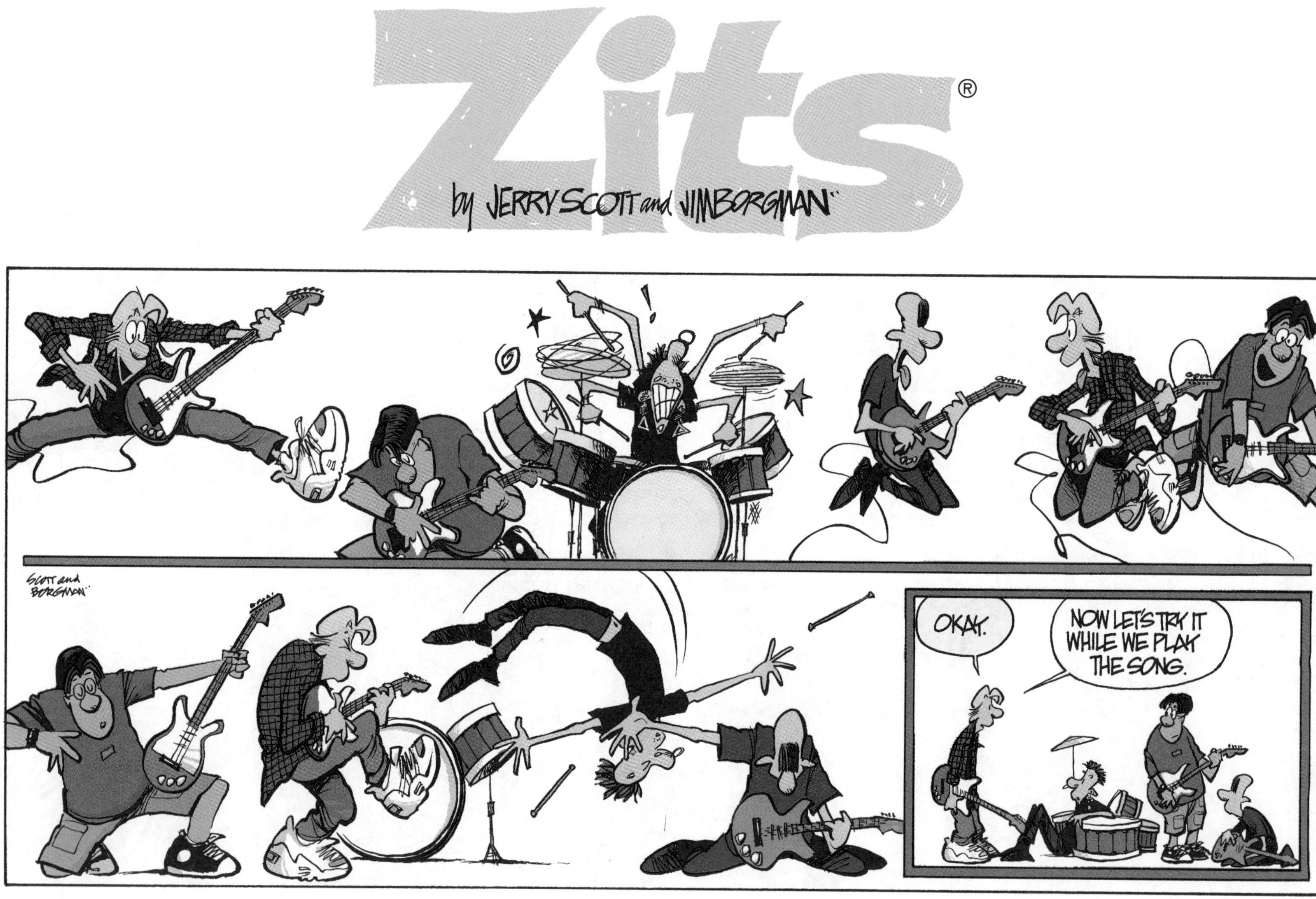
Zits®
by JERRY SCOTT and JIM BORGMAN
SCOTT and BORGMAN
OKAY.
NOW LET'S TRY IT WHILE WE PLAY THE SONG.

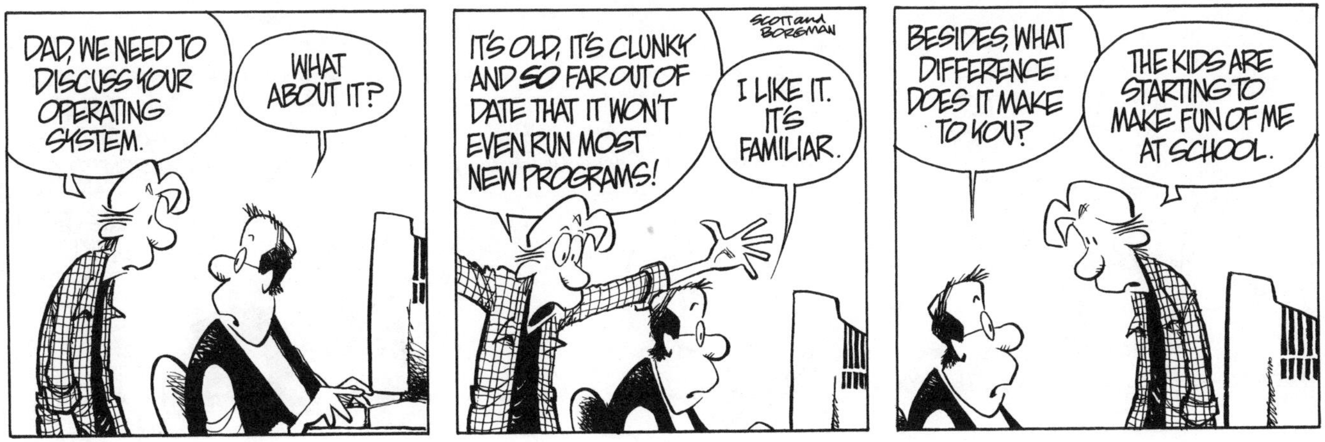
DAD, WE NEED TO DISCUSS YOUR OPERATING SYSTEM.
WHAT ABOUT IT?
SCOTT and BORGMAN
IT'S OLD, IT'S CLUNKY AND SO FAR OUT OF DATE THAT IT WON'T EVEN RUN MOST NEW PROGRAMS!
I LIKE IT. IT'S FAMILIAR.
BESIDES, WHAT DIFFERENCE DOES IT MAKE TO YOU?
THE KIDS ARE STARTING TO MAKE FUN OF ME AT SCHOOL.

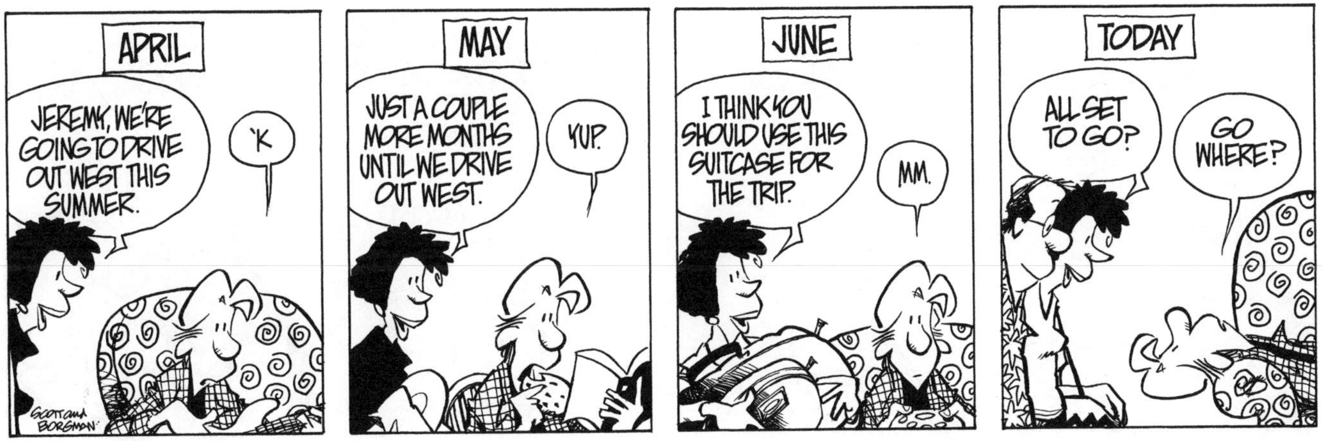
APRIL
JEREMY, WE'RE GOING TO DRIVE OUT WEST THIS SUMMER.
'K
SCOTT and BORGMAN
MAY
JUST A COUPLE MORE MONTHS UNTIL WE DRIVE OUT WEST.
YUP.
JUNE
I THINK YOU SHOULD USE THIS SUITCASE FOR THE TRIP.
MM.
TODAY
ALL SET TO GO?
GO WHERE?

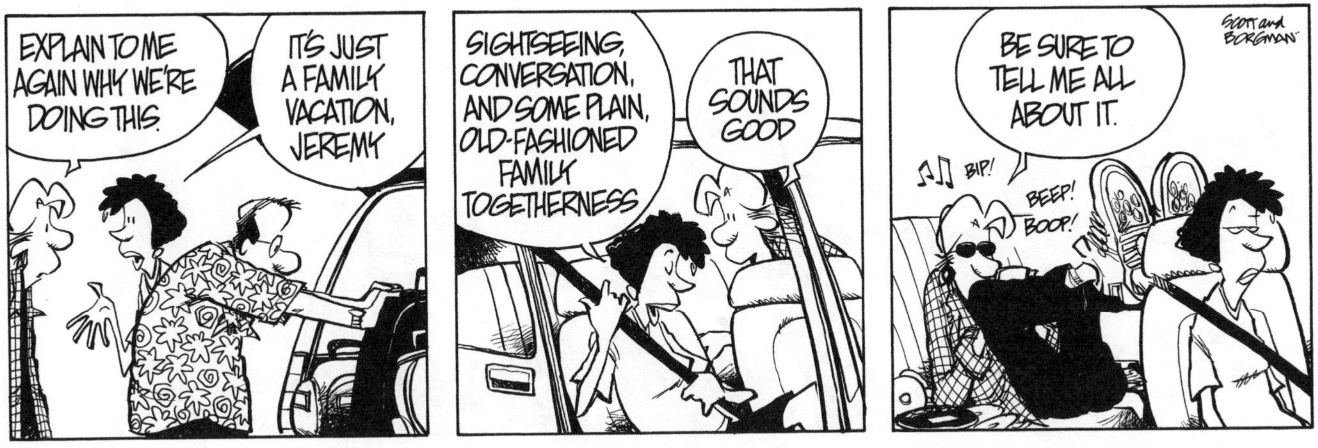
EXPLAIN TO ME AGAIN WHY WE'RE DOING THIS.
IT'S JUST A FAMILY VACATION, JEREMY
SIGHTSEEING, CONVERSATION, AND SOME PLAIN, OLD-FASHIONED FAMILY TOGETHERNESS
THAT SOUNDS GOOD
SCOTT and BORGMAN
BE SURE TO TELL ME ALL ABOUT IT.
BIP!
BEEP!
BOOP!

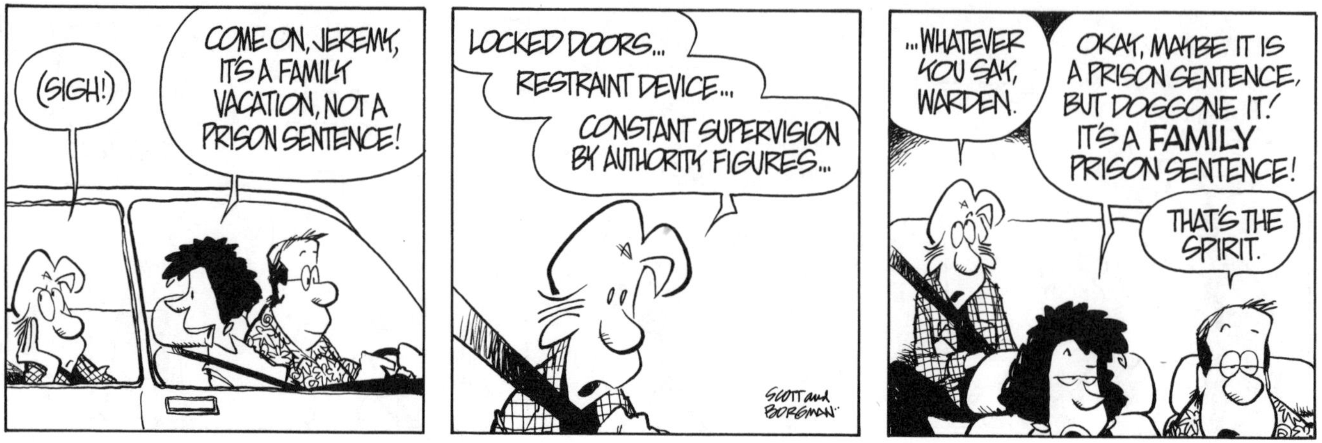
(SIGH!)
COME ON, JEREMY, IT'S A FAMILY VACATION, NOT A PRISON SENTENCE!
LOCKED DOORS...
RESTRAINT DEVICE...
CONSTANT SUPERVISION BY AUTHORITY FIGURES...
SCOTT and BORGMAN
...WHATEVER YOU SAY, WARDEN.
OKAY, MAYBE IT IS A PRISON SENTENCE, BUT DOGGONE IT! IT'S A **FAMILY** PRISON SENTENCE!
THAT'S THE SPIRIT.

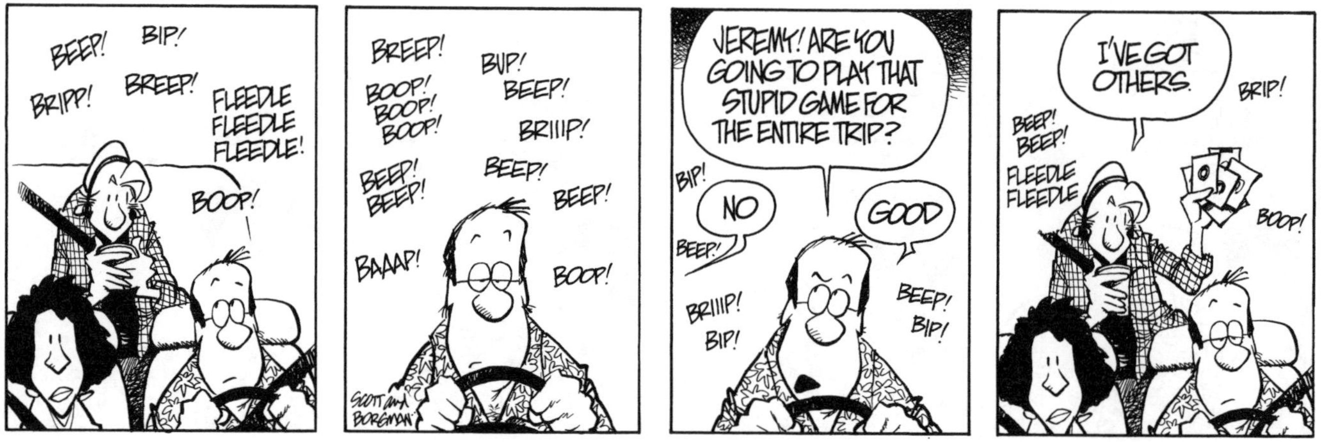
BEEP! BIP!
BRIPP! BREEP!
FLEEDLE FLEEDLE FLEEDLE!
BOOP!
BREEP! BIP! BEEP!
BOOP! BOOP! BOOP!
BRIIIP!
BEEP! BEEP! BEEP!
BEEP!
BAAAP! BOOP!
SCOTT and BORGMAN
JEREMY! ARE YOU GOING TO PLAY THAT STUPID GAME FOR THE ENTIRE TRIP?
BIP!
NO
BEEP!
GOOD
BRIIIP! BIP!
BEEP! BIP!
I'VE GOT OTHERS.
BRIP!
BEEP! BEEP!
FLEEDLE FLEEDLE
BOOP!

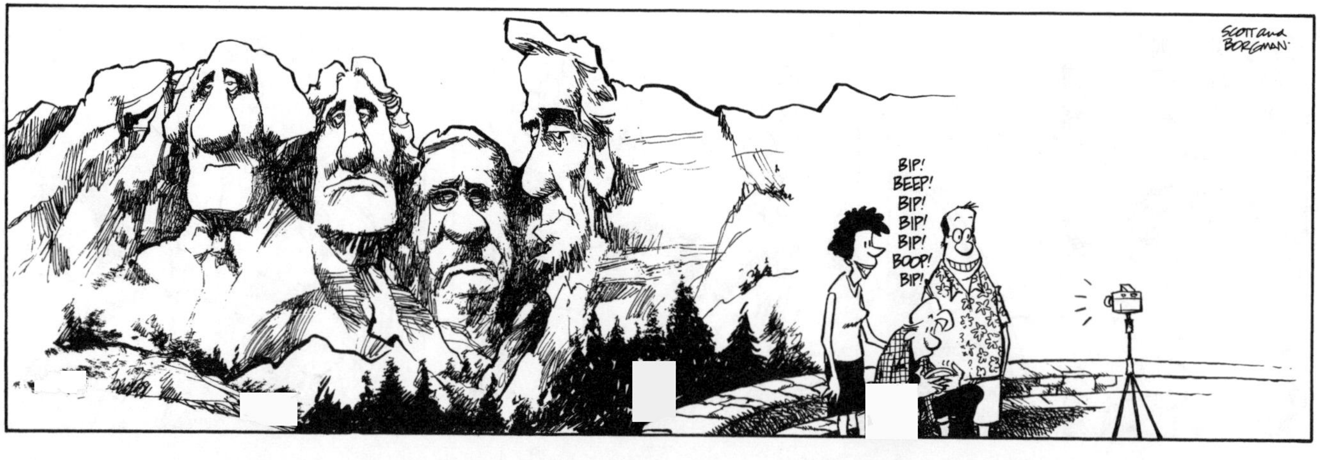
SCOTT and BORGMAN
BIP! BEEP! BIP! BIP! BIP! BOOP! BIP!

Zits®

by JERRY SCOTT and JIM BORGMAN

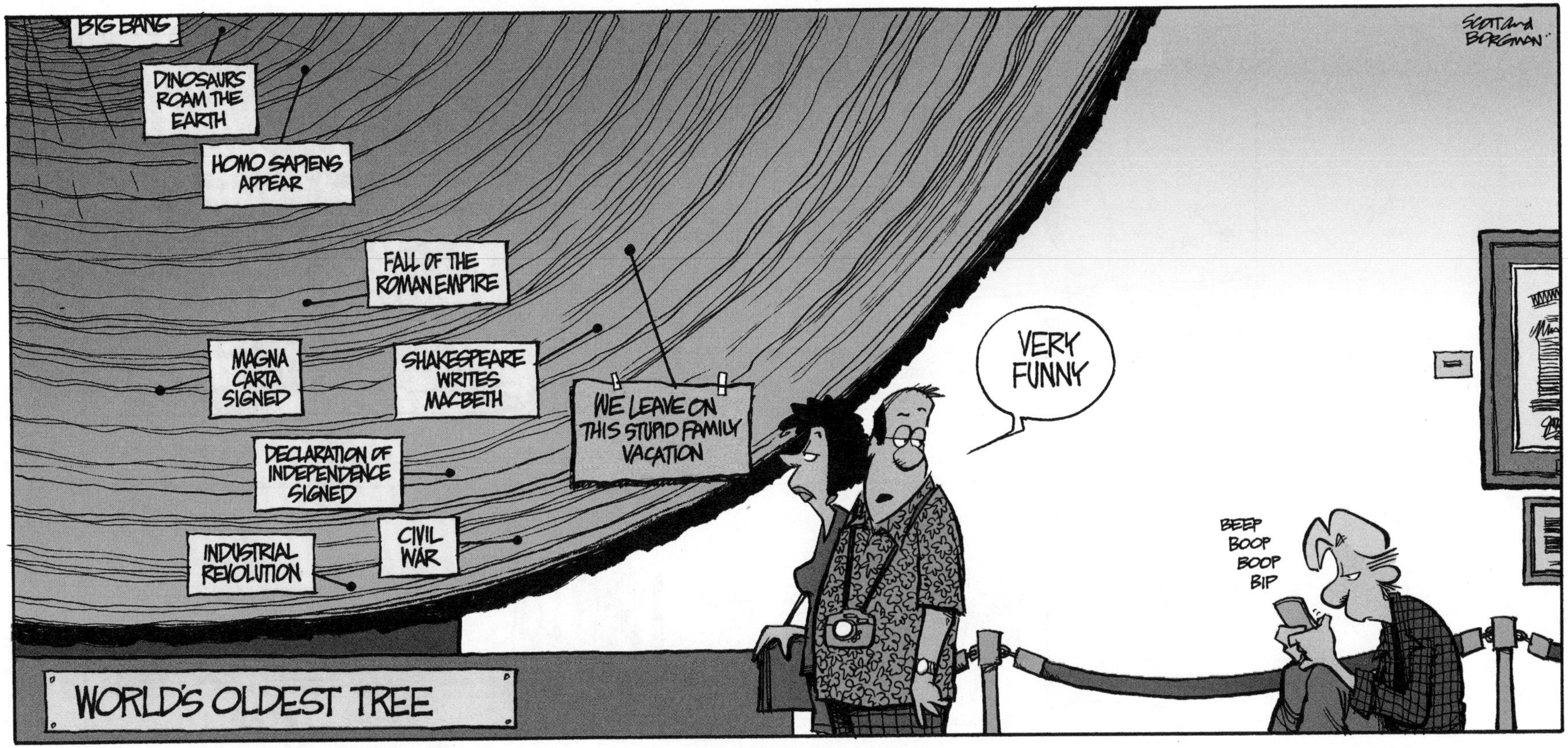
SCOTT and BORGMAN
BIG BANG
DINOSAURS ROAM THE EARTH
HOMO SAPIENS APPEAR
FALL OF THE ROMAN EMPIRE
MAGNA CARTA SIGNED
SHAKESPEARE WRITES MACBETH
WE LEAVE ON THIS STUPID FAMILY VACATION
DECLARATION OF INDEPENDENCE SIGNED
CIVIL WAR
INDUSTRIAL REVOLUTION
WORLD'S OLDEST TREE
VERY FUNNY
BEEP BOOP BOOP BIP

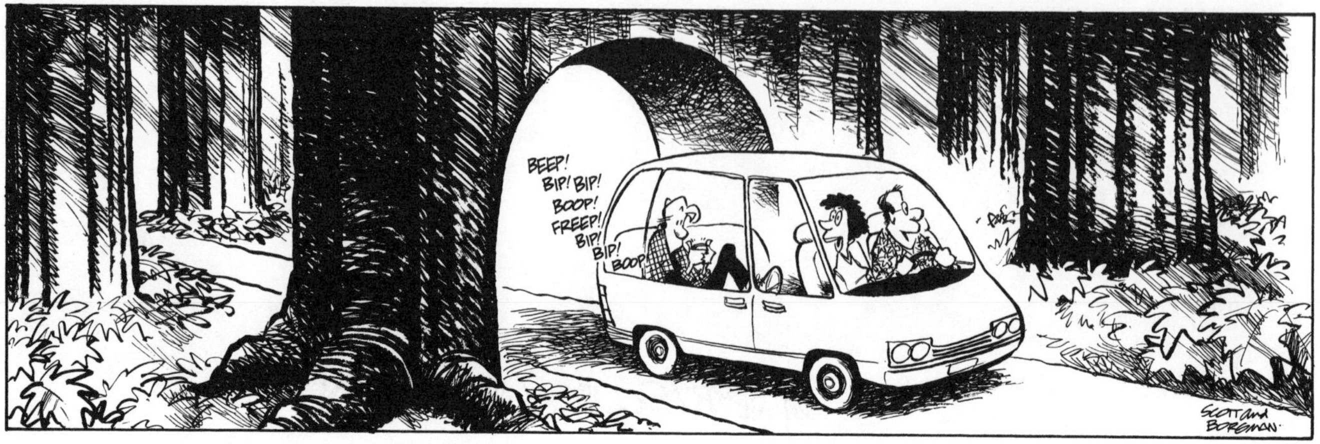
BEEP! BIP! BIP! BOOP! FREEP! BIP! BIP! BOOP
SCOTT and BORGMAN

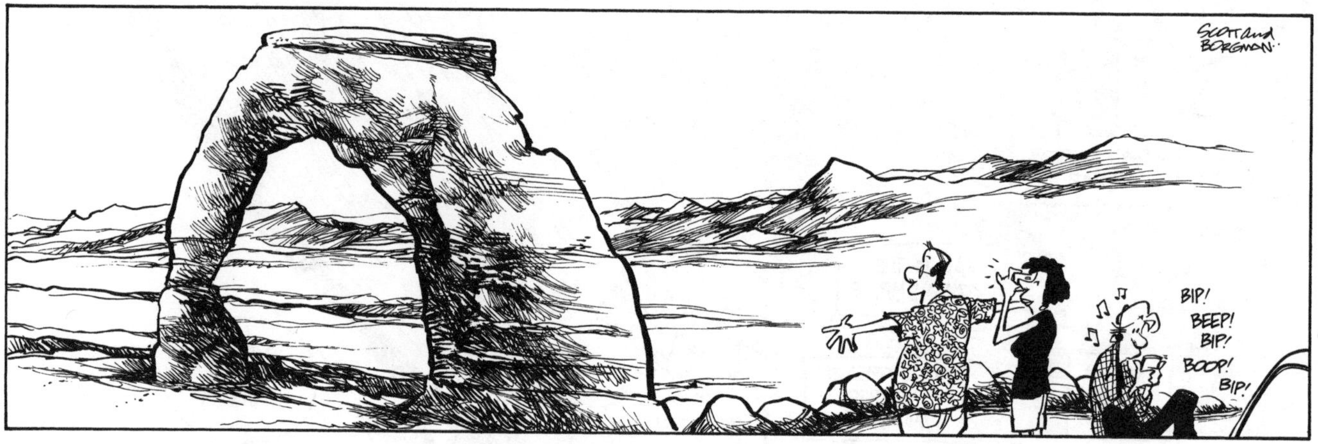
SCOTT and BORGMAN
BIP! BEEP! BIP! BOOP! BIP!

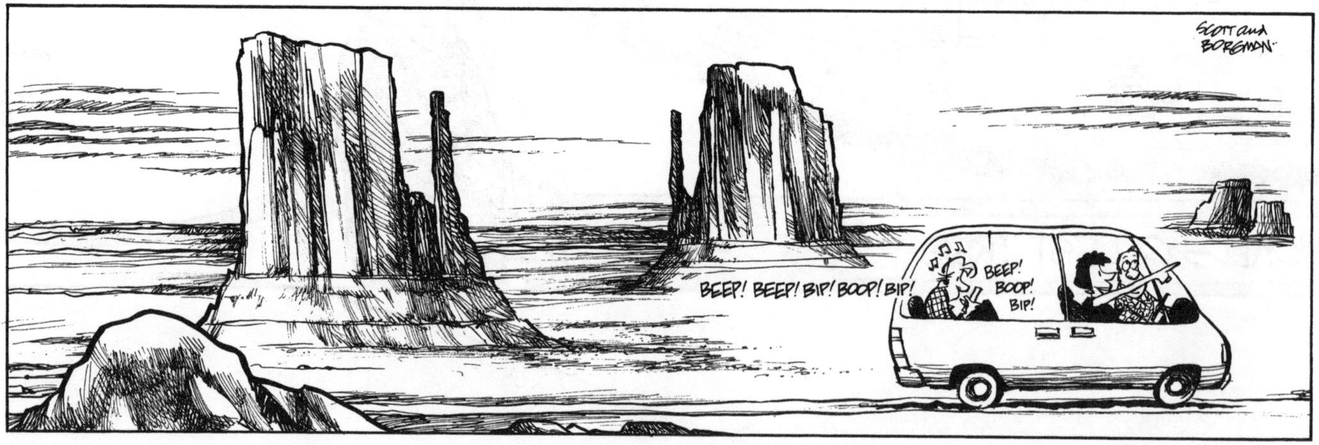
SCOTT and BORGMAN
BEEP! BEEP! BIP! BOOP! BIP!
BEEP! BOOP! BIP!

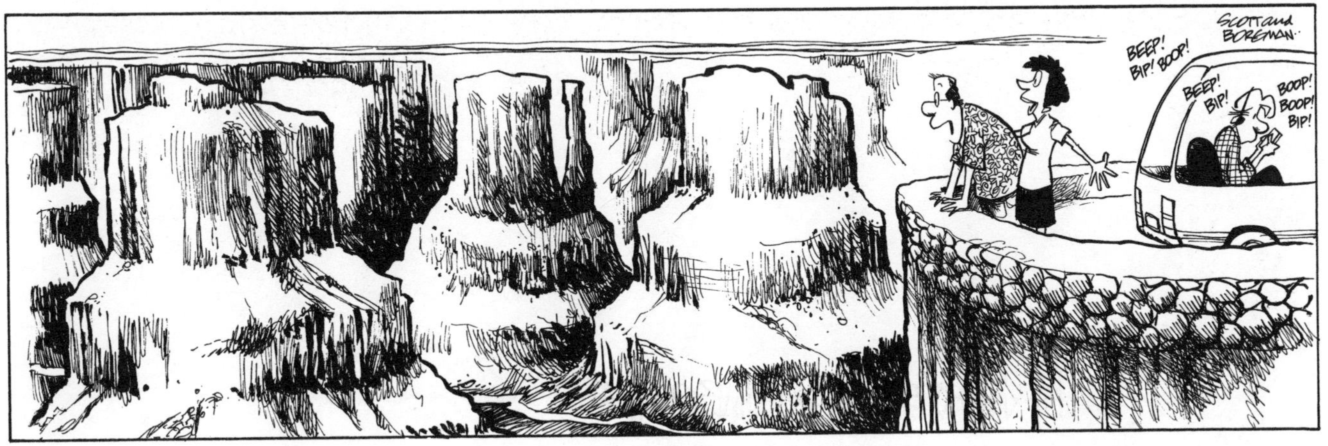
SCOTT and BORGMAN
BEEP! BIP! BOOP!
BEEP! BIP!
BOOP! BOOP! BIP!

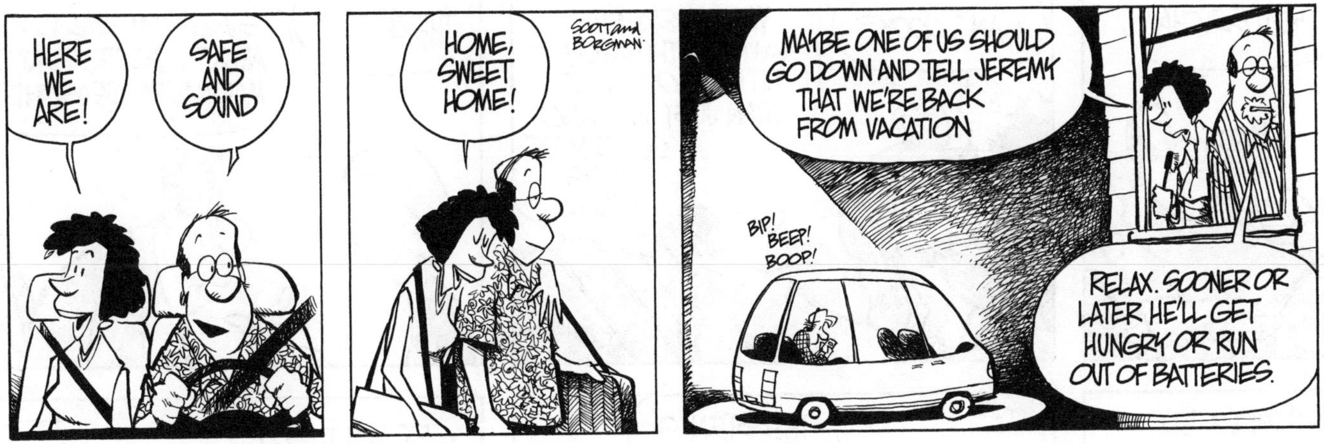
HERE WE ARE!
SAFE AND SOUND
HOME, SWEET HOME!
SCOTT and BORGMAN
MAYBE ONE OF US SHOULD GO DOWN AND TELL JEREMY THAT WE'RE BACK FROM VACATION
BIP! BEEP! BOOP!
RELAX. SOONER OR LATER HE'LL GET HUNGRY OR RUN OUT OF BATTERIES.

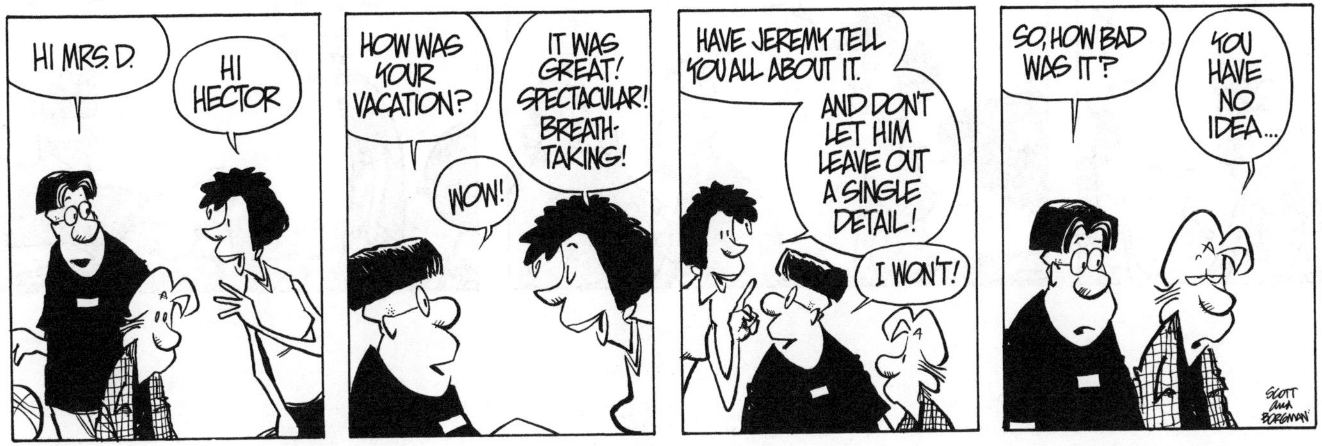
HI MRS. D.
HI HECTOR
HOW WAS YOUR VACATION?
IT WAS GREAT! SPECTACULAR! BREATH-TAKING!
WOW!
HAVE JEREMY TELL YOU ALL ABOUT IT.
AND DON'T LET HIM LEAVE OUT A SINGLE DETAIL!
I WON'T!
SO, HOW BAD WAS IT?
YOU HAVE NO IDEA...
SCOTT and BORGMAN

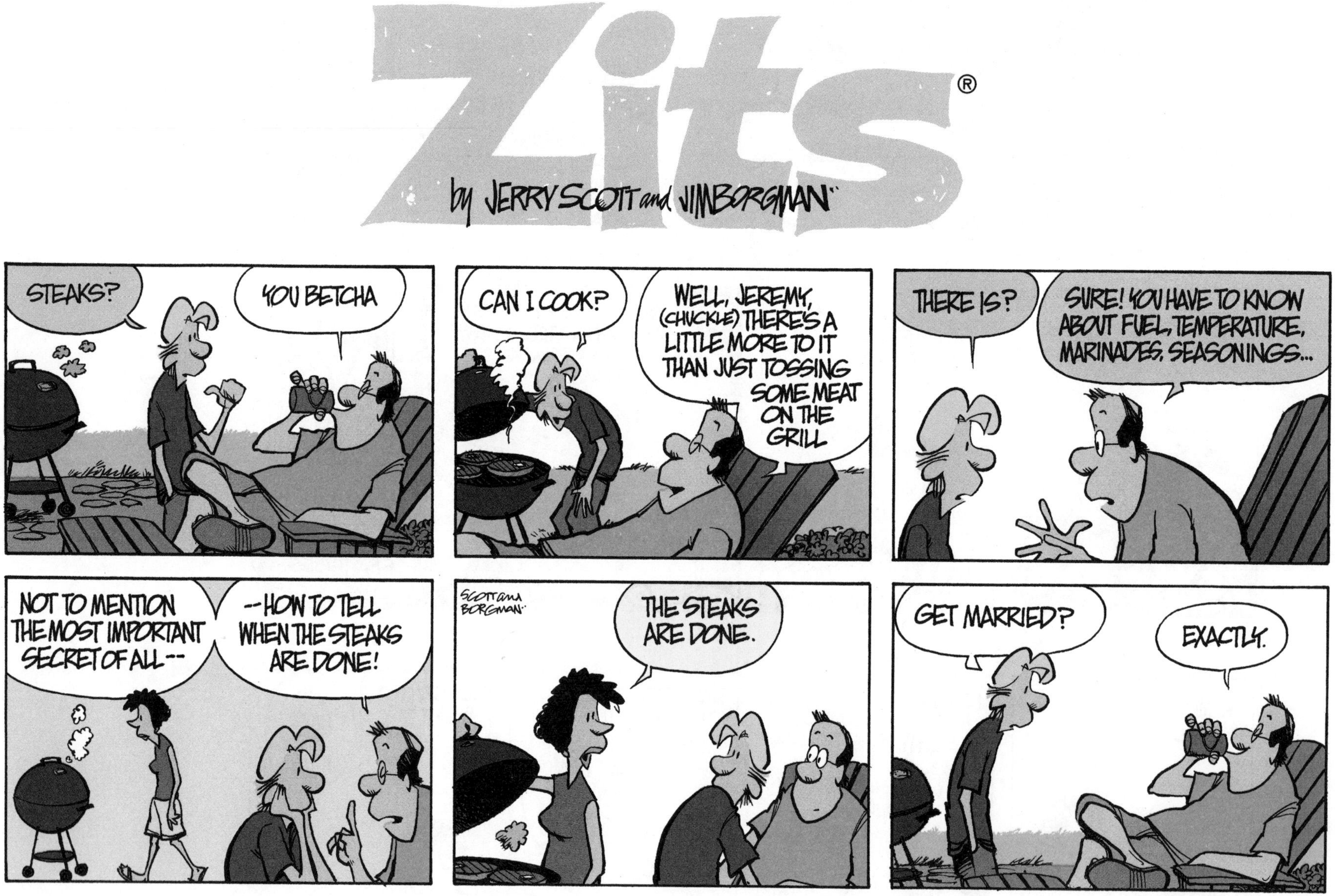
Zits®
by JERRY SCOTT and JIM BORGMAN
STEAKS?
YOU BETCHA
CAN I COOK?
WELL, JEREMY, (CHUCKLE) THERE'S A LITTLE MORE TO IT THAN JUST TOSSING SOME MEAT ON THE GRILL
THERE IS?
SURE! YOU HAVE TO KNOW ABOUT FUEL, TEMPERATURE, MARINADES, SEASONINGS...
NOT TO MENTION THE MOST IMPORTANT SECRET OF ALL--
--HOW TO TELL WHEN THE STEAKS ARE DONE!
SCOTT and BORGMAN
THE STEAKS ARE DONE.
GET MARRIED?
EXACTLY.

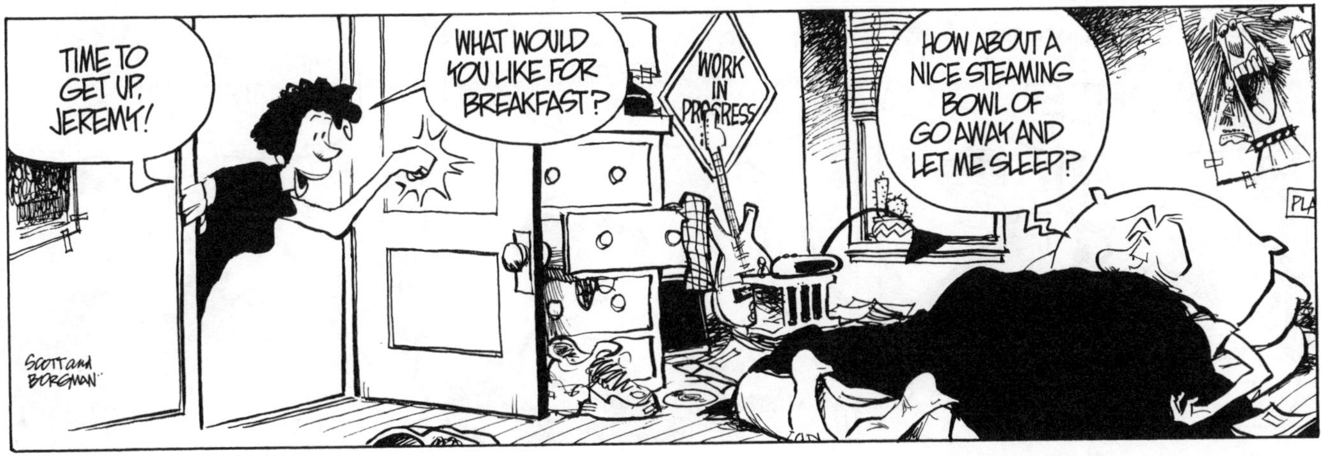
TIME TO GET UP, JEREMY!
WHAT WOULD YOU LIKE FOR BREAKFAST?
WORK IN PROGRESS
HOW ABOUT A NICE STEAMING BOWL OF GO AWAY AND LET ME SLEEP?
SCOTT and BORGMAN

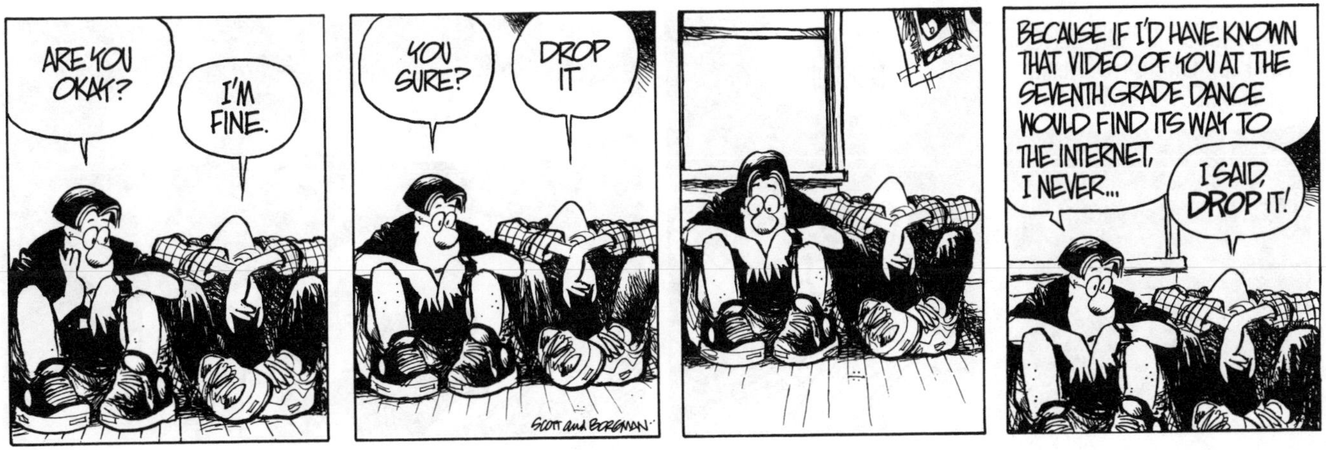
ARE YOU OKAY?
I'M FINE.
YOU SURE?
DROP IT
SCOTT and BORGMAN
BECAUSE IF I'D HAVE KNOWN THAT VIDEO OF YOU AT THE SEVENTH GRADE DANCE WOULD FIND ITS WAY TO THE INTERNET, I NEVER...
I SAID, DROP IT!

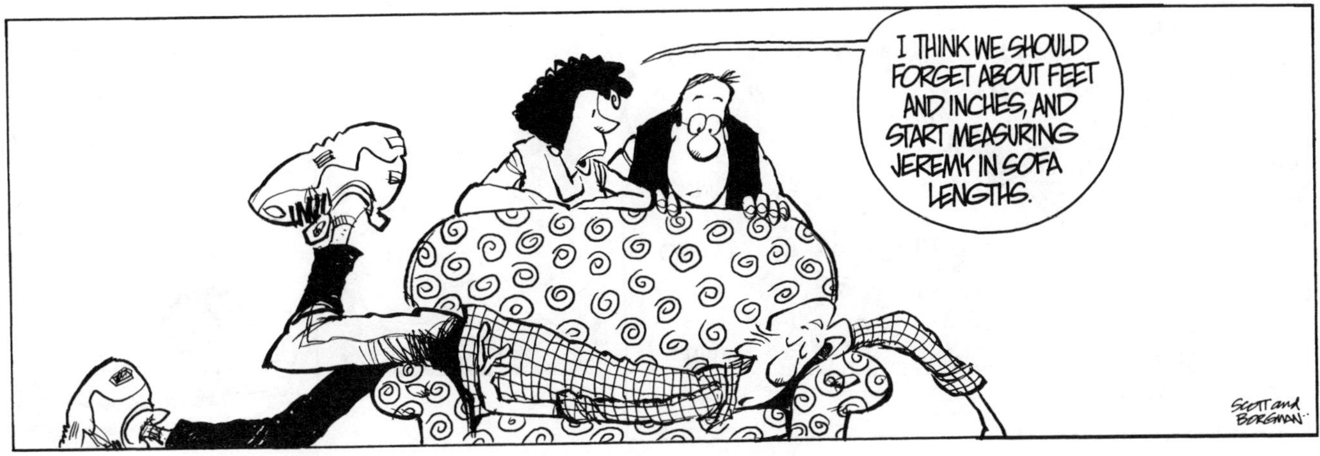
I THINK WE SHOULD FORGET ABOUT FEET AND INCHES, AND START MEASURING JEREMY IN SOFA LENGTHS.
SCOTT and BORGMAN

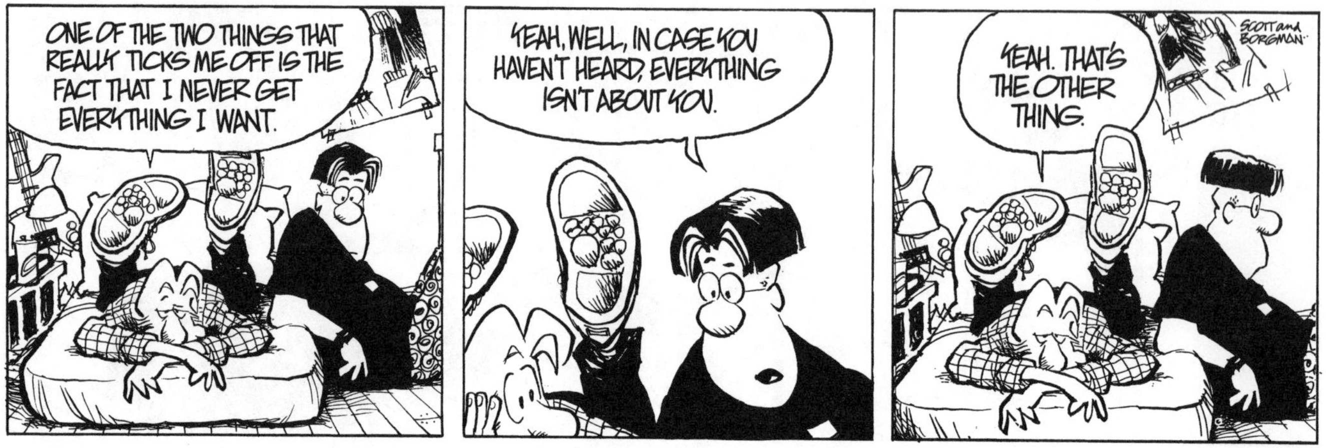
ONE OF THE TWO THINGS THAT REALLY TICKS ME OFF IS THE FACT THAT I NEVER GET EVERYTHING I WANT.
YEAH, WELL, IN CASE YOU HAVEN'T HEARD, EVERYTHING ISN'T ABOUT YOU.
YEAH. THAT'S THE OTHER THING.
SCOTT and BORGMAN

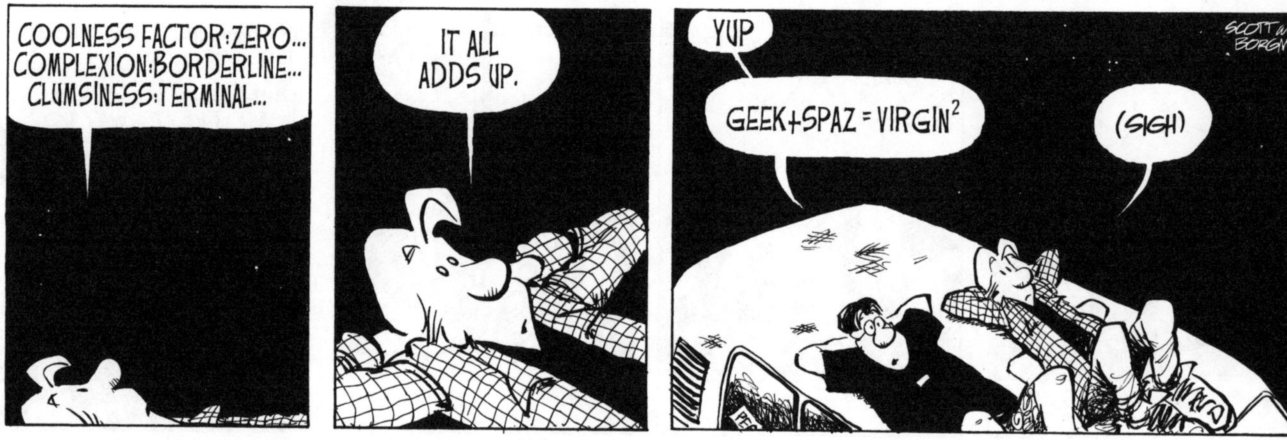
COOLNESS FACTOR: ZERO... COMPLEXION: BORDERLINE... CLUMSINESS: TERMINAL...
IT ALL ADDS UP.
YUP
GEEK + SPAZ = VIRGIN²
(SIGH)
SCOTT and BORGMAN

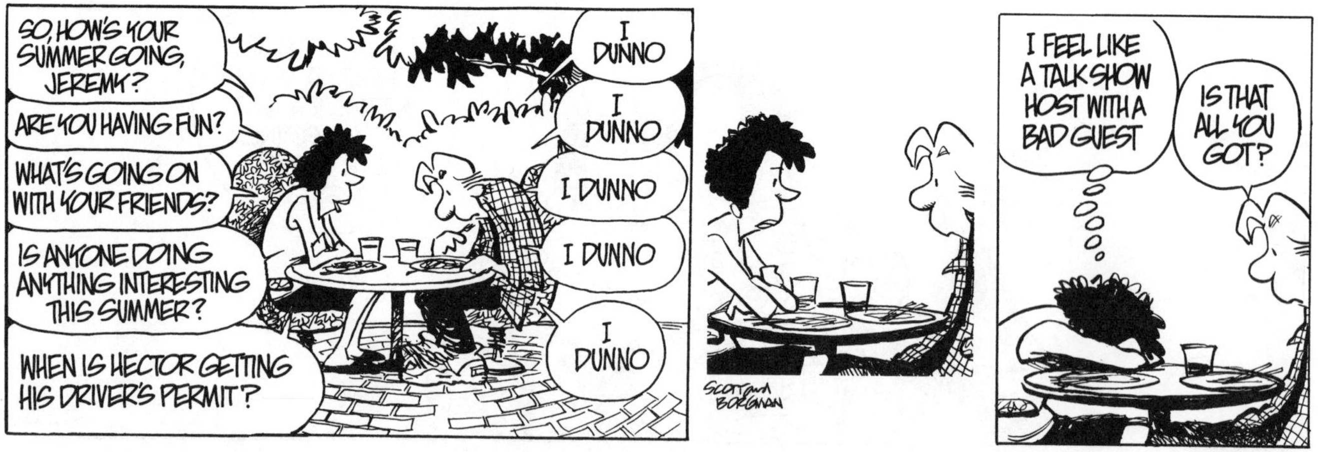
SO, HOW'S YOUR SUMMER GOING, JEREMY?
I DUNNO
ARE YOU HAVING FUN?
I DUNNO
WHAT'S GOING ON WITH YOUR FRIENDS?
I DUNNO
IS ANYONE DOING ANYTHING INTERESTING THIS SUMMER?
I DUNNO
WHEN IS HECTOR GETTING HIS DRIVER'S PERMIT?
I DUNNO
SCOTT and BORGMAN
I FEEL LIKE A TALK SHOW HOST WITH A BAD GUEST
IS THAT ALL YOU GOT?

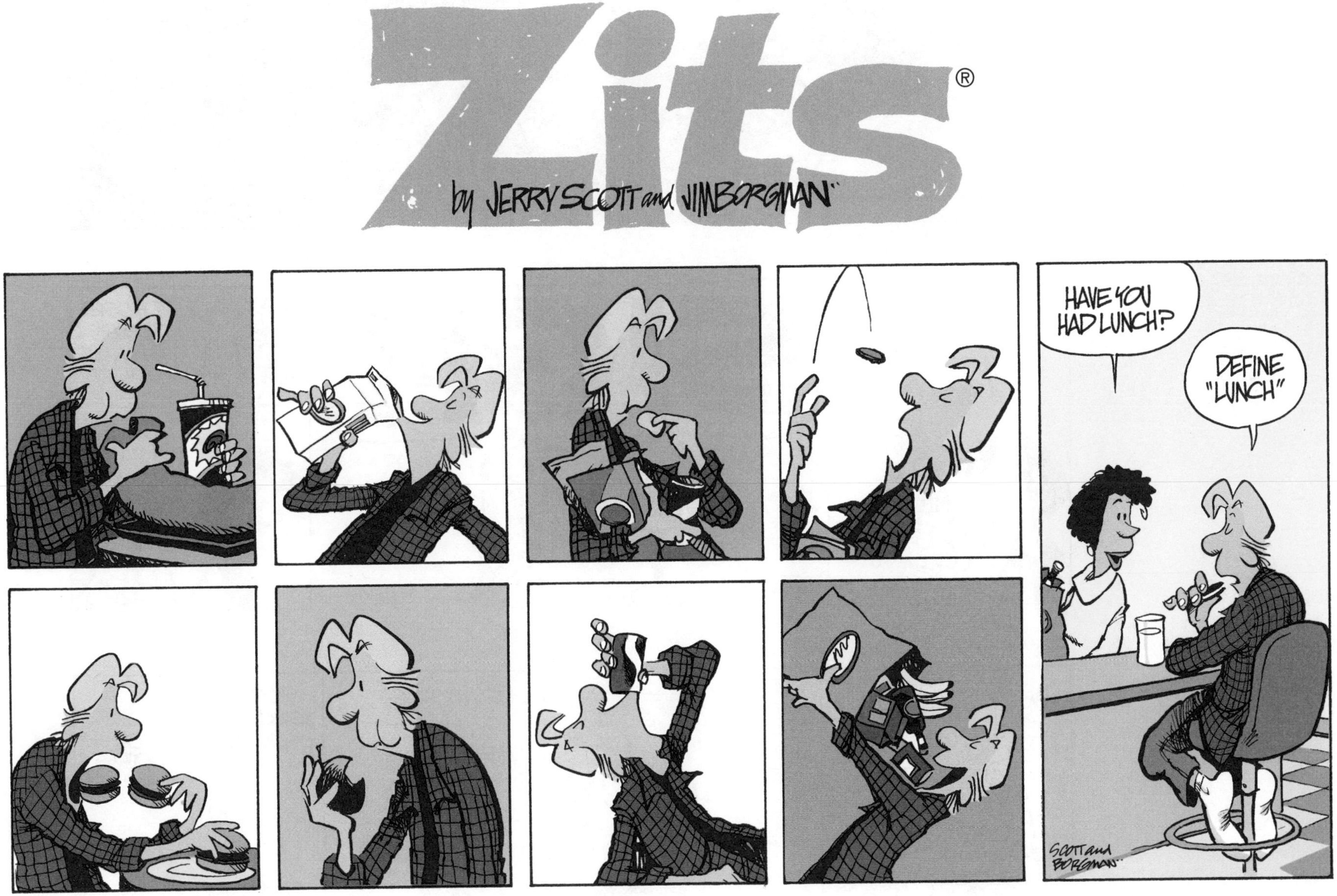
Zits®
by JERRY SCOTT and JIM BORGMAN
HAVE YOU HAD LUNCH?
DEFINE "LUNCH"
SCOTT and BORGMAN

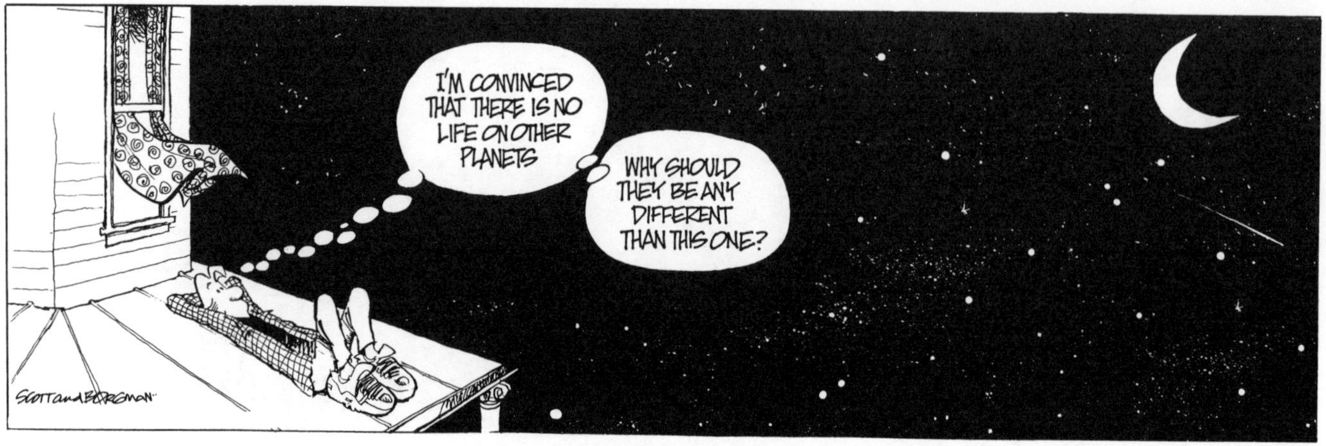
I'M CONVINCED THAT THERE IS NO LIFE ON OTHER PLANETS
WHY SHOULD THEY BE ANY DIFFERENT THAN THIS ONE?
SCOTT and BORGMAN

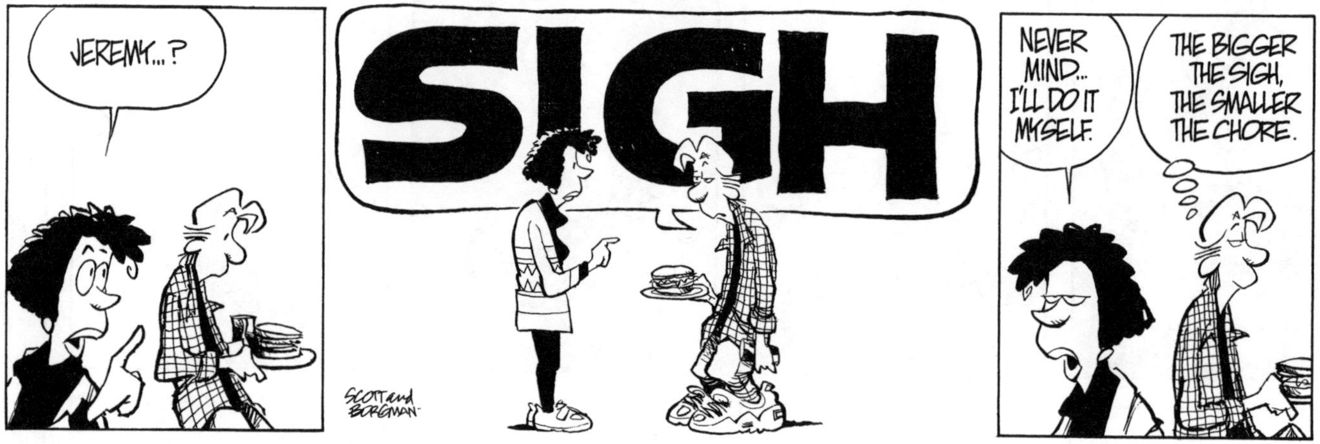
JEREMY...?
SIGH
SCOTT and BORGMAN
NEVER MIND... I'LL DO IT MYSELF.
THE BIGGER THE SIGH, THE SMALLER THE CHORE.

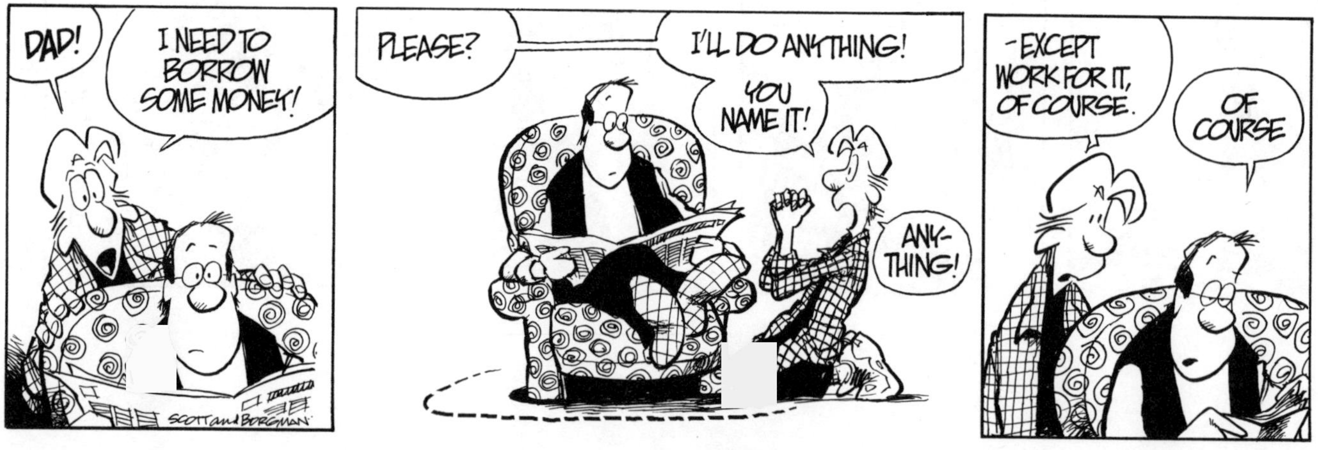
DAD!
I NEED TO BORROW SOME MONEY!
SCOTT and BORGMAN
PLEASE?
I'LL DO ANYTHING!
YOU NAME IT!
ANY-THING!
-EXCEPT WORK FOR IT, OF COURSE.
OF COURSE

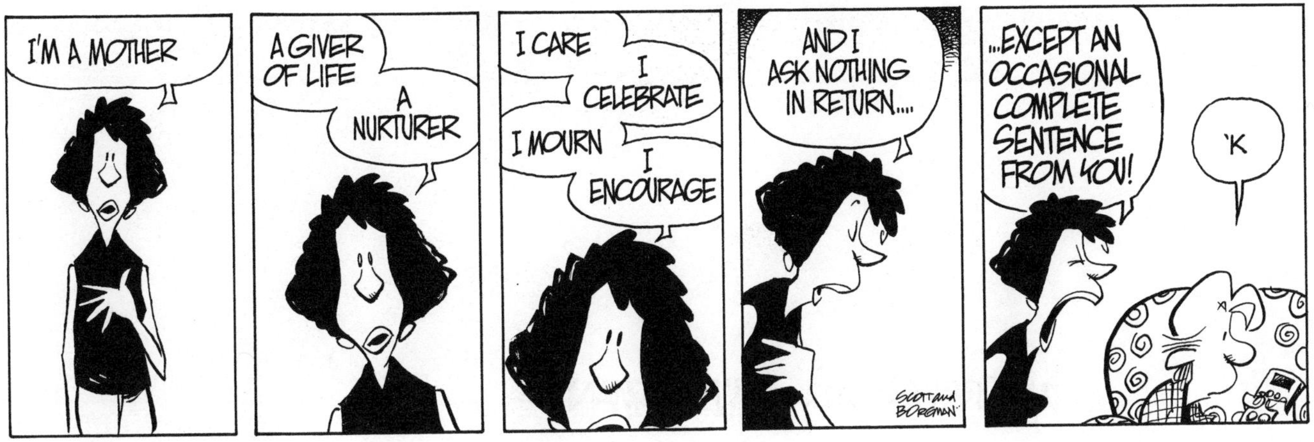
I'M A MOTHER
A GIVER OF LIFE
A NURTURER
I CARE
I CELEBRATE
I MOURN
I ENCOURAGE
AND I ASK NOTHING IN RETURN....
...EXCEPT AN OCCASIONAL COMPLETE SENTENCE FROM YOU!
'K
SCOTT and BORGMAN

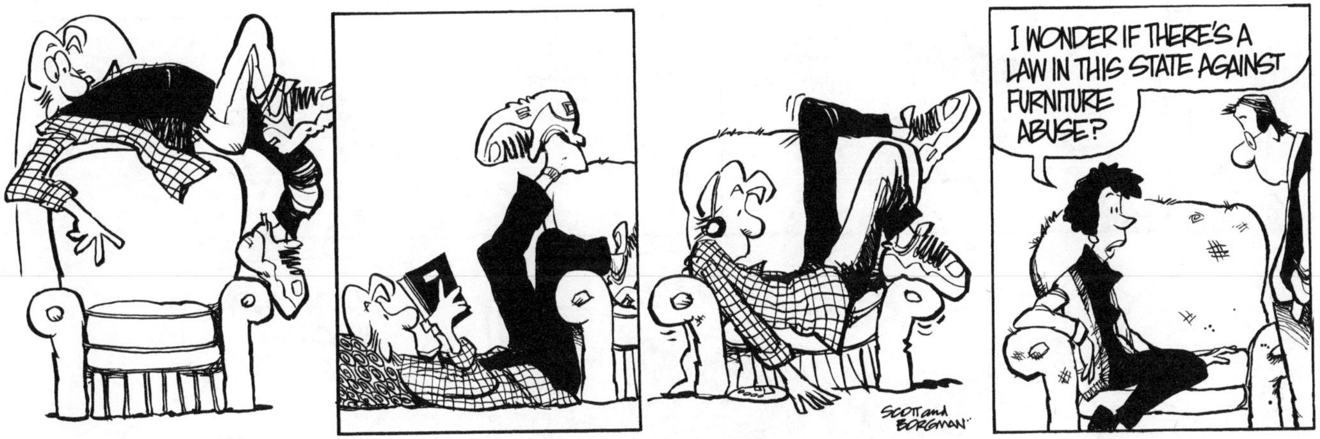
I WONDER IF THERE'S A LAW IN THIS STATE AGAINST FURNITURE ABUSE?
SCOTT and BORGMAN

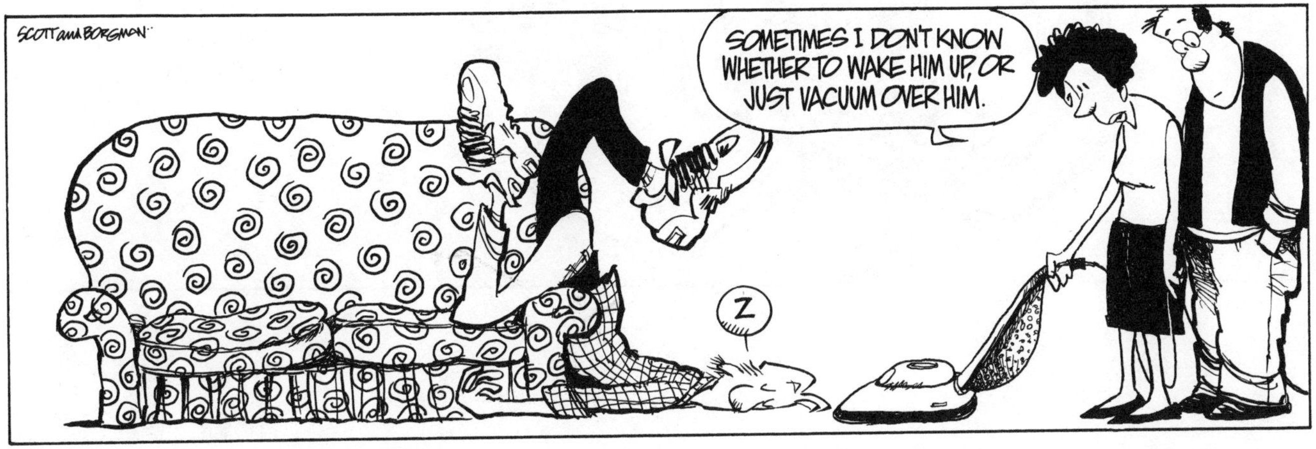
SCOTT and BORGMAN
SOMETIMES I DON'T KNOW WHETHER TO WAKE HIM UP, OR JUST VACUUM OVER HIM.
Z

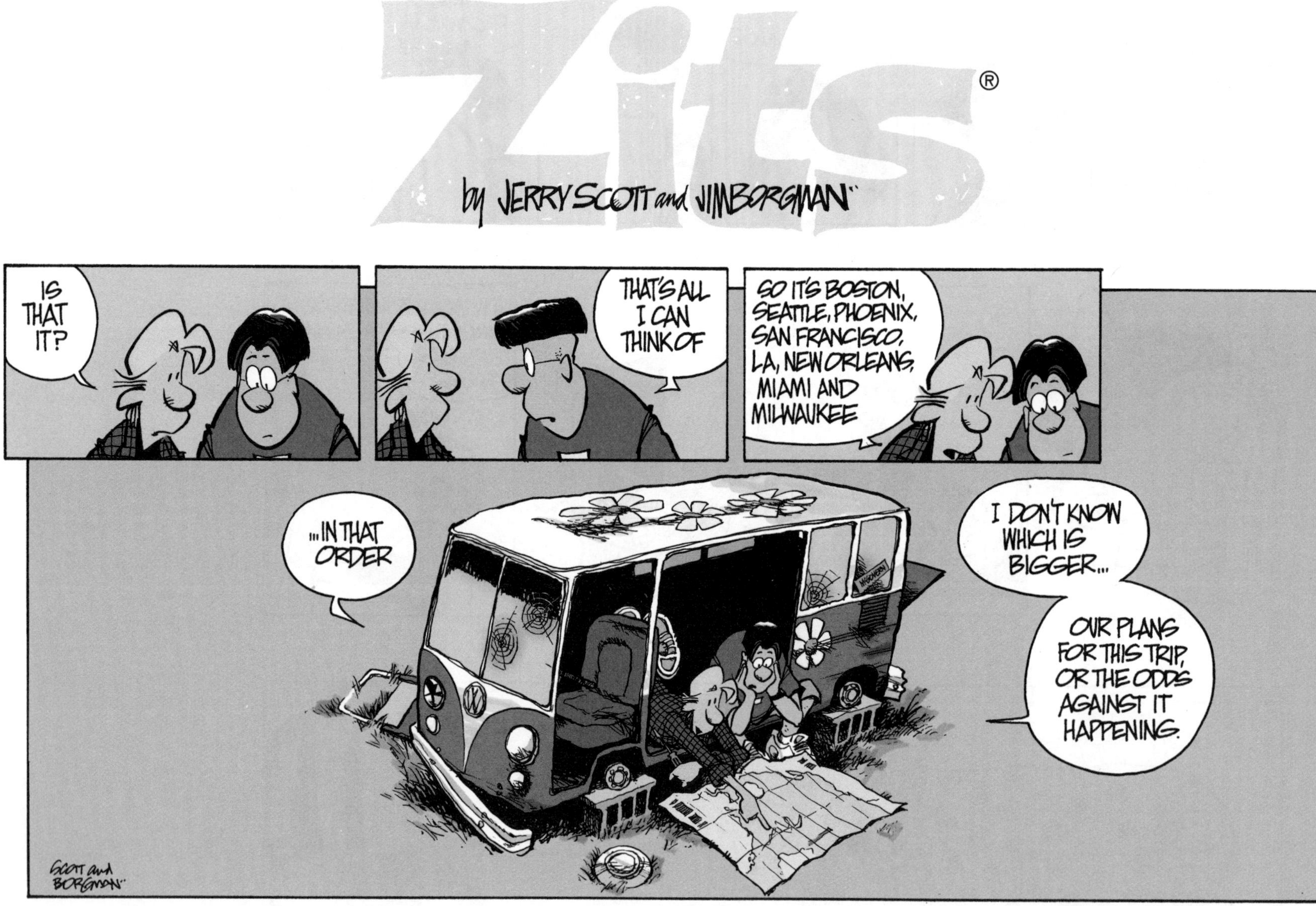
Zits®
by JERRY SCOTT and JIM BORGMAN
IS THAT IT?
THAT'S ALL I CAN THINK OF
SO IT'S BOSTON, SEATTLE, PHOENIX, SAN FRANCISCO, LA, NEW ORLEANS, MIAMI AND MILWAUKEE
...IN THAT ORDER
I DON'T KNOW WHICH IS BIGGER...
OUR PLANS FOR THIS TRIP, OR THE ODDS AGAINST IT HAPPENING.
SCOTT and BORGMAN

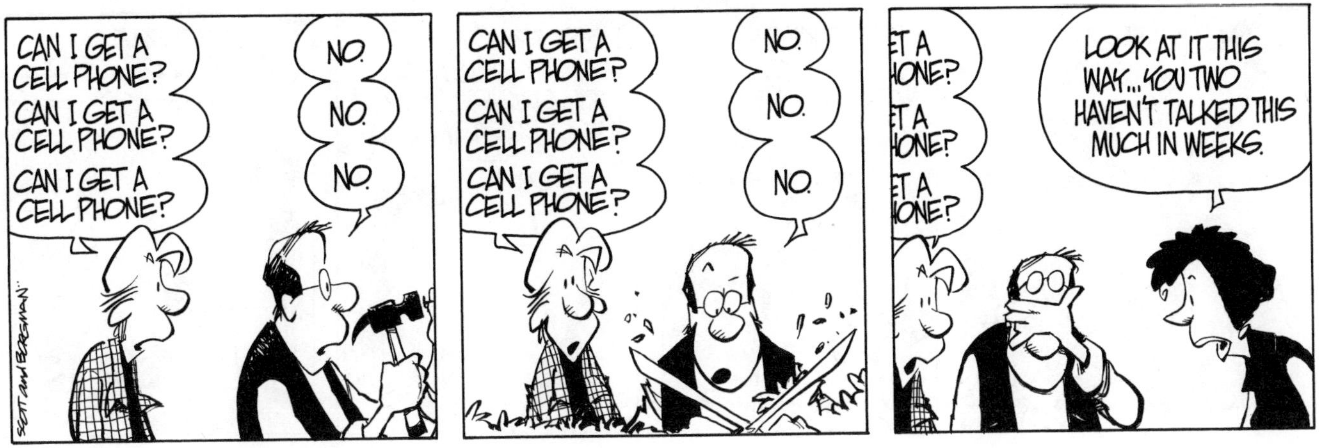
CAN I GET A CELL PHONE? CAN I GET A CELL PHONE? CAN I GET A CELL PHONE?
NO. NO. NO.
CAN I GET A CELL PHONE? CAN I GET A CELL PHONE? CAN I GET A CELL PHONE?
NO. NO. NO.
LOOK AT IT THIS WAY... YOU TWO HAVEN'T TALKED THIS MUCH IN WEEKS.

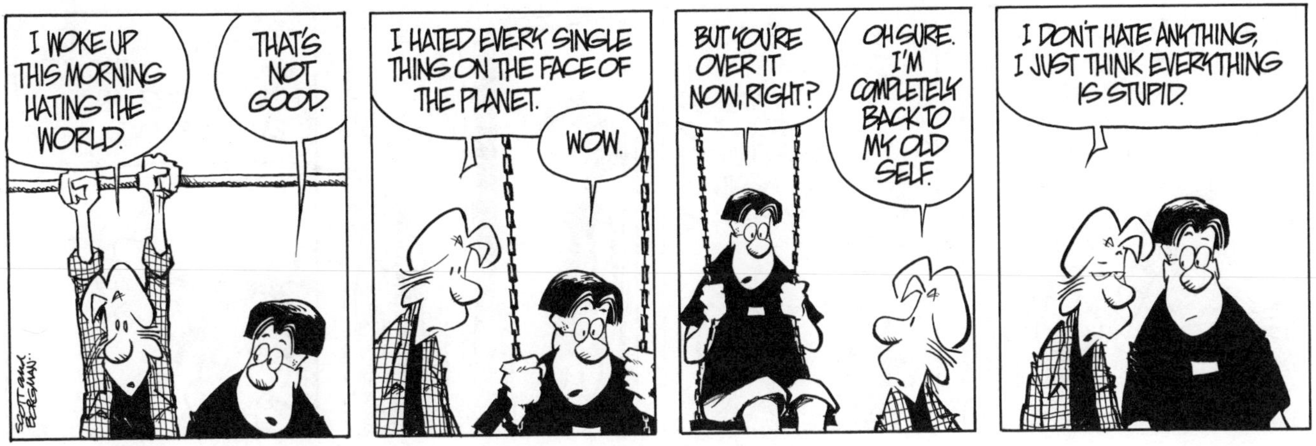
I WOKE UP THIS MORNING HATING THE WORLD.
THAT'S NOT GOOD.
I HATED EVERY SINGLE THING ON THE FACE OF THE PLANET.
WOW.
BUT YOU'RE OVER IT NOW, RIGHT?
OH SURE. I'M COMPLETELY BACK TO MY OLD SELF.
I DON'T HATE ANYTHING, I JUST THINK EVERYTHING IS STUPID.

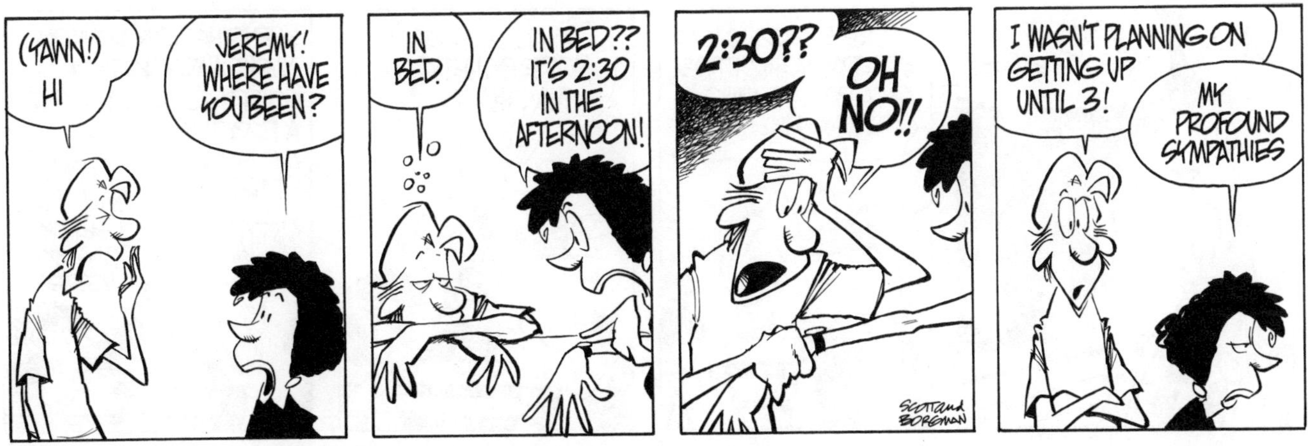
(YAWN!) HI
JEREMY! WHERE HAVE YOU BEEN?
IN BED.
IN BED?? IT'S 2:30 IN THE AFTERNOON!
2:30??
OH NO!!
I WASN'T PLANNING ON GETTING UP UNTIL 3!
MY PROFOUND SYMPATHIES

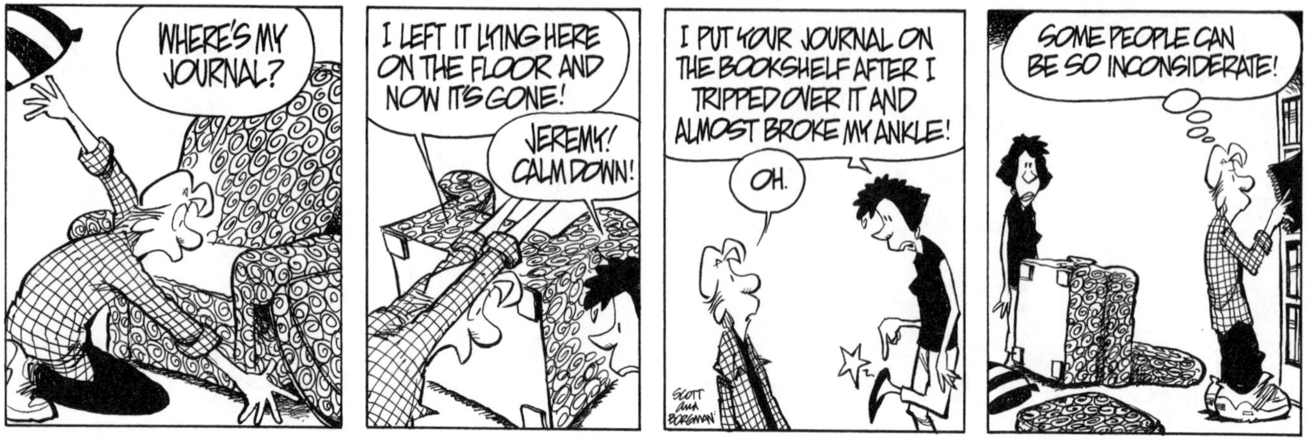
WHERE'S MY JOURNAL?
I LEFT IT LYING HERE ON THE FLOOR AND NOW IT'S GONE!
JEREMY! CALM DOWN!
I PUT YOUR JOURNAL ON THE BOOKSHELF AFTER I TRIPPED OVER IT AND ALMOST BROKE MY ANKLE!
OH.
SCOTT and BORGMAN
SOME PEOPLE CAN BE SO INCONSIDERATE!

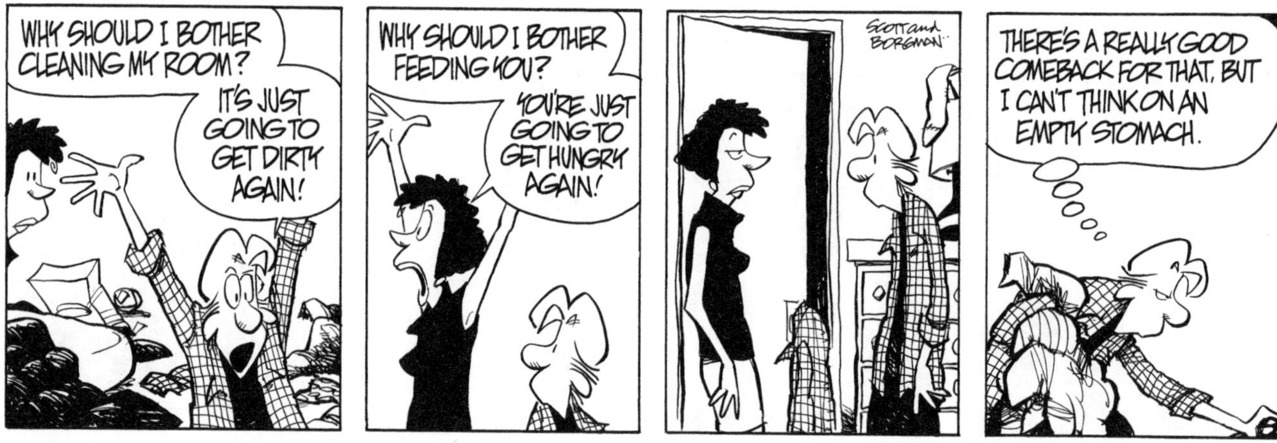
WHY SHOULD I BOTHER CLEANING MY ROOM?
IT'S JUST GOING TO GET DIRTY AGAIN!
WHY SHOULD I BOTHER FEEDING YOU?
YOU'RE JUST GOING TO GET HUNGRY AGAIN!
SCOTT and BORGMAN
THERE'S A REALLY GOOD COMEBACK FOR THAT, BUT I CAN'T THINK ON AN EMPTY STOMACH.

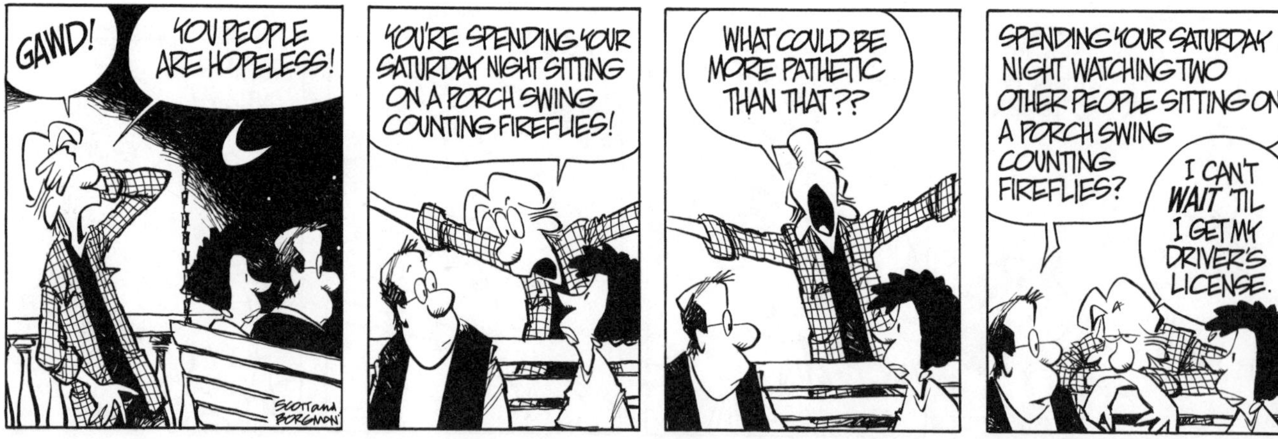
GAWD!
YOU PEOPLE ARE HOPELESS!
SCOTT and BORGMAN
YOU'RE SPENDING YOUR SATURDAY NIGHT SITTING ON A PORCH SWING COUNTING FIREFLIES!
WHAT COULD BE MORE PATHETIC THAN THAT??
SPENDING YOUR SATURDAY NIGHT WATCHING TWO OTHER PEOPLE SITTING ON A PORCH SWING COUNTING FIREFLIES?
I CAN'T WAIT 'TIL I GET MY DRIVER'S LICENSE.

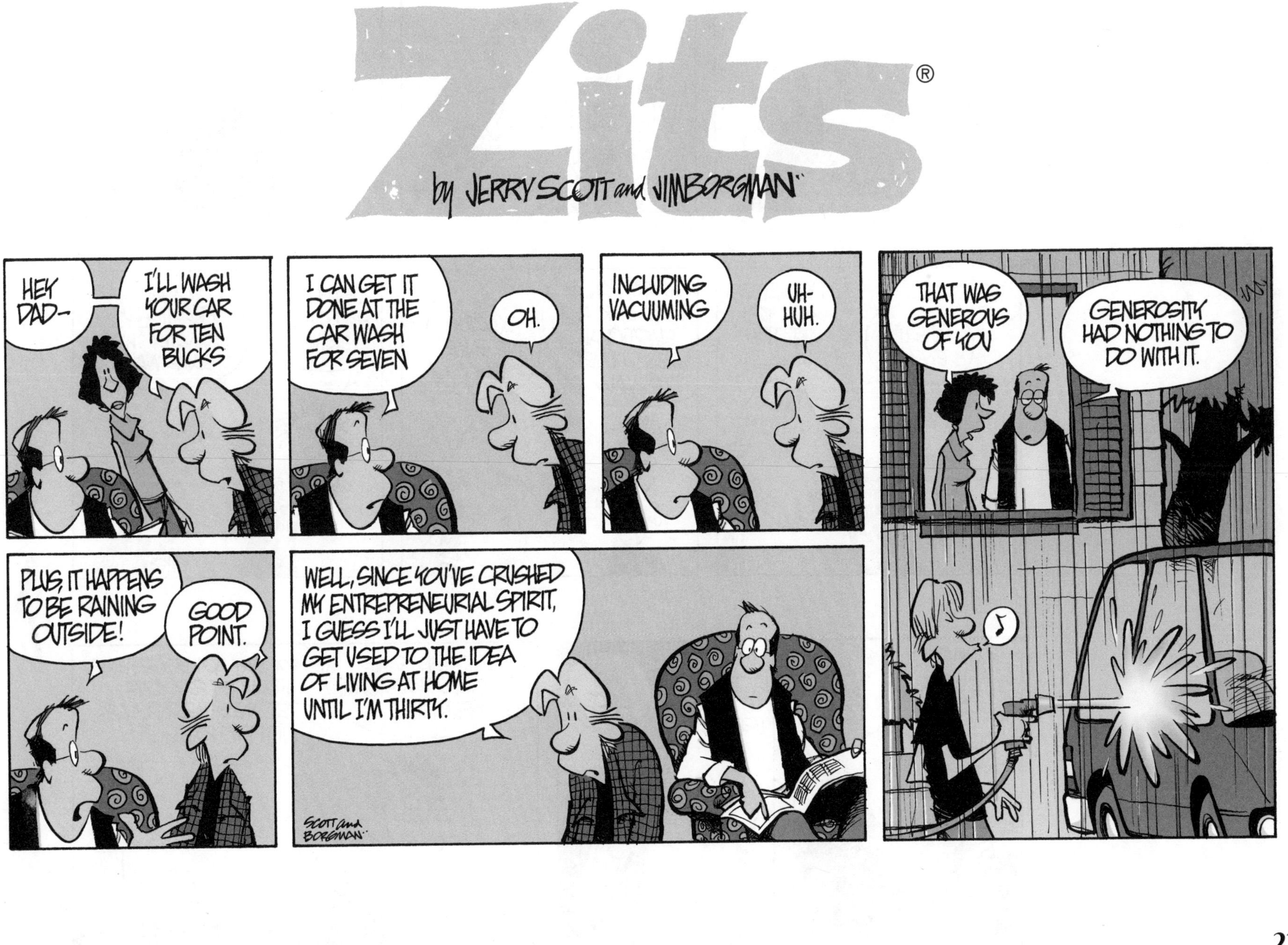
Zits®
by JERRY SCOTT and JIM BORGMAN
HEY DAD–
I'LL WASH YOUR CAR FOR TEN BUCKS
I CAN GET IT DONE AT THE CAR WASH FOR SEVEN
OH.
INCLUDING VACUUMING
UH-HUH.
THAT WAS GENEROUS OF YOU
GENEROSITY HAD NOTHING TO DO WITH IT.
PLUS, IT HAPPENS TO BE RAINING OUTSIDE!
GOOD POINT.
WELL, SINCE YOU'VE CRUSHED MY ENTREPRENEURIAL SPIRIT, I GUESS I'LL JUST HAVE TO GET USED TO THE IDEA OF LIVING AT HOME UNTIL I'M THIRTY.
SCOTT and BORGMAN

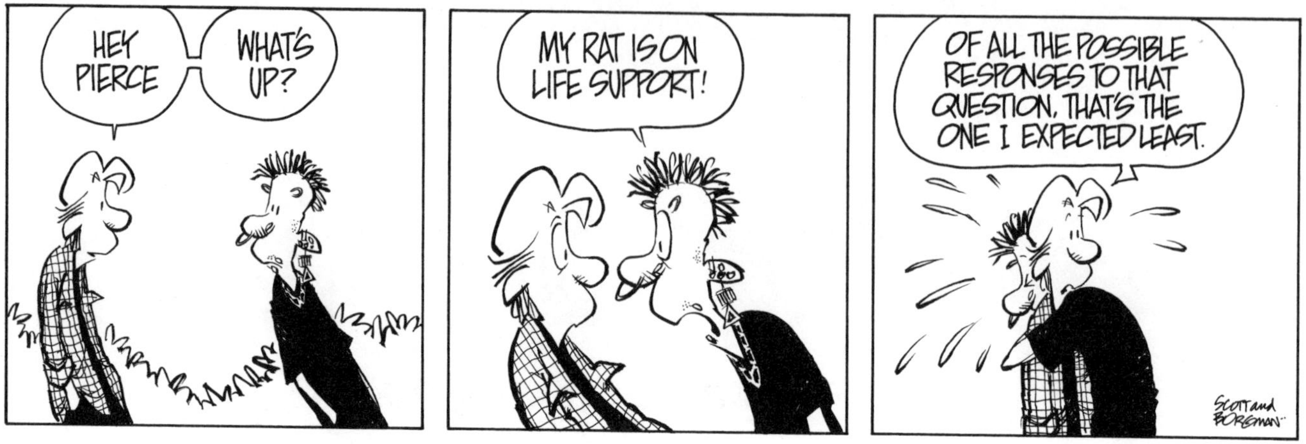
HEY PIERCE
WHAT'S UP?
MY RAT IS ON LIFE SUPPORT!
OF ALL THE POSSIBLE RESPONSES TO THAT QUESTION, THAT'S THE ONE I EXPECTED LEAST.
SCOTT and BORGMAN

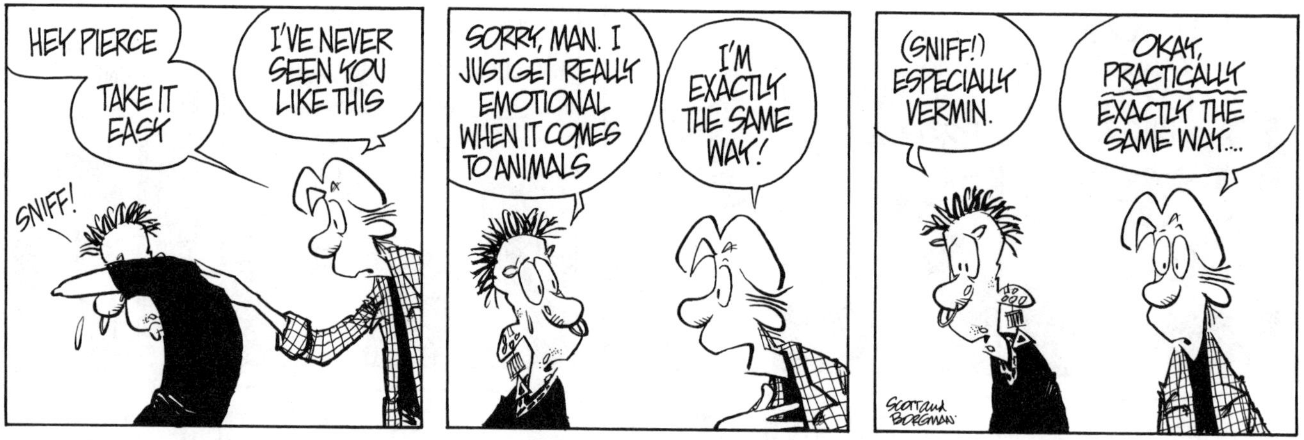
HEY PIERCE
TAKE IT EASY
I'VE NEVER SEEN YOU LIKE THIS
SNIFF!
SORRY, MAN. I JUST GET REALLY EMOTIONAL WHEN IT COMES TO ANIMALS
I'M EXACTLY THE SAME WAY!
(SNIFF!) ESPECIALLY VERMIN.
OKAY, PRACTICALLY EXACTLY THE SAME WAY....
SCOTT and BORGMAN

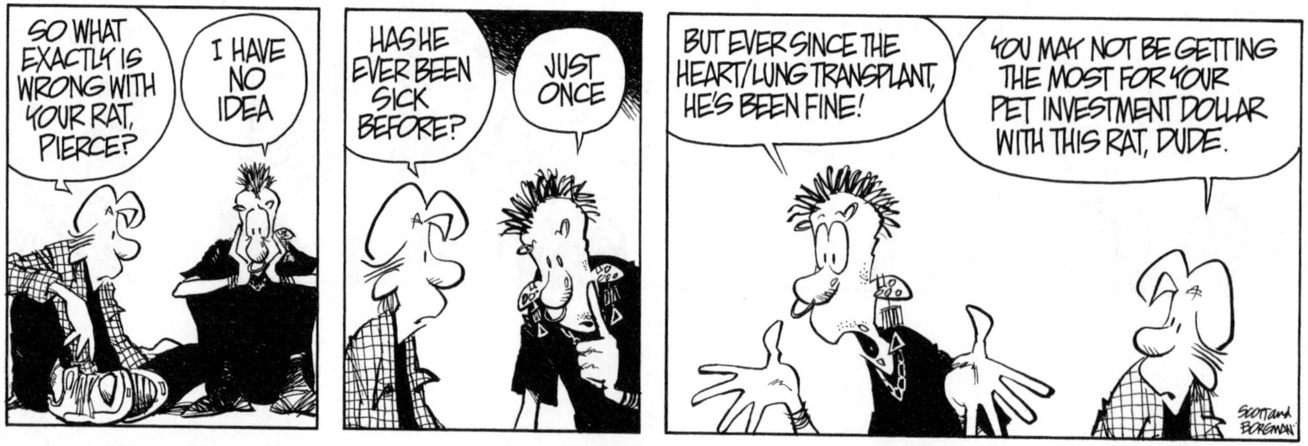
SO WHAT EXACTLY IS WRONG WITH YOUR RAT, PIERCE?
I HAVE NO IDEA
HAS HE EVER BEEN SICK BEFORE?
JUST ONCE
BUT EVER SINCE THE HEART/LUNG TRANSPLANT, HE'S BEEN FINE!
YOU MAY NOT BE GETTING THE MOST FOR YOUR PET INVESTMENT DOLLAR WITH THIS RAT, DUDE.
SCOTT and BORGMAN

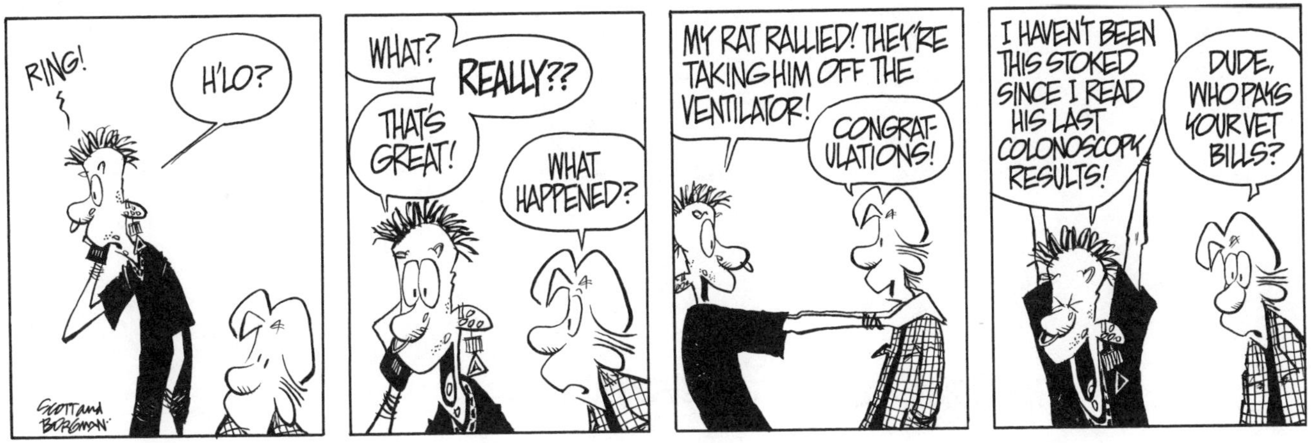
RING!
H'LO?
WHAT?
REALLY??
THAT'S GREAT!
WHAT HAPPENED?
MY RAT RALLIED! THEY'RE TAKING HIM OFF THE VENTILATOR!
CONGRAT-ULATIONS!
I HAVEN'T BEEN THIS STOKED SINCE I READ HIS LAST COLONOSCOPY RESULTS!
DUDE, WHO PAYS YOUR VET BILLS?
SCOTT and BORGMAN

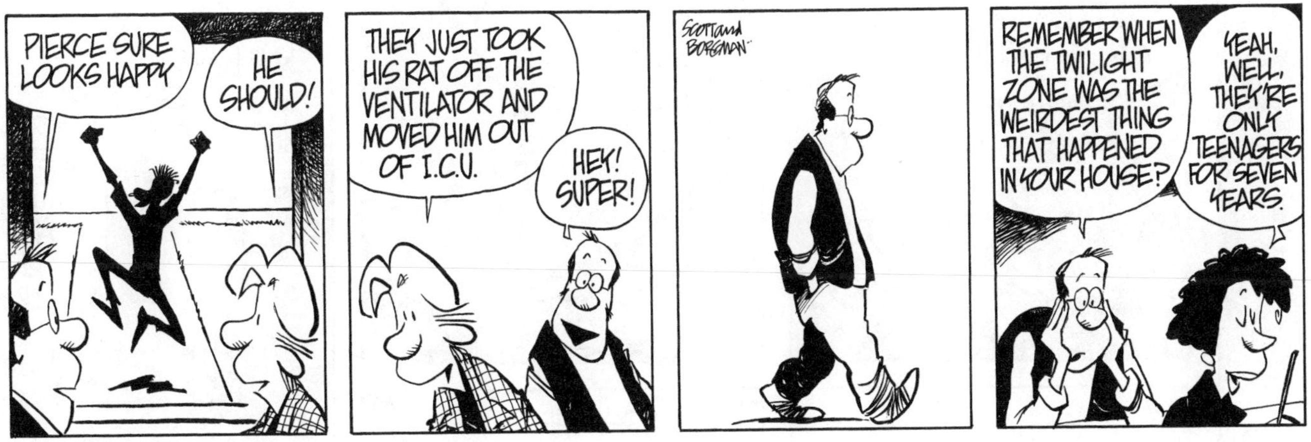
PIERCE SURE LOOKS HAPPY
HE SHOULD!
THEY JUST TOOK HIS RAT OFF THE VENTILATOR AND MOVED HIM OUT OF I.C.U.
HEY! SUPER!
SCOTT and BORGMAN
REMEMBER WHEN THE TWILIGHT ZONE WAS THE WEIRDEST THING THAT HAPPENED IN YOUR HOUSE?
YEAH, WELL, THEY'RE ONLY TEENAGERS FOR SEVEN YEARS.

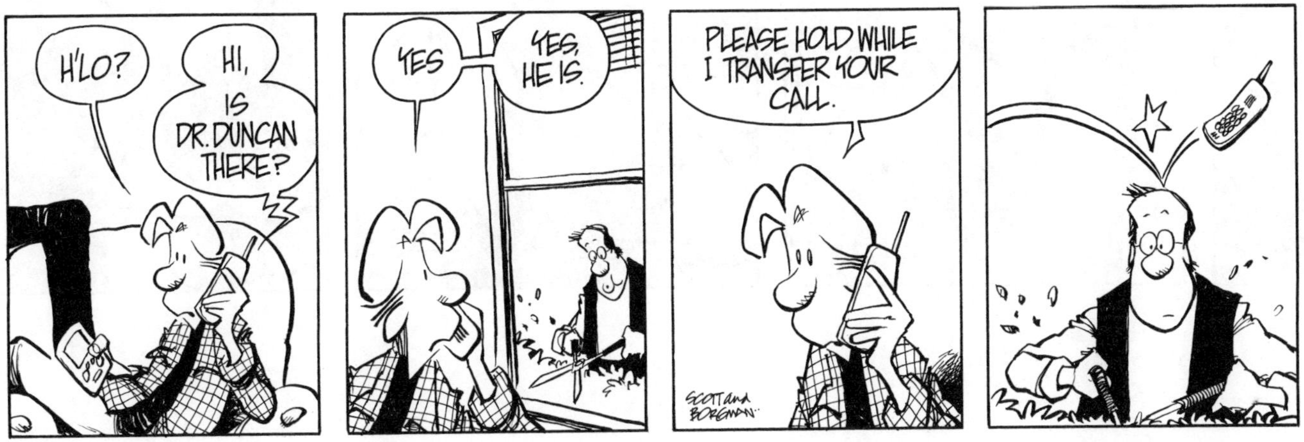
H'LO?
HI, IS DR. DUNCAN THERE?
YES
YES, HE IS.
PLEASE HOLD WHILE I TRANSFER YOUR CALL.
SCOTT and BORGMAN

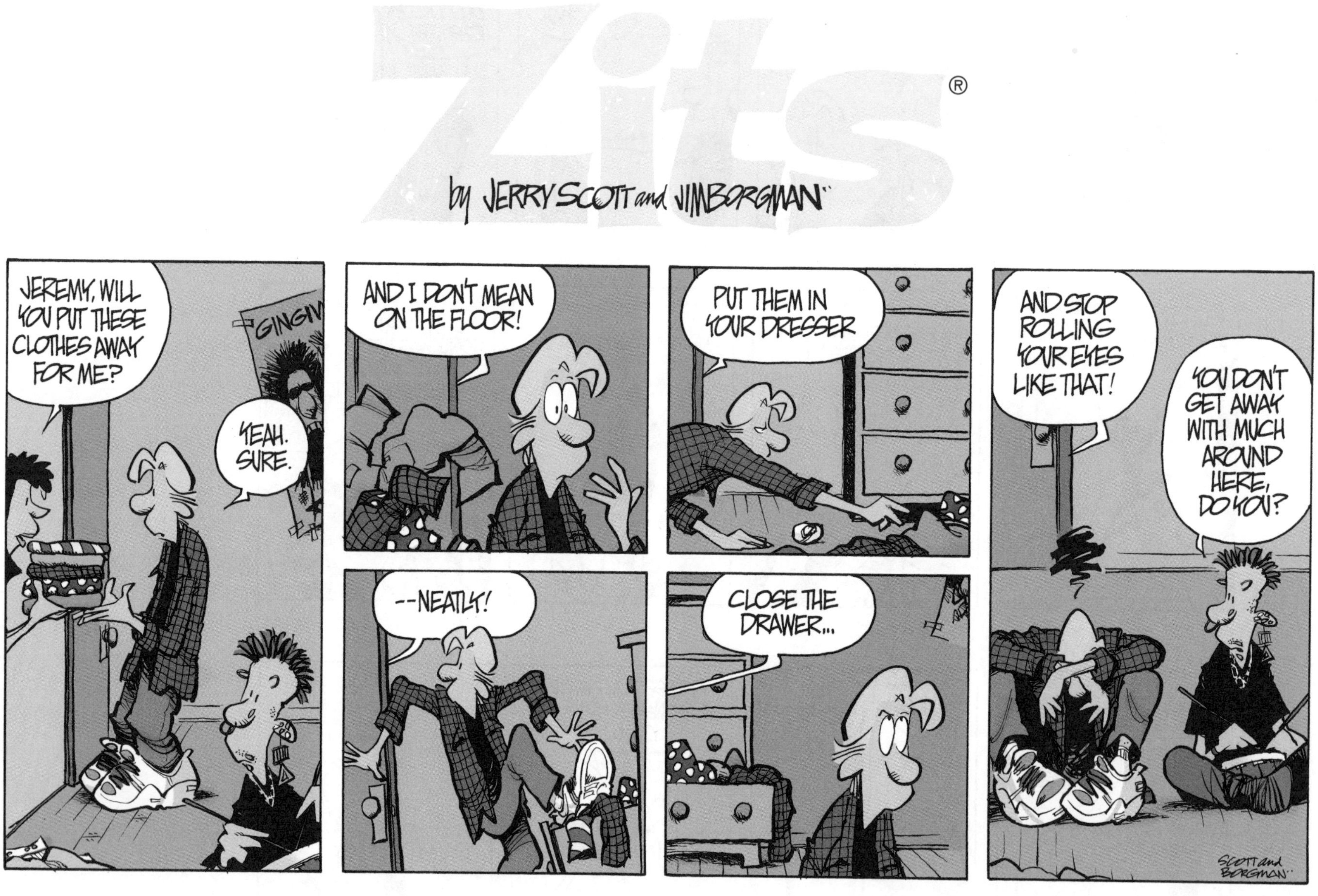

Zits®
by JERRY SCOTT and JIM BORGMAN
JEREMY, WILL YOU PUT THESE CLOTHES AWAY FOR ME?
YEAH. SURE.
AND I DON'T MEAN ON THE FLOOR!
--NEATLY!
PUT THEM IN YOUR DRESSER
CLOSE THE DRAWER...
AND STOP ROLLING YOUR EYES LIKE THAT!
YOU DON'T GET AWAY WITH MUCH AROUND HERE, DO YOU?
SCOTT and BORGMAN

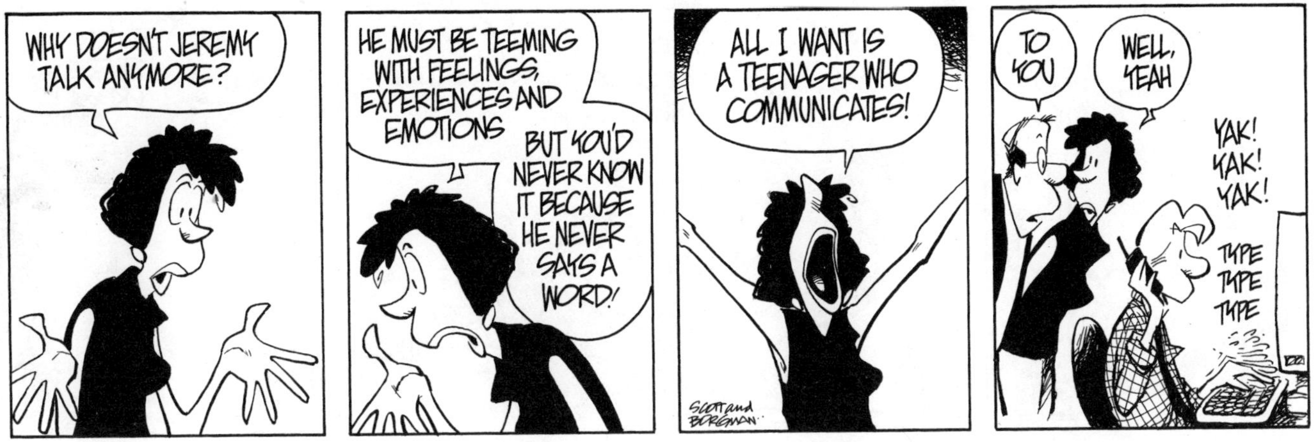

WHY DOESN'T JEREMY TALK ANYMORE?
HE MUST BE TEEMING WITH FEELINGS, EXPERIENCES AND EMOTIONS
BUT YOU'D NEVER KNOW IT BECAUSE HE NEVER SAYS A WORD!
ALL I WANT IS A TEENAGER WHO COMMUNICATES!
SCOTT and BORGMAN
TO YOU
WELL, YEAH
YAK! YAK! YAK!
TYPE TYPE TYPE

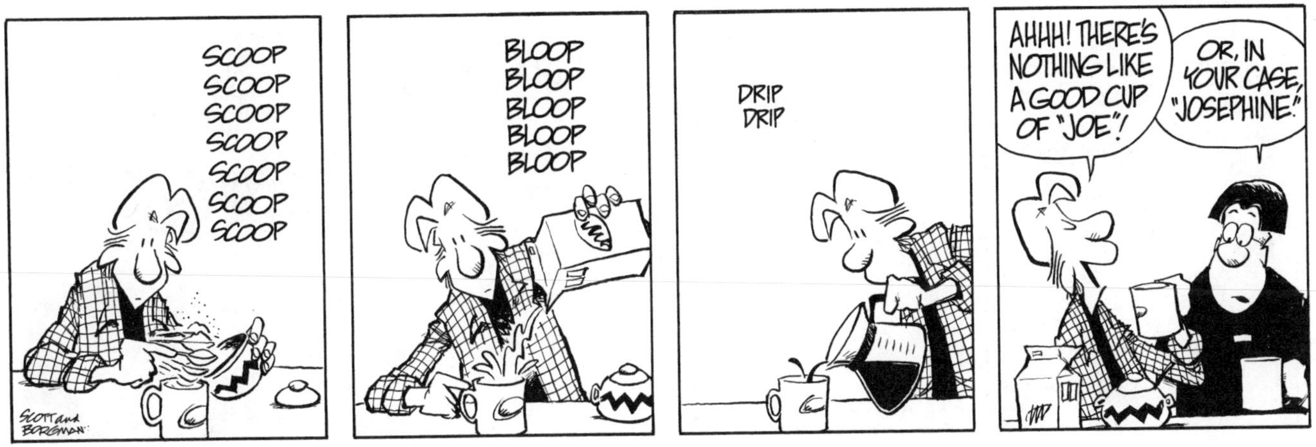

SCOOP SCOOP SCOOP SCOOP SCOOP SCOOP SCOOP
SCOTT and BORGMAN
BLOOP BLOOP BLOOP BLOOP BLOOP
DRIP DRIP
AHHH! THERE'S NOTHING LIKE A GOOD CUP OF "JOE"!
OR, IN YOUR CASE, "JOSEPHINE."

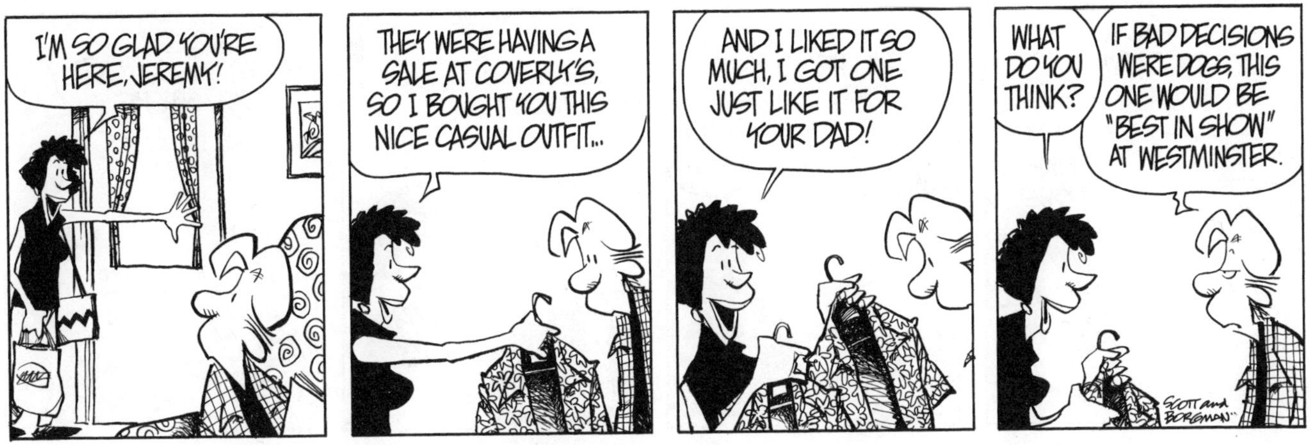

I'M SO GLAD YOU'RE HERE, JEREMY!
THEY WERE HAVING A SALE AT COVERLY'S, SO I BOUGHT YOU THIS NICE CASUAL OUTFIT...
AND I LIKED IT SO MUCH, I GOT ONE JUST LIKE IT FOR YOUR DAD!
WHAT DO YOU THINK?
IF BAD DECISIONS WERE DOGS, THIS ONE WOULD BE "BEST IN SHOW" AT WESTMINSTER.
SCOTT and BORGMAN

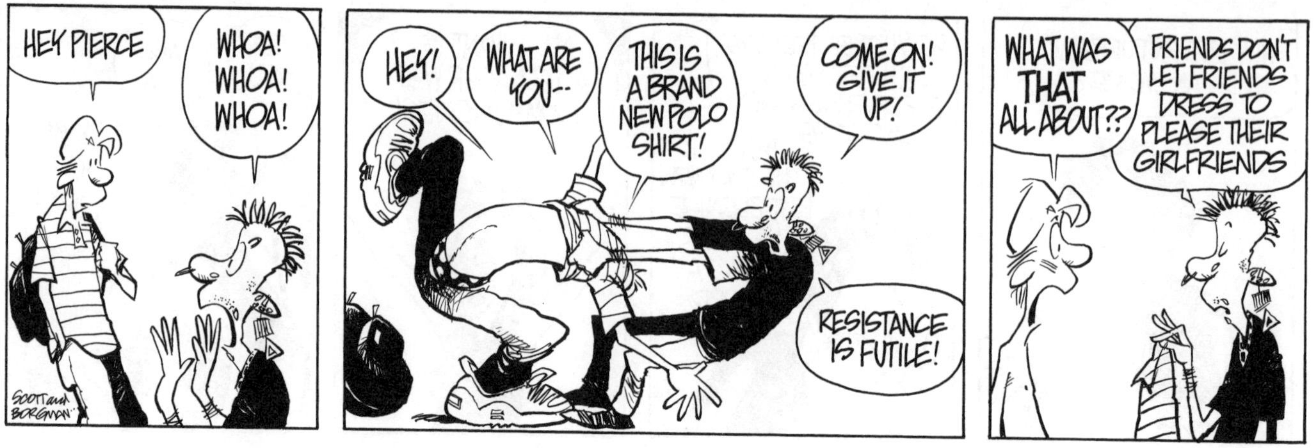
HEY PIERCE
WHOA! WHOA! WHOA!
HEY!
WHAT ARE YOU--
THIS IS A BRAND NEW POLO SHIRT!
COME ON! GIVE IT UP!
RESISTANCE IS FUTILE!
WHAT WAS THAT ALL ABOUT??
FRIENDS DON'T LET FRIENDS DRESS TO PLEASE THEIR GIRLFRIENDS
SCOTT and BORGMAN

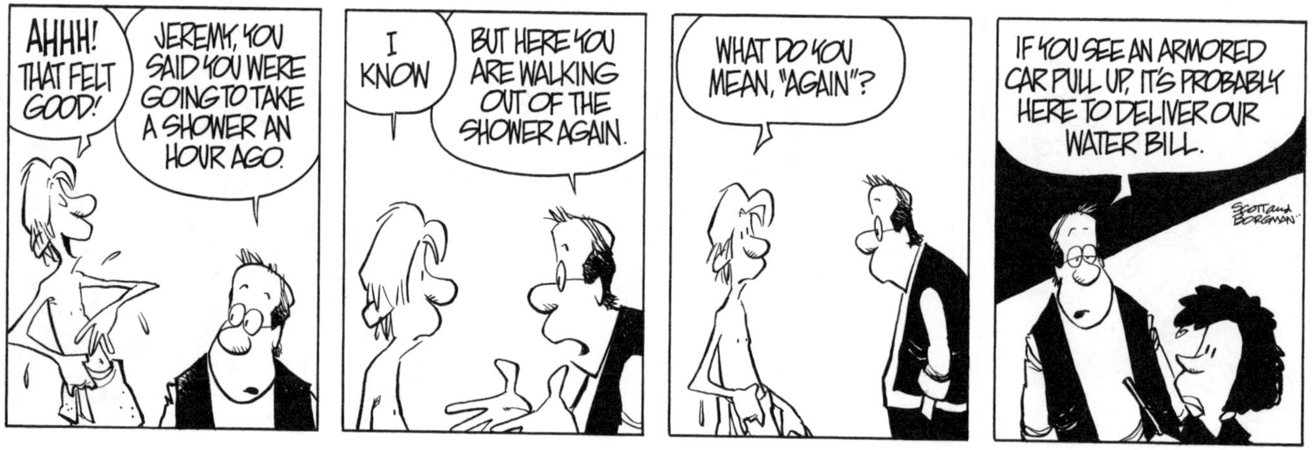
AHHH! THAT FELT GOOD!
JEREMY, YOU SAID YOU WERE GOING TO TAKE A SHOWER AN HOUR AGO.
I KNOW
BUT HERE YOU ARE WALKING OUT OF THE SHOWER AGAIN.
WHAT DO YOU MEAN, "AGAIN"?
IF YOU SEE AN ARMORED CAR PULL UP, IT'S PROBABLY HERE TO DELIVER OUR WATER BILL.
SCOTT and BORGMAN

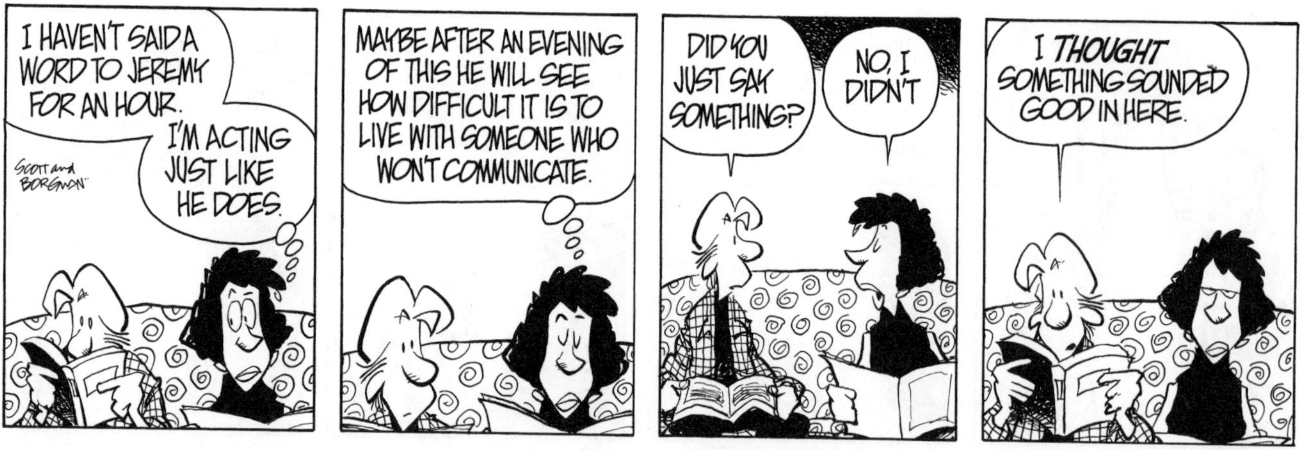
I HAVEN'T SAID A WORD TO JEREMY FOR AN HOUR.
I'M ACTING JUST LIKE HE DOES.
SCOTT and BORGMAN
MAYBE AFTER AN EVENING OF THIS HE WILL SEE HOW DIFFICULT IT IS TO LIVE WITH SOMEONE WHO WON'T COMMUNICATE.
DID YOU JUST SAY SOMETHING?
NO, I DIDN'T
I THOUGHT SOMETHING SOUNDED GOOD IN HERE.

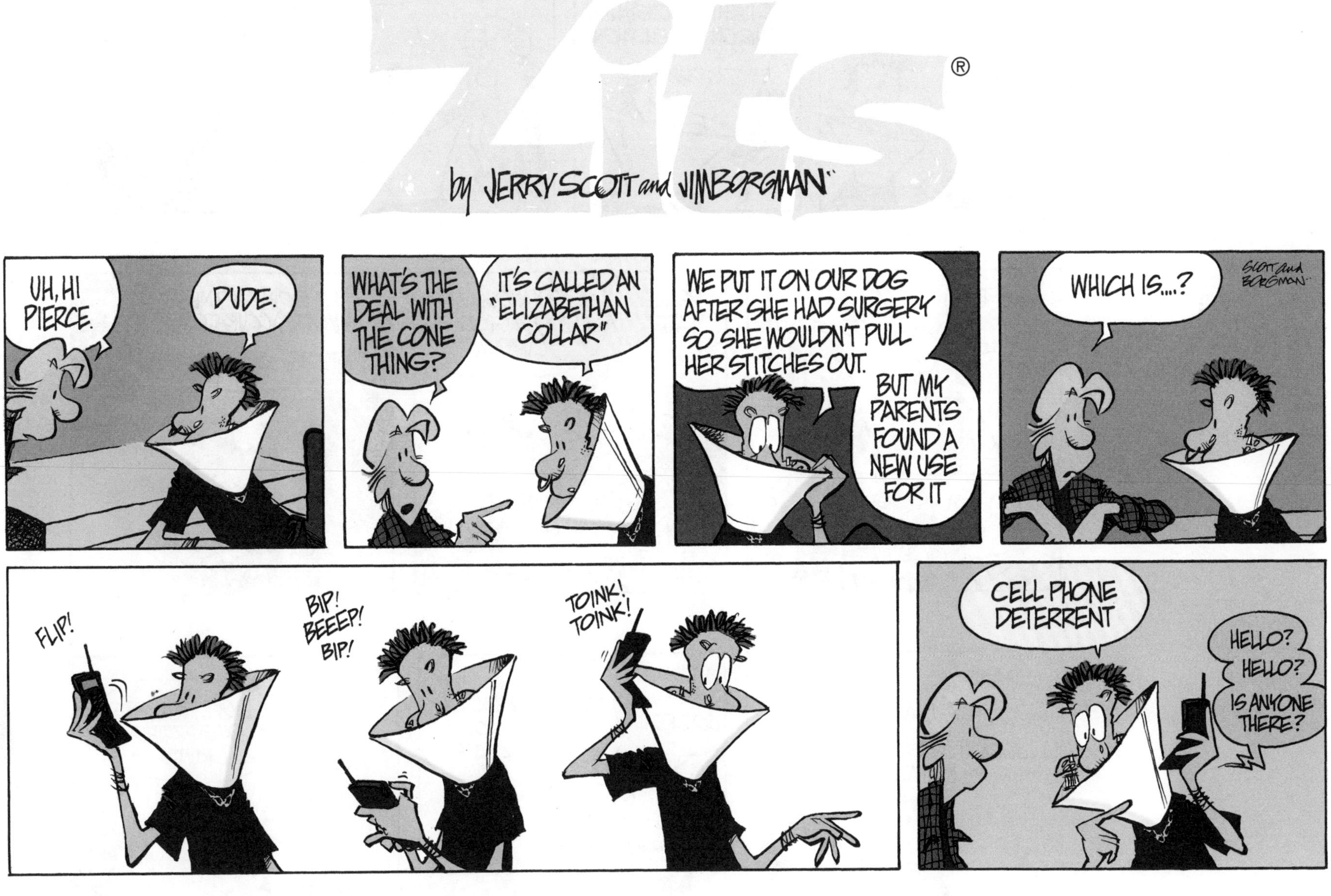
Zits®
by JERRY SCOTT and JIM BORGMAN
UH, HI PIERCE.
DUDE.
WHAT'S THE DEAL WITH THE CONE THING?
IT'S CALLED AN "ELIZABETHAN COLLAR"
WE PUT IT ON OUR DOG AFTER SHE HAD SURGERY SO SHE WOULDN'T PULL HER STITCHES OUT.
BUT MY PARENTS FOUND A NEW USE FOR IT
WHICH IS....?
SCOTT and BORGMAN
FLIP!
BIP! BEEEP! BIP!
TOINK! TOINK!
CELL PHONE DETERRENT
HELLO?
HELLO?
IS ANYONE THERE?

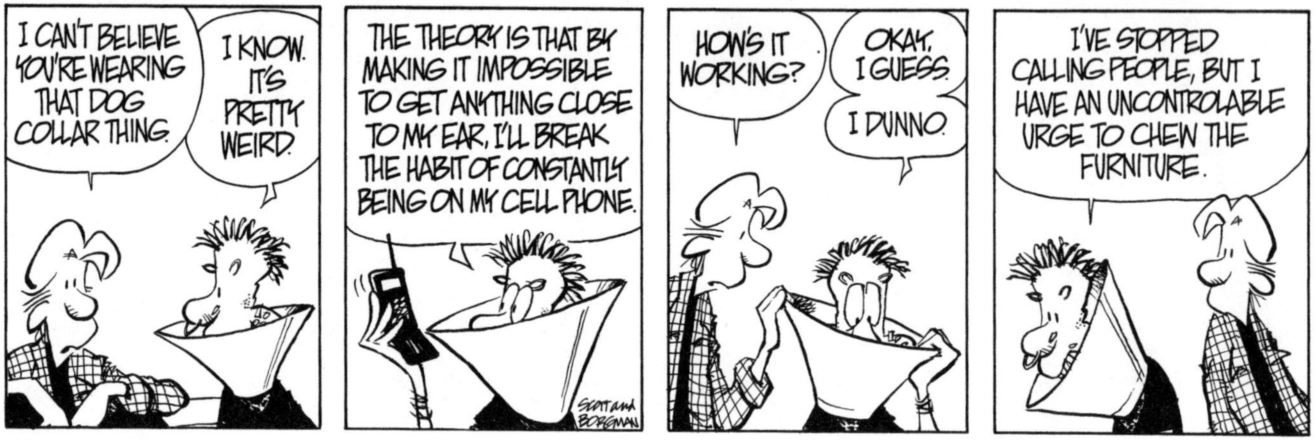
I CAN'T BELIEVE YOU'RE WEARING THAT DOG COLLAR THING.
I KNOW. IT'S PRETTY WEIRD.
THE THEORY IS THAT BY MAKING IT IMPOSSIBLE TO GET ANYTHING CLOSE TO MY EAR, I'LL BREAK THE HABIT OF CONSTANTLY BEING ON MY CELL PHONE.
SCOTT AND BORGMAN
HOW'S IT WORKING?
OKAY, I GUESS.
I DUNNO.
I'VE STOPPED CALLING PEOPLE, BUT I HAVE AN UNCONTROLABLE URGE TO CHEW THE FURNITURE.

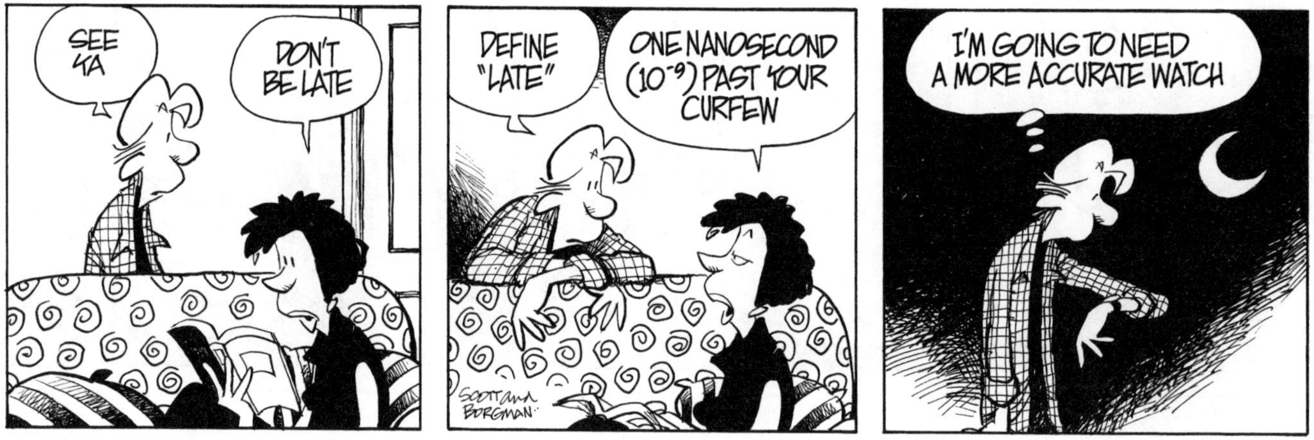
SEE YA
DON'T BE LATE
DEFINE "LATE"
ONE NANOSECOND (10⁻⁹) PAST YOUR CURFEW
SCOTT AND BORGMAN
I'M GOING TO NEED A MORE ACCURATE WATCH

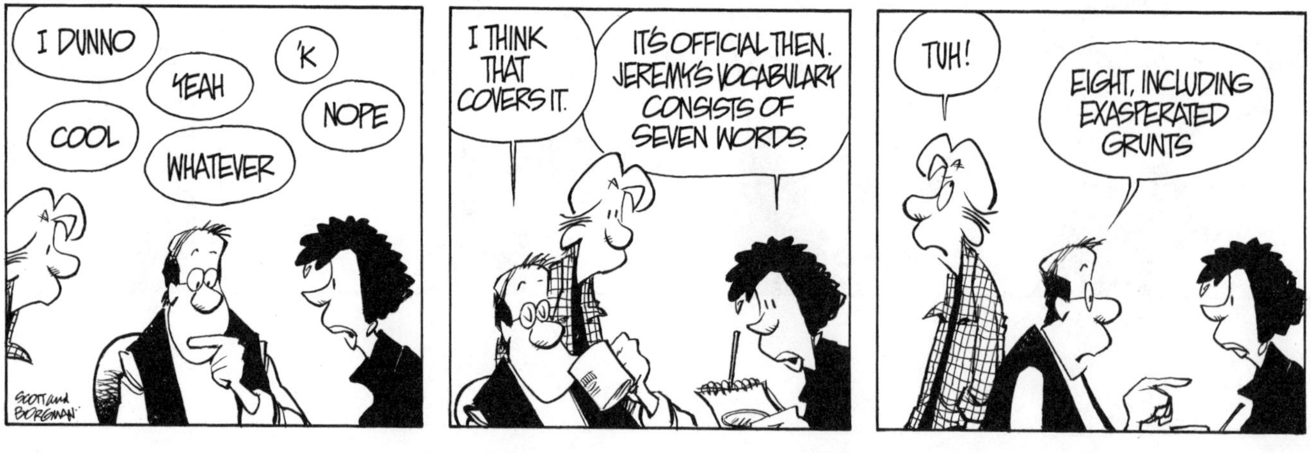
I DUNNO
YEAH
'K
COOL
NOPE
WHATEVER
SCOTT AND BORGMAN
I THINK THAT COVERS IT.
IT'S OFFICIAL THEN. JEREMY'S VOCABULARY CONSISTS OF SEVEN WORDS.
TUH!
EIGHT, INCLUDING EXASPERATED GRUNTS

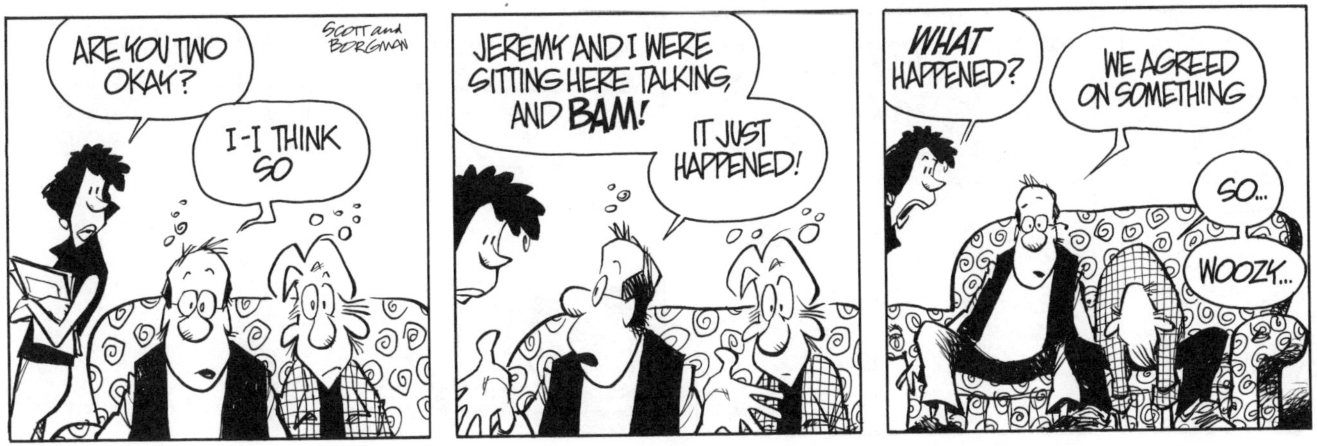
SCOTT and BORGMAN
ARE YOU TWO OKAY?
I-I THINK SO
JEREMY AND I WERE SITTING HERE TALKING, AND BAM!
IT JUST HAPPENED!
WHAT HAPPENED?
WE AGREED ON SOMETHING
SO...
WOOZY...

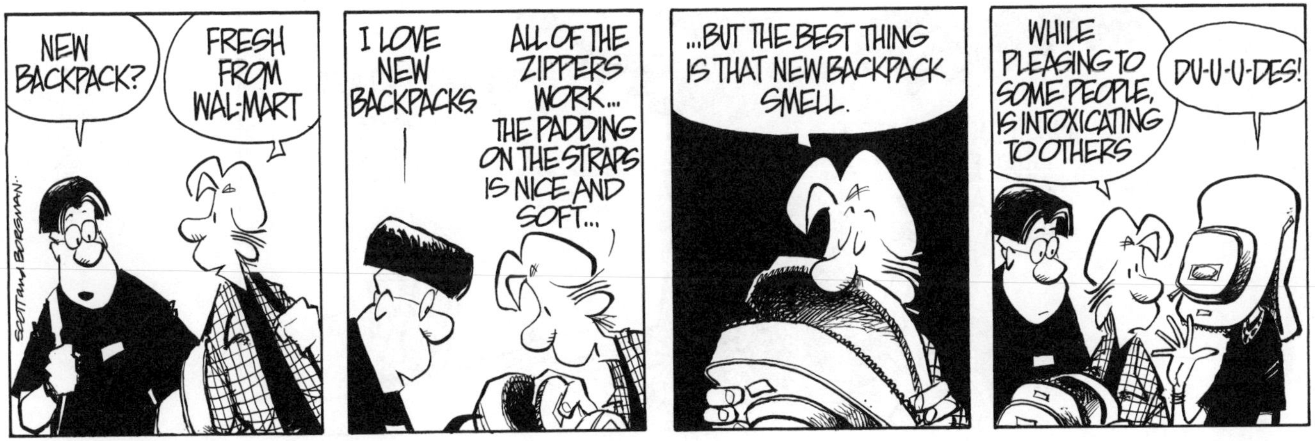
NEW BACKPACK?
FRESH FROM WAL-MART
SCOTT and BORGMAN
I LOVE NEW BACKPACKS
ALL OF THE ZIPPERS WORK... THE PADDING ON THE STRAPS IS NICE AND SOFT...
...BUT THE BEST THING IS THAT NEW BACKPACK SMELL.
WHILE PLEASING TO SOME PEOPLE, IS INTOXICATING TO OTHERS
DU-U-U-DES!

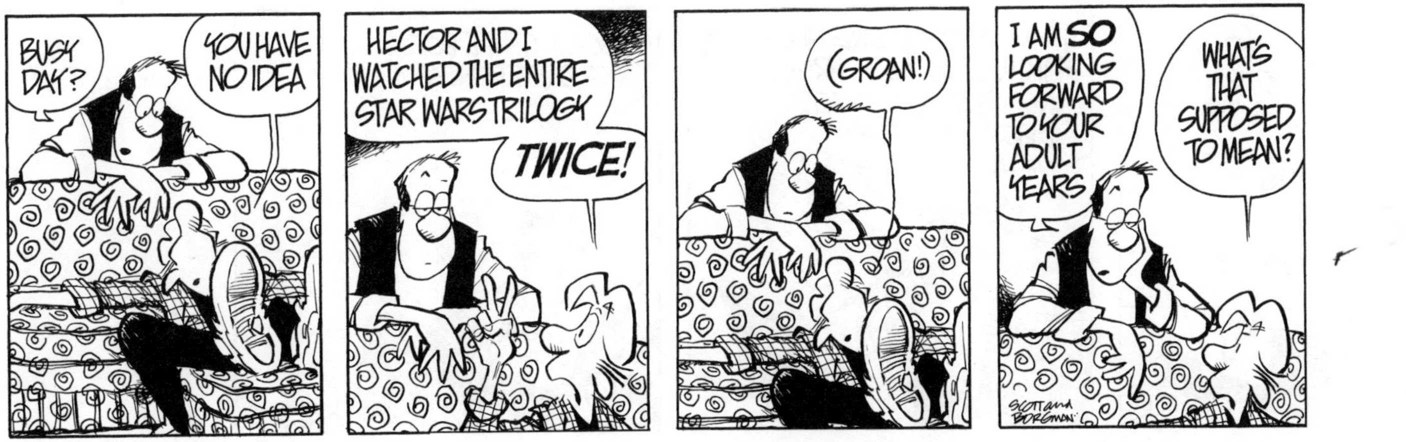
BUSY DAY?
YOU HAVE NO IDEA
HECTOR AND I WATCHED THE ENTIRE STAR WARS TRILOGY
TWICE!
(GROAN!)
I AM SO LOOKING FORWARD TO YOUR ADULT YEARS
WHAT'S THAT SUPPOSED TO MEAN?
SCOTT and BORGMAN

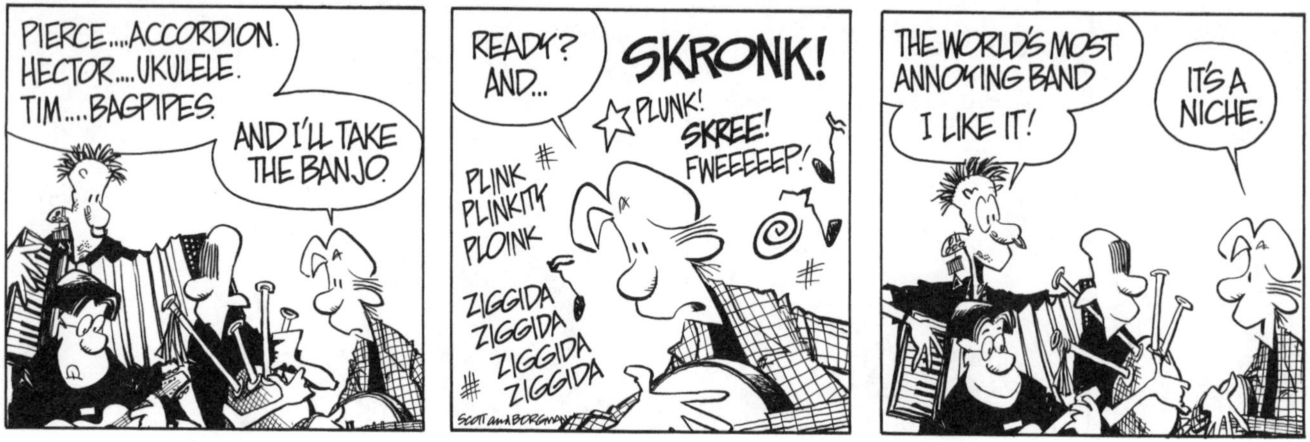
PIERCE....ACCORDION. HECTOR....UKULELE. TIM....BAGPIPES.
AND I'LL TAKE THE BANJO.
READY? AND...
SKRONK!
PLUNK!
SKREE!
FWEEEEEP!
PLINK PLINKITY PLOINK
ZIGGIDA ZIGGIDA ZIGGIDA ZIGGIDA
THE WORLD'S MOST ANNOYING BAND
I LIKE IT!
IT'S A NICHE.
SCOTT and BORGMAN

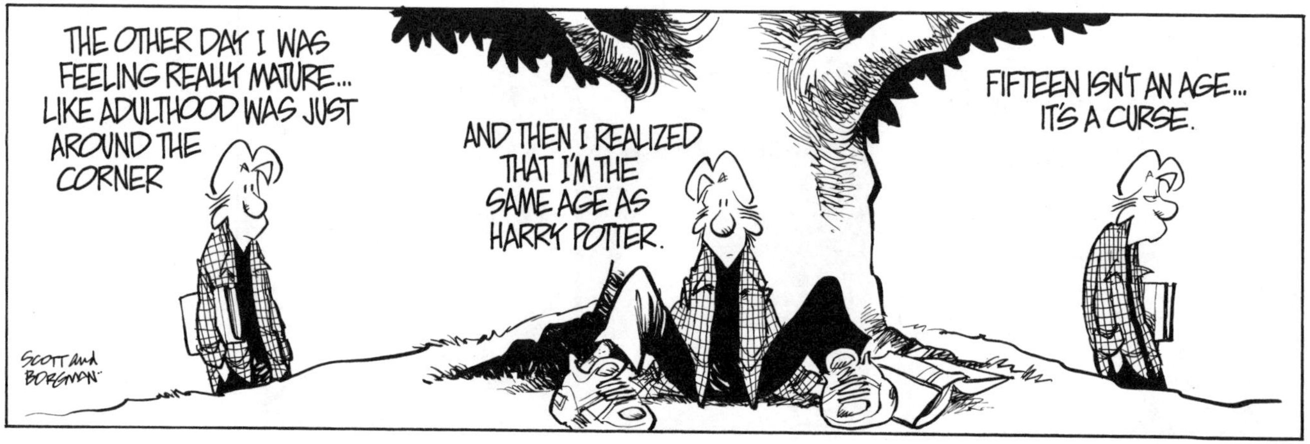
THE OTHER DAY I WAS FEELING REALLY MATURE... LIKE ADULTHOOD WAS JUST AROUND THE CORNER
AND THEN I REALIZED THAT I'M THE SAME AGE AS HARRY POTTER.
FIFTEEN ISN'T AN AGE... IT'S A CURSE.
SCOTT and BORGMAN

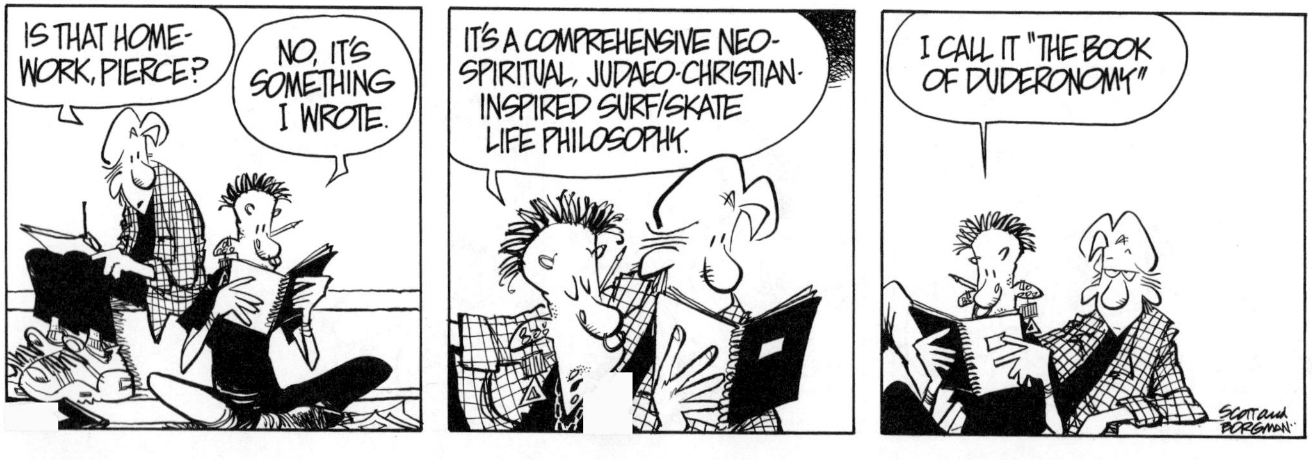
IS THAT HOME-WORK, PIERCE?
NO, IT'S SOMETHING I WROTE.
IT'S A COMPREHENSIVE NEO-SPIRITUAL, JUDAEO-CHRISTIAN-INSPIRED SURF/SKATE LIFE PHILOSOPHY.
I CALL IT "THE BOOK OF DUDERONOMY"
SCOTT and BORGMAN

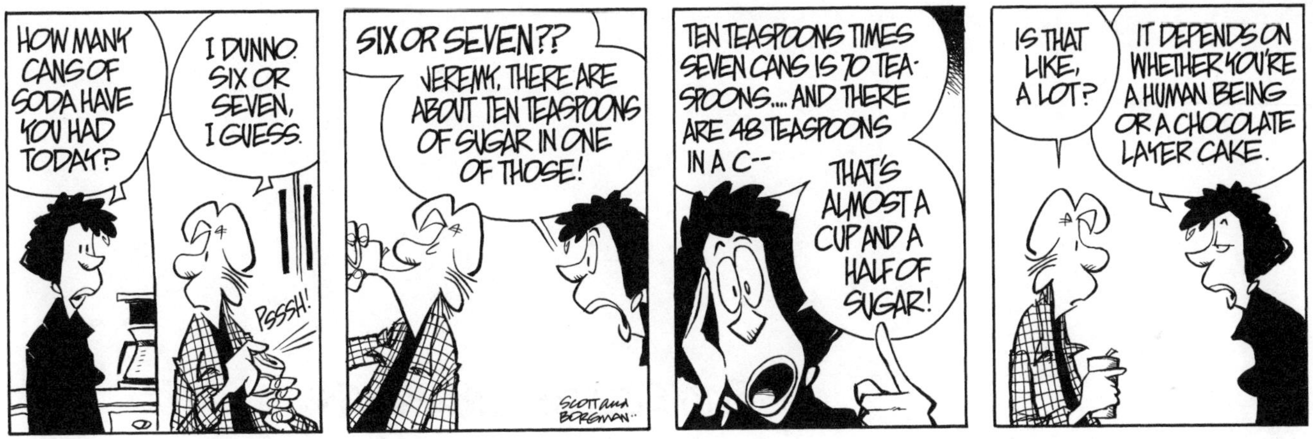
HOW MANY CANS OF SODA HAVE YOU HAD TODAY?
I DUNNO. SIX OR SEVEN, I GUESS.
PSSSH!
SIX OR SEVEN??
JEREMY, THERE ARE ABOUT TEN TEASPOONS OF SUGAR IN ONE OF THOSE!
SCOTT AND BORGMAN
TEN TEASPOONS TIMES SEVEN CANS IS 70 TEA-SPOONS.... AND THERE ARE 48 TEASPOONS IN A C--
THAT'S ALMOST A CUP AND A HALF OF SUGAR!
IS THAT LIKE, A LOT?
IT DEPENDS ON WHETHER YOU'RE A HUMAN BEING OR A CHOCOLATE LAYER CAKE.

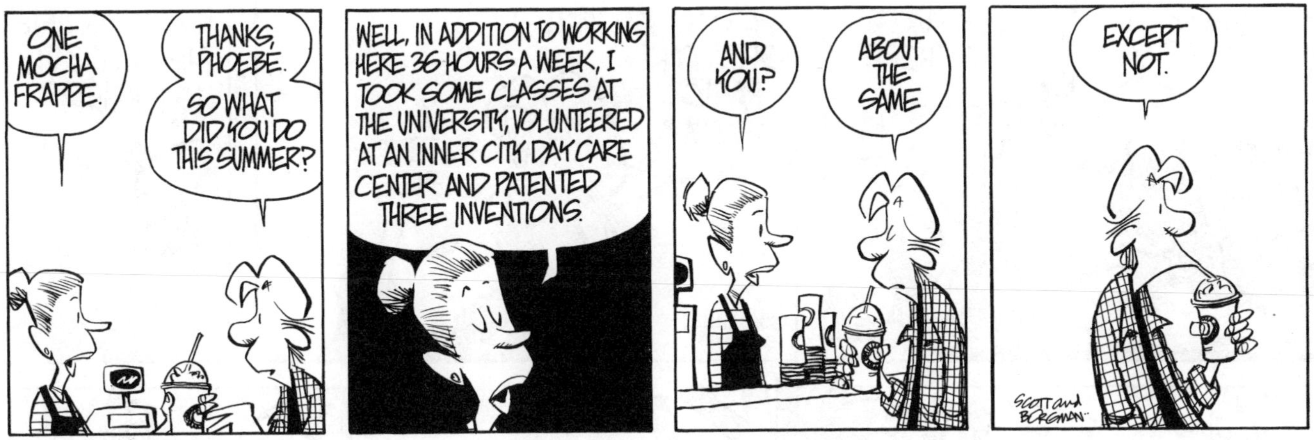
ONE MOCHA FRAPPE.
THANKS, PHOEBE.
SO WHAT DID YOU DO THIS SUMMER?
WELL, IN ADDITION TO WORKING HERE 36 HOURS A WEEK, I TOOK SOME CLASSES AT THE UNIVERSITY, VOLUNTEERED AT AN INNER CITY DAY CARE CENTER AND PATENTED THREE INVENTIONS.
AND YOU?
ABOUT THE SAME
EXCEPT NOT.
SCOTT AND BORGMAN

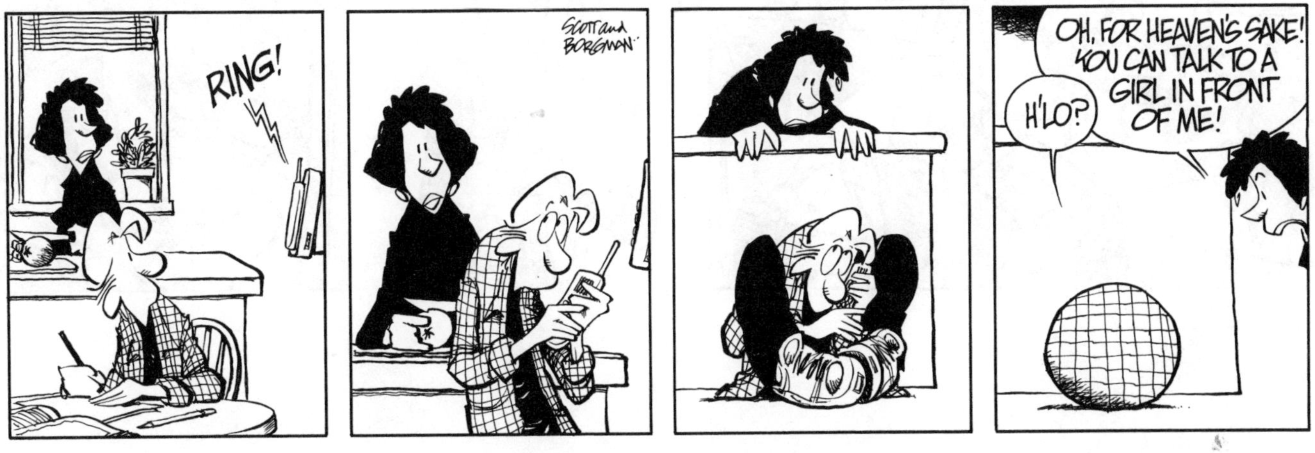
RING!
SCOTT AND BORGMAN
H'LO?
OH, FOR HEAVEN'S SAKE! YOU CAN TALK TO A GIRL IN FRONT OF ME!

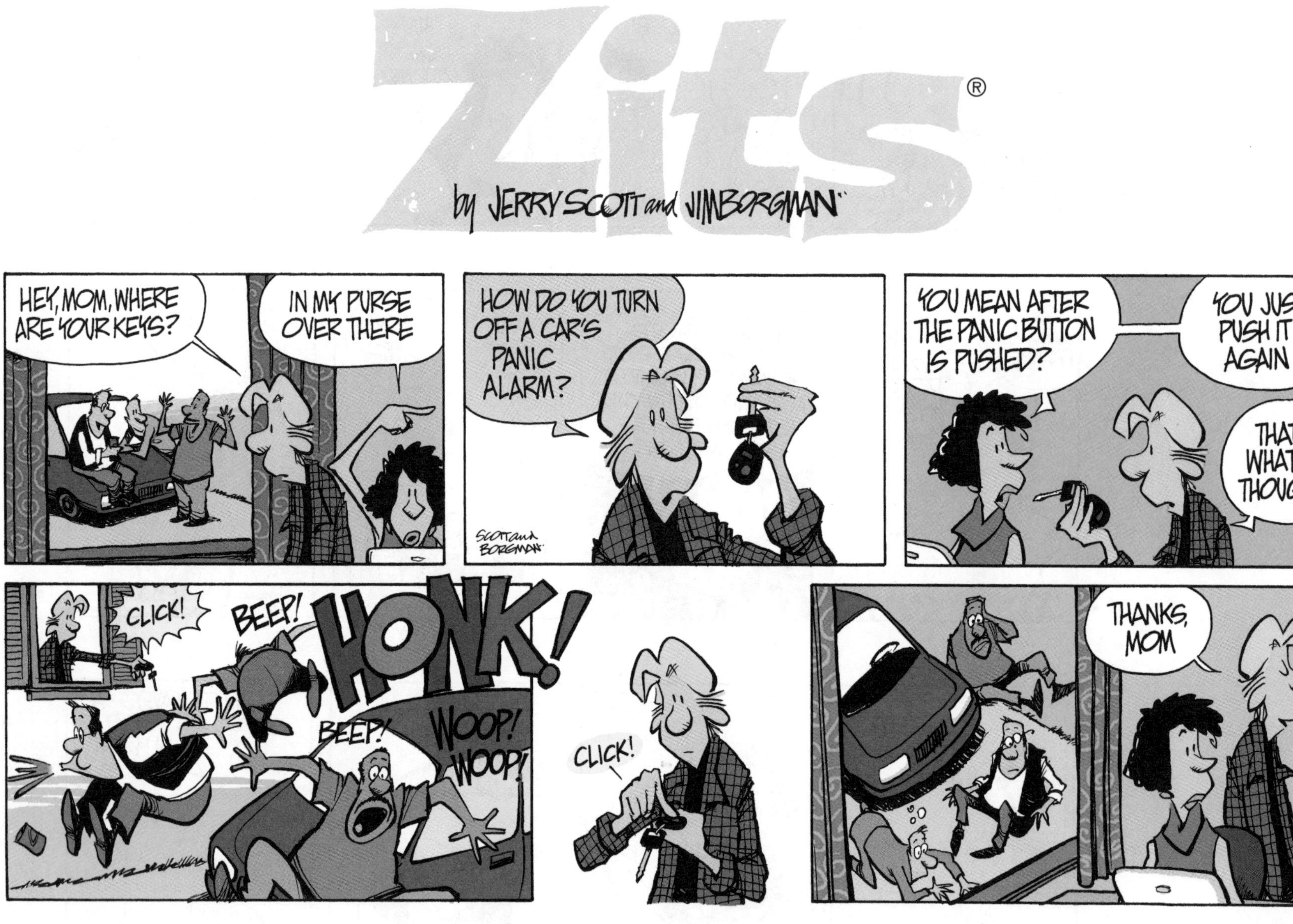
Zits®
by JERRY SCOTT and JIM BORGMAN
HEY, MOM, WHERE ARE YOUR KEYS?
IN MY PURSE OVER THERE
HOW DO YOU TURN OFF A CAR'S PANIC ALARM?
SCOTT and BORGMAN
YOU MEAN AFTER THE PANIC BUTTON IS PUSHED?
YOU JUST PUSH IT AGAIN
THAT'S WHAT I THOUGHT
CLICK!
BEEP!
HONK!
BEEP!
WOOP! WOOP!
CLICK!
THANKS, MOM

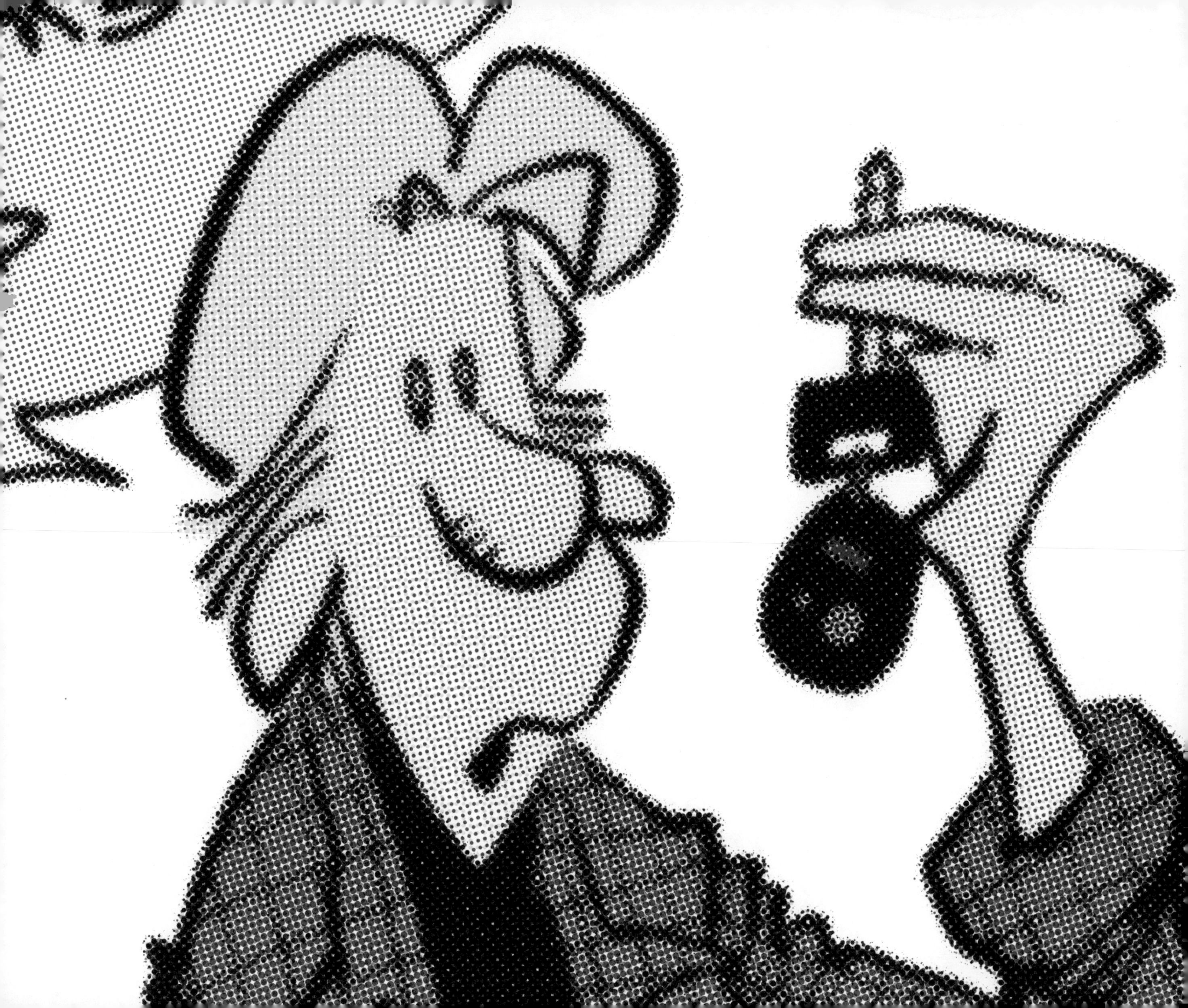

RANDOM Zits®

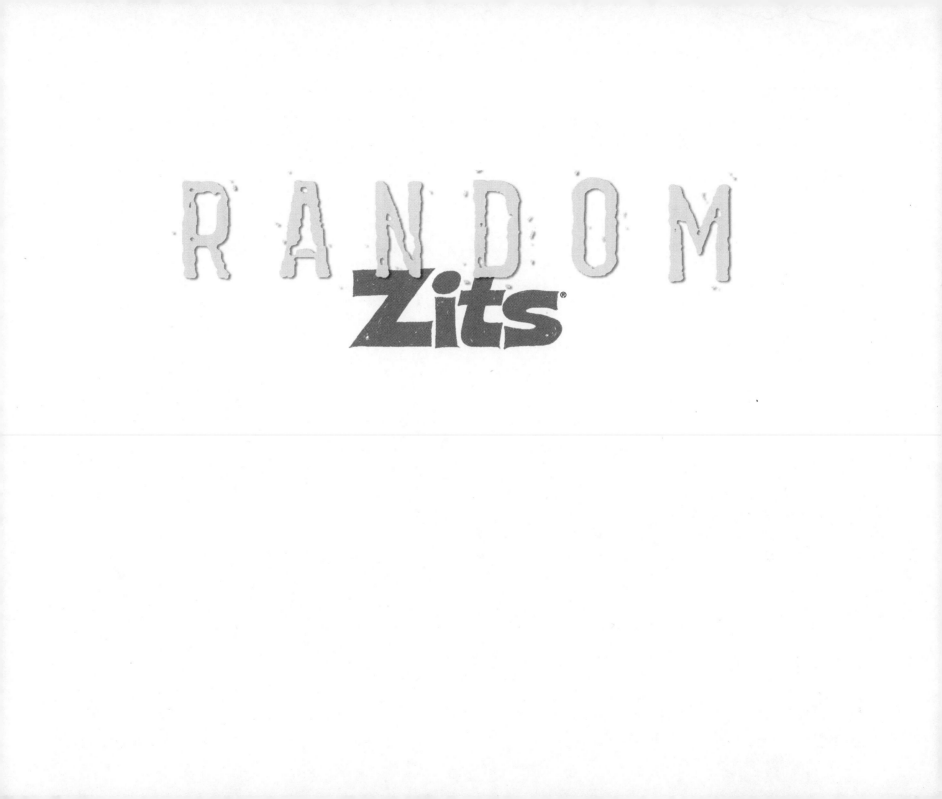

Also by Jerry Scott and Jim Borgman

Zits: Sketchbook 1
Growth Spurt: Zits Sketchbook 2
Don't Roll Your Eyes at Me, Young Man!: Zits Sketchbook 3
Are We an "Us"?: Zits Sketchbook 4
Zits Unzipped: Zits Sketchbook 5
Busted!: Zits Sketchbook 6
Road Trip: Zits Sketchbook 7
Teenage Tales: Zits Sketchbook 8

Treasuries
Humongous Zits
Big Honkin' Zits
Zits: Supersized